Communicate!

Fourteenth Edition

Kathleen S. Verderber

Northern Kentucky University

Rudolph F. Verderber

*Distinguished Teaching Professor of Communication,
University of Cincinnati*

Deanna D. Sellnow

University of Kentucky

WADSWORTH
CENGAGE Learning·

Australia • Brazil • Japan • Korea • Mexico • Singapore • Spain • United Kingdom • United States

WADSWORTH
CENGAGE Learning·

Communicate!, Fourteenth Edition
Kathleen S. Verderber, Rudolph F. Verderber, Deanna D. Sellnow

Editor-in-chief: Lyn Uhl

Publisher: Monica Eckman

Development Editor: Kassi Radomski

Editorial Assistant: Colin Solan

Media Editor: Jessica Badiner

Marketing Brand Manager: Ben Rivera

Marketing Communications Manager: Linda Yip

Content Project Manager: Rosemary Winfield

Art Director: Linda May

Print Buyer: Doug Bertke

Rights Acquisition Specialist: Ann Hoffman

Production Service: MPS Limited

Text Designer: Studio Montage

Cover Designer: Studio Montage

Cover Credits: Micro fiber, Fotosearch/© Getty Images; three people with phone, Kali9/© isctokphoto; video conference, Ariel Skelley/© Media Bakery; meeting with smart board, cultura/© Inmagine; man, Fotosearch/© Getty Images; two young women talking, Kristy-Anne Glubish/© Media Bakery

Compositor: MPS Limited

For product information and technology assistance, contact us at
Cengage Learning Customer & Sales Support, 1-800-354-9706

For permission to use material from this text or product, submit all requests online at **www.cengage.com/permissions**
Further permissions questions can be emailed to
permissionrequest@cengage.com

Library of Congress Control Number: 2012939050

Student Edition:
ISBN-13: 978-0-8400-2816-7
ISBN-10: 0-8400-2816-4

Wadsworth
20 Channel Center Street
Boston, MA 02210
USA

Cengage Learning is a leading provider of customized learning solutions with office locations around the globe, including Singapore, the United Kingdom, Australia, Mexico, Brazil, and Japan. Locate your local office at **international.cengage.com/region**

Cengage Learning products are represented in Canada by Nelson Education, Ltd.

For your course and learning solutions, visit **www.cengage.com**

Purchase any of our products at your local college store or at our preferred online store **www.cengagebrain.com**

Instructors: Please visit **login.cengage.com** and log in to access instructor-specific resources.

Printed in the United States of America
1 2 3 4 5 6 7 16 15 14 13 12

Brief Contents

Contents. iv

Preface xiii

Unit I: Foundations of Communication

Prequel: Foundations of Communication 2

Chapter 1: Communication Perspectives 4

Chapter 2: Perception of Self and Others 26

Chapter 3: Intercultural Communication 48

Chapter 4: Verbal Messages 72

Chapter 5: Nonverbal Messages. 92

Chapter 6: Listening 112

Sequel: What's Technology Got to Do with It? 132

Unit II: Interpersonal Communication and Relationships

Prequel: Interpersonal Communication and Relationships. 136

Chapter 7: Interpersonal Relationships 138

Chapter 8: Interpersonal Communication. 162

Sequel: What's Technology Got to Do with It? 188

Unit III: Group Communication

Prequel: Group Communication 192

Chapter 9: Communicating in Groups 194

Chapter 10: Group Leadership and Problem Solving 214

Sequel: What's Technology Got to Do with It? 240

Unit IV: Public Speaking

Prequel: Public Speaking 244

Chapter 11: Topic Selection and Development 246

Chapter 12: Organizing Your Speech. 276

Chapter 13: Presentational Aids 310

Chapter 14: Language 330

Chapter 15: Delivery 350

Chapter 16: Informative Speaking 386

Chapter 17: Persuasive Speaking. 412

Sequel: What's Technology Got to Do with It? 448

Appendix: Interviewing. 452

References 473

Index 492

Contents

Brief Contents iii

Preface xiii

Unit I. Foundations of Communication

Prequel: Foundations of Communication 2

Chapter 1: Communication Perspectives 4

    The Nature of Communication 7
        Canned Plans and Scripts 7

    Communication Contexts 8
        Communication Settings 9

    The Communication Process 10
        Sub-Processes of Communication 10
        Channels 11
        Interference/Noise 12
        A Model of the Communication Process 12

    Characteristics of Communication 14
        Communication Has Purpose 14
        Communication Is Continuous 15
        Communication Is Irreversible 15
        Communication Is Situated 15
        Communication Is Indexical 16
        Communication Is Learned 16
        Communication Messages Vary in Conscious Thought 17
        Communication Is Guided by Cultural Norms 17

    Communication and Ethics 17
        Ethical Principles 17
        Dark Side Messages 18

    Increasing Your Communication Competence 19
        Communication Competence 19
        Communication Apprehension 20

    Communication Improvement Plans 21

Chapter 2: Perception of Self and Others 26

    The Perception Process 28
        Attention and Selection 28
        Organization 29
        Interpretation 29
        Dual Processing 30

    Perception of Self 30
        Self-Concept 30
        Self-Esteem 32
        Cultural Norms and Self-Perceptions 32
        Accuracy and Distortion of Self-Perceptions 34
        Self-Perception and Communication 35
        Changing Self-Perceptions 38

Perception of Others 41
    Uncertainty Reduction 41
    Inaccurate and Distorted Perceptions of Others 42
    Improving Perceptions of Others 43

Chapter 3: Intercultural Communication 48

Culture and Communication 50
    Dominant Cultures, Co-cultures, and Cultural Identity 51

How Cultures Differ 55
    Individualism/Collectivism 56
    Context 57
    Chronemics 57
    Uncertainty Avoidance 58
    Power Distance 59
    Masculinity/Femininity 59
    Long-Term/Short-Term Orientation 60
    Cross-Cultural Adaptation 60

Developing Intercultural Communication
Competence 63
    Potential Barriers 63
    Competent Communication Strategies 65

Chapter 4: Verbal Messages 72

The Nature of Language 74
    What Is a Language? 75
    Characteristics of Language 77

The Relationship Between Language and Meaning 79
    Semantics 79
    Guidelines for Improving Semantics 80
    Pragmatics 82
    Guidelines for Improving Pragmatics 85
    Sociolinguistics 86
    Guidelines for Improving Sociolinguistic Understanding 89

Chapter 5: Nonverbal Messages 92

Characteristics of Nonverbal Communication 95

Types of Nonverbal Communication 96
    Use of Body: Kinesics 96
    Use of Voice: Paralanguage 99
    Use of Space: Proxemics 101
    Use of Time: Chronemics 102
    Physical Appearance 104

Guidelines for Improving Nonverbal Communication 107
    Sending Nonverbal Messages 107
    Interpreting Nonverbal Messages 107

Chapter 6: Listening 112

What Is Listening? 114

Challenges to Effective Listening 115
    Listening Style 115
    Listening Apprehension 116
    Processing Approach 118

Active Listening. 118
    Attending. 118
    Understanding. 119
    Remembering. 123
    Evaluating 124
    Responding 125

Communication Channels 132
    Media Richness. 133
    Synchronicity. 133
    Social Presence. 134
    Guidelines for Choosing a Channel. 134

Unit II: Interpersonal Communication and Relationships

Prequel: Interpersonal Communication and Relationships 136

Chapter 7: Interpersonal Relationships 138

Types of Relationships. 140
    Acquaintances. 140
    Friends 142
    Intimates. 144

Disclosure in Relationship Life Cycles 148
    Social Penetration 148
    The Johari Window 149

Stages of Relationships. 150
    Coming Together: Beginning Relationships. 150
    Coming Together: Developing Relationships. 151
    Relational Maintenance 152
    Coming Apart: Declining and Dissolving Relationships 155

Dialectics in Interpersonal Relationships 156
    Relational Dialectics 156
    Managing Dialectical Tensions. 158

Chapter 8: Interpersonal Communication. 162

Providing Emotional Support 164
    Comforting Guidelines 164

Managing Privacy and Disclosure 166
    Effects of Disclosure and Privacy on Relationships 168
    Disclosure Guidelines 169
    Privacy Management Guidelines 174

Expressing Desires and Expectations. 176
    Passive Communication Style 176
    Aggressive Communication Style. 176
    Passive-Aggressive Communication Style 177
    Assertive Communication Style 177
    Cultural and Co-cultural Considerations. 177

Managing Interpersonal Conflict 179
    Avoiding (Lose–Lose). 179
    Accommodating (Lose–Win) 180

Competing (Win–Lose). 180
Compromising (Partial Lose–Lose). 180
Collaborating (Win–Win) 181
Collaboration Guidelines 181

Unit III: Group Communication

Prequel: Group Communication. 192

Chapter 9: Communicating in Groups. 194

The Nature and Types of Groups 196
Families. 196
Social Friendship Groups 197
Support Groups 197
Interest Groups 198
Service Groups 198
Work Group Teams 199
Virtual Groups 200

Characteristics of Healthy Groups 201
Healthy Groups Have Ethical Goals. 201
Healthy Groups Are Interdependent 202
Healthy Groups Are Cohesive. 203
Healthy Groups Develop and Abide by Productive Norms 203
Healthy Groups Are Accountable 205
Healthy Groups Are Synergetic. 206

Stages of Group Development. 206
Forming. 207
Storming 207
Norming 207
Performing 208
Adjourning and Transforming. 208

Conflict in Groups 208
Pseudo-Conflict. 208
Issue-Related Group Conflict 209
Personality-Related Group Conflict. 209
Culture and Conflict. 209
Virtual Groups and Conflict 210

Chapter 10: Group Leadership and Problem Solving. 214

Effective Leadership 216
Task Roles. 217
Maintenance Roles 217
Procedural Roles 220
Shared Leadership Responsibilities 220

Effective Meetings. 221
Guidelines for Meeting Leaders/Conveners 221
Guidelines for Meeting Participants 224

Systematic Problem Solving 226
Step One: Identify and Define the Problem. 226
Step Two: Analyze the Problem 227
Step Three: Determine Criteria for Judging Solutions 228

Step Four: Identify Alternative Solutions 228
Step Five: Evaluate Solutions and Decide 229
Step Six: Implement the Agreed-Upon Solution and Assess It 230

Communicating Group Solutions 232
Written Formats 232
Oral Formats 232
Virtual Formats 233

Evaluating Group Effectiveness 234
Group Dynamics 234
Group Presentations 236

Unit IV: Public Speaking

Prequel: Public Speaking 244

Chapter 11: Topic Selection and Development 246

The Rhetorical Situation 248

Generate a List of Potential Topics 249
Subjects 249
Brainstorm and Concept Map 249

Analyze the Audience 250
Demographic Data 251
Subject-Related Data 251
Data-Gathering Methods 252
Ethical Use of Audience Data 253

Examine the Occasion 255

Select a Topic 256

Write a Speech Goal Statement 257
Understanding General and Specific Speech Goals 257
Phrasing a Specific Goal Statement 258

Locate and Evaluate Information Sources 260
Personal Knowledge and Experience 260
Secondary Research 260
Primary Research 266

Identify and Evaluate a Variety of Information 267
Factual Statements 267
Expert Opinions 268
Elaborations 269
Seek Information from Multiple Cultural Perspectives 269

Record Information 270
Annotated Bibliography 270
Research Cards 270

Cite Sources 271

Chapter 12: Organizing Your Speech 276

Developing the Body 279
Choose Main Points 279
Write the Thesis Statement 281
Outline the Speech Body 281
Create Transitions 288

Developing the Introduction. 290
   Get Attention 290
   Establish Relevance. 294
   Establish Credibility 294
   State the Thesis. 295

Developing the Conclusion 296
   Summarize Main Points. 296
   Clinch 296

Compiling the Reference List. 298

Reviewing the Outline 301

Chapter 13: Presentational Aids 310

Benefits of Presentational Aids 314

Types of Presentational Aids 314
   Visual Aids. 314
   Audio Aids 318
   Audiovisual Aids 319
   Other Sensory Aids 320

Choosing Presentational Aids 320

Preparing Presentational Aids 321

Displaying Presentational Aids. 323
   Posters 323
   Whiteboards or Chalkboards 324
   Flip Charts. 324
   Handouts. 324
   Document Cameras. 325
   Computers, CD/DVD Players, and LCD Projectors. 325

Chapter 14: Language 330

Oral Style 332

Speaking Appropriately 333
   Relevance 333
   Common Ground 334
   Speaker Credibility 335
   Linguistic Sensitivity 337
   Cultural Diversity. 338

Speaking Clearly. 340
   Specific Language. 341
   Familiar Terms. 341
   Details and Examples 342
   Vocalized Pauses. 343

Speaking Vividly 343
   Sensory Language. 343
   Rhetorical Figures and Structures of Speech 344

Chapter 15: Delivery 350

Public Speaking Apprehension 352
   Symptoms and Causes 352
   Management Techniques. 353

Effective Delivery Style 355
   Conversational. 355

Animated 355

Use of Voice 356
    Intelligibility 356
    Vocal Expression 357

Use of Body 357
    Appearance 357
    Posture 358
    Poise 358
    Eye Contact 358
    Facial Expressions 359
    Gestures 359
    Movement 362

Delivery Methods 362
    Impromptu Speeches 362
    Scripted Speeches 363
    Extemporaneous Speeches 363

Rehearsals 365
    Preparing Speaking Notes 365
    Handling Presentational Aids 368
    Rehearsing and Refining Delivery 369

Adapting While Delivering the Speech 370

Evaluating Speeches 372

Chapter 16: Informative Speaking 386

Characteristics of Effective Informative Speaking 388
    Intellectually Stimulating 388
    Relevant 389
    Creative 389
    Memorable 391
    Address Diverse Learning Styles 391

Methods of Informing 392
    Description 392
    Definition 394
    Comparison and Contrast 394
    Narration 395
    Demonstration 395

Common Informative Patterns 396
    Process Speeches 396
    Expository Speeches 396

Chapter 17: Persuasive Speaking 412

The Nature of Persuasion 414

Processing Persuasive Messages 414

Persuasive Speech Goals 415
    Types of Propositions 415
    Tailoring Propositions to Your Target Audience 416

Rhetorical Appeals to Logos 418
    Types of Logical Arguments 419
    Reasoning Fallacies 421

Rhetorical Appeals to Ethos 423
  Conveying Good Character 424
  Conveying Competence and Credibility 425

Rhetorical Appeals to Pathos 426
  Evoking Negative Emotions 426
  Evoking Positive Emotions 427

Persuasive Speech Patterns 429
  Statement of Reasons 429
  Comparative Advantages 429
  Criteria Satisfaction 430
  Refutative 430
  Problem–Solution 431
  Problem–Cause–Solution 431
  Motivated Sequence 432

Guidelines for Public Speaking in a Virtual World 449

Preface

We are delighted to share this revised version of *Communicate!* with you. We believe you will find the changes refreshing, relevant to current scholarship, and applicable to daily life. Most important is our deliberate effort to integrate examples of communication as it occurs through face-to-face and technology-driven channels, with friends and family, as well as across cultures and co-cultures. We can't wait to hear what you think of our approach.

To Students

Congratulations! You are beginning to study communication, a subject that is important and useful to you in all parts of your life. When you want to establish or improve a relationship, when you need to work with others on a group project for class or for a cause you support, or when you are required to make a public presentation, your success will depend on how effective you are at communicating in those settings.

Most of you have probably never studied communication formally. Rather, you've learned the communication skills and strategies you use every day informally, in your home and from your friends. By taking this communication course and learning tested communication skills, you'll strengthen your existing abilities and improve your relationships. You can improve the likelihood that your group projects are successful by understanding the predictable patterns of group process and communication. And you can more effectively overcome stage fright and give better presentations when you have studied public speaking and know how to plan and deliver a formal speech. So again, we say, congratulations! You'll find this course to be instantly relevant to your day-to-day living. We are confident that by the end of this term you will be glad you spent your time and money on it.

The textbook you're reading, *Communicate!*, was one of the first college texts published about human communication. A lot has changed since Rudy wrote that first edition. Over the years we have worked to make sure that students, like you, have a book that is easy and enjoyable to read and learn from. We have also worked hard to make sure that the information, theories, and skills discussed are relevant to the real relationships and communication situations you face. So every three years we examine the book in light of how the world has changed. Just ten years ago, cell phones were not in wide use, *texting* wasn't a verb, and sites like *Facebook, Twitter, and YouTube* didn't exist. Despite these huge changes in the way we communicate, this textbook is as up-to-date and useful as the first edition was because we work hard to make sure that the information we present reflects what it takes to be an effective communicator *today.*

Communicate! is written with six specific goals in mind:

1. **To explain important communication concepts, frameworks, and theories** that have been consistently supported by careful research so that you can understand the conceptual foundations of human communication.

2. **To teach specific communication skills** that facilitate the sharing of meaning in personal, group, and public speaking settings.

3. **To describe and encourage you to adopt the ethical frameworks** that can guide competent communication.

4. **To increase your ability to understand effective communication practices in different cultures.**

5. **To stimulate critical and creative thinking** about the concepts and skills you learn as they apply to face-to-face interactions as well as in technology-mediated ones.

6. **To provide tools to practice and assess** the communication concepts and skills you read about.

So we hope you will read and enjoy this textbook and that it will be a resource you will want to keep in your personal library.

To Instructors

Thank you for considering and using this new edition of *Communicate!* We believe the revisions will surprise and delight those of you who have used *Communicate!* in the past. We also believe that those of you who are looking for a new textbook will find *Communicate!* to be precisely the learning tool to encourage students to read and think about the important role of communication in their lives.

As we prepared this edition, we were acutely aware of how our students' lives are changing and how these changes are influencing their learning process and the nature of communication in their lives. So we have revised the text with these new realities in mind, while at the same time retaining the hallmarks that have made it useful to students and instructors in the past. And, as with every new edition, we have incorporated the suggestions of colleagues who use the text, and we've reviewed the latest scholarship so that this new edition reflects what users want and what recent scholarship has discovered about human communication. In the sections that follow, we detail what's new and highlight the pre-existing features that have made *Communicate!* a perennial favorite among students and faculty alike.

New to This Edition

- **New prequels at the beginning of each unit** provide an overview of the material in each chapter by introducing the fundamental concepts in them and explaining how the chapters relate to each other.

- **Increased emphasis on the role of social media.** Because technology and social media now play such a central role in our lives, we have integrated discussions of research findings and best practices into each chapter. These discussions focus on how specific communication concepts operate differently in technological and face-to-face environments. In addition, each unit ends with a **sequel** in which concepts unique to technological communication are discussed. For example, in the sequel to the unit on Public Communication, we discuss new forms of public discourse that occur over the Internet, such as webinars and narrated PowerPoint presentations.

- **A new chapter on presentational aids** (Chapter 13) expands our discussion of this increasingly important part of speechmaking.

- **A new "Media and Media Literacy" bonus chapter** written by Oakland University's Erin A. Meyer is included. Given the increasing pervasiveness of media in our lives, it has become more important than ever to understand what media is, how it effects and influences us, the components of media, and the principles of media literacy. (See the Instructor Resources section in this preface to find out more about bundling this chapter with *Communicate!* or speak to your Cengage sales representative.)

New features:

- At the beginning of each chapter, learning outcomes entitled **"What You'll Know"** and **"What You'll Be Able to Do"** help students preview the concepts and skills they will learn in the chapter.

- **"The Audience Beyond" boxes** found at the bottom of pages in the chapters provide brief examples illustrating how the fundamental communication principles being discussed play out through social media and technology-driven channels.

- **"Consider This" boxes** in the margins encourage readers to personalize what they are reading by reflecting on how a specific communication concept applies to their lives.

Revised features:

- **Updated "Pop Comm!" essays,** a popular feature introduced in the last edition, have been updated and expanded. These essays link communication concepts to specific exemplars and problems in popular culture. New topics include: Lady Gaga's construction of self in the article "Self-Monitoring and Celebrity Culture"; an examination of how pop culture art and entertainment can inadvertently encourage stereotypes in *The Help*: Race and Stereotyping in Popular Culture"; and how assessing the truthfulness of source material can be problematic in "Blurring the Lines: The Pragmatics of Tabloid and Mainstream Journalism."

- **Diverse Voices essays** have been added so that nearly every chapter now offers an essay illuminating cross-cultural communication challenges as told by real people who have experienced them.

- **Revised end-of-chapter material, now called** "*Communicate!* **Resource and Assessment Center,"** includes a brief summary of what you'll find on the Speech Communication CourseMate at cengagebrain.com, as well as **"Applying What You've Learned"** (critical thinking assessment activities), and **Skill-Building Exercises** designed to give students their first opportunity to practice new skills by writing responses to conversational prompts.

- The **Appendix on interviewing** has been updated and revised throughout. Additional information about the Appendix is provided on p. xvii.

Chapter-by-Chapter Revisions

- **Chapter 1, "Communication Perspectives,"** continues to focus on the fundamental processes of communication but is now organized so that students see the primacy of messages and the canned plans and scripts we use to encode and decode them in different communication settings and through various channels. The section on communication ethics has been expanded to address the *dark side* of communication.

- **Chapter 2, "Perception of Self and Others,"** introduces the notion of dual processing approaches in our thinking, specifically in how they affect what we perceive and how we make sense out of it. The chapter organization has been tightened and the role that perception processes play in social media interactions is explored.

- **Chapter 3** is now **"Intercultural Communication."** We have moved this chapter up in the text so that students understand how what is seen to be good and acceptable communication practice depends on one's culture. This heavily revised chapter now includes all of the foundational concepts that we use to differentiate cultural perspectives from each other. In addition, we focus on how cultural identity affects communication and guidelines for demonstrating empathy and respect when communicating with people from cultures other than your own.

- **Chapter 4, "Verbal Messages,"** has been revised with a more detailed discussion of the nature of language and how language and speech communities influence interpretation. We explain how message meanings are derived from the words themselves (semantics), the conversational context (pragmatics), and social and cultural contexts (sociolinguistics). Throughout the chapter, we propose specific guidelines for improving skills in constructing and interpreting verbal messages.

- **Chapter 5, "Nonverbal Messages,"** has been updated and we have expanded the discussion of how nonverbal messages are communicated in online environments.

- **Chapter 6, "Listening,"** has been reorganized by introducing how listening style, listening apprehension, and dual approaches to listening affect how well we understand what is being said. The chapter proposes active listening as a way to overcome these challenges.

- **Chapter 7, "Interpersonal Relationships,"** now includes a section on social penetration theory to help illustrate the role of disclosure in relationships and expands the section on the stages of coming together and coming apart to include current scholarship on relationship transformation.

- **Chapter 8, "Interpersonal Communication,"** introduces the role of communication in developing and maintaining a positive communication climate and a section on the passive-aggressive communication style of expressing wants, needs, desires, and expectations.

- **Chapter 9, "Communicating in Groups,"** offers updated examples of types of groups and effective communication within them. It also provides an expanded discussion of virtual groups and effective virtual group communication based on current research. Finally, we introduce an extended discussion about conflict in groups and how to manage it effectively when interacting in face-to-face or virtual environments.

- **Chapter 10, "Group Leadership and Problem Solving,"** focuses specifically on the nature of effective leadership and problem solving in meetings and on work group teams, which includes an expanded discussion about communicating group decisions in written, oral, and virtual formats.

- **Chapter 11, "Topic Selection and Development,"** continues to focus on topic selection, research, and speech development based on ongoing audience analysis and adaptation. New to this edition is an expanded discussion of ethics when analyzing audiences, evaluating sources and information, and when citing them. We also include a discussion of the role an annotated bibliography can play in documenting information and sources.

- **Chapter 12, "Organizing Your Speech,"** has a new sample outline on the abuses of the prescription drug, Adderall, among college students today. We also expanded the rhetorical strategies for gaining attention in the introduction to include action.

- **Chapter 13, "Presentational Aids,"** includes much of the material about visual aids from the previous edition but expands the discussion to illustrate the role of audio and audiovisual aids in speechmaking today. In doing so, we also devote special attention to computerized slideshows and how to prepare and integrate them effectively, thereby avoiding the consequence commonly referred to as "death by PowerPoint."

- **Chapter 14, "Language,"** is now devoted exclusively to effective formal oral language style used in public speaking as it differs from written style and casual conversational style. We added a discussion about why and how to convey verbal immediacy in public speeches.

- **Chapter 15, "Delivery,"** offers an expanded discussion about maintaining intelligibility for second-language speakers and those with an accent markedly different from the audience. We also added a section about adapting delivery during the speech based on audience feedback and analysis. And we introduce a new sample speech with commentary, "College Student Volunteering and Civic Engagement."

- **Chapter 16, "Informative Speaking,"** has been updated to include current examples and reflect current research. We also expanded our discussion of critical creative thinking and how to use it to develop interesting informative speeches.

- **Chapter 17, "Persuasive Speaking,"** now introduces the nature of persuasion as a form of argument and expands the discussion of logos, ethos, and pathos persuasive strategies to develop convincing arguments. And we offer a new sample student speech, "Together, We Can Stop Cyber-Bullying," another timely topic for readers today.

- The **Appendix on interviewing,** now located toward the end of the book, has been updated and revised to focus on that fact that many jobs are now posted and applied to online. We discuss types of questions to include in an effective interview protocol and some guidelines to follow when conducting an information-gathering interview, media interview, or employment interview as both interviewer and as interviewee. The chapter gives considerable attention to employment seekers and how to locate job openings through formal and informal networks, as well as how to prepare application materials, conduct the interview, and follow up afterward.

Hallmark Features

- **"Communication Skill" boxes** provide a step-by-step guide for each of the communication skills presented in the text. Each of these boxes includes the definition of the skill, a brief description of its use, the steps for enacting the skill, and an example that illustrates the skill.

- **"Speech Plan Action Steps"** in Chapters 11–15 guide students through a sequential speech-planning process. The activities that accompany each of these action steps guide students through an orderly process that results in better speeches.

- **Sample student speeches** appear in the text, each accompanied by an audience adaptation plan, an outline, and a transcript and analysis. Two new sample speeches are introduced in this edition: "Together We Can Stop Cyberbullying," and "College Student Volunteering and Civic Engagement." Students can use their online resources to view videos of these speeches, see the transcript and two different kinds of outlines and sample note cards, prepare their own critiques, and compare their critiques to the authors'.

- **"Communicate on Your Feet" speech assignments** in Parts I and II encourage students to begin building their public-speaking skills immediately while also addressing the needs of instructors who assign prepared speeches throughout the course. In Unit IV, these assignments correspond to the speech types discussed in Chapters 16 and 17.

- **"What Would You Do? A Question of Ethics"** are short case studies that appear near the end of chapters. These cases present ethical challenges and require students to think critically, sorting through a variety of ethical dilemmas faced by communicators. Conceptual material presented in Chapter 1 lays the groundwork for the criteria on which students may base their assessments, but each case focuses on issues raised in a specific chapter.

- *Communicate!* **online resources** provide students with the opportunity to view examples of each activity prepared by other students and to complete many of the action steps with Speech Builder Express. (See the section Student Resources for more about these online resources.)

Teaching and Learning Resources

Communicate! is accompanied by a full suite of integrated materials that will make teaching and learning more efficient and effective. **Note to faculty:** If you want your students to have access to the online resources for this book, please be sure to order them for your course. The content in these resources can be bundled with every new copy of the text or ordered separately. *If you do not order them, your students will not have access to the online resources.* Contact your local Wadsworth Cengage Learning sales representative for more details.

Student Resources

- **Speech Communication CourseMate for *Communicate!*** The more you study, the better the results. Make the most of your study time by accessing everything you need to succeed in one place. Speech Communication CourseMate includes: interactive learning tools, such as quizzes, flashcards, interactive video activities, Action Step activities, and an interactive eBook with highlighting, note-taking, and more—all for less than the price of a used book.

- Many of the Speech Plan Action Steps can be completed with the **Speech Builder Express 3.0 organization and outlining program.** This interactive Web-based tool coaches students through the speech organization and outlining process. By completing interactive sessions, students can prepare and save their outlines—including a plan for visual aids and a works cited section—formatted according to the principles presented in the text. Text models reinforce students' interactive practice.

- **InfoTrac College Edition.** This virtual library features more than 18 million reliable, full-length articles from 5,000 academic and popular periodicals that can be retrieved almost instantly.

- The **Cengage Learning Enhanced eBook** is a Web-based, interactive version of *Communicate!* that offers ease of use and maximum flexibility for students who want to create their own learning experience. The enhanced eBook includes advanced book tools such as a hypertext index, bookmarking, easy highlighting, faster searching, easy navigation, and a vibrant Web-based format. Students get access to the enhanced eBook with the printed text, or they can just purchase access to the stand-alone enhanced eBook.

- **Speech Studio™ Online Video Upload and Grading Program** improves the learning comprehension of public speaking students. This unique resource empowers instructors with a new assessment capability that is applicable for traditional, online, and hybrid courses. With Speech Studio, students can upload video files of practice speeches or final performances, comment on their peers' speeches, and review their grades and instructor feedback. Instructors create courses and assignments, comment on and grade student speeches with a library of comments and grading rubrics, and allow peer review. Grades flow into a gradebook that allows instructors to easily manage their course from within Speech Studio or download the grades to their LMS.

- **CengageBrain Online Store.** CengageBrain.com is a single destination for more than 15,000 new print textbooks, textbook rentals, eBooks, single eChapters, and print, digital, and audio study tools. CengageBrain.com provides the freedom to purchase Cengage Learning products à la carte—exactly what you need, when you need it. Visit **cengagebrain.com** for details.

- *A Guide to the Basic Course for ESL Students* can be bundled and is designed to assist the nonnative speaker. The *Guide* features FAQs, helpful URLs, and strategies for accent management and speech apprehension.

- *Service Learning in Communication Studies: A Handbook* is an invaluable resource for students in the basic course that integrates, or will soon integrate, a service-learning component. This handbook provides guidelines for connecting service-learning work with classroom concepts and advice for working effectively with agencies and organizations. It also provides model forms and reports and a directory of online resources.

Instructor Resources

- The **Instructor's Resource Manual with Test Bank** by Katrina Bodey, University of North Carolina, Chapel Hill, includes a sample syllabi, chapter-by-chapter outlines, summaries, vocabulary lists, suggested lecture and discussion topics, classroom exercises, assignments, and a comprehensive test bank with answer key and rejoinders. In addition, this manual includes the **"Spotlight on Scholars" boxes** that were in previous editions of the main text. These boxes feature the work of eight eminent communications scholars, putting a face on scholarship by telling each scholar's "story." These boxes can be used as discussion starters, as enrichment for students who are interested in communication scholarship, or in any other way instructors would like to integrate them into the course.

- **Special-topic instructor's manuals.** Written by Deanna Sellnow, University of Kentucky, these three brief manuals provide instructor resources for teaching public speaking online, with a service-learning approach, and with a problem-based learning approach that focuses on critical thinking and teamwork skills. Each manual includes course syllabi; icebreakers; information about learning cycles and learning styles; and public speaking basics such as coping with anxiety, outlining, and speaking ethically.

- *The Teaching Assistant's Guide to the Basic Course,* based on leading communication teacher training programs, covers general teaching and course management topics as well as specific strategies for communication instruction—for example, providing effective feedback on performance, managing sensitive class discussions, and conducting mock interviews.

- The **PowerLecture** CD-ROM contains an electronic version of the Instructor's Resource Manual, ExamView® Computerized Testing, predesigned Microsoft PowerPoint presentations, and JoinIn® classroom quizzing. The PowerPoint presentations contain text, images, and cued videos of student speeches and can be used as they are or customized to suit your course needs.

- **Communication Scenarios for Critique and Analysis** include the communication scenarios in the *Communicate!* interactive videos as well as additional scenarios covering interpersonal communication, interviewing, and group communication.

- The **BBC News and CBS News DVDs:** *Human Communication, Interpersonal Communication, and Public Speaking,* provide footage of news stories that relate to current topics in human and interpersonal communication, and footage of famous historical and contemporary public speeches, as well as clips that relate to current topics in speech communication.

- The **Student Speeches for Critique and Analysis** offer a variety of sample student speeches, including those featured in the *Communicate!* interactive videos, which your students can watch, critique, and analyze on their own or in class. All of the speech types are included, as well as speeches featuring nonnative English speakers and the use of visual aids.

- The *Media Guide for Interpersonal Communication* provides faculty with media resource listings focused on general interpersonal communication topics. Each listing provides compelling examples of how interpersonal communication concepts are illustrated in particular films, books, plays, Web sites, or journal articles. Discussion questions are provided.

- **CourseCare training and support.** Get trained, get connected, and get the support you need for the seamless integration of digital resources into your course. This unparalleled technology service and training program provides robust online resources, peer-to-peer instruction, personalized training, and a customizable program you can count on. Visit **cengage .com/coursecare/** to sign up for online seminars, first days of class services, technical support, or personalized, face-to-face training. Our online and onsite trainings are frequently led by one of our Lead Teachers, faculty members who are experts in using Wadsworth Cengage Learning technology and can provide best practices and teaching tips.

- **Flex-text customization program.** With this program you can create a text as unique as your course: quickly, simply, and affordably. As part of our flex-text program, you can add your personal touch to *Communicate!* with a course-specific cover and up to 32 pages of your own content—at no additional cost. The new Media and Media Literacy bonus chapter, discussed on p. xv, can also be added.

- **A single chapter on public speaking** is available through Cengage Custom Publishing for survey courses in which developing public speaking skills is not an emphasis. This chapter, written by the *Communicate!* authors, presents a concise overview of public speaking and the speech-making process. It is designed to substitute for Chapters 11–17 of *Communicate!* and to provide an overview, rather than a comprehensive guide to the speech-making process.

Acknowledgments

This fourteenth edition of *Communicate!* has benefitted from the work of many people we would like to recognize.

First, we thank our colleagues who reviewed the book and offered their insights and suggestions for this edition, including Norman Earls, Jr., Valdosta State University; James Floss, Humboldt State University; Angela Grupas, St. Louis Community College–Meramec; Darren Linvill, Clemson University; and Shellie Michael, Volunteer State Community College.

Second, early in the process of writing this edition, we happened upon the blog of a very talented communication professor with expertise in mass communication and popular culture. We were delighted when Erin A. Meyers of Oakland University agreed to write the Media and Media Literacy bonus chapter, as well as and update the PopComm! features. She was a delight to work with and is a talented author.

We are fortunate to work with the best editorial team in communication studies today. We are grateful for the support of Lyn Uhl, editor-in-chief; Monica Eckman, publisher; Colin Solan, editorial assistant; Jessica Badiner, media editor; Joanna Confalone, marketing manager; Linda Beckstrom Yip, senior marketing communications manager; Rosemary Winfield, senior content product manager; Linda May, art director; Lindsay Schmonsees, project manager at MPS Limited; Maura Brown, copy editor; Studio Montage, designer; Alexandra Ricciardi, rights acquisition specialist; Christina Ciaramella, image researcher; and Ellen Rasmussen, text permission researcher. We simply could not have produced the fourteenth edition this book without the encouragement and professionalism of Kassi Radomski, our development editor. She not only held our feet to the fire about manuscript length, but she also served as referee when we disagreed about changes in the content of the book. And her patience when we lagged behind on our deadlines demonstrated not only her character but her belief in our ability to pull through in the end.

We also thank our families for their continued patience, understanding, and support.

Finally, we would like to pay tribute to Rudolph (Rudy) Verderber, now author emeritus, for conceiving the first edition of *Communicate!* when the human communication course was in its infancy. His work then and through the years has shaped the course and the way it is taught throughout the discipline. During his forty-plus years of active authoring, he redefined what a basic communications textbook should be and the way that such a book should evolve as the theory and research base improves our understanding of communication processes and effectiveness. Today we ask you to keep Rudy in your thoughts and prayers as he continues his ongoing battle with Alzheimer's disease.

Finally, we thank God for the many ways that our lives have been blessed. We hope this book helps readers glimpse what Martin Buber called the I–Thou respect and love that we believe is central to our human relationships.

Kathleen S. Verderber
and
Deanna D. Sellnow

Communicate!

PREQUEL

Foundations of Communication

In the words of educational philosopher, Robert M. Hutchins, former dean of the Yale Law School and former president and chancellor of the University of Chicago,

> *A world community can only exist with world communication, which means something more than extensive software facilities scattered about the globe. It means common understanding, a common tradition, common ideas and common ideals.*

The title of the book you are about to read is *Communicate!* and from it you will gain skills designed to help you achieve what Hutchins describes. Before we embark on our journey, however, we ought to begin with a common understanding of what *communication* means. We know that communication has to do with things like reading, writing, talking, and listening, and that we begin learning to communicate from the day we are born. (Some even suggest that we begin learning to communicate while in the womb.) We also know that communication is a fundamental element of human thought, interaction, understanding, and persuasion. What people sometimes fail to realize, however, is that communication is something we can learn to do more effectively by studying the fundamentals of it and putting those skills into practice. Just as athletes improve their performance through study, practice, and skills training, so do effective communicators.

At its core, communication is the desire to share our thoughts, feelings, and ideas with others. We do this through the messages we send and receive every day. Messages are made up of a combination of verbal symbols (words), nonverbal cues (behaviors), and perhaps visual images. Through reflection and analysis, we interpret the messages of others—sometimes accurately and sometimes not.

New technologies provide new channels for communicating and new challenges. For example, e-mailing, texting, tweeting, blogging, Skyping, and Facebooking are expanding our ability to stay in touch with distant others. With these opportunities, however, comes an intensified need to improve our communication competence as we tailor our messages to be appropriate for the different communication channels we use. Still, communication at its core is based on messages and on the ways those messages are composed and interpreted. So this book focuses on effective communication (1) in various settings such as interpersonal encounters, small groups, and public forums, as well as (2) using a variety of channels ranging from flat print to face-to-face to mediated and technology-driven ones.

Chapter 1 The first unit, which is comprised of six chapters, is devoted to the fundamental elements of effective communication that remain constant across settings and channels. In Chapter 1, for example, we discuss the nature of communication and the communication process, the ethics of and the "dark side" of communication; that is, problems that surface when ethics are breached. And we explain what communication competence is, how communication apprehension affects it, and how to improve communication competence.

Chapter 2 Since the key to effective communication is mutual understanding, in Chapter 2, we discuss the basics of perception and social perception. We focus on the two most important social perceptions that affect communication: our perceptions of self and our perceptions of others. We also offer skills and guidelines to help you form more accurate social perceptions.

Chapter 3 Messages depend on language, which is derived from cultural groups. So in Chapter 3 we examine how cultures differ and how those differences affect what is viewed as appropriate and effective communication.

Chapter 4 Chapter 4 is devoted to verbal messages; that is, the words we use to express our thoughts and feelings. We explain how words come to mean something based on context, previous messages, and culture. We close by offering ways to improve your verbal messages.

Chapter 5 Chapter 5 focuses on nonverbal messages, which are essentially all messages that transcend written or spoken words. We discuss the characteristics and types of nonverbal messages and the ways they may compliment, contradict, or substitute for verbal messages. We also offer guidelines to improve your own nonverbal messages, as well as the accuracy of your interpretations of the nonverbal messages sent by others.

Chapter 6 Chapter 6 is devoted to the listening process. We describe the types of listening and provide specific suggestions for improving your listening skills.

We end this unit, as we will all others, with a sequel in which we describe the ways mediated and technology-driven communication channels affect these basic communication processes. By the time you finish this introductory unit, you will be ready—and we hope excited—to study how to apply these basic concepts in interpersonal, group, and public communication contexts.

Communication Perspectives

What you'll know

- The nature of communication and the communication process

- The characteristics of communication

- Major tenets of ethical communication

What you'll be able to do

- Create and evaluate messages using principles of ethical communication

- Develop a personal communication improvement plan

Jennifer was running late this morning. She stood at the kitchen counter eating a piece of toast while preparing a grocery list she would use on her way home from work. She noticed that the Weather Channel was forecasting heavy rain. She wondered where she left her umbrella and added "get umbrella" to her shopping list. Jennifer quickly texted Greta, a coworker she was driving with to work today, to ask if Greta had an extra one she could borrow.

As she was texting Greta, Jennifer's 16-year-old daughter, Hailey, bounded into the kitchen and asked, "Mom, can I get a tattoo? Kayla and Whitney are both getting them and we want to match."

"Not now, Hailey. I'm late for work. We can talk about it tonight."

"But mom. . . ."

"Yes, Hailey, yes, alright. We'll talk more tonight. . . ." Jennifer exclaimed as she headed to the door. Just then she heard her computer signal an incoming e-mail message. Jennifer thought, "I'd better just get going. I can check it on my phone on the way to pick up Greta."

As Hailey waited for the school bus, she quickly texted her friends, "Awesome! My mom said YES!"

Can you relate to Jennifer? We live in an era where multitasking has become a norm. Part of that multitasking includes communicating both to ourselves and with others. Like Jennifer, we get ready for work or school while checking voice messages and Facebook pages, answering texts and e-mails, as well as eating breakfast, monitoring the forecast, and getting dressed.

Some argue that the same technology that was supposed to simplify life has actually made it more complex. In fact, communication today extends across interpersonal, group, and public communication contexts and face-to-face and mediated channels. Jennifer, for example, composed her grocery list on *a piece of paper* while learning about the weather forecast on *television* and texting Greta about borrowing an umbrella. Then, when Hailey tried to talk to her face to face, Jennifer was so distracted that her communication signals implied to Hailey that she had granted Hailey permission to get a tattoo.

Unfortunately, one of the negative consequences of having so many modes through which to communicate is the false sense of competence it gives us about our ability to have several conversations at once. This chapter and the ones that follow focus on why it's important to improve your communication skills, *how* to improve them, and how to avoid the negative consequences of ineffective communication that can lead to misunderstandings and hurt our personal and professional relationships.

Our ability to make and keep friends, to be good members of our families, to have satisfying intimate relationships, to participate in or lead groups, and to prepare and present speeches depends on our communication skills. So what you learn about effective communication in this book and the specific skills you practice as a result is important because it will help you improve your relationships with others.

Not only that, but effective communication is crucial to success in the workplace. Time and time again, studies have concluded that, for almost any job, employers seek oral communication, teamwork, and interpersonal skills (College learning for the new global century, 2008; Hansen & Hansen, 2007; Young, 2003). For example, an article on the role of communication in the workplace reported that in engineering, a highly technical field, speaking skills were very important for 72 percent of the employers surveyed (Darling & Dannels, 2003, p. 12). A survey by the National Association of Colleges and Employers (Hart, 2006) reported the top 10 personal qualities and skills that employers seek from college graduates. The number one skill was communication, including face-to-face speaking, presentational speaking, and writing. Other "Top 10" skills, which you will learn about and practice in this course, include teamwork skills (number three), analytical skills (number five), interpersonal skills (number eight), and problem-solving skills (number nine). The employers also said these skills are, unfortunately, the ones many new graduates lack (Hart, 2010). Thus, what you learn from this book can significantly increase your ability to get a job and be successful in your chosen career.

We begin this chapter by describing the nature of communication and the communication process followed by several principles of communication and five tenets of ethical communication. Finally, we explain how to develop a personal communication improvement plan to hone your skills based on what you learn throughout the semester.

CONSIDER *THIS....*

Has anyone ever started multitasking by texting or checking e-mail during a conversation with you? How did that affect the conversation? If you ever check texts or e-mail while engaged in a conversation, how might it affect your ability to focus on the conversation and your relationship with others?

What are your career goals? How might effective communication help you achieve them?

Business meeting in an office

The Nature of Communication

Communication is a complex process through which we express, interpret, and coordinate messages with others in order to create shared meaning, meet social goals, manage personal identity, and carry out our relationships. At its core, communication is about messages.

Messages are the verbal utterances, visual images, and nonverbal behaviors used to convey thoughts and feelings. We refer to the process of creating messages as **encoding** and the process of interpreting them as **decoding**. So when the toddler points to her bottle and cries out "Ba-ba," her message (comprised of a nonverbal gesture—pointing—and a verbal utterance—"Ba-ba,") expresses her desire to have her father hand her the bottle of milk she sees on the table. How her father responds, however, depends on how he decodes it. He might respond by handing her the bottle or by saying, "Sorry, cutie, the bottle is empty." Or he may just look at her with a puzzled expression on his face. Either response is also a message. **Feedback** is a message that comes in response to a message indicating how it was interpreted.

Canned Plans and Scripts

How do we form and interpret messages? We do so, in part, based on our canned plans and scripts. A **canned plan** is a "mental library" of scripts each of us draws from to create messages based on what worked for us or others in the past (Berger, 1997). A **script** is an actual text of what to say and do in a specific situation. We have canned plans and scripts for a wide variety of typical interactions like greeting people, making small talk, giving advice, complimenting or criticizing someone, and persuading others. Suppose you spot a good friend sitting at a table across the room from you at a restaurant. What do you do? Your answer is based on your canned "greeting" plan.

We develop canned plans and scripts from our own previous experiences and by observing what appears to work for other people (even fictitious people we see on TV or in movies) (Frank, Prestin, Chen, & Nabi, 2009). Can you remember the first time you asked someone out on a date? How nervous were you? Did you mentally practice what you would say? How many different ways did you imagine bringing up the subject? Where did your ideas come from? In all likelihood they came from your canned plan of "ask for a date" scripts. We draw on scripts from our canned plans as we form a message and usually customize what we say based on the person and the situation. For example, you might have several canned "greeting" plan scripts to draw from when addressing a close friend, a parent, a supervisor, or a stranger.

communication

the process through which we express, interpret, and coordinate messages with others

messages

the verbal utterances, visual images, and nonverbal behaviors used to convey thoughts and feelings

encoding

the process of putting our thoughts and feelings into words and nonverbal behaviors

decoding

the process of interpreting another's message

feedback

reactions and responses to messages

canned plan

a "mental library" of scripts each of us draws from to create messages based on what worked for us in the past or that we have heard or used numerous times in similar situations

script

an actual text of what to say and do in a specific situation

THE AUDIENCE *BEYOND*

Patricia was crafting an e-mail to her instructor about the upcoming assignment. Because she wasn't sure whether her instructor had a Ph.D., she didn't want to use the title of "Dr." in her salutation because that would not be appropriate if her instructor did not have a doctorate. But she also wanted to demonstrate respect. So she used the canned salutation script of "Dear *Professor* Smith," which can be used for an instructor who may or may not hold a Ph.D.

Sometimes we develop canned plans and scripts by observing fictional characters or people on TV. What television programs might have influenced your canned plans and scripts? Why and how?

CONSIDER THIS....

What do you say when you greet (a) a stranger you pass on the sidewalk, (b) a casual friend, (c) a romantic partner, or (d) a family member? In what ways are the scripts similar and different? Why?

communication contexts

the values, attitudes, beliefs, orientations, and underlying assumptions prevalent among people in a society

physical context

a communication encounter's location, environmental conditions (temperature, lighting, noise level), distance between communicators, seating arrangements, and time of day

When we don't have a good script for a specific situation, we search for canned plans and scripts that are *similar to* the current situation and customize an appropriate message. For example, if you have never met a celebrity, you probably don't have a greeting script for doing so in your canned plan mental library. Suppose you are in line at a checkout counter and see Taylor Swift standing in front of you. What would you say? "Hi Taylor?" "Hi, Ms. Swift?" "OMG, are you really Taylor Swift?" "Hi, Taylor" is probably drawn from your "greet a friend" canned plan library, "Hi, Ms. Swift," from your "show-respect" canned plan library and "OMG..." from your "I-can't-believe-it" canned plan library.

The point here is that we don't usually start from scratch to form messages. Instead we recognize what type of message we want to form, search our mental canned plan library for an appropriate script, and then customize it to fit the unique parts of the current situation. All of this mental choosing happens in nanoseconds and somewhat automatically. We also use our canned plans and scripts when we interpret messages from others.

Obviously, the larger your canned plan library and the more scripts you have for each canned plan, the more likely you will be to form appropriate and effective messages, as well as understand and respond appropriately to the messages of others.

Communication Contexts

According to noted German philosopher Jürgen Habermas, the ideal communication situation is impossible to achieve, but considering its contexts as we communicate can move us closer to that goal (Littlejohn & Foss, 2010). The context in which a message is embedded affects the expectations of the participants, the meaning these participants derive, and their subsequent behavior. The **communication context** is made up of the physical, social, historical, psychological, and cultural situations that surround a communication event.

The **physical context** includes the location, the environmental conditions (temperature, lighting, noise level), and the physical proximity of participants to each other. Increasingly, however, communication occurs via smart phones and over the Internet. And while e-communication allows us to interact at a distance, our ability to share meaning may be affected by the media we use. For instance, when you telephone someone, you lose nonverbal cues like posture, gestures, eye contact, and facial expressions that are part of a face-to-face message. Without these cues, you have less information on which to base your interpretation. E-mail and text messages are missing even more of the nonverbal cues that help us interpret them accurately.

THE AUDIENCE *BEYOND*

Jonas gasped as he read the e-mail message from his instructor. Was his instructor actually accusing him of cheating? Angrily, he began to defend himself in a reply, but then stopped. Instead, he set up an appointment to meet with his instructor to discuss the issue face to face so that there would be less risk of misinterpreting each other.

The **social context** is the nature of the relationship that already exists between the participants. The better you know someone and the better relationship you have with them, the more likely you are to accurately interpret their messages.

The **historical context** is the background provided by previous communication between the participants. For instance, suppose Chas texts Anna to tell her he will pick up the draft of the report they had left for their manager. When Anna sees Chas at lunch later that day, she says, "Did you get it?" Another person listening to the conversation would have no idea what the "it" is to which Anna is referring. Yet Chas may well reply, "It's on my desk." Anna and Chas understand one another because of their earlier exchange.

The **psychological context** includes the moods and feelings each person brings to the encounter. For instance, suppose Corinne is under a great deal of stress. While she is studying for an exam, a friend stops by and asks her to take a break to go to the gym. Corinne, who is normally good-natured, may respond with an irritated tone of voice, which her friend may misinterpret as Corinne being mad at him.

The **cultural context** includes the beliefs, values, orientations, underlying assumptions, and rituals that belong to a specific culture (Samovar, Porter, & McDaniel, 2009). Everyone is part of one or more cultural groups (e.g., race, ethnicity, religion, age, sex, gender, sexual orientation, physical ability). When two people from different cultures interact, misunderstandings may occur because of their different cultural values, beliefs, orientations, and rituals. The *Pop Comm!* in this chapter (see p. 13) describes how the cultural ritual of mourning is changing in the United States today.

Communication Settings

The communication setting also affects how we form and interpret messages. **Communication settings** differ based on the number of participants and the level of formality in the interactions (Littlejohn & Foss, 2008, pp. 52–53). These settings are intrapersonal, interpersonal, small group, public, and mass.

Intrapersonal communication refers to the interactions that occur in our minds when we are talking to ourselves. We usually don't verbalize our intrapersonal communication. When you sit in class and think about what you'll do later that day or when you send yourself a reminder note as an e-mail or text message, you are communicating intrapersonally. A lot of our intrapersonal communication occurs subconsciously (Kellerman, 1992). When we drive into the driveway "without thinking," we are communicating intrapersonally on a subconscious level. The study of intrapersonal communication often focuses on its role in shaping self-perceptions and in managing communication apprehension, that is, the fear associated with communicating with others (Richmond & McCroskey, 1997). Our study of intrapersonal communication focuses on self-talk as a means to improve self-concept and self-esteem and, ultimately, communication competence in a variety of situations.

social context

the nature of the relationship that exists between participants

historical context

the background provided by previous communication episodes between the participants that influence understandings in the current encounter

psychological context

the mood and feelings each person brings to a conversation

cultural context

the beliefs, values, orientations, underlying assumptions, and rituals that belong to a specific culture

communication setting

the different communication environments within which people interact, characterized by the number of participants and the extent to which the interaction is formal or informal

intrapersonal communication

the interactions that occur in a person's mind when he or she is talking with himself or herself

We communicate intrapersonally when we talk to ourselves, reflect about people and events, and write in a journal. What are some examples of your own intrapersonal communication activities today?

interpersonal communication

informal interaction between two people who have an identifiable relationship with each other

small-group communication

three to 20 people who come together for the specific purpose of solving a problem or arriving at a decision

public communication

one participant, the speaker, delivers a message to a group of more than 20 people

CONSIDER THIS....

What are some forms of mass communication you have experienced already today?

mass communication

communication that is delivered by individuals and entities through mass media to large segments of the population at the same time

communication process

a complex set of three different and interrelated activities intended to result in shared meaning

message production

the steps you take when you wish to share your thoughts or feelings with others

Interpersonal communication is characterized by informal interaction between two people who have an identifiable relationship with each other (Knapp & Daly, 2002). Talking to a friend between classes, visiting on the phone with your mother, and texting or chatting online with your brother are all examples of interpersonal communication. In Part II of this book, our study of interpersonal communication includes the exploration of how we develop, maintain, improve, and end interpersonal relationships.

Small-group communication typically involves three to 20 people who come together to communicate with one another (Beebe & Masterson, 2006; Hirokawa, Cathcart, Samovar, & Henman, 2003). Examples of small groups include a family, a group of friends, a group of classmates working on a project, and a workplace management team. Small-group communication can occur in face-to-face settings, as well as online through electronic mailing lists, discussion boards, virtual meetings, and blogs. In Part III, our study of small groups focuses on the characteristics of effective groups, ethical and effective communication in groups, leadership, problem-solving, conflict, and group presentations.

Public communication is delivered to audiences of more than 20 people. Examples include public speeches, presentations, and forums we may experience in person or via mediated or technology-driven channels. For example, when President Barack Obama delivered his inaugural address some people were there, others watched on TV or the Internet as he spoke, and still others viewed it later in the form of televised snippets or a Web site video such as YouTube. The Internet is also becoming the medium of choice for posting job ads and résumés, for advertising and buying products, and for political activism. In Part IV, our study of public communication focuses on preparing, practicing, and delivering effective oral presentations in both face-to-face and virtual environments.

Mass communication is delivered by individuals and entities through mass media to large segments of the population at the same time. Some examples include newspaper and magazine articles and advertisements, as well as radio and television programs and advertisements. The bonus chapter on mass communication and media literacy focuses specifically on effective mass communication in both flat print and digital modalities.

The Communication Process

The **communication process** is a complex set of three different and interrelated activities intended to result in shared meaning (Burleson, 2009). These processes are affected by the channels used and by interference/noise.

Sub-Processes of Communication

Three sub-processes that must be performed to achieve shared meaning are message production, message interpretation, and interaction coordination.

First, **message production** is what you do when you *encode* a message. You begin by forming goals based on your understanding of the situation and your values, ethics, and needs. Based on these goals, you recall a canned plan and script that was effective in achieving similar goals and adapt it to the current situation. Then you share your message.

Second, **message interpretation** is what you do when you *decode* a message. The process begins when you notice someone is trying to communicate with you. You read or listen to their words, observe their nonverbal behavior, and take note of other visuals. You then interpret the message based on the canned plan scripts you remember that seem similar. Based on this interpretation, you prepare a feedback message, which leads into the third sub-process.

Interaction coordination consists of the behavioral adjustments each participant makes in an attempt to create shared meaning (Burgoon, 1998). For example, if your partner's message is more positive than what you expected, you might adjust your behavior by mirroring that positive behavior. If your partner's message is more negative than what you expected, you might behave in a more positive way in order to encourage your partner to reciprocate or you might respond in kind with a negative message of your own.

In what ways have you engaged in interaction coordination with an advisor, instructor, or supervisor?

message interpretation

the steps you take when you try to understand a message.

interaction coordination

the actions each participant takes to adjust their behavior to that of their partner

Let's look at an example of interaction coordination. Suppose you go to see your instructor about a paper that earned a lower grade than you expected. If you expect your instructor to be offended and defensive you might begin with a very assertive statement like, "I didn't deserve a C- on this paper." Perhaps your instructor's response to you is, "Well, I could have made a mistake, let's talk about what you thought I missed." Her openness to your point of view is more positive than what you expected, which might lead you to adjust what you were planning to say to match her tone. On the other hand, suppose your instructor mirrors your assertiveness with a response that is more negative than you expected. Suppose she says, "Well, you're not the one giving the grade, are you?" You may try to bring her into a more cooperative stance by becoming less assertive and more accommodating. So you might respond, "I'm sorry, I didn't mean to question your authority, but I don't understand what I did wrong." In so doing, you are inviting your instructor to match your conciliatory message with one of her own.

In sum, shared meaning occurs when the receiver's interpretation is similar to what the speaker intended. We can usually gauge the extent to which shared meaning is achieved by the sender's response to the feedback message. For example, Sarah says to Nick, "I dropped my phone and it broke." Nick replies, "Cool, now you can get a Droid™." To which Sarah responds, "No, you don't understand, I can't afford to buy a new phone." Sarah's response to Nick's feedback message lets Nick know he misunderstood her. The extent to which we achieve shared meaning can be affected by the channels we use and by the interference/noise that compete with our messages.

channel

the route traveled by the message and the means of transportation

Channels

Channels are both the route traveled by the message and the means of transportation. Face-to-face communication has three basic channels: verbal symbols, nonverbal cues, and visual images. Technologically mediated communication uses these same channels, though nonverbal cues such as movements, touch, and gestures are represented by visual symbols like **emoticons** (textual images that symbolize the sender's mood, emotion, or facial expressions) and **acronyms** (abbreviations that stand in for common phrases). For example, in a

emoticons

textual images that symbolize the sender's mood, emotion, or facial expressions

acronyms

abbreviations that stand in for common phrases

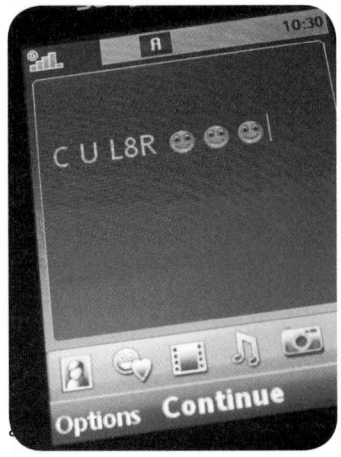

What emoticons and acronyms do you use in text messages and why?

interference (noise)

any stimulus that interferes with the process of sharing meaning

internal noise

thoughts and feelings that compete for attention and interfere with the communication process

semantic noise

distractions aroused by certain word choices that take our attention away from the main message

face-to-face interaction, Barry might express his frustration about a poor grade verbally by noting why he thought the grade was unfair, visually by showing the assignment along with the grading criteria for it, and nonverbally by raising his voice and shaking his fist. In an online interaction, however, he might need to insert a frowning-face emoticon (☹) or the acronym "POed" to represent those nonverbal behaviors.

Interference/Noise

Interference or **noise** can be external, internal, or semantic. **External noises** are sights, sounds, and other stimuli that draw people's attention away from the message. For instance, a pop-up advertisement may draw your attention away from a Web page or blog. Likewise, static or service interruptions can play havoc in cell phone conversations, the sound of a fire engine may distract you from a professor's lecture, or the smell of donuts may interfere with your train of thought during a conversation with a friend.

Internal noises are thoughts and feelings that draw people's attention away from the message. For example, you might lose track of a message because you are daydreaming or thinking about something you need to do later. **Semantic noises** are emotional distractions aroused by specific word choices. For instance, if someone describes a forty-year-old secretary as "the girl in the office," you may think "girl" is a condescending term for a forty-year-old woman and not hear the rest of what your friend has to say.

A Model of the Communication Process

In summary, let's look at a graphic model of a message exchange between two people presented in Figure 1.1. The process begins when one person who we will call Andy is motivated to share his thoughts with another person, Taylor. Andy reviews the communication situation, including the communication context, and sorts through the scripts in his canned plan library to find one he thinks will be appropriate. Based on this script, he encodes a customized message and shares it with Taylor.

Taylor decodes the message using her understanding of the situation and matching it to scripts in her canned plan library. She might misinterpret Andy's intended meaning because she is distracted by external, internal, or semantic interference/noise, or because her scripts don't match Andy's. Taylor encodes a feedback message using a script from her canned plan library as a guide. She then shares her feedback message and Andy decodes it. If Taylor understood what Andy was saying, he will extend the conversation. If, on the other hand, Andy believes Taylor misunderstood his meaning, he will try to clarify what he meant before extending the conversation. Finally, the communication process is not linear. In other words, both Andy and Taylor simultaneously encode and decode verbal and nonverbal messages throughout the message exchange.

THE AUDIENCE *BEYOND*

Clive shut down his computer and cell phone while participating in the conference call so he wouldn't be tempted to check messages while he should be focused on the conversation. Doing so reduced potential interference/noise that might distract him from the message at hand.

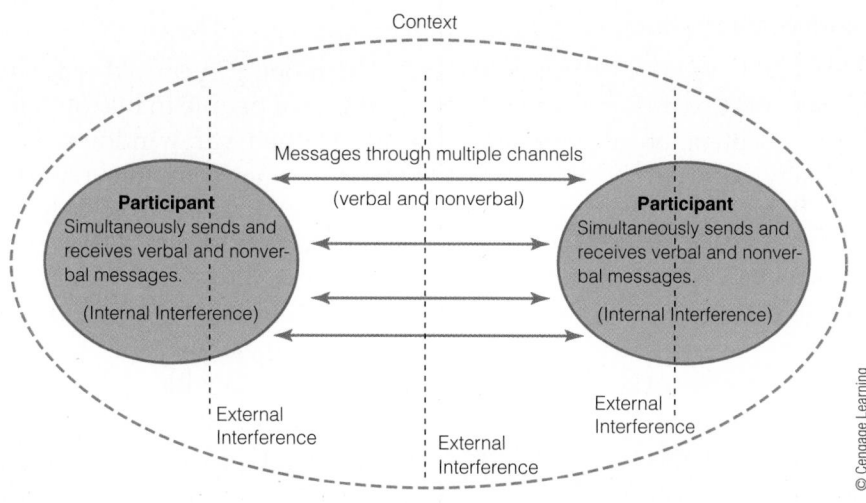

Context

Messages through multiple channels

(verbal and nonverbal)

Participant
Simultaneously sends and receives verbal and nonverbal messages.

(Internal Interference)

Participant
Simultaneously sends and receives verbal and nonverbal messages.

(Internal Interference)

External Interference

External Interference

External Interference

© Cengage Learning

Figure 1.1

Model of communication

POP COMM!

Mourning in the United States, 21st-Century Style

© Mydeathspace.com

Mourning is a universal human communication process of celebrating the life of someone while grieving his or her death. Mourning rituals and traditions vary by culture and religion and change over time. So it is not surprising that mourning in the United States in the 21st century is adapting past practices to modern life.

Mourning rituals include norms for how the body of the deceased is dealt with, burial and commemorative rituals, symbols of mourning, and comforting practices. In the past, personally washing, dressing, and preparing the body for burial enabled mourners to present the deceased as they would like the person to be remembered. Burial and commemorative rituals gave family and friends an opportunity to gather, exchange memories, comfort those closest to the deceased, and receive comfort in return. Graves were places where those close to the deceased could go to "talk" to the departed and recall memories. Family members would often withdraw into their homes for a period of time to grieve. Those closest to the person who died often wore symbols of

their status as mourners. Mourning clothes and tokens served as signals that the person was grieving and should be accorded extra gentleness.

Today in the United States, most families do not personally prepare the body of loved ones for burial or wear special mourning clothes. Instead, many of the rituals traditionally associated with funerals and memorial services often take place online.

Increasingly, one or more family members may prepare a commemorative Web page that memorializes the life of the departed. Web sites such as Legacy.com, MyDeathSpace.com, and Memory-Of.com facilitate the creation of these interactive online memorials. An article in the *Boston Globe* recounted the story of Shawn Kelley, who created a "moving tribute" to his brother Michael, a National Guardsman killed in Afghanistan. The 60-second video features a slide show of images of Michael growing up while quiet classical music plays softly and a voice-over recounts Michael's attributes and interests. Shawn reported that it made him feel good to be able to "talk" about his brother, and over a year later he was still visiting the site to watch the video and to view the messages left by family members and friends (Plumb, 2006).

Interactive memorial Web sites also have become a "place" where mourners can "visit" with their departed loved one and connect with other mourners, activities that traditionally occurred at a funeral or memorial service. Today, for example, Legacy.com hosts over 50,000 permanent memorials and reports being visited by over 10 million users each month (Plumb, 2009).

The somber mourning clothes of past generations have also given way to newer ways of marking oneself as in mourning. Today family members and friends may wear T-shirts imprinted with pictures of the deceased. This practice is most common when the departed is young and died a violent death. According to Montana Miller, professor of popular culture at Bowling Green State University, the tradition of wearing commemorative T-shirts originated with West Coast gangs in the early 1990s (Moser, 2005).

Not only do people use T-shirts to signal mourning, but they also design decals to place on cars and bikes. In a highly mobile society, decals are visual markers that can not only memorialize a loved one who died but can also connect mourners to others who have suffered a similar loss. When one 17-year-old was shot and killed, hundreds of people in his town put memorial decals in their car windows. Four years later the young man's mother reported that seeing those decals continued to help her with her grieving process (Moser, 2005).

Although we may no longer personally prepare the dead for burial or wear somber formal mourning clothes, we still need to connect and communicate with others as we grieve, and we continue to evolve new methods for doing so.

Questions to Ponder

1. How did you/do you mourn when someone you care about dies?

2. Do you mourn differently today than you did when you were younger? Explain.

3. Do you mourn differently based on your relationship with the deceased (e.g., friend, family member)? Explain.

4. Do you ever mourn a relationship that ends (e.g., romantic relationship, friendship), and if so, why and how?

Characteristics of Communication

Several communication characteristics provide a foundation for practicing and improving communication skills. In this section, we discuss eight of them.

Communication Has Purpose

Whenever we communicate, we have a purpose for doing so. The purpose may be serious or trivial, and we may or may not be aware of it at the time. Here we list five basic purposes we'll be addressing throughout the book.

1. **We communicate to develop and maintain our sense of self.** Through our interactions, we learn who we are and what we are good at.

2. **We communicate to meet our social needs.** Just as we need food, water, and shelter, so too do we need contact with other people. Two people may converse happily for hours, chatting about inconsequential matters that neither one remembers later. Still, their communication has functioned to meet the important need to simply talk with another human being.

3. **We communicate to develop and maintain relationships.** Not only do we communicate to meet simple social needs, but also to develop relationships. For example, when Beth calls Leah to ask whether she'd like to join her for

lunch to discuss a class project, her purpose actually may be to resolve a recent misunderstanding, because she wants to maintain a positive relationship with Leah.

4. **We communicate to exchange information.** Whether trying to decide how warmly to dress or whom to vote for in the next election, we all communicate to exchange information. We do so through observation, reading, and direct communication with others, whether face-to-face, via text messaging, or online through e-mail and social networking sites such as Facebook and Twitter.

5. **We communicate to influence others.** We may communicate to try to convince friends to go to a particular restaurant or to see a certain movie, a supervisor to alter the work schedule, or an instructor to change a grade.

Communication Is Continuous

We are always sending and interpreting messages. Even silence communicates if another person infers meaning from it. Why? Because our nonverbal behavior represents reactions to our environment and to the people around us. If we are cold, we might shiver; if we are hot or nervous, we might perspire; if we are bored, happy, or confused, our nonverbal language will probably show it.

Communication Is Irreversible

Once an exchange takes place, we can never go back in time and erase the communication. We might be able to repair damage we have done, but the message has been communicated. When you participate in an online discussion or leave a post on a blog, you are leaving an electronic "footprint" that others can follow and read. E-mails, IMs, and text messages are not always completely private either. Once you push the "send" button, not only can't you take it back, but you have little control over who the receiver might forward it to or how it might be used publicly.

Communication Is Situated

When we say that communication is situated we mean it occurs within a specific communication setting that affects how the messages are produced, interpreted, and coordinated (Burleson, 2009). Do you swear when you talk? For most of us the answer to that is "it depends." While we may occasionally use curse words when we are with friends or peers, many of us wouldn't consider swearing in front of our supervisors, teachers, grandmothers, or religious leaders. Similarly, the interpretation of the statement "I love you" varies depending on the setting. During a candlelit anniversary dinner, it may be interpreted as a statement of romantic feelings. If a mother says it as she greets her daughter, it may be interpreted as motherly love. If it is made in response to a joke delivered by someone in a group of friends gathered to watch a football game, it may be interpreted as

THE AUDIENCE BEYOND

Sarah thought about posting a picture of herself with her friends at the local pub on her Facebook page but ultimately decided not to since she had *friended* several work colleagues including her supervisor, and she didn't think doing so would be good for her professional image.

How might you signal trust and intimacy during a conversation?

index

measure of the emotional temperature of our relationship at the time

trust

the extent to which partners rely on, depend on, and have faith that their partners will not intentionally do anything to harm them

control

the degree to which one participant is perceived to be more dominant or powerful

complementary feedback

a message that signals agreement about who is in control

symmetrical feedback

a message that signals disagreement about who is in control

intimacy

the degree of emotional closeness, acceptance, and disclosure in a relationship

a complement for being clever. So what is said and what it means depends on the situation.

Communication Is Indexical

How we communicate is also an **index** or measure of the emotional temperature of our relationship at the time. For instance, when they are getting in the car to leave for a holiday, Laura says to Darryl, "I remembered to bring the map." She is not just reporting information. Through her tone of voice and other nonverbal cues, she is also communicating something about the relationship, such as, "You can always depend on me," or "You never remember to think of these things."

A message exchange can also signal the level of trust; who has control; and the degree of intimacy in a relationship (Millar & Rogers, 1987).

Trust is the extent to which partners rely on, depend on, and have faith that their partners will not intentionally do anything to harm them. For instance, Mark says, "I'll do the final edits and turn in the paper." Sandy replies, "Never mind, I'll do it so that it won't be late," which may signal that she doesn't trust Mark to get the group's paper in on time.

Control is the extent to which each person has power or is "in charge" in the relationship. When Tom says to Sue, "I know you're concerned about the budget, but I'll see to it that we have enough money to cover everything," through his words, tone of voice, and nonverbal behavior, he is signaling that he is "in charge" of the finances. In turn, Sue may respond by either verbally responding or nonverbally showing she agrees with him or by challenging him and asserting her desire to control the budget. In other words, control is communicated with either complementary or symmetrical feedback. **Complementary feedback** signals agreement about who is in control, whereas **symmetrical feedback** signals disagreement. If Sue says, "Great, I'm glad you're looking after it," her feedback complements his message. But if Sue responds, "Wait a minute, you're the one who overdrew our checking account last month," she is challenging his control with a symmetrical response. Relational control is not negotiated in a single exchange, but through many message exchanges over time. The point, however, is that control is negotiated through communication.

Intimacy is the degree of emotional closeness, acceptance, and disclosure in a relationship. When Cody asks Madison what she is thinking about, and Madison begins to pour out her problems, she is revealing the degree of intimacy she feels in the relationship. Or, should she reply, "Oh I'm not really thinking about anything important. Did you hear the news this morning about … ," her subject change signals that the relationship is not intimate enough to share her problems.

Communication Is Learned

Just as we learn to walk, so do we learn to communicate. Because communication is learned, we can always improve our ability to communicate.

Communication Messages Vary in Conscious Thought

Recall that creating shared meaning involves encoding and decoding verbal messages, nonverbal cues, and even visual images. Our messages may (1) occur spontaneously, (2) be based on a "script," or (3) be carefully constructed.

Many messages are **spontaneous expressions**, spoken without much conscious thought. For example, when you burn your finger, you may blurt out, "Ouch!" When something goes right, you may break into a broad smile. Some messages are *scripted* and drawn from our canned plan libraries. Finally, some are **constructed messages** that are formed carefully and thoughtfully when our known scripts are inadequate for the situation.

spontaneous expressions

spoken without much conscious thought

constructed messages

those that formed carefully and thoughtfully when our known scripts are inadequate for the situation

Communication Is Guided by Cultural Norms

Culture may be defined as a system of shared beliefs, values, symbols, and behaviors. How messages are formed and interpreted depends on the cultural background of the participants. We need to be mindful of our communication behavior as we interact with others whose cultural backgrounds differ from our own, so we don't unintentionally communicate in ways that are culturally inappropriate or insensitive.

culture

a system of shared beliefs, values, symbols, and behaviors

Throughout the history of the United States, we've experienced huge migrations of people from different parts of the world. According to the *New York Times Almanac* (Wright, 2002), at the turn of the 21st century, people of Latin and Asian decent constituted 12.5 percent and 3.8 percent, respectively, of the total U.S. population. About 2.4 percent of the population regards itself as multiracial. Combined with the approximately 13 percent of our population that is of African descent, these four groups account for nearly 32 percent of the total population. According to the U.S. Census Bureau, this figure is predicted to rise to nearly 50 percent by 2050 (retrieved from http://www.census.gov/population/www/projections/summarytables.html on December 20, 2011).

According to Samovar, Porter, and McDaniel (2007) "a number of cultural components are particularly relevant to the student of intercultural communication. These include (1) perception, (2) patterns of cognition, (3) verbal behaviors, (4) nonverbal behaviors, and (5) the influence of context" (p. 13). Because cultural concerns permeate all of communication, each chapter of this book points out when certain concepts and skills may be viewed differently by members of various cultural groups. And authors of the *Diverse Voices* feature found in many chapters explain how they or their culture *views* a concept presented in the text.

Communication and Ethics

Can people depend on you to tell the truth? Do you do what you say you will do? Can people count on you to be respectful? In any encounter, we choose whether to behave in a way others view as ethical. **Ethics** is a set of moral principles that may be held by a society, a group, or an individual. So an ethical standard does not tell us exactly what to do in any given situation, only what general principles to consider when deciding how to behave.

ethics

a set of moral principles that may be held by a society, a group, or an individual

Ethical Principles

Every field of study—from psychology and biology to sociology and history—has a set of ethical principles designed to guide the practice of that field.

Communication is no exception. Every time we communicate, we make choices with ethical implications. The general principles that guide ethical communication include:

1. **Ethical communicators are truthful and honest.** "An honest person is widely regarded as a moral person, and honesty is a central concept to ethics as the foundation for a moral life" (Terkel & Duval, 1999, p. 122). In other words, we should not intentionally try to deceive others.

2. **Ethical communicators act with integrity.** Integrity is maintaining consistency between what we say we believe and what we do. The person who says, "Do what I say, not what I do," lacks integrity, while the person who "practices what he or she preaches," acts with integrity. Integrity is basically the opposite of hypocrisy.

3. **Ethical communicators behave fairly.** A fair person is impartial. To be fair to someone is to gather all of the relevant facts, consider only circumstances relevant to the decision at hand, and not be swayed by prejudice or irrelevancies. For example, if two siblings are fighting, their mother exercises fairness if she allows both children to explain "their side" before she decides what to do.

4. **Ethical communicators demonstrate respect.** Respect is showing regard for someone else, their point of view, and their rights. We demonstrate respect through listening and understanding others' points of view, even when they differ from our own.

5. **Ethical communicators are responsible.** Responsible communicators recognize the power of words. Our messages can hurt others and their reputations. So we act responsibly when we refrain from gossiping, spreading rumors, bullying, and so forth.

Dark Side Messages

dark side messages

not ethical and/or appropriate

The "dark side" is a metaphor for inappropriate and/or unethical communication (Spitzberg & Cupach, 2011). It follows, then, that **dark side messages** are ones that are not ethical and/or appropriate (see Figure 1.2).

When Liz, who just spent a fortune having her hair cut and colored asks, "Do you like my new hairstyle?" and you think it is awful, how do you answer? The bright side answer would be one that is both ethical (honest, respectful, empathetic, etc.) and appropriate (sensitive to Liz's feelings and maintaining a good relationship). The hard side answer would be ethical, but it will likely hurt Liz and damage your relationship with her. The easy side would be unethical but would spare Liz's feelings. The evil dark side would be both unethical and inappropriate. Let's look at how someone might respond to Liz:

Bright side response: "Liz, it doesn't matter what I think. I can see that you really like how it looks and that makes me happy."

Hard dark side response: "Wow Liz, it's a dramatic change. I liked your hair long and I'd always admired the red highlights you had. But I'm sure it will grow on me."

Easy dark side response: "It looks great."

	Ethical	
Appropriate	Bright Side	Hard Side
	Easy Side	Evil Dark Side
	Unethical	**Inappropriate**

© Cengage Learning

Figure 1.2

Understanding dark side messages

Evil dark side response: "It doesn't matter what you do to your hair, you're still fat and ugly."

As you can see, relationships may benefit from bright, hard, and easy side responses depending on the situation. But dark side responses damage people and relationships.

We often face ethical dilemmas and must sort out what is more or less right or wrong. In making these decisions, we reveal our ethical communication standards. Each chapter in this book features "A Question of Ethics" case related to material in that chapter. Consider each case and the questions we pose based on these ethical communication principles.

Increasing Your Communication Competence

When we communicate effectively and ethically, it feels good. And when we experience the opposite, we may get frustrated and even angry. So let's look what it means to be a competent communicator, how communication anxiety can affect competence, and how to develop and use your own communication improvement plan to improve chances for success in your interactions with others.

Communication Competence

Communication competence is the impression that communicative behavior is both appropriate and effective in a given situation (Spitzberg, 2000, p. 375). Communication is *effective* when it achieves its goals and *appropriate* when it conforms to what is expected in a situation. Competence is a judgment people make about others. Our goal is to communicate in ways that increase the likelihood that others will judge us as competent.

Communication competence is achieved through personal motivation, knowledge acquisition, and skills practice (Spitzberg, 2000, p. 377). Motivation is important because we will only be able to improve our communication if we are *motivated*—that is, if we want to improve. Knowledge is important because we must know what to do to increase competence. The more knowledge we have about how to behave in a given situation, the more likely we are to convey competence. Skill is important because we must act in ways that are consistent with our communication knowledge. The more skills we have, the more likely we are to structure our messages effectively and appropriately.

In addition to motivation, knowledge, and skills, credibility and social ease also influence whether others perceive us to be competent communicators. **Credibility** is a perception of a speaker's knowledge, trustworthiness, and warmth. Listeners are more likely to be attentive to and influenced by speakers they perceive as credible. **Social ease** means managing communication apprehension so we do not appear nervous or anxious. To be perceived as a competent communicator, we must speak in ways that convey confidence and poise. Communicators that appear apprehensive are not likely to be regarded as competent, despite their motivation or knowledge.

communication competence

the impression that communicative behavior is both appropriate and effective in a given situation

credibility

a perception of a speaker's knowledge, trustworthiness, and warmth

social ease

communicating without appearing to be anxious or nervous

Does public speaking make you nervous? If so, you are like 75% of the population. Did you know that speaking effectively requires some nervousness?

Dennis MacDonald/PhotoEdit

Communication Apprehension

communication apprehension

fear or anxiety associated with real or anticipated communication with others

Communication apprehension is "the fear or anxiety associated with real or anticipated communication with others" (McCroskey, 1977, p. 78). Although most people think of public speaking anxiety when they hear the term *communication apprehension* (CA), there are actually four different types of CA. These are traitlike CA, audience-based CA, situational CA, and context-based CA. People who experience *traitlike communication apprehension* feel anxious in most speaking situations. About 20 percent of all people experience traitlike CA (Richmond & McCroskey, 2000). People who experience *audience-based communication apprehension* feel anxious about speaking only with a certain person or group of people. *Situational communication apprehension* is a short-lived feeling of anxiety that occurs during a specific encounter, for example, during a job interview. Finally, *context-based communication apprehension* is anxiety only in a particular situation, for example, when speaking to a large group of people. All these forms of communication anxiety can be managed effectively in ways that help convey social ease. Throughout this book, we offer strategies for managing communication apprehension in various settings.

The combination of motivation, knowledge, skills, perceived credibility, and social ease make up competent communication. The goal of this book is to help you become a competent communicator in interpersonal, group, and public speaking situations.

Peanuts: © United Feature Syndicate, Inc.

COMMUNICATE ON YOUR FEET

Introduce a Classmate

The Assignment

Following your instructor's directions, partner with someone in the class. Spend some time getting to know him or her and then prepare a short 2-minute speech introducing your partner to the rest of the class.

Questions to Ask

1. What is your background? (Where were you born and raised? What is the makeup of your family? What else do you want to share about your personal background?)

Speech Assignment

2. What are you majoring in and why?

3. What are some of your personal and professional goals after college?

4. What are two personal goals you have for this class and why?

5. What is something unique about you that most people probably don't know?

Speeches of Introduction

A speech of introduction is given to acquaint a group with someone they have not met. We make short "speeches" of introduction all the time. When a friend from high school comes to visit for a weekend, you may introduce her to your friends. Not only will you tell them her name, but you will probably mention other things about her that will make it easy for your friends to talk with her. Likewise, a store manager may call the sales associates together in order to introduce a new employee. The manager might mention the new team member's previous experience, interests, and expertise that will encourage the others to respect, help, and become acquainted with the new employee.

Speeches of introduction also often precede formal addresses. The goal of the introducer is to establish the credibility of the main speaker by sharing the speaker's education, background, and expertise related to the topic and to build audience interest.

Speech to Introduce a Classmate

Because your classmate will not be giving a formal address after you introduce him or her, we suggest you organize your speech as follows:

1. **The introduction:** Start with an attention catcher—a statement, story, or question tied to something about the speaker that will pique audience curiosity. Then offer a thesis and preview of main points, which can be as simple as "I'm here today to introduce [name of person] to you by sharing something about his personal background, personal and professional goals, and something unique about him."

2. **The body:** Group the information you plan to share under two to four main points. For example, your first main point might be "personal background," your second main point "personal and professional goals," and your third main point "something unique." Then offer two or three examples or stories to illustrate what you learned regarding each main point. Create a transition statement to lead from the first main point to the second main point, as well as from the second main point to the third main point. These statements should remind listeners of the main point you are concluding and introduce the upcoming main point. For example, "Now that you know a little bit about [name of person]'s personal background, let's talk about his personal and professional goals."

3. **The conclusion:** Remind listeners of the name of the classmate you introduced and the two to four main points you discussed about him or her. Then, end with a clincher—a short sentence that wraps the speech up by referring to something you said in the speech (usually in the introduction) that will encourage listeners to want to know him or her better.

Communication Improvement Plans

A communication improvement plan consists of setting a new goal to resolve a communication problem, identifying procedures to reach the goal, and determining a way to measure progress.

Before you can write a goal statement, you must first analyze your current communication skills repertoire. After you read each chapter and practice the skills described, select one or two skills to work on. Then write down your plan in four steps.

1. **Identify the problem.** For example: *"Problem:* Even though some of the members of my class project group have not produced the work they promised, I haven't spoken up because I'm not very good at describing my feelings."

2. **State the specific goal.** A specific goal identifies a measurable outcome. For example, to deal with the problem just identified, you might write: *"Goal:* To describe my disappointment to other group members about their failure to meet deadlines."

3. **Outline a specific procedure for reaching the goal.** To develop a plan for reaching your goal, first consult the chapter that covers the skill you wish to hone. Then translate the general steps recommended in the chapter to your specific situation. For example: *"Procedure:* I will practice the steps of

WHAT WOULD YOU DO?

A Question of Ethics

Molly has just been accepted to Stanford Law School and calls her friend Terri to tell her the good news.

MOLLY: Hi Terri! Guess what? I just got accepted to Stanford Law!

TERRI: [*Surprised and disappointed*]: Oh, cool.

MOLLY: [*Sarcastic*]: Thanks–you sound so enthusiastic!

TERRI: Oh, I am. Listen, I have to go–I'm late for class.

MOLLY: Oh, OK. See you.

The women hang up, and Terri immediately calls her friend Monica.

TERRI: Monica, it's Terri.

MONICA: Hey, Terri. What's up?

TERRI: I just got some terrible news–Molly got into Stanford!

MONICA: So, what's wrong with that? I think it's great. Aren't you happy for her?

TERRI: No, not at all. I didn't get in, and I have better grades and a higher LSAT score.

MONICA: Maybe Molly had a better application.

TERRI: Or maybe it was what was on her application.

MONICA: What do you mean?

TERRI: You know what I mean. Molly's black.

MONICA: Yes, and . . . ?

TERRI: Don't you see? It's called affirmative action.

MONICA: Terri, give it a rest!

TERRI: Oh, please. You know it, and I know it. She only got in because of her race and because she's poor. Her GPA is really low and so is her LSAT.

MONICA: Did you ever stop to think that maybe she wrote an outstanding essay? Or that they thought the time she spent volunteering in that free legal clinic in her neighborhood was good background?

TERRI: Yes, but we've both read some of her papers, and we know she can't write. Listen, Monica, if you're black, Asian, American Indian, Latino, or any other minority and poor, you've got it made. You can be as stupid as Jessica Simpson and get into any law school you want. It's just not fair at all.

MONICA [**Angrily**]: No, you know what isn't fair? I'm sitting here listening to my so-called friend insult my intelligence and my ethnic background. How dare you tell me that the only reason I'll ever get into a good medical school is because I'm Latino. Listen, honey, I'll get into medical school just the same way that Molly got into law school–because of my brains, my accomplishments, and my ethical standards. And based on this conversation, it's clear that Molly and I are way ahead of you.

Describe how well each of these women followed the ethical standards for communication discussed in this chapter.

Adapted from "Racism," a case study posted on the Web site of the Ethics Connection, Markkula Center for Applied Ethics, Santa Clara University. Retrieved from http://www.scu.edu/ethics/practicing/focusareas/education/racism.html *on May 1, 2012. Used with permission.*

describing feelings. (1) I will identify the specific feeling I am experiencing. (2) I will encode the emotion I am feeling accurately. (3) I will include what has triggered the feeling. (4) I will own the feeling as mine. (5) I will then put that procedure into operation when I am talking with my group members."

4. **Devise a method for measuring progress.** A good method points to minimum requirements for determining positive progress. For example: *"Test for Making Progress Toward Goal Achievement:* I will have made progress each time I describe my feelings to my group members about missed deadlines."

> **Problem:** When I speak in class or in the student senate, I often find myself burying my head in my notes or looking at the ceiling or walls.
>
> **Goal:** To look at people more directly when I'm giving a speech.
>
> **Procedure:** I will take the time to practice oral presentations aloud in my room. (1) I will stand up just as I do in class. (2) I will pretend various objects in the room are people, and I will consciously attempt to look at those objects as I am talking. (3) When giving a speech, I will try to be aware of when I am looking at my audience and when I am not.
>
> **Test for Achieving Goal:** I will have achieved this goal when I am maintaining eye contact with my audience most of the time.

Figure 1.3

Sample communication improvement plan

© Cengage Learning

Figure 1.3 provides another example of a communication improvement plan, this one relating to a public speaking problem.

Summary

Communication is the process of creating shared meaning, whether the setting is informal conversation, group interaction, public speaking, or mass communication. Regardless of whether the message is delivered via flat print text, in a face-to-face interaction, or through mass media technology, creating shared meaning about messages is at the core of all communication.

We develop and interpret messages based, in part, on our canned plan script library for different situations. When faced with a communication encounter for which we have no canned plan and script, we modify similar scripts to address the new situation.

As we attempt to reach shared meaning about a message, we engage in a three-fold process consisting of message production, interpretation, and coordination. Two potential constraints we need to account for include communication channels and interference/noise. This is especially true when trying to multitask by having different conversations with several people at the same time.

Our communication is guided by eight characteristics. Communication is purposeful, continuous, irreversible, situated, indexical, learned, varied in conscious thought, and guided by cultural norms. Cultural norms are so crucial to how we communicate today that we discuss them throughout this book and devote Chapter 3 entirely to the complexities of effective intercultural communication.

Communication also has ethical implications. The ethical standards that influence communication include truthfulness, integrity, fairness, respect, and responsibility. Not all communication is ethical and researchers have coined the term *the dark side* to describe such unethical communication. We hope to help you learn to make smart choices about where to draw the line when it comes to ethical standards and communication.

Communication competence is the perception by others that our communication behavior is appropriate and effective. Competent communication skills can be learned, developed, and improved, and you can do so by preparing and practicing your own personal communication improvement plan.

COMMUNICATE!

RESOURCE AND ASSESSMENT CENTER

Now that you have read Chapter 1, go to the Speech Communication Course-Mate at cengagebrain.com where you'll find an interactive eBook and interactive learning tools including quizzes, flashcards, sample speech videos, audio study tools, skill-building activities, action step activities, and more. Student Workbook, Speech Builder Express 3.0, and Speech Studio 2.0 are also available.

Applying What You've Learned

Impromptu Speech Activity

1. Identify one of your "heroes." Your hero may or may not be famous. Identify one of the five ethical principles of communication this hero's life adheres to and why. In your two to three minute impromptu speech, provide at least two incidents that serve as evidence regarding how this person demonstrates/demonstrated the principle.

Assessment Activity

1. Visit your Facebook page and then click on the "Home" tab. If you don't have an account, you might make one to observe while completing this course. Read through the postings and identify which of them adhere to and do not adhere to the ethical communication principles proposed in this chapter.

Skill-Building Activities

1. Identifying Elements of the Communication Process For the following interaction, identify the message, channels, contexts, interference (noise), and feedback:

Maria and Damien are meandering through the park, talking and drinking bottled water. Damien finishes his bottle, replaces the lid, and tosses the bottle into the bushes at the side of the path. Maria, who has been listening to Damien talk, comes to a stop, puts her hands on her hips, stares at Damien, and says angrily, "I can't believe what you just did!" Damien blushes, averts his gaze, and mumbles, "Sorry, I'll get it—I just wasn't thinking." As the tension drains from Maria's face, she gives her head a playful toss, smiles, and says, "Well, just see that it doesn't happen again."

1. Message

   _____

2. Channels

   _____

3. Contexts

   a. Physical _____

   b. Social _____

   c. Historical _____

   d. Psychological _____

4. Interference (noise) _____._____

5. Feedback _____

When you're done with this activity, compare your answers to the authors' on the CourseMate for *Communicate!* at cengagebrain.com.

2. Communicating Over the Internet Consider the advantages and disadvantages of communicating via the following Internet-based mediums: e-mail, newsgroups, iChat, Gchat, social networking sites (e.g., Facebook, Twitter), and blogs. Enter your thoughts into a two-column table, with advantages in the first column and disadvantages in the second. Did your analysis produce any discoveries that surprised you?

To help you complete this activity, you can use the table worksheet provided on the CourseMate for *Communicate!* at cengagebrain.com.

Perception of Self and Others

What you'll know

- How the perception process works
- How self-perception is formed and maintained
- How we form perceptions of others
- How to increase the accuracy of our perceptions
- How perception influences and is influenced by communication

What you'll be able to do

- Employ strategies to improve the accuracy of your self-perception
- Employ strategies to improve your perception of others
- Practice perception-checking skills

Donna approached her friend Camille and said, "David and I are having a really tough time. I think he's going to break up with me."

"I'm sorry to hear that, Donna," replied Camille. "What's up?"

"Well, did you notice how quiet he was at the restaurant last night? And, on top of that, he hasn't responded to any of my texts today. He must be really mad at me."

"Yeah, he was quiet, but I just thought he was tired from the all-nighter he pulled finishing his history paper. And didn't he have to go to work really early today? You know he can't respond to texts at work."

"Yeah."

"So, if his quietness at dinner is the only thing you noticed, I think you may be jumping to a wrong conclusion," Camille said.

"Really? Do you think so? I just can't figure out what he's thinking. What do you think I should do?"

D 2

social perception

who we believe ourselves and others to be

Two different women had two different interpretations of the same man's behavior. Who's right? Is David about to break up with Donna or is he just tired? **Social perception**—who we believe ourselves and others to be—influences how we communicate. To explain how, we begin this chapter by reviewing the basics of sensory perception. Then we explore how social perception influences self-concept and self-esteem and how these self-perceptions in turn influence communication. From there we offer suggestions for improving self-perceptions, explain how and why we perceive others as we do, and finally, offer guidelines for improving our perceptions of others.

The Perception Process

perception

the process of selectively attending and assigning meaning to information

Perception is the process of selectively attending and assigning meaning to information (Gibson, 1966). At times, our perceptions of the world, other people, and ourselves agree with the perceptions of others. At other times, our perceptions are significantly different from the perceptions of other people. For each person, however, our perception becomes our reality. What one person sees, hears, and interprets is real and considered true to that person. Another person may see, hear, and interpret something entirely different from the same situation and also regard his or her different perception as real and true. When our perceptions differ from those with whom we interact, sharing meaning becomes more challenging. So how does perception work? Essentially, the brain selects some of the information it receives from the senses (sensory stimuli), organizes the information, and then interprets it.

Attention and Selection

Although we are constantly exposed to a barrage of sensory stimuli, we focus our attention on relatively little of it. Just think about how many TV channels you watch regularly compared to the number of channels offered. Or consider how many Web sites pop up when you do an Internet search. Can you imagine visiting all of them? Because we cannot focus on everything we see and hear all the time, we choose what stimuli to concentrate on based on our needs, interests, and expectations.

Needs We choose to pay attention to information that meets our biological and psychological needs. When you go to class, how well you pay attention usually depends on whether you believe the information is relevant. Your brain communicates intrapersonally by asking such questions as, "Will what I learn here help me in school, in the work world, in my personal life?"

Interests We are likely to pay attention to information that piques our interests. For instance, you may not notice music playing in the background while dining at a restaurant until you suddenly find yourself listening to an old favorite. Similarly, when you are really attracted to a person, you are more likely to

THE AUDIENCE BEYOND

Martell decided to do his research project on the Ming dynasty. When he *Googled* "Ming dynasty," 5,110,000 results appeared. He decided to focus his attention by limiting his search to "Ming dynasty technology achievements" because that's what he really needed to know to complete the project.

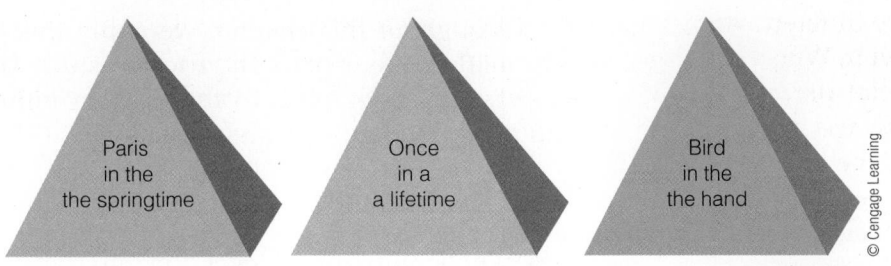

Figure 2.1

Expectations and Perception

© Cengage Learning

pay attention to what that person is saying. Likewise, when you get an e-mail from someone you don't like or don't recognize, you might simply delete it.

Expectations Finally, we are likely to see what we expect to see and miss what violates our expectations. Take a quick look at the phrases in the triangles in Figure 2.1. If you have never seen these triangles, you probably read "Paris in the springtime," "Once in a lifetime," and "Bird in the hand." But if you re-examine the words, you will see that what you perceived was not exactly what is written. Do you now see the repeated words? They are easy to miss because we don't *expect* to see the word repeated.

Organization

Through the process of attention and selection we reduce the number of stimuli our brains must process. Still, the number of stimuli we attend to at any moment is substantial. So our brains organize these stimuli using the principles of simplicity and pattern.

Simplicity If the stimuli we attend to are complex, the brain simplifies them into some commonly recognized form. Based on a quick look at what someone is wearing, how she is standing, and the expression on her face, we may perceive her as a business executive, a doctor, or a soccer mom. Similarly, we simplify the verbal messages we receive. For example, after an hour-long performance review in which his boss described four of Tony's strengths and two areas for improvement, Tony might say to Jerry, his coworker, "Well, I'd better shape up or I'm going to get fired!"

Pattern The brain also makes sense of complex stimuli by relating them to things it already recognizes. For example, when you see a crowd of people, instead of perceiving each individual, you may focus on sex and "see" men and women or on age and "see" children, teens, and adults.

Interpretation

As the brain selects and organizes information, it also assigns meaning to it. Look at these three sets of numbers. What are they?

A. 631 7348

B. 285 37 5632

C. 4632 7364 2596 2174

If you are used to seeing similar sets of numbers every day, you might interpret A as a telephone number, B as a Social Security number, and C as a credit card number. But your ability to interpret these numbers depends on your familiarity with the patterns. A French person may not recognize *631 7348* as a phone number since the pattern for phone numbers in France is: *0x xx xx xx xx.*

What assumptions do you make about this person based on how you organize and interpret what you see? Why?

automatic processing

a fast, top-down subconscious approach that draws on previous experience to make sense of what we are encountering

heuristics

short-cut rules of thumb *for understanding how to perceive something based on past experience with similar stimuli*

conscious processing

a slow deliberative approach to perceiving where we examine and reflect about the stimuli

self-perception

the overall view we have of ourselves, which includes both our self-concept and self-esteem

self-concept

the perception we have of our skills, abilities, knowledge, competencies, and personality

self-esteem

the evaluation we make about our personal worthiness based on our self-concept

Throughout this chapter, we apply this basic information about perception to the study of social perceptions of self and others as they influence and are influenced by communication.

Dual Processing

You may be thinking, "Hey, I don't go through all of these steps. I just automatically 'understand' what's going on." If so, you are right. Most of the perceptual processing we do happens subconsciously (Baumeister, 2005). This **automatic processing** is a fast top down subconscious approach of making sense of what we are encountering. In other words, we use **heuristics**, which are our short-cut *rules of thumb* for understanding how to perceive something based on past experience with similar stimuli. Consider, for example, sitting at a red light. When it turns green, you go. You probably don't consciously think about taking your foot off the brake and applying it to the gas pedal.

But what happens when we encounter things that are out of the realm of our normal experiences or expectations? Then we must exert conscious effort to make sense of what is going on. **Conscious processing** is a slow deliberative approach where we examine and reflect about the stimuli. Remember when you were first learning to drive? It took a lot of concentration to figure out what was happening on the road and how you were supposed to react. You probably thought carefully about doing things like taking your foot off the brake and applying it to the gas pedal when the light turned green.

Whether we engage in automatic or conscious processing, perception influences and is influenced by communication in a number of ways. The rest of this chapter is devoted to how we form our perceptions of self and others and the role communication plays in each.

Perception of Self

Self-perception is the overall view we have of ourselves, which includes both self-concept and self-esteem. **Self-concept** is the perception we have of our skills, abilities, knowledge, competencies, and personality (Baron, Byrne, & Branscombe, 2006). It is how we describe ourselves. **Self-esteem** is the evaluation we make about our personal worthiness based on our self-concept (based on Mruk, 2006). In this section, we explain how self-concept and self-esteem are formed and describe guidelines to improve self-perception.

Self-Concept

How do we decide what our skills, abilities, competencies, and personality traits are? We do so based on the interpretations we make about our personal experiences and how others react and respond to us.

Our personal experiences are critical to forming our self-concept. We cannot know if we are competent at something until we've tried doing it, and we cannot discover our personality traits until we uncover them through experience. We place a great deal of emphasis on our first experiences with particular phenomena (Centi, 1981). When we have a positive first experience, we are likely to believe we possess the competencies and personality traits associated with that experience. So if Sonya discovers at an early age that she does well on math problems and exams, she is likely to incorporate "competent mathematician" into her self-concept. If Sonya continues to excel at math throughout her life, that part of self-concept will be reinforced and maintained.

Similarly, when our first experience is negative, we are likely to conclude we do not possess that particular skill or trait. For instance, if you get anxious and draw a blank while giving a speech for the first time, you might conclude that you are a poor public speaker. When a negative first experience is not repeated, however, it is likely to take more than one contradictory additional experience to change our original perception. So even if you succeed the second time you give a speech, it will probably take several more positive public speaking experiences for you to change your original conclusion about not being a good public speaker.

Our self-concept is also shaped by how others react and respond to us in two important ways (Rayner, 2001). First, we use other people's comments to validate, reinforce, or alter our perceptions of who we think we are. For example, if during a brainstorming session, one of your co-workers says, "You're really a creative thinker," you may decide this comment fits your image of who you are, thus reinforcing your self-concept as someone who can think "outside the box."

Second, the feedback we receive from others may reveal abilities and personality characteristics we had never before associated with ourselves. For example, on the way back to campus after volunteering at the local Head Start Center, Janet commented to her friend Michael, "Gee, you're a natural with kids, they just flock to you." Michael thought about Janet's comment and similar ones he had received from others and decided to explore careers in early childhood education. Today he owns his own day care center and credits Janet with helping him recognize his natural ability to connect with preschoolers.

Not all reactions and responses we receive have the same effect on our self-concept. For instance, reactions and responses coming from someone we respect or someone we are close to tend to be more powerful (Aron, Mashek, & Aron, 2004; Rayner, 2001). This is especially important in families. Since self-concept begins to form early in life, information we receive from our family deeply shapes our self-concept (Demo, 1987). Thus, one major ethical responsibility of family members is to notice and comment on traits and abilities that help develop accurate and positive self-concepts in other family members. When Jeff's dad compliments him for keeping his bedroom clean because he is "so organized" or Carla's brother tells her she did a great job on her science project because she is "really smart," they are encouraging positive self-concepts.

As we interact with others, we also form an **ideal self-concept**, which is what we would like to be. For example, although Jim may know he is not naturally athletic, in his ideal self-concept he wants to be. So he plays on an intramural basketball team, works out at the gym daily, and runs in local 5k and 10k races regularly.

What three skills would *you* say you possess? What three skills would you say you do *not* possess? Consider what role positive and negative personal experiences played in determining each of them.

What are some characteristics of your self-concept and how did your family members help shape it?

ideal self-concept

what we would like to be

Our family members shape our self-concept. Can you recall a time when someone in your family praised you for something you did? Is that something you still consider yourself to be good at?

Self-Esteem

Self-concept and self-esteem are two different but related components of self-perception. Whereas self-concept is our perception of our competencies and personality traits, self-esteem is our positive or negative evaluation of those competencies and traits. So self-esteem is not just our perception of how well or poorly we do things (self-concept), but also the importance we place on what we do well or poorly (Mruk, 2006). For instance, Mitchell believes he is an excellent piano player, a faithful friend, and good with kids. But if he doesn't believe that these competencies and traits are valuable to have, then he will have low self-esteem. It takes both the perception of having a competency or personality trait and a belief that it is valuable to produce high self-esteem (Mruk, 2006). When we use our skills to achieve worthwhile endeavors, we raise our self-esteem. When we are unsuccessful in doing so, and/or when we use them in unworthy endeavors, we lower our self-esteem.

As is the case with self-concept, self-esteem depends not only on what each individual views as worthwhile but also on the ideas, morals, and values of the family and cultural group(s) to which the individual belongs. So if Mitchell comes from a family where athletic success is valued but artistic talents are not, if he hangs out with friends who don't appreciate his piano playing, and if he lives in a society where rock guitarists (not piano players) are the superstars, then his piano-playing ability may not raise his self-esteem and might actually lower it.

We've already noted that families are critically important to developing one's self-concept, but they are even more central to developing positive self-esteem. For example, when Jeff's dad pointed out that Jeff's room is always tidy, he also said he was proud of Jeff, which raised Jeff's self-esteem about being organized. And when Carla's brother said she did a great job on her science project, he reinforced the value their family places on being smart, which raised her self-esteem about that attribute of her self-concept. Unfortunately, in some families, negative messages repeatedly sent can create an inaccurate self-concept and damage self-esteem. Communicating blame, name-calling, and constantly pointing out shortcomings are particularly damaging to self-esteem and some people never fully overcome the damage done to them by members of their families.

Our self-esteem can affect the types of relationships we form and with whom. Individuals with high self-esteem tend to form relationships with others who reinforce their positive self-perception, and similarly, individuals with low self-esteem tend to form relationships with those who reinforce their negative self-perception (Leary, 2002, p. 130). This phenomenon plays out in unfortunate ways when a person (very often a woman) perpetually goes from one abusive relationship to another (Engel, 2005).

Bullying and cyberbullying, which are aggressive behaviors designed to intimidate others, also damage self-esteem. Children who are just forming their self-concepts and self-esteem, and adolescents whose self-concepts and self-esteem are in transition are particularly sensitive to bullying messages. The effects of bullying can have long-lasting effects on self-esteem. In fact, many years after bullying incidents that occurred during childhood, people may still have inaccurate self-perceptions (Hinduja & Patchin, 2010).

Cultural Norms and Self-Perceptions

Cultural norms play a critical role in shaping both our self-concept and self-esteem (Chen & Starosta, 1998). Two important ways they do so are in terms of independence/interdependence and masculinity/femininity.

In some cultures, such as the dominant American culture in the United States, people form and value independent self-perceptions. In other cultures, like the collectivist cultures of Japan and China, people form and value inter-dependent self-perceptions (Markus & Kitayama, 1991). **Independent self-perceptions** are based on the belief that traits and abilities are internal to the person and are universally applicable to all situations. The goal for someone with an independent self-perception is to demonstrate their abilities, competencies, characteristics, and personalities during interactions with others. For example, if you have an independent self-concept and believe that one of your competencies is your ability to persuade others, you gain self-esteem by demonstrating your skill, convincing others, and having others praise you for it.

Interdependent self-perceptions are based on the belief that traits and abilities are specific to a particular context or relationship. The goal of people with interdependent self-perceptions is to maintain or enhance the relationship by demonstrating the appropriate abilities and personality characteristics for the situation. People with interdependent self-perceptions don't think, "I'm really persuasive," but rather, "When I am with my friends I am able to convince them to do what is good for all of us. When I am with my father I do what he believes is best for the good of our family." High self-esteem comes from knowing when to be persuasive and when to be compliant.

Cultural norms also play a role in shaping self-perception around masculinity and femininity. In the dominant culture of the United States, for instance, many people continue to expect boys to behave in "masculine" ways and girls to behave in "feminine" ways (Wood, 2007). In the past, boys in the United States were taught to base their self-esteem on their achievements, status, and income, and girls learned that their culture valued their appearance and their relationship skills. So boys and girls developed high or low self-esteem based on how well they met these criteria (Wood, 2007).

Today these cultural norms about "appropriate" characteristics and behaviors for males and females are becoming less rigid, but they do still exist and are promoted incessantly in popular culture and entertainment media. Consider just about any television sitcom (e.g., *Two and a Half Men* and even *Modern Family*). Such programs continue to portray women as the "natural" caregivers for the family, and when men attempt to perform a caregiver behavior, they often make a mess of the situation. Think about your family experiences growing up. How do they compare? Similarly, in terms of appearance, you only need to flip through the pages of any popular magazine to see the narrowly defined perceptions of what is valued as "ideal" for women and men.

Some people are intimately involved in more than one cultural group. If one of the cultures encourages interdependent and/or gendered self-perceptions and the other encourages independent and/or gender neutral self-perceptions, these people may develop both types of self-perception and actually switch "cultural frames" based on the cultural group they are interacting within at a given time. They are more likely to do this well when they see themselves as part of and appreciate the strengths of both cultures (Benet-Martínez & Haritatos, 2005).

independent self-perceptions

based on the belief that traits and abilities are internal to the person and are universally applicable to all situations

interdependent self-perceptions

based on the belief that traits and abilities are specific to a particular context or relationship

Can you think of a television program that depicts men, rather than women, as competent caregivers for a family?

Mario Perez/AP Images

Who have you known that seems to have an over-inflated self-perception? Did you or do you enjoy interacting with him or her? Why or why not?

incongruence

a gap between self-perception and reality

self-fulfilling prophecy

an inaccurate perception of a skill, characteristic, or situation that leads to behaviors that perpetuate that false perception as true

Have you known someone who seems to have a deflated perception of self? Did you or do you enjoy interacting with him or her? Why or why not?

Accuracy and Distortion of Self-Perceptions

The accuracy of our self-concept and self-esteem depends on the accuracy of our perceptions of our own experiences and observations, as well as how we interpret others' reactions and responses to us. All of us experience successes and failures, and all of us hear praise and criticism. Since our perceptions are more likely than our true abilities to influence our behavior (Weiten, 1998), accurate self-perception is critical to competent communication. Self-perception may suffer from **incongruence** when there is a gap between self-perception and reality. For example, Sean may actually possess all of the competencies and personality traits needed for effective leadership, but if he doesn't perceive himself to have these skills and characteristics, he won't step forward when leadership is needed. Likewise, Yuri is ashamed to be too assertive at work. So she doesn't voice her opinion even when the problem is in her area of expertise and could help solve a serious problem. Unfortunately, individuals tend to reinforce these incongruent self-perceptions by behaving in ways that conform to them rather than attempting to break free from them.

If we are overly attentive to successful experiences and positive responses, our self-perception may become inflated. We tend to describe such individuals as "arrogant," "pompous," "haughty," or "snobbish." On the other hand, if we dwell on our failures and not our successes, remember only the criticism we receive, or focus on how we don't measure up to our ideal self-concept, we may have a deflated self-perception. Winnie the Pooh's friend Eeyore, the donkey who is always "having a bad day," is an example of someone with a deflated sense of self. We tend to describe such individuals as "depressed," "despondent," "sullen," or "gloomy." Neither the person with the inflated or deflated perception of self accurately reflects who they are. These incongruent and distorted self-perceptions are magnified through self-fulfilling prophecies, filtering messages, and media images.

Self-fulfilling prophecies A **self-fulfilling prophecy** is an inaccurate perception of a skill, characteristic, or situation that leads to behaviors that perpetuate that false perception as *true* (Merton, 1968). Self-fulfilling prophesies may be self-created or other-imposed.

Self-created prophecies are predictions you make about yourself. We often talk ourselves into success or failure. For example, when people expect rejection, they are more likely to behave in ways that lead others to reject them (Downey, Freitas, Michaelis, & Khouri, 2004, p. 437). So Aaron, who sees himself as unskilled in establishing new relationships, says to himself, "I doubt I'll know anyone at the party—I'm going to have a miserable time." Because he believes he'll have trouble interacting with others, he doesn't introduce himself to anyone, and just as he predicted, spends much of his time standing around alone thinking about when he can leave. In contrast, Stefan sees himself as quite social and able to get to know people easily. As a result, he looks forward to the party, and just as he predicted, makes several new acquaintances and enjoys himself.

Sometimes a self-fulfilling prophecy is other-imposed and based on what others say about us. When teachers act as if their students are bright, students buy into this expectation and learn more as a result. Likewise, when teachers act as if students are not bright, students may "live down" to these imposed prophecies and fail to achieve. A good example takes place in the popular book *Harry Potter and the Order of the Phoenix*. A prophecy was made that suggested Harry Potter would vanquish the Dark Lord (Voldemort). So the Dark Lord sets out to kill Harry Potter. Dumbledore explains to Harry that the prophecy is only true because the Dark Lord believes it. Still, because the Dark Lord will not rest until he kills Harry, it becomes inevitable that Harry will, in fact, have to kill Voldemort (or vice versa).

Moviestore collection Ltd/Alamy

How might media portrayals of "ideal" male and female figures distort self-perception?

Filtering messages Our self-perceptions can also become distorted through the way we filter what others say to us. We tend to pay attention to messages that reinforce our self-perception, and downplay or ignore messages that contradict this image. For example, suppose you prepare an agenda for your study group. Someone comments that you're a good organizer. If you spent your childhood hearing how disorganized you were, you may downplay or even ignore this comment. If, however, you think you are good at organizing, you will pay attention to the compliment and may even reinforce it by responding, "Thanks, I AM a pretty organized person. I learned it from my mom."

Media images Another way self-perception can become distorted is through our interpretation of what we see on television, in the movies, and in popular magazines. Social cognitive learning theory suggests that we strive to copy the characteristics and behaviors of the characters portrayed as perfect examples or "ideal types" (Bandura, 1977). Persistent media messages of violence, promiscuity, use of profanity, bulked-up males, and pencil-thin females have all been linked to distorted self-perceptions among viewers. One particularly disturbing study found that before TV was widely introduced on the Pacific island of Fiji, only 3 percent of girls reported vomiting to lose weight or being unhappy with their body image. Three years after the introduction of TV, that percentage had risen to 15 percent, and an alarming 74 percent reported being too big or too fat (Becker, 2004). Unfortunately, distorted body image perceptions lead to low self-esteem and, sometimes, to self-destructive behaviors such as anorexia and bulimia.

Self-Perception and Communication

Self-perception influences how we talk to ourselves, how we talk about ourselves with others, how we talk about others to ourselves, the self we present to others, and our ability to communicate with others.

Self-talk (a.k.a. intrapersonal communication) is the internal conversation we have with ourselves in our thoughts. People who have a positive self-perception are more likely to engage in positive self-talk, such as "I know I can do it" or "I did a really good job." People who have a negative self-perception

> **CONSIDER *THIS*....**
>
> Have you ever experienced a self-fulfilling prophecy based on what others have said? Consider how that influenced your self-concept and self-esteem.

self-talk

the internal conversation we have with ourselves in our thoughts

are more likely to engage in negative self-talk, such as "There's no way I can do that" or "I really blew it." Not surprisingly, a high level of speech anxiety (the fear of public speaking) is often rooted in negative self-talk.

Self-perception also influences how we talk about ourselves with others. If we have a positive self-perception, we are likely to convey a positive attitude and take credit for our successes. If we have a negative self-perception, we are likely to convey a negative attitude and downplay our accomplishments. Why do some people put themselves down regardless of what they have done? Perhaps people with a negative self-perception find it less painful to put themselves down than to hear criticism from others. Thus, to preempt the possibility that others will comment on their unworthiness, they do it first.

Some research suggests that the Internet can influence how we communicate about ourselves with others in unique ways. Some Internet discussion groups, for example, are designed to be online journals where the user engages in reflection and introspection. These users are actually communicating with themselves while imagining a reader. On the Internet, people can be more aware of themselves and less aware of the people to whom they are talking (Shedletsky & Aitken, 2004, p. 132).

Self-perception also influences how we talk about others to ourselves. First, the more accurate our self-perception, the more likely we are to perceive others accurately. Second, the more positive our self-perception is, the more likely we are to see others favorably. Studies show that people who accept themselves as they are tend to be more accepting of others; similarly, those with a negative self-perception are more likely to be critical of others. Third, our own personal characteristics influence the types of characteristics we are likely to perceive in others. For example, people who are secure tend to see others as equally secure. If you recall that we respond to the world as we perceive it to be (and not necessarily as it is), you can readily see how negative self-perception can account for misunderstandings and communication breakdowns.

social construction of self

phenomenon of presenting different aspects of our self-concept based on the situation and people involved

Our self-perceptions are the complete picture of how we view ourselves. When we communicate with others, however, most of us share only the parts we believe are appropriate to the situation. Research calls this phenomenon the **social construction of self**. For example, Damon presents his "manager self" at work where he is a serious task-oriented leader. When he is with his good friends, however, he is laid back, jovial, and more than happy to follow what the group wants to do. Which is the "real" Damon? Both are.

Do you have a Facebook page? Think of the time and effort you spend creating that "self." Does it accurately reflect all aspects of who you are? Do you pick and choose what to post on your page? Do you sometimes choose to "friend" certain people or not to "confirm" a friend request from others because of how you have constructed yourself on your Facebook page? These choices are based on the different aspects of ourselves we choose to highlight with different people. Social networking sites such as Facebook have added a new twist to the social construction of self because once we have posted

CONSIDER *THIS....*

How do you act or portray yourself differently with the various people you interact with, such as your siblings, parents, close friends, teachers, bosses, and so forth? These differences are an example of social construction of self.

THE AUDIENCE *BEYOND*

Margaret created two Facebook accounts. One she uses with close friends and the other with professional colleagues because the "self" she wants each group to see and not to see is different.

information on our page, others can co-opt our identity and actually reconstruct us in ways we never intended to do.

How effective we are at constructing different social selves depends on how actively we self-monitor. **Self-monitoring** is the internal process of being aware how we are coming across to others and adjusting our behavior accordingly. It involves being sensitive to other people's feedback and using that information to determine how we will respond (Gangestad & Snyder, 2000). If you have ever been in a situation where you made a remark and did not get the response you expected, you may have thought to yourself, "Ooh, I wish I hadn't said that. I wonder how to fix it." This is an example of self-monitoring. Some people are naturally high self-monitors, constantly aware of how they are coming across to others. But even low self-monitors are likely to self-monitor when they are in a new situation or relationship.

We all use self-monitoring to determine which "self" we choose to display in different situations and with different people. Celebrities use self-monitoring to decide which "self" to portray in public, which may be very different from the "self" they are in their private lives. The *Pop Comm!* feature that follows highlights how and why Lady Gaga does so.

self-monitoring

the internal process of being aware how we are coming across to others and adjusting our behavior accordingly

POP COMM!

Self-Monitoring and Celebrity Culture

Eduardo Munoz/Reuters Limited

From the moment she burst onto the pop music scene in 2009, Lady Gaga has been synonymous with outrageous performances and heavily stylized celebrity personas. From wearing a dress made of raw meat at the 2010 MTV Video Awards to showcasing over-the-top music videos to arriving in a giant egg to the 2011 Grammys, Gaga has built her celebrity image not just on her musical talent but on her ability to draw public attention to herself.

But is it all just an act? We all socially construct the selves we present in certain situations. But is that the same thing as Stefani Germonotta turning herself into Lady Gaga? Is there a "real" person beneath this celebrity image? For Gaga, as with all celebrities, being in the public eye means negotiating

perceptions of who she "really" is outside of her public image as a pop singer. Such self-presentation is largely done through the media, and the most successful celebrities manage to present audiences a glimpse of an authentic or "real" self that does not appear to be stage-managed or constructed for the sake of fame. Lady Gaga readily admits that such self-monitoring is a necessary part of her celebrity image. "[P]art of my mastering of the art of fame," she explained in an interview on *60 Minutes*, "is getting people to pay attention to what you want them to, and not pay attention to the things you don't want them to pay attention to." But we tend to be drawn to celebrities who, despite their fame, glamour and fortune, successfully present this self as "just like us," or the self we would like to be, not those who are "faking it" for fame.

For Lady Gaga, at first glance, this "behind-the-scenes self" appears to be just as constructed as her public celebrity persona. At the same time, however, she consistently frames this self as "real" in her songs and media appearances. Her celebrity persona is completely rooted in the idea that she is being her true self, even though that self is glamorous, constructed, extreme, over-the-top, and all the things that we already associate with her public image. She never takes off the makeup and fashion because being Lady Gaga is not simply a staged performance, but truly represents her sense of self. She told *Rolling Stone* "[B]eing myself in public was very difficult. I was being poked and probed and people would actually touch me and touch my clothes. . . . It was like I was being bullied by music lovers, because they couldn't possibly believe that I was genuine." Like all personas, what you see is constructed, but it is not "fake" or "inauthentic" just to be famous. But such careful self-monitoring also helps her protect some part of her private herself from the glare of the public eye. In the *60 Minutes* interview, she said, "[M]y philosophy is that if I am open with [my fans] about everything and yet I let art direct every moment of my life, I can maintain a sort of privacy in a way. I maintain a certain soulfulness that I have yet to give."

Gaga's "real" self remains self-consciously constructed in her physical appearance and how she behaves in public, but is not intended to be an act or something distinct from her "authentic" self. Songs like "Born This Way" and the press she's done surrounding the album of the same name foreground the idea that you should, like Gaga, be yourself no matter what, even if that self does not fit into dominant social expectations. In many ways, this consistent presentation of her public and private self has contributed to her success as a celebrity. She has become the icon of outsiders by claiming her outlandish identity as her "real" self. Anyone who has ever been on the outside can look to Gaga as someone who has been through the same ridicule and doubt that all outsiders experience. Gaga's persona explicitly invites audiences to connect not just with the pop diva but with the "real" person who is "just like us," even if we've never worn a meat dress.

Questions to Ponder

1. Do you believe Lady Gaga when she says her "public" and "private" selves are the same? Why or why not?

2. Do you think celebrities should maintain different public and private constructions of self? Explain.

Changing Self-Perceptions

Self-concept and self-esteem are fairly enduring characteristics, but they can be changed. Comments that contradict your current self-perception may lead you to slowly change it. Certain situations expedite this process, for example, when you experience a profound change in your social environment. When children begin school or go to sleep-away camp; when teens start part-time jobs; when young adults go to college; or when people begin or end jobs or relationships, become parents, or grieve the loss of someone they love, they are more likely to absorb messages that contradict their current self-perceptions.

Therapy and self-help techniques can help alter our self-concept and improve our self-esteem. In his analysis of numerous research studies, Christopher Mruk (1999) found that self-esteem is increased through "hard work and practice, practice, practice—there is simply no escaping this basic existential fact" (p. 112).

So why is this important to communication? Because our self-perception affects who we choose to form relationships with, how we interact with others, and how comfortable we feel when we are called on to share our opinions or present a speech. Essentially, improving self-perception improves how we interact with others, and improving how we interact with others improves self-perception. Emina's *Diverse Voices* story offers one example of how self-perception can change as a result of a profound change in one's social environment; in her case, in moving from Bosnia to the United States.

DIVERSE VOICES

Who Am I? The Self-Perception Struggles of a Bosnian American

by Emina Herovic

University of Kentucky

It was not until just this year, my 22nd year of life, that I began identifying myself as more American than Bosnian. I spent most of my childhood, adolescence, and young adulthood struggling with my cultural self-concept; just who was I? While most people experience periods of identity confusion, mine stemmed from my early life experiences living in several vastly different cultures.

Born in the Balkan region of Bosnia, I was not yet three years old when war broke out in my native country. To escape the tragedies of war, my parents moved our family to Turkey where we lived for the next two and a half years. When our temporary settlement in Turkey expired, my father boldly decided to move us again, this time to the United States. So by the time I was five years old, I had lived in three different countries on three different continents and had experienced three different cultures and languages.

Can you imagine my confusion and frustration? Just when I began speaking fluent Bosnian, we moved to Turkey. Then, just when I was becoming fluent in Turkish, I was thrown into a totally different cultural environment that used yet another language I didn't understand or speak. I remember walking into my kindergarten classroom on the first day of school in the United States. After observing the other kids for a few minutes, I remember turning to my mother saying, "These kids don't know how to talk!" I learned later that I was actually the oddball. I struggled for many years with whether to perceive myself as Bosnian or American.

There was very little diversity among the people at the school I attended in the States.

I was obviously the only "foreign" girl. I was surrounded by English-speaking teachers and peers and was exposed to American society at full force. When I was home, however, I was once again immersed in my native Bosnian cultural tradition and language: My parents would speak Serbo-Croatian around me; I ate Bosnian food; and I celebrated Bosnian traditions and customs. My religious practices also differed from those of my peers. Raised a Muslim, my family and I celebrated Islamic holidays. I remember as a little girl, when it was the month of Ramadan, I would go to the library at school during lunchtime to avoid the bombardment of questions from my peers as to why I was fasting. When I would explain that it was a religious practice, some of them did not understand. Experiences such as these differentiated me from my peers and created a greater divide between my bi-cultural identities.

Whenever I was asked as a young girl and adolescent, I always replied without hesitation that I was Bosnian. I did not perceive myself to be American at all. During the summer of my seventh grade year, my family and I went back to visit Bosnia. Despite the American accent I now used when I spoke Bosnian, my trip back was pleasant. I felt accepted and "at home" around the people of my native culture.

However, this strong Bosnian self-concept diminished as I got older. As I spoke, studied, and wrote in English every day at school and was exposed to Bosnian language only at home, I started to speak Bosnian less fluently. I also began to understand the American way of life, humor, and culture more. So year-by-year, I began to see myself as a bit more American.

Seven years after that first trip "home" to Bosnia, I returned to Bosnia at the age of 20. This time, I felt like a foreigner. The country, people, food, and overall experience did not feel "home-like" anymore. Looking back, I attribute this to my change in self-perception. It became clear to me that I no longer identified more with the Bosnian culture than the American one. I was beginning to identify more with the "American side" of my self-perception.

However, things did not immediately become easier for me when I returned to the United States. I realized I did not feel American either. In my interactions with my American friends, my Bosnian side was evident. My home life and cultural norms were different from those of my peers and, for this reason, it was hard for me to feel fully connected with them. I was not the typical "American girl." My experiences as an immigrant child that defined me in many ways were vastly different from my peers. My peers could not fathom many of the hardships, circumstances, and events I had experienced growing up. So I realized I had become too "American" to be Bosnian anymore, yet I was too "Bosnian" to be American. In this sense, my self-perception actually became more and more unclear as I got older.

The speed at which the acculturation process took effect was incredibly fast. Yet, every part of me fought it. I wanted to maintain my Bosnian identity because without it I believed I would no longer have a strong sense of self. What would I identify myself as if I wasn't "Bosnian" anymore? I felt like I wouldn't know who I was anymore. Would I then be fully American or would I be some mixture of both cultures? But, what would being a mixture of both cultures mean? This issue was especially pertinent to me because a strong sense of ethnic nationalism developed and grew steadily stronger amongst the Balkan people once the war ended. I was raised to be extremely proud of my nationality, culture, and country. Therefore, when I started feeling less Bosnian, I didn't understand what else I could be. I also felt a sense of guilt about losing the part of me that my parents had tried so hard to maintain in their children after we immigrated to the United States.

Now, at age 22, I have come to accept my self-perception based on my dual identification with Bosnia and the United States. I have also accepted that my American identity is now stronger than my Bosnian one. This was not something that just happened one morning, but rather, emerged over time. I have lived in the United States for most of my life. It is my home. I choose to acknowledge that being Bosnian will always be a part of me and I would never want to change that. It has educated me on the differences between the two cultures and I can look on the world more broadly and understand that everyone in the world has their own culture and customs. I know that other foreign-born Americans struggle with this aspect of self-perception. And that's why I have chosen to study this phenomenon in order to help others like me make successful self-perception transitions that honor their roots in more than one culture.

Source: Reprinted by permission of Emina Herovic.

COMMUNICATE ON YOUR FEET

Speech Assignment

Presenting Your Self-Concept

The Assignment

Jot down ten terms that describe your self-concept. Then create a short poem, rap, cheer, or song using those terms to present *who you see yourself as*. Perform it for the class. The presentation should take less than 2 minutes to perform.

Perception of Others

Now that you have a basic understanding of self-perception, let's look at how we perceive others and the role communication plays in that process. When we meet others for the first time, questions might arise such as: "What is this person like?" and "What is this person likely to do, and why?" We might wonder whether we have anything in common, whether they like us, whether we will get along, and whether we'll enjoy the experience or feel uncomfortable. Our natural reaction to such feelings is to say and do things that will reduce these uncertainties (Littlejohn & Foss, 2011).

Uncertainty Reduction

Uncertainty reduction (Berger & Bradac, 1982) is a communication theory that explains how individuals monitor their social environment in order to know more about themselves and others (Littlejohn & Foss, 2007). When people interact, they look for information to help them understand who their partner is and predict what their partner is likely to do. As we reduce uncertainty, we usually become more comfortable communicating (Guerrero, Andersen, & Afifi, 2007). To reduce uncertainty, we form impressions and make judgments about others as we interact with them.

Forming Impressions We engage in a variety of processes to form our perceptions about others. Researchers call these processes **impression formation**. Three of the most important ways we form impressions are based on physical appearance, perceived personality, and assumed similarity.

- **Physical Appearance.** The first thing we notice about other people is how they look. Although it may seem superficial, we form these first impressions very quickly. In fact, one study found that we assess how attractive, likeable, trustworthy, competent, and aggressive we think people are after looking at their faces for only 100 milliseconds (Willis & Todorov, 2006).

- **Implicit Personality Theory.** We also form impressions based on assumptions we make about another's personality. **Implicit personality theory** is our tendency to assume that two or more personality characteristics go together. So if we see someone displaying one trait, we assume they have the others we associate with it. For example, if you meet someone who is multilingual you might assume she is also intelligent. Or if you meet someone who volunteers at a homeless shelter, you might assume that he is compassionate.

- **Assumed Similarity.** We also form impressions about others by thinking that others who share one characteristic with us also share others. Researchers call this **assumed similarity**. We assume someone is similar to us in a variety of ways until we get information that contradicts this assumption. For instance, when Sam attended a campaign event for a city council candidate who belonged to the same political party, he expected the candidate's views on locating a new prison in the city to be the same as his. Sam was pleased to hear that the candidate agreed with his viewpoint, but he was shocked to hear the candidate's racist reasoning.

Making Attributions At the center of our quest to reduce uncertainty is the need to predict how others will behave. By it's nature predicting something depends on understanding the cause and effect relationship between

uncertainty reduction

communication theory that explains how individuals monitor their social environment to know more about themselves and others

impression formation

processes we use to form perceptions of others

implicit personality theory

tendency to assume that two or more personality characteristics go together

assumed similarity

assuming someone is similar to us in a variety of ways until we get information that contradicts this assumption

attributions

reasons we give for others and our own behavior

situational attribution

a reason that is beyond the control of the person

dispositional attribution

attributing behavior to some cause that is under the control of the person

CONSIDER THIS....

Visit an online dating Web site like Match.com or eHarmony. View a few profiles. What assumptions do you make based on what you see? How might you check the accuracy of your perceptions?

selective perception

the perceptual distortion that arises from paying attention only to what we expect to see or hear and ignoring what we don't expect

forced consistency

the inaccurate attempt to make several perceptions about another person agree with each other

prejudice

judging a person based on the characteristics of a group to which the person belongs without regard to how the person may vary from the group characteristic

stereotypes

exaggerated or oversimplified generalizations used to describe a group

two things. So when we see someone acting a certain way we try to figure out why. Then we use this explanation to predict how that person will act in similar situations in the future. **Attributions** are reasons we give for others and our own behavior. For instance, suppose a co-worker with whom you had a noon lunch date has not arrived by 12:30. How do you explain her tardiness? One way you might explain it is to make a **situational attribution**, a reason that is beyond the control of the person. So you might assume that your co-worker must have had an accident on the way to the restaurant. On the other hand you may have made a **dispositional attribution**, attributing behavior to some cause that is under the control of the person. So you may perceive that your co-worker is forgetful, self-absorbed, or insensitive to others. In any case, your attribution reduces your uncertainty by answering the question, "Why is my co-worker late?" But the type of attribution you make influences how you interact with your co-worker once she shows up. If you believe it is not her fault, you are likely to be concerned, understanding, and supportive. On the other hand, if you made a dispositional attribution, you are likely to be annoyed or hurt.

Inaccurate and Distorted Perceptions of Others

As we work to reduce uncertainty, we also must be careful to reduce perceptual inaccuracies. Because perception is a complex process, we use shortcuts to help us focus attention, interpret information, and make predictions about others. Selective perceptions, faulty attributions, forced consistency, and prejudice are shortcuts that can lead to perceptual inaccuracies.

Selective perception is the perceptual distortion that arises from paying attention only to what we expect to see or hear and ignoring what we don't expect. For instance, if Donna sees Nick as a man with whom she would like to develop a strong relationship, she will tend to see the positive side of Nick's personality and ignore the negative side. Similarly, if Dean thinks that his landlord is mean and unfair, he may ignore any acts of kindness or generosity offered by the landlord.

Forced consistency is the inaccurate attempt to make several perceptions about another person agree with each other. It arises from our need to eliminate contradictions. Imagine that Leah does not like her co-worker, Jill. If Jill supplies some information Leah missed on a form, Leah is likely to perceive Jill's behavior as interference, even if Jill's intention was to be helpful. If Leah likes Jill, however, she might perceive the very same behavior as helpful—even if Jill's intention was to interfere. In each case, the perception of "supplying missing information" is shaped by the need for consistency. It is consistent to regard someone we like as doing favors for us. It is inconsistent to regard people we don't like as doing favors for us. However, consistent perceptions of others are not necessarily accurate.

Prejudice is judging a person based on the characteristics of a group to which the person belongs without regard to how the person may vary from the group characteristic (Jones, 2002). Prejudices are based on **stereotypes**, which are exaggerated or oversimplified generalizations used to describe a group. A professor may see a student's spiked purple hair and numerous tattoos and assume the student is a rebel who will defy authority, slack off on classroom assignments, and seek attention. In reality, this person may be a polite, quiet, serious honor student who aspires to go to graduate school. Prejudice can lead to

discrimination, which is acting differently toward a person based on prejudice (Jones, 2002). Prejudice deals with perception and attitudes, while discrimination involves actions. For instance, when Laura meets Wasif and learns that he is Muslim, she may use her knowledge of women's roles in Islamic countries to inform her perception of Wasif and conclude that he is a chauvinist without really talking to him. This is prejudice. If based on this prejudice she refuses to be in a class project group with him she would be discriminating. Although he is an Iraqi American, Wasif may be a feminist, but Laura's use of the perceptual shortcut may prevent her from getting to know Wasif for the person he really is, and she may have cost herself the opportunity of working with the best student in class.

Racism, ethnocentrism, sexism, heterosexism, ageism, and **able-ism** are various form of prejudice, in which members of one group believe that the behaviors and characteristics of their group are inherently superior to those of another group. All people can be prejudiced and act on their prejudices by discriminating against others. Nevertheless, "prejudices of groups with power are farther reaching in their consequences than others" (Sampson, 1999, p. 131). Because such attitudes can be deeply ingrained and are often subtle, it is easy to overlook behaviors we engage in that in some way meet this definition. Prejudicial perceptions may be unintentional, or they may seem insignificant or innocuous, but even seemingly unimportant prejudices rob others of their humanity and severely impede competent communication.

discrimination

acting differently toward a person based on prejudice

racism, ethnocentrism, sexism, heterosexism, ageism, and able-ism

various form of prejudice in which members of one group believe that the behaviors and characteristics of their group are inherently superior to those of another group

Improving Perceptions of Others

Because perceptual distortions of others and their messages are common and because they influence how we communicate, improving perceptual accuracy is an important first step in becoming a competent communicator. The following guidelines can help you construct accurate impressions of others and assess your perceptions of others' messages.

1. **Question the accuracy of your perceptions.** Questioning accuracy begins by saying, "I know what I think I saw, heard, tasted, smelled, or felt, but I could be wrong. What other information should I be aware of?" By accepting the possibility that you have overlooked something, you will stop automatic processing and begin to consciously search out information that should increase your accuracy.

2. **Choose to use conscious processing as you get to know people.** When you mindfully pay attention to someone, you are more likely to understand the uniqueness of him or her. Doing so can increase the accuracy of your perceptions.

3. **Seek more information to verify perceptions.** If your perception is based on only one or two pieces of information, try to collect additional information. Note that your perception is tentative—that is, subject to change. The best way to get additional information about people is to talk with them. It's OK to be unsure about how to treat someone from another group. But rather than letting your uncertainty cause you to make mistakes, talk with the person and tell them you want to be respectful. Then ask them for the information you need to become more comfortable about interacting appropriately and respectfully with them.

4. **Realize that your perceptions of a person will change over time.** People often base their opinions, assumptions, and behaviors on perceptions that are outdated. So when you encounter someone you haven't seen for a while, let the person's current behavior rather than their past actions or reputation inform your perceptions. For example, a former classmate who was wild in high school may well have changed and become a mature, responsible adult.

5. **Seek clarification respectfully by perception checking.** One way to assess the accuracy of a perception is to verbalize it and see whether others agree with what you see, hear, and interpret. A **perception check** is a message that reflects your understanding of the meaning of another person's behavior. It is a process of describing what you have seen and heard and then asking for feedback from the other person. A perception check consists of three parts. First, you describe what you observed. Second, you offer two possible interpretations of it. Third, you ask for clarification.

perception check

a message that reflects your understanding of the meaning of another person's behavior

Recall Donna's predicament in the opening scenario of this chapter. She jumped to the conclusion that David was going to break up with her because he had been so quiet the night before and wasn't responding to any of her texts. Rather than jump to a conclusion and cause a defensive reaction when she does talk to David, she could employ a perception-checking message—something like this:

> *"When you didn't respond to my texts today"* (nonjudgmental description of the observed behavior), *"I thought you were mad at me"* (first interpretation), *"or maybe you were really busy at work"* (second interpretation). *"Is everything ok? Is it something else?"* (request for clarification).

Basically, perception checking is a tool to respectfully check for understanding of another's behavior without assuming your interpretation is correct. It helps you seek mutual understanding without directly threatening or attacking the other person.

COMMUNICATION SKILL

Perception Checking

Skill	Use	Procedure	Example
Making a verbal statement that reflects your understanding of another person's behavior.	To enable you to test the accuracy of your perceptions.	1. Offer a nonjudgmental description of the behavior that led to your perception. 2. Offer your interpretation of the behavior. 3. Offer a second possible interpretation. 4. Request clarification.	After taking a phone call, Shimika comes into the room with a completely blank expression and neither speaks to Donnell nor acknowledges that he is in the room. Donnell says, "Shimika, from your blank look, I get the feeling that you're in a state of shock. Or perhaps you are just tired. Has something happened? Is it something else?"

WHAT WOULD YOU DO?

A Question of Ethics

"There," exclaimed Ryan, "my résumé is done and ready to post on LinkedIn. Will you take a look at it and tell me what you think?"

"Sure," Shara replied. As she began to read, Shara gasped, "Ryan, it says here you have a degree in chemical engineering. But you don't."

"Well, that's my major. I'll have a degree in it eventually. Besides, everybody stretches the truth a little on their resumes."

"And what about this statement about your job responsibilities while working at LexCo," Shara continued. "I know you were a receptionist for two summers. You make it sound like you were a supervisor and that you actually worked there for two *years*."

"Well," Ryan replied, "remember how Professor Jarman said we need to sell ourselves if we want to get selected for the interview? I'm trying to make myself stand out as a leader."

"I'm not sure that's what he meant, Ryan. You need to be honest," Shara responded.

"Yeah, well I can clarify the details in the interview. I just want to make sure I actually get an interview."

1. What, if any, ethical principles is Ryan violating and how?

2. Some people justify exaggerating, or even lying, on their resumes by saying that everybody does it. In fact, according to CareerBuilder.com, 38 percent of those surveyed admitted to embellishing their job responsibilities on their resumes, and 18 percent admitted to lying about their skill sets. Given these numbers, are the justifications reasonable? Why or why not?

3. If you believe stretching the truth is acceptable in certain circumstances, how far can you go before you cross the line into unacceptable behavior?

Summary

Perception is the process of selectively attending and assigning meaning to information. Our perceptions are a result of our selection, organization, and interpretation of sensory information. We do so through dual processing.

Social perception consists of how we perceive ourselves and others. Perception of self is comprised of self-concept and self-esteem. Self-concept is the mental image we have about our skills, abilities, knowledge, competencies, and personality. Self-esteem is the value we place on the attributes of our self-concept. Cultural norms play a critical role in shaping our self-perceptions. Our self-perception can become distorted and magnified through self-fulfilling prophecies, filtering messages, and media images. Self-perception influences communication in terms of how we talk to ourselves, how with talk about ourselves with others, how we talk about others to ourselves, the way we present ourselves to others, and our ability to communicate competently with others.

When we meet others, we strive to reduce uncertainty through communication. We begin by forming impressions based on physical appearance, assumptions about their personality, and assumed similarity. We also reduce uncertainty by making attributions that may help us predict how others will behave.

Just as we make inaccurate and distorted perceptions of self, so do we make inaccurate assumptions about others based on selective perception, faulty attributions, forced consistency, and prejudice.

We can improve the accuracy of our perceptions of others and the messages they send by questioning the accuracy of our perceptions, choosing to use conscious processing as we get to know them, seeking more information about our perceptions, realizing that our perceptions will change over time, and practicing perception checking.

COMMUNICATE!

RESOURCE AND ASSESSMENT CENTER

Now that you have read Chapter 2, go to the Speech Communication Course-Mate at cengagebrain.com where you'll find an interactive eBook and interactive learning tools including quizzes, flashcards, sample speech videos, audio study tools, skill-building activities, action step activities and more. Student Workbook, Speech Builder Express 3.0 and Speech Studio 2.0 are also available.

Applying What You've Learned

Impromptu Speech Activity

1. Self-Concept Speech Prepare a 2- to 3-minute speech discussing how your initial impression of a friend has evolved over time.

Assessment Activities

1. For three days, record your roles in various situations such as "lunch with a friend" or "grocery store shopper at the checkout" or "meeting with a professor about an assignment." Describe the social construction of self you portray in each setting. Then, prepare a one-two page paper and/or two–three minute speech answering the following questions:

• To what extent did your "self" change across situations?

• What factors contributed to these differences?

• Are there certain roles you take on more than others?

• Are there roles you would like to modify?

• How satisfied are you with the "selves" you have enacted and why?

2. Who Am I? Complete this journal activity to help you assess how your self-concept aligns with how others see you.

First ask: *How do I see myself?* List the skills, abilities, knowledge, competencies, and personality characteristics that describe how you see yourself. To generate this list, try completing these sentences: "I am skilled at . . ."; I have the ability to . . ."; "I know things about . . ."; I am competent at doing . . "; and "One part of my personality is that I am . . .". List as many characteristics in each category as you can think of. What you have developed is an inventory of your self-concept.

Second ask: *How do others see me?* List the skills, abilities, and so on that describe how you think others see you by completing these sentences: "Other people believe I am skilled at . . .,"; "Other people believe I have the ability to . . ."; "Other people believe I know things about . . ."; "Other people believe I am competent at doing . . ."; and "One part of my personality is that other people believe I am . . .".

Compare your two lists. How are they similar? Where are they different? Do you understand why they differ? After you have thought about each, write a paragraph titled "Who I Am, and How I Know This."

3. Stereotypes and Media For a few days, catalog the stereotypes you come across as portrayed in mass media. Enter your research into a log broken down into the following categories: (1) medium of communication (TV, radio, magazines, newspapers, the Internet, signage/posters); (2) source (general content or advertising); (3) target (race, ethnicity/culture, religion, gender, sexual orientation, age, income, profession, hobby, appearance); and (4) connotation (positive or negative).

After you have completed your research, analyze the results. What target was most frequently stereotyped in your findings? Did some mediums of communication indulge in more stereotyping the others? Did regular programming or advertising employ more stereotyping than the other? Were the majority of the stereotypes positive or negative in connotation? Did anything in your research surprise you? Write a paragraph explaining what you learned in this activity.

Skill-Building Activities

1. Perception Checking Practice As an individual or with a partner, prepare a perception-checking response to each of the following scenarios. Be ready to share your response aloud if called upon by your instructor.

   a. Your neighbor Bill usually responds in kind to your "good morning" as each of you heads out for the day. He hasn't responded for the last three days. What would you say to him?

   b. You and your roommate have a deal: Whoever makes the evening meal also does the dishes. He made the meal last night. When you wake up in the morning, you see the dirty dishes still in the sink. When you see your roommate, what would you say?

   c. You haven't received a phone call from your mom in over a month. The last time you talked with her, you had an argument because you are not planning to go home for the holidays this year. What would you say to her when you call her?

   d. When you see your advisor in the hallway, you ask if you can make an appointment to talk about internship possibilities. He says, "Of course. I don't have my calendar with me. Let's set a date and time over e-mail." You haven't heard from him in two weeks, so you decide to e-mail him yourself. What do you say?

   e. Your boss has a quirky sense of humor, which you usually like. Today, however, when he praised you for a job well done, something about the way he said it made you think he was being sarcastic and really didn't think you'd done a good job at all. What do you say to him?

   f. As you vent to your good friend about how worried you are that you are going to flunk the exam you studied for all week, she simply smiles. What do you say to her?

2. Practicing Perception Checking Sentences For each of the following situations, write a well-phrased perception check.

   a. When Franco comes home from the doctor's office, you notice that he looks pale and his shoulders are slumped. Glancing at you with a sad look, he shrugs his shoulders. You say: _____

   b. As you return the basketball you borrowed from Liam, you smile and say, "Thanks, here's your ball." You notice Liam stiffen, grab the ball, and, turning abruptly, walk away. You say: _____

   c. Natalie, who has been waiting to hear about a scholarship, dances into the room with a huge grin on her face. You say: _____

   d. You see your advisor in the hall and ask her if she can meet with you on Wednesday afternoon to discuss your schedule of classes for next term. You notice that she pauses, frowns, sighs, turns slowly, and says, "I guess so." You say: _____

Compare your written responses to the guidelines for effective perception checking discussed earlier. Edit your responses where necessary to improve them. Now say them aloud. Do they sound "natural"? If not, revise them until they do.

Intercultural Communication

What you'll know

- What a culture is and the role of communication in it

- The relationship between dominant and co-cultures

- How cultural identity affects communication

- The inherent barriers in intercultural communication

What you'll be able to do

- Develop and implement a plan for acquiring accurate knowledge about various cultural groups

- Demonstrate empathy and respect when communicating interculturally

- Employ strategies to improve your intercultural communication competence

"Jack, I don't think we should take this flight," Alicia said. "Why don't we wait and take the next one?"

"What are you talking about?" Jack replied. "Our reservations are confirmed, our bags are probably on board by now, and why would we want to sit around here for two more hours?"

"But Jack, over there," Alicia muttered behind her hand while nodding to her far right. Jack turned his head. There on the end of the long bench sat a bearded man wearing a robe and a turban.

"Jack, I'm afraid," Alicia whispered urgently. "He could be a terrorist."

"Relax, Alicia," Jack said. "There is nothing to worry about. Anyway, what makes you think he's a terrorist? Is it because he's a Muslim? What makes you think all Muslims are terrorists? For that matter, anyone on our flight could be a terrorist."

3

How could we evaluate Alicia's assumptions? Are Jack's assumptions more accurate? In both cases, their judgments are based on perceptions of people who are culturally different from themselves.

Because culture has a profound impact on perception and communication, in this chapter we examine the relationship between culture and communication. We begin by explaining some basic concepts of culture and several ways cultures are unique. We end by proposing how to improve intercultural communication competence.

Culture and Communication

culture

system of shared values, beliefs, attitudes, and norms that guide what is considered appropriate among an identifiable group of people

values

commonly accepted standards of what is considered right and wrong, good and evil, fair and unfair, etc.

ideal values

values members profess to hold

real values

values that guide actual behavior

intercultural communication

interactions that occur between people whose cultures are so different that the communication between them is altered

culture shock

psychological discomfort when engaging in a new cultural situation

Culture is the system of shared values, beliefs, attitudes, and norms that guide what is considered appropriate among an identifiable group of people (Samovar, Porter, & McDaniel, 2009). In a real sense, culture is a way of life. It's the taken-for-granted *rules* for how and why we believe and behave as we do.

At the heart of any culture are its values. **Values** are the commonly accepted standards of what is considered right and wrong, good and evil, fair and unfair, just and unjust, and so on. Cultures have both ideal and real values. **Ideal values** are the ones that members profess to hold, whereas **real values** are the ones that guide actual behavior. For example, Israel is a democratic state whose constitution offers protections for members of religious minorities (ideal value). But the legal system's treatment of minorities (e.g., Muslims, Christians) sometimes falls short of this ideal. In other words, religious minorities are sometimes subject to legal hassles that their fellow Jewish citizens don't experience (real value in action). Similarly, the United States Constitution professes equal rights and opportunities for all (ideal value), yet some people are treated unfairly based on sex, race, ethnicity, age, disability, or sexual orientation (real value in action).

Intercultural communication refers to the interactions that occur between people whose cultures are so different that the communication between them is altered (Samovar, Porter, & McDaniel, 2009). To become effective intercultural communicators, we must begin by understanding what a culture is, then identifying how cultures differ from one another, and finally realizing how those differences influence communication.

We do not have to journey to other countries to meet people of different cultures. The United States is a multicultural society. Our population includes not only recent immigrants from other countries, but also descendents of earlier immigrants and of native peoples. So understanding how communication varies among cultural groups can help us as we interact with the people we encounter every day right here in the United States.

Because each of us is so familiar with our own customs, norms, and values, we may feel anxious when they are disrupted. We call this psychological discomfort when engaging in a new cultural situation **culture shock** (Klyukanov, 2005, p. 33). We are likely to feel culture shock most profoundly when thrust into an unfamiliar culture through travel, business, or studying abroad. In the film *Lost in Translation*, for example, Bill Murray's character struggles with culture shock while filming a commercial on location in Japan.

Culture shock can also occur when interacting with others within our own country. For example, Brittney, who is from a small town in Minnesota, experienced culture shock when she visited Miami, Florida, for the first time. She was overwhelmed as she noted the distinct Latin flavor of the city, heard Spanish spoken on the street, and saw billboards written in Spanish. Brittney was

CONSIDER *THIS....*

Have you ever visited another country or another state and experienced culture shock? If so, in what ways? How would you prepare for a future visit based on what you learned?

disoriented because what she witnessed seemed foreign to her. Likewise, if Maria, who lives in Miami, were to visit the small Minnesota town where Brittney grew up, she might also experience culture shock. She might feel uncomfortable because Brittney's hometown might seem a bit like the rural Minnesota towns whose values and customs are humorously highlighted on Garrison Keillor's public radio program *A Prairie Home Companion.*

Image Source/Getty Images

Culture shock can occur when visiting other countries, and even places here in the United States. When and where have you experienced culture shock?

Culture is both transmitted and modified through communication. In Western cultures, for example, most people eat using forks, knives, spoons, individual plates, and bowls. In many Eastern cultures, people may eat with chopsticks. In some countries, people use bread as a utensil, and in others, people use their fingers and share a common bowl. All of these dining rituals are culturally based and taught by one generation to the next through communication.

Communication is also the mechanism through which culture is modified. For example, several generations ago, most American children were taught to show respect by addressing adult family friends using a title and last name (e.g., Mr. Jones, Miss Smith). Today, children often address adult family friends by their first names. How did this cultural norm change? In earlier generations, adults corrected young children who addressed an adult by his or her first name. But toward the end of the 20th century, adults began giving children permission to use first names and, over time, the norm changed. So communication is both the means by which culture is transmitted and the way a culture is changed.

Dominant Cultures, Co-Cultures, and Cultural Identity

Dominant culture refers to the learned system of norms held by the majority group of empowered people in a society. The dominant culture of the United States has evolved over time. It once strictly reflected and privileged the values of white, western European, English-speaking, Protestant, heterosexual men. Before the 1960s, people immigrating to the United States were expected to embrace and adapt to this dominant culture in place of the culture of their native country. Immigrants even changed their names to sound more *American.* They were expected to learn English as quickly as possible and use it instead of other languages. Since the 1960s, however, the United States has begun to experience a gradual modification of the dominant culture to demonstrate respect and honor for the diverse cultures that co-exist here.

In addition to embracing the dominant American culture, then, many people also identify with one or more co-cultures. A **co-culture** is a group comprised

dominant culture

learned system of norms held by the majority group of empowered people in a society

co-culture

a group comprised of a smaller number of people who hold common values, beliefs, attitudes, and customs that differ from those of the dominant culture

THE AUDIENCE *BEYOND*

Thanks to technology, today we can prepare ourselves for potential culture shock by conducting online research before traveling to new places.

Code switchers vary their language to communicate with the dominant culture and to members of their co-culture. Do you ever code switch when conversing with members of a particular group to which you belong?

code switch

altering linguistic and nonverbal patterns to conform to the dominant or co-culture

cultural identity

the part of our self-concept that is based on how closely we associate with both the dominant culture and various co-cultures

of a smaller number of people who hold common values, beliefs, attitudes, and customs that differ from those of the dominant culture.

Co-culture also influences communication behavior. For example, co-cultural group members sometimes **code switch**, altering their linguistic and nonverbal patterns to conform to the dominant or co-culture depending on the topic and participants involved in a conversation (Bonvillain, 2003). So Linh may speak Vietnamese and defer to her older relatives while conversing at the dinner table. She may speak English and question her teachers openly during class discussions at school. And she may speak a mixture of Vietnamese and English (as well as slang and other accepted *in-group* jargon) when hanging out with friends. If you are familiar with the movie *Windtalkers,* you might know that the film is based on the real-life role Navajo code switchers played in Saipan during World War II (Jackson, 2004). You can see a short story about these Navajo code switchers at: http://navajocodetalkers.org/.

Cultural identity is the part of our self-concept that is based on how closely we associate with both the dominant culture and various co-cultures (Ting-Toomey et al., 2000). For example, you may be proud to be a third-generation Polish American who embraces the co-culture of your heritage through communication patterns, religion, food choices, and so on. Or you might identify more with the dominant American culture and rarely think about being Polish. If the dominant culture stigmatizes your co-culture, you might downplay this part of your identity to fit into the dominant culture or identify even more closely with the co-culture and become a vocal activist for it. For example, Cindy is a Polish American who hid that fact while growing up because her classmates often told jokes that stigmatized Polish Americans as foolish and unintelligent.

Some of the co-cultures that exist in the United States today are formed around shared beliefs and values related to, for example, race, ethnicity, sex and gender, sexual orientation, religion, socioeconomic status, age or generation, and disability.

Race Traditionally, the term "race" was used to classify people based on biological characteristics (e.g., skin and eye color, hair texture, body shape). However, scientific justifications for such divisions have proven elusive (Hotz, 1995). Nevertheless, people do experience the social effects of *perceived race* and form co-cultures based on similar experiences with respect to it. For example, the dominant American culture respects police officers as protectors. However, based on collective experiences of unjust treatment by some police officers, some African American co-cultures may not respect police officers as protectors, but instead view them with suspicion and perhaps even contempt.

ethnicity

a classification of people based on combinations of shared characteristics such as nationality, geographic origin, language, religion, ancestral customs, and tradition

Ethnicity Ethnicity is a classification of people based on combinations of shared characteristics such as nationality, geographic origin, language, religion, ancestral customs, and tradition. The degree to which people identify with their ethnic heritage can vary greatly. Generally, the further you are from your family's immigrant experience, the less likely you are to be influenced by your ethnic co-culture. For example, Maria and Juan are both Mexican Americans. Juan, who immigrated with his parents to the United States, identifies more with his ethnic heritage than does Maria, who is a fourth-generation Mexican American.

Native language (sometimes referred to as mother tongue) is the language of one's ethnic heritage and is typically the language a person learns from birth. Native language obviously influences communication. Even after learning English, many immigrants choose to speak their native language at home and to live in close proximity to others from their home country. Although the United States is considered an English-speaking country, it now has the third-largest Spanish-speaking population of any country in the world (Carlo-Casellas, 2002). In fact, 78 percent of Hispanic households report that Spanish is the primary language spoken at home (U.S. Census Bureau, 2010). So today most toll-free 800 and 888 numbers offer the option of conversing in English or Spanish; most cable and satellite television packages include Spanish-language channels; and Spanish radio stations can be heard across the country.

Sex and Gender In the dominant American culture, **sex** (which consists of biologically determined physical traits) and **gender** (which consists of the learned roles and communication patterns deemed "appropriate" for males and females in the dominant culture) tend to be intertwined. In other words, the dominant American culture expects men to communicate in masculine ways and women to communicate in feminine ways. If you have ever heard someone tell an outspoken young girl to "hush up and act like a lady," or a weeping boy to "buck up and act like a man," you have witnessed young people *learning gender* based on their sex. Generally, women who identify with the feminine gender co-culture may tend to speak more about their personal relationships, more easily describe their feelings, be more likely to include others in conversation, and actively respond to others (e.g., head nods, smiles). On the other hand, men who identify with masculine gender co-culture may focus more on tasks and outcomes, as well as emphasize control, competition, and status (Wood, 2007). Obviously, people differ in the extent to which they identify with these gendered co-cultures, and those who do not strongly identify with them may not behave in accord with these expectations at all.

Sexual Orientation The dominant American culture has historically valued and privileged heterosexuality. People who deviated from the heterosexual norm were severely mistreated. Although laws that reflect a change in attitude toward sexuality are gaining popularity, people who are not heterosexual still face discrimination, as well as legal and physical threats. Thus, co-cultures exist across the country based on the collective experiences of those who embrace a sexual orientation that is not heterosexual. Although many people are working hard to modify the dominant American culture with regard to sexual orientation,

native language (mother tongue)

the language of one's ethnic heritage; typically the language learned at birth

CONSIDER *THIS....*

Some people believe that Spanish should be a second official language in the United States. What do *you* think and why?

sex

consists of biologically determined physical traits

gender

consists of the learned roles and communication patterns deemed "appropriate" for males and females in the dominant culture

Many schools used to offer cheerleading as a "girls" sport. Today, both females and males compete in all kinds of sports, including cheer teams. What sports do or did you and your family members compete in? In what ways might gendered norms have influenced the decisions made?

Lance King/Getty Images

In the 1970s, Harvey Milk became the mayor of San Francisco and, by proxy, the first openly gay politician in America. This spurred a movement for others to stand up for their human rights as gay Americans. Milk was assassinated at the height of his popularity. Do you have friends or family members who are gay? How are their lives different from yours?

religion

belief system with a set of rituals and ethical standards based on a common perception of what is sacred or holy

socioeconomic status

the position of a person or family in the power hierarchy of a society based on income, education, and occupation

CONSIDER *THIS*....

What religion (if any) do you practice? How does this affiliation or lack of one (if you consider yourself atheist or agnostic) influence your communication with others?

and some progress has been made, much remains to be done.

Religion A **religion** is a belief system with a set of rituals and ethical standards based on a common perception of what is sacred or holy. Although the dominant culture in the United States values religious freedom, historically it has reflected monotheistic Judeo-Christian values and practices. However, many religious co-cultures exist harmoniously across the country today. Unfortunately, some people in the United States (like Alicia in our opening scenario) have become prejudiced against Muslims based on a misunderstanding that inaccurately equates Muslims with Al-Qaeda, the militant group responsible for the 9/11 terrorist attacks. Did you know that one-fifth of the world's population—that is, one billion people—is Muslim and that some of the core values of this religion are peace, mercy, and forgiveness (Faruqi, 2007)?

Socioeconomic Status (SES) **Socioeconomic status** is the position of a person or family in the power hierarchy of a society based on income, education, and occupation. SES is typically divided into three categories: high, middle, and low. Most Americans identify with the middle class even though they may really be members of a higher or lower class (Ellis, 1999). People develop co-cultures that reinforce distinct values, rituals, and communication practices based on SES. Although not true in all cases, parents in low-SES groups tend to emphasize obedience, acceptance of what others think, and hesitancy in expressing desires to authority figures. Middle-class parents tend to emphasize intellectual curiosity. Such differences based on SES may lead those from middle-class backgrounds to speak more directly and assertively than people from lower-class backgrounds. And, in terms of nonverbal communication, people of high SES backgrounds tend to perform more disengagement cues (e.g., doodling) and fewer engagement cues (e.g., head nods, laughs) than people from low SES backgrounds (Bornstein & Bradley, 2003; Kraus & Keltner, 2009). Finally, SES is at the heart of the American dream. Even in these tough economic times, a recent nationwide poll conducted by the *New York Times* revealed that nearly 80% believe their chances to move up to a higher class are the same or greater than they were 30 years ago (Leonhardt, 2005).

Age/Generation People born and raised in the same generation may identify with a co-culture distinct to it. Although not all people identify with their generational co-culture, generally speaking, people who grew up during the Great Depression tend to be frugal and those who grew up during World War II tend to value sacrifice of self for cause and country. Baby Boomers who came of age during the turbulent 1960s are likely to question authority. Many Generation Xers, who grew up as *latch-key kids* (with parents at jobs outside the home when they got home from school), are likely to be self-sufficient and adaptable. Millennials (a.k.a. Generation Y and Generation NeXt), who grew up during the 1990s and came of age after 9/11, have never known life without computers, became aware of the realities of school and world violence at an early age, and experienced globalization. They tend to be adept at using technology to multitask, be cautious about issues of safety, and appreciate diversity (Pew Research

Center, 2007). Finally, Generation Z (a.k.a. the Internet Generation or Digital Natives) were born after the Cold War era and the fall of the Soviet Union. They have never known a world without instant access to information via Internet searches on computers and smart phones, nor access to others via text messaging and social media sites like Facebook. They are adept at multitasking, as well as learning and using new technologies such as gaming (Prensky, 2001; Wallice, 2006).

When people from different generations interact, their co-cultural orientations can cause communication challenges. For example, when people from earlier generations interact with people who came of age after the 1960s, different expectations about how to demonstrate respect might cause misunderstandings and even conflict (Zemke, Raines, & Filipczak, 2000).

Many young people today prefer to text rather than call friends and family. How might that preference influence communication with people of earlier generations who might prefer conversing on the phone or in person?

disability

any physical, emotional, mental, or cognitive impairment that impacts how a person functions in society

Disability A **disability** is any physical, emotional, mental, or cognitive impairment that impacts how a person functions in society. A disability co-culture is a group of people who share a distinct set of shared values, beliefs, and attitudes based on their common experiences of living with a disability. Physically disabled veterans who may have lost a limb in a war, for example, sometimes form co-cultures where they share inside jokes and draw on common experiences to support each other during rehabilitation and afterward.

Recently, a number of feature films and documentaries have been produced to help people who do not live with a disability to both understand and respect various disability co-cultures. For example, HBO came out with a film about the real life of Temple Grandin (2010), a professor of animal science who improved the ethical treatment of animals, and who is also autistic. *Music Within* tells the story of what two Vietnam veterans did to help get the Americans with Disabilities Act passed, and *Front of the Class* focuses on the true story of a boy with Tourette syndrome who grew up to become a gifted teacher. Such films help to break through misinformed stereotypes and prejudiced thinking about the value and human potential of people who live with a disability.

CONSIDER THIS....

Who do you know that lives with a disability? How does the disability affect communication and interaction with others?

How Cultures Differ

We may be able to speculate as to which cultural groups people identify with based on their language, attire, or personal artifacts (e.g., religious markers worn as jewelry or placed in the home). Usually, however, such signs don't really tell us much beyond surface assumptions.

The early work of Edward T. Hall and more recently Gerard Henrik (Geert) Hofstede give us a way to understand how cultures are similar to and different from one another and to understand how these cultural variations may affect communication. Based on their work, we offer several dimensions for consideration: (1) individualism/collectivism, (2) context, (3) chronemics, (4) uncertainty avoidance, (5) power distance, (6) masculinity/femininity, and (7) long-term/short-term orientation.

Individualism/Collectivism

individualistic cultures

value personal rights and responsibilities, privacy, voicing one's opinion, freedom, innovation, and self-expression

Cultures differ in the extent to which individualism or collectivism is valued. Highly **individualistic cultures** value personal rights and responsibilities, privacy, voicing one's opinion, freedom, innovation, and self-expression (Andersen, Hecht, Hoobler, & Smallwood, 2003). People in highly individualistic cultures place primary value on the self and personal achievement. Competition is both desirable and useful, and the interests of others are considered primarily as they affect personal interests. If you come from an individualistic culture, you may consider your family and close friends when you make decisions, but only because your personal interests align with theirs. Cultures in the United States, Australia, Great Britain, Canada, and Northern and Eastern European countries are considered to be highly individualistic.

collectivist cultures

value community, collaboration, shared interests, harmony, the public good, and avoiding embarrassment

In contrast, highly **collectivist cultures** value community, collaboration, shared interests, harmony, the public good, and avoiding embarrassment (Andersen, Hecht, Hoobler, & Smallwood, 2003). Highly collectivist cultures place primary value on the interests of the group and group harmony. Decisions are shaped by what is best for the group, regardless of whether they serve an individual's personal interests. Maintaining harmony and cooperation is valued over competition and personal achievement. A variety of cultures throughout South and Central America, East and Southeast Asia, and Africa are considered to be highly collectivist.

Individualism and collectivism influence many aspects of communication (Samovar, Porter, & McDaniel, 2009). First, individualism and collectivism affect self-concept and self-esteem. People in individualist cultures form independent self-concepts and base their self-esteem on individual accomplishments. People in collectivist cultures form interdependent self-concepts and base their self-esteem on how well they work in a group. So, if LuAnne is raised in an individualistic culture and she is the highest-scoring player on her basketball team, she will probably identify herself as "winner," even if her team has a losing season. But if LuAnne is from a collectivist culture, the fact that her team had a losing season is more likely to influence her self-esteem than the fact that she is the highest-scoring player.

Second, emphasis on the individual leads members of highly individualistic cultures to be assertive and confront conflict directly, whereas members of highly collectivist cultures are more likely to engage in collaboration or to avoid conflict. In the United States, assertiveness and argumentation are skills used in personal relationships, small group situations, politics, and business. In Japan, a highly collectivist culture, common business practices are based on an elaborate process called *nemawashii* (a term that also means "binding the roots of a plant before pulling it out"). To maintain harmony and avoid confrontational argument, any subject that might cause conflict should be discussed among individuals before the group meets to ensure that interactions during the meeting will not seem rude or impolite (Samovar, Porter, & McDaniel, 2009).

Finally, individualism and collectivism influence how people make group decisions. In highly collectivist cultures, group members strive for consensus and may sacrifice optimal outcomes for the sake of group harmony. In highly individualistic cultures, optimal outcomes are paramount, even at the expense of disharmony. Groups comprised of members that come from both highly individualistic and highly collectivist cultures may experience difficulties because of these different cultural values related to individualism and collectivism.

Context

Another cultural distinction that affects intercultural communication is the extent to which members rely on contextual cues to convey the meaning of a message (Hall, 1976). In **low-context cultures**, speakers use words to convey most of the meaning. In low-context cultures like those of the United States, Germany, and Scandinavia, verbal messages are direct, specific, and detailed. Speakers are expected to say exactly what they mean and get to the point. In **high-context cultures**, much of the speaker's message is understood from the context. Much of the meaning is conveyed indirectly and can only be accurately interpreted by referring to unwritten cultural rules and subtle nonverbal behaviors. So in high-context cultures such as those of American Indian, Latin American, and Asian communities, verbal messages are ambiguous and understood by "reading between the lines" (Chen & Starosta, 1998).

As you can imagine, conducting a business meeting with professionals from both individualistic and collectivist cultures can prove quite challenging. Have you ever found yourself in such a situation? If so, how did communication work among members?

Effective communication between members of high- and low-context cultures can be challenging. When low-context communicators interact with high-context communicators, they should be mindful that building a good relationship first is important for long-term effectiveness. Also, nonverbal messages and gestures will probably be more important than what is actually said. When high-context communicators interact with low-context communicators, they should recognize that the verbal message should be taken at face value and direct questions, assertions, and observations are not meant to be offensive. Finally, they need to recognize that low-context communicators might not notice or understand indirect contextual cues.

low-context cultures

speakers use words to convey most of the meaning; verbal messages are direct, specific, and detailed

high-context cultures

much of the speaker's message is understood from the context

Chronemics

Chronemics is the study of how the perception of time differs among cultures (Hall, 1976). **Monochronic cultures** view time as a series of small units that occur sequentially. Monochronic cultures value punctuality, uninterrupted task completion, meeting deadlines, following plans, and doing things one at a time. For instance, when Margarite (who values a monochronic time orientation) is interrupted by her roommate, who wants to share some good news about her day, Margarite may respond, "I can't talk now. It's my study time!" The dominant culture of the United States values a monochronic orientation to time.

Polychronic cultures, for example, Latin American, Arab, and Southern European cultures, view time as a continuous flow. Thus, appointment times and schedules are perceived as approximate and fluid. People who abide by polychronic orientation to time are comfortable doing several things at once, having a flexible schedule or none at all, and disregarding deadlines to satisfy other needs (Chen & Starosta, 1998). Interruptions are not perceived as annoying but as natural occurrences.

Differences in time orientation can make intercultural communication challenging. In polychronic cultures, relationships are more important than schedules. So when Dante, who is polychronic, shows up for a noon lunch with Sean at 12:47 because a coworker had needed some help, he doesn't perceive this as

chronemics

the study of how the perception of time differs among cultures.

monochronic cultures

view time as a series of small units that occur sequentially

polychronic cultures

view time as a continuous flow

a problem. But Sean, who is monochronic, is annoyed because Dante arrived so "late," and quickly moves the discussion to the business they need to complete. Sean's attitude and immediate discussion of business seems rude to Dante.

Uncertainty Avoidance

uncertainty avoidance

the extent to which people desire to predict what is going to happen

low uncertainty-avoidance cultures

tolerate uncertainty and are less driven to control unpredictable people, relationships, or events

high uncertainty-avoidance cultures

low tolerance for uncertainty and a high need to control unpredictable people, relationships, or events

Cultures differ in their attitudes toward **uncertainty avoidance**, which is the extent to which people desire to predict what is going to happen. **Low uncertainty-avoidance cultures** such as those of the United States, Sweden, and Denmark tolerate uncertainty and are less driven to control unpredictable people, relationships, or events. People tend to accept unpredictability, tolerate the unusual, prize creative initiative, take risks, and think there should be as few rules as possible.

High uncertainty-avoidance cultures such as those of Germany, Portugal, Greece, Peru, and Belgium have a low tolerance for uncertainty and a high need to control unpredictable people, relationships, or events. These cultures often create systems of formal rules as a way to provide more security and reduce risk. They also tend to be less tolerant of people or groups with deviant ideas or behaviors. They often experience anxiety when confronted with unpredictable people, relationships, or situations (Samovar, Porter, & McDaniel, 2009).

How our culture teaches us to view uncertainty impacts communication. People from high uncertainty-avoidance cultures tend to value and use precise language to be more certain of what a person's message means. Imagine a teacher declaring to a class, "The paper must be well-researched with evidence cited appropriately and must look professional in format and appearance." Students from high uncertainty-avoidance cultures would probably ask a lot of questions about what kind of research is appropriate, how much evidence is needed and how to cite it, what writing style to use, and how long the paper should be. These students would probably welcome a specific checklist of the exact criteria by which the paper would be graded. By contrast, students from low uncertainty-avoidance cultures might be annoyed if given such a specific list of rules, viewing them as a barrier to creativity. As you can imagine, a teacher with students from both cultural orientations would face a difficult challenge when trying to explain an assignment.

Uncertainty avoidance also influences how people communicate in new and developing relationships. People from high uncertainty-avoidance cultures tend to be wary of strangers and may not seek out new relationships with people they perceive as different, and thus, unpredictable. They might prefer meeting people through friends and family. And in the early stages of a developing relationship, they might guard their privacy and refrain from self-disclosure. People from low uncertainty-avoidance cultures, on the other hand, are likely to initiate new relationships with people who seem unusual and unique, and might enjoy the excitement of disclosing personal information as a way to get to know one another earlier in the relationship.

THE AUDIENCE *BEYOND*

Zixue and Grant are college friends who are graduating this year. Both are hoping to meet the "right girl" and marry soon. Zixue, who comes from China, a low-uncertainty culture, enlists help from friends and family to meet potential partners. Grant, who grew up in the high-uncertainty U.S. culture, decides to post his profile on eHarmony and Match.com to see what possible "matches" show up.

Power Distance

Power distance is the extent to which members of a culture expect and accept that power will be equally or unequally shared. In a **high power-distance culture**, unequal distribution of power is accepted by both high and low power holders. Although no culture distributes power equally, people in high power-distance cultures (like many countries in the Middle East, Malaysia, Guatemala, Venezuela, and Singapore) view unequal power distribution as normal.

In a **low power-distance culture**, members prefer power to be more equally distributed. In the cultures of Austria, Finland, Denmark, Norway, and the United States, inequalities in power and status are muted. People know that some individuals have more clout, authority, and influence, but lower-ranking people are not in awe of or more respectful toward people in higher positions of power. Even though power differences exist, people value democracy and egalitarian behavior.

Our cultural beliefs about power distance naturally affect how we interact with others in authority positions. If you are a student or employee living in a high power-distance culture, you are not likely to argue with your teacher, supervisor, or boss. Rather, you will probably do what is ordered without question. In contrast, if you come from a low power-distance culture where status differences are muted, you might be more comfortable questioning or even arguing with those in authority.

Masculinity/Femininity

Cultures differ in how strongly they value traditional gender role distinctions. In a highly **masculine culture**, men and women are expected to adhere to traditional gender roles and behaviors. These cultures also value masculine roles more highly than feminine ones. If you come from a highly masculine culture (like those of Mexico, Italy, and Japan), you are likely to expect men to act in assertive and dominant ways and to expect women to be nurturing, caring, and service-oriented. You are likely to feel uncomfortable when you encounter people who don't meet these expectations. You are also likely to view masculine behaviors as more valuable, regardless of your sex. As a result, even though women are not supposed to enact such behaviors, you are likely to value the traditionally masculine characteristics of performance, ambition, assertiveness, competitiveness, and material success enacted by men more than you value traditionally feminine traits such as service, nurturing, relationships, and helping behaviors enacted by women embracing traditional gender roles and behaviors. (Hofstede, 2000).

In a highly **feminine culture**, people assume a variety of roles and are valued for doing so regardless of sex. In feminine cultures (like those of Sweden, Norway, and Denmark), both men and women are accustomed to being nurturing, caring, and service oriented and value those traits as much as performance, ambition, and competitiveness depending on the circumstances of a situation (Hofstede, 1998).

Whether you come from a highly masculine or feminine culture influences how you communicate with others. People from masculine cultures have strict definitions of what are appropriate behaviors for males and females and are

Spencer Grant/PhotoEdit

In the United States, a low power-distance culture, employers and employees often interact informally in many work settings. How have you interacted with your bosses? Has it varied from workplace to workplace?

power distance

extent to which members of a culture expect and accept that power will be equally or unequally shared

high power-distance culture

view unequal power distribution as normal

low power-distance culture

members prefer power to be more equally distributed

masculine culture

men and women are expected to adhere to traditional gender roles

feminine culture

people assume a variety of roles and are valued for doing so regardless of sex

rewarded for adhering to them. Men in these cultures tend to be unprepared to engage in nurturing and caring behaviors and women tend to be unprepared to be assertive or to argue persuasively. Both women and men in feminine cultures learn to nurture, empathize, assert, and argue, and are rewarded for doing so.

Long-Term/Short-Term Orientation

short-term oriented culture

tends to value static rewards in the here and now and emphasizes quick results

long-term oriented culture

emphasizes potential future rewards that will eventually be realized after slow and steady perseverance toward achieving a mutually acceptable result

Long-term and short-term orientations deal with how a culture values patience in arriving at rewards in the future or immediately in the here and now. A **short-term oriented** culture tends to value rewards in the here and now and, thus, emphasizes quick results, fulfilling social obligations, and getting to the bottom line efficiently. Cultures with a short-term orientation such as those found in the United States, Pakistan, Russia, Canada, Norway, and the United Kingdom tend to determine what result is desired at the outset of an experience and then do whatever it takes to achieve it. People in short-term oriented cultures also value keeping leisure time distinctly separate from working time. **Long-term oriented** cultures, such as those of China, Japan, Hong Kong, and Taiwan, emphasize potential future rewards that will be realized after slow and steady perseverance toward achieving a mutually acceptable result. Adaptability and honoring relationships are more important than quickly achieving the bottom line. And leisure time is not expected to be separate from working time.

Misunderstandings may arise when people from cultures with a long-term orientation interact with people from cultures with a short-term orientation. One of your authors experienced this on a business trip to Shanghai, China. Coming from a short-term oriented culture, when her hosts began discussing business ideas at dinner, she lightheartedly said, "No talking business at the dinner table." While this remark would have been quite appropriate in the United States, where a short-term orientation values leisure time as separate from working time, her hosts politely reminded her that they always talk business at the dinner table.

Cross-Cultural Adaptation

Understanding how cultures differ becomes critical when we interact with people whose cultural norms differ from ours, because it helps us empathize and adapt our communication patterns accordingly (Kim, 2001; 2005). Consequently, we end up demonstrating the ethical principles of respect and integrity. Perhaps one of the most illuminating ways to explain the cross-cultural adaptation process is through a personal narrative of someone who experienced it first-hand. Read Min Liu's story about moving from China to the U.S. in the *Diverse Voices* feature that follows.

THE AUDIENCE *BEYOND*

Historically, television sitcoms that do well in the United States often flop when aired in highly feminine cultures because the humorous anecdotes about men who fail as caregivers don't translate. Since men are just as likely as women to be nurturing caregivers, viewers can't relate and, thus, fail to see the humor.

DIVERSE
VOICES

My Story of Cross-Cultural Adaptation

by Min Liu

Assistant Professor of Communication Southern Illinois University at Edwardsville

I was born and raised in China, which is a collectivist country. China also rates high on context (we prefer indirect face-saving communication over direct verbal language), chronemics (we value nurturing relationships over deadlines and schedules), uncertainty avoidance (we like rules and predictability), power distance (we respect hierarchical authority), and long-term orientation (we value perseverance over quick problem-solving). So I was raised very differently from people in the dominant American culture of the United States.

I arrived in the United States for the first time in August of 2002 to begin the Ph.D. program at North Dakota State University (NDSU) in Fargo, North Dakota. I chose NDSU for a number of reasons, but one that really stands out in my mind is the fact that Fargo was listed as one of the safest cities in the United States at the time. You see, my family was concerned about sending their daughter to study in the most individualistic country in the world. They felt a bit more at ease knowing I would be studying in one of its safest cities. Even my decision to attend NDSU was influenced by my family and our collectivist ideals. Little did I know how much culture shock I would experience once I set foot on campus.

When I arrived, I felt prepared to study in the United States because I had been trained to be a college English instructor back in China. I had also aced the English proficiency test (TOEFL) required of international students. I remember feeling pretty confident about communicating with my American colleagues. As I walked across campus for my first day of orientation, I thought to myself, "Worst-case scenario, I'll forget how to say something in English and that's what my digital Chinese–English dictionary is for."

I would soon learn, however, that the issue of translating vocabulary was not the worst-case scenario. I could not find an answer for most of my communication struggles in the dictionary. For example, in one of my first graduate classes, the professor asked everyone to call her by her first name (Deanna). Without hesitation, all my American classmates began doing so. Calling a professor by her first name was unheard of for Chinese students like me! As a sign of respect for their power and authority, we always call our teachers by their titles—Dr. Sellnow, Professor Sellnow, or Teacher Sellnow. Wherever you are on a college campus in China, it's clear who is the teacher and who are the students. I thought, "How am I to call a professor by her first name?"

For a long time, I felt torn as to what to do—continuing to call her Dr. Sellnow may seem too distant and she might correct me. I want to honor her request out of respect for her authority. But everything in my Chinese norms and values suggested that calling her Deanna was disrespectful. So I simply avoided calling her anything. This solution worked fairly well in face-to-face communication situations—I would walk up to her, smile, and then start the conversation. This approach was working fairly well for me until the day came when I needed to e-mail her. I remember sitting in front of my computer for almost an hour trying to fine-tune a one-paragraph e-mail. Soon I realized the message was fine. The reason I couldn't bring myself to press "Send" was because I had begun with "Hello Deanna." I finally changed it to "Dr. Sellnow," followed by an apologetic explanation asking her to understand my dilemma and why I addressed her in this way. To my surprise, she responded by saying there was nothing wrong in addressing her as "Dr. Sellnow" and that I should continue to do so if that is what feels most appropriate to me.

In another class, I studied intercultural communication concepts. What I learned there proved helpful to me in reconciling some of the anxiety I was experiencing. As a Chinese, I grew up in a high power-distance culture. Professors and teachers are seen as having more power than students because, in my culture, people hold more or less power depending on where they are situated in certain formal, hierarchical positions. Students are to respect and honor their teachers by acknowledging their higher position of authority and status. The United States, however, is a low power-distance culture. People demonstrate respect for one another by addressing each other more as equals regardless of the formal positions they may hold. So, as uncomfortable as I felt, I tried to call my professors by their first names when they suggested it was appropriate to do so. I reminded myself that doing so was culturally appropriate and not a sign of disrespect.

Another culture shock experience I had to reconcile as a result of the differences between my Chinese norms and values and those of the United States had to do with disagreeing with my professor. In the United States, students learn to form opinions and defend their viewpoints and are rewarded for doing so in classroom presentations and debates. Professors perceive students who challenge viewpoints with evidence and reasoning as intelligent and motivated. Students who do so are perceived very differently in the Chinese culture, where public disagreement with an authority figure is not only rare, but also inappropriate. Because of this value clash, I found it difficult to express and defend my opinions in class, especially if they differed from something the professor said. Doing so, it seemed to me, would be extremely disrespectful. Yet I observed classmates doing so and being lauded for their comments. Many times, I chose not to say anything during a face-to-face meeting with a professor, but found the courage to write them in an e-mail later. In the online environment, I found I could be honest and explain my disagreement with respect. Fortunately, many of my professors soon realized my cultural-values dilemma and adapted their communication styles toward me. Still today, though, I prefer to present my viewpoints concerning controversial issues in a paper, a letter, an e-mail message, or an online post rather than in a meeting or other face-to-face discussion. I have found a way to honor my Chinese norms and values in a way that also allows me to express myself in an individualistic cultural setting.

Finally, I recall struggling with how to behave in groups as a result of cultural differences. When I first arrived in the United States, I was very conflict avoidant, probably because in collectivistic cultures that value a high power distance and long-term orientation, maintaining harmony is a priority. The approaches I had learned to value and enact in small group settings were actually perceived negatively by my peers and professors in the United States. My conflict avoidant style—which I engaged in as a sign of respect—would actually frustrate some of my group members. They perceived it as a sign that I did not care about the group's success and was a "slacker." I felt frustrated, too, as I tried to help the group become more cohesive and successful by avoiding conflict! I eventually learned that, to be successful, we all had to begin by being upfront about where we come from and our values. Once we all understood the differences, we could create a workable plan for success.

I have been in the United States for several years now, am married, and have a son. I have also earned my Ph.D. and am working as an assistant professor of communication at the University of Southern Illinois at Edwardsville. Even now, I continue to learn new things about how to communicate best in this individualistic, low uncertainty-avoidance, low power distance, and short-term orientation culture as compared to my home in China. Based on my experiences, I would have to say the most important thing for successful communication when interacting with people who come from different cultures is for all of us to always be mindful of those differences so we can both perceive communication by others correctly and acknowledge and adapt our own styles accordingly.

Source: By Min Liu, Assistant Professor of Communication Southern Illinois University at Edwardsville.

Developing Intercultural Communication Competence

We can develop intercultural communication competence by first acknowledging potential barriers and then by employing several strategies to overcome them.

Potential Barriers

Several of the most common barriers to effective intercultural communication include anxiety, assuming similarity or difference, ethnocentrism, stereotyping, incompatible communication codes, and incompatible norms and values.

Anxiety It is normal to feel some level of discomfort when entering a cultural setting whose norms and customs are unfamiliar to us. Most people experience fear, dislike, and distrust when first interacting with someone from a different culture (Luckmann, 1999).

Assumed Similarity or Difference When we cross into an unfamiliar cultural environment, we might assume that the norms that apply to our culture will also apply in the new one. When traveling internationally from the United States, for example, many people expect to eat their familiar hamburgers and fries and to be provided with rapid service when ordering. Likewise, they may be annoyed when shops and restaurants close during the early afternoon in countries that observe the custom of a siesta.

It can be just as great a mistake to assume that everything about an unfamiliar culture will be different. For example, Marissa, a Mexican-American student from California who is studying at a small private college in Vermont, may feel that no one understands her and her experiences. As she makes friends, however, she may learn that while Rachel, who is Jewish, didn't have a *quinceañera* party, she did have a bat mitzvah celebration, and Kate, who is Irish Catholic, had a big confirmation party. While these occasions are different, each rite celebrates a coming of age. As Marissa makes these and other connections, she will become more comfortable in her new environment.

Ethnocentrism Ethnocentrism is the belief that one's own culture is superior to others. The stereotype of the tourist in the host country, loudly complaining about how much better everything is back home, is the classic example of ethnocentrism. Ethnocentrism exists in every culture to some degree (Haviland, 1993) and can occur in co-cultures, as well. An ethnocentric view of the world leads to attitudes of superiority and messages that are condescending in content and tone.

ethnocentrism

the belief that one's own culture is superior to others

Stereotyping Recall that stereotyping is a perceptual shortcut in which people assume that everyone in a cultural group is the same. When we interact based on stereotypes, we risk engaging in inaccurate and even unethical communication that is likely to damage our relationships. The *Pop Comm!* feature focuses on the debate that arose about race and stereotypes in the critically acclaimed film, *The Help,* based on the bestselling book by Kathryn Stockett.

Incompatible Communication Codes When others speak a different language than we do, it is easy to see that we have incompatible communication codes. But even when people speak the same language, cultural variations can

Prejudice and stereotypes can negatively impact not only our relationships with people we know personally but also with our larger communities. How do you suppose this protester's sign affects the young girls in the photo?

result from belonging to different co-cultures. For example, people from Great Britain take a "lift" to reach a higher floor and eat "chips" with their fish. Americans ride an "elevator" and eat "french fries" with their burgers. Within the United States, many Midwesterners drink "pop" rather than "soda." Co-cultural groups will often purposefully develop "in-group" codes that are easily understood by co-culture members but are unintelligible to those from the outside. Just try having a conversation about a computer problem with your friend, Sam, who is a "techno geek." If you are not a "techno geek" yourself, Sam's vocabulary is likely to be as foreign to you as if he were speaking Icelandic.

Incompatible Norms and Values Sometimes what is considered normal or highly valued in one culture is offensive in another. To the Vietnamese, dog meat is considered a delicacy. Many Americans might find the practice of eating dog meat disgusting but think nothing of eating beef. However, practicing Hindus may not eat beef because the cow is sacred to their religion. Different norms and values can cause serious problems when communicating unless we are aware of and respect differences.

POP COMM!

The Help: Race and Stereotypes in Popular Culture

One of the most successful movies of the summer of 2011 was also one of the most controversial. Set in the South during the pre–Civil Rights era, *The Help*, based on Kathryn Stockett's 2009 best seller, depicts the relationships between upper-middle-class white women and working-class black women who took care of their homes and families. On the surface, the film seems to challenge racism and offer a richer view of the lives of the black domestic workers. However, it sparked debate among film critics and audiences about its representation of race, questioning whether or not the black maids and their co-cultural experiences within a dominant white culture were accurately depicted or if the film relied too heavily on stereotypes about race and racism that have long permeated popular culture.

The narrative of this film centers on the daily struggles of two black domestic workers, Aibileen (Viola Davis) and Minny (Octavia Spencer), employed in white households in Jackson, Mississippi, during the early 1960s. Their struggles as domestics are brought to light when Skeeter (Emma Stone), the white daughter of Aibileen's employer, writes a book based on interviews with Aibileen, Minny, and other black maids.

For many African American audiences, in particular, *The Help* resurrected negative stereotypes about black culture and life many have struggled to overcome. Prior to the release of the film, a statement issued by the Association of Black Women Historians challenged *The Help* on many levels, including its reliance on the "Mammy" stereotype that frames black women as "asexual, loyal, and contented caretakers of whites" who support the physical and emotional development of white children to the detriment of their own families. This stereotype, they argue, fails to recognize the economic realities that historically forced black women into such low-paying and often exploitative domestic work, as well as racist political and social discourses that framed relationships between black domestic workers and white families. By framing the film as "a progressive story of triumph over racial injustice," they argue, *The Help* distorts, ignores, and trivializes the experiences of black domestic workers."

These criticisms are rooted in the complexity of addressing and crossing the boundaries of cultural difference. Some expressed concern about the ability of a white woman (book author Stockett) and a white man (film director Tate Taylor) to tell the story of black women's experiences. Though both Stockett and Taylor grew up in Southern homes that employed black women as domestics, these critics challenge the assumption that their experiences as whites in the South match those of black women whose stories they try to tell. For example, black actor Wendell Pierce (*The Wire, Treme*) tweeted about taking his mother, who had worked as a domestic, to see the movie. He said they were both insulted by the film and its "passive segregation lite" that did not speak to the real experiences of black women in 1960s America. In other words, Pierce's mother's co-cultural experiences as a black domestic in the Jim Crow era did not resonate with the film's depiction, however well meaning, of those experiences. He tweeted, "Watching the film in UptownNewOrleans to the sniffles of elderly white people while my 80 year old mother was seething, made clear distinction."

This is not to say that all black audiences rejected *The Help*'s representation of race relations in the United States. Patricia Turner, African American studies professor and vice provost for undergraduate studies at the University of California–Davis, suggests that because the film in fact tackled the complex issue of race in America, it does indeed represent an important step toward successful intercultural dialogue in this country. As a black woman raised in the era of Civil Rights by a mother who, like the women in the film, worked as a maid, Turner argues that *The Help* creates the opportunity for an important public dialogue about race ("Dangerous White Stereotypes"). She challenges audiences to recognize the underlying messages about race and racism called up by the film and compare its fictionalized representation of black and white relationships to historical realities. Similarly, *Entertainment Weekly* film critic Owen Gleiberman calls on audiences to engage with the film and its problems rather than simply condemning it as "racist." He "envision[s] audiences, black *and* white, watching *The Help*, all sharing a greater understanding of our past" ("Is 'The Help' a condescending movie for white liberals?"). He hopes that instead of simply rejecting the film as "racist," audiences will use the potential problems of the film as a starting point for discussion about how this depiction of race in America's past speaks to our understanding of race in the present.

Questions to Ponder

1. What do you think? Can films like *The Help* offer audiences a way to challenge our own co-culturally ingrained stereotypes or do they simply reinforce them in the name of entertainment?

2. What other stories about co-cultural experience could or should be told in feature films? Explain.

Competent Communication Strategies

Unfortunately, there is no "silver bullet" strategy for communicating effectively across cultures. However, competent intercultural communicators work to overcome potential cultural barriers by acquiring accurate information about other cultures' values and practices, adopting an appropriate attitude, and developing culture-centered skills.

Acquire Accurate Knowledge The more we know about other cultures before we attempt to interact with people in them, the more likely we are to be competent intercultural communicators (Neuliep, 2006). There are several ways to learn about other cultures.

1. **Formal study.** You can learn about other cultures by reading books, periodicals, and Web sites about them. You can read personal accounts and ethnographic research studies, take courses, and interview members of the group.

2. **Observation.** You can learn about a culture or co-culture by watching as members interact with each other. We call this form of watching **nonparticipant observation**. As you watch, you can notice how certain values, rituals, and communication styles are similar to and different from your own.

3. **Immersion.** You can learn a great deal about another culture by actively participating in it. When you live or work with people whose cultural assumptions are different from yours, you not only acquire obvious cultural information, but you also learn nuances that escape passive observers and are not accessible through formal study alone. We call this form of immersion **participant observation**. One reason study-abroad programs often include home stays is to ensure that students become immersed in the culture of the host country.

nonparticipant observation

learning about a culture or co-culture by watching as members interact with each other

participant observation

learning about a culture or co-culture by living or working with people whose cultural assumptions are different from yours,

Adopt an Appropriate Attitude The right attitude involves one's motivations and flexibility in interacting with others (Neuliep, 2006). In other words, we must be willing to try and must have a genuine desire to succeed when communicating across cultures. We must be willing to adapt rather than expect the other person to adjust to our communication style. We must go into the experience following the motto of "assuming the best first" so as not to jump to wrong conclusions based on preconceived assumptions. We can begin to adopt an appropriate attitude by tolerating ambiguity, being open-minded, and acting altruistically.

1. **Tolerate ambiguity.** Communicating with strangers creates uncertainty, and when the stranger also comes from a different culture, we can become anxious about what he or she will expect of us. When communicating, we must be prepared to tolerate a high degree of uncertainty about the other person and to tolerate it for a long time. If you enter an intercultural interaction believing that it is OK to be unsure about how to proceed, you are likely to pay closer attention to the feedback you receive. You can then work to adjust your communication to demonstrate respect and to achieve mutual understanding.

When Jerome read the Partner Assignment List posted outside the lab, he discovered that his lab partner, Meena, was an exchange student from

THE AUDIENCE *BEYOND*

Rick was interested in China and Chinese history. To become interculturally competent, he began by Googling it. He studied everything he could find online before leaving for his study abroad immersion and observation experience. He also started a blog to which he would add entries throughout his study-abroad experience.

COMMUNICATE ON YOUR FEET

Speech Assignment

Acquiring Cultural Knowledge

The Assignment

Choose a culture you're not familiar with but are curious about. Prepare a 3- to 5-minute speech to deliver in class by gathering materials from (a) reviewing an online encyclopedia entry, (b) researching two or three academic sources about the culture, and (c) interviewing someone from that culture either face-to-face or online. Use what you learn from the encyclopedia and the academic sources to shape the questions you ask in the interview. In your speech discuss what you learned from each source, answering the following questions:

1. What did you know about the culture before you began your research?

2. What did you learn from the encyclopedia article that changed or deepened your knowledge?

3. How was your understanding enriched from the additional academic sources you read?

4. What did you learn from your interviewee, and how did the interview compare to your other sources?

Use Diverse Resources

When researching your topic, consult a variety of information sources. Whether online or in print, encyclopedias are a good jumping-off point. Specialized sources like books and articles by experts provide additional details. Finally, personal interviews with experts add another dimension or level of specificity. For example, in this assignment, when you interview someone from another culture, you can ask for specific examples about his or her experiences and about whether what you read in other sources is accurate.

Mumbai. Over the semester, Jerome worked hard to attune his ear to Meena's accent and Meena worked hard to understand him. As it turned out, Jerome was really happy to have Meena as a partner. She really had a much better grasp of chemistry than he did, and tutored him as they worked on assignments. Meena didn't mind tutoring Jerome because he demonstrated genuine respect for both her cultural values and her intelligence.

2. **Be open-minded.** Open-minded people are aware of their own cultural norms and values and recognize that other people's norms and values may be different, but not wrong. Resist the impulse to judge the values of other cultures in terms of your own culture. Also, avoid jumping to conclusions about what you think others mean by something they say or do. Instead, seek to learn from those you interact with by assuming their intentions are honorable and asking sincere questions about what they say and do differently and why.

3. **Be altruistic. Altruism** is a display of genuine and unselfish concern for the welfare of others. The opposite of altruism is **egocentricity**, a selfish interest in one's own needs to the exclusion of everything else. Egocentric people are focused on themselves, whereas altruistic people are focused on others. Altruistic communicators do not neglect their own needs, but they recognize that for a conversation to be successful, both parties must be able to contribute what they want and take what they need from the exchange. One way to demonstrate this is to learn some basic phrases in the language of your peer's culture and try to use them when possible. When people hear you say "please" and "thank you" in their native language, even if your pronunciation is imperfect, they are likely to perceive you as respectful and are likely to engage more openly with you as a result.

altruism

a display of genuine and unselfish concern for the welfare of others

egocentricity

a selfish interest in one's own needs to the exclusion of everything else

Develop Culture-Centered Skills To be effective in intercultural situations, you may need to adapt the basic communication skills you learn in this course to a particular culture. Three very useful skills are listening, empathy, and flexibility.

1. **Practice listening.** There are cultural differences in how people value and engage in listening. In the dominant culture of the United States, people listen closely for concrete facts and information and often ask questions while listening. In other cultures, such as those in Japan, Finland, and Sweden, listeners are more reserved and do not ask as many questions (Samovar, Porter, & McDaniel, 2009). Many cultures in East Asian countries value listening more than speaking.

   As you practice, remember to check your understanding about what you see and hear. One way you can do so is to ask them their name and then try to say it back as accurately as possible. One of your authors did this when visiting with college students at Shanghai University. Although each student first introduced himself or herself with an "English" name, your author also asked them to offer their Chinese name. Then she repeated it back to them. When the students heard her make this genuine attempt to honor them and their given Chinese names, they began to trust her and opened up more during the

WHAT WOULD YOU DO?

A Question of Ethics

Tyler, Jeannie, Margeaux, and Madhukar were sitting around Margeaux's dining room table working on a group marketing project. It was 2:00 A.M. They had been working since 6:00 P.M. and still had several hours of work remaining.

"Oh, the agony," groaned Tyler, "If I never see another photo of a veggie burger it will be too soon. Why didn't we choose a more 'appetizing' product to base our project on?"

"I think it had something to do with someone wanting to promote a healthy alternative to greasy hamburgers," Jeannie replied sarcastically.

"Right," Tyler answered. "I don't know what I could have been thinking. Speaking of greasy hamburgers, is anyone else starving? Anyone up for ordering a pizza or something?"

"Sorry, but no one will deliver up here so late," Margeaux apologized. "But I have a quiche that I could heat up."

"Oh, oui, oui," Tyler quipped.

"You wish," Margeaux said. "It came out of a box."

"Sure, it sounds great, thanks," Jeannie said. "I'm hungry too."

"It doesn't have any meat in it, does it?" asked Madhukar. "I don't eat meat."

"Nope, it's a cheese and spinach quiche," Margeaux answered.

Tyler and Margeaux went off to the kitchen to prepare the food. Tyler took the quiche, which was still in its box, from the refrigerator. "Uh-oh," he said. "My roommate is a vegetarian, and he won't buy this brand because it has lard in the crust. Better warn Madhukar."

"Shhh!" said Margeaux. "I don't have anything else to offer him, and he'll never know the difference anyway. Just pretend you didn't notice."

1. What ethical principles are involved in this case?

2. What exactly are Margeaux's ethical obligations to Madhukar in this situation?

3. What should Tyler do now?

classroom discussion. People who make a sincere effort to listen attentively and respond in an other-centered way find the most success when interacting with people from cultures that differ from their own.

2. **Practice intercultural empathy. Intercultural empathy** means imaginatively placing yourself in the other person's cultural world and attempting to experience what he or she is experiencing (Ting-Toomey, 1999). The saying "Don't judge a person until you have walked a mile in his or her shoes" captures this idea. Conveying intercultural empathy demonstrates that we sincerely respect the other person and their cultural norms even though those norms may not be ones upheld in our culture. Try to honor the practices of the host culture. If you are in an East Asian country, try to use the chopsticks rather than asking for a knife and fork. Similarly, learn whether shaking hands is appropriate when greeting others. Did you know, for instance, that Chinese people find it disrespectful to exchange business cards with one hand (rather than two) and extremely disrespectful to put the cards in your back pocket? Because business cards are considered an extension of the self, placing a person's business card in your back pocket is interpreted as something akin to sitting on their face.

intercultural empathy
imaginatively placing yourself in another person's cultural world and attempting to experience what he or she is experiencing

3. **Develop flexibility.** We discussed the concept of flexibility as part of an appropriate attitude toward intercultural encounters, but we can also provide concrete strategies for becoming more flexible while communicating. **Flexibility** is the ability to adjust your communication to fit the other person and the situation. With flexibility, you can use a wide variety of communication skills during an interaction and modify your behavior within and across situations. Being flexible means analyzing a situation, making good decisions about how to communicate in that situation, and then modifying your communication when necessary as you go along.

flexibility
the ability to adjust your communication to fit the other person and the situation

Summary

Culture is the system of shared values, beliefs, attitudes, and norms that guide what is considered appropriate among an identifiable group of people. Intercultural communication involves interactions that occur between people whose cultures are so different that the communication between them is altered. Culture shock refers to the psychological discomfort people have when we attempt to adjust to a new cultural situation. Both dominant and co-cultures exist in a society. A shared system of meaning exists within the dominant culture, but meanings can vary within co-cultures based on race, ethnicity, sex and gender, sexual orientation, religion, socioeconomic status, age/generation, and disability. Cultural identity is formed based on how closely we identify with the dominant culture and each of the co-cultural groups to which we belong.

Cultures are unique among a variety of dimensions. These include: individualism/collectivism, context, chronemics, uncertainty avoidance, power distance, masculinity/femininity, and long-term/short-term orientation. To become interculturally competent, we need to acknowledge and overcome common intercultural communication barriers, which include anxiety, assumptions about differences and similarities, ethnocentrism, stereotyping, incompatible communication codes, and incompatible norms and values. We also need to employ the competent communication strategies of acquiring accurate knowledge, adopting an appropriate attitude, and developing culture-centered skills (e.g., listening, intercultural empathy, and flexibility).

COMMUNICATE!

RESOURCE AND ASSESSMENT CENTER

Now that you have read Chapter 3, go to the Speech Communication CourseMate at cengagebrain.com where you'll find an interactive eBook and interactive learning tools including quizzes, flashcards, sample speech videos, audio study tools, skill-building activities, action step activities and more. Student Workbook, Speech Builder Express 3.0 and Speech Studio 2.0 are also available.

Applying What You've Learned

Impromptu Speech Activity

1. Select a photograph of a person or people from a magazine advertisement provided by your instructor. Prepare an impromptu speech about the assumptions you make about their cultural norms and values based on what you see in the photograph. Close by explaining what you would do to check the accuracy of your assumptions.

Assessment Activities

1. Consider your family as a co-cultural group. First, describe the scope of your family unit. Are you considering your nuclear family, extended family, etc? Who are the people who make up your family group? Now describe some generally held stories that everyone knows. What do these stories tell you about your family co-culture's norms and values? What sorts of beliefs and behaviors does your family group consider normal/not normal, desirable/undesirable, appropriate/inappropriate? How do you know? Describe events/interactions and the consequences of them that have helped shape your family's set of norms and values. Finally, describe your family along the dimensions discussed in this chapter and explain why you have assessed your family this way.

2. Visit a toy store and see if you can identify what are being promoted as "toys for boys" and "toys for girls," as well as how the rows of "toys for boys" and "toys for girls" are arranged differently, if at all. What do your observations suggest about what and how children are being taught *gender*? Prepare a short paper to articulate your observations and analysis.

Skill-Building Activity

1. Acquiring Accurate Cultural Knowledge For the next week, conduct research into a distinct culture with which you have little or no familiarity. This can be a co-culture based on race, religion, ethnicity, sex and gender, socioeconomic status, sexual orientation, age/generation, disability, or some combination; just be sure you can access it locally. First, arrange to observe members of the culture engaged in a typical activity and note as many of their individual communication behaviors as you can. Take your notes respectfully, being careful not to offend those you observe. Second, spend some time formally researching publications about the culture and its communication behaviors. Finally, observe members of the culture once more and then write a paragraph in which you answer these questions: What were your impressions of the culture's communication behaviors the first time you observed its members? How were these first impressions altered, if at all, by your formal research into the culture? How did your formal research affect your second observation of the culture?

To help you complete this activity, look for the Chapter 3 Skill-Building activities on the CourseMate for *Communicate!* at cengagebrain.com.

Verbal Messages

What you'll know

- What is a language, a dialect, and an idiolect

- The characteristics of language

- How word choices and sentence structure shape meaning

- How conversational social, and cultural contexts shape meaning

What you'll be able to do

- Form verbal messages using clear and precise language

- Form appropriate verbal messages for different social and cultural contexts

As Anthony, Lauren, and Carla began to settle in for their work session, Anthony noticed that Bethney hadn't arrived yet and said: "Hey, maybe we should wait a few minutes for Bethney before we get started."

Lauren responded, "No, I don't think she's coming. She texted me this afternoon. Here, look at this."

Lauren showed the text message chain to Anthony and Carla:

LAUREN: "U coming to study tonight?"

BETHNEY: "In 2 hrs, right?"

LAUREN: "Yep, Union coffee shop at 7."

BETHNEY: "Argh . . . gotta go to the store. . . . Forgot to make cupcakes. . . . Addie's turn to bring snacks."

LAUREN: "Hang in there. I ♥ U!"

Carla said, "I really don't know how Bethney does it all, I mean school and kids and work. I know I couldn't do it."

"Yeah, I know," Lauren responded, "but I'm sure you understand now why she's not coming tonight."

4.

Swahili = English

mtoto = a child

mwanadamu = a man

mwanamke = a woman

mtoto mchanga = baby

jamaa = family

"Absolutely," Carla replied.

Anthony jumped in, "Hey, wait a minute. Bethney never said she wasn't going to make it, just that she had a lot to do first."

"You think so, Anthony?" Lauren remarked. "I thought she was letting us know why she wouldn't be joining us."

Just then Bethney hurried over to the table and said, "Sorry I'm late. Thanks for waiting. What a day! Oh well. Hey, I can't wait to show you the research I found last night for our project. Check this out!"

What just happened? Why did Lauren, Carla, and Anthony interpret Bethney's texts differently? After all, each of them read the very same words. As you'll learn in this chapter, there are many reasons for such different interpretations, which can lead to serious misunderstandings that affect our relationships.

We begin by explaining the nature of language. Then we describe the relationship between language and meaning and offer suggestions for improving your ability to communicate both face-to-face and online.

utterance

complete unit of talk bounded by the speaker's literal or figurative silence

turn-taking

verbal and nonverbal messages and exchanging utterances

In what ways do we use language to compare or judge?

© mediacolor's/Alamy

The Nature of Language

When you hear the word "language," what comes to mind? If you're like most people, you probably think of English, Spanish, French, Chinese, Hindi, Swahili, and so forth. While each language is certainly different from the others in some ways, their purposes and fundamentals are the same.

In terms of purposes, we use language to label, compare, and define. So when we label some music as hip hop, we do so to differentiate it from other musical genres such as rock, pop, country, and classical. We also use language to compare and judge things as better or worse. Television programs like *What Not to Wear* and *American Idol* are based on this very principle. We also use language to discuss and learn from the experiences of others. We might do so by taking a course, attending a lecture, visiting with a friend, watching a TV program, or surfing the Internet.

In terms of fundamentals, all languages are based on utterances and exchanging them. An **utterance** is a complete unit of talk bounded by the speaker's silence (Arnoff & Rees-Miller, 2001). "Silence" can be literal, as during a face-to-face or telephone conversation, or it can be figurative as when waiting for a response to a text message. Exchanging utterances is known as **turn-taking**. With these purposes and fundamentals in mind, let's turn now to a more specific discussion about what a language is and the characteristics of it.

THE AUDIENCE *BEYOND*

Although Karlie had never been to Panama, she learned a lot about it by reading her friend's blog and Facebook page.

What Is a Language?

A **language** is a system of symbols used by people to communicate. Verbal languages communicate thoughts and feelings. Each verbal language is comprised of a **lexicon**, the collection of words and expressions; a **phonology**, the sounds used to pronounce words; and **syntax** and **grammar**, the rules for combining words to form sentences and larger units of expression.

All people who understand a particular language are part of a **language community**. For example, the English language is spoken by people who live in Australia, Scotland, Ireland, Canada, India, and America, among others. The five largest language communities in the world, in order, are Chinese, Spanish, English, Arabic, and Hindi (Lewis, 2009).

If all people in a particular language community knew all the words, pronounced them the same way, and used the same rules of grammar and syntax, communication would be easy. Unfortunately, however, this is not the case. The English spoken in England is not the same as the English spoken in the United States. And the English spoken in Boston is not the same as the English spoken in Biloxi, Mississippi, or in Fargo, North Dakota.

Languages are really collections of dialects. A **dialect** is a unique form of a more general language spoken by a specific culture or co-culture (O'Grady, et al., 2001). These smaller groups that speak a common dialect are known as **speech communities**. Dialects exist on a continuum. The more commonalities shared by two dialects, the closer they are on the continuum. This is why Americans can generally understand Canadians more easily than they can understand Scots or Aussies.

No one dialect is better or worse than another. Each just uses different lexicons, phonology, grammar, and syntax. However, some dialects are *perceived* to be "better" than others because they are spoken by the power elite of a language community. This dialect tends to be promoted as the "proper" form.

As is demonstrated in the cases of the former Yugoslavia and China, what is called a *language* and what is called a *dialect* are usually rooted in politics. When Yugoslavia was a country, its official language (Serbian-Croatian) was comprised of many similar dialects among various regions. Since the collapse of Yugoslavia in the 1990s, however, each region is now a separate country and many of these regional dialects are also considered the official languages of each country. Serbian is spoken in Serbia, Croatian in Croatia, Bosnian in Bosnia, and Montenegrin in Montenegro (Cvetkovic, 2009).

On the other hand, the official language of China is Chinese and all literate people use this same written symbol system. Thus, people from one part of the country can easily read compositions written by someone in other parts of the country. But the written symbols do not have commonly shared pronunciations. So although the regional tongues of Mandarin, Wu, Cantonese, and Min are dialects of Chinese, speakers of one dialect often can't understand someone speaking another (Wright, 2010). In the *Diverse Voices* feature that follows, Raj shares his story about how Indian English differs from American English spoken in the United States.

language

a system of symbols used by people to communicate

lexicon

collection of words and expressions

phonology

sounds used to pronounce words

syntax and grammar

rules for combining words to form sentences and larger units of expression

CONSIDER *THIS....*

If you know more than one language, how are the lexicons, phonology, syntax, and grammar similar and different? How and why does this make learning a language difficult?

language community

all people who can speak or understand a particular language

dialect

a unique form of a more general language spoken by a specific culture or co-culture that shares enough commonality so that most people who belong to the larger language community can still understand it

speech communities

smaller groups that speak a common dialect

THE AUDIENCE *BEYOND*

It had been three hours since Brian texted Greta to apologize for poking fun at her and he still hadn't received a reply. He figured Greta's "silence" meant she was still upset with him.

DIVERSE VOICES

Raj Gaur, Ph.D.

University of Kentucky

"Mommy, Why Does Raj Talk Funny?"

I grew up in India. In my home we spoke Hindi, but from the time I began school at five years old, I was also taught English. By the time I was fourteen years old I was fluent in English—at least what I thought of at the time as English. Ten years ago, I came to the United States and have since learned that the English I speak is somewhat different from the English spoken here in the United States. These differences sometimes make it difficult for me to be understood by some Americans. You see, the English I learned as a child is a *nativization* of English that might more accurately be called "Indian English." What is nativization?

Nativization is the unconscious process of adapting a foreign language so it conforms to the linguistic style and rhetorical patterns of the native language spoken in a particular culture. You are familiar with the ways American English differs between regions and among groups within the U.S., as well as differences between British English and American English. If there are differences among native English speakers, imagine what happens when a cultural group like Indians, whose native language is Hindi, adopts English as a second language! As you would probably expect, they adapt English to include some of the grammar, syntax, and pronunciation rules that characterize their first language, as well as by adopting some of the rhetorical and idiomatic expressions that they use in their mother tongue. It's not that Indians consciously decide to make these changes. Rather, the changes simply occur as the new language, in this case English, is used in everyday conversations with other Indians.

Prior to coming to the U.S., most of the people I knew spoke English just like I did, and I had no problem understanding them or being understood by them. So imagine my consternation when after arriving in the U.S. some of my American colleagues, professors, and students had trouble understanding me when I spoke. What made this particularly interesting was that they didn't seem to have trouble understanding what I wrote. Rather, it was when I spoke that I got quizzical looks and requests to repeat myself.

What I now understand is that there are major differences between the way certain words are pronounced by those speaking American English and those speaking Indian English. Some of these differences are due to the rules each type of English uses for accenting the syllables within a word. In American English, as a general rule, words with more than one syllable alternate between accented and unaccented syllables. So if the first syllable is accented the second is not and vice versa. But in Hindi, whether a particular syllable is accented or not depends on the sounds in the word. Some sounds always receive an accent and others do not regardless of their position in a word. So in Indian English, "pho" is pronounced the same whether the speaker is using the word *photo* or *photography*. If you speak American English, you are used to hearing "pho·TOG·gra·phy," but when I pronounce it in Indian English, I say "PHO·to·GRAPH·y." If you're an American English speaker and you hear me say this, you may not understand me or may think, "Oh he just mispronounced that word." But to me, your pronunciation sounds just as strange because in India, that is how we pronounce the word.

There are also syntactic differences between Indian and American English. You will recall that syntax is the rules of a particular language for how words are supposed to be put together to form complete ideas. The syntactic issue that I have struggled most with is the use of articles (a, an, the, etc.). In Hindi, we may or may not use articles, and this practice also guides our Indian English. So an Indian English student may say, "I go to university in city of Mumbai," rather than

"I go to *the* university in *the* city of Mumbai. Another syntactic difference that is common to speakers of Indian English is to form questions without using an auxiliary verb (do, should, can, must, etc.). In Hindi, auxiliary verbs are not required when forming an interrogatory sentence. So in Indian English I may ask: "I know you?" Rather than "*Do* I know you?" or "I finish it?" rather than "*Should* or *can* or *must* I finish it?"

Nativization of English can also be perceived at the idiomatic level when I attempt to express Indian sensibilities and Indian realities to my American friends. To clarify, as a speaker of Indian English, I sometimes exploit the syntactic structures of the language by directly translating Hindi idioms to English. For example, I might say "wheatish complexion" in Indian English to mean "not dark skinned, tending toward light." Or I might use the phrase "out of station" to mean "out of town," which has its origins to denote army officers posted to far-off places during the British rule. Indians also commonly substitute "hotel" for "restaurant," "this side" and "that side" for "here" and "there," "cent per cent" for "100 percent," and "reduce weight" for "lose weight."

Any one of these English adaptations might not pose problems, but taken together they make the brand of English that I speak very different from that of my American friends. Indian English has evolved over a long period of time, and English is now integrated into much of Indian culture. English is taught in schools, business is conducted in English, and English is used in government dealings. Nonetheless, the English of Delhi is not the English of London, or Berlin, or New York, or Lexington, Kentucky. And I find it ironic that after living in the United States for nearly ten years now and struggling to be understood by Americans, my friends in India now complain about my English too. They say it's too American!

References

Don't care for Nano or No-No: Mamta. (2009, March 23). Hindustan Times. http://www.hindustantimes.com; Kachru, B.B. (1992). The other tongue: English across cultures. Urbana, IL: University of Illinois Press; Kachru, B. B. (1986). The alchemy of English: The spread, functions, and models of non-native Englishes. Oxford: Pergamon Press; Guj riots a national shame, not IPL going abroad: PC. (2009, March 23). The Financial Express. Retrieved from http://www.expressindia.com; Patrolling intensified in sea, on shores in Tamil Nadu. (2009, March 23). Press Trust of India. Retrieved from http://www.ptinews.com; Wiltshire, C., & Moon, R. (2003). Phonetic stress in Indian English vs. American English. World Englishes, 22(3), 291–303; Zardari is 5th biggest loser in world: Foreign policy magazine. (2009, March 23). NDTV. Retrieved from http://www.ndtv.com.

Source: By Raj Gaur, Ph.D., University of Kentucky.

In addition to language and dialect, each of us uses our own personal symbol system called an **idiolect**, which includes our active vocabularies and our unique pronunciations, grammar, and syntax (Higginbotham, 2006). We may have words in our personal lexicon that are understood by very few people as well as words understood by large numbers of people. Likewise, we may pronounce some words or use grammar or syntax in idiosyncratic ways. Those who talk with us most understand our idiolect best. That's why parents can understand toddlers whose speech is unrecognizable to others.

idiolect

our own personal symbol system that includes our active vocabularies and our unique pronunciations, grammar, and syntax

Characteristics of Language

Sharing meaning can be difficult because we speak different languages and use different dialects and idiolects than those with whom we are communicating.

CONSIDER THIS....

Do you have difficulty understanding certain dialects? If so, how do you try to overcome it?

Sharing meaning can also be difficult because language is arbitrary, abstract, and constantly changing.

words

arbitrarily chosen symbols used to represent thoughts and feelings

1. **Language is arbitrary.** The **words** used to represent things in any language are arbitrary symbols. In other words, there is not necessarily any literal connection between a word and the thing it represents. For a word to have meaning, it must be recognized by members of the language or speech community as standing for a particular object, idea, or feeling. The word D-O-G is nothing more than three letters used together unless members of a community agree that it stands for a certain four-legged animal. Different language communities use different word symbols to represent the same phenomenon. In Spanish, for instance, *el perro* stands for the same thing as *dog* does in English. Different speech communities within a language community may also use different words to represent the same phenomenon. For example, the storage compartment of an automobile is called a "trunk" in the United States and called a "boot" in England.

2. **Language is abstract.** Not only is language arbitrary, but it is also abstract. For example, in the United States, the word "pet" is commonly understood to be an animal kept for companionship. Still, if Rema refers simply to her "pet," Margi may think of a dog, cat, snake, bird, or hamster. Even if Rema specifically mentions her cat, Margi still might think of cats of various breeds, sizes, colors, and temperaments.

3. **Language changes over time.** New words are constantly being invented and existing words abandoned or assigned new meanings. Just think, for example, of the words that have been invented to represent new technologies, such as *texting, Googling, cyberbullying, sexting, tweeting, retweeting, netiquette, webinar, emoticon,* and *blogging.* Some of the new words most recently added to English dictionaries include *vanity sizing* (the deliberate undersizing of clothes), *twirt* (flirt via Twitter), *mankle* (the male ankle), and *cougar* (an older woman in a romantic relationship with a younger man). Did you know that the *Oxford English Dictionary* now also includes *OMG, LOL,* and *<3* as actual words?

Some words become obsolete because the thing they represent is no longer used. For example, today we use *photocopiers* and *computers* to make multiple copies of print documents rather than *mimeographs* (low-cost printing presses) and *stencils*. We record audio and video data using *smartphones* rather than using *tape recorders, cassette tapes,* and *videotapes*. And we take notes on *iPads* and *laptops* rather than on paper that we organize in a *Trapper Keeper* (a loose-leaf binder used by school children in the United States during the 1970s and 1980s).

Sometimes the meanings of existing words change. For example, in the United States, *gay* once meant *happy* and only that. Today, its more common usage references one's sexual orientation. In some communities, *bad* might mean *not good*, in others it might mean *naughty*, and in others it might mean *really great*

Depending on where you live, you might call a knitted hat like this one a tuque, a bobble hat, a burglar beanie, a stocking cap, or a toboggan. What do you call it? Did you know of these other names for it?

Ursula Alter/iStockphoto.com

(e.g., "That movie was really bad."). And, language can change as a result of melding aspects of multiple languages. *Tex-Mex* and *Spanglish* for instance, both blend English and Spanish and we don't think twice about the fact that children go to *kindergarten,* a word absorbed by the United States from German immigrants.

As you can see, language is an imprecise and complex way to transfer meaning from one person to another. That is why we must consider not only the words themselves, but also how they are used in the conversational, social, and cultural contexts where they are used.

The Relationship Between Language and Meaning

On the surface, the relationship between language and meaning seems pretty simple. We select words, structure them using the rules of grammar and syntax of a language community, and people will understand what we mean when we say them. Because communicating verbally is more complicated than that, in this section, we focus specifically on the relationship between language and meaning in terms of semantics (meanings derived from the words themselves), pragmatics (meanings derived from the conversational context), and sociolinguistics (meanings derived from social and cultural contexts).

Semantics

Semantic meaning is derived from the words themselves and how they are arranged into sentences. Recall that *words* are the arbitrarily chosen symbols used to represent thoughts and feelings (Saeid, 2003). Although we learn new words everyday, our ability to express our thoughts and feelings and understand others is limited by the size and accuracy of our vocabulary.

Identifying the meaning of a word is tricky because words have two types of meanings. **Denotation** is the direct, explicit meaning found in the dictionary of a language community. However, different dictionaries may define words in slightly different ways and many words have multiple denotative definitions. For instance, the *Random House Dictionary of the English Language* lists 23 definitions for the word *great.* Not only that, the lexicon of our personal idiolect rarely corresponds precisely to the definitions found in formal dictionary definitions. Thus, your definition of a word may be different from mine. So when your friend says your performance was *great*, he might mean it was very good, exceptional, powerful, or that it lasted a long time. All are denotative dictionary definitions of *great.*

Connotation, the feelings or evaluations we associate with a word, also influences meaning. For example, think of the different meanings people might associate with the word "family," based on their experiences growing up. To one person, a "family" may connote a safe place where one is loved

semantic meaning

derived from the words themselves and how they are arranged into sentences

denotation

direct, explicit meaning found in the dictionary of a language community

connotation

feelings or evaluations associated with a word

THE AUDIENCE *BEYOND*

Chloe's aunt is just learning how to text. So, for now, she spells out words rather than using abbreviations such as *OMG* and *LOL.*

Michael Klenetsky/Shutterstock

Our connotative definitions are influenced by previous experiences. How might your experiences with a family pet, an attack dog, or a hunting dog influence your connotative feelings about dogs?

unconditionally. To another, it might connote a dangerous place where people must fend for and protect themselves. Word denotation and connotation are important because the only message that counts is the message that is understood, regardless of whether it is the one you intended.

Semantic meaning is based on both the words themselves and how they are combined into meaningful phrases, sentences, and larger units of expression For example, you might communicate the same message by saying:

"When he went to the pound he adopted a 3-pound puppy."

"He went to the pound and adopted a 3-pound puppy."

"Upon arriving at the pound, he adopted a 3-pound puppy."

These three sentences use slightly different syntax and grammar to convey the same semantic meaning. But notice how the semantic meaning can change by deleting one word:

"He, the 3 pound adopted puppy, went to the pound."

Now the semantic meaning is that an adopted three-pound premature canine went to the place where unclaimed animals are kept. Next consider how the semantic meaning can change based on its position in a sentence. The word *pound* is used twice in each sentence but in one instance it signifies a unit of weight and in the other it signifies a place. We knew which meaning to apply based on syntax. With this in mind, let's consider several semantics guidelines for forming effective verbal messages.

Guidelines for Improving Semantics

To improve semantics, choose words and arrange them in ways that both improve clarity and demonstrate respect. You can do so by using specific, concrete, and familiar words, by embellishing them with descriptive details and examples, and by demonstrating linguistic sensitivity. In terms of clarity, compare the language used in the following two descriptions of the same incident:

"Some nut almost got me a while ago."

"About 1:00 p.m. last Saturday afternoon, an older man in a banged-up Honda Civic ran through the red light at Calhoun and Clifton and came within inches of hitting my car while I was in the intersection waiting to turn left."

In the second description, the speaker used specific, concrete language, as well as descriptive details and examples, to improve semantic clarity. Let's look closer at each one.

CONSIDER THIS....

Have you ever been misunderstood or misunderstood someone else based on how you or they phrased the verbal message? If so, how did it affect your relationship and how did you resolve the misunderstanding?

1. **Use specific language. Specific language** refers to precise words that clarify semantic meaning by narrowing what is understood from a general category to a particular item or group within that category. The first words that come to mind are often general, abstract, and imprecise. The ambiguity of these words forces the receiver to choose from many possible images rather than the precise one we have in mind. To improve semantics, use specific language. For example, saying "a banged-up Honda Civic" is more specific than saying "a car."

specific language

precise words that clarify semantic meaning by narrowing from a general category to a particular item or group within it

2. **Use concrete language. Concrete language** clarifies semantic meaning by appealing to the senses (e.g., seeing, hearing, feeling, tasting, smelling). Instead of saying Jill "speaks in a weird way," we might say, Jill *mumbles, whispers, blusters,* or *drones.* Each of these words provides a more concrete description of the sound of Jill's voice.

concrete language

words that clarify semantic meaning by appealing to the senses

3. **Use familiar language.** We also need to use words our receivers will understand, which includes using jargon and slang only when we are certain the meaning will be clear or by defining it clearly the first time we use it. Overusing and misusing abbreviations and acronyms can also hinder understanding.

4. **Use descriptive details and examples.** Sometimes semantic meaning can be improved by using descriptive details or examples. Suppose Lucy says, "Rashad is very *loyal.*" Since the meaning of *loyal* (faithful to an idea, person, company, and so on) is an abstract word, Lucy might add, "I mean, he never criticizes friends behind their backs." By following up the abstract concept of loyalty with an example, Lucy clarifies what she means as it applies to Rashad.

5. **Demonstrate linguistic sensitivity. Linguistic sensitivity** is achieved by using language that is inclusive and demonstrates respect for others.

linguistic sensitivity

inclusive word choices that demonstrate respect for others

Inclusive language does not use words that apply only to one sex, race, or other group as though they represent everyone. In the past, English speakers used the masculine pronoun *he* to represent all humans regardless of sex. This approach is not inclusive because it excludes half of the population. Instead, use plurals or both male and female pronouns (Stewart, Cooper, Stewart, & Friedley, 1998, p. 63). So rather than saying, "When *a person* shops, *he* should have a clear idea of what *he* wants to buy," say "When *people* shop, *they* should have a clear idea of what *they* want to buy."

inclusive language

use of words that do not apply only to one sex, race, or other group

To be inclusive, we also need to avoid words that indicate a sex, race, age, or other group distinction. For example, rather than saying *fireman, mailman, stewardess,* or *mankind,* saying *firefighter, postal carrier, server,* and *humankind* is more inclusive and semantically accurate.

Why does referring to these people as policemen fail to demonstrate linguistic sensitivity?

Demonstrating linguistic sensitivity also means avoiding potential offensive humor, profanity, and vulgarity. Dirty jokes and racist, sexist, or other "-ist" remarks may not be intended to be offensive, but if someone perceives them to be offensive, then that person will likely lose sight of your intended meaning and focus on the offensive remark instead. The same thing can happen when you pepper your message with profanity and vulgar expressions. Listeners may be offended and focus on those words rather than on the semantic meaning of your intended message.

Pragmatics

pragmatic meaning

understanding a message related to the conversational context of it

Pragmatic meaning comes from understanding a message related to the conversational context of it. Whereas semantic meaning focuses on what the *words* mean (Korta & Perry, 2008), pragmatic meaning focuses on what *people* mean. So, pragmatic meaning changes across speakers and situations.

speech act

utterance of a verbal message by a speaker and what it implies about how the listener should respond

A **speech act** is the utterance of a verbal message by a speaker and what it implies about how the listener should respond. In other words, when we *speak*, we *do*. Although our speech acts are usually explicit, what we are doing is often implied. To discover pragmatic meaning, we ask ourselves, "What is the speaker *doing* by saying these words to me right now?" Similarly, as we form a message, we choose language intended to evoke a certain response. For example, if I say, "Karen, pass me the bowl of potatoes," I have directly ordered Karen to pick up the bowl of potatoes and hand them to me. Instead, suppose

COMMUNICATE ON YOUR FEET

Speech Assignment

What Does It Mean?

The Assignment

Following your instructor's instructions, work alone, partner with someone in the class, or form a small group. Make up a nonsensical word and then develop a short speech clarifying its meaning using the tools you have learned in this chapter. If you work with a partner or in a small group, identify a representative to present the speech to the class. After each speech has been

presented, ask a volunteer from the audience to paraphrase the meaning of the word.

Guidelines

1. Be sure to follow the speech organization directions provided by your instructor.

2. Be sure to incorporate the concepts for clarifying semantic meaning in ways that are specific, concrete, descriptive, and linguistically sensitive.

I ask, "Karen, would you mind passing me the potatoes?" At the semantic level, this question appears to give Karen a choice. At the pragmatic level, however, what I am doing is the same. I am directing her to pass the bowl of potatoes to me. So, we can accomplish the same pragmatic goal with either a direct/explicit or indirect/implicit speech act.

What is meant by a speech act also depends on the context. Let's look at a simple example. When Harry's car wouldn't start one morning, he made three phone calls:

Phone Call 1:

Harry: The car won't start.

Katie: Sorry about that. I'll just take the bus.

Phone Call 2:

Harry: The car won't start.

AAA Customer Service Representative: Where is the car, sir? I'll send a tow truck right away.

Phone Call 3:

Harry: The car won't start.

Previous owner who recently sold the car to Harry: Wow, that never happened to me. But I told you I was selling the car "as is."

AP Photo/Toby Talbot

What indirect or implied meanings are being communicated in this advertisement?

In all three cases, the verbal utterance and the semantic meaning of Harry's message is the same. In terms of pragmatic meaning, however, Harry performed three different speech acts. What he was *doing* when he was talking to Katie was different from what he was *doing* when he was talking with the customer service representative at AAA and different still from what he was *doing* when he made the statement to the person who sold him the car. He expressed his feelings by apologizing to Katie and implied that Katie should understand and release him from his obligation to take her to school. With the AAA representative, Harry's speech act was a demand for assistance. When Harry called the previous owner of the car, he was complaining and implying that the previous owner should accept responsibility. In each case, Harry used the same words and syntax, but three different speech acts.

The feedback from each person illustrates that each had understood Harry's pragmatic meaning. Katie's response showed that she understood and would need to find another way to get to school. The AAA representative expected the call to be about car trouble so she responded by asking where the car was located. The previous owner also understood Harry's speech act when he responded by refusing to accept responsibility for the problem.

Sometimes the media use the principles of pragmatics to get the attention of and even mislead us about what the facts are in a given situation. The *Pop Comm!*

POP
COMM!

Blurring the Lines: The Pragmatics of Tabloid and Mainstream Journalism

The tabloids that line the checkout aisles claim to bring us the latest juicy details about the private lives of our favorite celebrities. Headlines pasted over photos of famous women like Angelina Jolie, Jennifer Aniston, and Jennifer Lopez often proclaim: "I'm having a baby!," "Yes, I'm pregnant!," or "Countdown to baby!" Yet more often than not, the featured celebrity isn't pregnant. Most of us understand that what is shouted in the headline of a tabloid will be a far cry from what is actually reported in the actual article. Because of the context, we question the accuracy of the headline and become curious about the "real story." This achieves the tabloids' purpose, which is to entice us to buy the magazine. Because of the pragmatics of tabloid speech acts, we're not surprised when the actual story turns out to be very different from what was touted on the cover. Still, we seek out the "truth" in the article because of our assumptions about the role of the press to present accurate facts.

Historically, the purpose of mainstream journalism has been to provide important unbiased information about substantial topics to a democratic society. Even if we are skeptical about tabloids' accuracy, we do expect "serious" news articles and stories to present facts that have been rigorously checked and editorial and opinion pieces that have been labeled as such. Given this context, when we view a headline in the daily paper or hear a news anchor's before-break-lead-in to the story, we trust that the headline is an accurate representation of the facts. As we read the item or listen to that news story, we assume that the facts presented are typical, accurate, unbiased, and can be trusted. In other words, we take the message at face value. So when a mainstream headline proclaims that Jennifer Aniston is pregnant, we have a context that

prompts us to assume that the story will contain facts verifying that the actress is, in fact, "with child."

But celebrity tabloids and gossip blogs rely on language and pragmatic context more than facts to shape the meaning behind their stories. A candid photo of Jennifer Aniston touching her stomach does not, on its own, necessarily provide any proof that she is pregnant. But when captioned with the words "a baby at last?" or "is that a baby bump?" the magazine influences audiences to believe that Aniston is pregnant. Thus, the pragmatic goal of tabloids is to make a rumor seem true, even when the inside story doesn't contain any facts that validate the headline and may actually provide evidence to the contrary. Although most tabloid readers know that we should scrutinize photos and question headlines, we enjoy the entertainment value of them. The fun of these gossip magazines is the invitation to negotiate meaning and "truth" by judging the facts promised by the headlines against the information within the text of the articles rather than accepting them at face value.

Though we may expect such gossip-oriented reporting from tabloids and take such stories with a grain of salt, there is increasing concern about the "tabloidization of the mainstream press" and biased reporting from sources we historically turned to for facts and evidence. Driven in part by financial considerations, traditional media sources are reporting more sensational stories and using the same sorts of embedded sensationalism as the tabloids (Slattery, Doremus, & Marcus, 2001). Celebrity stories were once largely confined to the tabloids, but in this hyper-competitive media market, the so-called "serious" news outlets now spend more time reporting on celebrity deeds and misdeeds than in times past, and articles and stories in general focus more on rumors and innuendos. For example, mainstream media frequently "report" stories that appear in tabloids without confirming the information reported in the original article ("The Star reports that Jen is pregnant"). Meanwhile, stories about political candidates increasingly use "facts" to speculate about the underlying motivation for a candidate's position rather than digging up the facts that would reveal the validity of the position itself (e.g., speculating that Mitt Romney's wealth puts him "out of touch" with middle-class Americans rather than examining his position and arguments or focusing on rumors about President Obama's place of birth instead of his policy initiatives).

This blurring of lines between tabloid journalism and mainstream journalism has been going on for some time. In fact, in an article published in 1999, reporter Lynn Washington, Jr., commented on "the shallowness of mainstream media coverage of matters of public substances." As evidence he cited "the increasing focus of political campaign coverage on polls and candidate faux pas rather than in-depth reporting of the difference in candi-dates' positions." Further, he noted, "the intimacies of celebrity lifestyles receive wider coverage than the intricacies of public and corporate policies that affect quality of life issues." It appears from recent campaigns and elections that Washington's critique is still relevant today.

Questions to Ponder

1. Given these changes, how should we approach mainstream media stories?

2. Should we discount the headlines and expect the stories to be sensationalized as we do stories in tabloids, assuming the same pragmatics apply?

3. If we no longer can trust mainstream media to supply us with unbiased, fact-checked information (*Is* Jen pregnant?), how does this impact our understanding of substantive policy issues?

4. Where do we go for this information and how do we know that the sources we find can be trusted or believed?

illustrates how tabloids do so to entice potential readers to buy magazines and how the practice is being adopted by mainstream media outlets today.

As you can imagine, accurately conveying and interpreting the pragmatic meaning and what is being implied in verbal messages can be challenging. Let's consider several guidelines to improve your use of pragmatics in verbal messages.

Guidelines for Improving Pragmatics

We understand pragmatic meaning based on an assumption that both partners want to achieve mutual understanding (Grice, 1975). With this in mind, we suggest the following guidelines.

1. **Tell the truth.** This guideline seems pretty self-explanatory. Fully disclose all that you know about something. Say only what you believe to be true

THE AUDIENCE *BEYOND*

Linda read her sister's Facebook status that read, "20 below and 10 inches of snow. I think HELL just froze over and I'm in it. Isn't America great!?" Linda wondered if her sister was implying that she was feeling depressed. Linda decided to give her a call to make sure she was all right.

Have you ever witnessed someone going on and on about something unrelated to the question you asked? How did that influence your judgment of their ethical communication behavior?

based on evidence to support your position. Sometimes we tell partial truths and rationalize that we are "protecting" our listeners or ourselves. For example, when your friend asks you what you think of her new boyfriend you may offer a noncommittal response that masks your immediate dislike for the guy. You might say, "Well, he certainly appears to like you." Your friend may interpret your remark as approval rather than as your attempt to spare her feelings. Obviously, this makes it more difficult to correctly understand what you truly believe. You can tell the truth by adding a comment about something you don't particularly like about him.

2. **Provide the right amount of information.** Include all the information needed to fully answer the question and refrain from adding irrelevant information. For instance, when Sam is getting ready to leave for work, he asks Randy where he parked the car. Randy answers "down the street." In this case, Randy does not provide enough information because Sam needs to know exactly where to find the car. If Randy responds with, "You just wouldn't believe the trouble I had finding a parking space . . ." followed by a five-minute monologue about trying to find a parking space after midnight, he would be providing too much irrelevant information.

3. **Relate what you say to the topic being discussed.** Link your messages to the purpose of the conversation and interpret the messages of others in line with the topic at hand. For example, Barry asks, "Who's going to pick up Mom from work today?" His brother answers, "I've got a big test tomorrow." Barry assumes that his brother's remark is relevant to the topic at hand and interprets it as, "I can't; I have to study." Barry was able to correctly understand the pragmatic meaning of his brother's answer because he assumed that it was relevant to figuring out how to get their mother home.

4. **Acknowledge when your message violates a guideline.** When you violate one of these guidelines, you should tell your partner that you are breaking it. Doing so will help your partner interpret what you are saying accurately. For example:

   • If you violate guideline #1, you might say "I don't know if this is true, but my sister said…,"
   • If you violate guideline #2, you might say "If I told you, I'd have to kill you…,"
   • If you violate guideline #3, you might say "This may be beside the point, but…,"

5. **Assume the best first.** At times, you or your partner may intentionally break one of these guidelines and not signal beforehand. In these instances, rather than take offense, employ perception-checking in an attempt to come to mutual understanding.

sociolinguistic meaning

varies according to the norms of a particular culture or co-culture

Sociolinguistics

Sociolinguistic meaning varies according to the norms of a particular culture or co-culture. Sociolinguistic misunderstandings occur when we interact with someone who operates using different norms regarding how words are combined, how to say what to whom and when, and verbal style.

First, cultures have norms that assign meaning to specific words and combinations of words that may be different from their semantic meaning. For example, in English we associate the word "pretty" with women and "handsome" with men, even though both refer to physical beauty. So choosing to say "She is a pretty woman" sends a different message than saying, "She is a handsome woman (Chaika, 2008). All cultures also use **idioms**, which are expressions whose meaning is different from the literal meanings associated with the words used in them. So imagine how confusing it is to someone learning English when we say, "That test was *a piece of cake*." Similarly, when Janelle attempted to impress the new guy in her life by asking her 7-year-old sister to "Bring me the trophy on my dresser," Janelle expected her sister to return with the award she won at a recent swim meet. Instead, her sister returned with an 8 X 10 picture of Janelle's last boyfriend that her father jokingly referred to as her "trophy."

idioms

expressions whose meanings are different from the literal meanings associated with the words used in them

Second, cultures develop different norms about what is appropriate to say to whom, by whom, when, and about what. For example, the "appropriate" way to compliment others and accept compliments can vary from culture to culture. In the dominant culture of the United States, you might compliment your Japanese friend by saying, "Miki, this is the *best* miso soup I have ever tasted." To Miki, however, your compliment might sound insincere because in Japanese culture the language of compliments is more humble. So she might reply, "Oh, it's nice of you to say that, but I am sure that you have had better miso soup at sushi restaurants in the city." Similarly, Midwesterners often smile and say "Hi" to strangers on the street as a sign of being friendly. In China, acknowledging a stranger in this way typically assumes an unwarranted familiarity and is likely to be considered rude.

Third, preferred verbal style differs from culture to culture, particularly in terms of how direct or indirect one ought to be (Ting-Toomey & Chung, 2005). A **direct verbal style** is characterized by language that openly states the speaker's intention in a straightforward and unambiguous way. An **indirect verbal style** is characterized by language that masks the speaker's true intentions in a roundabout and ambiguous way. Consider the following example of how these different styles can create communication challenges.

direct verbal style

language that openly states the speaker's intention in a straightforward and unambiguous way

indirect verbal style

language that masks the speaker's true intentions in a roundabout and ambiguous way

Jorge and Kevin are roommates at college who come from the same hometown as Sam, who lives across the hall and has a car. Thanksgiving is fast approaching and both men need to find a ride home. One night while watching a football game in Sam's room, the following conversation occurs:

Jorge says to Sam: "Are you driving home for Thanksgiving?" [Maybe he'll give me a ride.]

Sam: "Yep." [If he wanted a ride he'd ask.]

THE AUDIENCE *BEYOND*

Alex *tweeted* that the food at a local restaurant was "so awful they should be paying the customers to eat there." The message quickly went viral and Alex was painted as rude and wrong. Alex apologized for his *tweet* and that he didn't mean it the way it sounded. He also vowed to "count to 10" before *tweeting* about negative experiences in the future.

Kevin: "Well I'd like a ride home."

Sam: "Sure no problem."

Jorge: "Are you taking anyone else?" [I wonder if he still has room for me.]

Sam: "Nope. I'm leaving early, after my last class on Tuesday and not coming back until late Sunday evening." [I guess Jorge already has a ride home.]

Jorge: "Well, enjoy Thanksgiving!" [If he wanted to give me a ride I gave him plenty of opportunities to offer. I guess I'll take the bus.]

In this conversation, Jorge used an indirect style he learned growing up in Nicaragua. His questions were meant to prompt Sam to offer him a ride home. But Sam, who grew up in New York, used a direct style and completely misses Jorge's intent. As a result, Jorge rode the bus even though Sam would have gladly given him a ride if their preferred verbal styles had not gotten in the way of mutual understanding.

> **CONSIDER *THIS*....**
>
> Do you operate using a direct or an indirect verbal style? Have you ever experienced misunderstandings when communicating with someone who uses a different style?

WHAT WOULD YOU DO?

A Question of Ethics

As Abbie was adding sweetener to her latte, she spied her friends Ethan and Nate sitting at a table in a corner of the coffee shop. She popped a top on her drink and strolled over to join them.

"Hi guys. What are you doing?" Abbie asked.

"Not much. Ethan and I were just comparing our biology notes. How about you?"

"I'm just heading over to my philosophy class," Abbie replied. "But, I've got to say I don't know why I even bother going."

"Why not? What's up?" asked Nate.

"Well," responded Abbie, "Professor Miller is so mean. The other day, I offered my opinion and she told me I was wrong. Can you believe it? I mean, she could have praised me for offering my opinion. What makes her opinion so 'right' anyway? She is so narrow-minded and *obviously* doesn't care about her students."

Ethan asked, "Well, were you?"

"Was I what?" Abbie asked.

"Wrong."

"Well, I guess so. But that's not the point," Abbie contested.

"Actually, I think it *is*," Ethan replied. "Maybe she said you were wrong because she *does* care about her students and wants you to learn. Maybe she sets high standards and wants to help you achieve them."

"Whatever. That's *your* opinion. I bet you'd feel differently if she embarrassed *you* in front of the other students," Abbie retorted.

"Maybe you should go talk to her about it during her office hours," suggested Nate. "She probably doesn't even realize she embarrassed you."

"Oh, she knows," replied Abbie. "And there is *no way* am I going to talk to her about it. I'm just going to get through the semester and then tell her *exactly* what I think on the end-of-semester evaluations. See you later!"

1. What ethical principles if any are at issue in this case?

2. What do you think about the issues Abbie raises and why?

3. Based on what you have learned about language in this chapter, what could you say to Abbie that might help her?

Guidelines for Improving Sociolinguistic Understanding

1. **Develop intercultural competence.** The more you learn about other cultures, the better you will be able to convey and interpret messages when communicating with those whose sociolinguistic verbal styles differ from yours.

2. **Practice mindfulness. Mindfulness** is the practice of paying attention to what is happening at any given moment during a conversation (Langer & Moldoveanu, 2000). If we are mindful when interacting with others, we will constantly attend to how our cultural norms, idioms, scripts, and verbal styles are similar to and different from our conversational partners.

3. **Respect and adapt to the sociolinguistic practices of others.** The old saying, "When in Rome, do as the Romans do" captures the essence of this guideline. For example, if you are invited to your Indonesian American friend's home for the weekend, you should adapt your verbal style to that of your hosts. Or if you are from a low-context culture and are talking with someone from a high-context culture, be sensitive to the indirect meanings in their verbal messages. If you are fluent in more than one language or dialect, you can even codeswitch and converse in the language or use the dialect of your conversational partner.

mindfulness

paying attention to what is happening at any given moment during a conversation.

Summary

Although many different languages are spoken throughout the world, all of them share the same purposes and are based on the same fundamental principles. All are symbol systems used to communicate by labeling, comparing, and defining. And all are based on utterances bounded by silences. Verbal language is made up of a symbol system that includes a lexicon, phonology, and syntax and grammar. Sharing meaning can be difficult because we may speak different languages, dialects, and idiolects. Doing so can also be challenging because language is arbitrary, abstract, and constantly changing.

Since meanings are in people rather than the words themselves, verbal symbols convey semantic, pragmatic, and sociolinguistic meanings. Semantic meaning is derived from the words and how they are arranged into sentences. We can improve semantic meaning by using specific, concrete, and familiar words, descriptive details and examples, and linguistic sensitivity. Pragmatic meaning comes from understanding a message within the context of the conversation. We can improve pragmatic meaning by telling the truth, providing the right amount of information, relating what we say to the topic being discussed, acknowledging when we are violating one of these guidelines, and assuming the best first. Sociolinguistic meaning varies according to the norms of a particular culture or co-culture. We can improve sociolinguistic meaning by developing intercultural competence, practicing mindfulness, and respecting and adapting to the sociolinguistic practices of others.

RESOURCE AND ASSESSMENT CENTER

Now that you have read Chapter 4, go to the Speech Communication Course-Mate at cengage.brain.com where you'll find an interactive eBook and interactive learning tools, including quizzes, flashcards, sample speech videos, audio study tools, skill-building activities, action step activities, and more. Student Workbook, Speech Builder Express 3.0, and Speech Studio 2.0 are also available.

Applying What You've Learned

Impromptu Speech Activity

1. Draw a slip of paper from a container provided by your instructor. On it, you will find the name of a superhero, cartoon character, or comic strip character. Prepare and deliver a 2–3 minute impromptu speech making a case for him or her as either a positive or negative example of effective verbal communication. Be sure to draw on the principles offered in this chapter to make your case.

Assessment Activities

1. Pick an article from a favorite magazine. Read through it, highlighting instances in which the writer uses specific language, concrete language, and familiar language, and identify passages in which the writer might improve in each area. Then look for examples of the writer's linguistic sensitivity and find places where the writer might have done a better job. Write a 400–500-word essay identifying strengths and suggestions for improvement based on your assessment.

2. Select one of these popular TV sitcoms: *Two and a Half Men, How I Met Your Mother, The Office, 30 Rock, Modern Family, The Big Bang Theory, Family Man, or Parks & Recreation.* Watch an episode and record the following for each of the main characters: (a) use of profanity and vulgarity, (b) use of biased (not inclusive) language, and (c) use of offensive humor. Based on your analysis, would you consider each of them a model of ethical or unethical communication behavior? Why or why not?

Skill-Building Activities

1. Reword the following messages using more specific, concrete, and familiar words:

   a. You know that I really love baseball. Well, I'm practicing a lot because I'm hoping to get a tryout with the pros.

   b. I'm really bummed out. Everything with Corey is going down the tubes. We just don't connect anymore.

   c. She's just a pain. She's always doing stuff to tick me off. And then just acting like, you know.

   d. My neighbor has a lot of animals in her yard.

   e. My sister works for a large newspaper.

2. Reword the following sentences to demonstrate linguistic sensitivity:

   a. Margaret is a fantastic waitress.

   b. Mark, a Jewish fireman, is going to the Bahamas next week.

   c. I believe in equal rights and opportunities for all of mankind.

   d. I can't figure out why Mrs. B makes us learn how to calculate these damned math problems by hand.

   e. Geez. It really bugs me when Erin acts like such a dumb blonde. She's actually a pretty smart girl.

Nonverbal Messages

What you will know

- Characteristics of nonverbal messages
- Types of nonverbal messages we send through our bodies
- Types of nonverbal messages we send through our voices
- Types of nonverbal messages we send through use of space and time
- Types of nonverbal messages we send through appearance

What you'll be able to do

- Improve the nonverbal messages you send
- More accurately interpret the nonverbal messages you receive

Take I: The Verbal Exchange

Amber enters the suite.

Amber: "I'm home. Are we going to dinner soon?"

Louisa: "Uh huh."

Amber: "Good, because I'm starving. I worked so long in Chem lab that I completely missed lunch and had to make do with a stale granola bar I found at the bottom of my backpack. "

Louisa: "Uh huh."

Amber: "Hey, I've been thinking about spring break. What would you think about doing an alternative spring break? Student government is sponsoring three different trips and one is to Haiti. I thought we could do some good and get some sun. What do you think?"

Louisa: "Whatever,"

Amber: "Wow. What'd I do wrong this time? Sometimes I just don't understand her."

5

What just happened? From the verbal transcript it's hard to tell because it only records the verbal message part of each of these utterances. Let's look at a different account of the conversation.

Take II: The Nonverbal and Verbal Exchange

As Amber enters the suite, Louisa is sitting cross-legged on the bed typing furiously on her laptop.

"I'm home. Are we going to dinner soon?" Amber asks, smiling brightly as she drops her backpack on the floor and flops down on the futon across the room.

"Uh huh," mumbles Louisa as she furrows her eyebrows and continues staring at the screen and typing furiously.

"Good, because I'm starving," Amber says. "I worked so long in Chem lab that I completely missed lunch and had to make do with a stale granola bar that I found at the bottom of my backpack," Amber continued wrinkling her nose.

"Uh huh," Louisa mutters. She exhales loudly as she turns her back to Amber and continues typing, her eyes focused intently on the screen.

"Hey, I've been thinking about spring break," Amber says. "What would you think about doing an alternative spring break? Student Government is sponsoring three different trips and one is to Haiti. I thought we could do some good and get some sun. What do you think?" Amber asks excitedly as she gets up from the futon, and plops down on the bed in front of Louisa sending books and papers flying.

"Whatever," Louisa shouts as she bangs her laptop closed, gathers her papers, and storms out of the room.

"Wow," Amber thinks as she stares wide-eyed at the door Louisa just slammed shut. "What'd I do wrong this time? Sometimes I just don't understand her."

After reading Take II, you probably recognized what Amber had completely ignored in the first scenario: the nonverbal messages Louisa was sending via eye contact, tone of voice, and body language. The last chapter focused on the verbal messages we send to communicate thoughts and feelings. This chapter is dedicated to **nonverbal communication**, which consists of all the messages we send in ways that transcend spoken or written words (Knapp & Hall, 2006). More specifically, **nonverbal messages** are cues we send with our body, voice, space, time, and appearance to support, modify, contradict, or even replace a verbal message.

Nonverbal messages play an important role in communication. In fact, nonverbal messages convey as much as 65 percent of the meaning communicated in face-to-face interactions (Burgoon and Bacue, 2003, p. 179). In other words, the meaning we assign to any utterance is based on our interpretation of both the verbal message and the nonverbal messages that accompany it. As we can see from Amber and Louisa's conversation, interpreting nonverbal messages accurately is critical to understanding and responding appropriately to what our partner is "saying."

The widespread use of social media to communicate today (e-mail, Facebook, texting) emphasizes the important role of nonverbal messages when communicating. Because these modes force us to rely only on words, chances for misunderstanding skyrocket (Olaniran, 2002; 2003). So we often use emoticons, all capital letters, and acronyms like LOL to represent the emotional tone that nonverbal messages do in face-to-face communication.

nonverbal communication

all the messages we send in ways that transcend spoken or written words

nonverbal messages

cues we send with our body, voice, space, time, and appearance to support, modify, contradict, or even replace a verbal message

We begin this chapter by briefly describing the characteristics of nonverbal communication. Next, we identify the types of nonverbal messages we use to communicate with others, including use of body (kinesics), use of voice (paralanguage), use of space (proxemics), use of time (chronemics), and appearance (including clothing and grooming). Finally, we offer suggestions for improving clarity when sending nonverbal messages and accuracy when interpreting the nonverbal messages we receive from others.

Ei Katsumata-CMC/Alamy Limited

Nonverbal communication is so important that we have developed emoticons, acronyms, and avatars to represent it in computer-mediated and text messages.

Characteristics of Nonverbal Communication

We use nonverbal messages to provide unique information by emphasizing, substituting for, or contradicting a verbal message. Nonverbal messages can also regulate our interactions. In other words, we can cue a sender to continue, repeat, elaborate, or hurry up and finish what he or she is saying through shifts in eye contact, slight head movements, posture changes, and raised eyebrows. And nonverbal messages can convey a particular image of ourselves through our choice of clothing, grooming, jewelry, and body art. Even when we don't consciously choose to do so, our nonverbal messages give people an impression of who we are. Sometimes we use nonverbal messages to express our status in a situation or a relationship. For example, managers may dress more formally than their employees. The challenge of conveying and interpreting nonverbal messages accurately is rooted in four fundamental characteristics.

1. **Nonverbal communication is *inevitable*.** The phrase "We cannot NOT communicate" (Watzlawick, Bavelas, & Jackson, 1967) captures the essence of this characteristic. If you are in the presence of someone else, your nonverbal messages (whether intentional or not) are communicating. When Austin yawns and stares off into the distance during class, his classmates may notice this behavior and assign meaning to it. One classmate may interpret it as a sign of boredom, another might see it as a sign of fatigue, and yet another may view it as a message of disrespect. Meanwhile, Austin may be oblivious to all of the messages his behavior is sending.

2. **Nonverbal communication is the primary conveyer of emotions.** We interpret how others feel about what they are communicating based almost entirely on their nonverbal messages. In fact, some research suggests that an overwhelming 93 percent of the emotional meaning of messages is conveyed nonverbally (Mehrabian, 1972). So, when Janelle frowns, clenches her fists, and forcefully says, "I am NOT angry!" her sister Renée ignores the verbal message and believes the contradicting nonverbal messages, which communicate that Janelle is actually very angry.

3. **Nonverbal communication is *multi-channeled*.** We perceive meaning from a combination of different nonverbal behaviors including, for example,

posture, gestures, facial expressions, vocal pitch and rate, and appearance. So, when Anna observes her daughter Mimi's failure to sustain eye contact, her bowed head, and her repetitive toe-stubbing in the dirt, she may decide that Mimi is lying when she says she did not hit her brother. The fact that nonverbal communication is multi-channeled is one reason people are more likely to believe nonverbal communication when nonverbal behaviors contradict the verbal message (Burgoon, Blair, & Strom, 2008).

4. **Nonverbal communication is *ambiguous*.** Very few nonverbal messages mean the same thing to everyone. The meaning of one nonverbal behavior can vary based on culture, sex, gender, and even context or situation. For example, in the dominant American culture, direct eye contact tends to be understood as a sign of respect. That's why parents often tell their children, "Look at me when I'm talking to you." In other cultures, however, direct eye contact might be interpreted as disrespectful if the speaker is a superior and averting one's eyes might signal respect. Not only can the meaning of nonverbal messages vary among different cultures, but the meaning of the same nonverbal message also can differ based on the situation. For example, a furrowed brow might convey Byron's confusion when he did not understand his professor's explanation of the assignment, or Monica's anger when she discovered she did not get the internship she had worked so hard for, or Max's disgust when he was dissecting a frog during biology lab.

Types of Nonverbal Communication

We use various types of nonverbal messages to communicate. These include the use of body (kinesics), voice (vocalics/paralanguage), space (proxemics), time (chronemics), and appearance.

Use of Body: Kinesics

kinesics

technical name for the interpretation of what and how body motions communicate

Of all the research on nonverbal behavior, you are probably most familiar with **kinesics**, the technical name for the interpretation of what and how body motions communicate (Birdwhistell, 1970). These include gestures, eye contact, facial expression, posture, and touch.

gestures

movements of our hands, arms, and fingers to replace or clarify a verbal message

Gestures Gestures are the movements of our hands, arms, and fingers to replace or accompany a verbal message. Some people gesture more than others. Unfortunately, "talking with our hands" too much can actually distract listeners from the message we are trying to convey. **Emblems** are gestures that substitute entirely for a word or words. For example, when you raise your finger and place it vertically across your lips, it signifies "Be quiet." Other gestures called **illustrators**, clarify the verbal message. When you say "about this high" or "nearly this round," your listeners expect to see a gesture

emblems

gestures that substitute entirely for a word or words

illustrators

type of gesture that serves to clarify the verbal message

THE AUDIENCE *BEYOND*

Jo was worried. She had just read Aaron's tweet about the brawl that took place after the big game with a cross-town basketball rival, and she couldn't tell whether Aaron was angry, frightened, or just disgusted about what had happened.

accompanying your verbal description. Sometimes, these gestures augment the verbal message by conveying the emotional stance of the sender. Still other gestures, called **adaptors**, are unconscious responses to physical or psychological needs. For example, you may scratch an itch, adjust your glasses, or rub your hands together when they are cold. You do not mean to communicate a message with these gestures, but others may notice and attach meaning to them.

The use and meaning of gestures can vary greatly across cultures. For example, the American hand sign for "OK" has an obscene sexual meaning in some European countries, means "worthless" in France, is a symbol for money in Japan, and stands for "I'll kill you" in Tunisia (Axtell, 1998). When communicating with people who come from different cultures, be especially careful about the gestures you use; their meaning is not necessarily universal.

Christian Steinhausen/Taxi/Getty Images

The same nonverbal cue can mean very different things in different cultures. What does this gesture mean to you?

Eye Contact The technical term for **eye contact** is oculesics. It has to do with how and how much we look at others when communicating. Eye contact can signal that you are paying attention and that you respect the person you are speaking with, as well as a variety of different emotions. So, when your professor sees that most of her students are not looking at her while she is lecturing, she might conclude that they are not paying attention. Or if you mention to your friend's parents that he plans to drop a history class, something he shared with you in confidence, your friend may glare at you to signal your transgression. Intense eye contact may also be an attempt to dominate (Pearson, West, & Turner, 1995). That's why we sometimes say things like "if looks could kill" when we see someone glare at someone else.

What is considered appropriate eye contact varies across cultures. Studies show that in Western cultures, talkers hold eye contact about 40 percent of the time and listeners nearly 70 percent of the time (Knapp & Hall, 2006). In Western cultures people also generally maintain more eye contact when discussing topics they are comfortable with, when they are genuinely interested in what another person is saying, and when they are trying to persuade others. Conversely, they tend to avoid eye contact when discussing topics that make them feel uncomfortable, when they aren't interested in the topic or the person talking, or when they are embarrassed, ashamed, or trying to hide something.

A majority of people in the United States and other Western cultures expect those with whom they are communicating to "look them in the eye." But direct eye contact is not universally considered appropriate (Samovar, Porter, & McDaniel, 2009). For instance, in Japan, prolonged eye contact is considered rude, disrespectful, and threatening. Similarly, in China and Indonesia, too much direct eye contact is a sign of bad manners. In many Middle Eastern countries, people tend to use continuous and direct eye contact with others to demonstrate keen interest.

CONSIDER THIS....

Do you know anyone who tends to use a lot of gestures when they talk to you? Does it help or hurt message clarity? Why?

adaptors

unconscious responses to physical or psychological needs

eye contact (oculesics)

how and how much we look at others when communicating

Comedic actors often use lots of facial expression to convey emotions. What is being communicated here?

Various co-cultural groups within the United States use eye contact differently, as well. For instance, African Americans tend to use more continuous eye contact than European Americans when they are speaking, but less when they are listening (Samovar, Porter, & McDaniel, 2009). Native Americans tend to avoid eye contact when communicating with superiors as a sign of respect for their authority. And women tend to use more eye contact during conversations than men do (Wood, 2007).

facial expression

arranging facial muscles to communicate emotions or provide feedback

Facial Expression **Facial expression** is arranging facial muscles to communicate. Facial expressions are especially important in conveying the six basic emotions of happiness, sadness, surprise, fear, anger, and disgust. For example, we may furrow our brows and squint our eyes when we are confused, or purse our lips and raise one eyebrow to convey skepticism. Facial expressions are so important for communicating emotional intent that we often use smiley face ☺, sad face ☹, and winking face ☺ emoticons to represent emotions when texting, sending e-mail, or posting comments on Facebook (Walther & Parks, 2002).

Studies show that there are many similarities across cultures with regard to the meaning of certain facial expressions (Samovar, Porter, & McDaniel, 2009). For instance, a slight raising of the eyebrow communicates recognition and wrinkling one's nose conveys repulsion (Martin & Nakayama, 2006). However, whether or not doing so is appropriate varies across cultures and co-cultures. For instance, in some Eastern cultures, people downplay facial expressions like frowning and smiling; whereas members of other cultures amplify their displays of emotion through facial expressions. In the United States, women who identify with the feminine co-culture tend to smile more frequently when communicating than do men who identify with the masculine co-culture.

posture

how we position and move our body

body orientation

how we position our body in relation to other people

Posture **Posture** is how we position and move our body. Posture can communicate attentiveness, respect, and dominance. **Body orientation** refers to how we position our body in relation to other people. *Direct body orientation* is when two people face each other squarely and *indirect body orientation* is when two people sit or stand side-by-side. In many situations, direct body orientation signals attentiveness and respect and indirect body orientation shows inattentiveness and disrespect. In a job interview, for example, you

THE AUDIENCE *BEYOND*

After reading Aaron's tweet about the brawl at the basketball game, Jo responded by tweeting to him, "Are you OK?" to which Aaron replied, "Sure, I just have a broken arm and a black eye." Jo knew he was kidding because he ended the tweet with a winking emoticon.

AF archive/Alamy Limited

are likely to sit up straight and face the interviewer directly because you want to communicate your interest, attentiveness, and respect. Yet in other situations, such as talking with friends, a slouched posture and indirect body orientation may be appropriate and may not carry messages about attention or respect. **Body movement** is changing body position. It can be motivated (movement that helps clarify meaning) or unmotivated (movement that distracts listeners from the point being made). When making a speech, an upright stance and squared shoulders communicates poise and confidence. Taking a few steps to the left or right can signal a transition from one main point to the next, but pacing actually distracts listeners from the message.

body movement

changing body position

Touch **Haptics** is the technical term for what and how touch communicates. We use our hands, arms, and other body parts to pat, hug, slap, kiss, pinch, stroke, hold, embrace, and tickle others.

haptics

the technical term for what and how touch communicates

There are three types of touch: spontaneous touch, ritualized touch, and task-related touch. *Spontaneous touch* is automatic and subconscious. Patting someone on the back when you hear that he or she has won an award is an example of spontaneous touch. *Ritualized touch* is scripted rather than spontaneous. Handshakes and high-fives, are examples of ritualized touch. *Task-related touch* is used to perform a certain unemotional function. For instance, a doctor may touch a patient during a physical examination or a personal trainer may touch a client during a gym workout. There is also a type of touch that combines spontaneity and task-related touch to convey messages of closeness. For example, when someone adjusts your coat collar or removes some lint from your clothing in a public place, the person may not only be doing a task-related favor for you but also may be signaling a degree of closeness between the two of you.

People differ in their touching behavior and in their reactions to unsolicited touch from others. Some people like to touch and be touched; other people do not. Although American culture is relatively non–contact oriented, the kinds and amounts of touching behavior within our society vary widely. Touching behavior that seems innocuous to one person may be perceived as overly intimate or threatening to another. Moreover, the perceived appropriateness of touch differs with the context. Touch that is considered appropriate in private may embarrass a person when done in public.

Differences in touching behavior are highly correlated with culture (Gudykunst & Kim, 1997). In some cultures, frequent touching is considered normal; in other cultures, it is considered inappropriate. Some countries in South and Central America, as well as many in southern Europe, encourage contact and engage in frequent touching (Neuliep, 2006). In many Arabic countries, for example, two grown men walking down the street holding hands is a sign of friendship. In the United States, however, it might be interpreted as a sign of an intimate relationship. Because the United States is a country of immigrants, however, the degree of touching behavior considered appropriate varies widely from individual to individual based on family heritage and norms.

Use of Voice: Paralanguage

Paralanguage (also known as *vocalics*) is the voiced part of a spoken message that goes beyond the actual words. Six vocal characteristics of paralanguage are pitch, volume, rate, quality, intonation, and vocalized pauses.

paralanguage (vocalics)

the voiced part of a spoken message that goes beyond the actual words

pitch

highness or lowness of vocal tone

volume

loudness or softness of vocal tone

rate

the speed at which a person speaks

quality

the sound of a person's voice that distinguishes it from others

intonation

the variety, melody, or inflection in one's voice

vocalized pauses

extraneous sounds or words that interrupt fluent speech

Pitch Pitch is the highness or lowness of vocal tone. People raise and lower vocal pitch to emphasize ideas and emotion, as well as to signal a question. We sometimes raise our pitch when feeling nervous or afraid. We may lower our pitch to convey peacefulness or sadness (as in a speech given at a funeral), or when trying to be forceful. When parents scold a child for misbehaving, they often lower their pitch to convey force.

Volume Volume is the loudness or softness of vocal tone. Whereas some people have booming voices that carry long distances, others are normally soft-spoken. Regardless of our normal volume level, however, we also tend to vary our volume depending on the situation, the topic of discussion, and emotional intent. For example, we might talk louder when we wish to be heard in noisy settings and when we are angry. We might speak softer when we are being reflective or romantic. There are also some cultural variations in the meanings attached to volume. For example, Arabs tend to speak with a great deal of volume to convey strength and sincerity; whereas soft voices are preferred in Britain, Japan, and Thailand (Samovar, Porter, & McDaniel, 2009).

Rate Rate is the speed at which a person speaks. Most people in the USA naturally speak between 100 and 200 words per minute. People tend to talk more rapidly when they are happy, frightened, nervous, or excited and more slowly when they are problem-solving out loud or are trying to emphasize a point. People who speak too slowly run the risk of boring listeners, and those who speak too quickly may not be intelligible.

Quality (Timbre) Quality is the sound of a person's voice that distinguishes it from others. Voice quality may be breathy (Marilyn Monroe or Kathleen Turner), strident (Joan Rivers or Marge Simpson), throaty (Nick Nolte or Jack Nicholson), or nasal (Fran Drescher in *The Nanny*). Although each person's voice has a distinct quality, too much breathiness can make people sound frail, too much stridence can make them seem hypertense, too much throatiness can make them seem cold and unsympathetic, and too much nasality can make them sound immature or unintelligent.

Intonation Intonation is the variety, melody, or inflection in one's voice. Voices that use very little or no intonation are described as monotone and tend to bore listeners. If you've ever seen the movie *Ferris Bueller's Day Off*, you may recall the teacher (played by Ben Stein) who is portrayed as boring via a monotone voice as he questions the class: "Anyone? Anyone? Bueller? Bueller?" Other voices that use a lot of intonation may be perceived as ditzy, sing-songy, or childish. People prefer to listen to voices that use a moderate amount of intonation.

In the United States, there are stereotypes about masculine and feminine voices. Masculine voices are expected to be low-pitched and loud, with moderate to low intonation; feminine voices are expected to be higher-pitched, softer in volume, and more expressive. Although both sexes have the option to portray a range of masculine and feminine paralanguage, most people usually conform to the expectations for their sex (Wood, 2007).

Vocalized Pauses Vocalized Pauses are extraneous sounds or words that interrupt fluent speech. They are essentially "place markers" designed to fill in momentary gaps while we search for the right word or idea. The most common vocalized pauses that creep into our speech include "uh," "er," "well," "OK," "you know," and "like."

Occasional vocalized pauses are generally ignored by listeners. However, when used excessively, vocalized pauses can give others the impression that we are unsure of ourselves or our ideas are not well thought out. Sometimes speakers use so many vocalized pauses that listeners are distracted by them to the point of not being able to concentrate on the meaning of the message.

We can interpret the paralinguistic part of a message as complementing, supplementing, or contradicting the meaning conveyed by a verbal message. So when Joan says, "Well, isn't that an interesting story," how we interpret her meaning will depend on her paralanguage. If she alters her normal voice so that "Well" is varied both in pitch and tone and the rest of her words are spoken in a staccato monotone, we might perceive her message as sarcasm because we interpret the paralanguage to contradict the words. But if her pitch rises with each word, we might perceive the paralanguage as supplementing the message and understand that she is asking a question.

Use of Space: Proxemics

Proxemics is the formal term for how space and distance communicate (Hall, 1968). Some of the ways we do so include our use of personal space, territorial space, acoustic space, and artifacts.

Personal space Personal space is the distance we try to maintain when interacting with others. How much space we perceive as appropriate depends on our individual preference, the nature of our relationship to the other person or people, and our cultural norms. With these variations in mind, the amount of personal space we view as appropriate generally decreases as the intimacy of our relationship increases. For example, in the dominant U.S. culture, four distinct distances are generally perceived as appropriate and comfortable, depending on the nature of the conversation and relationship. *Intimate distance* is defined as up to 18 inches and is appropriate for private conversations between close friends. *Personal distance*, from 18 inches to 4 feet, is the space in which casual conversation occurs. *Social distance*, from 4 to 12 feet, is where impersonal business such as a job interview is conducted. *Public distance* is anything more than 12 feet (Hall, 1968).

Of greatest concern to us is intimate distance—that which we regard as appropriate for intimate conversation with close friends and family. Americans usually become uncomfortable when "outsiders" violate this intimate distance. For instance, in a movie theater that is less than one-quarter full, people will tend to leave one or more seats empty between themselves and others they do not know. If a stranger sits right next to us in such a setting, we are likely to feel uncomfortable and may even move to another seat. Intrusions into our intimate space are acceptable only in certain settings and then only when all involved follow the unwritten rules.

proxemics

the formal term for how space and distance communicate

personal space

the distance we try to maintain when we interact with other people

Although you might find it rude for someone who was not an intimate friend to get this close to you, these men would find it rude if you backed away.

Robert Azzi–Woodfin Camp

territorial space

the physical space over which we claim ownership

acoustic space

the area over which your voice can be comfortably heard

artifacts

the objects we use to adorn our territory

chronemics

how we interpret the use of time

So, we tolerate being packed into a crowded elevator or subway and even touching others we do not know by following unwritten rules, such as standing rigidly, looking at the floor or above the door, and not making eye contact or talking with others.

Territorial Space **Territorial space** is the physical space over which we claim ownership. As with personal space, we expect others to respect our territory and may feel annoyed or even violated when they do not. Sometimes we do not realize how we are claiming or "marking" our territory. For example, Graham may have subconsciously marked "his chair" in the family room and others just "know" not to sit in it when Graham is around. Other times we mark our territory quite consciously. People consciously mark territory, for example, by using locks, signs, and fences.

Not only can we understand someone's ownership of space by the territorial markers they use, but also their status. For instance, higher-status people generally claim larger and more prestigious territory (Knapp, 2006). In business, for example, the supervisor is likely to have the largest and nicest office in the unit.

Acoustic space **Acoustic space** is the area over which your voice can be comfortably heard. Competent communicators protect acoustic space by adjusting the volume of their voices to be easily heard by their conversational partners and not overheard by others. Loud cell phone conversations occurring in public places violate acoustic space. With the invention of Bluetooth technology, this problem has become even more pronounced. This is why some communities have ordinances prohibiting cell phone use in restaurants, hospitals, and theaters.

Artifacts **Artifacts** are the objects we use to adorn our territory. We display things on our desks and in our offices and homes, not just for their function but also because we find them pleasing in some way. Other people observe these artifacts to make interpretations about us.

We use artifacts to achieve certain effects including signaling what we expect to happen in the space. The chairs and couch in your living room may approximate a circle that invites people to sit down and talk. Classroom seating may be arranged in theater style, which discourages conversation. A manager's office with a chair facing the manager across the desk encourages formal conversation and signals status. It says, "Let's talk business—I'm the boss and you're the employee." A manager's office with a chair placed at the side of her desk encourages more informal conversation. It says, "Don't be nervous—let's just chat."

Use of Time: Chronemics

Recall that **chronemics** is how we interpret the use of time; it is largely based on cultural norms. Just as cultures tend to be more monochronic or polychronic, so too are individuals. If your approach to time is different from those with whom

THE AUDIENCE *BEYOND*

Margie was expecting an important call from her dad regarding the results of her mom's surgery. To respect the acoustic space of her classmates, she turned her phone to vibrate and stepped out of the room to take her dad's call.

you are interacting, your behavior could be viewed as inappropriate and put strains on your relationship. When Carlos, who is polychronic, regularly arrives late to meetings with his monochromic teammates, they might resent his tardiness and perceive him to be full of himself, disrespectful, or perhaps as a slacker. In this chapter's *Diverse Voices* on p. 103, Charles Okigbo talks about moving from what he calls "African time" to "American time."

 **DIVERSE VOICES**

Changing Times

by Charles Okigbo

Professor of Communication, North Dakota State University and Head, Policy Engagement & Communication African Population and Health Research Center Nairobi, Kenya

It is ironic that time is universal in the sense that every society understands the passage of time as it is connected to growth, aging, and transitions from one life stage to another. And yet, the concept of time is so varied from one society to another. I have experienced this similar, yet varying sense of time in my own life, as I grew up in Nigeria, came to the United States for higher education, and have traveled between the United States and different African countries. In much of Africa, there are two time modes—cultural time, which is imprecise, and Western, or as we call it in Nigeria, "English" time. In Nigeria, we call this precise clock-based accounting for time "English time" because the British colonized us. Other African countries that had different colonists might call it by a different name.

Time in much of traditional Africa is seen as an inexhaustible resource that flows endlessly and is hardly in short supply. Growing up in my Igbo village in southeastern Nigeria, the setting for Chinua Achebe's novel, *Things Fall Apart*, I saw my people mark time with the rising and setting of the sun. Longer periods were marked by the rainy and dry seasons, which could come late or early, and people's ages were gauged by historic events such as the world wars, the invasion of locusts, or the British colonialists' confiscation of all guns. Such loose characterization meant that precision was not possible. I vividly remember my people saying with utmost imprecision that a morning meeting would start "after sunrise" or "at the first cockcrow" or "after the morning market." Whereas this would appear confusing and imprecise to Western time observers, to us, it presented no problems at all.

My first experience with Western time was when I went to kindergarten and later elementary school. We were taught to be punctual, and tardiness exacted strict sanctions, usually severe flogging. The severity of the punishment depended on how late one came to school.

When I came to the United States in 1978 for the first time for graduate studies at Ohio University, I was already comfortable with Western time and never had any problem with punctuality. In fact, many Africans in the United States who come from backgrounds of cultural time are often hypersensitive about punctuality issues and tend to be too punctual. This may be a case of overcompensating to avoid relapsing to cultural time. The adjustment to Western time can present some challenges, especially in situations when we have exclusive African events in the United States. For example, I remember as an African student and teacher in the United States, many meetings organized by Nigerian or other African students hardly ever started "on time" by Western standards because we often relapsed to our cultural time for exclusively African events.

So, we seem capable of successfully weaving in and out of cultural time depending on our expectation of whether the occasion is for Africans only or for Africans and "others." When the "others" are people with Western time orientation, we make every effort to be punctual. But when they are people who seem to share our sense of time, we respond accordingly. This represents a chronemics co-orientation, by which I mean that unconsciously we size up the other to know where to position them on the continuum of "cultural" and "Western" time. If they are closer to the former, we expect them to have a more relaxed approach to time, but if they are closer to the latter, we try to be punctual and seriously time conscious in dealing with them.

The tendency is for people to adjust their sense of time depending on the situation or the expectation of the audience. Professional meetings, conferences, even appointments with doctors or lawyers are loosely treated depending on one's expectations of how the other side sees time.

I must say that we Africans are not the only ones who could benefit from engaging in chronemics co-orientation. People who are usually Western in their approach to keeping appointments may decide not to be so punctual if they expect the other party will keep them waiting. For example, in the 1960s my village, Ojoto, was so small that we had no resident priest for the local church. Every Sunday, an Irish priest came from the cathedral in Onitsha to conduct mass. Whereas many priests observed Western time and were usually punctual and expected us to be as well, Revered Father Nicholson was so native in his sense of time that the joke became that if Father Nicholson was the celebrant for the Sunday mass, you could go to the market and do five other chores and you still would not be late for Sunday mass! So, we could say that whereas sometimes Africans may need to adjust to the precision of Western time, at other times, Europeans and Americans who are dealing with exclusive African groups should consider adjusting to cultural time.

I have noticed that many African Americans in the United States are similar to Africans from the continent with respect to time consciousness, and many Native Americans in North Dakota and Minnesota share a similar cultural time orientation. So when African Americans host a party where most of the guests are also African American, the invitation may state that the party starts at 7:00 p.m., but the host may not expect most guests to arrive until after 9:30 p.m.

While both cultural time and Western time continue to guide human behavior, increasing globalization and the information technological revolution are dictating a global approach to time that runs by the precision of the clock rather than by the natural rhythms of the rising or setting of the sun or the beginning or ending of seasons. Whether this move is ultimately in the best interest of humankind remains to be seen.

Source: By Charles Okigbo, Professor of Communication, North Dakota State University. Used with permission.

Physical Appearance

physical appearance

how we look to others and is one of the first things others notice and judge

Physical appearance is how we look to others and is one of the first things others notice and judge. American society places so much emphasis on physical appearance that entire industries are devoted to changing it. Options for changing our physical appearance range from surgical procedures to weight loss programs and products to cosmetics and clothing lines.

Today, more than ever, people use clothing choices, body art, and other personal grooming to communicate who they are and what they stand for. Likewise, when we meet someone, we are likely to form our first impression of them based on how they are dressed and groomed. Because clothing and grooming can be altered to suit the occasion, we can influence how others are likely to perceive us by our clothing and grooming choices. For example, Marcus, a successful sales representative, typically wears dress slacks and a collared shirt to the office, a suit and tie when giving a formal presentation, and a graphic T-shirt and jeans when hanging out with friends. Body art (such as piercings and tattoos) has become quite popular in the United States today. Although body art can be an important means of self-expression, we often make choices about how much of it to display based on the situation and how others are likely to judge us based on it. For example, when Tiffany is at work she dresses conservatively and covers the tattoo on her arm by wearing long-sleeved blouses. But on evenings and weekends, she does not. The *Pop Comm!* feature that follows points out some important considerations regarding body art and how it communicates.

"Tell me about yourself, Kugelman—your hopes, dreams, career path, and what that damn earring means."

POP COMM!

The Meanings and Messages of Body Art: Then and Now

Since ancient times, people have been painting, piercing, scarring, tattooing, and shaping their bodies. In fact, there is no culture that didn't or doesn't use body art to signal people's place in society, mark a special occasion, or just make a fashion statement (American Museum of Natural History, 1999). The body art you see today is simply an extension of ancient human practice that has been adapted to our 21st-century definitions of status, ritual, and beauty.

Body painting is a temporary means of creating a different identity or celebrating a particular occasion. For centuries, Eastern cultures have used henna to dye hands and other body parts to celebrate rites of passage such as marriages. Traditionally in India, married women wore a *bindi*, a red spot or a piece of jewelry, between their eyebrows. Native Americans used a variety of natural dyes to paint their bodies in preparation for war. Today, women use cosmetics, sports fans decorate their faces and bodies before big games, and children have their faces painted at community festivals.

Roman soldiers voluntarily underwent body piercings as a sign of strength. Some tribal cultures had a rite of passage calling for a person to hang from large piercings in the limbs or body trunk. Some societies used piercings as a sign of slavery, and others viewed them as signs of beauty or royalty (Schurman, n.d.). Today piercing is voluntary, and common parts of the body to be pierced are the ears and nose. Some people choose to pierce other body parts including eyebrows, tongues, navels, and genitals. Others practice stretching or gauging, the process of slowly expanding the size of a piercing to accommodate increasingly larger pieces of jewelry. Often, piercings are a rite of passage signaling some personal milestone. At a certain age, girls may have their ears pierced. Less traditional piercings or multiple piercings may be undertaken as a sign of rebellion or to express membership in a particular subculture.

Scarification is the deliberate cutting or burning of the skin in such a way as to control the scarring and create a pattern or picture. Sometimes the freshly made cuts are purposely irritated so that they form raised or keloid scars. Scarification was widely practiced in Africa, where facial scars could identify a person's ethnic group or family, or just be an individual statement of beauty. The Jewish rite of circumcision practiced since the time of Abraham is a form of scarification. Today, scarification may be part of a fraternity or gang initiation rite. Some individuals use cutting to escape from feeling trapped in an intolerable psychological and emotional situation (Jacobs, 2005). The scars that result from this type of cutting are seen as badges of survival.

Tattooing is the oldest form of body art; tattooed mummies have been found in various parts of the world. Tattoos are permanent alterations to the body using inks or dyes, and they are symbolic in nature. Like other body art, tattoos can be either a statement of group solidarity or an expression of individuality. They can be sources of shame or pride. They can be public statements of outsider status or privately enjoyed personal symbols.

Like piercings, tattoos have also been used to mark people who were considered property or inferior in some other way. African American slaves were often tattooed. During World War II, the Nazis tattooed a five-digit number on the inner forearm of Jews and other "undesirables" in concentration camps to strip them of their individual identities. Unlike self-initiated tattoos, which are a source of pride for the wearer, these tattoos were a source of shame. For years after their ordeal, many Holocaust survivors covered their forearms and refused to talk about their experiences. The number on their arm was a grim reminder that they had survived while others had perished.

Today, tattoos are losing their outsider status. Celebrities, soccer moms, corporate executives, star athletes, and high school students sport tattoos as statements of individuality and personal aesthetic. Teenagers may "rebel" by having a small butterfly tattooed on their shoulder blade or a Native American–patterned band tattooed on their bicep. Some people have tattoos strategically placed so that they can choose to display them or hide them from view depending on the self they want to portray.

Shaping, another type of body art, is altering the silhouette or shape of the body based on a culturally validated aesthetic (Australian Museum, 2009). Cranial shaping, neck stretching, foot binding, and corsetry have been practiced in various cultures at various times. Native American and African tribes practiced head shaping. In Africa, Burma, and Thailand rings or beaded necklaces are used to give the appearance of an elongated neck ("African Neck Stretching," 2008–2009). In a practice that lasted two thousand years, Chinese girls' feet were bound to achieve the ideal of tiny feet; this would help them to marry well (Lim, 2007). Corsetry began in ancient times as a means of protecting the wearer from hernias and other body damage that occurs during strenuous activity. By the time of the Romans, wearing a corset became a sign of lower status. Slaves, who did manual labor, wore corsets while their owners wore flowing garments. In the 16th century, fashionable French women cinched their corsets to achieve a 13-inch waist (Wilson, 2002). When Madonna donned a merry widow corset in the 1980s, she may not have realized that she was following a practice that is several centuries old. The Spanx undergarments that many women wear today have their origins in body shaping. Excessive exercising and weight lifting, cosmetic surgery addiction, and even eating disorders allow us to change our body and conform to current definitions of beauty. When it comes to body art, everything old is new again.

Questions to Ponder

1. At least in the United States, it appears that some types of body art have become extremely popular again. Why do you suppose this is?

2. Do you have any body art? If so, reflect on when and why you chose to do it.

3. When you see someone who has taken body art to an extreme, what do you think? How does this affect your interaction with this person?

Guidelines for Improving Nonverbal Communication

Because nonverbal messages are inevitable, multi-channeled, ambiguous, and sometimes unintentional, interpreting them accurately can be tricky. Add to this the fact that the meaning of any nonverbal behavior can vary by situation, culture, and gender, and the reasons we so often misinterpret the behavior of others becomes clear. The following guidelines can help improve the likelihood that your nonverbal messages will be perceived accurately and that you will accurately interpret the nonverbal messages of others.

Be mindful of the distracting nonverbal messages you display. What might this person's nonverbal messages be saying?

Sending Nonverbal Messages

1. **Consciously monitor your nonverbal messages.** Try to be more consciously aware of the nonverbal messages you send through your use of body, voice, space, time, and appearance. If you have difficulty doing this, ask a friend to point them out to you.

2. **Align your nonverbal messages with your purpose.** When nonverbal messages contradict verbal messages, people are more likely to believe the nonverbal messages, so it is important align your nonverbal messages with your purpose. For instance, if you want to be persuasive, you should use direct eye contact, a serious facial expression, an upright posture, a commanding vocal tone with no vocalized pauses, and professional clothing and grooming. If you want to be supportive and convey empathy, you might use less direct eye contact, a more relaxed facial expression, a softer voice, a nonthreatening touch, and a lean inward towards your partner.

3. **Adapt your nonverbal messages to the situation.** Just as you make language choices to suit different situations, so should you do so with nonverbal messages. Assess what the situation calls for in terms of use of body, voice, space, time, and appearance. For example, you would not dress the same way for a wedding as you would for a workout.

4. **Reduce or eliminate distracting nonverbal messages.** Fidgeting, tapping your fingers on a table, pacing, mumbling, using lots of pauses, and checking your phone often for texts and e-mails can distract others from the message you are trying to convey. Make a conscious effort to learn what distracting nonverbal messages have become habitual for you and work to eliminate them from your communication with others.

Interpreting Nonverbal Messages

1. **Remember that the same nonverbal message may mean different things to different people.** Most nonverbal messages have multiple meanings that vary from person to person and culture to culture. Just because you

THE AUDIENCE *BEYOND*

Larissa read her brother's text, "CALL ME!" and immediately stepped into the hall and called him. She interpreted his use of all capital letters and an exclamation point as nonverbal messages to do so immediately, rather than just whenever she had time.

fidget when you are bored, doesn't mean that others are bored when they fidget. What you perceive as an angry vocal tone might not be intended as such by the person talking. So always try to consider multiple interpretations of the nonverbal messages you receive, particularly when your first interpretation is negative. As you interact more with someone, you will learn to "read" their nonverbal messages accurately.

2. **Consider each nonverbal message in context.** Because any one nonverbal message can mean different things in different contexts, take the time to consider how it is intended in a given situation. Also realize that you might not understand all the details of the situation. For example, if you see a classmate sleeping during your speech, you might interpret the nonverbal message as boredom or disrespect. What it might be communicating, however, is utter exhaustion because your classmate just finished back-to-back 12-hour shifts at work while trying to keep up with homework for a full load of courses.

3. **Pay attention to the multiple nonverbal messages being sent and their relationship to the verbal message.** In any one interaction, you are likely to get simultaneous messages from a person's appearance, eye contact, facial expressions, gestures, posture, voice, and use of space and touch. By taking into consideration all nonverbal messages in conjunction with the verbal message, you are more likely to interpret the messages of others accurately.

COMMUNICATE ON YOUR FEET

Speech Assignment

Communicating Emotions Nonverbally: Encoding and Decoding Skill and Practice

The Assignment

Your instructor will display a simple sentence for you to recite to your classmates while attempting to convey a particular emotion nonverbally. First, you will use only your voice; then you will use your voice and face; and finally you will use your voice, face, and body. The sentence could be as simple as "I had bacon and eggs for breakfast this morning."

1. To find out the emotion you will convey, draw a card from a stack offered by your instructor. Without letting your classmates see, turn the card over to read what emotion is written on the front. Some possible emotions include *anger, excitement, fear, joy, worry*, and *sadness*. Consider how you will use vocalics and kinesics to convey that emotion.

2. When your instructor calls on you, go to the front of the classroom and shield your face with a piece of paper

(so that your classmates cannot see your face). Try to convey that emotion with only your voice while saying the sentence with your back to the class.

3. The class might make some guesses about the emotion you are conveying and give some reasons for their guesses. You should not tell them whether they are correct at this point.

4. Turn around to face your classmates and say the sentence again, this time trying to reinforce the emotion with your face and eyes.

5. The class might again make some guesses.

6. Repeat the sentence once more, this time using your voice, face, and body to convey the emotion.

7. The class might again make some guesses.

8. Tell them the emotion that was on the card and what you did with your voice, face, and body to convey it.

9. Your instructor may lead a discussion about what worked and didn't, as well as how you could have made the emotional message more clear.

WHAT WOULD YOU DO?

A Question of Ethics

After the intramural mixed-doubles volleyball games on Tuesday evening, most of the players went to the campus grill for a drink and a chat. Marquez and Lisa sat down with their competitors Brad and Elana, to whom they had lost due to Elana's ability to land killer spikes. Although Marquez and Lisa were only friends through volleyball, Brad and Elana had been going out together for much of the year.

After some general conversation about the game, Marquez said, "Elana, your spikes today were awesome!"

"Yeah, I was really impressed," Lisa added.

"And you're getting so high at the net," Marquez added.

"Thanks, guys," Elana said in a tone of gratitude, "I've really been working on it."

"Well, aren't we getting the compliments today?" sneered Brad in a sarcastic tone. Then after a pause, he said, "Oh, Elana, would you get my sweater? I left it on that chair by the other table."

"Come on, Brad. You're closer than I am," Elana replied.

Brad moved slightly closer to Elana and looked at her sternly with piercing eye contact.

Elana quickly backed away from Brad as she said, "OK, Brad. It's cool." She then quickly got the sweater for him.

"Gee, isn't she sweet?" Brad said to Marquez and Lisa as he grabbed the sweater from Elana.

Lisa and Marquez both looked down at the floor. Then Lisa glanced at Marquez and said, "Well, I'm out of here. I've got a lot to do this evening."

"Let me walk you to your car," Marquez said as he quickly stood up and grabbed her jacket for her.

"See you next week," they both said in unison as they hurried out the door, leaving Brad and Elana alone at the table.

1. What do you think Brad's nonverbal messages were attempting to achieve?

2. How would you interpret Lisa's and Marquez's nonverbal reactions to Brad?

3. Do you think Brad's nonverbal communication was ethical? Explain.

4. **Use perception checking.** The skill of perception checking lets you see if your interpretation of another person's message is accurate. By describing the nonverbal message you notice, sharing your interpretation of it, and asking for clarification, you can get confirmation or correction of your interpretation.

Summary

Nonverbal communication consists of all the messages that transcend spoken or written words. Nonverbal messages may emphasize, substitute for, or contradict a verbal message. They can regulate our conversations and project an image about who we are to others. Nonverbal communication is inevitable, multi-channeled, and ambiguous. It is also the primary way we convey our emotions. We communicate nonverbal messages through our bodies (gestures, eye contact, facial expression, posture, and touch), our voices (pitch, volume, rate, quality, intonation, and vocalized pauses), our use of space (personal space, territorial space, acoustic space, and artifacts), use of time, and physical appearance. We can become more adept at sending and interpreting nonverbal messages by following several guidelines.

COMMUNICATE!

RESOURCE AND ASSESSMENT CENTER

Now that you have read Chapter 5, go to the Speech Communication Course-Mate at cengagebrain.com where you'll find an interactive eBook and interactive learning tools including quizzes, flashcards, sample speech videos, audio study tools, skill-building activities, action step activities, and more. Student Workbook, Speech Builder Express 3.0, and Speech Studio 2.0 are also available.

Applying What You've Learned

Impromptu Speech Activity

1. Select a card from a stack provided by your instructor. Each card identifies a different emotion. Using no words, go to the front of the room and attempt to convey the emotion using only your body (including your hands and eyes). Ask the class to identify the emotion you are conveying and then discuss what you did to try to convey it.

Assessment Activities

1. Read this scenario and answer the questions that follow by applying the concepts of nonverbal communication we discussed in this chapter:

> Jesa and Madison were lounging on a blanket in the park one spring afternoon, enjoying the sunshine as they reviewed for an upcoming test. Jesa looked into the distance, then jerked her head around, bolted upright, quickly gathered her things, and quietly said, "See you back at the apartment." With that she took off at a fast clip.
>
> Madison quickly glanced in the direction that Jesa had been looking just before she took off, then shouted, "Wait a sec, I'm coming too."
>
> Once they were back in their apartment Madison sighed and said, "Okay, Jesa, what's really going on with you? Who was that guy you saw in the park? And why are you acting so scared?"
>
> "What guy? I don't know what you're talking about," Jesa mumbled, looking down at her feet. "And I'm not scared," she added as she turned to the window pulled back the corner of the curtain and peeked outside.

- How is each of the characteristics of nonverbal communication exemplified in this scene?

- Do you think Jesa was telling the truth? What about her nonverbal communication led you to this conclusion?

2. Go to a public place (for example, a restaurant or coffee shop) where you can observe two people having a conversation. You should be close enough so that you can observe their eye contact, facial expression, and gestures, but not close enough to hear what they are saying.

Carefully observe the interaction, with the goal of answering the following questions: What is their relationship? What seems to be the nature of the conversation (social chitchat, plan making, problem solving, argument, intimate discussion)? How does each person feel about the conversation? Do feelings change over the course of the conversation? Is one person more dominant? Take note of the specific non-verbal behaviors that led you to each conclusion, and write a paragraph describing this experience and what you have learned.

3. Enter a crowded elevator and face the back. Make direct eye contact with the person you are standing in front of. When you disembark, record the person's reactions. On the return trip, introduce yourself to the person who is standing next to you and engage in an animated conversation. Record the reaction of the person and others around you. Then get on an empty elevator and stand in the exact center. Do not move when others board. Record their reactions. Be prepared to share what you have observed with your classmates.

Skill-Building Activities

1. Provide a perception check for each of the following nonverbal messages:

   a. Larry walks into the cubicle, throws his report across the desk, smiles, and loudly proclaims, "Well, that's that!"

   Perception Check:

   b. Christie, dressed in her team uniform, with her hair going every which way, charges into the room and announces in a loud voice, "I'm here, and I'm ready."

   Perception Check:

   c. It was dinnertime and Anthony was due home from work at any minute. Suddenly the door flew open, banging against its hinges and Anthony stomped in, crossing the room in three long strides, plopped onto the sofa, crossed his arms, and with a sour expression stared straight ahead.

   Perception Check:

Listening

What you'll know

- What listening is and why it is important to effective communication

- Three challenges to effective listening

- Five steps in the active listening process

What you'll be able to do

- Employ specific strategies to willfully attend to the messages you receive

- Employ specific strategies to understand the messages you receive

- Employ specific strategies to successfully remember the messages you receive

- Critically evaluate information in the messages you receive

- Provide appropriate feedback about the messages you receive

"Beth, do you have my car keys? I can't find them and I have to take the car or I'll be late for class."

"No, but it doesn't matter because . . ."

"I can't believe it. I was sure I left them here on the counter last night."

"Bart, it's okay . . ."

"It just figures. Just because I'm in a hurry, I can't find them."

"Bart, I've been trying to tell you, the . . ."

"I swear I put them here on the counter. Did you stuff them in a drawer when you were cleaning the kitchen or something?"

"Bart, chill out. The car's . . ."

"Chill out? If I'm late, I won't be able to do my presentation and it's worth 50 percent of the course grade! I won't pass the class and I need at least a B to declare my major. Beth, this is a very big deal."

"Bart, I've been trying to tell you . . ."

6

"Oh, sure—I just go into Professor Harrington's office and say, 'By the way, the reason I wasn't in class was that I couldn't find my car keys. Can I please do my presentation tomorrow?' I'll sound like a slacker who wasn't ready. There's no way he'll buy that argument even though it's true."

"Bart, listen! I've been trying to tell you—I went out to get milk this morning and knew you would be leaving soon, so I left the keys in the car for you."

"Geez, Beth, why didn't you tell me?"

Are you a good listener? Or, like Bart, do you occasionally find yourself jumping to conclusions before hearing others out, particularly when you're under pressure? We shouldn't underestimate the importance of listening; it can provide clarification, help us understand and remember material, improve our personal and professional relationships, and increase our ability to evaluate information effectively (Donoghue & Siegel, 2005).

Of the basic communication skills (reading, writing, speaking, and listening), we use listening the most. In fact, although we spend more than 50 percent of our communication time listening, many of us can remember only about 25 percent of what we heard 48 hours later (Janusik & Wolvin, 2006). A survey of *Fortune* 500 firms conducted jointly by the American Society for Training and Development and the U.S. Department of Labor showed listening to be one of the "top five" most important basic workplace skills expected of employees. What is somewhat troubling, however, is the fact that fewer than 2 percent of us have had any formal listening training (Listening Factoid, 2003). So the skills you learn and apply from this chapter will set you apart in ways that will benefit you both personally and professionally.

We begin with a discussion of what listening is and some of the challenges we must overcome to listen effectively. Then, we describe the steps involved in the active listening process and propose some specific guidelines you can follow to improve your listening skills during each step in the process. Finally, we suggest strategies for responding appropriately in different listening situations.

What Is Listening?

People sometimes make the mistake of thinking listening and hearing are the same, but they're not. Hearing is a physiological process, whereas listening is a cognitive one. In other words, listening occurs only when we choose to focus on and attach meaning to what we hear. According to the International Listening Association, **listening** is the process of receiving, constructing meaning from, and responding to spoken and/or nonverbal messages (International Listening Association, 1996).

listening

the process of receiving, constructing meaning from, and responding to spoken and/or nonverbal messages

We choose to listen for various reasons depending on the situation. For example, sometimes we listen to learn about something new. Other times we might listen to provide emotional support as others work through their feelings about an emotionally charged experience. Still other times we listen to make discerning inferences beyond the surface message by "listening between the lines," so to speak. And other times, we listen not only to understand but also to evaluate and assign worth to a message. To become effective listeners, we must first consciously overcome three key challenges.

Challenges to Effective Listening

The three challenges to effective listening are rooted in listening style, apprehension, and processing approach.

Listening Style

Listening style is our favored and usually unconscious approach to listening (Watson, Barker, & Weaver, 1995). Each of us favors one of four listening styles and only a few people can switch effectively between styles based on the situation (Weaver & Kirtley, 1995).

Content-oriented listeners focus on and evaluate the facts and evidence. Content-oriented listeners appreciate details and enjoy processing complex messages that may include a good deal of technical information. Content-oriented listeners are likely to ask questions to get even more information.

People-oriented listeners focus on the feelings their conversational partners may have about what they are saying. For example, people-oriented listeners tend to notice whether their partners are pleased or upset and will encourage them to continue based on nonverbal cues like head nods, eye contact, and smiles.

Action-oriented listeners focus on the ultimate point the speaker is trying to make. Action-oriented listeners tend to get frustrated when ideas are disorganized and when people ramble. Action-oriented listeners also often anticipate what the speaker is going to say and may even finish the speaker's sentence for them.

Finally, **time-oriented listeners** prefer brief and hurried conversations and often use nonverbal and verbal cues to signal that their partner needs to be more concise. Time-oriented listeners may tell others exactly how much time they have to listen, interrupt when feeling time pressures, regularly check the time on smart phones, watches, or clocks, and may even nod their heads rapidly to encourage others to pick up the pace.

Each of these styles has advantages and disadvantages. Content-oriented listeners are likely to understand and remember details, but may miss the overall point of the message and be unaware of the speaker's feelings. People-oriented listeners are likely to understand how the speaker feels, empathize, and offer comfort and support. However, they might become so focused on the speaker's feelings that they miss important details or fail to evaluate the facts offered as evidence. Action-oriented listeners may notice inconsistencies but, because they tend to anticipate what will be said rather than hearing the speaker out, may miss important details. Finally, time-oriented listeners are prone to only partially listen to messages while also thinking about their time constraints; thus, they might miss important details and be insensitive to their partner's emotional needs. In our opening scenario, Bart fell victim to the consequences of being too action-oriented and time-oriented when listening to Beth.

Preferred listening style may also be influenced by cultural and co-cultural identity. For example, women who identify with the feminine co-culture are more likely to describe themselves as person-oriented. Similarly, men who identify with the masculine co-culture are more likely to be time-oriented (Salisbury & Chen, 2007). People from collectivist cultures where maintaining group harmony is highly valued are more likely to have a people-oriented listening style and people from individualistic cultures to have an action-oriented listening style (Kiewitz et al., 1997). People from high-context cultures tend to favor a person-oriented listening style and people from low-context cultures tend to prefer an action-oriented style (Harris, 2003).

listening style
our favored and usually unconscious approach to listening

content-oriented listeners
focus on and evaluate the facts and evidence

people-oriented listeners
focus on the feelings their conversational partners may have about what they're saying

action-oriented listeners
focus on the ultimate point the speaker is trying to make

time-oriented listeners
prefer brief and hurried conversations and use nonverbal and verbal cues to signal that their partner needs to be more concise

CONSIDER THIS....

Which listening style do you engage in most often? Can you think of a time when it would have been better to use one of the other styles? Why or why not?

Have you ever felt your anxiety increase because you really wanted to understand an explanation of difficult information or directions?

Listening Apprehension

Listening apprehension is the anxiety we feel about listening. Listening apprehension may increase when we are worried about misinterpreting the message, or when we are concerned about how the message may affect us psychologically (Brownell, 2006). For example, if you are in an important meeting or job training session, you may worry about trying to absorb all the important technical information needed to do your job well. Or you might feel anxiety when the material you need to absorb is difficult or confusing. Likewise, your anxiety may increase when you feel ill, tired, or stressed about something else going on in your life at the time. Listening apprehension makes it difficult to focus on the message. In the *Diverse Voices* selection, "How I Learned to Shut Up and Listen," Eileen describes how her apprehension actually taught her the value of listening.

DIVERSE VOICES

How I Learned to Shut Up and Listen

By Eileen Smith

Bearshapedsphere.com

Living in the "wrong" country for nearly seven years, Elieen calls Chile home now. She bikes, photographs, writes, eats, and talks about language. She was raised in Brooklyn, New York.

I sat at a table of no fewer than fifteen people on the street Pio Nono, entry to Bellavista, the down-home party section of Santiago, Chile. I'd been invited to go out for a beer after the monthly critical mass bike ride. We sat at a long series of card tables extending down the street, serving ourselves beer from the liter bottles of Escudo on the center of the tables. Some drinkers mixed theirs with Fanta. I drank mine plain and listened.

I arrived to Chile in 2004, with way more than a passing knowledge of Spanish. Between high school and a couple of travel and study stints in the *mundo hispanohablante* (Spanish-speaking world), I could express myself fairly well, if not cleverly. Hadn't I explained the electoral college to a group of teachers in Antigua, Guatemala, in the 1990s? Wasn't it me who grabbed other travelers by the hand to take them to the post office, the bus station, or to get their hair cut? I enjoyed helping, expressing, being in charge. I could get you a seat on the bus, a doorstop, tape to fix a book—you name it. I could ask for it directly or circumlocute it. I spoke, and people understood. At the time, I felt that this was the only necessary linguistic accomplishment. You, listen to me. And then it was over.

While output was the feather in my linguistic cap, my listening wouldn't have won any awards. Still, I was skilled enough (or so I thought). Ask a predictable question while travelling, and get a predictable answer. "Where" questions should lead to a location. "When" questions should yield a time or day. "I don't know" might come up at any time, so be prepared. Other times you might get a "probably," or "No, we're out of that (on the menu), what about this?" These little sayings are repetitive, predictable, often accompanied by hand and head motions, and occasional pointing. Understandable.

But what happens when you get out of the predictable, and put fifteen of your new closest friends on a loud sidewalk, add an unfamiliar accent, country-specific slang, and not just a touch of cheap beer? As an ESL teacher I'd seen students reduced to frustration, to squinching their eyes shut against visual input while they leaned their heads closer to the audio, hoping that the problem wasn't their ear for English, but their hearing. Try as I might there on the sidewalk, no matter of eye squinching or head leaning was going to fix the fact that I was simply not up to the task. My Chilean friends could understand me, but of the reading/writing/listening/speaking quadrifecta that make up second-language learning, clearly my listening was the weakest. I'm loquacious at the best of times, grate-on-your-nerves chatty when it's worse. But here, on the street in Santiago, 5,000 miles from a place where I could understand easily (and foolishly had taken this for granted), I was relegated to good listener status. I could understand enough to follow, kind of, but not fast enough to say anything relevant to the conversation while the topic was still hot.

I was also in Chile, which, with the exception of not letting people off the metro before getting on, is one of the most polite places I'd ever been. What this means is that any time I so much as appeared to want to say anything, a hush would fall over the string of tables. People knew they might not understand me easily, so they wanted to give me their complete attention.

Between the hot topic issue and the *plancha* (embarassment) I felt at having all eyes on me, the venerable communicator, I simply had to take a different tact. No longer was I Eileen, wordsmith extraordinaire. I was Aylín, the good listener. I was polite and people described me as quiet.

Not being able to participate in a conversation is like being in disguise. For the first time in my life I was getting to know the patient people, the ones that reach out to quiet ones. I'd never met them before because I was so busy with my soundtrack. It made people want to take me into their confidence, their inner circle. I was not a person who repeated private information. As far as they could tell, I didn't even speak.

After several months of more listening than speaking, I took it up as a new challenge: To follow every conversation with surgical precision, and say nothing, or nearly nothing. I could feel the cloud of wonder and panic lifting, and still I chose to stay quiet. I learned about body language and turn-taking, Chilean social niceties, and watched the other quiet people to see what they were doing. They weren't bland, just quiet. It was a revelation.

Nearly five years later, I don't have to just listen any more. I can exchange jokes and fling around slang with abandon. But what I've found is that I often don't want to. I'm often happy to let events take place without interrupting them, just listening to people say what they have to, what they want to. I don't interrupt as much and I've discovered this whole new world, even among my very own family, the self-professed masters of interrupting and simultaneous yammering (I blame Brooklyn). Sometimes I just try to let them talk themselves out before chiming in. Because when people are talking, they tend not to be great listeners. I'd rather have their attention before saying something.

I'm often told I've changed quite a bit since being in Chile. Years have passed, and in that time we've all changed. But what I learned there is that you don't have to be on your game at every possible second. You can watch from the sidelines and participate at the same time. Sometimes the story we tell when we're not saying a word is the most important story of all.

Originally posted April 2, 2009, at Travelblogs.com.

Source: Reprinted by permission of Eileen Smith.

When we listen passively, we usually miss important parts of the message. When have you felt the consequences of failing to listen actively?

passive listening

the habitual and unconscious process of receiving messages

active listening

the deliberate and conscious process of attending to, understanding, remembering, evaluating, and responding to messages

attending

the process of willfully perceiving selected sounds

Processing Approach

You may recall from Chapter 2 that we use one of two approaches to process information. The approach we use depends, in part, on how we listen. **Passive listening** is the habitual and unconscious process of receiving messages. When we listen passively, we are on automatic pilot. We may attend only to certain parts of a message and assume the rest. We tend to listen passively when we aren't really interested or when we are multitasking. By contrast, **active listening** is the deliberate and conscious process of attending to, understanding, remembering, evaluating, and responding to messages. Active listening requires practice. The rest of this chapter focuses on helping you become a better active listener.

Active Listening

Active listening is a complex process made up of five steps. These steps are (a) attending, (b) understanding, (c) remembering, (d) evaluating, and (e) responding to the messages we receive.

Attending

Active listening begins with attending. **Attending** is the process of willfully perceiving selected sounds (O'Shaughnessey, 2003). Poor listeners have difficulty exercising control over what they attend to, often letting their minds drift to thoughts unrelated to the topic. One reason for this is that people typically speak at a rate of about 120–150 words per minute, but our brains can process between 400 and 800 words per minute (Wolvin & Coakley, 1996). This means we usually assume we know what a speaker is going to say before he or she finishes saying it. So our minds have lots of time to wander from the message.

The first step to becoming a good active listener, then, is to train ourselves to focus on or attend to what people are saying regardless of potential distractions. Let's consider five techniques that can help improve attending skills.

1. **Get physically ready to listen.** Good listeners create a physical environment conducive to listening and adopt a listening posture. It is easier to pay attention when we eliminate possible sources of distraction. For example, you can turn music down or off. You can silence your cell phone and

THE AUDIENCE *BEYOND*

Seth didn't want his mind to wander while using Facebook to chat with his brother about the seriousness of their dad's illness. So he deliberately put away his cell phone, turned off the television, and moved from the couch to the kitchen table for the conversation.

even put it away so you won't be tempted to check messages when you are supposed to be listening. Good listeners also adopt a listening posture by sitting upright in the chair or moving closer to the speaker and by making direct eye contact. You have probably noticed that when a professor tells the class that the next bit of information will be on the test, students often sit upright in their chairs, lean forward slightly, and look directly at the professor.

2. **Resist mental distractions.** Work consciously to block out wandering thoughts that might come from a visual distraction (e.g., a classmate who enters the room while the professor is lecturing), an auditory distraction (e.g., coworkers chatting beside you while your supervisor is giving in-structions), or a physical distraction (e.g., wondering what you'll eat for lunch because your stomach is growling).

3. **Make the shift fully from speaker to listener.** In conversation, we may find it difficult to completely make the shift from speaker to listener. When we fail to do so, instead of fully attending to the speaker, we might rehearse what we plan to say next or even interrupt them before they've finished. This is especially true when engaged in a heated conversation. During such exchanges, consciously stop yourself from preparing a response or interrupting the speaker. Shifting completely from the role of speaker to listener requires constant conscious effort.

4. **Observe nonverbal cues.** We interpret messages more accurately when we observe the nonverbal behaviors that accompany the words. For instance, when your friend says, "Don't worry about me. I'm fine, really," actively attend to nonverbal cues such as tone of voice, body actions, and facial expression to tell whether she is really fine or whether she is upset but re-luctant to tell you about it.

5. **Hear a person out.** Far too often, we stop listening before the person has fin-ished speaking because, relying on our scripts library, we think we "know" what they are going to say. But what we think they are going to say is only a guess. Active listeners cultivate the habit of hearing the speaker out. The *Pop Comm!* feature in this chapter highlights the lost art of listening that is evident all too often in political debates today as candidates interrupt and talk over others rather than attending fully to one another's remarks before planning what to say themselves.

Understanding

Understanding results from accurately decoding a message. We offer four sets of guidelines to help you make sense of the messages you receive.

1. **Identify the main point.** As you listen, ask yourself, "What does the speak-er want me to understand?" and "What is the point being made?" In addi-tion to the surface message, you might also need to consider the pragmatic meaning couched within it. For example, when Marlee, who is running for city council, asks Joanna what she thinks about the plans for the new arts center and begins to talk about some of its pros and cons, Joanna un-derstands that, beneath the surface, Marlee is also attempting to persuade Joanna to vote for her.

2. **Ask questions.** A **question** is a statement designed to clarify informa-tion or get additional details. Effective questioning begins by identifying

CONSIDER *THIS....*

Think of a time when you were in a heated argument with a friend or colleague. Did you consciously hear them out before responding? How did you feel about the exchange afterward and why?

understanding

results from accurately decod-ing a message

question

a statement designed to clarify information or get additional details

Presidential "Debates": The Lost Art of Listening and the Future of Civil Democratic Discourse in the United States

Eric Gay-Pool/Getty Images

Political debates have always been a key part of American democracy, exercising free speech in order to promote a national dialogue on important political issues. Though political debates are, ideally, moments of civil discourse intended to enhance a listener's understanding of a topic or viewpoint, the debates held in fall 2011 mattered more for what they revealed about the continuing decline of civil discourse in political culture.

For example, during a debate in September 2011, moderator Brian Williams asked Texas Governor Rick Perry about "the 234 executions of death row inmates over which Perry has presided," and the mere mention of the executions was met with loud cheers from some members of the audience before the governor could even respond (Greenwald, 2011). Though the cheers were clearly an instance of partisan support for Perry's position on the death penalty, many criticized this response as inappropriate; saying it shut down any meaningful public conversation about this difficult issue. *Salon* columnist Glenn Greenwald wrote, "Wildly cheering the execution of human beings as though one's favorite football team just scored a touchdown is primitive, twisted and base."

Similarly, in another debate that same month, when an openly gay member of the military asked former Senator Rick Santorum about his position on "Don't Ask, Don't Tell," members of the audience booed loudly at the question and cheered wildly as Santorum spoke of his opposition of the repeal of the policy (Wolf, 2011). Again, the crowd showed its support for Santorum and his views, but at the cost of shutting down a legitimate policy question from the soldier. Jesse Jackson argues that "a full and fair discussion is essential to democracy." Does limiting free speech on one side of the debate meet this standard?

The candidates themselves also participated in the debates using emotionally charged language and cutting one another off mid-sentence. Former Massachusetts Governor Mitt Romney struggled to get his message out in the face of attacks and interruptions from the other candidates. Rick Perry labeled Romney's stance on illegal immigration as "the height of hypocrisy," claiming Romney had knowingly employed illegal workers at his Utah home. As Romney attempted to defend himself and his policy, Perry frequently tried to interrupt. During the same debate, Rick Santorum also continually interrupted and spoke over Romney's attempts to answer criticisms of the health insurance legislation he signed while governor of Massachusetts. Santorum declared "You're out of time. You're out of time" when Romney asked for more time to fully explain his views in light of the continued interruptions (Morrison, 2011). Are these the types of political debate that serve our democracy?

Professor Dale Harrison of Auburn University suggests emotion plays an important role in our political process, "Rants add passion to news events and inspire people to take sides on issues" (Johnson, 2006). This is certainly not a new phenomenon. As journalist James Maguire (2007) points out, as far back as 80 B.C., the Roman philosopher Cicero speculated that people are more convinced by pathos (emotion) than by logos (logic). But is the purpose of democratic dialogue lost when politicians refuse to listen to one another and instead interrupt and engage in emotional rants?

One research study showed that, in debates that are less than civil, viewers are less likely to remember the actual arguments underlying the positions than in more civil ones (Mutz, Reeves, & Wise, 2003). According to the National Institute for Civil Discourse, a bipartisan organization chaired by former presidents

George H. W. Bush and Bill Clinton, this has important consequences for our political lives. They suggest the decline of civil discourse in politics and the media's focus on the loudest and most extreme voices over rational and substantive debate "impairs the development of sound policy, making government less effective" and ignores "the multiplicity of opinions and approaches" needed to address the complex political problems facing our nation. In the midst of the political theater of debates and the media's focus on bickering, Americans are losing interest in the political process. Survey data from the Pew Research Center for the People and the Press (2011) shows that Americans are becoming increasingly frustrated with elected officials for their poor performance and increasingly dissatisfied with the potential Presidential candidates.

Questions to Ponder

1. Given the decline of civil discourse in political debates today, should they be eliminated from the campaigning process?

2. What could be done to restore civil discourse in political debates?

the kind of information you need to increase your understanding. Suppose Chris says to you, "I am totally frustrated. Would you stop at the store on the way home and buy me some more paper?" You may be a bit confused by his request and need more information to understand. Yet if you simply respond, "What do you mean?," Chris, who is already frustrated, may become defensive. Instead, you might think about what type of information you need and form a question to meet that need. To increase your understanding, you can ask one of these three types of questions:

- *To get details*: "What kind of paper would you like me to get, and how much will you need?"

- *To clarify word meanings*: "Could you tell me what you mean by *frustrated*?"

- *To clarify feelings*: "What's frustrating you?"

3. **Paraphrase. Paraphrasing** is putting your interpretation of the message into words. For example, during an argument with her sister, Karen paraphrased what she thought she heard her sister saying: "You say that you are tired of me talking about work and that you feel that I'm trying to act like I'm better than you when I talk about my successes." Paraphrases may focus on content, on feelings underlying the content, or on both. A **content paraphrase** focuses on the denotative meaning of the message. The first part of the example above ("You say that you are tired of me talking about work") is a content paraphrase. A **feelings paraphrase** is a response that captures the emotions attached to the message. The second part of the example ("you feel that I'm trying to act like I'm better than you") is a feelings paraphrase.

By paraphrasing, you give the speaker a chance to verify your understanding. The longer and more complex the message, the more important it is to paraphrase. When the speaker appears to be emotional or when the speaker is not using his or her native language, paraphrasing is essential to understanding.

To paraphrase effectively, (1) listen carefully to the message, (2) notice what images and feelings you have experienced from the message, (3) determine

paraphrasing

putting your interpretation of the message into words

content paraphrase

focuses on the denotative meaning of the message

feelings paraphrase

a response that captures the emotions attached to the message

COMMUNICATION SKILL

Paraphrasing

Skill	Use	Procedure	Example
A response that conveys your understanding of another person's message.	To increase listening efficiency; to avoid message confusion; to discover the speaker's motivation.	1. Listen carefully to the message. 2. Notice what images and feelings you have experienced from this message. 3. Determine what the message means to you. 4. Create a message that conveys these images or feelings.	Grace says, "At two minutes to five, the boss gave me three letters that had to be in the mail that evening!" Bonita replies, "If I understand, you were really resentful that your boss dumped important work on you right before quitting time when she knows you have to pick up the baby at day care."

empathy

intellectually identifying with or vicariously experiencing the feelings or attitudes of another

empathic responsiveness

occurs when you experience an emotional response parallel to another person's actual or anticipated display of emotion

perspective taking

occurs when we use everything we know about sender and his or her circumstances to understand their feelings

Sometimes effective listening means demonstrating empathy for someone who is obviously distressed. Who do you typically go to for empathy and support when you feel stressed, and why?

Bruce Ayres/The Image Bank/

what the message means to you, and (4) create a message that conveys these images or feelings.

4. **Empathize. Empathy** is intellectually identifying with or vicariously experiencing the feelings or attitudes of another. Three approaches are empathic responsiveness, perspective taking, and sympathetic responsiveness (Weaver & Kirtley, 1995, p. 131).

- **Empathic responsiveness** occurs when you experience an emotional response parallel to, and as a result of observing, another person's actual or anticipated display of emotion (Omdahl, 1995, p. 4; Stiff, Dillard, Somera, Kim, & Sleight, 1988, p. 199). For instance, when Jackson tells Janis that he is in real trouble financially, and Janis senses the stress and anxiety that Jackson is feeling, we would say that Janis has demonstrated empathic responsiveness.

- **Perspective taking** occurs when we use everything we know about the sender and his or her circumstances to understand their feelings. For example, suppose that Jackson tells James that he is in serious financial trouble. James, who has known Jackson since grade school, understands that Jackson was raised by parents who were very frugal and paid their bills on time. Because of what he knows about Jackson, James understands that Jackson must be very worried about his rising debts.

- **Sympathetic responsiveness** is feeling concern, compassion, or sorrow for another's situation. Sympathy differs from the other two approaches. Rather than attempting to experience the feelings of the other, we translate our intellectual understanding of what the speaker has experienced into feelings of concern, compassion, and sorrow for that person. In our previous example, Janis has sympathy for Jackson when she understands that Jackson is embarrassed and worried, but instead of trying to feel those same emotions herself, she feels concern and compassion for her friend.

"Cheer up, Nicole! What does Princeton know? Say, you got any plans for that last bit of cobbler?"

How well we empathize also depends on how observant we are of others' behavior and how clearly we read their nonverbal messages. To improve these skills, develop the habit of silently posing two questions to yourself: "What emotions do I believe the person is experiencing right now?" and "On what cues from the person am I basing this conclusion?"

To further increase the accuracy of reading emotions, you can also use perception checking. This is especially helpful when the other person's culture is different from yours. Let's consider an example. Atsuko, who was raised in rural Japan and is now studying at a university in Rhode Island, may feel embarrassed when her professor publicly compliments her work. Her friend Meredith might notice Atsuko's reddened cheeks and downcast eyes and comment, "Atsuko, I noticed that you looked down when Professor Shank praised you. Did the compliment embarrass you, make you feel uncomfortable, or was it something else?"

sympathetic responsiveness

feeling concern, compassion, or sorrow for another's situation

Remembering

Remembering is the process of moving information from short-term to long-term memory. Several things can make remembering difficult. We filter out information that doesn't fit our listening style, our listening anxiety prevents us from recalling what we have heard, we engage in passive listening, we practice selective listening and remember only what supports our position, and we fall victim to the primacy-recency effect of remembering only what is said at the beginning and end of a message. Let's look at three techniques to improve our ability to remember information.

remembering

the process of moving information from short-term to long-term memory

THE AUDIENCE *BEYOND*

When Allie's friend posted on Facebook that he had lost his job, Allie was able to understand her friend's pain because she knew that he had been working at his dream job and loved going to work each day.

Some people remember the color spectrum using the mnemonic device "Roy G. Biv" for red, orange, yellow, green, blue, indigo, and violet.

repetition

saying something aloud or mentally rehearsing it two, three, or more times

mnemonic device

a technique that associates a special word or very short statement with new and longer information

1. **Repeat the information. Repetition**—saying something aloud or mentally rehearsing it two, three, or four times— helps store information in long-term memory (Estes, 1989). If information is not reinforced, it will be held in short-term memory for as little as 20 seconds and then forgotten. So when you are introduced to a stranger named Jon McNeil, if you mentally think, "Jon McNeil, Jon McNeil, Jon McNeil," you increase the chances that you will remember his name. Likewise, when a person gives you directions to "go two blocks east, turn left, turn right at the next light, and it's the second apartment building on the right," you should immediately repeat the directions to yourself to help remember them.

2. **Construct mnemonics.** A **mnemonic device** is a learning technique that associates a special word or very short statement with new and longer information. One of the most common mnemonic techniques is to form a word with the first letters of a list of items you are trying to remember. For example, a popular mnemonic for the five Great Lakes is HOMES (*H*uron, *O*ntario, *M*ichigan, *E*rie, *S*uperior). Most beginning music students learn the mnemonic "*e*very *g*ood *b*oy *d*oes *f*ine" for the notes on the lines of the treble clef (E, G, B, D, F) and the word *face* (F, A, C, E) for the notes on the spaces.

3. **Take notes.** Although note taking may not be an appropriate way to remember information when engaged in casual interpersonal encounters, it is a powerful tool for increasing recall during lectures, business meetings, and briefing sessions. Note taking provides a written record that you can go back to later. It also allows you to take an active role in the listening process (Wolvin & Coakley, 1996).

What constitutes good notes varies depending on the situation. Useful notes may consist of a brief list of main points or key ideas plus a few of the most significant details. Or they may be a short summary of the entire concept (a type of paraphrase). For lengthy and detailed information, however, good notes are likely to consist of a brief outline, including the overall idea, the main points, and key developmental material. Good notes are not necessarily long. In fact, many classroom lectures can be reduced to a one-page or shorter outline.

Evaluating

evaluating

critically analyzing what you hear

facts

statements whose accuracy can be verified as true

inferences

assertions based on the facts presented

Evaluating is the process of critically analyzing what you hear to determine how truthful, authentic, or believable you judge the message to be. This may involve ascertaining the accuracy of facts, the amount and type of evidence used, and how a position relates to your personal values. Here are some suggestions to help you evaluate messages effectively.

1. **Separate facts from inferences. Facts** are statements whose accuracy can be verified as true. If a statement is offered as a fact, you need to determine if it is true. Doing so often requires asking questions that probe the evidence. For example, if Raoul says, "It's going to rain tomorrow," you might ask, "Oh, did you see the weather report this morning?" **Inferences** are assertions based on the facts presented. When a speaker makes an inference, you need to determine whether the inference is valid. You can ask: (1) What are the

facts that support this inference? (2) Is this information really central to the inference? (3) Is there other information that would contradict this inference? For example, if someone says, "Better watch it—Katie's in a really bad mood today. Did you catch the look on her face?" you should stop and think, is Katie really in a bad mood? The support for this inference is her facial expression. Is this inference accurate? Is Katie's expression one of anger, or unhappiness, or something else? Is the look on her face enough to conclude that she's in a bad mood? Is there anything else about Katie's behavior that could lead us to believe that she's not in a bad mood? Separating facts from inferences helps us realize the difference between a verifiable observation and an opinion related to that observation. Separating facts from inferences is important because inferences may be false, even if they are based on verifiable facts.

Effective managers understand the value of making notes about problems that employees point out. How can you use note taking at work to improve your performance?

2. **Probe for information.** Sometimes we need to encourage the speaker to delve deeper into the topic in order to truly evaluate the message critically. For example, suppose that Jerrod's prospective landlord asked him to sign a lease. Before signing it, Jerrod should probe for more information. He might ask about the term of the lease and the consequences for breaking the lease early. He might also ask about a deposit and what he will need to do to get the deposit back when the lease is up. He may have noticed inconsistencies between the rental ad on Craigslist and something the landlord says. In that case he might say, "Your ad said that utilities would be paid by the landlord, but just now you said the tenant pays the utility bill. Which one is correct?" With questions like these, Jerrod is probing to accurately evaluate the message.

Responding

The final step in active listening is **responding**, the process of providing feedback. When we respond to a friend or family member who appears emotionally upset, to a colleague's ideas, or to a public speech, we need to do so in ways that demonstrate respect for the speaker even when we disagree with him or her. Let's take a look at some general guidelines for responding effectively and then some specific guidelines to follow when offering emotional support, when critiquing others, and when evaluating public speeches.

responding

providing feedback

1. **General response guidelines.** Regardless of the situation, you should respond by providing appropriate feedback cues, only after the speaker has finished, and do so before changing the subject.

THE AUDIENCE *BEYOND*

When Valerie read Scott's tweet claiming that all flights out of O'Hare were delayed at least an hour, she called her carrier to verify whether what he said was true so that she could plan for a later departure that day.

126　Unit 1　|　Foundations of Communication

/

COMMUNICATE ON YOUR FEET

Speech Assignment

Active Listening to and Evaluating a Speech

Attend a formal public presentation on campus or in your community. Your goal is to listen actively to understand, remember, and critically evaluate what you hear. Be sure to take notes as you listen. Afterward, analyze what you heard using the following questions to guide your thinking:

- What was the purpose of the speech? What was the speaker trying to explain to you or convince you about?

- Was it easy or difficult to identify the speaker's main ideas? What did you notice about how the speaker developed each point she or he made?

- Did the speaker use examples or tell stories to develop a point? If so, were these typical examples, or did the speaker choose examples that were unusual but seemed to prove the point?

- Did the speaker use statistics to back up what was said? If so, did the speaker tell you where the statistics came from? Did the statistics surprise you? If so, what would you have needed to hear that would have helped you to accept them as accurate?

- Do you think that the speaker did a good job? If so, why? If not, what should the speaker have done to be more effective?

When you have finished your analysis, follow your instructor's directions. You may be asked to deliver a short speech about what you have learned.

---

feedback cues

verbal and nonverbal signals used to signal that you are attending to and understanding the message

- **Provide feedback cues. Feedback cues** are the verbal and nonverbal signals you use to signal that you are attending to and understanding the message. These cues include nodding, smiling, laughing, head cocking, frowning, eyebrow furrowing, or even saying "huh?," "uh huh," or "yeah." Feedback cues are appropriate when they communicate to the speaker without becoming distractions.

- **Respond only after the speaker has finished.** Except for feedback cues, respond only after the speaker has finished. One of the most common signs of poor listening is interrupting (Halone & Pecchioni, 2001). Learning to wait can be especially challenging for those of us with a time-oriented listening style, when there is a group of people talking, when we are in a heated conversation, or when we are excited and enthusiastic about what we have just heard.

supportive responses

create an environment that encourages the other person to talk about and make sense of a distressing situation

It is especially challenging to hear a speaker out when engaged in a heated argument. What might you do to keep from interrupting another person on these occasions?

Nina Shannon/princessdlaf/iStockphoto.com

- **Respond to the message before changing the subject.** Abrupt topic changes are inappropriate because they don't acknowledge what the speaker has said. Acknowledge your partner's message before changing the subject by asking questions, paraphrasing, offering emotional support, or critiquing.

2. **Emotional support response guidelines.** Sometimes the appropriate response is to reassure, encourage, soothe, console, or cheer up. **Supportive responses** create an environment that encourages the other person to talk about and make sense of a distressing situation. Supporting does not mean making false statements or telling someone only what he or she wants to hear. Figure 6.1 summarizes research-based guidelines for forming supportive messages (Burleson, 2003, pp. 565–568).

Guideline	Example
1. Clearly state that your aim is to help.	*I'd like to help you, what can I do?*
2. Express acceptance or affection; do not condemn or criticize.	*I understand that you just can't seem to accept this.*
3. Demonstrate care, concern, and interest in the other's situation; do not give a lengthy recount of a similar situation.	*What are you planning to do now?* OR *Gosh, tell me more; what happened then?*
4. Indicate that you are available to listen and support the other without intruding.	*I know that we've not been that close, but sometimes it helps to have someone to listen and I'd like to do that for you.*
5. State that you are an ally.	*I'm with you on this* OR *Well, I'm on your side; this isn't right.*
6. Acknowledge the other's feelings and situation, and express your sincere sympathy.	*I'm so sorry to see you feeling so bad; I can see that you're devastated by what has happened.*
7. Assure the other that their feelings are legitimate; do not tell the other how to feel or to ignore those feelings.	*Hey, it's OK, man. With all that has happened to you, you have a right to be angry.*
8. Use prompting comments to encourage elaboration.	*Uh-huh, Yeah,* OR *I see. How did you feel about that?* OR *Tell me more.*

© Cengage Learning 2014

Figure 6.1

Guidelines for supportive responses

CONSIDER THIS....

Think of a situation in which someone disagreed with you in a disrespectful manner. Then think of a situation where someone respectfully disagreed with you. How did you feel in each situation and how did it affect your relationship? If you unintentionally disagree with or critique someone in a disrespectful manner, what might you do to repair the damage?

3. **Critique Response Guidelines.** When you cannot agree with what a speaker has said, or when it is appropriate for you to offer a critique, your messages will be most effective if they clearly demonstrate respect for the speaker. Figure 6.2 provides some guidelines to help you demonstrate respect when disagreeing with or critiquing others.

4. **Public Speech Evaluation Response Guidelines.** You may be asked to respond to a speech given by one of your classmates in this course or by a colleague in the workplace. If so, you will want to remember that your goal is to be respectful, honest, and helpful. Since you will be critiquing them, you will want to use "I" language, be specific and use examples, and make statements about what was done well before offering suggestions for improvement. Good speech critiques also address each primary element of an effective speech: the content, structure, and delivery, as well as the construction and integration of presentational aids if used.

Effective supportive messages are in touch with the facts and provide emotional encouragement.

David R. Frazier/Photoresearchers/First Light

- When critiquing content, you can comment on the appropriateness of the speech for that particular audience and the use of facts and inferences; you can also analyze the logic of the arguments and the evidence used to support ideas.

- When critiquing structure, you can focus on the introduction, the use of transitions, the choice of organizational pattern, and the concluding remarks.

Guidelines	Example
1. Use "I" language to clearly own the comments you make. Do not ascribe them to others.	*Carla, I really like the way you cited the references for your opening quotation.*
2. Use specific language and specific examples to point out areas of disagreement and areas for improvement.	*I can't agree to this plan because I cannot afford a 15% reduction in my personnel budget. I could probably live with a 10% decrease.*
3. Find a point to agree with or something positive to say before expressing your disagreement or offering a negative critique.	*I really appreciate what you have to say on this topic and agree that we need to support our co-workers who need after school care for their children. I wonder, though, if we should brainstorm additional potential solutions before settling on one.*

Figure 6.2

Guidelines for demonstrating respect when disagreeing with or critiquing others

© Cengage Learning 2014

WHAT WOULD YOU DO?

A Question of Ethics

Janeen always disliked talking on the phone—she thought it was an impersonal form of communication. Thus, college was a wonderful respite. When friends called her, instead of staying on the phone, she could quickly meet them in a dorm room or a café.

One day while studying for final exams, Janeen received a phone call from Barbara, an out-of-town friend. When she answered, she found herself bombarded with information about old high school friends and their whereabouts. Not wanting to disappoint Barbara, who seemed eager to talk, Janeen tucked her phone under her chin and returned to studying her notes, answering Barbara with the occasional "uh-huh," "hmm," or "wow, that's cool!" After a few minutes, she realized Barbara was no longer talking. Suddenly very ashamed, she said, "I'm sorry, what did you say? The phone . . . uh, there was just a lot of static."

Barbara replied with obvious hurt in her voice, "I'm sorry I bothered you. You must be terribly busy."

Embarrassed, Janeen muttered, "I'm just really stressed, you know, with exams coming up and everything. I guess I wasn't listening very well; you didn't seem to be saying anything really important. I'm sorry. What were you saying?"

"Nothing 'important,'" Barbara answered. "I was just trying to figure out a way to tell you. I know that you are friends with my brother Billy, and you see, we just found out yesterday that he's terminal with a rare form of leukemia. But you're right; it obviously isn't really important." With that, she hung up.

1. Which of the ethical principles did Janeen violate by how she listened to Barbara? Explain how each of these principles apply specifically to active listening.

2. Although Barbara was hurt by Janeen's comment about the "importance" of the call, did she violate any ethical principles in how she ended the call?

3. How has this case influenced the way you view ethical listening, if at all, and why?

	Ineffective critique	Effective critique
Content	"The sources you cited are old and no longer represent current thinking on the topic."	"I noticed you relied heavily on Johnson's 1969 essay about global warming. For me, your argument would be more compelling if you were to cite research that has been published in the last five years."
Structure	"You were really hard to follow."	"I really appreciate what you had to say on this topic. I would have been able to follow your main points better if I had heard clear transitions between each one. Transitions would have helped me notice the switch from one topic to the next."
Delivery	"You talk too fast!"	"I was fascinated by the evidence you offered to support the first main point. It would have been even more compelling for me if you were to slow down while explaining that information. That would give me time to understand the material more fully before we moved on to the next main point."

© Cengage Learning 2014

Figure 6.3

Examples of effective and ineffective speech critiques

- When critiquing delivery, you can comment on use of voice, face, and gestures, as well as whether the tone was appropriately conversational or formal.

- When critiquing presentational aids, you can talk about whether they were easy to see, were professional in appearance, and enhanced the verbal message by using a visual symbol system such as charts, graphs, or photos. You can also mention how the speaker referenced them during the speech.

When you critique a speech, remember that it is important to point out things you thought the speaker did particularly well and why, as well as specific things you believe they could do differently to improve the content, structure, delivery, and presentational aids. Figure 6.3 provides examples of ineffective and effective speech critique statements.

CONSIDER *THIS*....

Have you ever received a speech evaluation that focused only on the things you should do to improve? How helpful (or unhelpful) was this critique and why?

Summary

Listening is the process of receiving, constructing meaning from, and responding to spoken and/or nonverbal messages. We must overcome three major challenges based on our personal listening style, listening apprehension, and processing approach to become effective listeners. Our listening style might be content-oriented, people-oriented, action-oriented, or time-oriented. Listening apprehension is the anxiety we feel when trying to listen effectively, which can interfere with our success. And our approach to listening may be unconscious and passive or conscious and active. Active listening is the process of attending, understanding, remembering, evaluating, and responding to the messages we hear.

COMMUNICATE!

RESOURCE AND ASSESSMENT CENTER

Now that you have read Chapter 6, go to the Speech Communication Course-Mate at cengagebrain.com where you'll find an interactive eBook and interactive learning tools including quizzes, flashcards, sample speech videos, audio study tools, skill-building activities, action step activities, and more. Student Workbook, Speech Builder Express 3.0, and Speech Studio 2.0 are also available.

Applying What You've Learned

Impromptu Speech Activity

1. Draw a slip of paper from a stack provided by your instructor. Read the scenario and formulate an appropriate response based on the information provided in the chapter. Deliver a short impromptu speech where you (a) read the scenario aloud, (b) identify which response you think is most appropriate (emotional support, critique, speech evaluation) and why, and (c) articulate the response based on the guidelines for it from this chapter. Be sure to structure your message using a thesis, preview, transitions, summary, and clincher.

Assessment Activities

1. Personal Listening Style Profile Go to the Speech Communication CourseMate at cengagebrain.com and complete the Personal Listening Style Profile in the Chapter 6 materials. Then write a short essay in which you report how you scored on this profile, whether you agree with the styles that the profile indicates are your dominant ones, and explain how your style helps and hinders your ability to actively listen. Then, based on what you have learned in this chapter, describe two or three steps you can take to improve your listening.

2. Conversation and Analysis Damien and Chris. Go to the CourseMate for *Communicate!* at cengagebrain.com and access the Damien and Chris Dialogue in the Chapter 6 materials. Watch the video of this conversation between Damien and Chris and note examples of the participants using the active listening process. Be sure to note which specific skills and guidelines each follows, as well as any challenges or problems you see in their listening behavior. How is this conversation affected by the use of active listening?

Skill-Building Activities

1. Writing Questions and Paraphrases Provide an appropriate question and paraphrase for each of the following statements. To get you started, the first prompt has been completed for you.

    a. **Luis:** "It's Dionne's birthday, and I've planned a *big* evening. Sometimes, I think Dionne believes I take her for granted—well, I think after tonight she'll know I think she's something special!"

    Question: What specific things do you have planned?

    Content paraphrase: If I'm understanding you, you're planning a night that's going to cost a lot more than what Dionne expects on her birthday.

Feelings paraphrase: From the way you're talking, I get the feeling you're really proud of yourself for making plans like these.

b. **Angie:** "Brother! Another nothing class. I keep thinking one of these days he'll get excited about something. Professor Romero is a real bore!"

Question:

Content paraphrase:

Feelings paraphrase:

c. **Jerry:** "Everyone seems to be talking about that movie on Channel 5 last night, but I didn't see it. You know, I don't watch the 'idiot box' very often."

Question:

Content paraphrase:

Feelings paraphrase:

d. **Kaelin:** "I don't know if it's something to do with me or with Mom, but lately we just aren't getting along."

Question:

Content paraphrase:

Feelings paraphrase:

e. **Aileen:** "I've got a report due at work and a paper due in management class. On top of that, it's my sister's birthday, and so far I haven't even had time to get her anything. Today's going to be a disaster."

Question:

Content paraphrase:

Feelings paraphrase:

2. Creating Mnemonics Practice remembering the four personal listening styles and the steps in the active listening process by creating a mnemonic for each. Record your mnemonics. Tomorrow morning while you are dressing see whether you can recall the mnemonics you created. Then see how many of the personal listening styles and active learning steps you can recall using the cues in your mnemonics.

3. Listening to Remember On the CourseMate for *Communicate!* at cengagebrain. com for Chapter 6, take an online listening test to see how well you can remember what you hear. First, listen as you usually do and take the test. Then listen a second time but take notes and try to create mnemonics. Put your notes away and take the test again. Did your score improve when you used notes and mnemonics?

WHAT'S TECHNOLOGY GOT TO DO WITH IT?

Foundations of Mediated Communication

On her way to the grocery store, Kendell received a text message from her new roommate, Tasha.

"Can U PU bread, yogurt, and lettuce 4 me?"

Kendell texted back: "OK." When she returned to the apartment and began unpacking the groceries, Tasha seemed annoyed. When Kendell asked if anything was wrong, Tasha huffed, "You know I am really conscious about what I eat. So I'm surprised you bought me white bread. And everybody knows that Greek yogurt has way less sugar and twice as much protein, and it's the only kind you've seen me eat since I moved in. As far as the lettuce goes, iceberg is the worst; you know you've only seen me eat arugula because it's high in fiber, beta carotene, and vitamins!"

Kendell threw up her hands and replied, "Fine, next time do your own shopping."

Thanks to smartphone and Internet technology, we can now communicate 24/7 without conversing face-to-face. Yet, as the opening vignette illustrates, the very technologies that allow us to do so can also lead to greater chances for misunderstandings. In this sequel, we look at the basic characteristics of message channels (e.g., face-to-face, e-mail, phone calls, text messages, etc.) and how they affect our ability to understand each other. Specifically, we explain three important ways in which the channel affects our ability to achieve mutual understanding and, ultimately, how these mediated exchanges can affect our relationships.

Communication Channels

You'll recall from Chapter 1 that a communication channel is both the route traveled by the message and the means of transportation. We can talk face-to-face or through a variety of technology-mediated channels (MC), many of which are computer mediated (CMC). So if we can't or prefer not to talk with someone in person, we might:

- call them on the phone (MC),
- send a text message (MC),
- talk with them through Skype (CMC),
- e-mail them (CMC),
- send them a fax (MC), or
- post on their Facebook page (CMC).

Because each of these channels has different potential benefits and drawbacks, understanding how they function can help us make informed choices about which one to use at a particular time. Three characteristics that differentiate these communication channels are media richness, synchronicity, and social presence (see Figure S1.1).

ASYNCHRONOUS					SYNCHRONOUS	
Bulk Letters	Posted Letters	Facebook	Interactive	Telephone	Skype	Face-to-Face
Posters	Email	My Space	Chat		iChat	
Email Spam	Text	Other social			Other video	
	Messages	media websites			conferencing	
LEAN						RICH
LOW SOCIAL PRESENCE					HIGH SOCIAL PRESENCE	

© Cengage Learning 2014

Figure S1.1

Continuum of communication channels

Media Richness

Media richness refers to how much and what kinds of information can be transmitted via a particular channel. Media richness theory suggests that some media are better suited than others for communicating the meaning of different types of messages (Daft & Lengel, 1984). Face-to-face is generally the richest channel and the standard against which other channels are measured. When we communicate face-to-face, we not only hear the verbal message content, but we also observe the nonverbal cues and physical context to interpret a speaker's meaning. Sometimes, however, communicating face-to-face is either impossible or not a good use of time. Other times, we may want time to carefully compose and revise our message, as well as time to carefully ponder the feedback we receive.

Although mediated channels allow us to communicate across distances, they often cannot do so as richly as in face-to-face interaction. The less information offered via a given channel, the leaner it is. The leaner the channel, the greater the chances become for misunderstanding. For example, text messages are very lean since they do not include nonverbal cues and context information and because they use as few characters as possible to convey a single message. On the other hand, videoconferencing channels such as Skype are richer than text messaging because we can observe nonverbal cues and contextual information almost as much as in a face-to-face setting.

Synchronicity

A second distinguishing characteristic of mediated channels is **synchronicity**, or the extent to which a channel allows you to get immediate feedback (Kiesler, Zubrow, Moses, & Geller, 1985). **Synchronous channels** (like telephone calls, conference calls, and video chats) allow communicators to exchange messages in "real time." Although communicators are physically separated from one another when communicating via any mediated channel, synchronous channels allow all to be "present" in virtual time and space with little or no lag between sending, receiving, and responding to messages. Messages conveyed through synchronous channels allow for immediate feedback to clarify potential misunderstandings before they are acted upon or damage the relationship (Condon & Čech, 2010).

In **asynchronous channels** (such as e-mails and letters), message exchanges are separated by both time and space. When you e-mail your friend, for example, there is usually lag time between sending a message and receiving a response. With the exception of voicemail recordings, asynchronous channels rely only on written verbal messages. However, most messages delivered via

media richness

how much and what kinds of information can be transmitted via a particular channel

synchronicity

the extent to which a channel allows you to get immediate feedback

synchronous channels

allow communicators to exchange messages in "real time"

asynchronous channels

message exchanges are separated by both time and space

asynchronous channels replace the careful composition process normally associated with written communication with "talking by writing." In other words, language choices are similar to those used in oral, synchronous conversations even though the messages are actually written (Spitzer, 1986). Unfortunately, however, when "talking by writing," we often fail to consider emotional tone and the possible ways our partner may interpret that tone. Thus, the chances for misunderstanding are high. For example, a message we intend to be clear and direct might be interpreted as intimidating, cold, or angry because the nonverbal cues that would soften the tone if conveyed orally are missing. To account for this limitation, we have developed acronyms like "LOL" and emoticons like ☺ to represent the emotional tone that is more readily conveyed in rich and synchronous channels.

Social Presence

Have you ever "talked back" to someone on the TV or radio or "coached" your favorite team while watching a televised game? If so, you perceived yourself as in some way "present" with those on the screen, even though you knew they could not actually see or hear you. **Social presence** is the sense of being "there" with another person in a particular moment in time. Social presence is also the extent to which you believe you can sense what another person is thinking and feeling and the extent to which you believe your partner also knows that you are "there." When we interact face-to-face, we are fully aware of the social presence of one another.

When we interact with others through a mediated channel, however, social presence is filtered through technology. So instead of experiencing another's physical presence, we experience their "mediated presence." In other words, we sense that someone is immediately available to us in a particular moment—even if they are not (Biocca & Harms, 2002). Experiencing someone's social presence is easier through some mediated channels (such as phone calls and text messages) than others (e-mails, blogs, and Facebook posts). When we communicate through mediated channels, we usually realize that our partner is not really physically present; however, when we communicate through richer and more synchronous channels, we are more likely to perceive others as socially present. For example, when we read an e-mail message, we may be able to conjure up a mental image of the person that wrote it, but we don't generally perceive them to be present with us as we read. In fact, the time stamp may indicate that the message was written hours, days, or weeks earlier. However, when we Skype with someone, we experience them as more socially present since we can talk back and forth and interpret nonverbal cues to understand their emotional tone.

Refer back to Figure S1.1 again, which displays common forms of social media by degrees of richness, synchronicity, and social presence. Notice the position of face-to-face communication along the right side of the continuum and how mediated messages become leaner as you scan further and further to the left.

Guidelines for Choosing a Channel

The following guidelines can help you decide which channels are best suited for the message you want to convey about certain topics, to various audiences, and in different situations.

Use the richest channel available if your message is complicated. If your message is complicated, you should try to communicate in a face-to-face setting where you can interpret verbal and nonverbal messages, as well as engage in exchanges to clarify cognitive meaning and emotional intent. Text messages and tweets are most appropriate when the message is very straightforward. For example, if you are running late to pick up your sister, a quick text that says, "Running 5 min late. Sorry" is appropriate since the information you want to share is simple and straightforward. But suppose you and your sister want to decide what present to buy your mother for her birthday. In this case, a text message would not be as effective because the communication issues are more complex. Since the two of you will need to reach agreement on multiple issues like the amount of money to spend, the type of gift your mother would appreciate, and who will do the shopping, a telephone call or a face-to-face conversation would be a better choice. In the opening scenario, Kendall's shopping errors were the result of the leanness of the text message channel. Had Tasha telephoned Kendall instead, she could have provided more specific details about the particular items she wanted Kendall to buy.

1. *Use more synchronous channels when communicating about difficult or controversial topics.* When we anticipate that our partner may have a strong emotional reaction to our message, we should use a synchronous channel. That way we can observe our partner's feedback and respond to it in real time. When it is impossible to have these conversations face-to-face, our relationships will be best served if do so via a phone call or a video chat.

2. *Use richer and synchronous channels when you want to feel socially present with your partner.* We are more likely to feel connected to our partners when we can hear and see them and when they can respond to us in real time. So, when we want to feel that our partner is "there" with us, we should choose channels such as instant messaging, iChat, telephone calls, and videoconferencing.

3. *Use lean channels when you merely want to convey simple and emotionally neutral information.* A good way to determine when lean channels (such as texting) are not the best choice is if it will take more than two turns to complete the conversation.

4. *Use an asynchronous channel when you need extra time to carefully organize and word your message.* Although asynchronous messages like letters and e-mail don't provide for immediate feedback, they do allow us to plan and edit our messages. The lack of synchronicity allows our partners to re-read and think about our messages before they respond.

Interpersonal Communication and Relationships

President Franklin Delano Roosevelt once said:

> *if civilization is to survive, we must cultivate the science of human relationships . . . the ability of all peoples, of all kinds, to live together, in the same world, at peace."*

This unit focuses on that very thing: how to use communication to cultivate positive human relationships. In other words, we discuss the nature of interpersonal relationships, how they are formed and maintained, and what role communication plays in them.

Although communicating to form and maintain personal relationships is as old as humankind itself, the formal study of interpersonal communication did not emerge until the 1960s. Interestingly, however, one of the very first books devoted to interpersonal communication and relationships was actually Dale Carnegie's *How to Win Friends and Influence People*, published in 1936. The fact that this book has sold more than 15 million copies worldwide illustrates the degree to which people want to develop positive relationships and the role effective communication plays in achieving that goal.

Interpersonal communication emerged as a formal area of communication studies in response to three major social issues of the 1960s: the proliferation of manipulative messages being delivered through the mass media, the social unrest felt about civil rights issues, and U.S. involvement in the armed conflict in Vietnam (Knapp & Miller, 1985, p. 8). Interpersonal communication presented itself as an alternative by focusing instead on developing personal awareness and improving personal relationships. One of the most significant scholarly books grounding the formal study of interpersonal communication is *Pragmatics of Human Communication* written by Paul Watzlawick, Janet Beavin Bavelas, and Don D. Jackson and published in 1967. Based on their extensive studies of dysfunctional family relationships, they formulated five principles that continue to influence our understanding of interpersonal communication today. These are (in no particular order):

- We cannot <u>not</u> communicate. In other words, everything we say and do, including silence, communicates something to others. Healthy relationships are those in which partners learn to interpret one another's messages accurately.

- Every communication interaction has both a content and relational aspect to it. When we communicate, we do more than share information by *what* we say. We also indicate how we feel about the relationship by *how* we say it.

- The nature of a relationship depends on how participants *punctuate* the interactions between them. In other words, each participant believes our communication is a reaction to (or *caused by*) the other's behavior.

- Human communication is both digital (spoken words) and analogic (nonverbal behaviors).

- All communication exchanges are *symmetrical* (based on *equal power* between participants) or *complementary* (based on *power differences*). A simple way to understand the general nature of this principle is to think of your relationship with a friend, classmate, or coworker compared to one with a parent or guardian (when you were a child), a teacher, or a supervisor/boss.

These five principles of human communication have been reinforced, challenged, and expanded upon by interpersonal scholars since they were first coined over forty years ago. Still, several common themes persist. Among them is the notion that interpersonal communication is comprised of both intentional and unintentional verbal and nonverbal behavior. Moreover, interpersonal communication is an ongoing and ever-changing process. Also, interpersonal communication in any interaction is a result of the reciprocal relationship between behavior and human thought (e.g., intepretations). And, interpersonal communication must be understood in relation to the context in which it occurs. Finally, an inherent goal of interpersonal communication is to influence (i.e., control, persuade) our partner in some way. In essence, ordinary everyday conversations matter (e.g., Berger, 2005; Knapp & Daly, 2011; Knapp & Miller, 1985; LeBaron, Mandelbaum, & Glenn, 2003; Littlejohn & Foss, 2011).

Since the 1960s, numerous academic journals and books (including handbooks, textbooks, scholarly books, trade books, and popular press books) devoted exclusively to interpersonal communication and relationships have been and continue to be published. This unit obviously cannot capture all that we know about interpersonal communication and relationships. Rather, in it, we merely introduce you to the field via an overview comprised of two chapters.

Chapter 7 The first chapter, "Interpersonal Relationships," focuses on the different types of interpersonal relationships and how they are formed, maintained, and ended or redefined. We explain some of the major theories grounding the study of interpersonal relationships such as Altman and Taylor's social penetration theory, Luft and Ingham's Johari window, Knapp and Vangelisti's stages of coming together and coming apart, and Montgomery and Baxter's theory of relational dialectics. Finally, we offer several guidelines for communicating effectively when forming and maintaining healthy relationships, as well as when disengaging, ending, or transforming relationships.

Chapter 8 In the next chapter, "Interpersonal Communication," we turn our attention to the messages themselves and specific guidelines to follow and skills to practice when constructing and interpreting them. More specifically, we describe specific communication strategies for offering emotional support to a distraught friend or family member. We also offer suggestions for making informed decisions about how to manage privacy and disclosure based on Petronio's understanding of privacy management theory. And we provide recommendations for expressing your relationship desires and expectations in ways that promote a healthy communication climate. Finally, we suggest effective ways to manage the interpersonal conflict that inevitably occurs in any interpersonal relationship.

These two chapters do not provide you with all there is to know about effective interpersonal communication and healthy interpersonal relationships. However, we hope they provide a solid grounding for developing your skills and piquing your curiosity to learn more about this area of communication as it can inform your personal and interpersonal interactions and relationships.

Interpersonal Relationships

Jenna was headed to the Student Center to grab a quick lunch before her next class. On the way, she spotted Morgan, a classmate from her history course.

"Hey Morgan. How are you doing?"

"Ok," Morgan replied. "What did you think of that history test we took yesterday?"

"Argh. Not good. It was so hard! I definitely didn't study right for it," Jenna responded with a nervous laugh.

"I know what you mean," said Morgan. "I hope we get them back tomorrow so I can see what it will take to bounce back from that one. Well, I'd better get going or I'll be late to biology. See you tomorrow."

Jenna watched Morgan cross the street. She was still thinking about her performance on the history test, so she was startled when she heard, "Hey, pretty lady!"

"Zach!" Jenna said to her boyfriend with a big smile on her face. "What are you doing on campus? I thought you had to work today."

"Yeah, I was supposed to, but they called me this morning to say I didn't have to come in," Zach replied. "So, I figured I'd better get to the library and get some work done where it's quiet, but I need to grab some lunch first. Want to join me?"

"Of course!" Jenna exclaimed. "Let's get some lunch and then we can go study together."

interpersonal communication

all those interactions that occur between two people to help start, build, maintain, and sometimes end or redefine the relationship

interpersonal relationship

defined by sets of expectations two people have for each other based on their previous interactions

healthy relationship

ones in which the interactions are satisfying and beneficial to all those involved

Interpersonal communication is all those interactions that occur between two people to help start, build, maintain, and sometimes end or redefine our interpersonal relationships. **Interpersonal relationships** are defined by the sets of expectations two people have for each other based on their previous interactions (Littlejohn & Foss, 2010). We form interpersonal relationships as we communicate overtly and covertly through face-to-face and online interactions. Interpersonal relationships help satisfy our innate human need to feel connected with others and run the gamut from impersonal acquaintances (like Jenna and Morgan) to intimate friends (like Zach and Jenna). Regardless of the level of intimacy, we want to be involved in **healthy relationships**, ones in which the interactions are satisfying and beneficial to all those involved. How we communicate is central to achieving that goal.

We begin this chapter by describing three types of interpersonal relationships and providing guidelines for healthy communication in each of them. Next, we explain the role of disclosure in the stages of relationship life cycles. Finally, we talk about the dialectical tensions that exist in any interpersonal relationship and ways to manage them.

Types of Relationships

We communicate differently based on the level of intimacy we feel toward our partner. Moving on a continuum from impersonal to personal (Dindia & Timmerman, 2003), we can classify our relationships as acquaintances, friends, and intimates.

Acquaintances

acquaintances

people we know by name and talk with when the opportunity arises, but with whom our interactions are largely impersonal

impersonal communication

interchangeable polite chitchat involving no or very little personal disclosure

Acquaintances are people we know by name and talk with when the opportunity arises, but with whom our interactions are limited. For example, we become acquainted with those who live in our apartment building or dorm or the house next door, sit next to us in class, go to our church, or belong to our club. Thus Whitney and Paige, who meet in calculus class, may talk with each other about class-related issues but make no effort to share personal ideas or to see each other outside of class. Most conversations with acquaintances can be defined as **impersonal communication**, which is essentially interchangeable chit-chat (Buber, 1970). In other words, I may talk about the same thing—for instance, the weather—with the grocery clerk, the sales associate, the bank teller, and the restaurant server. If you have an online social networking profile on *Facebook*, *Twitter*, or *LinkedIn*, many of your online "friends" are probably acquaintances if your online conversations with them are primarily surface-level ones.

Our goals when communicating with acquaintances are usually to reduce uncertainty and maintain face. We attempt to reduce uncertainty by seeking information that may reveal similar beliefs, attitudes, and values (Berger, 1987). In doing so, however, we may say or do something that offends the other person or is taken the wrong way. So, our second goal is to help one another save face. **Saving face** is the process of attempting to maintain a positive self-image in a relational situation (Ting-Toomey, 2004).

Acquaintanceship guidelines To meet other people and develop acquaintance relationships, it helps to be good at starting and developing conversations. The following guidelines can help you develop scripts to become more competent in doing so:

Which of your online "friends" would you describe as acquaintances and why?

- **Initiate a conversation** by introducing yourself, referring to the physical context, referring to your thoughts or feelings, referring to another person, or making a joke. For example:

    WHITNEY: "Do you think it's hot in here, or is it just me? By the way, I'm Whitney."

- **Make your comments relevant** to what has previously been said before you change subjects:

    PAIGE: "My name's Paige. Yes, I'm burning up. I wonder if the air conditioner is broken. Do you know if this class meets for 75 or 90 minutes today?"

saving face

the process of attempting to maintain a positive self-image in a relational situation

- **Develop an other-centered focus** by asking questions, listening carefully, and following up on what has been said. For example:

    WHITNEY: "I'm pretty sure it's only a 75-minute session. Have you ever taken a class from this professor?"

    PAIGE: "Yeah, I took algebra from her."

    WHITNEY: "What was she like?"

    PAIGE: "She was pretty good. Her tests were hard, but they were fair. I learned a lot."

    WHITNEY: "Did she offer study guides?"

    PAIGE: "Yes, and we reviewed as a class by playing what she called 'algebra *Jeopardy*.' That worked well for me."

    WHITNEY: "Sounds like I'm going to like this class and this instructor!"

- **Engage in appropriate turn-taking** by balancing talking with listening and not interrupting. In his best-selling book, *How to Win Friends and Influence People,* Dale Carnegie (1936) put it this way: "Listen first and let them finish. Do not resist, defend or debate. This only raises barriers. . . . Remember that the people you are talking to are a hundred times more interested in themselves and their wants and problems than they are in you and your problems" (pp. 98, 127).

- **Be polite.** Consider how your conversational partner will feel about what you say and work to phrase your comments in a way that allows your partner to save face. For example:

CONSIDER *THIS....*

Have you ever been in a conversation with someone who made it difficult for you to get a word in? If so, how did that make you feel about the other person and your relationship with them and why?

WHITNEY:	"I wish I wouldn't have signed up for this section that meets right at noon. I'm famished. Here, do you want some M&Ms?"
PAIGE:	"No thanks."
WHITNEY:	"Are you sure? I don't mind sharing. A little sugar never hurt anyone."
PAIGE:	"I'm diabetic."
WHITNEY:	"Oh, I'm so sorry. I'll save these for later."

Friends

friends

people with whom we have voluntarily negotiated more personal relationships

Over time, some acquaintances become friends. **Friends** are people with whom we have voluntarily negotiated more personal relationships (Patterson, Bettini, & Nussbaum, 1993, p. 145). As friendships develop, people move toward interactions that are more interpersonally satisfying. For example, Whitney and Paige, who are acquaintances, may decide to get together after class to work out at the gym. If they find that they enjoy each other's company, they may continue to meet outside of class and eventually become friends.

We often refer to friends according to the context in which we interact with them. For example, we may have tennis friends, office friends, or neighborhood friends. These context friendships may fade if the context changes. For instance, your friendship with a person at the office may fade if you or your friend takes a job with a different company.

Friendship guidelines Several key communication behaviors will help you maintain your friendships whether you live close to one another or are separated by a distance and can only communicate remotely via e-mail, *Facebook, Skype,* or mobile phone (Sampter, 2003; Walther & Parks, 2002).

- **Initiation.** Be proactive in setting up times to spend together. One person must get in touch with the other. A friendship is not likely to form or endure between people who rarely interact.

- **Responsiveness.** Each person must listen. Listen to others and respond to what they say. It is difficult to form or maintain friendships with people who focus only on themselves or their issues, and it is equally difficult to maintain relationships with people who are uncommunicative altogether.

- **Self-disclosure.** Friends share thoughts and feelings with each other. Although acquaintances can be maintained by conversations that discuss surface issues, a friendship is based on the exchange of more personal and specific information including personal history, opinions, and feelings. For example, after Paige and Whitney start to spend more time together outside of class, they might have this conversation:

CONSIDER *THIS....*

How many of your "high school friends" do you still interact with regularly? Consider how your interactions with each other and the topics you discuss have changed since high school. Why do you think this change has (or has not) occurred?

 THE AUDIENCE *BEYOND*

Because Charles valued his relationship with his brother, who was serving in the Peace Corps and stationed in Tanzania, he initiated a regular weekly Skype session on Friday afternoons. That way they could catch up on *what* one another had been doing and *how* they had been doing, which would help to maintain their relationship.

PAIGE: "Can I tell you something and trust you to keep it between us?"

WHITNEY: "Of course."

PAIGE: "Well, you know I've been seeing David for a while now."

WHITNEY: "Yeah, he seems like a nice guy."

PAIGE: "Well, the other night we got into a little fight and he pushed me onto the couch. I actually have a bruise here on my arm from it."

- **Emotional support.** Provide comfort and support when needed. When we are emotionally or psychologically vulnerable, we expect to be helped by those we consider our friends. When your friends are hurting, they need you to support them by clarifying your supportive intentions, confirming their feelings, helping them make sense of what has happened, and giving advice (Burleson, 2002; Burleson & Goldsmith, 1998).

WHITNEY: "Oh, no. I'm here to help in any way I can."

PAIGE: "He said he was sorry and I believe him, but I just don't feel comfortable around him now."

WHITNEY: "I understand. I'm not sure I would feel comfortable either. Is there anything I can do?"

PAIGE: "No, not really. I guess I just wanted someone to confirm that I'm not overreacting."

WHITNEY: "Well, I don't think you're overreacting at all. Please let me know what I can do to help, OK?"

PAIGE: "OK. I'm so lucky to have you for a friend."

- **Conflict management.** Friends will sometimes disagree about ideas or behaviors. Healthy friendships handle these disagreements effectively through conversation.

WHITNEY: "Maybe you should talk to a campus counselor about this."

PAIGE: "No, I don't want to make a big deal out of it."

WHITNEY: "Paige, you got a bruise. That seems like a big deal to me."

PAIGE: "Actually, I bruise really easily. I don't want to see a counselor. Maybe I shouldn't have even told you about it."

WHITNEY: "Oh, Paige. I'm so glad you did and I totally respect your decision. If anything like this happens again, though, will you please talk to someone?"

PAIGE: "OK, if something happens again, I promise I will."

Original Artist/CSL, CartoonStock Ltd

"Jerkins and I worked it out. He can have the office with the window."

RANDY TEPPER/CBS/Landov

We have intimate relationships with romantic partners and platonic friends. Who would you identify as your close intimate friends and why?

intimates

people with whom we share a high degree of interdependence, commitment, disclosure, understanding, affection, and trust

platonic relationship

an intimate relationship in which the partners are not sexually attracted to each other or do not act on an attraction they feel

romantic relationship

an intimate relationship in which the partners act on their sexual attraction

trust

placing confidence in another in a way that almost always involves some risk

CONSIDER *THIS....*

Have you or someone you've known ever tried to meet a potential romantic partner online? If so, how did it work out?

Intimates

Intimates are those close, personal friends with whom we share a high degree of interdependence, commitment, disclosure, understanding, affection, and trust. We may have countless acquaintances and many friends, but we are likely to have only a few truly intimate relationships. Unfortunately, the percentage of Americans who identify having even just one intimate relationship beyond family members declined from 80% in 1985 to 57% in 2006 (McPherson, Smith-Lovin, & Beshears, 2006). Today, most Americans report having no more than two intimate friends, including family members (Bryner, 2011). This dramatic decline is particularly troubling given that these close personal relationships help define who we are (Aron, Aron, Tudor, & Nelson, 2004; Moore, 2003; Fiske, Gilbert, & Lindzey, 2010). Empirical research reports a direct relationship between intimate relationships and a strong self-concept and positive self-esteem (Prager & Buhrmester, 1998). And many studies suggest that intimate relationships are the most important predictor of life satisfaction and emotional well-being (Moore, 2003; Peterson, 2006).

Intimacy is not synonymous with "love" or exclusivity, and intimate relationships can be platonic or romantic. A **platonic relationship** is one in which the partners are not sexually attracted to each other or do not act on an attraction they feel. If you're familiar with the television series *Will and Grace*, the relationship between the title characters is platonic. Although Will and Grace live together and are intimate friends, Will is a homosexual man and Grace is a heterosexual woman. Other examples include the relationship between Leslie and Ron on *Parks and Recreation* and Alex and Meredith on *Grey's Anatomy*. Conversely, a **romantic relationship** is one in which the partners act on their sexual attraction. Today, many people use matchmaking sites to find romantic relationship partners. In fact, some research suggests that as many as 1 in 5 romantic relationships today begin online. Sometimes people also use ghostwriters to help create their matchmaking profile. The *Pop Comm!* feature on p. 145 talks about the role of ghostwriters and the ethical decisions to consider when using matchmaking sites to find romantic partners.

Regardless of whether the relationship is platonic or romantic, both partners must trust each other for it to become and remain intimate. **Trust** is placing confidence in another in a way that almost always involves some risk. As we share private information and feelings, we monitor how well our partner keeps our confidence. If our partner keeps our confidence, we share more and the relationship becomes more intimate. If our partner proves untrustworthy, we share less and, as a result, and over time intimacy decreases. When there is a severe breach of trust, we may even abruptly end the relationship altogether.

Cultural and Co-cultural Influences on Intimacy Research shows that intimate relationships are based on one or more of four types of interactions. The first comes from physical touch, which may include holding hands, hugging, being held, kissing, and engaging in sexual relations. The second comes from the intellectual sharing of important ideas and opinions and the

"Why Don't You Speak for Yourself, John?": Using Ghostwritten Online Dating Profiles

Michael Kemp/Alamy

Throughout history—in life, literature, and the media—people hoping to find love have solicited help from others. In Henry Wadsworth Longfellow's poem "The Courtship of Miles Standish," the shy Miles asks his friend John Alden to plead his case with the beautiful Priscilla Mullins. John complies, but in a classic love triangle scenario, Priscilla asks John, "Why don't you speak for yourself, John?" And most of us remember at least one occasion in junior high when we asked a best friend to find out if that cute classmate was interested in us.

Today we've expanded our search for love to online dating services, but advanced technologies don't eliminate the need some of us have to seek outside help in expressing ourselves. A quick Amazon search produces several results promising online dating success: *I Can't Believe I'm Buying This Book: A Commonsense Guide to Successful Internet Dating* by Evan Marc Katz; *Online Dating for Dummies* by Judy Silverstein and Michael Lasky; *Fine, I'll Go Online!: The Hollywood Publicist's Guide to Successful Internet Dating* by Leslie Oren; and *Romancing the Web: A Therapist's Guide to The Finer Points of Online Dating* by Diane M. Berry.

Personal coaching for online dating is also on the rise. Online services such as Dating-Profile.com, ProfileHelper.com, and E-Cyrano.com help singles write their profiles for a fee ranging from $29 to $2,000 (Alsever, 2007). Dating coaches claim their services are not aimed at helping clients lie, but rather, to more effectively communicate their true identities in a virtual dating world. On the ProfileHelper.com home page, the founder, Eric Resnic, says:

"Everyone has something unique that makes them special. Together we will figure out that special thing that attracts people to you and exactly what qualities you are looking for in a partner. Then, I will create or enhance your profile so that it is one of a kind, charming, entertaining and impossible to resist."

Similarly, Laurie Davis, founder and CEO of eFlirt Expert, suggests online dating should be approached as "the same thing as a personal branding campaign" and encourages clients to use her site to help make "the ultimate virtual first impression and transition their digital selves into meaningful, in-person dating experiences." (Wang, 2011; eFlirt homepage). Her site helps clients create and manage profiles for online dating sites as well as for other social networking platforms, like Facebook and Twitter. According to the services page of the site, eFlirt coaches will even ghostwrite tweets, IMs, or e-mails for clients in order to "take your online flirtation IRL."

Opinions vary on the ethics of using such ghostwriting services on dating profile sites. Jenny Cargile, a Match.com user, says hiring someone to help write her profile would obscure who she truly is. "I'm not a person who is put together or always knows the right thing to say," she says. "I would feel like if I went out on a date with someone, I would have to be what they read instead of myself" (Alsever, 2007). Mark Brooks of Online Personals Watch warns that such misrepresentation and the use of ghostwriters can have even deeper impacts on the potential development of "real" relationships through these online sites. He says, "[I]magine if everyone started hiring proxies. . . . Then you'd just have virtual dating assistants chatting up other virtual dating assistants, and what a mess that would be" (Ianotti, 2010).

However, online dater Jim West sings the praises of ProfileHelper.com, where he learned to be more specific and inquisitive when communicating on online dating sites (Alsever, 2007). In his case, a profile-writing coach stressed basic communication principles that helped West more accurately convey the kind of person he was, pinpointing the types of things he enjoyed, and what he was looking for in a potential partner. Likewise, eFlirt client Monica Astley says, "I only use [the ghostwriter's] stuff for the initial contact. After that, it's all me. . . . [S]omeone else just writes it up for you, and you approve it" (Ianotti, 2010). Given the busy lives of many of today's singles, such sites are seen by supporters as ways to save time and energy in the search for love, not as a way to trick potential suitors. Steve Zologa, founder of a similar company in Washington, D.C., looks at it as a simple matter of marketing: "My hypothesis is that there are many great men and women in the D.C. area who can't market themselves. You have about seven seconds to make a good impression, then you're done" (McCarthy, 2008).

However you feel about profile-writing coaches, most would agree that communication on online dating sites is tricky. An article in *Skeptic* explores the pros and cons of self-disclosing when dating online (King, Austin-Oden, & Lohr, 2009): On one hand, information presented online is easy to manipulate and control, so people can present themselves in any way they like—even if what they present isn't 100 percent accurate. On the other hand, the relative anonymity of online communication "accelerates intimacy through increased openness about aspects of the self." When what we disclose about ourselves is true, self-disclosure is an important step in making a successful relationship.

Questions to Ponder

1. What do you think—is true self-disclosure encouraged or obscured by online dating?

2. Is it ethical to use a ghostwriter for your online dating profile?

3. Do you present yourself differently in online settings than "in real life"?

third comes from sharing important feelings. The final type comes from participating in shared activities. Such activities can include anything from working together on the job or on a class project to participating on a sports team or in a civic club, getting together regularly for coffee or lunch, going to a movie or dinner, or going shopping.

Research suggests that our cultural identity may influence which type of interactions we are most likely to engage in to foster intimacy. For example, women who identify with the feminine co-culture tend to be more willing to share their thoughts and feelings than men (Dindia, 2000). Men who identify with the masculine co-culture tend to foster intimate relationships by participating in shared activities (Bowman, 2008; Morman & Floyd, 1998; Stafford, Dainton, & Haas, 2000; Swain, 1989). Of course, since masculine and feminine co-cultural norms are socialized, these generalizations may not be true for all men or for all women. Frankly, recent research suggests that such differences are increasingly becoming less prominent (Morman & Floyd, 2002).

Intimacy development norms also vary across cultures. In collectivist cultures such as China, Taiwan, and Japan, for example, people do not typically reach out to acquaintances until properly introduced and then take care to keep private information about close friends and family to themselves. In individualistic cultures such as the United States, people are likely to share more private information and personal feelings with acquaintances (Triandis, 1994). As with gender, however, such differences are becoming increasingly less pronounced as the world becomes more connected through travel, media, and technology (Hatfield & Rapson, 2006).

COMMUNICATE ON YOUR FEET

Speech Assignment

Relationships Speech

The Assignment

Prepare a 3- to 5-minute speech about your friends. Identify one person you have known for some time that you would consider an acquaintance, one that you would consider a friend, and one that you would consider an intimate or best friend. Describe each person and your relationship, as well as why you placed them in the category you did. Identify the kinds of topics you typically discuss with them and the kinds you would not be likely to talk about with them. Be sure to follow the Speech Organization Guidelines as you prepare. At your instructor's request, deliver your speech for your classmates.

Speech Organization Guidelines

Introduction

1. Catch attention
2. Provide listener relevance and speaker credibility
3. State thesis with preview of main points

Body

1. Acquaintance
2. Friend
3. Best friend

Conclusion

1. Restate thesis with summary of main points
2. Clincher

Even within the United States, some research suggests that the ways in which intimate relationships develop can vary according to co-cultural identity based on race, ethnicity, religion, and socioeconomic status. As with other cultural differences, however, such distinctions are becoming increasingly less prominent as we interact more frequently across cultures in both our personal and professional relationships.

Intimacy guidelines Regardless of the type(s) of interaction you rely on to foster intimacy, the following guidelines can help you establish and maintain affection, understanding, trust, and commitment in your intimate relationships (Boon, 1994, pp. 97–101):

- **Be dependable** so your partner learns that he or she can rely on you. Of course, nobody is perfect. But striving to be dependable will provide a foundation for understanding when something does come up.

- **Be responsive** in meeting your partner's needs. At times, this will require you to put their needs before your own.

- **Be collaborative** in managing conflict. Doing so includes saying you're sorry for something you've done or said, agreeing to disagree, and letting go of the need to be "right."

THE AUDIENCE *BEYOND*

Risha was supposed to meet her husband for dinner at a restaurant where they had a 6:30 p.m. reservation. When her meeting ran late, she texted him to explain why she would not arrive until 6:45 or 7:00. Doing so demonstrated respect for him and their relationship with regard to being dependable.

- **Be faithful** by maintaining your partner's confidential information and by abiding by sexual or other exclusivity agreements between you and your partner. If your partner tells you something in confidence, honor that request.

- **Be transparent** by honestly sharing your real ideas and feelings with your partner.

- **Be willing** to put your relationship first. This is not to say you should give up all other activities and relationships. Rather, healthy, intimate relationships are characterized by a balance between doing things together and doing things apart (Baxter & Montgomery, 1996).

Disclosure in Relationship Life Cycles

Relationships are not something we *have,* but rather are something we *make* as we communicate with others (Parks, 2006). Even though no two relationships develop in exactly the same manner, all relationships tend to move through identifiable and overlapping phases of coming together and coming apart (Knapp & Vangelisti, 2005). This moving back and forth among the phases is known as the **relationship life cycle**.

How we move among the phases depends on how we communicate with one another (Duck, 2007). We do so through **disclosure**, which is the process of revealing confidential information, and feedback, which includes the verbal and nonverbal responses to such information. Disclosure can come in the form of **self-disclosure**, which is the confidential information we deliberately choose to share about ourselves, and **other-disclosure**, which is the confidential information shared about someone by a third party (Petronio, 2002). **Social penetration theory** describes the different kinds of self-disclosure we use in our relationships and the **Johari window** explains how these various forms of disclosure and feedback operate in them. Knowing these processes can help us make wise disclosure decisions depending on the type and life cycle stage of our relationship.

Social Penetration

Not all self-disclosure is equally revealing. By that we mean some messages reveal more about our thoughts and feelings than others. Irwin Altman and Dalmas Taylor (1973; 1987) conceptualized a model of self-disclosure based on breadth and depth of information shared. *Breadth* has to do with the range of different subjects you discuss your partner. *Depth* has to do with the quality of information shared, which can range from relatively impersonal and "safe" to very confidential and "risky." For example, when Whitney and Paige first met, the breadth of subjects they discussed focused on their families, hometowns, and things they were learning in class. As their relationship became more intimate they added subjects about career ambitions, feelings about people they were dating, and feelings about their own relationship. The depth of disclosure also deepened. For example, in addition to sharing impersonal information, such as how many siblings they each have, they also disclosed characteristics they liked and did not like about their brothers and sisters. Discussions about their hometowns became deeper as they shared personal stories about positive and negative experiences they had growing up. And discussions about class grew to include opinions each had about whether what they were learning would help

relationship life cycle

moving back and forth among the relationship phases

disclosure

the process of revealing confidential information

self-disclosure

sharing biographical data, personal ideas, and feelings that are unknown to the other person

other-disclosure

the confidential information shared about someone by a third party

social penetration theory

describes the different kinds of self-disclosure we use in our relationships

johari window

a tool for examining the relationship between disclosure and feedback in the relationship

them achieve their career goals. Paige and Whitney's social penetration model is illustrated in Figure 7.1.

The Johari Window

Whereas we once believed that more disclosure between partners naturally resulted in increased intimacy, today we realize that relational closeness depends on appropriate self-disclosure along with appropriate feedback and other-disclosure. One way to understand the nature of disclosure and feedback in interpersonal relationships is through the Johari window. The Johari window, named after its two originators, Joe Luft and Harry Ingham (1970), consists of four panes that comprise all information about you. You and your partner each know some (but not all) of this information (see Figure 7.2).

The Open Pane The first quadrant is called the "open" pane because it represents the information about you that both you and your partner know. It includes information you have self-disclosed and observations about you that your partner has shared with you. It might include mundane information that you share with most people, such as your college major, but it also may include information that you disclose to relatively few people. Similarly, it could include simple observations that your partner has made, such as how you doodle when you're bored, or more serious ones such as how you behave when you're angry.

The Secret Pane The second quadrant is called the "secret" pane. It contains all those things that you know about yourself but that your partner does not yet know about you. Secret information is made known through the process of self-disclosure. The information moves into the open pane of the window once you share it with your partner. For example, suppose you were once engaged to be married, but on the day of the wedding your fiancé(e) backed out. You may not want to share this part of your history with casual acquaintances, so it will be in the secret pane of your window in many of your relationships. But when you disclose this fact to a friend, it moves into the open part of your Johari window with this person. As you disclose information, the secret pane becomes smaller and the open pane grows larger.

The Blind Pane The third quadrant is called the "blind" pane. This is the place for information that the other person knows about you, but about which you are unaware. They may have discovered it by observing you or from other-disclosure shared by a mutual friend or acquaintance. Information moves from the blind area of the window to the open area through feedback. When someone gives you an insight about yourself and you accept the feedback, then the information moves into the open pane. Thus, the open pane of the Johari window becomes larger and the blind pane becomes smaller.

The Unknown Pane The fourth quadrant is called the "unknown" pane. It contains information that neither you nor your partner knows about you. Obviously, you cannot develop a list of this information. So how do we know that it exists? Well, because

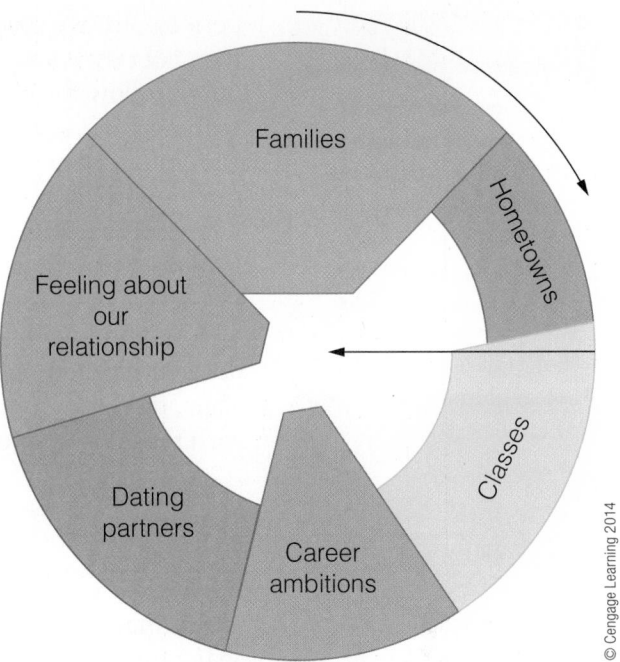

Figure 7.1

Social penetration model

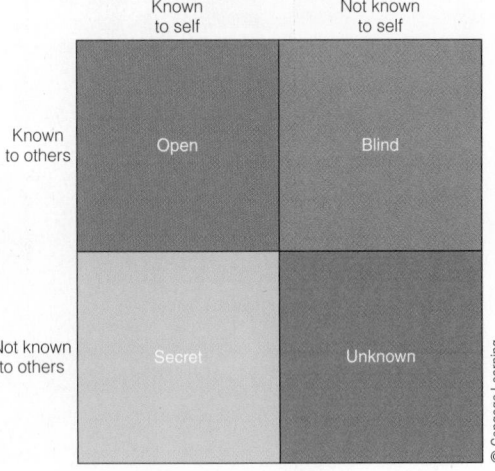

Figure 7.2

The Johari window

periodically we discover it. If, for instance, you have never tried hang gliding, then nobody knows how you will react at the point of takeoff. You might chicken out or follow through, do it well or crash, love every minute of it or be paralyzed with fear. But until you try it, this information is unknown. Once you try it, you gain information about yourself that becomes part of the secret pane, which you can move to the open pane through disclosure. Also, once you have tried it, others who observe your flight will have information about your performance that you may not know unless they give you feedback.

As you and your partner disclose information with each other, the sizes of the various windowpanes change. And, the panes of the Johari window you have with different friends will vary in size depending on the nature of that relationship. Thus, disclosure and feedback are the communication processes through which each relationship moves back and forth through phases in its life cycle.

Stages of Relationships

Regardless of whether your relationship is with an acquaintance, a friend, or an intimate partner, every relationship develops and changes with time. Researchers have identified ten stages within the three phases of coming together, relational maintenance, and coming apart (Dindia, 2003; Knapp & Vangelisti, 2005). Our relationships move among these stages based on the *information* we share with our partners and "by the *interpretation* of such things" by them (Duck, 2007, p. 80).

Coming Together: Beginning Relationships

The stages in the coming together phase focus on beginning and developing relationships. Communication during the stages of coming together focuses on reducing uncertainty by increasing your knowledge of the other person. Your goal is to understand how he or she sees the world (Berger, 1987). Noted interpersonal communication scholar Steve Duck (1999) conceived the *Relationship Filtering Model* to explain the process that relationships go through in the beginning stages. When you first meet someone, the model suggests you assume they are similar to you until what they say or do tells you otherwise. You begin by communicating very generally about noncontroversial topics and asking questions about surface information such as where they grew up and if they have any hobbies. Based on what you learn, you make inferences about their general attitudes, values, and ways of thinking. If you decide you have enough common interests and attitudes, you will choose to develop the relationship by disclosing more about yourself.

Let's look again at Whitney and Paige, who have decided to become college roommates. At first, they are nervous, wondering if they will be compatible. To reduce this uncertainty, they get to know each other better through disclosure and feedback. They may talk about what they did in high school, what major each is pursuing, what hobbies they like, and their favorite foods, movies, and music. As they learn more about each other, they find that although Whitney is majoring in fine arts and Paige is pre-med, both are passionate

One exciting thing about the college experience is the opportunity to meet new people and form new friendships. What new relationships have you begun since you arrived on campus?

David Young-Wolff/PhotoEdit

environmentalists and vegetarians. As they learn more, they begin to relax and find that although they have many differences, they like and respect each other. Over the semester, they each socialize with different friends, but they continue to have evening meals in the dining hall together. Life in the room they share begins to take on a predictable pattern. When Whitney is working on a class project, materials are strewn all over the room, so Paige accommodates her by studying in the library. When Paige is freaking out over her midterm exam in chemistry, Whitney gets her a Red Bull from the Quick Mart and then goes to the lounge to watch TV while Paige studies.

Relationships can begin in face-to-face or online environments. Increasingly, the beginning stage may occur online (Ward & Tracy, 2004). Online communication may present a potentially less difficult way to meet others than traditional face-to-face interactions. The initial interaction can occur in the comfort of your own home and at your own pace. You need not be concerned about physical aspects of the self or the other, and you can more precisely select what you are going to say (Ward & Tracy, 2004).

David Young-Wolff/PhotoEdit

If you have ever initiated a relationship with someone online, what did you say and do to reduce uncertainty and what were the results?

Coming Together: Developing Relationships

As the relationship develops, you continue coming together by disclosing more to one another, engaging in more physical contact, and feeling a deepening psychological closeness (Duck, 1999). Through disclosure and feedback, partners identify and capitalize on their similarities and tolerate or negotiate their differences.

Partners also tend to share greater physical contact during this developing relationship stage. Physical contact may involve sitting closer together, leaning toward each other, and engaging in more eye contact and touch. Such physical behaviors may or may not involve romantic feelings. Even platonic friends increase physical contact with each other as the relationship develops, for example, through hugs, high-fives, and fist bumps. Let's say the relationship between Whitney and Paige is working out well. They spend time together, get to know each other well, and consider themselves to be intimate friends. By second semester, they hug each other when they return from spring break, share clothes, and do each other's hair, makeup, and nail polish.

What forms of physical contact do you engage in with acquaintances, friends, and intimates?

Of course, cultural norms also affect how people engage in physical contact in relationships. In some cultures, for instance, male friends who are not romantic partners may hold hands in public or kiss to greet one another. In contrast, for orthodox Jews and observant Muslim women, touching men is abhorred. Take a moment to read the *Diverse Voices* article by Saba Ali on page 153 in which she recounts how holding hands with a man she considered marrying influenced her decision.

As a relationship develops, partners will feel psychologically closer as well (Duck, 1999). Partners who do not feel relaxed and comfortable will remain casual acquaintances and may even decide

Getty Images/Jupiter Images

to avoid having any relationship with one another. If you share no common interests, attitudes, or ways of interpreting the world, you are not likely to choose to develop a deeper relationship. Think about the people you met during your first weeks on campus. Which ones did not become your friends and why? Most likely, during your initial encounters you gathered information that reduced uncertainty about them, but what you learned was that they did not share enough common interests or attitudes to warrant developing a relationship.

We know that relationships can develop via face-to-face or online interactions; it may come as a surprise that some people report that they achieve more closeness in online relationships than in equivalent face-to-face relationships (Brooks, 2011). Indeed, rapid and exaggerated intimacy can be part of the fun of online relationships (Rabby & Walther, 2003).

Relational Maintenance

relationship maintenance

communication strategies used to keep a relationship operating smoothly and satisfactorily

Once a relationship has developed into what others identify as a relationship, we employ communication strategies to maintain it. **Relational maintenance** consists of those communication strategies used to keep a relationship operating smoothly and satisfactorily (Dindia, 2003). Maintaining a relationship means both people continue to invest emotionally in the relationship in ways that demonstrate an ongoing commitment to their partner. Researchers have catalogued many relational maintenance strategies (Rusbult, Olsen, Davis, & Hannon, 2004). Some of them include continuing to engage in prosocial behaviors like being friendly and polite, observing ceremonial occasions (e.g., birthdays, anniversaries, regular "date nights," and memorable shared experiences), and not becoming overly critical or taking the other for granted. For example, Paige and Whitney celebrate one another's birthdays by going bowling and then to dinner at a favorite restaurant. Paige also tries not to be overtly critical when Whitney strews papers around while working on a big project, knowing that Whitney will tidy things up when she is finished. Instead, Paige admires Whitney for having such a serious work ethic.

Other strategies include spending time together (both with one another and with mutual friends), communicating honestly and frequently about both deep and everyday topics, and offering words and actions that demonstrate affection and respect for one another. Whitney and Paige, for example, gave each other "best friend" status on their *Facebook* pages, decided to join some of the same clubs and, even visited each other's hometowns to meet each other's families and high school friends.

sacrifice

putting one's needs or desires on hold to attend to the needs of one's partner or the relationship

Partners also **sacrifice** by putting their needs or desires on hold to attend to the needs of their partner or the relationship. For example, when Whitney was ill, Paige sacrificed a date in order to stay home and take care of her sick roommate. Because all relationships involve give and take, being willing to do what is best for the other person or for the relationship itself can help maintain it.

Finally, because conflict is inevitable in developed relationships, we may do or say things that hurt our partner. If not handled properly, such transgressions can harm the relationship and move it to a less intimate level.

THE AUDIENCE *BEYOND*

When Ruth was going through a difficult time, she sent an e-mail to her mother telling her, "Stay out of my business. I can handle it myself," which hurt her mother's feelings. Ruth later apologized, and her mother forgave her because she valued their close relationship and wanted to maintain that closeness.

DIVERSE
VOICES

Close Enough to Touch Was Too Far Apart

by Saba Ali

Saba Ali lives in upstate New York.

Who knew that holding hands, the very act that signals the start of so many relationships, would be the end of mine? Growing up Muslim, I missed out on the *Dawson's Creek* method of courtship. For scarf-wearing Muslims like me, premarital interaction between the sexes (touching, talking, even looking) is strictly controlled. Men and women pray, eat, and congregate separately. At private dinner parties, women exit the dining room so the men can serve themselves. Boys sit on one side of the hall, girls on the other, and married couples in the middle.

My friends and I had high expectations for marriage, which was supposed to quickly follow graduation from college. That's when our parents told us it was time to find the one man we would be waking up with for the rest of our lives, God willing. They just didn't tell us how.

There were no tips from our mothers or anyone else on how to meet the right man or to talk to him. It's simply expected that our lives will consist of two phases: unmarried and in the company of women, and then married and in the company of a man.

It's all supposed to start with a conversation, but not a private one. My friends and I call them "meetings." The woman comes with her chaperone, a family member, and the man comes with his. Talking points include such questions as "What do you expect from your husband?" and "Would you mind if my parents were to move in with us after the reception?"

Yet now, at 29, despite all of my "meetings," I remain unmarried. And in the last five years I've exhausted the patience of my matchmaking aunties and friends who have offered up their husbands' childhood playmates.

All I wanted was to feel secure, to look forward to spending my days and nights with my match. Which is why my interest

was piqued last year when a friend from college told me about a radiologist in his early 30s who was also frustrated by the challenges of the contemporary Muslim hookup. Our first get-together was for brunch at a little French café near Central Park. I listened as he talked about his past relationships. Not the most appropriate topic for a first date, perhaps, but more comfortable for me than the typical pressurized questions: "Do you cook?" and "How many children do you want?" As he talked about the girls who either broke his heart, or whose hearts he had broken, I watched his hands, wondering what they would feel like to touch.

After brunch, we walked through the park. I spoke with ease about my own confusions, ambitions, faith, and fear of making the wrong decision about marriage. I told him I wanted someone who liked eating out, prayed five times a day and didn't drink alcohol, and who made eye contact when talking with girls. He said he wanted a wife who wasn't conservative and could fit in with his non-Muslim friends. He had most of the items on my mental checklist.

We kept getting to know each other by phone, often talking for hours at a time. If I was driving when he called, I would roam around aimlessly just so our exchange wouldn't end when I reached my destination. I hadn't yet told my parents about him, not wanting to get my mother's hopes up.

Our lingering problem, however, was the difference in how religious we each were; he hadn't planned on marrying someone who wore the traditional head scarf. His ideal woman was less strict, more secular. But I reveled in the recognition. Covering was a choice I had made in high school, partly out of a need for identity, and partly out of fear from what I had heard at Muslim summer camp. Instead of ghost stories, we had "judgment day" stories about the terrible things that would happen if you strayed from God, which scared me enough to start covering and praying.

In the years since, that fear has evolved into understanding. Most girls will say the scarf is for modesty. I see it as a protection. It keeps me from making stupid decisions. To me, the scarf is more than a piece of fabric—it's a way of life. On my wedding night, going topless would mean unpinning my scarf and letting it fall down.

In order to get him over his hesitation, I planned our dates to take place in very public places. We played miniature golf, ate out at restaurants, and went blueberry picking. I looked at his objection as a challenge, a project. I wanted to convince him that even though I did stand out with my hijab, it didn't matter because no one really took notice of the scarf after the first glance.

And I had my own doubts, although I was afraid to admit them: Namely, why should I push forward with this when we weren't aligned in terms of our faith? How could we be a good match if he didn't approve of my hijab? Would I have to change? Should I?

One evening he called to tell me he had gone to a lounge with a few of his buddies. "I visualized what it would feel like to have you sitting next to me," he told me.

"And how did I feel?" I asked.

"Pretty good," he said. "Manageable."

After, I finally called my mother and told her about him.

Before him, I had never gone past the second date. But by now he and I were approaching our fourth date—plenty of time, in my mind, to decide whether a man is right for you.

And then came the night of the movie, his idea. I'm a movie fanatic and remember the details of almost every movie I've ever seen. I can't remember the title of the one we saw that night. I looked over at him and smiled, convincing myself that the weightiness I felt was because I was in uncharted territory. We were moving forward, talking about meeting each other's families. So when he leaned over and asked, "Can I hold your hand?" I didn't feel I could say no. I liked him for taking the risk.

Nearly 30 years old, I had thought about holding hands with a boy since I was a teenager. But it was always in the context of my wedding day. Walking into our reception as husband and wife, holding hands, basking in that moment of knowing this was forever.

Non-Muslim girls may wonder about their first kiss or, later, about losing their virginity. I thought I was running the same risk, though for me it would be the first time actually touching the hand of a potential husband. How would it feel? Would it convince me that he was the one?

A lifetime's worth of expectations culminated in this single gesture in a dark theater over a sticky armrest. I'm not sure it's possible to hold hands wrong, but we were not doing it right. It felt awkward with my hand under his, so we changed positions: my arm on top, his hand cradling mine. It was still uncomfortable, and soon my hand fell asleep, which was not the tingling sensation I was hoping for. Finally, I took it away.

But the damage had been done. We had broken the no-contact rule, and in doing so, I realized I wasn't willing to be the kind of girl he wanted. I believe in my religion, the rules, the reasons, and even the restrictions. At the same time, I've always wanted to be married, and the thought of never knowing that side of myself, as a wife and a mother, scares me. Being with him made me compromise my faith, and my fear of being alone pushed me to ignore my doubts about the relationship.

When we took it too far, I shut down. It wasn't supposed to happen that way. So after the date, I split us up. And I never saw him again.

Source: New York Times, October 12, 2007

By forgiving minor transgressions, we can keep a relationship at the desired level of closeness. For example, Whitney and Paige each have little habits that annoy the other, but they choose not to let these annoyances get in the way of a good friendship.

Coming Apart: Declining and Dissolving Relationships

When one or both partners fail to engage actively in relational maintenance strategies, the relationship may begin to come apart and could eventually even end altogether. Relationships between acquaintances, casual friends, coworkers, and neighbors are more likely to end than highly developed ones (Parks, 2007). The communication in declining relationships is marked by four stages: circumscribing, stagnating, avoiding, and terminating.

Circumscribing The first sign that a relationship is coming apart is known as the **circumscribing stage**, which is where communication decreases in both quantity and quality. Rather than discuss a disagreement, for example, both parties ignore it outwardly even if it troubles them inside. Even though Whitney and Paige were close during their first two years of college, they drifted apart as they each met people with more aligned personal and professional interests. They found they had less and less to talk about when they were together, so they started spending less time with each other.

circumscribing stage

the stage during which communication decreases in both quantity and quality

Stagnating If circumscribing continues, it may eventually lead to **stagnating**, which is the stage at which partners just go through the motions of interacting with each other routinely without enthusiasm or emotion. When employees reach this stage, we say they have "job burnout" as they go through the motions without joy or passion. Because Whitney and Paige share a dorm room, they continue to engage in the routines they had developed for studying, cleaning, and entertaining friends there. But they often do so in silence, neither of them wanting to make the effort to initiate a conversation about meaningless topics.

stagnating

the stage at which partners just go through the motions of interacting with each other routinely without enthusiasm or emotion

Avoiding When remaining in a relationship that has stagnated becomes too painful, partners begin to **avoid** one another by creating physical distance between them and by making excuses not to do things together. They communicate about "safe" topics if they even interact at all. The overriding tone is usually not marked by hostility but by indifference. When Whitney tells Paige she is moving into an apartment with other friends, Paige responds with "Whatever."

avoiding

creating physical distance by making excuses not to do things with the other person in the relationship

Terminating Of course, not all relationships end. However, when partners decide the relationship is no longer satisfying and no longer worth trying to maintain, it will end. Basically, a relationship has ended when the people no longer interact with each other. People give many reasons for terminating relationships, including poor communication, lack of fulfillment, differing

THE AUDIENCE *BEYOND*

When DeMarcus decided to break up with his girlfriend, Larissa, he thought about just ignoring her e-mails, texts, and voice mail messages hoping she would "get the hint." Instead, he invited her to coffee and explained his feelings honestly and respectfully. To his surprise, she thanked him for telling her in person, rather than via text like her last boyfriend.

How relationships end depends on the interpersonal competence of both people. Do you know people who are amicably divorced? How do they differ from people with hostile divorces?

grave-dressing

attempts to explain why the relationship failed

relationship transformation

the process of changing a relationship from one level of intimacy to another

lifestyles and interests, rejection, outside interference, absence of rewards, and boredom (Cupach and Metts, 1986). Research calls these attempts to explain why the relationship failed **grave-dressing** (Duck, 1982).

Unfortunately, partners sometimes look for reasons to blame each other rather than trying to find equitable ways of bringing the relationship to an acceptable conclusion. They do so by using strategies of manipulation, withdrawal, and avoidance (Baxter, 1982). Though misguided and inappropriate, manipulation involves being indirect and failing to take any responsibility for ending the relationship. Manipulators may purposely sabotage the relationship in hopes that the other person will break it off. Withdrawal and avoidance, also less than competent ways to terminate a relationship, are passive approaches, which lead to the slow and often painful death of the relationship.

The most competent way to end a relationship is to be direct, open, and honest. Clearly state your wish to end the relationship while being respectful of the other person and sensitive to the resulting emotions. If two people have had a satisfying and close relationship, they owe it to themselves and to each other to be forthright and fair about communicating during the terminating stage of the relationship.

Even when partners agree that their relationship in its current form is over, they may continue to interact and influence each other through a different type of relationship. This is called **relationship transformation**. Romantic relationships may transform into friendships, best friends may become casual friends, and even marriages may continue on friendly terms or as a type of business relationship where child-rearing practices and expenses are coordinated (Parks, 2006). After Whitney and Paige graduate, their friendship may be transformed into that of acquaintances who enjoy seeing each other at reunions.

Dialectics in Interpersonal Relationships

Have you ever felt ambivalent about a relationship? On the one hand, you really wanted to become close to someone but at the same time you wanted your "space." Or have you met someone who seemed a bit too nosy but you really wanted to get to know the person? Have you ever enjoyed the stability of a long-term relationship, but at the same time longed for the same excitement as when you first met? If so, you were experiencing what scholars call a relational dialectic. A **dialectic** is a tension between conflicting forces. **Relational dialectics** are the competing psychological tensions that exist in any relationship. At any one time, one or both people may be aware of these tensions. Let's take a look at some specific relational dialectics and then discuss some ways to manage these inevitable tensions in our relationships.

dialectic

a tension between conflicting forces

relational dialectics

the competing psychological tensions in a relationship

Relational Dialectics

Three dialectics common to most relationships are the tugs between autonomy and connection, openness and closedness, and novelty and predictability (Baxter & Montgomery, 1996; Baxter & West, 2003). How these tensions are dealt with can alter the stage and life cycle of a relationship.

Autonomy/Connection **Autonomy** is the desire to do things independent of your partner. **Connection** is the desire to link your actions and decisions with your partner. Joel and Shelly have been dating for about a year. At this point in their relationship, Shelly wants to spend most of her free time with Joel and enjoys talking with him before acting or making decisions, but Joel has begun to feel hemmed in. For example, he wants to be able to play basketball with the guys without having to clear it first with Shelly. At the same time, however, he doesn't want to hurt Shelly's feelings or ruin the closeness of their relationship. Shelly is happy with their relationship and may not recognize any tension between autonomy and connection. On the other hand, Joel is feeling the tension between wanting to be more autonomous without jeopardizing his connection to Shelly. If Joel begins to act autonomously, he may relieve his own tension but at the same time create tension in the relationship.

autonomy

the desire to do things independent of one's partner

connection

the desire to do things and make decisions with one's partner

Openness/Closedness **Openness** is the desire to share intimate ideas and feelings with your partner. **Closedness** is the desire to maintain privacy. Let's say that Joel discloses quite a bit to Shelly. He believes it is important to divulge his feelings to Shelly, and he expects her to do the same. In other words, the open quadrant of Joel's Johari window in his relationship with Shelly is quite large. Shelly, however, is a more private person. She does disclose to Joel, but not as much as he would like. The secret pane of her Johari window is larger than Joel would like it to be. The fact that Shelly and Joel differ in their preferred levels of self-disclosure is one source of tension in their relationship. But Joel does not want complete openness all the time. He realizes it is sometimes appropriate to refrain from self-disclosure. So he seeks both openness and closedness in this relationship. Likewise, Shelly, although wanting more closedness than Joel does, still wants some openness. So, like Joel, she wants both forces to occur simultaneously in this relationship.

openness

the desire to share intimate ideas and feelings with one's partner

closedness

the desire to maintain one's privacy in a relationship

Novelty/Predictability **Novelty** is the desire for originality, freshness, and uniqueness in your own or your partner's behavior or in the relationship. **Predictability** is the desire for consistency, reliability, and dependability. People experience tension between their desires for novelty and predictability. Because Shelly and Joel have been dating for a year, much of the uncertainty is gone from their relationship. But they do not want to eliminate uncertainty altogether. With no uncertainty at all, a relationship becomes so predictable and so routine that it is boring. Although Shelly and Joel know each other well, can predict much about each other, and have quite a few routines in their relationship, they also want to be surprised and have new experiences with each other. Shelly and Joel may differ in their needs for novelty and predictability. Shelly may yearn for Joel to surprise her with a mystery date, or she may shock Joel by spontaneously breaking into their favorite song in the middle of the mall. At this point in their relationship, Joel may be comfortable operating by the routines they have established and may be embarrassed and shocked by Shelly's song. This is another tension between the two that must be managed in their relationship. But they must also cope with the fact that they each need some amount of both novelty and predictability in the relationship.

novelty

originality, freshness, and uniqueness in the partner's behaviors or in the relationship

predictability

consistency, reliability, and dependability in a relationship

Although our example of Shelly and Joel is an intimate relationship, it is important to remember that dialectical tensions exist in all relationships—and they are always in flux. Sometimes these dialectical tensions are active and in the foreground; at other times they are in the background. Nevertheless, when we experience them, they influence the nature of our relationship (Wood, 2000).

Managing Dialectical Tensions

You may be wondering how you can cope with dialectical tensions in relationships. How do people satisfy opposite needs at the same time? Several researchers (Baxter & Montgomery, 1996; Wood, 2000) have studied how people manage dialectical tensions in relationships. Four strategies for doing so include temporal selection, topical segmentation, neutralization, and reframing.

Temporal selection is the strategy of choosing one desire and ignoring the other for the time being. Perhaps you and a friend realize that you have spent too much time apart lately (autonomy), so you make a conscious decision to pursue connection. That is, you agree that over the next few months, you will make a point of spending more time together. You schedule lots of activities together so that you can be more connected. Over time, however, you may feel that you are spending too much time together, and so you may find yourself cancelling dates. Seesawing back and forth like this is one way to temporarily manage a relational dialectic.

Topical segmentation is the strategy of choosing certain topics with which to satisfy one desire and other topics for the opposite desire. You and your mom may practice openness by sharing your opinions and feeling about certain topics such as school, work, and politics, but maintain your privacy

temporal selection

the strategy of choosing one dialectical tension and ignoring its opposite for a while

topical segmentation

the strategy of choosing certain topics with which to satisfy one dialectical tension and other topics for its opposite

WHAT WOULD YOU DO?

A Question of Ethics

Jeff and Magda, seniors at a small rural college, had been dating each other since they were freshmen. Jeff loved Magda, and he planned to propose to her after they graduated in the spring. At the same time, though, he reluctantly recognized that their relationship had fallen into a bit of a rut over the previous six months, and he missed the excitement and romance of their first year together. Although he was troubled by these conflicting feelings, Jeff was unsure what to do about them.

One day while he was surfing MySpace.com, Jeff decided, on a whim, to create a fake user profile for the person he wanted to be in his fantasies. He spent quite a bit of time researching and designing the profile of his imaginary persona, a rap singer/flamenco guitarist/snowboarder/kung fu expert who went by the user name "MoonDog13." Jeff inserted photos of an obscure young Romanian actor he found online into MoonDog13's user profile. He posted lyrics to rap songs he wrote on MoonDog13's page and joined online user groups for those interested in flamenco

guitar, snowboarding, and kung fu. In very little time, MoonDog13 had made a number of online friends, many of whom were admiring young women. MoonDog13 loved to flirt with these girls.

Jeff told Magda nothing about MoonDog13, even when the time he spent online managing the fictitious life of his alter ego began to interfere in his relationship with her. He justified this decision with the belief that MoonDog13 was an imaginary figure who existed only in cyberspace. As long as fantasy didn't cross into reality, there was no reason Jeff had to feel guilty about anything MoonDog13 said online.

1. How is Jeff acting ethically or unethically in this situation?

2. Like Jeff, most people act differently in cyberspace than they do in the real world. Are the ethics of cyberspace any different from those of the real world? What about fantasy—are the ethics of our private desires different from the real world? Are we ethically obliged to disclose our fantasies to our loved ones?

concerning your sex lives. This segmentation satisfies both your needs for balance in the openness/closedness dialectic.

Neutralization is the strategy of compromising between the desires of one person and the desires of the other. Neutralization partially meets the needs of both people but does not fully meet the needs of either. A couple might pursue a moderate level of novelty and spontaneity in their lives, which satisfies both of them. The amount of novelty in the relationship may be less than what one person would ideally want and more than what the other would normally desire, but they have reached a middle point comfortable to both.

Reframing is the strategy of changing your perception about the level of tension. Reframing involves looking at your desires differently so that they no longer seem quite so contradictory. Maybe you are tense because you perceive that you are more open and your partner is more closed. So, you think about how much you disclose to him and how little he discloses to you. You might even discuss this issue with your partner. Perhaps during the conversation, you begin to realize the times that you have held back (closedness), as well as the instances when he was open. After the conversation, you no longer see as strong a contradiction. You see yourselves as more similar than different on this dialectic. You have reframed your perception of the tension.

In most cases when you are developing, maintaining, or trying to repair a deteriorating relationship, it helps to openly talk with your partner about the tensions you are feeling and come to an agreement about how you will manage the dialectic going forward. Through self-disclosure and feedback, you and your partner may be able to negotiate a new balance that satisfies both of you. At times, however, partners will be unable to resolve the tensions. When this happens, one or both of you will probably experience dissatisfaction and the relationship may deteriorate or end.

neutralization

the strategy of compromising between the desires of the two partners

reframing

the strategy of changing one's perspective about the level of tension

Summary

Interpersonal communication is the process through which relationships move through their unique life cycles. Healthy interpersonal relationships are mutually satisfying and beneficial to both parties. We engage in three types of relationships. Acquaintances are people we know by name and talk with, but with whom our interactions are limited in quality and quantity. Friends are those people with whom we have voluntarily negotiated more personal relations. Intimates are those with whom we share a high degree of commitment, trust, interdependence, disclosure, and enjoyment. Relationships are influenced by communication disclosure and feedback processes. These include both self-disclosure and other-disclosure about a breadth and depth of topics.

Relationship life cycles may occur in a series of stages that include coming together in beginning and developing relationships, relational maintenance in developed relationships, and perhaps coming apart by declining or dissolving in ending relationships. Sometimes terminated relationships are transformed into something new as people interact in different ways.

Partners must negotiate inevitable dialectical tensions in interpersonal relationships. These tensions focus on autonomy/connectedness, openness/closedness, and novelty/predictability. We can manage them through temporal selection, topical segmentation, neutralization, and reframing. Competent communicators talk openly, honestly, and respectfully with their partners in any relationship type, regarding disclosure of confidential information, during any stage, and in ways that manage dialectical tensions appropriately.

COMMUNICATE!

RESOURCE AND ASSESSMENT CENTER

Now that you have read Chapter 7, go to the Speech Communication Course-Mate at cengagebrain.com where you'll find an interactive eBook and interactive learning tools including quizzes, flashcards, sample speech videos, audio study tools, skill-building activities, action step activities, and more. Student Workbook, Speech Builder Express 3.0, and Speech Studio 2.0 are also available.

Applying What You've Learned

Impromptu Speech Activities

1. Select a scenario from a stack of options provided by your instructor. Each one will describe a relationship that is experiencing a dialectical tension. Together with a classmate, create a role-play where you effectively manage the tension. If called upon to do so, enact the scenario and your solution in front of the class.

2. Draw a slip of paper from a stack provided by your instructor. The paper will identify one of the relationship types or stages we have discussed in this chapter. Together with a partner, enact a script in the form of a role-play in front of your classmates that demonstrates this relationship type or stage. Then see if the class can identify which one you and your partner were displaying and why.

Assessment Activities

1. Dialectics in Your Relationships Choose one of your current close friendships or intimate relationships. It can be with a friend or family member. Briefly explain this assignment and ask your relationship partner if she or he is willing to help you with this assignment and to have what you discuss become part of a short paper you are doing for this class. Only if your partner consents should you proceed; otherwise, find another friend or intimate.

- Briefly explain the concept of relationship dialectics to your partner. You may want to have them read the section of this chapter that explains these.

- Once your partner understands the concepts, have a conversation about how each of you has experienced each of these tensions over the course of your relationship. Can you each think of specific instances when you were "out of sync"? How did this play out in the relationship? Be specific and be sure to talk about each of the three dialectical tensions.

- Based on your conversation, write a short paper/journal entry in which you describe what you learned. How has hearing your partner talk about how he or she experienced these changed your understanding?

- Given what you have learned in this conversation, how can you use this to improve this relationship going forward.

2. Distinguishing between Relationship Types

- List five people you have known for some time that you consider to be acquaintances. Why do you consider these people to be acquaintances rather than friends? What do you talk about with each of these people? What subjects do you avoid? Do any of these relationships have the potential to become friendships? If so, what would you have to do to make that transition?

- List five people you have known for some time whom you consider to be friends. Why do you consider each of these people to be a friend? How does your relationship with each differ from your relationships with your acquaintances? What do you talk about with each of these people? What subjects do you avoid? Do any of these relationships have the potential to become best friendships or intimate relationships? If so, what would you have to do to make the transition?

- List one to three people you have known for some time whom you consider to be your best friends or intimates. Why do you consider each of these people to be best friends or intimates? What do you talk about with each of these people? What subjects do you avoid? How does each of these relationships differ from those you have with your friends?

- Write a short essay in which you describe what you have learned about your relationships.

3. Johari Window Select five or six adjectives from the Johari Window grid provided on p. 149, which you feel accurately describe yourself. Enter your name (or an alias if you'd prefer) and save your grid. Then ask a few of your friends, relatives, or colleagues to access your grid and pick out five or six adjectives from that grid that they feel describe you. When you have finished, write a paragraph discussing what you have learned. Did the adjectives other people picked to describe you match the adjectives you picked for yourself? How does this information explain your experiences in developing and sustaining relationships? Does this suggest any changes you need to make to improve your relationships?

4. Conversation and Analysis: Trevor and Meg After you have watched the video of Trevor and Meg on the CourseMate for *Communicate!* at cengagebrain. com answer the following questions.

- How do Trevor and Meg disclose their feelings and offer feedback?
- What stage of their relationship life cycle do they seem to be in and why?
- What dialectical tensions are they dealing with and what strategies are they, or should they be, using to manage them?
- What is Meg's real fear?

Interpersonal Communication

What you'll know

- The characteristics of emotional support messages

- Why and how we manage privacy and disclosure in interpersonal relationships

- Ways to express desires and expectations

- Different conflict management styles

What you'll be able to do

- Offer effective emotional support messages

- Make informed choices regarding what, when, and with whom to disclose your thoughts and feelings

- Practice direct and indirect strategies for maintaining privacy

- Express your personal desires and expectations assertively

- Manage conflict by using an appropriate conflict management style

"Chuck, when that interviewer at the movie theatre asked whether you'd rather see a comedy or a thriller, you said 'thriller'! We've been dating for four years, and I'm just now learning that you'd rather see a thriller? We've *never* gone to a thriller in all the time we've been dating," Susan said, her voice becoming shrill.

"Gosh, I'm sorry, Susan," Chuck said sheepishly. "But truthfully, I didn't want to upset you. I know you don't like thrillers and so I've never suggested seeing one with you. If I do want to see one, I just go with my friend Larry."

"Chuck, it's not that I don't like them. In fact, I wanted to see *Twilight: Breaking Dawn*." Susan asks, "Are there other things you like or don't like that you haven't told me about?"

"Well, um, probably."

"Probably? Why haven't you been leveling with me?"

"Well, I don't know. I guess I just didn't think they were all that important."

"Not important? Chuck, I thought we trusted each other enough to be honest. Now I find out you keep things from me. I just don't know what to think!"

communication climate

overall emotional tone of your relationship

positive communication climate

one where partners feel valued and supported

confirming communication messages

convey that we care about our partner

disconfirming communication messages

signal a lack of regard for our partner

"Sue, why didn't you ever tell me that you wanted to see *Twilight: Breaking Dawn*?"

"Well I, uh, uh. . . ."

Poor Chuck, poor Susan! In the last chapter, you learned about how we begin, maintain, and end relationships and the dialectical tensions that pull partners between competing desires. As you and your partner interact, you create the **communication climate**—the overall emotional tone of your relationship—through the messages you exchange (Cissna & Seiberg, 1995). A **positive communication climate** is one where partners feel valued and supported. We use **confirming communication messages** to convey that we care about our partner (Dailey, 2006). We can say "you're important to me" and "you matter to me" verbally through skillfully wording our messages. At the same time, we need to avoid **disconfirming communication messages**, which signal a lack of regard for our partner. In this chapter, we look at how to create confirming messages when we want to: (1) respond to a partner who is experiencing emotional distress, (2) share or keep private some of our personal information, (3) express a personal desire or expectation, and (4) resolve a conflict.

Providing Emotional Support

Can you recall a time when you were emotionally distraught? Perhaps someone close to you died unexpectedly, or the person you thought you would spend the rest of your life with dumped you, or someone you trusted betrayed you, or you were treated unjustly by someone with power over you. If so, you probably appreciated the emotional support you received from some friends and family members and might have been perplexed or even angered by inappropriate statements made by others. Most likely, you have also helped those close to you during times of distress. **Comforting** is helping others feel better about themselves, their behavior, or their situation by creating a safe space to express feelings and to work out a plan for the future. Comforting can also help those doing the comforting by improving self-esteem and their relationship with the person being comforted (Burleson, 2002). Comforting usually occurs over several turns in a conversation or over several conversations that may span weeks, months, or even years.

comforting

helping people feel better about themselves, their behavior, or their situation by creating a safe conversational space where they can express their feelings and work out a plan for the future

Many people believe that women expect, need, and provide more emotional support than men. However, a growing body of research suggests that both men and women value emotional support from their partners in a variety of relationships, including same-sex friendships, opposite-sex friendships, romantic relationships, and sibling relationships (Burleson, 2003). Providing emotional support is also generally valued across cultural and co-cultural groups (p. 574).

Comforting Guidelines

The following guidelines can help you succeed when providing emotional support.

1. **Clarify supportive intentions.** When people are experiencing emotional turmoil, they may have trouble trusting the motives of those wanting to help. You can clarify your supportive intentions by openly stating that your goal is to help. Notice how David does this:

CONSIDER *THIS....*

Identify a time when someone offered emotional support to you. What did that person say and do? How did it make you feel about the distressing situation and about your relationship with the comforter?

DAVID: *(noticing Paul sitting in his cubicle with his head in his lap and his hands over his head)* Paul, is everything OK?

PAUL: *(sitting up and looking miserable and then defiant)* Like you should care. Yeah, everything is fine.

DAVID: Paul, I do care. You've been working for me for five years. You're one of our best technicians. So if something is going on, I'd like to help, even if all I can do is listen. So, what's up?

Can you recall a time when you were upset and someone comforted you? Did you feel closer to this person as a result?

2. **Buffer face threats with politeness. Face** is the perception we want others to have of our worth (Ting-Toomey & Chung, 2005). **Positive face needs** are the desires we have to be appreciated, liked, and honored. **Negative face needs** are the desires we have to be free from imposition and intrusion. The very act of providing comfort can threaten your partner's face needs. For example, your partner might worry that you will respect, like, or value him or her less because of the situation. Or, your partner might worry that you will think he or she cannot handle the situation independently. So effective comforting messages must be phrased in ways that address the other person's positive and negative face needs. **Buffering messages** cushion the effect by using both positive and negative politeness skills. When David says to Paul, "You're one of our best technicians," he attends to Paul's positive face need to be valued. When David says, all he "can do is listen," he attends to Paul's negative face need for independence.

3. **Encourage understanding through other-centered messages. Other-centered messages** encourage those feeling emotional distress to talk about what happened and how they feel about it. Other-centered messages can be questions encouraging others to elaborate or simply be vocalized encouragement (e.g., um, uh-huh, wow, I see). Other-centered messages are the most highly valued type of comforting message among most cultural and co-cultural groups (Burleson, 2003).

4. **Reframe the situation.** When people are emotionally distressed, we might **reframe the situation** by offering ideas, observations, information, or explanations that help them understand the situation in a different light. For example, imagine that Travis returns from class and tells his roommate, Abe, "Well, I'm flunking calculus. It doesn't matter how much I study, I just can't get it. I might as well just drop out of school before I flunk out completely. I can ask for a full-time schedule at work and not torture myself with school anymore." To reframe the situation, Abe might remind Travis that he has been putting in many hours of overtime at work and ask Travis if he thinks the heavy work schedule might be cutting into his study time. Or he might suggest that Travis seek help at the tutoring center, a resource many of their mutual friends found helpful. In each case, Abe has provided new observations and information that can help Travis reframe the situation from the seemingly impossible to the manageable.

5. **Give advice.** We can also comfort by **giving advice**—presenting relevant suggestions for resolving a problem or situation. You should not give advice, however, until your supportive intentions have been understood, you have attended to your partner's face needs, and you have sustained an other-centered conversation for some time. Even then, always ask

face

the perception we want others to have of our worth

positive face needs

the desire to be appreciated, liked, and honored

negative face needs

the desire to be free from imposition and intrusion

buffering messages

comforting messages that are phrased very politely in ways that address another person's face needs

other-centered messages

comforting messages that encourage relational partners to talk about and elaborate on what happened and how they feel about it

reframing the situation

offering ideas, observations, information, or alternative explanations that might help a relational partner understand a situation in a different light

giving advice

presenting relevant suggestions that a person can use to resolve a situation

permission before offering advice and always acknowledge that your advice is only one suggestion. Present the potential risks or costs associated with your advice and affirm that it's OK if your partner chooses not to follow it.

Managing Privacy and Disclosure

As you recall from chapter seven, people in relationships experience dialectical tensions, one of which is the tension between openness and closedness. When we want more openness, we use disclosure skills to share information and feelings. When we want more closedness, we manage privacy to limit what others know about us.

Disclosure is revealing confidential or secret information about you (self-disclosure) and about others (other-disclosure) (Petronio, 2002). Suppose Jim tells Mark that he wet the bed until he was 12 years old (self-disclosure), but had never told anyone because he had always been afraid of being teased. If Mark later tells a friend that Jim was once a bed wetter, Mark is also disclosing, but he is disclosing Jim's private information, not his own (*other-disclosure*).

Privacy management is maintaining confidential or secret information in order to enhance autonomy or minimize vulnerability (Margulis, 1977, p. 10). The concept of *privacy* assumes that people *own* their personal information and have the right to control it by determining whether or not to communicate it (Petronio, 2002). Like Jim, you can choose whether to reveal or conceal personal information to your partner. Then, either of you can choose to reveal that sensitive information to others or maintain it within the privacy of your relationship.

If your partner has your permission to share some of your personal information, then disclosing it to others is unlikely to affect your relationship. However, if you have not given your partner permission to disclose certain information and you expect it to remain between the two of you, then disclosure is likely to damage your relationship. So when Jim hears that Mark told a mutual friend that Jim is a former bed wetter, he may feel embarrassed, hurt, and betrayed if he believes Mark breached his confidentiality. If he doesn't care that others know, he may be unaffected. Controlling who has access to your personal information is becoming more complicated with our ever-increasing use of technology. For example, Web providers like *Google* routinely track our searches. And, according to a recent article published in the *New York Times*, a "bug" in Apple software allowed people to access photos stored on personal cell phones (Bilton, 2012). Similarly, whenever we post something to a Facebook page, that comment or image can quickly become viral when a friend decides to comment on it or tag it for another network of friends to see. In addition, information posted on the Web has no expiration date. So before you post, you should consider whether the information is something you are

Gossip is a form of disclosing somebody else's private information, which may or may not be true, without permission. Have you ever been the victim of gossip? What were the consequences for you? For others?

disclosure

revealing confidential or secret information about others as well as yourself

privacy management

exercising personal control over confidential information in order to enhance autonomy or minimize vulnerability

THE AUDIENCE *BEYOND*

David posted an album of New Year's Eve party photos to Facebook. Gretchen then tagged a photo of Ellen and David dancing on a table at the party. When Ellen saw it, she sent a private message asking David to remove it because she was on the job market and knows that potential employers look at what people post on their social networking sites.

comfortable sharing not only with your friends and your friends' friends, but also to potential employers and strangers today and in the future.

Effective communicators choose to disclose or withhold information and feelings based on their relational motive, the situation, and a careful risk–benefit analysis. For example, we may disclose information or feelings to someone in an attempt to get to know them better, or to a therapist in an attempt to sort out personal issues, or to someone we mentor in an attempt to help them make an informed life choice.

One of the most important criteria we use to decide whether to disclose information or keep it private is the risk–benefit analysis. That is, we weigh the advantages we might gain by disclosing or maintaining private information against the disadvantages of doing so. Common benefits of disclosing include building the relationship, coping with stress, and emotional or psychological catharsis. Common benefits of maintaining privacy include control and independence. The risks of disclosing include loss of control, vulnerability, and embarrassment. Risks of maintaining privacy include social isolation and being misunderstood.

In the *Diverse Voices* feature "Long Overdue," Naomi Shihab Nye describes her experiences with anti-Arab prejudice. As you read this excerpt, consider her courage in disclosing information about herself and her feelings.

DIVERSE VOICES

Long Overdue

by Naomi Shihab Nye

Poets like Naomi Shihab Nye devote their lives to using words to communicate their feelings and ideas, yet when Shihab Nye, who is of Palestinian descent, encountered anti-Arab prejudice, she was unable to disclose her Arab roots and to respond.

The words we didn't say. How many times? Stones stuck in the throat. Endlessly revised silence. What was wrong with me? How could I, a person whose entire vocation has been dedicated one way or another to the use of words, lose words completely when I needed them? Where does vocal paralysis come from? Why does regret have such a long life span? My favorite poet, William Stafford, used to say, "Think of something you said. Now write what you *wish you* had said."

But I am always thinking of the times I said nothing.

In England, attending a play by myself, I was happy when the elderly woman next to me began speaking at intermission.

"Smashingly talented," she said of Ben Kingsley, whose brilliant monologue we'd been watching. "I don't know how he does it—transporting us so effortlessly; he's a genius. Not many in the world like him." I agreed. But then she sighed and made an odd turn. "You know what's wrong with the world today? It's Arabs. I blame it all on the Arabs. Most world problems can really be traced to them."

My blood froze. Why was she saying this? The play wasn't about Arabs. Ben Kingsley was hardly your blue-blooded Englishman, either, so what brought it up? Nothing terrible about Arabs had happened lately in the news. I wasn't wearing a keffiyeh [traditional Arab headdress] around my neck.

But my mouth would not open.

"Why *did* so many of them come to England?" she continued, muttering as if she were sharing a confidence. "A ruination, that's what it is."

It struck me that she might be a landlady having trouble with tenants. I tried and tried to part my lips. She chatted on about something less consequential, never seeming to mind our utterly one-sided conversation, till the lights went down. Of course, I couldn't concentrate on the rest of the play. My precious ticket felt wasted. I twisted my icy hands together while my cheeks burned.

Even worse, she and I rode the same train afterwards. I had plenty of time to respond, to find a vocabulary for prejudice and fear. The dark night buildings flew by. I could have said, "Madam, I am half Arab. I pray your heart grows larger someday." I could have sent her off, stunned and embarrassed, into the dark.

My father would say, "People like that can't be embarrassed."

But what would he say back to her?

Oh I was ashamed for my silence and I have carried that shame across oceans, through the summer when it never rained, in my secret pocket, till now. Years later, my son and I were sitting on an American island with a dear friend, the only African American living among 80 or so residents. A brilliant artist and poet in his seventies, he has made a beautiful lifetime of painting picture books, celebrating expression, encouraging the human spirit, reciting poems of other African American heroes, delighting children and adults alike.

We had spent a peaceful day riding bicycles, visiting the few students at the schoolhouse, picking up rounded stones on the beach, digging peat moss in the woods. Our friend had purchased a live lobster down at the dock for supper. My son and I were sad when it seemed to be knocking on the lid of the pot of boiling water. "Let me out." We vowed quietly to one another never to eat a lobster again.

After dinner, a friend of our friend dropped in, returned to the island from her traveling life as an anthropologist. We asked if she had heard anything about the elections in Israel— that was the day Shimon Peres and Benjamin Netanyahu vied for prime minister and we had been unable to pick up a final tally on the radio.

She thought Netanyahu had won. The election was very close. But then she said, "Good thing! He'll put those Arabs in their places. Arabs want more than they deserve."

My face froze. Was it possible I had heard correctly? I didn't speak another word during her visit. I wanted to. I should have, but I couldn't. My plate littered with red shells.

After she left, my friend put his gentle hand on my shoulder. He said simply, "Now you know a little more what it feels like to be black."

So what happens to my words when the going gets rough? In a world where certain equalities for human beings seem long, long, long, overdue, where is the magic sentence to act as a tool? Where is the hoe, the tiller, the rake?

Pontificating, proving, proselytizing leave me cold. So do endless political debates over coffee after dinner. I can't listen to talk radio, drowning in jabber.

But then the headlines take the power. "Problem is, we can't hear the voices of the moderates," said the Israeli man, who claimed his house was built on a spot where Arabs had never lived. "Where are *they*? Why don't they speak *louder*?"

(They don't like to raise their voices.)

(Maybe they can't hear you either.)

Excerpt from Naomi Shihab Nye, "Long Overdue," Post Gibran: An Anthology of New Arab American Writing (Syracuse University Press, 2000), p. 127. Reprinted by permission of the author.

Effects of Disclosure and Privacy on Relationships

Privacy and disclosure decisions affect relationships in three major ways. They affect intimacy level, reciprocity expectations, and information co-ownership.

Intimacy Because disclosure is the mechanism for increasing intimacy, you might think people move in a clear-cut way toward deeper disclosure as relationships develop. However, people actually move back and forth between periods of choosing to disclose and choosing to maintain privacy (Altman, 1993). We may choose privacy over disclosure to protect the other person's feelings, avoid unnecessary conflict, protect the relationship, or re-establish a boundary of independence (Petronio, 2002). For example, disclosing an infidelity to a romantic partner may do irreparable damage to the relationship and opting for privacy may actually preserve intimacy (Hendrick, 1981) and avoid conflict (Roloff & Ifert, 2000).

Reciprocity Whether your disclosure is matched by similar disclosure from your partner also can affect your relationship. Although you may expect immediate reciprocity, research suggests there can be a long time lag after one person discloses before the other reciprocates (Dindia, 2000b). After their fourth date, for instance, Tom might proclaim, "Sam, I love you and I know that I'm going to marry you." Sam, who thinks she loves Tom but wants to make sure she is not just taken with the idea of being in love, may not voice her feelings for many more months. Nevertheless, the two of them may continue dating, building common history, and sharing other personal information even though Sam did not reciprocate at the moment when Tom first declared his love for her.

Information Co-Ownership A third way disclosure and privacy can affect relationships has to do with how partners treat the private information they know about one another. When we disclose private information, the person with whom we share it becomes a co-owner of it. When a partner shares confidential information without permission, it is likely to damage our relationship at least temporarily.

As we rely more and more on technology to develop and maintain relationships, the lines between what is public and what is private are blurring (Kleinman, 2007). For example, we may use mobile phones and Bluetooth technology to carry on even the most private conversations in public spaces. Similarly, when we e-mail a friend, we can't be sure that friend won't forward the message to others. The same problem exists on social networking sites. Once we post information, it is there for others to take and share with anyone. The *Pop Comm!* feature, "Our Right to Privacy in a Mediated Society," describes some of the ethical issues we must confront in our brave new mediated world.

Disclosure Guidelines

The following guidelines can help you make wise decisions regarding disclosure when sharing personal information, sharing feelings, and providing feedback.

CONSIDER *THIS*....

Describe a conversation you have experienced where TMI (too much information) was disclosed. What happened and why?

CONSIDER *THIS*....

How would you feel if someone shared something that you told them in confidence? How might it affect you, them, and your relationship?

Information co-ownership is increasingly prevalent on online social networking sites. How do you try to manage your privacy online?

Monkey Business Images/Shutterstock

The Right to Privacy in a Mediated Society

moodboard/Cultura/Jupiter Images

For over a century, celebrities have complained that the media invades their privacy, but it was the death of Princess Diana in 1997 that focused worldwide attention on the extent to which some public figures are denied any right to privacy. Whether it's the paparazzi hounding Princess Diana to her death, or the media scrutinizing Republican presidential candidate Herman Cain's private life in 2011 following sexual harassment allegations, some might conclude that public figures can no longer expect even a basic right to privacy. Certainly, public figures such as Cain expect to be scrutinized regarding their professional lives and should be held accountable for misconduct, but the current cult of celebrity has created a situation in which the media also prys into their private lives—for reasons that often have little or nothing to do with their professional careers. The debate over invasive media coverage was particularly relevant in 2009 when the celebrity Web site *TMZ.com* posted a photo of pop star Rihanna after she had been assaulted by her then-boyfriend, R&B artist Chris Brown. The photo had been leaked by someone at the Los Angeles Police Department, and in embarrassment, the department opened an internal investigation saying it "takes seriously its duty to maintain the confidentiality of victims of domestic violence" (Itzkoff, 2009). *TMZ.com*'s executive producer, Harvey Levin, defended the publication of the photo, saying it helped put a face to the victims of domestic abuse ("TMZ Responds," 2009). Even people who fight for the rights of victims of domestic abuse hesitantly supported the decision to publish the photo. Chicago author and advocate for victims of domestic abuse Susan Murphy-Milano speculated, "Maybe it is a good idea, if it's her, if young girls see this." She added that she hoped it would make young women think

"Is the next picture going to be of her in a morgue?" (McCartney, 2009).

But what about Rihanna's right to privacy? *PR Week* points out that typical standards of journalism prevent reporters and editors from publishing names of victims. However, in the case of Rihanna, David Hauslaib, former editorial director of the now-defunct *Jossip.com*, says, "We have this appetite for celebrity culture and it brings down any sort of safeguards we, as a media industry, have implemented to protect people" (Maul, 2009). Celebrity news blog *Gawker.com* added, "Critics say running the picture humiliates Rihanna at a time when she's already in emotional agony, that it pierces a zone of emotional and physical privacy already grossly violated in the apparent attack on her" (Tate, 2009). Nonetheless, profit-seeking publishers know that publishing such a shocking image will increase their traffic hits, and they simply choose to run the risk of exploitation accusations.

In the age of new media, celebrities are not the only ones who have to worry about such issues of privacy. Social networking sites, e-mail, and text messaging have made it easier and faster to communicate with others, but they also open some important questions about how we control our identities, protect our privacy and manage relationships online. A recent controversy has arisen regarding the Web site IsAnyoneUp.com, launched in 2010, which features thousands of explicit photos submitted by users. These amateur nude photos often began as private photos exchanged between partners, but are submitted to the site as a form of "revenge" by jilted exes or former friends without the consent of those pictured (Chen, 2011). The pictures are accompanied by the subjects' real names and screenshots of their Facebook profiles and Twitter feeds, further exposing the private lives of those pictured across the Internet. Even though they did not submit the photos nor consent to having them posted, under current communication law, those pictured have little recourse. Site founder, Hunter Moore, defends his posting of the pictures by suggesting it teaches people a valuable lesson about privacy. "[I]t might sound rough, but how else are you going to learn not to do this again?" Moore says. "It's like you're playing Russian roulette like, oh, let's hope this doesn't get out" (Gold, 2011).

Questions to Ponder

1. Is the media justified in exposing the private moments of celebrities' lives, no matter how personal or painful, if doing so raises public awareness?

2. Do celebrities have a right to control their personal information and maintain a level of privacy? Why or why not?

3. Do different standards exist for "everyday people"? Why or why not?

Sharing personal information

1. **Self-disclose the kind of information you want others to disclose to you.** How do you determine whether certain information is appropriate to disclose? You can do so by asking yourself whether you would feel comfortable if the other person were to share similar information with you.

2. **Self-disclose private information only when doing so represents an acceptable risk.** Some risk is inherent in any self-disclosure. The better you know your partner, the more likely a difficult self-disclosure will be well received.

3. **Move gradually to deeper levels of self-disclosure.** Because receiving self-disclosure can be as threatening as giving it, most people become uncomfortable when the level of disclosure exceeds their expectations. So we should disclose surface information early in a relationship and more personal information in a more developed relationship (Dindia, Fitzpatrick, & Kenny, 1997).

4. **Continue self-disclosing only if it is reciprocated.** Although a self-disclosure may not be immediately reciprocated, when it is clearly not being returned, you should consider limiting the amount of additional self-disclosure you make. Failure to reciprocate suggests that your partner does not feel comfortable with that level of intimacy.

5. **Reserve very personal self-disclosure for ongoing intimate relationships.** Disclosures about intimate matters are appropriate in close, well-established relationships. Making intimate self-disclosures before a bond of trust is established risks alienating the other person.

Sharing personal feelings

Sharing personal feelings At the heart of intimate self-disclosure is sharing personal feelings. Doing so demonstrates a bond of trust. Effective communicators share by **describing feelings**. Doing so teaches others how to treat us by explaining how what has happened affects us. For example, if you tell Paul that you enjoy it when he visits you, this description of your feelings should encourage him to visit you again. Likewise, when you tell Gloria that it bothers you when she borrows your iPad without asking, she may be more likely to ask the next time. To practice describing feelings, follow these three guidelines:

describing feelings

the skill of naming the emotions you are feeling without judging them

1. **Identify what *triggered* the feeling.** What did someone specifically say or do?

Describing feelings is difficult for many people because it makes them feel vulnerable. Can you recall a feeling in which you masked your feelings because you didn't trust the other person? Was your fear justified?

2. **Identify the *specific emotion* you feel as a result.** If what you are feeling is similar to anger, try to be more specific. Are you annoyed, betrayed, cheated, crushed, disturbed, furious, outraged, or shocked? Each of these words more richly describes the feeling.

3. **Frame your response as an "I" statement.** For example, "I feel happy/sad/ irritated/excited/vibrant." "I" statements help neutralize the impact of an emotional description because they do not blame the other. Be careful, however, not to couch a blaming statement as an "I" statement. For example, "I feel like you don't respect me" is actually a blaming statement because it doesn't let the other person know how you feel (e.g., hurt, angry, betrayed) about what happened. These two examples describe feelings effectively:

> *"Thank you for the compliment [trigger]; I [the person having the feeling] feel gratified [the specific feeling] that you noticed my efforts."*

> *"I [the person having the feeling] feel hurt and unappreciated [the specific feelings] when you criticize my cooking after I've worked all afternoon to prepare it [trigger]."*

Providing personal feedback When personal feedback about what our partner says or does is shared with sensitivity, it can help develop a more accurate self-concept and increase openness in the relationship. The following three guidelines can help you provide feedback effectively:

1. **Describing specific behavior.** As when sharing feelings, be descriptive rather than evaluative and specific rather than vague. Statements like "You're so mean" and "You're a real friend," are ineffective because they are evaluative and vague.

   Instead, **describing behavior** accurately recounts the specific behaviors of another without commenting on appropriateness. What led you to conclude someone was *mean*? Was it something the person said or did? If so, what? Once you identify the specific behaviors, actions, or messages that led to your conclusion, you can share that information as feedback. For example, "You called me a liar in front of the team knowing I have no way to prove that I told the truth." "When Tyrone died, you stayed with me and even babysat my son so I could job hunt. You're a real friend."

describing behavior

accurately recounting the specific behaviors of another without commenting on their appropriateness

2. **Praising positive behavior. Praise** is describing a specific positive behavior of another person and its effect on others. Praise is not the same as flattery. When we flatter someone, we use insincere compliments to ingratiate ourselves to that person. Praise compliments are sincere.

   Sincere praise doesn't cost much, is usually appreciated, can develop positive self-concept and build self-esteem, and often deepens relationships. To praise effectively, identify the specific behavior you want to reinforce and then describe any positive feelings you or others experienced as a result.

   So if your sister, who tends to be forgetful, remembers your birthday, saying something like "Thanks for the birthday card; I really appreciate

praise

describing the specific positive behaviors or accomplishments of another and the effect that behavior has on others

Jetta Productions/Iconica/Getty Images

that you remembered my birthday" describes the specific behavior you want to reinforce and the effect it had on you.

3. **Giving constructive criticism. Constructive criticism** is describing specific behaviors that hurt you or someone else and that person's relationships with others. Although the word *criticize* can mean judgment, constructive criticism does not condemn but is based on empathy and a sincere desire to help someone understand the impact of his or her behavior. Use the following guidelines when providing constructive criticism:

constructive criticism

describing specific behaviors of another that hurt the person or that person's relationships with others`

- *Ask for permission.* A person who has agreed to hear constructive criticism is more likely to be receptive to it than someone who was not accorded the respect of being asked beforehand.
- *Describe the behavior and its consequences precisely.* Your objective description allows the other to maintain face while receiving accurate feedback about the damaging behavior. For example, DeShawn asks, "What did you think of the visuals I used when I delivered my report?" If you reply, "They weren't very effective," you would be too general and evaluative to be helpful. In contrast, you might say, "Well, the small font size on the first two made it hard for me to read." Notice this constructive criticism does not attack DeShawn's competence. Instead, it describes the font size and its consequences, and in so doing, enables DeShawn to see how to improve.
- *Preface constructive criticism with an affirming statement.* Remember, even constructive criticism threatens the innate human need to be liked and admired. So, preface constructive criticism with statements that validate your respect for the other person. You could begin your feedback to DeShawn by saying, "First, the chart showing how much energy we waste helped me see just how much we could improve. And the bold colors you used really helped me focus on the main problems. I think using a larger font size on the first two PowerPoint slides would have made it easier for me to see from the back of the room."
- *When appropriate, suggest how the person can change the behavior.* Because the goal of constructive criticism is to help, you can do so by providing suggestions that might lead to positive change. In responding to DeShawn's request for feedback, you might also add, "In my communication class, I learned that most people in a small audience should be able to read 18-point font or larger. You might want to give that a try." By including a positive suggestion, you not only help the person by providing useful information, you also show that your intentions are respectful.

THE AUDIENCE *BEYOND*

Stephen was furious when he read the e-mail from his boss saying that Stephen needed to update his sales forecast by the next morning instead of the original deadline of next week. Before sending his e-mail response, Stephen reread it and determined that his attempt at constructive criticism could easily be misconstrued. So, he deleted the message, and walked down the hall to see if his manager was available to meet face-to-face instead.

COMMUNICATION SKILL

Describing Feelings

Skill	Use	Procedure	Example
Naming the emotions you are feeling without judging them.	For self-disclosure; to teach people how to treat you.	1. Identify the behavior that has triggered the feeling. 2. Identify the specific emotion you are experiencing as a result of the behavior. Anger? Joy? Be specific. 3. Frame your response as an "I" statement. "I feel ____" 4. Verbalize the specific feeling.	"I just heard I didn't get the job, and I feel cheated and bitter" or "Because of the way you defended me when I was being belittled by Leah, I feel both grateful and humbled."

Privacy Management Guidelines

Because reciprocity is a way to develop a relationship, maintaining privacy without damaging the relationship can be difficult. We offer three indirect strategies and one direct strategy you can use when being pressed to disclose something you do not want to share.

Indirect strategies You may choose to maintain privacy by deflecting attention or by practicing strategic ambiguity.

Learning to give constructive criticism can help you avoid a defensive reaction when you describe a person's negative behavior.

- **Change the subject.** Observant partners will recognize changing the subject as a signal that you don't want to disclose. For example, as Pat and Eric leave economics class, Pat says to Eric, "I got an 83 on the test, how about you?" If Eric doesn't want to share his grade, he might redirect the conversation by saying, "Hey, that's a B. Good going. Did you finish the homework for calculus?"

- **Mask feelings.** If you decide that sharing your personal feelings is too risky, you might mask your emotions. For example, Alita masks her feelings of betrayal and embarrassment by laughing along with the others as Manny makes fun of her. On occasion, masking feelings can be an effective strategy. If we make it a regular habit, however, we might experience health problems as a result of repressing our feelings. We also run the risk of damaging our relationships because our partners won't really know or understand us.

- **Tell a white lie.** A white lie is an ambiguous or misleading statement that might be acceptable if telling the truth would embarrass you or your partner and if the untruth will not cause serious harm to either person or to the relationship. So when Pat asks Eric about his grade on the test, Eric might respond, "I'm not sure. I got a few tests back this week."

Direct strategy Changing the subject, masking feelings, and telling white lies are indirect ways to maintain privacy and generally work in one-time situations. But these strategies will eventually damage your relationships if used repeatedly. So you might decide to use a more direct approach. **Establishing a personal boundary** is a direct approach for responding to people who expect you to disclose information or feelings you prefer to keep private.

To do so, begin by **recognizing why you choose not to share the information.** For example, when Pat asks Eric about the grade he received on a history paper, Eric may tell Pat he feels uncomfortable doing so. Then **identify your privacy policy that guided this decision.** Eric, who has been teased for getting good grades, has developed a rule that he does not disclose the grades he receives. Next, **preface your personal boundary statement with an apology or other face-saving statement.** Eric might tell Pat that he values the fact that Pat is interested in Eric's achievement. Finally, **form an "I"-centered message that briefly establishes a boundary.** For example, Eric might say:

> *"I'm sorry. I know that everyone's different, and I don't mean to be rude, but I'm not comfortable sharing my grades. It's been my policy not to ask other people about their grades or to discuss my own ever since getting teased about grades when I was a kid. I value you and our friendship and hope my policy doesn't offend you."*

establishing a personal boundary

a direct approach for responding to people who expect you to disclose something you would rather keep private

COMMUNICATE ON YOUR FEET

Speech Assignment

Personal Narrative

The Assignment

Prepare a 3- to 5-minute speech that is a story about something that happened to you and is not generally known by others. Your story might be humorous, serious, or somewhere in between. It might be about something that happened recently or about an event from your past.

Begin by making a list of stories you might tell. As you think about the stories on your list, use the privacy and disclosure guidelines in this chapter to determine whether the story is appropriate for a classroom setting. Remember to consider not only your own privacy, but also the privacy of others who are part of the story.

As you prepare your speech, think about how to tell the story so that your audience can easily follow what you are saying. We tell most stories in chronological order, introducing people in the story as they make their appearance in the events. You can help your audience follow your story if you divide it into two, three, or four sequential parts, similar to the chapters of a book. For example, if you are going to tell a story about a cake-baking disaster, you could divide your story into three parts: problems with ingredients, problems with mixing, and problems with baking.

Briefly introduce your story in a way that piques the interest of your audience members. End your story by summarizing what you learned from the experience.

Phrasing his response this way lets Pat know that Eric's decision is based on a personal boundary rule rather than an indication of his trust in Pat or their relationship.

Expressing Desires and Expectations

Even two people in a mutually satisfying, intimate relationship have different needs, desires, and expectations (Alberti & Emmons, 2008). How they choose to express them to their partner will affect the relationship's communication climate. Let's look at four such communication styles and how each can affect the climate of a relationship.

Passive Communication Style

passive communication style

not expressing personal preferences or defending our rights

A **passive communication style** is submitting to another's demands and concealing, rather than voicing, your needs, rights, desires, and expectations. For example, Aaron and Katie routinely go to the gym at 10 a.m. on Saturday mornings. Aaron's Friday work schedule has recently changed and now he doesn't get home until 3 a.m. on Saturdays. Aaron behaves passively if he doesn't say anything to Katie and drags himself out of bed even though he'd much rather sleep. We tend to choose a passive approach when we value our relationship with the other person more than we value asserting our own particular need. If used habitually, however, passive communication will eventually damage the relationship because we will begin to resent our partner as we continually ignore our own needs, desires, and expectations.

aggressive communication style

belligerently or violently confronting another with your preferences, feelings, needs, or rights with little regard for the situation or for the feelings or rights of others

Aggressive Communication Style

Have you ever engaged in or been the victim of aggressive road rage? Was it effective in achieving its goal? Were there any unanticipated consequences?

An **aggressive communication style** is attacking another person's self-concept and/or expressing personal hostility in order to inflict psychological pain (Rancer & Avtgis, 2006). Verbally aggressive messages disregard a partner's right to be treated with dignity and respect. Examples of aggressive communication range from yelling, badgering, and name calling to sarcasm, put-downs, and taunting. Suppose Aaron continues to meet Katie at the gym on Saturdays at 10 a.m. without telling her about his work schedule change. If Katie suggests they meet even earlier next week, Aaron may explode and aggressively reply, "No way! We always do what you want when you want. I'm sick of it. You are so selfish and inconsiderate. In fact, I don't care if I ever work out on Saturday again!" Katie, who has no context for understanding

this aggressive outburst, may be startled, hurt, and confused. People may use verbal aggression when they perceive themselves to be powerful, do not value the other person, lack emotional control, or feel defensive. Studies have found that verbally aggressive messages can lead to less satisfying relationships, family violence, divorce, and loss of credibility (Hample, 2003). Unfortunately, the fact that some people today use technology to convey verbally aggressive messages has become so prevalent that we coined the term cyberbullying to describe it (Kleinman, 2007).

Passive-Aggressive Communication Style

A **passive-aggressive communication style** is exhibited in messages where hostility is expressed indirectly. For example, you may say yes when you want to say no or complain about others behind their backs. Suppose Aaron apologizes for his outburst and then tells Katie about his work schedule change. Although Katie claims to accept the apology and tells Aaron "It's no big deal," the next week she doesn't call him and instead goes alone to the gym. When Aaron shows up and asks for an explanation, Katie shrugs her shoulders and says, "Well I thought you said you were sick of always doing things 'my way.'" Over time, passive-aggressive behavior damages relationships because it undercuts mutual respect.

passive-aggressive communication style

submitting to another's demands and concealing your needs, rights, desires, and expectations

Assertive Communication Style

An **assertive communication style** uses messages that describe personal needs, rights, desires, and expectations honestly and directly in ways that also demonstrate respect and value for you, your partner, and the relationship. Assertive messages teach partners how to treat us as we stand up for ourselves and express legitimate concerns without denying the worth of our partners.

An effective assertive message (1) describes the behavior or event as objectively as possible, (2) proposes your interpretation of it, (3) names the feeling you have as a result, (4) identifies potential consequences for you, your partner, or others, and (5) suggests your intentions regarding how you will act and/or what you expect in the future. For example, Aaron could have responded to Katie's suggestion to go to the gym at 8 a.m. assertively in this way:

assertive communication style

expressing your personal preferences and defending your personal rights while respecting the preferences and rights of others

> "I understand that you want to work out at 8 a.m. starting next week (description). I am guessing you want more time to run errands, do chores, or study (interpretation). The thought of working out at 8 a.m. frustrates me (feeling) because my work schedule changed and I don't even get home until 3 a.m. I can't imagine having the energy to exercise at 8 a.m. (consequence). But I really like working out together and would like to keep doing so on Saturdays. So maybe we could start at 9 a.m. instead, or you could start earlier and I could join you at 9 a.m. (intention)."

Notice how Aaron honestly and directly communicates his desires in confirming ways that demonstrate respect for Katie and his relationship with her.

Cultural and Co-cultural Considerations

Assertiveness is typically valued in individualistic cultures, such as in the United States where direct communication is preferred. This style is not necessarily the norm across the world (Holt & DeVore, 2005). For example, collectivist cultures such as China and Japan that value accord and harmony may tend to prefer passive behavior (Samovar, Porter, & McDaniel, 2012). In fact, those who abide by traditional collectivist norms may even find what North Americans interpret as appropriate assertive communication to be rude and insensitive (Alberti & Emmons, 2008). In Latino or Hispanic societies where traditional norms are followed, men may exercise a form of self-expression called "machismo" that goes beyond the guidelines presented here for assertive behavior (Ukashah, Arboleda-Florez & Sartorius, 2000).

Co-cultural groups within the United States may also prefer different communication styles. For example, females who have been socialized to embrace feminine gender norms are likely to use passive or passive-aggressive communication styles (Hess & Hagen, 2006). In fact, numerous books and workshops exist today to help women learn to replace passive and passive-aggressive communication styles with assertive ones. Similarly, males who embrace masculine gender norms tend to use aggressive communication styles and similarly benefit from learning to replace them with assertive messages, as well.

Although differences exist across cultures and co-cultures, the distinctions are becoming less dramatic. Still, when talking with people whose cultural or co-cultural norms differ from your own, you may need to observe their behavior and their responses to your statements before you can be sure about how best to communicate your needs, rights, desires, and expectations.

CONSIDER THIS....

Have you ever experienced a disagreement over competing rights, desires, or expectations with someone whose cultural norms clash with yours? How did your conversation end? Did it satisfy you? Why or why not?

COMMUNICATION SKILL

Assertive Communication Style

Skill	Use	Procedure	Example
Messages that describe your needs, rights, desires, and expectations in an honest and direct way that demonstrates respect and value for both you and your partner.	To stand up for yourself and express legitimate concerns without denying the worth of your partner.	(1) Describe the behavior or event as objectively as possible. (2) Propose your interpretation of it. (3) Name the feeling(s) you have as a result. (4) Identify potential consequences for you, your partner, or others. (5) Suggest your intentions regarding how you will act and/or what you expect of them in the future.	When you refer to us as "girls" after I explained we want to be called "women" (behavior), I feel disrespected (feeling) because it seems like you don't appreciate how important the difference is to me (interpretation). Because this really bothers me, it is hurting the intimacy I feel for our relationship (consequences). I'll keep bringing it up if you keep using "girls" to refer to us (intention).

Managing Interpersonal Conflict

Interpersonal conflict is an expressed struggle between two interdependent people who perceive incompatible goals, scarce resources, and interference from the other in achieving their goals (Wilmot & Hocker, 2010). Let's untangle this definition. To be an *expressed struggle,* both people must be aware of the disagreement. To be *interdependent,* achieving a satisfactory outcome for each person depends on the actions of the other. By *perceived incompatible goals* we mean both people believe they have something to lose if the other person gets their way. *Perceived scarce resources* assumes there isn't enough of something to go around and *perceived interference* is the belief that the other person is forcing us to do or not to do something. For example, when sixteen-year-old Darla's mother (interdependence) told her she would not waste money (scarce resources) on a tattoo (perceived interference), she claimed Darla would regret it when she grew up (perceived incompatible goals), and they argued (expressed struggle). In conflict situations such as this one, participants have choices about how they communicate with each other to manage, and hopefully, to resolve it.

Conflict is not necessarily a bad thing. In fact, conflict is a natural part of interpersonal relationships, and when managed effectively, can actually strengthen them (Cupach & Canary, 1997). When not managed effectively, however, conflict can hurt people and relationships (Brake, Walker, & Walker, 1995). The consequences of poorly managed conflict can be particularly devastating when communicating across cultures (Ting-Toomey, 2006). In this section, we discuss five conflict management styles and how to skillfully initiate and respond to conflict situations that arise in your relationships. These five styles are avoiding, accommodating, competing, compromising, and collaborating (Thomas, 1976; Thomas & Kilmann, 1978; Thomas, 1992). Figure 8.1 is a visual representation of these styles as they relate to assertiveness and cooperativeness.

interpersonal conflict

when the needs or ideas of one person are at odds with the needs or ideas of another

CONSIDER *THIS*....

Think about the last time you experienced a conflict. Did you react by trying to avoid it, by giving in or by forcing the other person to see or do it your way? Or did the two of you try to work together to find a mutually acceptable solution? Looking back, how satisfied are you with your actions?

Avoiding (Lose–Lose)

Avoiding involves physically or psychologically removing yourself from the conflict. It is both unassertive and uncooperative and is typically characterized as a lose–lose approach. Avoiding may be appropriate when hot tempers need to cool down or when either the issue or the relationship isn't important to us.

avoiding

physically or psychologically removing yourself from the conflict

Figure 8.1

Conflict management style taxonomy

For instance, imagine Eduardo and Justina get into an argument about their financial situation. Eduardo may say, "I don't want to talk about this" and physically walk out the door. Or he may psychologically withdraw by simply ignoring Justina. We risk damaging our relationships when avoiding becomes a habit because doing so doesn't deal with or resolve the conflict and usually makes it more difficult to deal with later on.

Accommodating (Lose–Win)

accommodating

managing conflict by satisfying others' needs or accepting others' ideas while neglecting our own

Accommodating is satisfying the needs or accepting the opinions of our partner while neglecting our own needs or opinions. It is unassertive and cooperative and is typically characterized as a lose–win approach. Accommodating may be appropriate when the issue is not important to us, but the relationship is. For instance, Anthony doesn't particularly enjoy romantic movies but knows Marianne has her heart set on seeing *The Vow*. He suggests going to see it because he doesn't really care which movie they see and wants to please her because he values his relationship with her.

Competing (Win–Lose)

competing

satisfying our own needs or with little or no concern for the needs of the other or for the harm it may do to the relationship

Competing is satisfying our own needs or desires with little or no concern for the desires of the other or for the relationship. It is assertive and uncooperative and is typically characterized as a win–lose approach. It may be appropriate when quick and decisive action must be taken to ensure your own or another's welfare or safety. For example, David knows that, statistically speaking, the likelihood of death or serious injury increases dramatically if one does not wear a helmet when riding a motorcycle. So he insists that his sister wear one when she rides with him.

If one partner uses competing and the other responds by avoiding or accommodating, the conflict may seem to have resolved even though it has not. And if both partners engage in competing, the conflict is likely to escalate. Finally, although competing may result in getting your way, when you use it repeatedly, it will usually hurt your partner and damage the relationship.

Compromising (Partial Lose–Lose)

compromising

managing conflict by giving up part of what you want, to provide at least some satisfaction for both parties

Compromising occurs when each partner gives up part of what they desire to satisfy part of what their partner wants. It is partially assertive and cooperative and is typically characterized as a partial lose–lose approach. Neither partner is completely satisfied, but it seems to be the best solution either can hope for.

Compromising may be appropriate when the issue is moderately important, when there are time constraints, when doing so will buy credits for future negotiations, and when attempts at collaborating have not been successful. For example, if Heather and Paul need to meet outside of class to complete a class project but both have busy schedules, they may compromise to meet at a time that isn't ideal for either of them.

THE AUDIENCE *BEYOND*

When Karna finished reading Jeremy's tweet, she could tell he was upset but just needed to vent, and the issue wasn't really important to her. So she chose not to respond right away to let him cool down.

1995 Baby Blues Partnership. Reprinted by permission of King Features Syndicate, Inc.

Collaborating (Win–Win)

Collaborating occurs when people work through the problem together to discover a mutually acceptable solution. It is assertive and cooperative and is typically characterized as a win–win approach. Collaborating may be appropriate when the issue is too important for a compromise, when the relationship is important, and when we want to come up with a creative solution to a problem. We collaborate by discussing the issues, describing feelings, and identifying the characteristics of a solution that will satisfy everyone. For example, Fadi really wants to vacation alone with Aliana and Alaina wants to invite their friends, Greg and Shelly. Aliana may explain how she thinks that vacationing with friends would lower the cost of the trip. Fadi may describe his desire to have "alone time" with Aliana. As they discuss their vacation goals, they arrive at a plan that meets both of their needs. For example, they may decide to vacation alone, but camp rather than stay in hotels to lower their expenses. Or they may share a condo with their friends, but schedule alone time each day.

collaborating

managing conflict by fully addressing the needs and issues of each party and arriving at a solution that is mutually satisfying

Collaboration Guidelines

When you decide that collaboration is the best strategy for resolving a conflict, several guidelines can help assist you:

- **Identify the problem and own it as your own:** "Hi, I'm trying to study and I need your help."

- **Describe the problem in terms of behavior, consequences, and feelings:** "When I hear your music, I listen to it instead of studying, and then I get frustrated and behind schedule."

- **Refrain from blaming or accusing:** "I know you aren't trying to ruin my study and are just enjoying your music."

- **Find common ground:** "I would guess that you have had times when you became distracted from something you needed to do, so I'm hoping that you can help me out by lowering the volume a bit."

- **Mentally rehearse so that you can state your request briefly.**

THE AUDIENCE *BEYOND*

Micah really wanted to get the vintage motorcycle he saw on *e-Bay*. He ended up paying more than he intended to spend but less than what the seller had hoped to get. In the end, Micah and the seller ended up compromising.

It is more difficult to collaborate when you have to respond to a conflict that someone initiates in a confrontational manner. But you can shape the conversation toward collaboration by following these guidelines:

- **Disengage:** Mentally "put up your shield" and avoid a defensive response by emotionally disengaging." Remember your partner has a problem and you want to help.

- **Respond with genuine concern:** Sometimes you need to allow your partner to vent before the partner will be ready to problem solve: "I can see that you're angry. Tell me about it."

- **Paraphrase and ask questions:** "Is it the volume of my music or the type of music that is making it difficult for you to study?"

- **Seek common ground:** "I can understand that you would be upset about losing precious study time."

- **Ask for alternative solutions:** "Can you give me a couple of ideas about how we could resolve this so your study is more effective?"

WHAT WOULD YOU DO?

A Question of Ethics

Ronaldo sat in the study hall cramming for a final examination when two of his classmates, Chauncey and Doug, walked up to his table.

"Studying hard?" Chauncey asked.

"Yeah. I'm really stressing over this final," said Ronaldo. "What about you guys?"

"Hardly studying," said Chauncey.

Doug laughed.

Ronaldo looked at the two and saw that they both seemed relaxed and confident. "Something's not right with this picture," he said. "You're not going to tell me you guys are ready for this thing, are you?"

"Yep," said Chauncey.

Doug nodded.

"I don't get it," said Ronaldo. "You mean you've already gone back and studied everything we've covered this semester?"

"Hey, you only need to study what's actually on the test," said Chauncey.

"And how would you know that when McAllister didn't even give us a study guide?"

asked Ronaldo. He was beginning to put the puzzle together.

Doug placed his hand on Chauncey's arm and said, "Don't tell him anything else, man."

"No, it's all right. Ronaldo's cool," said Chauncey. "He knows how to keep a secret. Don't you?"

"I guess," Ronaldo said uneasily.

"It's like this," said Chauncey. "Doug's little brother hacked into McAllister's system and downloaded a copy of the final exam. You interested in getting a head start?"

1. Assuming that Ronaldo declines Chauncey's offer to cheat, what other ethical issues must he grapple with? Which would be more ethically compromising: letting Chauncey and Doug get away with cheating, or betraying their trust by notifying the professor?

2. When, if ever, is it ethically acceptable to divulge information that you have sworn not to share with others?

Summary

We develop and maintain interpersonal relationships through communication. We do so by: (1) providing emotional support, (2) dealing with competing needs for privacy and disclosure, (3) expressing different desires and expectations, and (4) managing conflict.

We can provide emotional support by clarifying our supportive intentions, buffering face threats with politeness, using other-centered messages, reframing the situation, and giving advice.

The openness-versus-closedness dialectical tension gives rise to our needs to disclose or maintain privacy in our relationships. We are most effective at disclosing when we describe feelings. We can also effectively disclose feedback by describing behavior, offering praise, and giving constructive criticism. When we want to maintain privacy, we can use three indirect methods (change the subject, mask feelings, tell "white lies") or one direct method (establishing a personal boundary).

Finally, relationship satisfaction depends on our ability to express our personal desires and expectations. We can do so using a passive, aggressive, passive-aggressive, or assertive communication style. When our competing desires and expectations produce a conflict situation, we can employ one of five conflict management styles. These are avoiding, accommodating, competing, compromising, and collaborating. Each style may be most appropriate under certain circumstances; however, when we want to maintain a good relationship and our differences are serious, collaborative methods are often the best choice.

RESOURCE AND ASSESSMENT CENTER

Now that you have read Chapter 8, go to the Speech Communication Course-Mate at cengagebrain.com where you'll find an interactive eBook and interactive learning tools including quizzes, flashcards, sample speech videos, audio study tools, skill-building activities, action step activities, and more. Student Workbook, Speech Builder Express 3.0, and Speech Studio 2.0 are also available.

Applying What You've Learned

Impromptu Speech Activity

1. Communication Negotiation Styles Identify a recent incident in which you behaved either passively, aggressively, or passive aggressively. Now analyze the situation. What type of situation was it? Did someone make a request? Did you need to express a preference or right? What type of relationship did you have with the person (stranger, acquaintance, friendship, intimate)? How did you feel about how you behaved? If you had used an assertive message, what might you have said? Prepare a short, well-organized speech (2-3 minutes) describing your analysis and be prepared to deliver it to the class if called upon by your instructor.

Assessment Activities

1. Self-Disclosure and Popular Media American popular culture has a reputation for promoting self-disclosure that probably exceeds that of any other culture in the world. Yet clearly, as the phrase "TMI" (too much information) indicates, inappropriate self-disclosure still happens. Of course, what may be inappropriate for one person can be appropriate for another. Find three instances of self-disclosure in popular media (film, television, radio, magazines, newspapers, or the Internet) and write a paragraph on each, explaining why you think the particular instance of self-disclosure is appropriate or inappropriate.

2. Your Conflict Profile Go to the CourseMate for *Communicate!* at cengagebrain. com to access and print out your conflict profile, which is the article "How Do You Manage Conflict?" by Dawn M. Baskerville. Fill out and score the self-assessment questionnaire and graph your results. Read the description of each pattern. Study these results. Do they seem to capture your perception of your conflict profile accurately? Which are your dominant styles? Are your scores close together, or are there one or two styles that seem to dominate and other styles you prefer not to use? How does this pattern equip you to handle the conflicts you have experienced? Based on the information from this self-assessment, what do you need to do to become better able to handle conflict in your relationships? Write a paragraph in which you describe what you have learned about your conflict profile.

3. Conversation and Analysis: Jan and Ken After you've watched the video of Jan and Ken on the CourseMate for *Communicate!* at cengagebrain.com to answer the following questions.

- How does each person handle this conflict?

- How well does each person listen to the other?

- Are Jan and Ken appropriately assertive?

- Comment on how well each provides feedback and describes feelings?

When you're done with this activity, compare your answers to the authors' at the CourseMate Web site for *Communicate!*

Skill-Building Activities

1. Describing Feelings and Communicating Boundaries Each of the statements below expresses feelings. Rephrase each to describe feelings or where appropriate to communicate a boundary.

    a. Expressed: *"I can't believe you told that story without my permission!"*

Described:

    b. Expressed: *"Growing up without a dad was hard. But it's really none of your business."*

Described:

    c. Expressed: *"It's not fair to expect me to share our dorm room with your boyfriend."*

Described:

    d. Expressed: *"All you've done this whole lunch is text. I don't know why I bothered to come!"*

Described:

2. Describing Behavior Rephrase each statement so that it describes the behavior(s) that might have led you to this generalization.

    a. *"You're a really good friend."*

Described:

    b. *"You're always picking on me."*

Described:

    c. *"I can't believe that you stabbed me in the back."*

Described:

    d. *"One of the things I admire about you is that you are so thoughtful."*

Described:

3. Disclosing Personal Feedback For each of the following situations, write an appropriate feedback message.

    a. You have been car pooling to school for about three weeks now with a fellow student referred by the school transportation office. Everything about the situation is great (e.g., he's on time, your schedules match, and you enjoy your conversations), except he drives ten to fifteen miles per hour faster than the speed limit, and this scares you.

Feedback:

    b. A good friend has a habit of saying "like" and "you know" more than once every sentence. Although she is an "A" student, you believe this habit makes her sound uneducated. She is about to graduate and has been doing on-campus job interviews. So far every potential employer she has interviewed with has rejected her. She asks why you think she is having such a hard time.

Feedback:

c. Your professor has asked you for feedback on his or her teaching style. Based on your experience in this class, write a message of praise and one of constructive criticism.

Feedback:

4. Assertive Messages Write an assertive message for each of the following situations. Indicate what type of assertion you are making: a complaint, a personal request, or a refusal.

a. You come back to your dorm, apartment, or house to finish a paper that is due tomorrow, only to find that someone else is using your computer.

Assertive response:

b. You work part-time at a clothing store. Just as your shift is ending, your manager says to you, "I'd like you to work overtime, if you would. Martin's supposed to replace you, but he just called and can't get here for at least an hour." You have tickets to a concert that starts in an hour.

Assertive response:

c. You and your friend made a date to go dancing, an activity you really enjoy. When you meet, your friend says, "I don't feel like dancing tonight. Let's go to Joey's party instead."

Assertive response:

d. You're riding in a car with a group of friends on the way to a party when the driver begins to clown around by swerving the car back and forth, speeding up to tailgate the car in front, and honking his horn. You believe this driving is dangerous, and you're becoming scared.

Assertive response:

5. Initiating a Conflict Prepare a message that would effectively initiate a conflict for each of the following situations.

a. Situation: *You observed your long-time romantic partner flirting with another person. Your partner's arm was around this person's waist and they were quietly talking, laughing together, and periodically whispering in each other's ear.*

Initiating Message:

b. Situation: *Your roommate borrowed your iPod and returned it late last night. You put it on your desk without really looking at it. This morning when you grabbed it to use at the gym, you noticed that the display was cracked. You are certain it was not damaged before your roommate borrowed it.*

Initiating Message:

c. Situation: *Halfway through your shift, your manager called you into her office and told you that someone had called in sick and that you would have to stay until closing. You have a test tomorrow and need to study.*

Initiating Message:

6. Responding to Conflict Prepare a response that would move the conflict toward a collaboration for each of the following situations.

a. Initiating Message: *"I saw you yesterday and, boy, were you enjoying yourself. So I hope you really had fun because, it's over between you and me. You can't cheat on me and expect me to take it."*

Your Response:

b. Initiating Message: *"I can't believe that you broke my iPod and then didn't have the guts to tell me."*

Your Response:

c. Initiating Message: *"There's no way I'm staying late again to close the store. You never even consider the fact that some of us have other things to do besides cover your ass."*

Your Response:

WHAT'S TECHNOLOGY GOT TO DO WITH IT?
Mediated Interpersonal Communication in Relationships

VStock/Alamy

"Hi, Aaron. What's new?"

"Well, actually I met an incredible woman."

"Yeah, do you work with her?"

"No."

"Oh, she's in one of your classes?"

"No."

"Well, where did you meet her?

"Uh...online."

"Oh come on Aaron! Don't tell me you've been on one of those online dating sites. That's so lame!"

"No. I met her on World of Warcraft. We've been questing together for at least six months and a few weeks ago we decided to talk outside the game so we friended each other on Facebook. And it was a really cool way to get to know her by seeing her friends and what they talked about. Of course we also exchanged private messages. Then we began to talk on the phone. We have so much in common. So we've done a couple of Skype sessions. And she's just so easy to be with. The only bummer is that she lives about 800 miles away. But next week we're meeting in Austin for the first time. And I'm so jazzed. She could be the one."

"Wow, you must be serious about this. . . ."

Have you ever met someone online, used the Internet to keep connected to a friend or loved one who lives far away, or used e-mail and text messaging to "converse" with friends and family? Today, the widespread use of Internet technology and social media are changing how we build and maintain our relationships in several important ways.

First, today people can begin friendships and even meet their soul mates online. Sometimes these relationships stem from shared interests, like Aaron's new relationship that began by playing WOW.

Second, when we meet online, our partners usually respond to our verbal messages rather than our physical appearance or nonverbal cues. As a result, we are more likely to develop "pure relationships" based on mutual interests unconstrained by pressures to maintain the social order. This increases the likelihood that we will form relationships that cross boundaries of race, class, and sex (e.g., Baym & Ledbetter, 2009; Clark, 1998; Giddens, 1993; Mesch & Talmad, 2006; Rawlings, 1992).

Third, social media makes it very easy to stay connected and maintain our existing relationships. When we are temporarily in different physical locations, we can still be together in cyberspace. In addition, we can communicate with our partners whenever it is convenient for us, regardless of the time. If I want to communicate with my sister who lives in Japan, I can send her an e-mail in my early afternoon that she can read when she wakes up in the morning.

Finally, we can either increase or decrease risk compared to relationships that begin face-to-face. To clarify, meeting people online can sometimes be riskier than meeting in person since we don't know whether the "cyber-self" being presented is an accurate reflection of who the person really is. On the other hand, online relationships can also be less risky because we can get to know people at a distance before meeting face-to-face. With these changes in mind, let's look at how technology can affect interpersonal communication and relationships.

When people meet online, they don't experience what we traditionally call interpersonal communication. Rather, they experience **hyperpersonal communication**, which differs from face-to-face interaction in that senders have a greater capacity to strategically manage their self-presentation because nonverbal and relevant contextual cues are more limited (Walther, 1996). As you would expect, they "put their best foot forward." So, hyperpersonal communication receivers are left to fill in the blanks. They do this by assuming that their partner is similar to them and by using implicit personality theory. Thus partners who begin their relationships online seem to like each other more than partners who first meet face-to-face (Walther, 1996).

Relationships that begin online show a predictable pattern of adding additional media as they develop, each bringing more nonverbal and contextual cues into play. Partners who meet in an online group, like a class blog, may begin to exchange private e-mails, exchange pictures, then make phone calls, conduct video chats, and finally arrange face-to-face meetings. In one study, over 50 percent of the people who met online had followed this progression through to a face-to-face meeting (McKenna, et al., 2002).

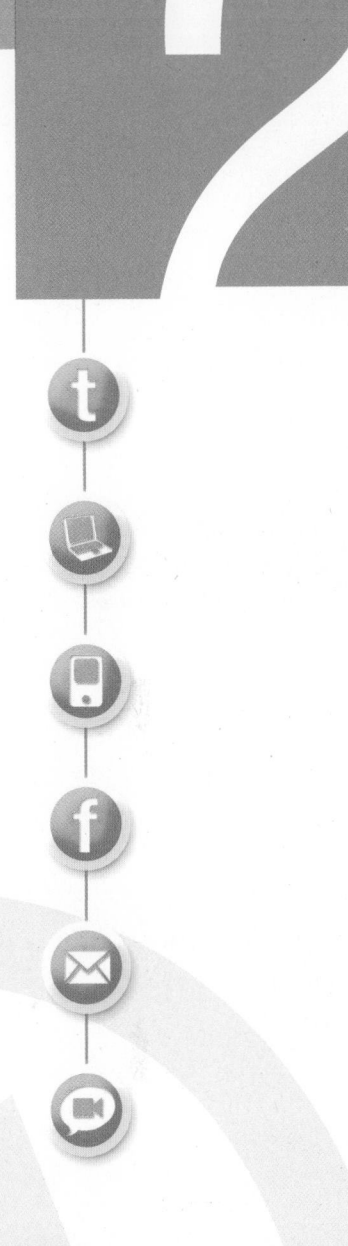

hyperpersonal communication

hyperpersonal communication the ability to strategically manage one's self-presentation that is unique to online communication

Relationships that begin in face-to-face settings may also use digital technology and social media as the relationship develops. Research suggests, in fact, that many of us find self-disclosure and feedback easier online (McKenna, et al., 2002). In addition, one study found that Americans reported being more honest with family members online than they are in face-to-face encounters (Rainie, et al., 2000). As we interact online, we also develop new "rites of passage" that signal important relationship transitions. For example, giving your partner the passwords to your social networking pages and e-mail accounts might signal a deepening bond of trust (Gershon, 2010).

We also use digital technology to maintain relationships. Most of our ongoing relationships are characterized by **media multiplexity**, which simply means that we use more than one medium to maintain our relationships. Interestingly, research has found that closer relationships use more media (Haythornthwaite, 2005). Although you are likely to e-mail or call your co-workers, you are more likely to also text and video chat with close friends and family members. We also maintain our relationships using social networking sites (SNS) like Facebook (Gilbert, et al., 2008; Golder, et al., 2007).

Finally, not only do we begin, develop, and maintain our relationships online, but we also often use mediated technology to disengage from relationships. Just as we distance ourselves physically in face-to-face relationships, digitally connected partners signal a desire to disengage by exchanging fewer e-mails, texts, and phone calls. For example, Brian began letting phone calls from Ruth go to voice mail rather than picking up. He also began ignoring her e-mails and texts. Ruth, who was not ready to let go of the relationship, began checking Brian's Facebook page more frequently to figure out why he wasn't responding to her messages. Some research suggests that young adults today choose to "break up" using technology rather than by having a face-to-face conversation even though they believe it is an inappropriate way to end a relationship (Gershon, 2010).

media multiplexity

using more than one medium to maintain relationships

Digital media is certainly changing the way we conduct our relationships. As we try to squeeze our interactions into Twitter messages, or convey the complexity of our feelings in an e-mail, or try to connect with a loved one who lives across the country via weekly phone calls or video chat sessions, we also realize our interactions are not identical to face-to-face conversations. To be honest, we are still experimenting with how to use these technological channels in our interpersonal relationships and don't yet have enough research to identify a set of best practices. But interpersonal communication and relationship scholars are at work trying to help us understand not only what we do in our mediated relationships, but also, how we can use the new technologies to improve our communication practices in them.

Group Communication

In the words of famous American cultural anthropologist, Margaret Mead:

"Never doubt that a small group of thoughtful, committed people can change the world. Indeed, it is the only thing that ever has."

When groups of people work together effectively to achieve a common goal, the results of their collective efforts can be profound. On the other hand, when groups of people function ineffectively, the results can range from meaningless to disastrous. This unit provides you with communication skills to function effectively within a group.

Although we participate in many different types of groups (e.g., families, friends, teams) every day, group communication research did not emerge until the 20th century (Forsyth & Burnette, 2005). In fact, most of the research on groups conducted in the first half of the 20th century came from analysts working in business and industry, rather than academics (Cartwright & Zander, 1968).

It wasn't until about 1950 that the formal study of groups and group communication found its home in colleges and universities across the country. Today, new technologies are generating renewed interest in group communication research and practice. For example, a growing number of communication researchers have discovered the principles and processes of group communication found in face-to-face settings may or may not hold true in virtual environments. However, as you will read in the chapters that follow, many group communication fundamentals are still considered best practices in either environment.

Although we cannot provide you with all that is known about the nature of groups and group communication in two chapters, we can introduce you to some major themes, fundamental theories and principals, and practical guidelines to make your group communication interactions both effective and rewarding.

Chapter 9, "Communicating in Groups," introduces you to the nature and types of groups and the role of communication in them. We also discuss the characteristics of healthy groups as a rationale for working with others rather than alone. We explain educational psychologist Bruce Tuckman's (1965/1977) theory of group formation and development and expand on it to include the role communication plays in a group's movement through them. And we clarify the important role of conflict and conflict management in effective groups.

In Chapter 10, "Group Leadership and Problem Solving," we turn our attention more specifically to communication in work group teams. We begin with a robust discussion of leadership as it is currently understood in the communication field. We acknowledge classic theories that conceive of leadership as a role enacted by one person, but maintain that effective leadership is shared among group members, even when a formal "leader" is designated or elected. Because meetings are such a common occurrence and are often unproductive and even unpleasant to endure, we spend a good deal of time providing guidelines for effective communication both when you are the meeting leader/facilitator and when you are a meeting participant. We also guide you through the six-step systematic problem-solving process John Dewey first described in 1933, which remains relevant and effective today, as well as provide strategies for communicating results of group work effectively in a variety formats. We close by suggesting tools to evaluate and, thus, improve group communication effectiveness.

We believe the *best practices* provided in these chapters will improve your group experiences in a variety of settings. We also hope these principles and strategies will encourage you to learn more about the nature of groups and group communication as a rich, fascinating, and practical field of study. In doing so, perhaps you will help accomplish what Margaret Mead suggests you can: *change the world*.

Communicating in Groups

What you'll know

- What makes a group different from a mere assembly of people

- Different types of groups

- Characteristics of healthy groups

- How groups develop

- The nature of conflict in groups

What you'll be able to do

- Communicate effectively during the various stages of group development

- Employ communication strategies to manage conflict effectively

"Hi, Mom. I'm just calling to tell you that I'm not going to make it home for the family dinner you're having tonight. The gang at work really needs me to close because Jennifer just called in sick."

"I can't believe it! Tonight is Sarah's last night at home before she deploys, and you know that your Grandma, Grandpa, Uncle Bill, and Aunt Vivien are all coming over for a big family dinner. What's wrong with you, Darla? Two nights ago you weren't home because you were playing softball with your friends; last night you begged off, claiming you had some team meeting for a class project; and now you're going to miss your sister's going-away family dinner? I just don't understand you. Isn't your family important to you at all? I mean, where do we fall in your priorities? It seems to me that you have a lot of commitments to other groups of people and we are always last."

"But, Mom. . . ."

group

a collection of about three to 20 people who interact and attempt to influence each other in order to accomplish a common purpose

group communication

all the verbal and nonverbal messages shared among members of the group

family

a group of intimates who through their communication generate a sense of home and group identity, complete with strong ties of loyalty and emotion, and also experience a history and a future

CONSIDER THIS....

Think about several different groups you belong to or belonged to at some point. Which ones do/did you most enjoy being part of and which ones do/did you least enjoy? Why?

Like Darla in the opening scenario, you probably belong to many formal and informal groups. Each group has different purposes and different expectations of you. But one thing all groups have in common is that their effectiveness depends on communication. In fact, year after year, surveys conducted by the National Association of Colleges and Employers report "the ability to work well in groups" is one of the top ten skills sought in college graduates. Although students are often asked to do group projects, very few graduate from college with any formal training in how to communicate effectively in groups.

In this chapter and the one that follows, we discuss how groups function and how to communicate most effectively within them. We begin by defining the nature and types of different groups, as well as some of the communication challenges you are likely to face when interacting in each of them. Then we describe key characteristics of healthy groups and the stages of development groups often follow over the course of their existence. We end this chapter with a discussion about conflict in groups and provide guidelines for managing conflict effectively.

The Nature and Types of Groups

Take a moment to think about the groups of people you interact with consistently. Examples may range from student clubs to friendship groups to family groups to study groups to online networking groups. What makes each of these a group rather than a mere assembly of people? Scholars generally agree that a **group** is a collection of about three to 20 people who feel a sense of belonging and attempt to influence each other in order to accomplish a common purpose. **Group communication**, which consists of all the verbal and nonverbal messages shared among members, is what makes participating in groups a positive or negative experience. Let's look at some of the most common group types and the role communication plays in them.

Families

A **family** is "a group of intimates who through their communication generates a sense of home and group identity, complete with strong ties of loyalty and emotion, and experiences a history and a future" (Galvin, Byland, & Brommel, 2007). Families can be nuclear (consisting of two parents who live together with their biological or adopted children), single parent (consisting of one adult living with his or her children), extended (consisting of a parent or parents and children living with grandparents, cousins, aunts and uncles, or other relatives), blended (consisting of committed or married adults living with the children of their previous marriages and relationships as well as the children of their union), as well as unrelated by either blood or marriage.

Research suggests that families typically function using one of four family communication patterns (Koerner & Fitzpatrick, 2002). In protective families, for example, issues are not discussed and are decided solely by the family authority figure. In the movie *The Sound of Music*, prior to Maria's arrival, the Von Trapp family exemplified this family dynamic. In consensual families, all members engage in conversation about an issue but a family authority figure still makes the final decision. Many television sitcoms from the 1950s and 1960s such as *Father Knows Best*, *Leave It to Beaver*, and *The Brady Bunch* portray families with a benevolent and self-sacrificing father filling this role. In pluralistic families, all members engage in conversation about an issue and everyone participates in the decision making. These families may have formal family meetings to decide important family issues. The popular 1980s television sitcom *Full House,* in which three men raised children together, operated as a pluralistic family. Finally, in laissez-faire families, members may converse about an issue, but each member makes his or her own decision and is responsible for its consequences. The cartoon family portrayed on *The Simpsons* tends to function this way.

We initially learn how to communicate in groups based on how our family members communicated with each other while we were growing up. Healthy family communication builds self-concept and self-esteem through messages of (1) praise (e.g., "awesome job on that painting"), (2) acceptance (e.g., "whether you decide to go to college or get a full time job, just know that we support you"), and (3) love (e.g., "I love you no matter what"). Unfortunately, however, not all families engage in healthy communication.

Social Friendship Groups

A **social friendship group** is composed of people who genuinely care about each other's welfare and enjoy spending time together. Their interactions are characterized by "interpersonal ties and positive, amiable preexisting relationships among members" (Thompson, 2003, p. 239). Most of us belong to more than one social friendship group. You may have had a group of friends you were close to in high school, a group of buddies you were close to when you served in the military, or a group of friends you play golf or softball with regularly. Sometimes people who work together evolve into a social friendship group when they begin to get together for social activities outside of work. Popular TV programs such as *New Girl, How I Met Your Mother,* and *Sex in the City* provide examples of social friendship groups.

Because social friendship groups fill our needs to be accepted and to belong, communication in these groups should (1) encourage quieter members to participate in conversations ("Hey, Jules, you haven't had a chance to catch us up on how your Dad is doing"); (2) protect members from playful harassment ("Hey Jenna, back off, you've been picking on Pam all evening"); and (3) provide opportunities for friends to disclose problems and receive support ("Hey, Zach, I heard that your sister was in a bad accident. How's she doing?").

Support Groups

A **support group** is composed of people who come together to provide encouragement, honest feedback, and a safe environment for expressing deeply personal feelings about a problem common to the members. Support groups include, for example, addiction recovery groups like AA (Alcoholics Anonymous), grief counseling support groups, survivor or caregiver support groups, and, abuse recovery groups such as the ASCA (Adult Survivors of Child Abuse). Until recently, support groups met face-to-face, but today

social friendship group

a group comprised of friends who have a genuine concern about each other's welfare and enjoy spending time together

support group

a group comprised of people who come together to provide encouragement, honest feedback, and a safe environment for expressing deeply personal feelings about a problem common to the members

Can you identify ways that this social friendship group was similar to a family and ways in which it was different?

NBC/Getty Images

there are thousands of online support groups connecting people who have never met face-to-face.

Support groups must create an environment in which members feel safe to disclose highly personal information. So members need to make sure that their messages follow guidelines for comforting (see Chapter 8), which include clarifying supportive intentions, buffering face threats, using other-centered language, framing, and selectively offering advice.

Interest Groups

interest group

a group comprised of individuals who come together because they share a common concern, hobby, or activity

An **interest group** is composed of individuals who come together because they share a common interest, hobby, or activity. These groups may be formal with defined goals and tasks (such as a 4-H club or community theater troupe) or they may be informal (like a neighborhood book or gardening club). They may be part of a larger organization like La Raza, the Urban League, or the Houston Area Apple Users Group. Some interest groups are externally focused on a common political or social issue and adopt an agenda to achieve change. MADD (Mothers Against Drunk Driving) is an example. Other interest groups are internally focused on increasing skills or knowledge of their members. Toastmasters, for instance, is focused on helping its members improve their public speaking skills. Some interest groups meet online. Meetup.com is an Internet site that helps people find others who share their interests.

Because interest group members share some passion, all members ought to have an opportunity to communicate their expertise by (1) encouraging members to share success stories ("I'm really glad that Brian was able to get Ace Hardware to donate all the bathroom fixtures for our project. Brian, can you tell us what you said and did?"), and (2) allowing all members to highlight what they know without demeaning the knowledge or opinions of others ("I really liked hearing Brian's story and I'd like to know how other people approach getting donations.").

Service Groups

service group

a group comprised of individuals who come together to perform hands-on charitable works or to raise money to help organizations that perform such work

A **service group** is composed of individuals who come together to perform hands-on charitable works or to raise money to help organizations that perform such work. Service groups may be local affiliates of larger secular or religious service organizations like Lions Club International, the Red Cross, the Salvation Army, and Habitat for Humanity. Other service groups are local and function independently. Examples include small soup kitchens and community beautification groups.

Because service groups are both voluntary and task-oriented, they need to be dedicated to the task as well as sensitive to the emotional needs of members. So communication should (1) be clear about individual tasks, roles, and responsibilities ("Jim, as I recall, you agreed to work on patching the roof"); (2) encourage and praise member accomplishments ("I was really impressed with

THE AUDIENCE *BEYOND*

Although Shelly's friends were very supportive after her husband's unexpected death, she also joined an online grief support group to connect with others who were going through a similar loss.

how sensitive you were when you said no to her"); and (3) be polite ("Mary, it would be really helpful if you would stuff envelopes today. Thanks so much!"

Work Group Teams

A **work group team** is a collection of three or more people formed to work together to solve a problem or accomplish a specific task. Examples of work group teams include class project groups (established to create a joint presentation, paper, or other learning project) and workplace teams (established as needed to perform specific activities in the workplace). Effective work group teams have an appropriate number of members with diverse skills and viewpoints, clearly defined goals, and explicit roles and rules for members (Katzenbach & Smith, 2003).

What is the best size for a work group team? In general, research suggests that the ideal size for most work group teams is five to seven members (Bonito, 2000; Henley & Price, 2002). However, the best size is the smallest number of people capable of effectively achieving the goal (Sundstrom, DeMeuse, & Futrell, 1990). As the size of the group increases, the time spent discussing also increases. Smaller groups can make decisions more quickly than larger ones. However, if the goals and issues are complex, a group with more members is more likely to have the breadth of information, knowledge, and skills needed to make high-quality decisions (Bonito, 2000; Henley & Price, 2002).

More important than the number of people is the right combination of people on the team. Effective work group teams are composed of people who offer different but relevant knowledge and skills (Valacich, George, Nonamaker, & Vogel, 1994). A **heterogeneous group** is usually better than a **homogeneous group**. In homogeneous groups, members are likely to know the same things, come at the problem from the same perspective, and consequently, are likely to overlook some important information or take shortcuts in the problem-solving process. In contrast, heterogeneous teams are more likely to have diverse information, perspectives, and values, and consequently, discuss issues more thoroughly before reaching a decision. For example, a group composed of seven nurses who are all young white females would be considered a homogeneous group; a group composed of nurses, doctors, nutritionists, and physical therapists differing in age, race, and sex would be considered a heterogeneous group. The heterogeneous medical group would probably make a more comprehensive decision about a patient's care than the homogeneous group of nurses.

What are the elements of an effective work group team goal? An effective **work group team goal** is a clearly stated objective desired by enough members to motivate the group to work toward achieving it (Johnson & Johnson, 2003). Effective work group team goals meet four important criteria.

1. **Effective goals are specific.** For example, the crew at a local fast-food restaurant that began with the goal of "increasing profitability" made it more specific in this way: "During the next quarter, the crew will increase profitability by reducing food costs by 1 percent. They will do so by throwing away less food due to precooking."

2. **Effective goals serve a common purpose.** Achieving one goal must not prevent achieving another. For the fast-food crew, all members must believe that reducing the amount of precooked food on hand will not hinder their current level of service.

work group team

a collection of three or more people formed to solve a problem

heterogeneous group

a group in which various demographics, levels of knowledge, attitudes, and interests are represented

homogeneous group

group in which members have a great deal of similarity

work group team goal

a future state of affairs desired by enough members to motivate the group to work toward its achievement

3. **Effective goals are challenging.** Achieving them will require hard work and team effort.

4. **Effective goals are shared.** People tend to support things they help create. So group members who participate in setting the goals are likely to exert high effort to achieve them as well.

Finally, effective work group teams develop explicit member roles and rules (Katz & Koenig, 2001). Because the goals of work group teams are typically quite challenging, all members must understand and perform their specific roles for the group to succeed (LaFasto & Larson, 2001). These roles and rules are always discussed and sometimes even written down in a formal or informal contract.

Most work group team communication focuses on task-related issues and should (1) update other members on the status of individual efforts ("I thought you all should know that I will be about two days late with that feasibility report because the person providing me with the cost data is on vacation"); (2) appropriately credit the contributions of other team members ("Today I am presenting the conclusions, but Len did the initial research and Mavis did the quantitative analysis that led to them"); (3) keep the discussion focused on the task ("Georgia, let's talk more about your party after the meeting, ok?"); and (4) seek collaboration to resolve conflicts ("Felicia, I'm stuck and I really need your help.").

Virtual Groups

virtual group

a group whose members "meet" via technological media from different physical locations

Until recently, group communication occurred almost exclusively in face-to-face settings. A **virtual group** is a group whose members "meet" via technological media from different physical locations. We can interact with our families, social friendship groups, support groups, interest groups, service groups, and work group teams from different physical locations through e-mail, teleconferences and videoconferences, online social networks such as *Linked In, Facebook,* and *Twitter,* and other technologies (Timmerman & Scott, 2006). We can also form groups through technology without ever meeting other members in person.

virtual group communication

communication that occurs in virtual groups

Since many of these technologies are relatively new and continue to evolve, research about how communication functions in them is also only just beginning. We do know, however, that effective **virtual group communication** follows the same fundamental principles as effective communication in face-to-face groups but is also unique in several ways. Technology makes virtual group communication possible (1) at the same time and location, (2) at the same time but from different locations, (3) at different times but from the same

location, and (4) at different times and from different locations (Becker-Beck, Wintermantel, & Borg, 2005). Teleconferences and videoconferences are examples of virtual group communication taking place in **real time**, which means at the same time. Communication in videoconferences most closely resembles group communication in face-to-face settings because participants can interact using both verbal and nonverbal messages. Social networking sites, blogs, and Web sites are examples of virtual group communication that occurs at the same location (on a particular Internet page), but not necessarily at the same time. E-mail is an example of virtual group communication that typically occurs at different times. A group member can send a message and wait hours or days before getting a reply.

> **real time**
>
> *at the same time*

Now that we have illustrated some of the different types of groups you are likely to belong to and the role communication plays in them, let's turn to a discussion of the similarities among healthy groups regardless of type.

Characteristics of Healthy Groups

Healthy groups are formed around a constructive purpose and are characterized by ethical goals, interdependence, cohesiveness, productive norms, accountability, and synergy.

> **healthy group**
>
> *a group formed around a constructive purpose and characterized by ethical goals, interdependence, cohesiveness, productive norms, accountability, and synergy*

Healthy Groups Have Ethical Goals

Sometimes the actual goal of a group is unethical and other times fulfilling the goal would require some or all group members to behave in unethical ways. For example, criminal gangs can be highly effective but unethical groups. They may make lots of money, but do so at the expense of society at large and often by risking the welfare of members. In this chapter's *Pop Comm!* feature, "The Dark Side of Online Social Groups," you can read about online groups

POP COMM!

The Dark Side of Online Social Groups

AP Photo/Eckehard Schulz

Imogen D'Arcy was only 13 years old when she hanged herself in her bathroom, because despite being described as fit and well-liked, she felt fat and ugly (Stokes, 2008). Laura Dunnegan developed an eating disorder at age seven. Sixteen years later, she sees her disorder as a "lifestyle option" rather than as a disease that may kill her (Croucher, 2008). What do these girls have in common? Both regularly visited Web sites where they received encouragement and reinforcement of their distorted self-images.

The Internet provides a new space for individuals to form social groups with others who share interests or concerns. However, these technological spaces do not necessarily demonstrate the characteristics of healthy groups. For example, the "pro-ana" (promoting anorexia nervosa) sites, such as the types D'Arcy visited before she died and that Dunnegan frequently visits, are online spaces where people with eating disorders can find support and share their experiences without judgment. Although initially these sites may seem to provide a positive environment, they often encourage people to develop and continue dangerous behaviors. For example, pro-ana sites often feature advice on how to starve effectively or photos of extremely underweight women as "thinspiration" for members.

C. J. Pascoe (2008), a sociologist who studies teenagers and digital media at the University of California, Berkeley, explains that, before the Internet, anorexics had to check into a psychiatric hospital to find others like themselves. Now, they can find community without seeking treatment. In the *British Journal of Social Psychology*, David Giles (2006) suggests that pro-ana Web sites—and other sites that promote unhealthy behaviors such as unsafe sex, smoking, and self-harm—may have no offline equivalent, saying, "The Internet offers a perfect sanctuary for people with interests that are unacceptable to the general public. By serving as a counter-culture to official discourse around health and illness, the Web may serve to undermine the professionals so that more and more people find ways of opting out of conventional society (e.g., health care) if they can locate supportive communities online" (p. 2).

On the other hand, online outlets for co-cultural groups can be a good thing,

too (Pascoe, 2008). One example is the vast online community of gay, lesbian, bisexual, and transgendered (GLBT) teenagers. These teens, who can have a difficult time finding friends or dates in their physical communities, can easily find other GLBT teenagers online on sites like the It Gets Better project (http://www.itgetsbetter.org). Originally created by syndicated columnist and author Dan Savage in response to a rash of bullying-related suicides among GLBT youth, the site features over 30,000 user-created videos of support for GLBT teens facing harassment to "show young LGBT people the levels of happiness, potential, and positivity their lives will reach—if they can just get through their teen years" ("What Is the It Gets Better Project?"). It Gets Better provides a place where GLBT youth, adults, and straight allies can come together to share their stories without judgment and find support from other members, showing that the Internet can be a place where healthy groups can be created. "It's a double-edged sword when it comes to subcultures," says Pascoe. "For better or for worse, kids who are marginalized can find community online " (p. 2).

Questions to Ponder

1. Do you think the pros of online social groups outweigh the cons? Why or why not?

2. What online social groups have you or do you participate in and why?

with unethical goals. By contrast, healthy groups have goals that benefit the members and the larger society. Fulfilling these goals may require sacrifice and hard work, but accomplishing them does not depend on any illegal or unethical behavior.

Healthy Groups Are Interdependent

interdependent group

a group in which members rely on each other's skills and knowledge to accomplish the group goals

In **interdependent groups**, members rely on each other's skills and knowledge to accomplish the ultimate group goal(s). One concrete way to understand interdependence is to observe a musical group, for instance, a symphony orchestra. One reason the music we hear is so beautiful has to do with the fact that the violins, violas, cellos, and basses not only sound different but each perform a different part made up of different notes. If any of the musicians did not perform their part well, the beautiful sound would be compromised. Likewise, in any group, if one person tries to do all the "work," or if anyone performs their work poorly, or if everyone does the same piece of "work" while other pieces are left unattended, that group is not interdependent and also not as effective as it could be.

HANK MORGAN/Getty Images

Most clubs follow a set of norms to keep meetings on track. What norms might this group follow and why?

Healthy Groups Are Cohesive

Cohesiveness is the force that brings group members closer together (Eisenberg, 2007). In a highly cohesive group, members genuinely respect each other and work cooperatively to reach the group's goals (Evans & Dion, 1991). Because cohesiveness is such an important characteristic of healthy groups, many newly formed groups often engage in **team-building activities** designed to build rapport and develop trust among members (Midura & Glover, 2005). Research suggests that five factors help foster cohesiveness in groups (Balgopal, Ephross, & Vassil, 1986; Widmer & Williams, 1991; Wilson, 2005). First, members are attracted to its purpose. Daniel, for example, joined the local Lions Club because he was attracted to its community service mission. Second, groups are generally more cohesive when membership is voluntary. If Daniel had joined the Lions Club because he felt obligated to do so, cohesiveness would have suffered. Third, members feel safe expressing themselves even when they disagree with others. Fourth, members support, encourage, and provide positive feedback to each other. Finally, members perceive the group to be achieving its goals and celebrate their accomplishments. For example, when the local chapter of the Lions Club surpassed its previous fundraising record for the annual Journey for Sight 5K Community Run, the group celebrated the accomplishment with a picnic in the park.

cohesiveness

the force that brings group members closer together

team-building activities

activities designed to build rapport and develop trust among members

CONSIDER *THIS*....

Did your family have formal ground rules about going out on school nights or curfews?

Healthy Groups Develop and Abide by Productive Norms

Norms are expectations about the way group members are to behave. Healthy groups develop norms that help them achieve their goals (Shimanoff, 1992) and foster cohesiveness (Shaw, 1981). Norms can be developed through formal discussions or informal group processes (Johnson & Johnson, 2003, p. 27). Some groups choose to formulate explicit **ground rules**, prescribed behaviors designed to help the group meet its goals and conduct its conversations. These may include sticking to the agenda, refraining from interrupting others, making brief comments rather than lengthy monologues, expecting everyone to participate, focusing on issues rather than personalities, and sharing decision making.

norms

expectations for the way group members are to behave while in the group

ground rules

prescribed behaviors designed to help the group meet its goals and conduct its conversations

In most groups, however, norms evolve informally. When we join a new group, we act in ways that were considered appropriate in the groups we participated in previously. When members of our new group respond positively to our actions, an informal norm is established. For example, suppose Daniel and two others show up late for a Lions Club meeting. If the latecomers are greeted with disapproving glares, then Daniel and the others will learn that this group has an on-time norm. A group may never actually discuss informal norms, but members understand what they are, behave in line with them, and educate new members about them.

We sometimes find ourselves struggling to act appropriately in different groups because each seems to have different norms. This can be especially true for people who move from one country to another, as was the case for Dr. Mina Tsay, an assistant professor at Boston University who emigrated from Taiwan to the United States and maintains strong ties with groups in both countries. Her story is detailed in this chapter's *Diverse Voices* feature.

DIVERSE VOICES

Managing Competing Group Norms

by Mina Tsay, Ph.D.

Assistant Professor of Communication
Boston University

Although I emigrated from Taiwan to the United States when I was only two years old, my memories are still surprisingly vivid. What I remember most is clinging to my mother as we faced our first blustery winter in Boston, Massachusetts. As a naturalized Chinese American growing up in Boston, I faced numerous challenges in managing competing group norms. I can probably best illustrate these challenges by focusing on my experiences (a) speaking Chinese at home and English at school, (b) attending both American and Chinese schools while growing up, (c) traveling to Taiwan to visit my extended family, and (d) engaging in rich interactions with Chinese international students at college.

The first conflicting norm I remember struggling with was whether to speak English or Mandarin, which is my native language and the most common Chinese dialect. I always spoke Mandarin at home but was expected to speak English at school. My parents made it very clear that they did not

want me to forget how to speak Mandarin. In fact, this norm was so important to them that they enrolled my sister and me in a Chinese school in a Boston suburb when I was in third grade.

I must admit I did not fully appreciate the workload at Chinese school during my early years. But, I developed several close friendships and gradually came to enjoy learning calligraphy, diabolo, literature, and dance. Being involved in these activities exposed me to Chinese art, culture, traditions, and rituals. Learning these customs was exceptionally rewarding, but being enrolled in both schools made it difficult for me to shift from the norms of one school setting to those of another, primarily in terms of linguistic expectations, standards of discipline, and social values. I often felt conflicted. In Chinese school, I became grounded in and celebrated my cultural roots. Then, when I went to American school, I found myself compromising some of my Chinese cultural norms to be accepted by my peers.

At home and at Chinese school, I adhered to norms focused on discipline, a strong work ethic, and respect for elders. At American school, I had to adjust my norms in ways that seemed to conflict with those of my cultural heritage in order to fully engage in activities and to "fit in" with my American friends there.

Adjusting to competing norms at Chinese and American schools here in the United States was demanding, but I also faced this challenge when I traveled to Taiwan to visit relatives. In Taiwan, I would often sense a strong pull to adhere to norms in the other direction. On one hand, it was comforting to know that my extended family held similar politeness, spiritual, and collectivist norms. On the other hand, my relatives would sometimes say that I was acting more American than Chinese. At times like these, I again felt the struggle of trying to adhere to competing norms.

Back in the United States as a college student at the University of Michigan and then at Pennsylvania State University, I also recall feeling torn between competing norms when Chinese international students would make remarks that I had become "Westernized." Those

comments made me feel apprehensive about whether I was losing aspects of my cultural identity. Such realizations encouraged me to seek ways to consciously integrate the norms of two worlds in order to maintain my unique sense of self. As a result, I have negotiated standards and customs to both preserve my own Chinese norms and assimilate to American norms with regard to independence, discipline, religion, group identification, and life goals.

As a Chinese American, I continue to negotiate between competing norms, trying my best to integrate norms of both cultural worlds. When I meet new people and encounter new situations, I consciously try to adapt my behavioral norms in order to "fit in." Although these cultural negotiations are challenges, I choose to view them as opportunities to develop and cultivate a more refined sense of self. After all, I am a Chinese American, which means I honor and value both sets of norms, those grounded in my Chinese roots and those I have acquired as an American naturalized citizen.

Used with permission.

Healthy Groups Are Accountable

Accountability means all group members are held responsible for adhering to the group norms and working toward the group's goal. This means a group will sanction a member who violates a group norm. The severity of the sanction depends on the importance of the norm, the extent of the violation, and the status of the person who violated it. Violating a norm that is central to a group's performance or cohesiveness will generally receive a harsher sanction than violating a norm that is less central. Violations by a newcomer also generally receive more lenient sanctions. As a new Lions Club member, for example, Daniel's sanction for arriving late was merely a stern look from the others. Group members who have achieved higher status in the group also tend to receive more lenient sanctions or even escape sanctioning altogether.

accountability

group members being held responsible for adhering to the group norms and working toward the group's goal

THE AUDIENCE *BEYOND*

Elisia was troubled about the way her colleagues used the company listserv to banter about non-work-related issues. Sorting through the messages was hurting her productivity. So, she suggested changing the norm by creating another listserv for those kinds of discussions.

When underdog teams win championships, it is often because the combined efforts of individual players resulted in synergy. Have you ever been on an underdog team that went on to win a big game or championship? Do you think synergy played a role? Why or why not?

Being accountable can also mean changing counterproductive norms. For example, suppose a few folks tell jokes, stories, and generally ignore attempts by others to begin more serious discussion about community service issues at the Lions Club meetings. If the group does not effectively sanction this behavior, then it could become a counterproductive group norm. As a result, work toward the group's goals could be delayed, set aside, or perhaps even forgotten. If counterproductive behavior continues for several meetings and becomes a norm, it will be very difficult (though not impossible) to change.

What can a group member do to try to change a norm? You can help your group change a counterproductive norm by (1) observing the norm and its outcome, (2) describing the results of the norm to the group, and (3) soliciting opinions of other members of the group (Renz & Greg, 2000, p. 52). For instance, Daniel observed that every Lions Club meeting began 15–20 minutes late and that this was making it necessary to schedule additional meetings. When members became frustrated about holding extra meetings, he could bring up his observations and the consequences and ask the group for their reaction.

Healthy Groups Are Synergetic

synergy

the multiplying force of a group working together that results in a combined effort greater than any of the parts

The old saying "two heads are better than one" captures an important characteristic of healthy groups. **Synergy** is the multiplying force of a group of individuals working together that results in a combined effort greater than any of the parts (Henman, 2003). For instance, the sports record books are filled with "no-name teams" that have won major championships over opponents with more talented players. A healthy group can develop a collective intelligence and a dynamic energy that translate into an outcome that exceeds what even a highly talented individual could produce. When a group has ethical goals and is interdependent, cohesive, and held accountable to productive norms, the group is well on its way toward achieving synergy.

Stages of Group Development

Just as interpersonal relationships go through identifiable life cycles, so too do groups move through overlapping stages of development. Although numerous models have been proposed to describe these stages, psychologist, Bruce Tuckman's (1965) model has been widely accepted because it identifies central issues facing a group at each stage. In this section, we describe each of these stages and the nature of communication during each one.

Forming

Forming is the initial stage of group development, and is characterized by orientation, testing, and dependence. Members try to understand precisely what the goal is, what role they will play in reaching the goal, and what the other group members are like. As the goal becomes clearer, members assess how their skills, talents, and abilities might be used in accomplishing it. Group interactions are typically polite and tentative as members become acquainted with each other and find their place in the group. Any real disagreements between people often remain unacknowledged during this stage because members want to be perceived as flexible and likable. During the forming stage, you should communicate a positive attitude; refrain from making abrasive or disagreeable comments; self-disclose appropriately benign information and feelings; and demonstrate open-minded and genuine interest in others (Anderson, 1988).

Why is storming an important stage of group development?

forming

the initial stage of group development characterized by orientation, testing, and dependence

Storming

As members figure out the goal and become comfortable with each other, they begin to express their honest opinions and vie for power and position. This signals the beginning of the second stage. The **storming** stage is characterized by conflict and power plays as members seek to have their ideas accepted and to find their place within the group's power structure. Constructive disagreements help the group clarify its goal and the resolution of power plays clarifies the group structure. During this storming stage, the politeness exhibited during forming may be replaced by pointedly aggressive exchanges between some members. While storming, members may also take sides and form coalitions. Although storming occurs in all groups, some groups manage it better than others. When storming is severe, it can threaten the group's survival. However, if a group does not storm, it may experience **groupthink**, a deterioration of mental efficiency, reality testing, and moral judgment that results from in-group pressure to conform (Janis, 1982, p. 9). To avoid groupthink, communicate in ways that encourages constructive disagreement, avoid name-calling and inflammatory language, and use active listening skills with an emphasis on paraphrasing and honest questioning (Anderson, 1988).

storming

the stage of group development characterized by conflict and power plays as members seek to have their ideas accepted and to find their place within the group's power structure

groupthink

a deterioration of mental efficiency, reality testing, and moral judgment that results from in-group pressure to conform

Norming

Norming is characterized by increased cohesion, collaboration, emerging trust among members, and motivation to achieve the group goal. Having expressed honest opinions, resolved major differences, and sorted out specific roles, members become loyal to each other and to the group goal. During this stage, members come to appreciate their differences, strengthen their relationships, and freely

norming

the stage of group development during which the group solidifies its rules for behavior, resulting in greater trust and motivation to achieve the group goal

express their ideas and opinions. Members accept the norms established by the group and provide positive and constructive feedback to each other.

Performing

performing

the stage of group development when the skills, knowledge, and abilities of all members are combined to overcome obstacles and meet goals successfully

Performing is characterized by harmony, productivity, problem solving, and shared leadership. During this stage, the group capitalizes on the skills, knowledge, and abilities of all members to work toward achieving its goal; conversations are focused on sharing task-related information and problem-solving. Groups cannot achieve their full potential in this stage unless they have successfully resolved storming conflicts and developed productive norms.

Adjourning and Transforming

adjourning

the stage of group development in which members assign meaning to what they have done and determine how to end or maintain interpersonal relations they have developed

transforming

occurs when a group continues to exist with a new goal

Adjourning is characterized by celebrating goal accomplishment and disengagement. The group usually engages in some type of formal or informal celebration during which they recognize their accomplishment and the role each member played. They may rehash parts of their work and try to capture what they learned about group process or their own behavior. Finally, group members will begin to disengage from their relationships with each other. Sometimes the group will formally disband but a few members will continue to interact interpersonally with one another. Other times, rather than adjourn and disband, the group will engage in **transforming** and continue to exist with a new goal. The new goal will inevitably cause the members to revisit the earlier stages of group development, but the cohesion, trust, and norms developed earlier are likely to help the group move quickly and more smoothly through them.

> **CONSIDER *THIS*....**
>
> Think about a group you recently joined. What stage is the group in and why do you think so?

Conflict in Groups

Just as conflict is inevitable in interpersonal relationships, so is it to be expected in group interactions (Kraus, 1997). As we discussed earlier, groups that experience no conflict are likely to engage in groupthink. Groups that experience conflict but fail to manage it effectively are likely to stall out and never achieve their goal (Nussbaum, Singer, Rosas, Castillo, Flies, Lara, & Sommers, 1999). The key is to manage conflict effectively. Conflict can be directed toward other members (interpersonal conflict) or ideas (issues) or both (Li & Hambrick, 2005; Wilmot & Hocker, 2007). Let's look at three types of conflict that will inevitably occur during group interactions and reveal some communication strategies you can employ to manage the disagreements effectively.

Pseudo-Conflict

pseudo-conflict

occurs when group members who actually agree about something believe they disagree due to poor communication

Pseudo-conflict occurs when group members who actually agree about something believe they disagree due to poor communication. Since *pseudo* means *fake*, the perceived conflict is essentially a misperception. So, to manage or resolve pseudo-conflict, employ the effective listening, perception-checking, and paraphrasing skills we discussed in Chapters 6, 7, and 8. Doing so will reveal misinterpretations and result in a moment of revelation that you are actually on the same page after all.

Issue-Related Group Conflict

Issue-related group conflict occurs when two or more group members' goals, ideas, or opinions about the topic are incompatible. One major advantage of collaboration is the synergy that occurs as a result of expressing diverse points of view. So issue-related conflict is actually a good thing when handled appropriately. To manage issue-related conflict effectively, begin by clarifying your position and the position of the other group member using perception-checking and paraphrasing skills. Then, as we discussed in Chapter 8, express your position using assertive communication supported with facts rather than opinions or feelings. Finally, make the conflict a group discussion by asking others for input regarding it, and if possible, postpone making a final decision until a later date. Doing so provides time for doing additional research to make an informed decision and for tensions among members to lessen.

issue-related group conflict

occurs when two or more group members' goals, ideas, or opinions about the topic are incompatible

Personality-Related Group Conflict

Personality-related group conflict occurs when two or more group members become defensive because they feel like they are being attacked. Typically, personality-related conflicts are rooted in a power struggle (Sell, Lovaglia, Mannix, Samuelson, & Wilson, 2004).

Personality-related conflicts sometimes emerge from poorly managed issue-related conflict. For example, Jack thought the group should do something fun to celebrate the end of finals. Jill thought they should do a service project to give something back to the community before everyone headed home for the summer. What began as an issue-related conflict turned sour as Jill exclaimed, "Jack, all you ever think about is yourself. You are so cold-blooded and self-centered!" and Jack retorted with, "You are such a square, Jill. You don't even know HOW to have fun. That's why you end up sitting alone in your room so much!" Factions emerged and, ultimately, some group members sided with Jill and others with Jack. The group ended up doing nothing to mark the successful completion of the semester. Had the group handled the issue-related conflict effectively, they could probably have done both. Instead, they did neither and departed feeling frustrated and dissatisfied.

To manage personality-related conflict effectively, try to turn the conflict into an issue-related problem to be solved rather than a conflict someone has to win and someone has to lose. Develop rules that allow for differences of opinion. Be descriptive rather than evaluative. Use "I" language and perception-checking. Finally, if the conflict isn't central to the group's goal, agree to disagree and move on.

personality-related group conflict

occurs when two or more group members become defensive because they feel like they are being attacked

Culture and Conflict

As we discussed in Chapter 3, as well as throughout this book, people belonging to different cultural and co-cultural groups tend to abide by unique communication norms. Keep in mind that cultural differences may exist when managing conflict in groups, as well. For instance, people who identify with individualistic cultural norms tend to use direct verbal methods to manage conflict whereas those who identify with collectivist norms tend to use indirect nonverbal methods for doing so (Ting-Toomey & Oetzel, 2003). Knowing that

WHAT WOULD YOU DO?

A Question of Ethics

The community service and outreach committee of Students in Communication was meeting to determine what cause should benefit from their annual fund-raiser, a talent contest.

"So," said Mark, "does anyone have any ideas about whose cause we should sponsor?"

"Well," replied Glenna, "I think we should give it to a group that's doing literacy work."

"Sounds good to me," replied Mark.

"My aunt works at the Boardman Center as the literacy coordinator, so why don't we just adopt them?" asked Glenna.

"Gee, I don't know much about the group," said Reed.

"Come on, you know, they help people learn how to read," replied Glenna sarcastically.

"Well, I was kind of hoping we'd take a look at sponsoring the local teen runaway center," offered Angelo.

"Listen, if your aunt works at the Boardman Center," commented Leticia, "let's go with it."

"Right," said Pablo, "that's good enough for me."

"Yeah," replied Heather, "let's do it and get out of here."

"I hear what you're saying, Heather," Mark responded, "I've got plenty of other stuff to do."

"No disrespect meant to Glenna, but wasn't the Boardman Center in the news because of questionable use of funds?" countered Angelo. "Do we really know enough about them?"

"OK," said Mark, "enough discussion. I've got to get to class. All in favor of the literacy program at the Boardman Center indicate by saying aye. I think we've got a majority. Sorry, Angelo—you can't win them all."

"I wish all meetings went this smoothly," Heather said to Glenna as they left the room. "I mean, that was really a good meeting."

1. What did the group really know about the Boardman Center? Is it good group discussion practice to rely on a passing comment of one member?

2. Regardless of whether the meeting went smoothly, is there any ethical problem with this process? Explain.

cultural differences may exist can help you select communication strategies for managing group conflict effectively and for interpreting the messages of others accurately, as well.

Virtual Groups and Conflict

Managing conflict effectively in virtual groups poses an additional set of challenges because it can be more difficult to catch the subtle meanings of group members' messages. This is due, in part, to the fact that most technology channels reduce our ability to send and receive nonverbal messages, particularly emotional and relational cues. Most of us use emoticons and acronyms to represent missing nonverbal cues, however, a smiley face can be offered sincerely or sarcastically and it can be difficult for the receiver to ascertain the difference. Unfortunately, conflict goes unresolved more often in virtual groups than in face-to-face groups because in most virtual settings we cannot see the nonverbal reactions of frustration that are visible when interacting in person (Bordia, DiFonzo, & Chang, 1999). However, when communication is effective, the bonds among members of virtual groups can be even stronger than those in face-to-face ones (Jiang, Bazarova, & Hancock, 2011; Wang, Walther, & Hancock, 2009).

So, to manage potential conflict effectively in virtual groups, work to overcome its limitations by making a conscious effort to communicate both what you *think* and how you *feel* about a topic. You can do so most clearly in your verbal messages although emoticons and acronyms can also help when used deliberately for such purposes.

Summary

A group is more than a mere assembly of people. A group is a collection of three or more people who share a common purpose or goal. We all interact in many different types of groups including families, social friendship groups, support groups, interest groups, service groups, and work group teams. We may participate in any of these groups in person or virtually through the use of a variety of electronic technologies.

Although some groups form around purposes that have negative consequences, we focus on the characteristics of healthy groups—groups that are formed around a constructive purpose. These characteristics are ethical goals, interdependence, cohesiveness, productive norms, accountability, and synergy.

Just as interpersonal relationships move through life cycles, so do groups move through stages of development. These stages are forming, storming, norming, performing, and adjourning or transforming.

Finally, constructive conflict is necessary in effective groups. In fact, groups that arrive at decisions without engaging in constructive conflict risk engaging in groupthink. Several guidelines can help you manage conflict regarding misperceptions, issues, and personalities effectively. You can also manage conflict effectively by following some additional guidelines when communicating in virtual groups.

COMMUNICATE!

RESOURCE AND ASSESSMENT CENTER

Now that you have read Chapter 9, go to the Speech Communication Course-Mate at cengagebrain.com where you'll find an interactive eBook and interactive learning tools including quizzes, flashcards, sample speech videos, audio study tools, skill-building activities, action step activities, and more. Student Workbook, Speech Builder Express 3.0, and Speech Studio 2.0 are also available.

Applying What You've Learned

Impromptu Speech Activity

1. Identify a group you enjoy being a part of. Prepare and present a 2- to 3-minute speech describing the group and why you enjoy being part of it based on the characteristics of healthy groups discussed in this chapter.

Assessment Activities

1. Group Membership Identify two groups (for example, a sports team, study group, community group, or work group team) to which you belong; one should have a homogeneous membership and the other a heterogeneous membership.

Analyze the demographic differences in each group. When you have completed this analysis, write a paragraph that discusses cohesiveness in each group. How cohesive is each group? Are both groups equally cohesive? Was it easier to establish cohesiveness in one of the groups? What real or potential pitfalls result from the level of cohesiveness in each group? Prepare a short 400- to 500-word essay explaining what you discovered.

2. Group Formation and Development Think of a group to which you have belonged for less than three months. If you have an assigned group in this course, you may use it. Now, write a 400- to 500-word essay that begins by identifying the stage of development the group is currently in and then describe how this group transitioned through each of the previous stages of group development. What event(s) do you recall as turning points, marking the group's movement from one stage to another? Has the group become stuck in a stage, or has it developed smoothly? What factors contributed to that? What can you do to help this group succeed in the stage it is in and to transition to the next stage?

Skill-Building Activity

1. Classroom Norms Identify 4–5 communication norms for this class. They may be verbal or nonverbal, as well as explicit or implicit. Then on a scale of 1 through 5 (with 5 being "excellent"), rate yourself. For each rating lower than "5," write down a specific strategy you will employ to improve your rating.

2. Nonverbal Cues This activity is designed to help you make conscious decisions about nonverbal cues in face-to-face groups and virtual groups. For each emotion or message listed, identify how you will demonstrate it when communicating with a group in a face-to-face setting and in a virtual setting.

Emotion/Message	Face-To-Face Group	Virtual Group
Agreement		
Disagreement		
Frustration		
Pleasure		
Excitement		
Boredom		
Hurt feelings		

Group Leadership and Problem Solving

What you'll know

- How leadership functions in problem-solving work group teams

- Group member responsibilities when participating in meetings

- The six steps in the systematic problem-solving process

What you'll be able to do

- Practice effective communication when leading or participating in meetings

- Engage in systematic group problem solving

- Communicate group decisions and solutions to others

- Evaluate group effectiveness

Members of the campus chapter of the Public Relations Student Society of America (PRSSA) chatted while Dolores, the chapter president, distributed the agenda. The recession had taken its toll on the chapter's membership, and the original budget was now unrealistic. They would have to cut corners somewhere to make ends meet. When all the members had received a copy of the agenda, Dolores began, "Well, we all know why we're here this evening. We've got to decide what to do to balance our budget. It's not going to be fun, but let's get started." After a few seconds of silence, Dolores asked, "Drew, what have you been thinking?"

"Well, I don't know," Drew replied, "I haven't really given it much thought." (*There were nods of agreement all around the table.*)

"Well," Jeremy said, "I'm not sure I even remember what our projected expenses are."

"But when I sent you the e-mail reminder, I attached a detailed spreadsheet and some questions to think about before this meeting," Dolores replied.

"Oh, is that what that was?" Bethany asked. "I read the part about the meeting, but I guess I didn't get a chance to look at the attachment."

10

Hill Street Studios/Blend Images/Getty Images

Dolores responded, "We've got some tough decisions to make. Do we cut our donations to the food pantry? Do we cut travel support for those planning to attend the annual convention? Do we stop printing our monthly newsletter and just offer the online version? Do we raise our dues? Do we add another fundraising project?"

"Anything you think would be appropriate is OK with me," Dawn said.

"Well, I'm not comfortable making these decisions alone. Let's each of us plan to review the materials I sent and meet again tomorrow night with some ideas, okay?" Dolores suggested. (*There were nods of agreement around the table.*) "Meeting adjourned."

As the group dispersed, Dolores overheard Drew whisper to Dawn, "These meetings sure are a waste of time, aren't they?"

Perhaps you have attended a meeting like this one and felt just as frustrated. When group meetings are ineffective, it is easy to point the finger at the leader. But as was the case with this group, the responsibility for the "waste of time" lies not with one person; instead, it is part of the complex nature of making decisions in groups. Although working in groups can have its disadvantages, it is the preferred approach in business and industry today (Katzenbach & Smith, 2003; O'Hair, O'Rourke, & O'Hair, 2001; Snyder, 2004; Teams, 2004). Business leaders realize that when groups work effectively to solve problems, they generate greater breadth and depth of ideas, promote positive group morale, and increase productivity. You can expect to work in groups many times throughout your professional life (Tullar & Kaiser, 2000). You will also work to make decisions and solve problems in community groups, in service groups, and even in your family.

This chapter focuses on effective leadership and problem solving in groups. We begin by discussing what effective group leadership means and the responsibilities of every group member in achieving it. Then we illustrate how shared leadership and effective communication plays out before, during, and after group meetings. From there we turn our attention specifically to problem solving and take you through a systematic problem-solving process. Finally, we propose methods for communicating your results with others and evaluating group effectiveness.

Effective Leadership

leadership
a process whereby an individual influences a group of individuals to achieve a common goal

formal leader
a person designated or elected to facilitate the group process

informal emergent leaders
members who help lead the group to achieve different leadership functions

shared leadership functions
the sets of roles that group members perform to facilitate the work of the group and help maintain harmonious relationships between members

Leadership is a process "whereby an individual influences a group of individuals to achieve a common goal" (Northouse, 2007, p. 3). When we think of leadership, we typically think of a person who is in charge (Gardner, 2011). In fact, scholars once thought that leaders were "born"—that some people inherited traits that made them naturally suited to be leaders. This trait theory approach was called "The Great Man Theory of Leadership" (Kippenberger, 2002). Later, scholars believed that different leadership styles were more or less effective based on the goal and situation. These classic theories suggest that *leadership* is enacted by one *person*. Today, however, we understand leadership as a set of communication functions performed by any group member at various times based on each one's unique strengths and expertise (Fairhurst, 2001; Frey & Sunwulf, 2005). So, although a group may have a **formal leader**, a person designated or elected to oversee the group process, a series of **informal emergent leaders**, members who help lead the group to achieve different leadership functions, make for effective leadership in groups.

Shared leadership functions are the sets of roles you and other members perform to facilitate the work of the group and help maintain harmonious relationships among members. A **role** is a specific communication behavior that group members perform to address the needs of the group at a given point in time. When these roles are performed effectively, the group functions smoothly. The three sets of shared leadership functions can be categorized as task, maintenance, and procedural roles.

Task Roles

Task leadership roles help the group acquire, process, or apply information that contributes directly to completing a task or goal.

- Information or opinion givers provide content for the discussion. People who perform this role are well informed on the content of the task and share what they know with the group. Your ability to assume this role depends on your command of high-quality information that the group needs in order to complete its task. "Well, the articles I read seem to agree that . . ." and "Based on how my sorority raised money for the Ronald McDonald House, we could . . ." are statements typical of information and opinion givers.

- Information or opinion seekers probe others for their ideas and opinions during group meetings. Typical comments by those performing this role include "Before going further, what information do we have about how raising fees is likely to affect membership?" or "How do other members of the group feel about this idea?"

- Information or opinion analyzers help the group to scrutinize the content and the reasoning of discussions. They may question what is being said and help members understand the hidden assumptions in their statements. Information or opinion analyzers make statements such as "Enrique, you seem to be generalizing from only one instance. Can you give us some others?"

Maintenance Roles

Maintenance leadership roles are the sets of behaviors that help the group to develop and maintain cohesion, commitment, and positive working relationships.

- Supporters encourage others. When someone contributes an idea or opinion, supporters may smile, nod, or vigorously shake their heads. They might also say things like "Good point, Ming," "I really like that idea, Paolo," or "It's obvious you've really done your homework, Janelle."

- Interpreters use their knowledge about the different social, cultural, and gender orientations of group members to help group members understand each other (Jensen & Chilberg, 1991). For example, an interpreter might say, "Paul, Lin Chou is Chinese, so when she says that she will think about your plan she might mean that she does not support your ideas, but she doesn't want to embarrass you in front of the others." When groups do not have a member to serve in the interpreter leadership role and members come from different cultures, effective group process can suffer. This was the case for Lily Herakova when she came to the United States from Bulgaria to study. You can read Lily's story in the *Diverse Voices* feature in this chapter.

- Harmonizers intervene when conflict is threatening to harm group cohesiveness or a relationship between specific group members. Harmonizers are likely to make statements such as "Tom, Jack, hold

role

a specific communication behavior that group members perform

task leadership roles

sets of behaviors that help a group acquire, process, or apply information that contributes directly to completing a task or goal

maintenance leadership roles

sets of behaviors that help a group develop and maintain cohesion, commitment, and positive working relationships

CONSIDER THIS....

Which task roles do you believe yourself to be good at and not-so-good at? Why?

Some members provide information to the group, others help maintain harmonious relations among the group members, and still others help the group stay on track. When you are part of a problem-solving group, which roles do you usually assume?

Nita Winter Photography

it a second. I know you're on opposite sides of this, but let's see where you might have some agreement" or "Cool it, everybody, we're coming up with some good stuff; let's not lose our momentum by name-calling."

- Mediators are impartial arbiters who guide the discussion to help find a mutually acceptable (win–win) resolution. Mediators do this by maintaining their own neutrality, keeping the discussion focused on issues and not personalities, helping to identify areas of common ground, and working to find a mutually satisfying solution to the disagreement using paraphrasing and perception checking.

- Tension relievers recognize when group members are stressed or tired and intervene to relieve the stress and reenergize the group usually through humor. We know that humor "facilitates communication, builds relationships, reduces stress, provides perspective, and promotes attending and energizes" (Sultanoff, 1993, para 2). *Fortune* 500 companies such as General Electric, AT&T, Lockheed, and IBM all emphasize the value of workplace humor in their training programs. People who are effective in this leadership role might tell a joke, kid around, or tell a lighthearted story. A single well-placed one-liner can get a laugh, break the tension, and jolt the group out of its lethargy. Although the tension reliever momentarily distracts the group from its task, this action helps the group remain cohesive.

CONSIDER *THIS*....

Which maintenance roles do you believe yourself to be good at and not-so-good-at? Why?

DIVERSE VOICES

The Effects of Cultural Diversity When Problem Solving in Groups

by Lily Herakova

Ph.D. student, University of Massachusetts, Amherst

I'll never forget the day—it must have been early October—the rural Minnesota town where I had arrived from Bulgaria to pursue my dreams of attaining a diverse and challenging education was still holding on to the warm traces of summer. In history class that day, the professor assigned us to work in what he called "problem-solving groups." We were to review each other's papers and offer suggestions for improvement. He said, "Use this not only as an editing exercise, but as a problem-solving activity. I want you to rely on your group partners' responses to move toward solutions of problems you might be having in your papers." Because I was not sure I understood the professor, I asked for clarification. One of my classmates explained that we were to identify problem areas in the papers and make suggestions for improvement to the author. Then, through further discussion with group members, the author was to make sense of the comments and use the ones he or she

agreed with to improve the manuscript. I realize today that the professor's definition of a problem-solving group was pretty loosely defined. We would not be working together as a group to arrive at a solution to one problem. However, we did have to work in groups to solve problems. So, to be most effective, it would be important to engage in shared leadership.

The bright sunshine outside the classroom window carried me away and, in my mind, I was back in my parents' bedroom in Bulgaria. That was where our family computer was and where, consequently, I did a lot of my paper writing and editing. (Nostalgia has a strange way of creeping in to the most mundane activities.) Although I hadn't ever been asked to do so in a class with my peers before, I thought to myself: "I know how to do this. I've done it plenty of times. In fact, it's kind of cool that professors here in the United States allow us time in class to 'problem-solve' and learn from each other." Confident in my understanding, I began reading my classmates' papers. I was going to help "solve problems" and help my group mates improve their papers.

I was fairly confident because back home in Bulgaria my friends and I often reviewed each others' papers and offered suggestions for improvement. Although I had never heard of the concept of "problem solving in groups," it seemed to me I actually had experience in doing so. You see, in Bulgaria computers and printers were scarce and it cost a lot of money to hire someone to type and print your term paper. So my parents agreed to let my friends use our computer to type and print their papers. Because classes in Bulgaria were usually large lectures where we rarely knew our professors, our insecurities about expectations abounded. Our collaborative paper writing was our way of checking perceptions in terms of identifying and defining the goals (e.g., problem) of the assignment, getting information from each other (e.g., analyzing the problem), and developing papers that met the assignment guidelines (e.g., solution). So, we did actually solve problems in groups. It was just something my friends and I did informally as opposed to as an in-class activity.

My friends and I would assemble in my parents' sunny bedroom to help each other prepare papers that met the goal. One of us dictated the draft of her paper while another typed using only her two pointer-fingers. The other group members listened and offered on-the-spot suggestions for revising the essay in ways that more clearly met the goal (at least what we believed it to be) of the assignment. In our informal problem-solving sessions, my Bulgarian classmates and I would offer conflicting opinions, argue, and laugh about our "mistakes." We straightforwardly pointed out when we thought something in the text was wrong, and quietly swallowed our pride as the others made candid comments and offered constructive criticism. For example, members might say, "This sentence doesn't make any sense," "It's grammatically weird," "It's completely missing a verb," or "How is this even relevant?" Responses to this feedback ranged from anger—"I give up! No one seems to get me!"—to much quieter resignation—"Fine, I'll just do it your way. . . ." Most of the time, though, reactions fell somewhere in between. We often dove into long conversations about what someone actually wanted to say and why it wasn't coming through that way on paper.

Though sometimes painful to hear, more often than not, these group sessions helped me. Comments sometimes hurt my pride but often deepened the analysis and always clarified my writing. Ultimately, we all benefitted because we produced papers that usually met and often exceeded the expectations of the instructor.

So, in history class that day in rural Minnesota, I felt I had the proper experience to participate effectively in what he called "problem-solving" groups! I proceeded confidently to read the papers. When I read one of the papers and it was mostly composed of incomplete sentences, I said to the author, "This will make so much more sense if you would write in complete sentences. It's kind of hard to get what you mean when you're missing verbs." In retrospect, I only remember what I said because of the reaction that followed. She immediately raised her hand to call the instructor over to our group and said, "I don't know why you let her respond to our papers. She's not even a native English speaker, and she's telling me I don't know how to write! I want someone else to read my paper." I believed I was acting appropriately in my role as an information analyzer, which was what our instructor expected us to do. My group member, however, was unwilling to listen (regardless of whether I may have been correct) because English was not my first language.

To this day, I don't know for certain if her reaction was due to cultural differences (perhaps ethnocentrism), an inability to accept feedback (especially accepting constructive criticism), or some other issue. Throughout the years, however, this experience has stayed with me as an unresolved confusion—why did my nationality matter in terms of functioning as an analyzer in the group? Did it somehow automatically disqualify me from having a good command of the English language or a good understanding of history? I could have taken her response personally and been hurt by it, but, interestingly, this was not my reaction. Instead, I keep this question in the forefront of my mind when asked to work in a group to solve problems: How can we problem solve together without creating new problems out of our good-natured attempts to "help," especially when cultural diversity might play a role?

Used with permission of author.

A good logistics coordinator leads by providing for the physical needs of the group and its members. Can you think of a group experience you have had in which no one provided this type of leadership?

procedural leadership roles

sets of behaviors that directly support a group process

Procedural Roles

Procedural leadership roles are sets of communication behaviors that provide logistical support, keep the group focused on the task, and record the group's accomplishments and decisions.

- Logistics coordinators arrange for appropriate spaces for group meetings, procure the supplies and equipment needed, and manage other details to meet the group's physical needs. The logistics coordinator's leadership role is usually carried out behind the scenes, but is crucial to a group's success.

- Expediters keep track of the group's objectives and help move the group through the agenda. When the group strays, expediters make statements like "I'm enjoying this, but I can't quite see what it has to do with resolving the issue" or "Let's see, aren't we still trying to find out whether these are the only criteria that we should be considering?"

- Gatekeepers manage the flow of conversation so that all members have an opportunity to participate. If one or two members begin to dominate the conversation, the gatekeeper acknowledges this and invites other group members to participate. Gatekeepers also notice nonverbal signals that indicate that a member wishes to speak. The gatekeeper is the one who sees that Juanita is on the edge of her chair, eager to comment, and says, "We haven't heard from Juanita, and she seems to have something she wants to say."

- Recorders take careful notes of group decisions and the evidence upon which they are based. Recorders usually distribute edited copies of their notes to group members prior to the next meeting. Sometimes these notes are published as minutes, which become a public record of the group's activities.

Shared Leadership Responsibilities

For shared leadership to work, all members must do their part. We propose five key shared leadership responsibilities (see Figure 10.1) that all members must abide by for the group to function effectively.

1. **Be committed to the group goal.** Being committed to the group goal means finding a way to align your expertise with the agreed-upon goal of the group. In addition to demonstrating responsibility, doing so also conveys both integrity and respect. So, for a class project, this might mean working

CONSIDER *THIS....*

Which procedural roles do you believe yourself to be good at and not-so-good at? Why?

 **THE AUDIENCE *BEYOND***

Because their schedules were all so full, Carla, Troy, Molly, and Mike decided to schedule regular virtual meetings via teleconferencing to update each other on progress made and next steps along with a shared "Drop Box" online where they could see each others' documents and drafts.

together on a topic that wasn't your first choice. Once the decision has been agreed upon, however, it is no longer appropriate to dredge up old issues that have already been settled.

2. **Keep discussions on track.** It is every member's responsibility to keep the discussion on track by offering only comments that are relevant and by gently reminding others to stay focused if the discussion starts to get off track. It is unproductive to talk about personal issues during the team's work time. Moreover, it is unethical to try to get the discussion off track because you disagree with what is being said.

3. **Complete individual assignments on time.** One potential advantage of group work is that tasks can be divided among members. However, each member is responsible for completing his or her tasks thoroughly and on time.

4. **Encourage input from all members.** All too often, quiet members are overshadowed by extroverts. Sometimes, outspoken members interpret this silence as having nothing to contribute or not wanting to contribute. If you are an extrovert, you have a special responsibility to refrain from dominating the discussion and to ask others for their opinions. Likewise, if you tend to be an introvert, make a conscious effort to express yourself. You might write down what you want to share or even raise your hand to get the attention of other members in an unobtrusive way.

5. **Manage conflict among members.** As you learned in Chapter 9, all small groups experience some *conflict*—disagreement or clash among ideas, principles, or people. If managed appropriately, conflict can actually be beneficial to the group goal by stimulating thinking, fostering open communication, encouraging diverse opinions, and enlarging members' understanding of the issues (Rahim, 2001). So do your part to manage pseudo-conflict, issue-related conflict, and personality-related conflict effectively when it arises.

Figure 10.1

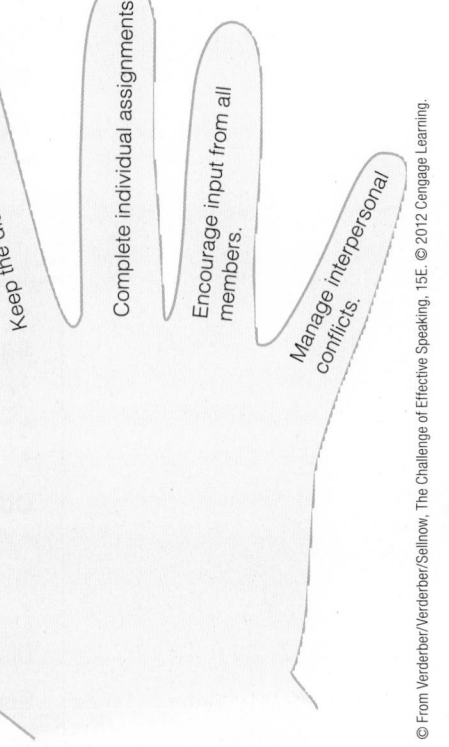

Now that we have a clear understanding of effective leadership in groups, let's turn our attention to one of the most common group communication workplace events—meetings.

Effective Meetings

The disastrous meeting experience in the chapter opener stemmed from poor communication skills by both the meeting facilitator and the participants. In a survey of managers, business consultant Mike Drummond (2004) discovered that over 50 percent of managers spend at least six hours per week in meetings and these same managers feel 50 percent of their meeting time is wasted! To ensure that your meetings are not a waste of time, let's look at several guidelines for meeting leaders and meeting participants.

Guidelines for Meeting Leaders/Conveners

Most of us will be responsible for convening a group meeting at some point in our lives. Whether you are the designated formal leader for a class project, a task force at work, or substituting for your manager at the monthly department meeting, knowing how to effectively plan for, facilitate, and follow up after meetings are useful skills.

Before the meeting

1. **Prepare and distribute an agenda.** An **agenda** is an organized outline of the information and decision items to be covered during a meeting. It is a road map that lets the members know the purpose of the meeting and what they are expected to accomplish as a result of attending. Agenda items should move the group toward its goals. You can identify the items for your agenda by

   • reviewing your notes and the formal minutes of the previous meeting;
   • clarifying what the group decided to accomplish between meetings; and
   • identifying what decisions it expected to make in this next session.

   Then you can structure the agenda into information items and decision items. In other words, you can have members report on their assignments (information items), then make decisions and determine next steps.

   It is critical to distribute the agenda at least 24 hours before the meeting so that members have time to prepare. You can e-mail the agenda, post it to the group's Web page, or hand-deliver it. None of us likes to come to a meeting and be embarrassed because we forgot to complete an assignment or be called on to make decisions about something we have not had time

---

March 1, 2013

To: Campus computer discussion group

From: Janelle Smith

Re: Agenda for discussion group meeting

Meeting Date: March 8, 2013

Place: Student Union, Conference Room A

Time: 3:00 p.m. to 4:30 p.m.

Meeting objectives
• We will familiarize ourselves with each of three courses that have been proposed for Internet-based delivery next semester.
• We will evaluate each course against the criteria we developed last month.
• We will use a consensus decision process to determine which of the three courses to offer.

Agenda for group discussion
• Review and discussion of Philosophy 141 (Report by Justin)
• Review and discussion of Art History 336 (Report by Marique)
• Review and discussion of Communication 235 (Report by Kathryn)

Consensus building discussion and decision
• Which proposals fit the criteria?
• Are there non-criteria-related factors to consider?
• Which proposal is more acceptable to all members?

Discussion of next steps and task assignments

Set date of next meeting

Figure 10.2

Agenda for Internet course committee

© Cengage Learning

to think about. As the meeting leader/convener, you are responsible for providing the information members need to come prepared. Figure 10.2 shows an agenda for a group meeting to decide which one of three courses to offer over the Internet next semester.

2. **Decide who should attend the meeting.** In most cases, all group members will attend meetings. Occasionally, one or more members may not need to attend a particular meeting but merely be informed of the outcomes later.

3. **Manage meeting logistics.** You may choose to enact this role or ask another group member to do so. But even if you delegate, it remains your responsibility to confirm that the meeting arrangements are made and appropriate. If the group is meeting face to face you will want a room that is appropriate for the size and work of the group, and you will want to make sure that any equipment the group needs is available and operational. The room should be set up so that it encourages group interaction. This usually means that members can sit around a table or in a circle with plenty of desk/table space for writing. If the entire group or some group members are attending the meeting from remote locations, you will need to make sure that the technology needed is available and in working order. Because groups become less effective in long meetings, a meeting should last no longer than ninety minutes. For those meetings that require more time, schedule breaks every ninety minutes to avoid fatigue.

4. **Speak with each participant prior to the meeting.** As the leader, you need to understand members' positions and personal goals. Time spent discussing issues in advance allows you to anticipate conflicts that might emerge during the meeting and plan how to manage them effectively if they do.

During the meeting

1. **Review and modify the agenda.** Begin the meeting by reviewing the agenda and modifying it based on members' suggestions. Reviewing the agenda ensures that the group will be working on items that are still relevant and gives members a chance to provide input into what will be discussed.

2. **Monitor member interaction.** If other group members are assuming the task-related, maintenance, and procedural leadership functions, you need do nothing. But when there is a need for a particular role and no one is assuming it, you should do so. For example, if you notice that some people are talking more than their fair share and no one is trying to draw out quieter members, you should assume the gatekeeper role and invite reluctant members to comment. Similarly, if a discussion becomes too heated, you may need to take on the role of harmonizer or tension reliever.

3. **Monitor the time.** Although another group member may serve as expediter, it is ultimately your responsibility to make sure the group stays on schedule.

4. **Praise in public and reprimand in private.** Meetings provide an excellent opportunity to praise individuals or the entire group for jobs well done. Being recognized among one's peers often boosts self-esteem and group morale. Conversely, criticizing individuals or the entire group during a meeting has the opposite effect. The humiliation of public criticism can deflate self-esteem, group morale, and motivation.

5. **Check periodically to see if the group is ready to make a decision.** You should listen carefully for agreement among members and move

© 2002 Ted Goff

"At 10:01, Mr. Holtz fell asleep. At 10:17, Ms. Sommer fell asleep. At 10:31, everyone else fell asleep. Those are the minutes of our last meeting."

the group into its formal decision-making process when the discussion is no longer adding insight.

6. **Implement the group's decision rules.** You are responsible for executing the decision-making rule the group has agreed to use. If the group is deciding by consensus, for example, you must make sure all members feel they can support the chosen alternative. If the group is deciding by majority rule, you call for the vote and tally the results.

7. **Summarize decisions and assignments.** You should summarize what has been and is left to accomplish, as well as assignments tasked to various members.

8. **Set the next meeting.** Clarify when future meetings will take place if necessary.

Following up

1. **Review the meeting outcomes and process.** A good leader learns how to be more effective by reflecting on how well the meeting went. Did the meeting accomplish its goals? Was group cohesion improved or damaged in the process? What will you do differently next time to improve the experience?

2. **Prepare and distribute a meeting summary.** Although some groups have a designated recorder, many groups rely on their leader to do so. If your group has a designated recorder, be sure to review the minutes and compare them to your notes before they are distributed. Summaries are most useful when they are distributed within two or three days of the meeting when everyone's memories are still fresh.

3. **Repair damaged relationships.** If any heated debate occurred during the meeting, some members may have left angry or hurt. You should help repair relationships by seeking out these participants and talking with them. Through empathic listening, you can soothe hurt feelings and spark a recommitment to the group.

4. **Conduct informal progress reports.** When participants have been assigned specific task responsibilities, you should periodically check to see if they have encountered any problems in completing those tasks and how you might help them.

Guidelines for Meeting Participants

Just as there are guidelines for effective conveners/formal leaders to follow before, during, and after meetings, there are also guidelines for meeting participants.

Before the meeting As the chapter opener illustrated, too often people think of group meetings as a "happening" that requires attendance but no preparation. Countless times we have observed people arriving at a meeting unprepared even though they come carrying packets of material they received in advance. Here are some important preparation guidelines for meeting participants.

1. **Study the agenda.** Consider the meeting's purpose and determine what you need to do to be prepared. If you had an assignment, make sure you are ready to report on it.

2. **Study the minutes.** If this is one in a series of meetings, read the minutes and your own notes from the previous meeting. Doing so should provide the basis for what you need to prepare for the next one.

3. **Do your homework.** Read the material distributed prior to the meeting and do what is necessary to be informed about each agenda item. Bring with you any materials that may help the group accomplish its objectives.

4. **List questions.** Make a list of questions related to any agenda items that you would like to have answered during the meeting.

5. **Plan to play a leadership role.** Consider which leadership functions and roles you are best at and decide what you will do to enact them during the meeting.

Some people wait until the last minute to prepare for meetings. Do you find it annoying to attend meetings at which people arrive unprepared to participate?

During the meeting Go into the meeting planning to be a full participant.

1. **Listen attentively.** Concentrate on what others say so you can complement, supplement, or counter what is presented.

2. **Stay focused.** It is easy to get off track during meetings. Keep your comments focused on the specific agenda item under discussion. If others get off the subject, do what you can to get the discussion back on track.

3. **Ask questions.** Honest questions, whose answers you do not already know, help stimulate discussion and build ideas.

4. **Take notes.** Even if someone else is responsible for providing the official minutes, you'll need notes to remember what occurred and any tasks you agreed to take on after the meeting.

5. **Play devil's advocate.** When you think an idea has not been fully discussed or tested, be willing to voice disagreement or encourage further discussion.

6. **Monitor your contributions.** Especially when people are well prepared, they have a tendency to dominate discussion. Make sure that you are neither dominating the discussion nor abdicating your responsibility to share insights and opinions.

Following Up When meetings end, too often people leave and forget about what took place until they arrive at the next meeting. Instead:

1. **Review and summarize your notes.** Do this soon after the meeting while the discussion is still fresh in your mind. Make sure your notes include what you need to do before the next meeting.

2. **Evaluate your effectiveness.** How effective were you in helping the group move toward achieving its goals? Where were you strong? Where were you weak? What should you do next time to improve and how? For example, if you didn't speak up as much as you would have liked to, perhaps you'll decide to write down questions or topics when they come to you and use them as notes to encourage you to speak up next time.

3. **Review decisions.** Make notes about what your role was in making decisions. Did you do all that you could have done? If not, what will you do differently next time, why, and how?

4. **Communicate progress.** Inform others who need to know about information conveyed and decisions made in the meeting.

5. **Complete your tasks.** Make sure you complete all assignments you agreed to take on in the meeting.

6. **Review minutes.** Compare the official meeting minutes to your own notes and report any discrepancies to the member who prepared them.

Sometimes the goal of a workplace meeting is to regroup and refocus as we perform the regular duties assigned to us. Other times, however, we will meet as part of a work group team charged with a specific problem-solving challenge. In these situations, we will be most successful if we work through the problem or issue using a systematic problem-solving process.

Systematic Problem Solving

When a work group team is charged with tackling a problem together, they may use an orderly series of steps or a less-structured spiral pattern in which they refine, accept, reject, modify, combine ideas, and circle back to previous discussion as they go along.

Whether the deliberations are linear or spiral, groups that arrive at high-quality decisions accomplish the six tasks that make up what is known as the Systematic Problem-Solving Process. This process, first described by John Dewey in 1933 and since revised by others, remains a tried and true approach to individual or group problem solving (Duch, Groh, & Allen, 2001; Edens, 2000; Levin, 2001; Weiten, Dunn, & Hammer, 2011).

Step One: Identify and Define the Problem

The first step is to identify the problem and define it in a way that all group members understand and agree with. Even when a group is commissioned by an outside agency that provides a description of the problem, the group still needs to understand precisely what is at issue and needs to be resolved. Many times what appears to be a problem is only a symptom of a problem, and if the group focuses on solutions that eliminate only a symptom, the underlying problem will remain. For example in the opening vignette, the group's budget crisis was described as stemming from a recession-related membership drop. How does the group know that the inability to fund the budget is the problem and not just a symptom of the problem? What if their membership drop has some other cause? If that is the case, then cutting the budget may be a temporary fix but will not solve the problem. One way to see if you have uncovered the root cause or real problem is to ask, "If we solve this problem, are we confident that the consequences of the problem will not reoccur?" In other words: If you cut the budget, are you confident that you won't have to cut it further? If not, then you probably need to look further for the root problem. You will need to look more closely at causes for the drop in membership and other ways besides dues for funding the budget. The real problem may be how to fund the budget.

Once your group agrees about the nature of the root problem, you will want to draft a **problem definition**, which is a formal written statement describing the problem. An effective problem definition is stated as a question of fact, value, or policy; it contains only one central idea; and it uses specific, precise, and concrete language. **Questions of fact** ask the group to determine what is true or to what extent something is true. "What percentage of our projected expenses can be covered with our existing revenue?" is a question of fact. **Questions of value** ask the group to determine or judge whether something

problem definition

a formal written statement describing a problem

question of fact

a question asked to determine what is true or to what extent something is true

question of value

a question asked to determine or judge whether something is right, moral, good, or just

is right, moral, good, or just. Questions of value often contain words such as *good, reliable, effective, or worthy*—for instance, "What is the most effective way to recruit new members?" **Questions of policy** concern what course of action should be taken or what rules should be adopted to solve a problem—for example, "Should we sponsor an annual fund-raising event with the local Public Relations Society of America (PRSA) chapter in order to help fund our budget?" After some discussion, the student chapter decided that the problem they needed to solve was a policy question that could be best stated: "How can we increase our revenues in order to meet our budget in the current economic conditions?"

question of policy

a question asked to determine what course of action should be taken or what rules should be adopted to solve a problem

Step Two: Analyze the Problem

Analysis of a problem entails finding out as much as possible about the problem. Most groups begin this process with each member sharing information he or she already knows about the problem. Then the group needs to determine what additional questions they need to answer and search for additional information to answer them. Members may be assigned to collect and examine information about the problem that is published in materials available at the library and on the Internet. Other members may interview experts, and still others may conduct surveys to gather information from particular target groups. The information gathered by group members should help the group to answer key questions about the nature of the problem such as those listed in Figure 10.3.

The PRSSA chapter, for example, might interview the Dean of Student Affairs to understand how other campus groups increased their revenues and to learn of any campus policies that govern fund-raising by student groups. Some group members might network with other student groups on campus and PRSSA chapters at other schools. Finally, the group could survey former members to understand why they dropped out of the group and what might entice them to rejoin, as well as survey eligible students who are not members to find out what would entice them to join.

During the information gathering and analysis step, it is important to consciously encourage members to share information that is new or contradicts the sentiments or preferences expressed in the group. A group that is willing to consider new and unexpected information will more deeply analyze the problem and, therefore, will likely come to a more effective solution.

* What are the symptoms of this problem?
* What are the causes of this problem?
* Can this problem be subdivided into several smaller problems that each may have individual solutions?
* What have others who have faced this problem done?
* How successful have they been with the solutions they attempted?
* How is our situation similar and different from theirs?
* Does this problem consist of several smaller problems? If so, what are their symptoms, causes, previously tried solutions, and so forth?
* What would be the consequences of doing nothing?
* What would be the consequences of trying something and having it fail?

© Cengage Learning

Figure 10.3

Questions to guide problem analysis

- What are the quantitative and qualitative measures of success that a solution must be able to demonstrate?
- Are there resource constraints that a good solution must meet (costs, time, manpower)?
- Is solution simplicity a factor?
- What risks are unacceptable?
- Is ease of implementation a consideration?
- Is it important that no constituency be unfairly harmed or advantaged by a solution?

© Cengage Learning

Figure 10.4

Questions to guide discussion of solution criteria

Step Three: Determine Criteria for Judging Solutions

criteria

standards or measures used for judging the merits of proposed solutions

Criteria are standards used for judging the merits of proposed solutions. They provide a blueprint for how the group will evaluate the virtues of each alternative solution. Research suggests that when groups develop criteria before they think about specific solutions, they are more likely to come to a decision that all members can accept (Young, Wood, Phillips, & Pedersen, 2007). Without clear criteria, group members may argue for their preferred solution without regard to whether it will adequately address the problem and whether it is feasible. Figure 10.4 provides a list of questions that can help a group think about the types of criteria that a solution might need to meet.

Once you've agreed on the list of solution criteria, the group needs to prioritize the list. Although rank ordering the list from most to least important may be unwieldy and counterproductive, it is probably useful to agree which criteria are major (must meet) and which are minor (would like to see).

The PRSSA chapter agreed on three major criteria and one minor criterion. A good plan must comply with the university's policy on fund-raising by student groups. It must cost less than $500 to implement. It must raise at least $4,000. And ideally (minor criterion), it should not require more than 20 hours of work from each member.

Step Four: Identify Alternative Solutions

brainstorming

an uncritical, non-evaluative process of generating possible solutions by being creative, suspending judgment, and combining or adapting ideas

Ending up with a good solution depends on having a wide variety of possible solutions to choose from. So one of the most important activities of problem solving is coming up with solution ideas. Many groups fail at generating solution ideas because they criticize the first ideas expressed; this discourages members from taking the risk to put their ideas out for the group to consider. One way to encourage everyone's ideas is to use the technique of brainstorming. **Brainstorming** is an uncritical, non-evaluative process of generating possible solutions by being creative, suspending judgment, and combining or adapting ideas. When brainstorming, the group agrees to a freewheeling session when members offer ideas without censoring themselves. During this time other members may build on ideas that have been presented, combine two or more ideas, or even offer off-the-wall thoughts. What members may not do is criticize, poke fun at, or in any other way evaluate the ideas. While the group is brainstorming, one member should be recording the ideas, preferably in a manner that allows all members to see them (on a white board, smart board, or projector, for instance).

When members trust each other to abide by the rules, brainstorming is fun and productive and a group can quickly generate 20 or more solution ideas.

The PRSSA chapter brainstormed and came up with these ideas:

- Place an ad on the Communication Department's Web site to recruit members.

- Place an ad on the college Web site to recruit members.

- Ask faculty to allow PRSSA members to do 2-minute "testimonials" in classes as a way of recruiting members.

- Text-message and tweet all the people we know about upcoming PRSSA events.

- Run a monthly raffle at the PRSA meetings. The winning ticket would get 4 hours of work from a PRSSA member.

- Find PRSA chapter members whose businesses would sponsor student scholarships to the national convention.

- Set up a consulting program to provide public relations help to other student groups for a fee.

- Set up a consulting program to provide public relations help to small businesses for a fee.

- Do a virtual newsletter instead of a printed one.

- Double membership dues.

- Cosponsor a golf outing with the local PRSA chapter.

- Raffle off a spring break getaway for six to St. Thomas.

Step Five: Evaluate Solutions and Decide

With a list of potential solutions in hand, the group must then sort through them to find the one or ones that will best solve the problem. To do this, the group needs to compare each alternative to the decision criteria established earlier. If a lot of solutions were generated during brainstorming, the group will probably want to quickly review the list and eliminate those that obviously do not meet the criteria. Then it can concentrate on evaluating the remaining solutions, talking about how well each meets specific criteria and comparing the positive features of each. This discussion may result in only one solution that meets all the criteria, but often there will be more than one viable solution.

Decision making is the process of choosing among alternatives. Sometimes your group will not be responsible for choosing among the remaining alternatives. Instead you will present the results of your work to others who will make the final decision. At other times your group will make the decision. Five methods are commonly used to reach a group decision.

decision making

the process of choosing among alternatives

1. **The expert opinion method.** Once the group has eliminated those alternatives that do not meet the criteria, the group asks the member who has the most expertise to make the final choice. Obviously, this method is quick and useful if one member is much more knowledgeable about the issues or has a greater stake in the implementation of the decision. The PRSSA chapter, for instance, might ask its president to make the final choice.

2. **The average group opinion method.** In this approach, each group member ranks each of the alternatives that meet all the criteria. Their rankings are then averaged, and the alternative receiving the highest average becomes the choice. This method is useful for routine decisions or when a decision

needs to be made quickly. It can also be used as an intermediate straw poll so the group can eliminate low-scoring alternatives before moving to a different process for making the final decision.

3. **The majority rule method.** In this method, the group votes on each alternative, and the one that receives a majority of votes (a minimum of 50 percent + 1) is selected. Although this method is considered democratic, it can create problems. If the majority voting for an alternative is slight, then nearly as many members oppose the choice as support it. If these minority members strongly object to the choice, they may sabotage implementation of the solution either actively or passively.

4. **The unanimous decision method.** In this method, the group must continue deliberation until every member of the group believes that the same solution is the best. As you would expect, it is very difficult to arrive at a truly unanimous decision, and to do so takes a lot of time. When a group reaches unanimity, however, each member is likely to be committed to selling the decision to others and helping to implement it.

5. **The consensus method.** This method is an alternative to the unanimous decision method. In consensus, the group continues deliberation until all members of the group find an acceptable solution, one they can support and are committed to helping implement. Some group members may believe there is a better solution than the one chosen, but all feel they can live with the chosen solution. Arriving at consensus, although easier than reaching unanimity, is still difficult. Although the majority rule method is widely used, the consensus method is a wise investment if the group needs everyone's support to implement the decision successfully.

Sometimes a group will choose only one solution. But frequently a group will decide on a multi-pronged approach that combines two or three of the acceptable solutions. The PRSSA chapter, for instance, reached consensus on a plan to place ads on both the college and department Web sites and to launch a text-message and tweeting campaign 24 hours before their next meeting. They also decided to approach PRSA chapter members and ask them to sponsor student members to the national convention. Finally, they decided to explore the feasibility of setting up a consulting program.

Step Six: Implement the Agreed-Upon Solution and Assess It

Finally, the group may be responsible for implementing the agreed-upon solution or, if the group is presenting the solution to others for implementation, making recommendations for how the solution should be implemented. The group has already considered implementation in terms of selecting a solution, but now must fill in the details. What tasks are required by the solution(s)? Who will carry out these tasks? What is a reasonable time frame for implementation generally and for each of the tasks specifically? Because the agreed-upon solution may or may not prove effective, the group should determine a point at which they will revisit and assess its success. Doing so builds in an opportunity to revise or replace the solution if warranted.

We discussed unique communication challenges when interacting in a virtual group in Chapter 9. The *Pop Comm!* feature in this chapter, "Problem Solving in Cyberspace: *Dungeons & Dragons* and *World of Warcraft*," points to some unique opportunities in virtual group communication, more specifically, in online gaming.

POP
COMM!

Problem Solving in Cyberspace: *Dungeons & Dragons* and *World of Warcraft*

AP Photo/Eckehard Schulz

For some, mention of games like *Dungeons & Dragons* and *World of Warcraft* might conjure up the stereotypical image of a teenage boy typing away at his computer, alone. But role-playing games are actually social interactions that encourage successful group problem solving, incorporating the six steps we discuss in this chapter: identifying and defining the problem, analyzing the problem, developing criteria for evaluation solutions, brainstorming possible solutions, selecting one, and implementing it.

Dungeons & Dragons, the first modern role-playing game of its kind (Williams, Hendricks, & Winkler, 2006), is typically played among a group of friends at a table, without a computer. A Dungeon Master narrates and creates rules for a fantasy story, and people at the table act as the story's characters. Together, the players work to defeat monsters, find treasure, gain experience, and face other challenges. One of the creators of *Dungeons & Dragons*, Gary Gygax, said in a 2006 telephone interview, "The essence of a role-playing game is that it is a group, cooperative experience. There is no winning or losing" (Schiesel, 2008). *Newsweek's* Patrick Enright remembers his own *Dungeons & Dragons* experiences as a boy (Ebeling, 2008):

If you suddenly wanted to attack your traveling companions with a broadsword or a Finger of Death spell, there was nothing stopping you. The amazing thing is how rarely that happened. Unless the neighborhood bully joined in (and almost never did those tanned, skinned-kneed fellas venture into our dank lairs), we all helped each other and together defeated whatever dragon or monster we were battling. Yes, I'll say it:

Dungeons & Dragons taught me everything I need to know about teamwork.

Dungeons & Dragons inspired *World of Warcraft*, a popular MMORPG (massively multiplayer online role-playing game). *World of Warcraft* differs from *Dungeons & Dragons* in that it is played online, and the game, instead of a human Dungeon Master, regulates the story and the rules. To advance in the game, players must still work with others to defeat monsters, find treasure, and gain experience, but they communicate with one another using text or voice chat programs (Newman, 2007).

In a *BusinessWeek* Online article, researcher John Seely Brown and business consultant John Hagel (2009) argue that many aspects of *World of Warcraft* encourage group problem solving and can even be applied as innovative workplace strategies. These aspects include

- Creating opportunities for teams to self-organize around challenging performance targets.

- Providing opportunities to develop tacit knowledge without neglecting the exchange of broader knowledge.

- Encouraging frequent and rigorous performance feedback.

Based on these benefits, some MMORPGs are actually being developed for a range of "real-life" applications. For example, the Bill and Melinda Gates Foundation recently awarded a $3 million grant to the MIT Education Arcade to develop games that help high school students learn math and biology. Professor Eric Klopfer, director of the Education Arcade says, "This genre of games is uniquely suited to teaching the nature of science inquiry because they provide collaborative, self-directed learning situations. Players take on the roles of scientists, engineers and mathematicians to explore and explain a robust virtual world."

But beyond the application to real-life situations, many fans of role-playing find that the complexities of group problem solving make things more interesting and more exciting. In *The Escapist*, an online magazine about video games, Ray Huling (2008) writes of *Dungeons & Dragons*, "Players can mitigate the chaos inherent in a game's dice by agreeing to ignore rolls, but they can also intensify chaos by pissing off (or on!) huge barbarians. The group decides whether encouraging mischief-makers adds to the game." He adds, "Group dynamics produce unforeseen complications, which often maximize fun."

Questions to Ponder

1. Do you think online gaming is a good teaching method? Why or why not?

2. What if any role-playing games do you play and why?

"MIT's Education Arcade uses online gaming to teach science" (2012, Jan 17). [Press release] Retrieved from: http://education.mit.edu/blogs/louisa/2012/pressrelease

Communicating Group Solutions

deliverables

tangible or intangible products of work that must be provided to someone else

Once a group has completed its deliberations, it is usually expected to communicate its results. **Deliverables** are tangible or intangible products of your work that must be provided to someone else. Although some deliverables are objects, typically the deliverables from problem-solving groups are communications of the information gathered, analyses, decisions, and recommendations of the group. These kinds of intangible deliverables can be communicated in written formats, oral formats, or virtual formats.

Written Formats

written brief

a very short document that describes a problem, background, process, decision, and rationale so that a reader can quickly understand and evaluate a group's product

1. **Written brief.** A **written brief** is a very short document that describes the problem, background, process, decision, and rationale so that the reader can quickly understand and evaluate the group's product. Most briefs are one or two pages long. When preparing a brief, begin by describing your group's task. What problem were you attempting to solve and why? Then briefly provide the background information the reader will need to evaluate whether the group has adequately studied the problem. Present solution steps and timelines for implementation as bullet points so that the reader can quickly understand what is being proposed. Close with a sentence or very short paragraph that describes how the recommendation will solve the problem, as well as any potential side effects.

comprehensive report

a written document that provides a detailed review of the problem-solving process used to arrive at a recommendation

2. **Comprehensive report.** A **comprehensive report** is a written document that provides a detailed review of the problem-solving process used to arrive at the recommendation. A comprehensive report is usually organized into sections that parallel the problem-solving process.

executive summary

a one-page synopsis of a comprehensive report

Because comprehensive reports can be very long, they usually include an executive summary. An **executive summary** is a one-page synopsis of the report. This summary contains enough information to acquaint readers with the highlights of the full document without reading it. Usually, it contains a statement of the problem, some background information, a description of any alternatives, and the major conclusions.

oral brief

a summary of a written brief delivered to an audience by a group member

Oral Formats

1. **Oral brief.** An **oral brief** is essentially a summary of a written brief delivered to an audience by a group member. Typically, an oral brief can be delivered in less than 10 minutes.

2. **Oral report.** An **oral report** is similar to a comprehensive report. It provides a more detailed review of a group's problem-solving process. Oral reports can range from 30 to 60 minutes.

3. **Symposium.** A **symposium** is a set of prepared oral reports delivered sequentially by group members before a gathering of people who are interested in the work of the group. A symposium may be organized so that each person's speech focuses on one step of the problem-solving process, or it may be organized so that each speaker covers all of the steps in the problem-solving process as they relate to one of several issues or recommendations that the group worked on or made. In a symposium, the speakers usually sit together at the front of the room. One member acts as moderator, offering the introductory and concluding remarks and providing transitions between speakers. When introduced by the moderator, each speaker may stand and walk to a central spot, usually a lectern. Speakers who use a computerized slideshow should coordinate their slides so that there are seamless transitions between speakers. Symposiums often conclude with a question-and-answer session facilitated by the moderator, who directs one or more of the members to answer based on their expertise. Questions can be directed to individuals or to the group as a whole.

4. **Panel discussion.** A **panel discussion** is a structured problem-solving discussion held by a group in front of an audience. One member serves as moderator, introducing the topic and providing structure by asking a series of planned questions that panelists answer. Their answers and the interaction among them provide the supporting evidence. A well-planned panel discussion seems spontaneous and interactive but requires careful planning and rehearsal to ensure that all relevant information is presented and that all speakers are afforded equal speaking time. After the formal discussion, the audience is often encouraged to question the participants. Perhaps you've seen or heard a panel of experts discuss a topic on a radio or television talk show like *Sports Center* or *The Doctors*.

Virtual Formats

1. **Remote access reports**. A **remote access report (RAR)** is a computer-mediated audiovisual presentation of the group's process and outcome that others can receive through e-mail, Web posting, and so forth. Prepared by one or more members of the group, the RAR is prepared using PowerPoint or some other computer slideshow software and provides a visual overview of the group's process, decisions, and recommendations. Effective RARs typically consist of no more than 15 to 20 slides. Slides are titled and content is presented in outline or bullet-point phrases or key words (rather than complete sentences or paragraphs), as well as through visual representations of important information. For example, a budget task force might have a slide with a pie chart depicting the portions of the proposed budget that are allocated to operating expenses, salaries, fundraising, and travel (see Figure 10.5). RARs may be self-running so that the slides automatically forward after a certain number of seconds, but it is better to let the viewer choose the pace and control when the next slide appears. RARs can be silent or narrated. When narrated, a voice-over accompanies each slide, providing additional or explanatory information.

2. **Streaming videos.** A **streaming video** is a recording that is sent in compressed form over the Internet. You are probably familiar with

---

oral report

a detailed review of a group's problem-solving process delivered to an audience by one or more group members

symposium

a set of prepared oral reports delivered sequentially by group members before a gathering of people who are interested in the work of the group

panel discussion

a structured problem-solving discussion held by a group in front of an audience

remote access report (RAR)

a computer-mediated audiovisual presentation of a group's process and outcome that others can receive electronically

streaming video

a recording that is sent in compressed form over the Internet

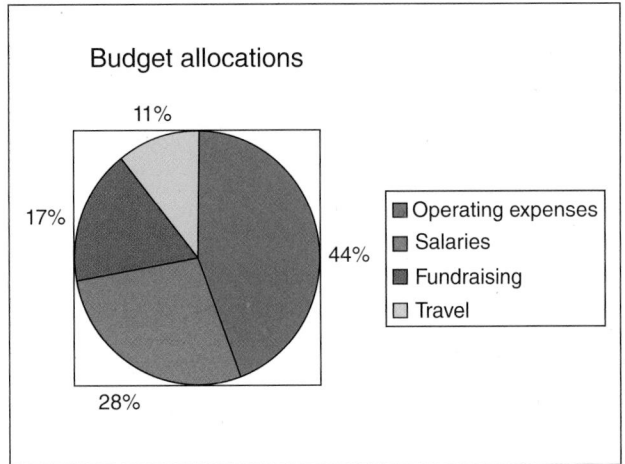

Budget allocations

11%

17%

44%

28%

- Operating expenses
- Salaries
- Fundraising
- Travel

© Cengage Learning

Figure 10.5

Example of a slide in a remote access report

group dynamics

the way a group interacts to achieve its goal

streaming video from popular Web sites such as *YouTube*. Streaming videos are a great way to distribute oral briefs, but they also can be used to distribute recordings of oral reports, symposiums, or panel presentations. Streaming videos are useful when it is inconvenient for some or all the people who need to know the results of the group's work to meet at one time or in one place.

Evaluating Group Effectiveness

As with any communication skill, group communication can improve over time based on practice, reflective assessment, and revision. In this section, we offer some guidelines for evaluating the group communication process and a group presentation.

Group Dynamics

Group dynamics is the way a group interacts to achieve its goal. Effective groups periodically stop and evaluate how their interactions are affecting what they are accomplishing and how members perceive themselves and others. At times you may be asked to provide a formal evaluation of the group dynamics of a class project group or other work team. One way you might evaluate members is to describe how each member performed his or her specific tasks and how well his or her communication contributed to the cohesiveness, problem solving, and conflict resolution processes in the group. Figure 10.6 is one example you can use for evaluating class project group member participation. Alternatively, in a class project group, members could prepare a "reflective thinking process paper," which details in paragraph form

COMMUNICATE ON YOUR FEET

Panel Discussion

The Assignment

Form a small group with 3–5 classmates. As a group, decide on a social issue or problem you would like to study in depth. Then select one group member to serve as moderator and the others as expert panelists. Each member should do research to find out all they can about the issue, why it is a problem, how it affects people and to what degree, as well as potential ideas for solving it. The moderator's role is to come up with 4–6 good questions to ask the panelists. The panelists should prepare notes about the research they discovered.

On the day determined by the instructor, you will engage in a 15-to 20-minute panel discussion in front

Speech Assignment

of your classmates. The moderator will guide the discussion by asking questions of the panelists, as well as asking for questions from the class.

Suggested Format

1. Moderator thanks audience for coming and introduces the panelists and the topic.
2. Moderator asks panelists a series of questions, letting a different panelist respond first each time.
3. Moderator asks follow-up questions when appropriate.
4. Moderator asks for questions from the audience.
5. Moderator thanks the panelists and the audience members for participating.

Group Dynamics Evaluation Form

Meeting date: ——————————————————————

Your name: ———————————————————————

Directions

After each required group meeting, provide ethical critiques for both your group members and yourself. Rate each individual on his or her performance in the group. Justify the rating with specific examples. As you rate each member, consider the following:

- commitment to the group goal
- fulfills individual assignments
- manages interpersonal conflicts
- encourages group participation
- helps keep the discussion on track

Yourself ——————————————————————————

Circle overall individual rating

0   1   2   3   4   5   6   7

(poor)   (met requirements)   (excellent)

Tasks accomplished:

Tasks assigned:

Ethical critique:

Group member ——————————————————————

Circle overall individual rating

0   1   2   3   4   5   6   7

(poor)   (met requirements)   (excellent)

Tasks accomplished:

Tasks assigned:

Ethical critique:

Group member ——————————————————————

Circle overall individual rating

0   1   2   3   4   5   6   7

(poor)   (met requirements)   (excellent)

Tasks accomplished:

Tasks assigned:

Ethical critique:

Group member ——————————————————————

Circle overall individual rating

0   1   2   3   4   5   6   7

(poor)   (met requirements)   (excellent)

Tasks accomplished:

Tasks assigned:

Ethical critique:

Group member ——————————————————————

Figure 10.6

Group dynamics evaluation form

(Continued)

Figure 10.6

(Continued)

Circle overall individual rating

0	1	2	3	4	5	6	7

(poor)   (met requirements)   (excellent)

Tasks accomplished:

Tasks assigned:

Ethical critique:

what each member did well and could improve upon as well as a self-analysis of their own contributions and what they could do to improve.

Like the performance evaluations business managers make of employees, these evaluations serve to document the efforts of group members. They can be submitted to the instructor, just as they would be submitted to a supervisor. In business, these documents provide a basis for determining promotion, merit pay, and salary adjustments. In the classroom, they can provide a basis for determining one portion of each member's grade.

Group Presentations

Effective group presentations depend on quality individual presentations as well as overall group performance. So evaluations of group presentations should consist of both an individual and a group component (see Figure 10.7). And, if you are serious about improving your individual presentation skills, you will also evaluate yourself to discover areas where you can improve (see Figure 10.8).

Group Member Name: _____

Critic (your name): _____

Directions: Evaluate the effectiveness of each group member according to each of the following criteria for effective presentations individually and as a group.

Rating Scale:

1	2	3	4	5	6	7

(poor)   **(excellent)**

__INDIVIDUAL PERFORMANCE CRITIQUE__

_____ **Content** (Breadth and depth and listener relevance)

(rating) Critique (Provide a rationale for the rating you gave):

_____ **Structure** (Macrostructure and microstructure/language)

(rating) Critique (Provide a rationale for the rating you gave):

_____ **Delivery** (Use of voice and use of body)

(rating) Critique (Provide a rationale for the rating you gave):

__GROUP PERFORMANCE CRITIQUE__

_____ **Content** (Thematic? Focused? Thorough? Construction of presentational aids?)

(rating) Critique (Provide a rationale for the rating you gave):

_____ **Structure** (Balanced? Transitions? Flow? Attn/Clincher?)

(rating) Critique (Provide a rationale for the rating you gave):

_____ **Delivery** (Teamwork? Cooperation? Fluency? Use of aids?)

(rating) Critique (Provide a rationale for the rating you gave):

Overall Comments:

Figure 10.7

Sample evaluation form for group presentations

Directions: Complete the items below with regard to your presentation in the group symposium.

1. If I could do my portion of the oral presentation over again, I would do the following things differently:
   a.
   b.

2. In terms of content, I did the following things well in my oral presentation:
   a.
   b.

3. In terms of structure, I did the following things well in my oral presentation:
   a.
   b.

4. In terms of delivery, I did the following things well in my oral presentation:
   a.
   b.
   c.

5. In terms of my role as a group member, I am most proud of how I:

6. In terms of my role as a group member, I am least proud of how I:

7. Overall, I would give myself a grade of _____ for the group speech because:

Figure 10.8

Sample self-critique form for group presentations

© From Verderber/Verderber/Sellnow. The Challenge of Effective Speaking, 15E. © 2012 Cengage Learning.

WHAT WOULD YOU DO?

A Question of Ethics

"You know, Sue, we're going to be in deep trouble if the group doesn't support McGowan's resolution about dues reform."

"Well, we'll just have to see to it that all the arguments in favor of that resolution are heard, but in the end it's the group's decision."

"That's very democratic of you, Sue, but you know that if it doesn't pass, you're likely to be out on your tail."

"That may be, Heather, but I don't see what I can do about it."

"You don't want to see. First, right now the group respects you. If you would just apply a little pressure on a couple of the members, you'd get what you want."

"What do you mean?"

"Look, this is a good cause. You've got something on just about every member of the group. Take a couple of members aside and let them know that this is payoff time. I think you'll see that some key folks will see it your way."

1. Should Sue follow Heather's advice? Why or why not?

2. Is it appropriate to use personal influence to affect the outcome of group decisions? Why or why not?

Summary

Many leadership skills are needed to communicate effectively and achieve positive results when participating on a work group team. These shared leadership skills focus on task, maintenance, and procedural roles.

Group meeting leaders and participants must follow several guidelines before, during, and after meetings to be effective.

An effective six-step systematic problem-solving process that consists of identifying and defining the problem, analyzing the problem, developing criteria for evaluating solutions, brainstorming possible solutions, selecting a solution, and implementing it.

Finally, there are several different formats to choose from when sharing solutions with others. These formats can be written, oral, or virtual.

COMMUNICATE!

RESOURCE & ASSESSMENT CENTER

Now that you have read Chapter 10, go to the Speech Communication Course-Mate at cengagebrain.com where you'll find an interactive eBook and interactive learning tools, including quizzes, flashcards, sample speech videos, audio study tools, skill-building activities, action step activities, and more. Student Workbook, Speech Builder Express 3.0, and Speech Studio 2.0 are also available.

Applying What You've Learned

Impromptu Speech Activity

1. Draw a slip of paper from a pile provided by your instructor. The paper will have the name of a famous real-life person (e.g., Snooki from Jersey Shore, Eminem; Jimmy Kimmel, NFL quarterback Tom Brady) or fictional character (e.g., Bugs Bunny, Scooby-Doo, Homer Simpson, Liz Lemon from *30 Rock*, Harry Potter) on it. Prepare a 2- to 3-minute speech about why you think the person would or would not be an effective work group team leader.

Assessment Activity

1. Analyze a situation in which a group to which you belong attempted to solve a problem. Write a paragraph in which you answer the following questions. Did the group use all six of the problem-solving steps listed in this chapter? If not, which steps did the group overlook? Were there any steps the group should have placed more emphasis on? Was the group successful in its efforts to solve the problem? Prepare a 400- to 500-word essay explaining why you think this was or was not the case.

Watch a recent episode of one of the popular CBS Survivor series. Select one tribe and identify the dominant roles that each member of the group seems to play in that episode. Who is vying for informal leadership? How are they trying to gain or maintain their leadership? What do you think will happen to each leader candidate? Write a short 400- to 500-word essay explaining your answers.

Skill-Building Activity

1. Identifying Roles Match the typical comment to the role of which it is most characteristic.

> #### Roles
>
> a. aggressor
>
> b. analyzer
>
> c. expediter
>
> d. gatekeeper
>
> e. harmonizer
>
> f. information or opinion giver
>
> g. information or opinion seeker

    h. interpreter

    i. supporter

    j. tension reliever

Comments

1. "Did anyone discover if we have to recommend only one company?"

2. "I think Rick has an excellent idea."

3. "Stupid idea, Katie. Why don't you stop and think before you open your mouth?"

4. "Kwitabe doesn't necessarily agree with you, but he would consider it rude to openly disagree with someone who is older."

5. "Josiah, in your plan, weren't you assuming that we'd only need two days rest for rehearsal?"

6. "Lisa, I understand your point. What do you think about it, Paul?"

7. "Okay, so we've all agreed that we should begin keeping time logs. Now shouldn't we be thinking about what information needs to be on them?"

8. "Wow, it's getting tense in here. If we don't chill out soon, we're likely to spontaneously combust. And, hello, that'll be a problem because we're the only engine company in this area of town, right?"

9. "Barb, I don't think that your position is really that different from Saul's. Let me see if I can explain how they relate."

10. "I've visited that home before, and I found that both the mom and dad are trying very hard to help their son."

WHAT'S TECHNOLOGY GOT TO DO WITH IT?
Communicating in Virtual Groups

"Boy, was that frustrating," said Jerome as he exhaled loudly.

"What?" queried Alicia from the next cubicle. "What was frustrating?"

"Well, I just read the latest posts from the threaded discussion among procurement managers around the world, and we're no closer to agreeing on an organization-wide procurement policy than we were when we began. So far, I've spent 20 hours posting and reading, and that's time I could have spent negotiating with our local vendors. I don't understand why they don't just fly us all to headquarters, put us in a room together, and let us hash it out until we come to consensus. This process is not working and it's sure costing the company more than a face-to-face meeting would."

Have you ever participated in a threaded online discussion? Perhaps you have done so as part of a course requirement or, like Jerome, as part of a work team. Or have you ever held a three-way telephone conversation with your friends to decide where to go on a Friday night? If so, you have been part of a virtual group. Some types of virtual groups include:

- **computer conferences** (a.k.a. threaded discussions): asynchronous virtual forums in which comments related to an issue are organized by topic and available for all group members to read and comment upon

- **online social networks** (e.g., Facebook, Twitter): Internet sites that focus on building social relationships among people who share interests, activities, and backgrounds

- **teleconferences:** multiperson telephone meetings using telephone conferencing technology

- **video chats (**e.g., Skype, iChat): synchronous informal meetings using personal computer video capabilities

- **videoconferences** (e.g., Adobe Connect, gotomeeting.com): synchronous formal meetings using video conferencing technology provided at various sites

As was discussed in Chapters 9 and 10, we sometimes choose to meet virtually as a way to overcome many time and space constraints inherent in face-to-face meetings. Communicating effectively in virtual groups, however, also poses unique challenges. We provide several recommendations for communicating in virtual groups in ways that capitalize on the benefits and address the challenges.

Virtual groups and virtual group meetings have become popular for a number of reasons. First, members need not be physically present to communicate. Before these technologies, group members had to meet face-to-face to exchange information or make a decision. But today, group members can interact while in different cities, states, and countries. Second, asynchronous virtual groups allow people to participate across time. Busy people often struggle to find a meeting time that works with everyone's schedule. So a group can "meet" and communicate using a threaded discussion instead. Third, virtual meetings can save money. Before these technologies, meeting participants often had to travel to a meeting site. To do so, they might have to pay for travel, accommodations, meals, parking, and even meeting space rental. Because virtual group meetings can be conducted over the phone or Internet, meeting costs can be reduced for both meeting participants and meeting hosts.

These benefits also come with potential costs. For example, research has found that communication problems can impact both task and relationship outcomes (Andre, 2002). Face-to-face groups are often more dedicated to task (Olsen, et al., 1996), and the rich communication environment leads to more effective interactions and results than virtual teams. Face-to-face groups are also better at maintenance functions. They are more cohesive (Huang, et al., 2003), have stronger social ties (Warkentin, et.al., 1997), and are more dedicated to other team members (Olsen, et al., 1996).

Because virtual groups are becoming increasingly popular in both education and industry, improving communication in them can increase work quality and member satisfaction. We offer several guidelines for doing so.

1. **Train members to use the technology**. First and foremost, all members must be skilled in appropriately using the technology. Provide training if needed. Also, don't assume that someone who has used a particular technology before understands all of its capabilities or how it can be used with the current situation. And just because someone has used a similar program (e.g., Skype) doesn't necessarily mean he or she will be able to comfortably use another (e.g., iChat) without training.

netiquette

etiquette rules when communicating over comptuer networks.

2. **Create opportunities for members to become acquainted as the group is forming.** Just as members of face-to-face groups take time to socialize to get to know each other when forming, so must members of virtual groups. For example, many successful virtual groups encourage members to develop and share personal Web pages with pictures, self-descriptions, and places to update what is happening in their lives. To be successful, you may even need to allow more time to form social bonds before turning to task considerations in virtual groups.

3. **Use the richest form of technology available.** While e-mails and threaded discussions allow people the freedom to do group work at their own convenience, these asynchronous technologies also convey the fewest social cues. So whenever possible, use scheduled synchronous audio or video meetings along with text-based technologies.

4. **Develop group ground rules.** Functional norms are crucial for effective group communication in both face-to-face and virtual settings. Set ground rules such as how quickly members should respond to messages, turn-taking, and **netiquette** (etiquette rules when communicating over computer networks). These include being courteous and respectful, using emoticons, keeping messages short, refraining from the use of all capital letters, thinking before posting, being patient with new users, obeying copyright laws, and keeping personal information private (Shoemaker-Galloway, 2007).

5. **Create opportunities to meet outside the virtual environment.** Members of virtual groups can feel closer if they can also have side conversations. One way to accomplish this is to set up an instant messaging system that allows members to contact each other for short "conversations," much like those that can occur when we are physically present in face-to-face settings.

6. **Provide clear structure.** Virtual groups perform better when there is a clear plan guiding their tasks. So the leader should develop a series of threaded discussions that clearly outline the expected outcomes and process.

7. **Create regular opportunities to evaluate the technology and use of it.** Regularly scheduled surveys of virtual group members can identify emerging problems members are experiencing in order to correct them before they undermine the group's work.

Public Speaking

Unlike interpersonal and group communication, which didn't emerge and blossom as areas of study in the communication field until the middle of the twentieth century, the study and practice of public speaking has a long and rich history dating back more than 2000 years to ancient Greek (e.g., Aristotle and Plato) and Roman (e.g., Cicero and Isocrates) philosophers. They were the ones, who coined the terms *rhetoric* and *oratory* to describe the processes of preparing and delivering effective public speeches.

Public speaking was the primary means by which to conduct business, debate public issues, make public decisions, and gain and maintain power. Fundamental to effective public speaking then and now is *audience*. The ancient Greek philosopher, public speaker, and teacher Aristotle is often credited with saying, "The audience is the end and object of the speech." Frankly, whether conveyed in written, oral, or visual form, or some combination of them, a message is only effective if it is understood and internalized by the people being addressed. So understanding our audience and tailoring the message accordingly is key to effective public speaking.

Audiences are motivated to listen to, understand, and believe what we say when we appeal to them using strategies of logos, ethos, and pathos. Appeals to **logos** come from logical arguments supported with evidence and reasoning. Appeals to **ethos** foster a perception of us as competent, credible, and of good character. Appeals to **pathos** motivate audience members to listen and internalize our speeches by tapping into emotions.

These ancient orators also conceptualized the process of speechmaking based on five rhetorical canons. These canons—(1) invention, (2) arrangement, (3) style, (4) delivery, and (5) memory—have also withstood the test of time. The chapters comprising this unit take you through a five-step speech preparation process based on these canons. These speechmaking action steps are:

1: Select a speech goal that is adapted to the rhetorical situation.

2: Gather and evaluate information.

3: Organize ideas into a well-structured outline.

4: Identify, prepare, and use appropriate presentational aids.

5: Practice oral language and delivery style

Chapter 11, "Topic Selection and Development," focuses on the first two action steps, which flesh out what the ancient rhetoricians called the "invention" canon. We discuss strategies for selecting a speech topic and adapting your specific goal to address the needs and expectations of both the audience and occasion. We also focus on how to develop your topic by conducting primary and secondary research, evaluating information and sources, and citing external research in your speeches.

Chapter 12, "Organizing Your Speech," is devoted to the third action step, which is based on the second rhetorical canon, "arrangement." In this chapter, we provide guidelines for organizing your ideas into a well-structured outline that audiences will be able to follow.

Chapter 13, "Presentational Aids," focuses on how to identify, prepare, and use appropriate presentational aids. Effectively prepared and integrated presentational aids address both the fourth (delivery) and fifth (memory) canons. Whereas we once considered presentational aids to merely embellish the verbal message, today we realize they often function in a much more integral way. Thus, effective speakers consider possible presentation aids to help present their content throughout the research and topic development process. We also focus specifically on how to create and integrate your presentational aids effectively in ways that avoid audience tune-out as a result of what is often referred to today as "death by PowerPoint."

In Chapter 14, "Language," we narrow the discussion we provided in Chapter 4 ("Verbal Communication") to focus on specific language guidelines unique to public speaking. Thus, this chapter addresses the "style" canon identified by the ancient rhetoricians. We clarify how oral style differs from written style, as well as how oral public speaking style differs from the more casual style we use in everyday conversations. We also discuss how to convey verbal immediacy in a formal public speaking situation and language strategies that will help your audience pay attention to, understand, and remember your ideas long after the speech is over.

Like Chapter 14, Chapter 15, "Delivery," also focuses on Action Step 5 and the "style" canon. However, we turn our attention here specifically to delivery style. We discuss the symptoms and causes of public speaking apprehension and propose methods for managing it effectively. We also discuss how to be both conversational and animated in your speech delivery. Finally, we discuss how to rehearse your speech strategically to ensure successful delivery.

Chapters 16 and 17 focus respectively on informative and persuasive speeches, two of the most common speech types used today. Chapter 16, "Informative Speaking," focuses on the characteristics and methods of informing, as well as the major elements in process speeches and expository speeches. Chapter 17, "Persuasive Speaking," hones in on the challenges of effective persuasive speaking, how to phrase your speech goal as a proposition, and the heightened role of logos, ethos, and pathos in such messages. The chapter closes with an explanation of different persuasive speech patterns you can use to arrange your ideas when attempting to convince audiences to agree with your proposition or to incite them to act.

If you read these chapters thoughtfully and apply the concepts and guidelines offered in them diligently as you prepare, practice, and present your public speeches, you will be a successful public speaker. Not only that, you will discover that effective public speaking skills will catapult you into leadership roles in both your personal and professional life.

Topic Selection and Development

- How to identify an appropriate speech topic
- How to adapt your speech to meet the needs and expectations of your audience
- Three different types of sources you can draw from to develop your speech
- How to locate, evaluate, and cite sources

- Select an appropriate speech topic and goal based on audience analysis
- Collect audience demographic and subject-related data
- Write an effective specific speech goal statement
- Conduct secondary and primary research
- Record information and sources effectively
- Correctly cite sources orally during your speech

Donna is a marine biologist. She knows her audience wants to hear her talk about marine biology, but she doesn't know what aspect of the topic she should focus on.

Romeo has been invited to speak to a student assembly at the inner-city middle school he attended years ago. He really wants the students to understand what they need to do *now* to have a shot at going to college *later*. He wonders how to make sure they realize how relevant the topic is for them today.

Alyssa, who is taking a public speaking class, is scheduled to give a speech in two weeks. She volunteers regularly at the local homeless shelter and wants to focus on the value of doing community service as college students. She doesn't have the foggiest idea where to find good information beyond her own personal experiences and opinions.

P11

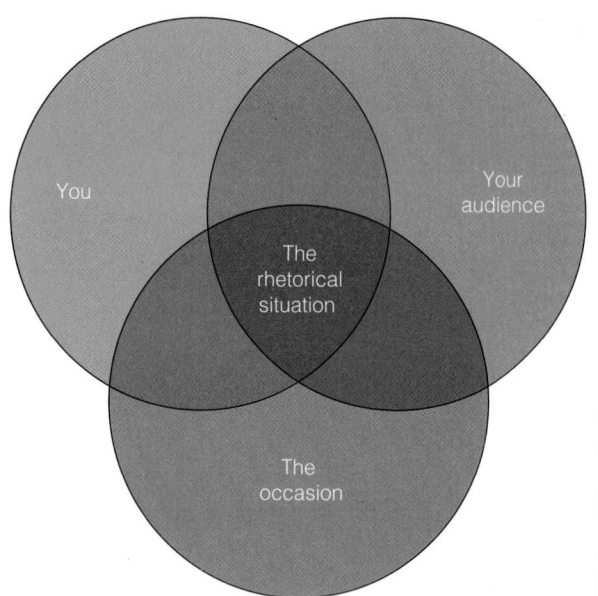

© Challenge of Effective Speaking

Figure 11.1

The rhetorical situation

Do any of these situations sound familiar? Do you identify with Alyssa? You may be taking this course as part of a graduation requirement and the thought of giving a speech can be overwhelming. However, developing effective public speaking skills is empowering. Effective speakers can influence the thinking of others and effective public speaking skills are essential to advancing your career. Whether giving a "job talk" speech during an interview, presenting oral reports and proposals, responding to questions, or training other workers, you will spend a good portion of your work life in activities that require effective public speaking skills. This chapter focuses on the first steps in effective speechmaking: (1) selecting a specific speech goal that is adapted to the rhetorical situation and (2) gathering and evaluating information to develop your speech.

Sometimes people like Donna are invited to speak because they have expertise on a particular subject. Sometimes people like Romeo are asked to speak because they have some relationship to the audience. Nevertheless, choosing exactly what to speak about is usually left to the speaker. So, although Donna and Romeo may have an idea about what they will talk about, like Alyssa, they need to begin by determining a speech goal that is adapted to the rhetorical situation.

The Rhetorical Situation

rhetorical situation

a state in which you, the audience, and the occasion overlap

exigence

the reason the speech needs to be given

audience analysis

the study of the intended audience for your speech

audience adaptation

the process of tailoring your speech to the needs, interests, and expectations of your audience

uncertainty reduction theory

explains the processes we go through to get to know strangers

As Figure 11.1 illustrates, the **rhetorical situation** is a state in which you (and your knowledge and intentions), the audience (and their knowledge and expectations), and the occasion (and the constraints of it) overlap. Effective speakers address all three throughout the speech preparation and presentation process. Lloyd Bitzer (1968), an esteemed professor and rhetorician, coined the term **"exigence"** to capture this notion of speeches that address a real or perceived need, in other words, *the reason the speech needs to be given.* Because audience is so crucial to a successful speech, your specific speech goal must be based on **audience analysis**, the study of the intended audience for your speech, and **audience adaptation**, the process of tailoring your speech to the needs, interests, and expectations of them. Audience analysis and adaptation is rooted in what communication scholars refer to as **uncertainty reduction theory**, which explains the processes we go through to get to know strangers (Berger & Calabrese, 1975). Although effective speakers adapt their speech to the audience throughout the speech preparation and presentation process, they begin doing so at the point of selecting a topic and speech goal.

To determine a specific speech goal that is adapted to the rhetorical situation, begin by identifying lots of subjects and topics that interest you. Then, based

ACTION STEP   **1**

Select a specific speech goal that is adapted to the rhetorical situation.

on your analysis of both the audience and the occasion, you narrow your list of topics to an appropriate one. Ultimately, a good speech is one that interests you, is adapted to address the needs, interests, and expectations of the audience, and is appropriate for the occasion.

Generate a List of Potential Topics

Good speech topics come from subject areas that you have some knowledge about and interest in. A **subject** is a broad area of knowledge, such as contemporary cinema, renewable energy, computer technology, or Middle Eastern politics. A **topic** is a narrow, specific aspect of a subject. So, if your broad subject area is contemporary cinema, you might feel qualified to speak on a variety of topics such as how the Academy Awards nomination process works; the relationships between movie producers, directors, and distributors; or how technology is changing movie production. Let's look at how you can identify subject areas that interest you and then topics you might use for an upcoming speech.

When you brainstorm, you will come up with many subjects from one topic. Try it!

Subjects

You can identify subjects by listing those that (1) are important to you and (2) you know something about. Subjects may be related to careers that interest you, your major area of study, special skills or competencies you have or admire, your hobbies, as well as your social, economic, or political interests. So if your major is marketing, favorite hobbies are skateboarding and snowboarding, and special concerns are substance abuse and childhood obesity, then these are *subjects* from which you can identify potential speech topics.

At this point, you might be thinking, "What if my audience isn't interested in the subjects that interest me?" In reality, topics in any subject area can be of interest when they are adapted to address the needs and expectations of the audience. Figure 11.2 contains a list of subjects that Holly, a beginning communication student, identified as she began thinking about her upcoming speech. She chose to organize her subject areas under three headings: (1) career interests, (2) hobbies, and (3) issues of concern.

Brainstorm and Concept Map

Because a topic is a specific aspect of a subject, you can identify many topics related to one subject. Two methods for identifying topics are brainstorming and concept mapping.

> **CONSIDER THIS....**
>
> What do you know a lot about? What has interested you enough so that you have gained some expertise in it? Do you think any of them might make a good speech topic? Why or why not?

subject
a broad area of knowledge

topic
some specific aspect of a subject

Career interests	Hobbies	Issues of concern
teacher	social networking	endangered birds
Web site designer	rowing	child pornography on the Internet
information systems specialist	Big Brothers Big Sisters organizations	personal privacy and the Internet
technology trainer	birding	water pollution
public relations	photography	global warming/ climate change

Figure 11.2

Holly's subject lists

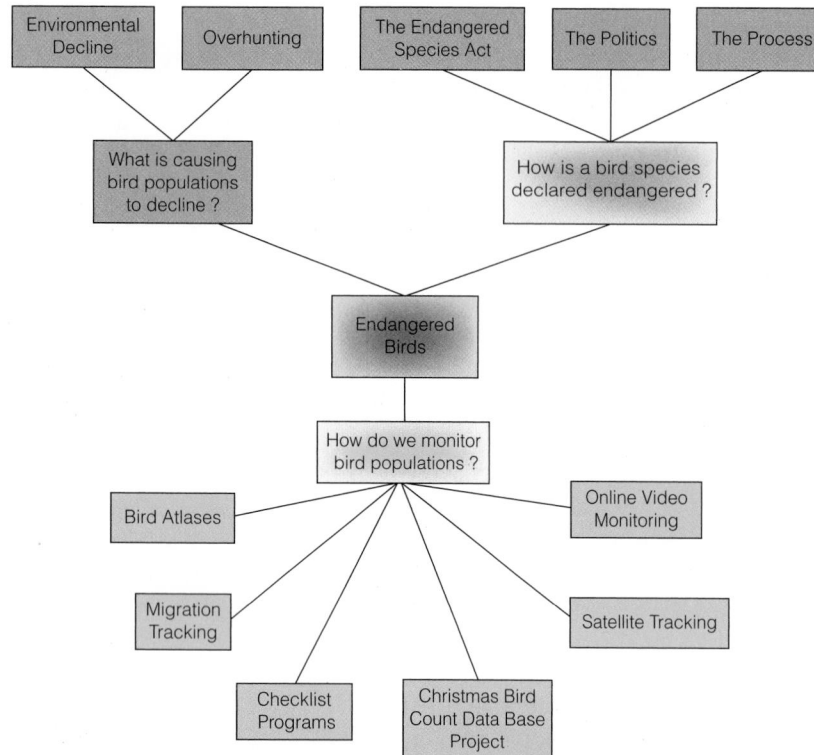

Brainstorming is an uncritical, nonevaluative process of generating associated ideas. When you brainstorm, you list as many ideas as you can think of without evaluating them. Holly, for example, decided she wanted to give a speech on the subject of social networking. By brainstorming, she came up with a list of potential topics that included: the history of social networking, future trends in social networking, comparisons between popular social networking sites, the downside of social networking, and the social impacts of online social networks.

Concept mapping is a visual means of exploring connections between a subject and related ideas (Callison, 2001). To generate connections, you might ask yourself questions about your subject, focusing on who, what, where, when, and how. In

© Cengage Learning

Figure 11.3

Holly's endangered birds concept map

brainstorming

an uncritical, non-evaluative process of generating associated ideas

concept mapping

a visual means of exploring connections between a subject and related ideas

Figure 11.3, you can see Holly's concept map on the subject of endangered birds.

Analyze the Audience

Because addressing the specific needs and expectations of your intended audience is integral to the rhetorical situation, you need to conduct an audience analysis about their demographic characteristics and subject-specific knowledge in order to select an appropriate topic. You will use the information you learn from audience analysis to inform your topic selection and throughout the speechmaking process.

ACTION STEP   1.A

Brainstorm and Concept Map for Topics

1. Develop a subject list.

  a. Divide a sheet of paper into three columns. Label column 1 "career interests," column 2 "hobbies," and column 3 "issues of concern."

  b. Working on one column at a time, identify subjects that interest you. Try to identify at least three subjects in each column.

  c. Place a check mark next to one subject in each column you might enjoy speaking about.

  d. Keep these lists for future use in choosing a topic for an assigned speech.

2. For each subject you checked, brainstorm a list of potential speech topics related to it.

3. Then, for each subject you checked, develop a concept map to identify potential speech topics.

Age: What is the average age range of your audience members?

Educational Level: What percentage of your audience has a high school, college, or postgraduate education?

Sex: What percentage of your audience is male? Female?

Occupation: Is a majority of your audience from a single occupational group, industry, or major? Or do they come from a variety of occupations, industries, or majors?

Socioeconomic status: What percentage of your audience comes from high-, middle-, or low-income families?

Race: Are most members of your audience of the same race, or is there a mixture of races represented?

Ethnicity: What cultural and co-cultural groups do your audience members identify with?

Religion: What religious traditions are represented?

Geographic Uniqueness: Are audience members from the same state, city, or neighborhood?

Language: What language (if any) is spoken by all audience members? What are the most common primary languages?

Figure 11.4

Demographic and subject-specific audience analysis questions

Demographic Data

Helpful demographic information includes, for example, each person's approximate age, education, sex, income, occupation, race, ethnicity, religion, geographic uniqueness, and language. Figure 11.4 presents a list of questions that will help you uncover important demographic information.

Subject-Related Data

You also want to collect subject-related audience data, including: how knowledgeable audience members are about the subject area and potential topics you are considering, as well as their initial level of interest in and attitude toward them. Once you determine what your audience already knows about the subject area, you can use a process of elimination to choose a topic that will offer new information and insight. Similarly, when you understand their initial level of interest regarding your subject, you can choose a topic that builds on that interest or adapt your material in order to capture their interest. Understanding your audience's attitude toward your subject is especially important when you want to influence their beliefs or move them to action. Knowing your audience members' attitudes toward your subject will help you choose a topic and tailor it in ways that influences them without alienating them.

Suppose, for example, you want to give a speech on blogging. If you're not sure your audience understands what blogging is, you may infer what they know by examining demographic data. Are most of the audience members young, educated, and from a middle class background? If so, you can infer that they will have heard about blogging and know some of the basics. So you might adapt your speech topic to offer insight they might not know

CONSIDER THIS....

Select a topic you are considering for your next speech. How might you adapt your focus based on demographic characteristics of your audience and their possible attitude toward your topic?

Two-sided question

Are you _____ a man _____ a woman?

Question with multiple responses

Which is the highest educational level you have completed? _____ less than

high school _____ high school _____ attended college _____ associate's degree

_____ bachelor's degree _____ master's degree _____ doctorate degree _____

postdoctorate

Scaled items

How much do you know about Islam? _____ not much _____ a little _____ some

_____ quite a lot _____ detailed knowledge

Open-ended item

What do you think about labor unions?

Figure 11.5

Sample survey questions

© Cengage Learning

about blogging, such as the dangers or "dark side" of blogging. But if your audience is from different demographic groups, then you might need to collect subject-related data to learn what they know about blogging and then pick an appropriately focused topic within the general subject area of blogging. If you discover that most of your audience members have never written or even read a blog, then you may need to adapt your topic to introduce them more generally to what blogging is.

Data-Gathering Methods

You can use several different methods to gather data about your audience.

survey

an examination of people to gather information about their ideas and opinions

1. **Conduct a survey.** Although it is not always possible, the most direct way to collect audience data is to survey them A survey is an examination of people to gather information about their ideas and opinions. Some surveys are done as interviews; others as written questionnaires. The four most common items used in a survey are two-sided, multiple-response, scaled, and open-ended. *Two-sided items* force respondents to choose between two answers (e.g., yes/no, for/against). *Multiple-response items* give respondents several alternatives from which to choose. *Scaled items* measure the direction of intensity of respondents' feelings or attitudes toward something (e.g., on a scale from 1 to 5, with 5 being "very likely," . . .). *Open-ended items* encourage respondents to elaborate on their opinions without forcing them to answer in a predetermined way. Figure 11.5 above gives examples of each type.

2. **Observe informally.** If you are familiar with the members of your audience (as you are with members of your class audience), you can learn a lot

THE AUDIENCE *BEYOND*

Darius wanted to survey his classmates about their knowledge and attitudes about social networking sites like Facebook and Twitter. So he created an online survey in *Qualtrix* and posted a link to it on the class Web site.

through informal observation. For instance, after being in class for even a couple of sessions, you should be able to estimate the approximate age or age range and the ratio of men to women. As you listen to your classmates talk, you will learn more about their interest in, knowledge of, and attitudes about many issues.

3. **Question a representative.** When you are invited to speak to a group you are unfamiliar with, ask your contact person for demographic and subject-related audience data. You should specifically ask for data that are somewhat important for you as you choose a topic or work to adapt your material. For the blogging speech, for example, you would want to know if the audience members have a basic understanding of what a blog is.

You can learn a lot about an audience through informal observation.

4. **Make educated guesses.** If you can't get information in any other way, you can make educated guesses based on indirect data such as the general makeup of the people who live in a certain community, belong to a certain organization, or who are likely to attend a speech of this nature.

Ethical Use of Audience Data

Once you have collected audience data you can use it to tailor your speech to their interests, needs, and expectations. But, adapting to your audience also means creating a speech that all audience members can relate to. So you will want to avoid two potential pitfalls: marginalizing and stereotyping.

Marginalizing is the practice of ignoring the values, needs, interests, and subject-specific knowledge of some audience members, leaving them to feel excluded. For example, if you find out that most of your audience members have blogged, you want to avoid marginalizing the few members who have never blogged. So you might provide a quick definition of blogging and show an example as a visual aid before going into your speech about the dangers of blogging.

Stereotyping is assuming all members of a group have similar knowledge, behaviors, or beliefs simply because they belong to that group. If, for instance, you find out that the average age of your audience is 65, you might stereotype and assume that most of them know nothing about blogging when, in fact, many of them not only know about blogs, but have created them. To avoid stereotyping based on demographic data, you need to collect subject-related data from them, as well.

You also can reduce your chances of marginalizing or stereotyping by identifying and acknowledging the diversity represented in your audience. **Audience diversity** is the range of demographic characteristics and subject specific differences represented in an audience. So while the average age of your audience may be 65, there may also be some in the audience who are much younger. This chapter's *Diverse Voices* feature, "Considering Cultural Differences When Speaking," serves as a reminder of the diversity that might be represented in your audiences and to avoid making hasty (and possibly wrong) assumptions about them.

marginalizing

ignoring the values, needs, interests, and subject specific knowledge of some audience members

stereotyping

assuming all members of a group have similar knowledge levels, behaviors, or beliefs simply because they belong to that group

audience diversity

the range of demographic characteristics and subject specific differences represented in an audience

DIVERSE VOICES

Considering Cultural Differences When Speaking

by Sheila Wray Gregoire

So often we assume that those to whom we're speaking are just like us, but they're not. When my husband and I speak at marriage conferences, we're often paired with another couple where the man is a real man's man. My husband hunts. He fishes. He kills stuff. And his stories about hunting are side-splittingly funny. He tells them so well. And they illustrate some great points in marriage.

But one conference just happened to occur in Montreal. You don't talk about hunting in Montreal. My husband realized that after the first night fell flat, and then changed his talk for the next day.

In the same way, we need to be really sensitive about our audiences. Let me give you another example. I think the biggest difference [between] Canadian and American audiences is that Canadians don't see it as a plus to sell yourself. We don't brag about ourselves; we tend to brag about others. Saying good things about yourself sounds odd.

So, when an American is speaking to a Canadian audience, for example, you should use yourself as an anecdote, for sure, but don't do "I have arrived, or God has blessed me, and He will bless you, too." That comes off as bragging and that's a huge no-no. I see American speakers—even [best]-selling authors—do this all the time up here in Canada and they lose the whole audience. When you tell your own story, you must do it with humility, and with "here's what God is still teaching me," rather than "I'm so glad God taught me this. Now you should learn it, too." Perhaps that sounds like I'm being mean to Americans, and I don't mean to be, but in general Canadians are much more low-key about sharing our own successes. And it's important to know this about your audience if you're going to communicate effectively.

Another big difference: we're not as dramatic. Twice I have seen American speakers actually get down on the floor and act out a horrible experience from their past, thrashing around down there and everything. Canadians would NEVER do this. (Note: both these speakers were speaking before audiences of thousands, and were headlining large events up here). When we tell our sad or difficult stories, we tell them quietly. We never act them out. It looks fake.

Where we do get loud and boisterous is in our humorous parts of our stories. So it's not that we're monotone; it's just that adding drama to the difficult parts of life is seen as gauche.

Canadians, when we're with American audiences, need to learn to turn it up a notch. Americans, when you're with Canadian audiences (and European ones) need to learn to turn it down.

Speaking is a form of communication. You are saying something that you want others to hear. But communication is a two-way street: you put it out there, but your listeners have to take a hold of it. And that means understanding and researching your niche.

Whenever I speak, I ask who is going to be in the audience. Are they married? Single? A blend? What [are] their ages? Do they work outside the home? Is it multicultural? Are they mostly Christians, or not? You have to know these things, or your talk may go right over their heads. If I find out, for instance, that many in the audience aren't married, I will always choose at least one anecdote that has nothing to do with marriage or children, and focuses more on one's workplace or something.

So know your audience. Don't assume they are just like you. Make sure you communicate in a way that they understand. And then your message is much more likely to get through!

Source: Gregoire, S. W. (2009, December 8). Considering cultural differences when speaking. Becoming a Christian Woman's Speaker: With author and Speaker Sheila Wray Gregoire. Retrieved April 7, 2012, from http://christianwomensspeaker.wordpress.com/2009/12/08/considering-cultural-differences-when-speaking/

ACTION STEP 1.B

Analyze Your Audience

1. Decide on the audience characteristics (demographic and subject-related data) you want to research in order to adapt your topic and speech effectively.

2. Choose a method for gathering audience information.

3. Collect the data.

Examine the Occasion

The **occasion** is made up of the expected purpose for the speech and the setting where it will be given. Answers to several questions about the occasion should guide you when selecting your topic and throughout the speech-making process.

1. **What is the intended purpose of the speech?** In other words, why does the audience think this speech is being given? At a Sunday church service the congregation expects the minister's sermon to have a religious theme. At a national sales meeting, the field representatives expect to hear about new products. For your classroom speeches, a major expectation is that your speech will meet the assignment criteria.

2. **What is the expected length?** Time limits for classroom speeches are usually quite short, so you will want to choose a topic that is narrow enough to be accomplished in the brief time allotted. For example, "Three Major Causes of the Declining Honeybee population" could probably be covered in a 5-minute speech; however, "A History of Human Impact on the Environment" could not. Speakers who speak for more or less time than what has been allotted can seriously interfere with event programming and lose the respect of both their hosts and their audience.

3. **Where will the speech be given?** Rooms vary in size, shape, lighting, and seating arrangements. Some are a single level, some have stages or platforms, and some have tiered seating. The space affects the speech. For example, in a long, narrow room, you may have to speak loudly to be heard in the back row. If you are speaking in an auditorium to a large group of people, you will need to speak loudly and perhaps use a microphone. You will also need to use large gestures and presentational aids that can be seen and heard easily in all parts of the room. The brightness of the room and the availability of shades may affect what kinds of visual aids you can use. So you will want to know and consider the layout of the room as you plan your speech. At times, you might request that the room be changed or rearranged so that the space is better suited to your needs.

4. **When will the speech be given?** A speech given early in the morning requires a different approach from one given right after lunch or in the

occasion

the expected purpose and setting for the speech

CONSIDER *THIS....*

What examples of audience diversity exist among your classmates? What will you do to avoid marginalizing or stereotyping in your upcoming speech?

CONSIDER *THIS....*

Consider a time when an instructor kept you beyond the allotted class time. How did you feel and why? Did it influence your attitude about that instructor? If so, how?

ACTION STEP 1.C

Analyze the Occasion

Hold a conversation with the person who arranged for you to speak and get answers to the following questions:

1. What is the intended purpose of the speech?

_____

2. What is the expected length for the speech?

_____

3. Where will the speech be given and to how many people?

_____

4. When will the speech be given?

_____

5. What equipment is necessary to give the speech?

_____

Write a short paragraph discussing which aspects of the occasion are most important to consider for your speech and why.

How does the setting and the occasion dictate what a speaker will talk about at a graduation ceremony?

evening. If a speech is scheduled after a meal, for example, the audience may be lethargic, mellow, or even on the verge of sleep. So you may want to plan more material that gains and regains their interest throughout the speech. Similarly, where you are placed on the schedule of events should influence your speech planning. For example, if you are first, you may need to "warm up" the audience and be prepared to deal with the distraction of latecomers entering the room while you are speaking. If you speak later in the program, you will need to integrate attention-catching material to keep the interest of a weary audience.

5. **What equipment is necessary and available?** Would you like to use a microphone, lectern, flip chart, smart board, computer and LCD projector, or Internet during your speech? If so, you need to check with your host to make sure that the equipment can be made available to you. In some cases, the unavailability of equipment may limit your topic choice. Regardless of what arrangements have been made, however, experienced speakers expect that something may go wrong and always prepare a backup plan. For example, although computer slide shows can be very effective, technological glitches can sometimes interfere with their use. So it's a good idea to bring handouts as a backup.

Select a Topic

As you review your topic list, compare each to your audience profile. Are any topics too simple or too difficult for this audience's knowledge base? If so, eliminate those topics. Are some topics likely to bore the audience and you can't think of any way to pique their interest? Eliminate those, as well. How might the audience's age range, ethnicity, and other demographic characteristics mesh with each topic? By asking these and similar questions,

ACTION STEP 1.D

Select a Topic

Use your responses to Action Steps 1.a, 1.b, and 1.c to complete this step.

1. Write each of the topics that you checked in Action Step 1 on the lines below:

———   ———   ———

———   ———   ———

———   ———   ———

2. Using the information you compiled in Action Step 1.b (audience analysis), compare each topic to your audience profile. Draw a line through topics that seem less appropriate for your audience.

3. Using the information you compiled in Action Step 1.c (analysis of the occasion), compare the remaining topics to the expectations of the occasion. Draw a line through topics that seem less suited to the occasion.

4. From the remaining topics, choose one that you would find enjoyable preparing and sharing in your speech.

you will be able to identify topics that are appropriate for the audience. Also consider the occasion. Are some topics inappropriate for the intended purpose? Are some too broad to cover adequately in the time allotted? Would any require equipment that cannot be made available where you will be speaking? Answers to these kinds of questions will help you identify topics appropriate to the occasion. Finally, the topics that remain should be appropriate for the rhetorical situation. Choose one that you would enjoy preparing and sharing with the audience.

Write a Speech Goal Statement

Once you have chosen your topic, you are ready to identify the general goal of your speech and then to write your specific goal statement tailored to the audience and occasion.

Understanding General and Specific Speech Goals

The **general goal** is the overall intent of the speech. Most speeches intend to entertain, inform, or persuade, even though each type can include elements of the others. Consider the following examples. Jimmy Kimmel's opening monologue on *Jimmy Kimmel Live* is generally intended to entertain, even though it may include persuasive material. Presidential campaign speeches are intended to persuade, even though they also include informative material. The general goal is usually dictated by the occasion. (In this course, your instructor is likely to specify it.)

general goal

the overall intent of the speech

Although the general goal of Jimmy Kimmel's opening monologues is to entertain, he may also include informational and persuasive material in them.

Ethan Miller/Getty Images Entertainment/Getty Images

Informative Goals

Increasing understanding: I want my audience to understand the three basic forms of a mystery story.

Increasing knowledge: I want my audience to learn how to light a fire without a match.

Increasing appreciation: I want my audience to appreciate the intricacies of spider-web designs.

Persuasive Goals

Reinforce belief: I want my audience to maintain its belief in drug-free sports.

Change belief: I want my audience to believe that SUVs are environmentally destructive.

Motivation to act: I want my audience to join Amnesty International.

© Cengage Learning

Figure 11.6

Informative and persuasive speech goals

specific speech goal

a single statement of the exact response the speaker wants from the audience

Whereas the general goal is typically determined by the occasion, the **specific goal** (or specific purpose) is a single statement that identifies the desired response a speaker wants from the audience. For a speech about "vanishing honeybees," you might state a specific goal as, "I want my audience to understand the four reasons honeybees are vanishing" if your general goal is to inform. If you general goal is to persuade, you might state as your specific goal, "I want my audience to donate money to *Honeybee Advocacy International,* a group trying to solve the problem and stop the crisis." Figure 11.6 offers additional examples of informative and persuasive speech goals.

Phrasing a Specific Goal Statement

A specific speech goal statement must be carefully crafted because it lays the foundation for organizing your speech. The following guidelines can help you do so.

1. **Write a first draft of your specific speech goal statement.** Julia, who has been concerned with and is knowledgeable about the subject of illiteracy, drafts the following: "I want my audience to understand the effects of illiteracy." Julia's draft is a complete sentence, and it specifies the response she wants from the audience: *to understand* the effects of illiteracy. Thus, she is planning to give an informative speech.

2. **Make sure the goal statement contains only one central idea.** Suppose Julia had written: "I want the audience to understand the nature of illiteracy and innumeracy." This would need to be revised because it includes two distinct ideas: illiteracy and innumeracy. It would be difficult to adequately address both within one speech. If your goal statement includes the word *and*, you probably have more than one idea and need to narrow your focus.

3. **Revise the statement until it clearly articulates the desired audience response.** The draft "I want my audience to understand illiteracy" is a good start, but it is fairly broad. Julia narrows the statement to: "I want my audience to understand three effects of illiteracy." This version is more specific, but still does not clearly capture her intention, so she revises it again to: "I would like the audience to understand three effects of illiteracy

ACTION STEP 1.E

Write a Specific Speech Goal Statement

General speech goal

_____

1. Write a draft of your specific speech goal, using a complete sentence that specifies the type of response you want from the audience: *to learn about, to understand,* or *to appreciate* the topic.

2. Review the specific goal statement. If it contains more than one idea, select one and redraft your specific goal statement.

Write out your revised specific speech goal statement:

_____

_____

_____

COMMUNICATION SKILL

Crafting an Effective Specific Speech Goal Statement

Skill	Use	Procedure	Example
The process of identifying a speech purpose that draws on the speaker's knowledge and interests and is adapted to the audience and occasion.	To identify a specific goal that matches speaker interest and expertise with audience and occasion.	1. Identify topics within subject areas in which you have interest and expertise. 2. Analyze audience demographics, interests, and attitudes toward your subject. 3. Understand the expectations and location for the speech. 4. Select a topic that meets the interests and expectations of the audience and occasion. 5. Write a specific speech goal that clearly states the desired response you want from your audience.	Ken first writes, "I want my audience to know what to look for in adopting a dog." As he revises, he writes, "I want my audience to understand four important considerations in adopting the perfect dog." Once Ken has a goal with a single focus and a clearly specified, desired audience reaction, he tests his first version by writing two differently worded versions.

in the workplace." Now the goal is limited by Julia's focus not only on the specific number of effects but also on a specific situation.

ACTION STEP 2

Gather and Evaluate Information to Develop Your Speech

To use the most effective information to support your speech goal, you must be able to locate and evaluate appropriate sources, identify and select relevant information, and cite information and sources appropriately during your speech.

secondary research

the process of locating information about your topic that has been discovered by other people

primary research

the process of conducting your own study in the real world

credentials

your experiences or education that qualifies you to speak with authority on a subject

Locate and Evaluate Information Sources

How can you quickly find the best information related to your specific speech goal? You can start by assessing your own knowledge and experience. Then you can move to **secondary research**, which is the process of locating information discovered by other people. This includes doing Internet and library searches for relevant books, articles, general references, and Web sites. If the information you find from secondary sources doesn't answer all your questions, you may need to conduct **primary research**, which is the process of collecting data about your topic directly from the real world.

Personal Knowledge and Experience

Because you will be speaking on a topic you know something about, you can include examples from your personal experiences. For instance, a saxophone player knows how to select and care for a reed. Likewise, entrepreneurs know the key features of a business plan, and dieticians have a wealth of information about healthy diets. So Diane, a skilled long-distance runner, can draw from her own knowledge and experience to develop her speech on "How to Train for a Marathon." If you have personal knowledge and experience about the topic, however, you should also share your **credentials**—your experiences or education that qualifies you to speak with authority on a subject. For Diane, establishing her credentials means briefly mentioning her training and expertise as a long-distance runner before she launches into her speech about training for a marathon.

What expert knowledge or experience do you have that could make for good speech topics?

Secondary Research

Even if you are an expert on your topic, you may need to do secondary research as you adapt the information for your intended audience. To conduct secondary research, you'll need to know

Christopher Futcher/iStockphoto.com

THE AUDIENCE *BEYOND*

For his speech on bioluminescence, Dan consulted a blog maintained by the Association of Biogenetic Engineers. He was able to research several issues being debated by experts in the field even before their works had been published.

how to locate sources, what types of sources you can draw from, as well as how to skim and evaluate them.

Locating sources Begin by locating potential sources. Today we usually start searching for potential sources online. Because there is so much material available on the Internet, we can quickly access many sources from which to collect general facts about a topic, as well as quickly identify some of the outlets that tend to publish material on it. We can also locate relevant material found on personal and commercial Web sites, blogs, and discussion boards, as well as original content created by people on sites such as *YouTube*.

You can also do online library searches to locate secondary sources about your topic. Some of these materials will be available digitally. Others may require you to visit a library to pick up hard copies. When you locate a source that is not available digitally or in your local library, you may be able to get it through interlibrary loan.

Visiting the library can prove helpful when you get stuck trying to locate information for your speech. Although you can ask librarians for help online via an "ask the librarian" link, visiting with them face-to-face affords you their undivided attention until you are satisfied with the sources they've helped you locate. Librarians are free resources, experts who can demystify thorny research problems. Helping you is their job, so you're not imposing on them when you seek their advice.

Types of sources You'll want to draw from a variety of source types. You can find pertinent information in encyclopedias, books, articles in academic journals and magazines, newspapers, statistical sources, biographies, quotation books and Web sites, and government documents.

1. *Encyclopedias* Encyclopedia entries can serve as a good starting point by providing an overview acquainting you with the basic terminology associated with a topic. But because encyclopedias provide only overviews, they should never be the only source you rely on. General encyclopedias contain short articles about a wide variety of subjects. In addition, specialized encyclopedias focus on areas such as art, history, religion, philosophy, and science. For instance, a college library is likely to have the *African American Encyclopedia, Latino Encyclopedia, Asian American Encyclopedia, Encyclopaedia Britannica, Encyclopedia Americana, World Book Encyclopedia, Encyclopedia of Computer Science, Encyclopedia of Women, Encyclopedia of Women in American Politics*, and many more.

The online collaborative encyclopedia, Wikipedia, has become a popular research tool, but it is also a controversial source of information. Because there is no way to confirm the credibility of the people posting information in Wikipedia entries, you might use it as a starting point but not as a primary source. You can also use the *Notes* section at the end of the articles to find links to published sources that inform the entry. Then you can locate those articles to determine if they provide relevant and reliable evidence for your speech. To understand the controversy about *Wikipedia*, read the *Pop Comm!* feature "To Wikipedia or Not to Wikipedia? That's a Good Question."

THE AUDIENCE *BEYOND*

Diane wanted to find information on the subject "training for marathons." She searched several keywords such as "long-distance running" and "marathon training" and came up with a number of "hits" revealing secondary sources she could consider.

POP COMM!

To Wikipedia or Not to Wikipedia?: That's a Good Question

www.wikipedia.org

The Office's Michael Scott opined, "Wikipedia is the best thing ever. Anyone in the world can write anything they want about any subject, so you know you are getting the best possible information." Funny, right? Not for John Seigenthaler, a well-respected journalist who was a friend and aide to President John F. Kennedy and Attorney General Robert F. Kennedy in the 1960s. Seigenthaler was a victim of a hoax article posted to Wikipedia that falsely claimed he had been suspected in the assassinations of John and Robert Kennedy. The hoax upset Seigenthaler not only because the article defamed his character, but also because Wikipedia editors didn't discover and correct it for over four months (Seigenthaler, 2005). Shortly after Seigenthaler published an article in *USA Today* about the incident, Wikipedia announced that it had barred unregistered users from creating new articles, and later the site enacted a policy that prevented the public from creating new articles about living people without editorial review (Helm, 2005; Cohen, 2009). These moves signaled a change from Wikipedia's initial desire to provide a free online encyclopedia that the public could create collaboratively.

Wikipedia is one of the top ten Web sites used worldwide, offering over 18 million articles in 279 different languages, with the English language section alone featuring 3.77 million articles (Cohen, 2011; Kirkpatrick, 2011) Nonetheless, the Seigenthaler hoax and other incidents have spurred a "credibility" backlash against the site. For example, U.S. courts have begun ruling that Wikipedia cannot be used as legal evidence. In April 2009, a New Jersey judge reversed an initial ruling that Wikipedia could be used to plug an evidentiary gap, saying that because "anyone can edit" the online encyclopedia, it is not a reliable source of information (Gallagher, 2009). In October of 2011, Wikipedia member (or "Wikipedian") Sven Manguard reported the community was facing a huge backlog of editorial work with over 250,000 articles lacking even a single citation to support them (Manguard, 2011). Though Wikipedia and its community planned to take steps to address the problem and ensure more quality content in the future, these sorts of issues have led many educators to discourage their students from using Wikipedia as a research tool, and some schools have even banned access to it completely.

But some educators argue that to simply dismiss Wikipedia as a "bad" source misses the opportunity for students to think critically about how to do authoritative research. A study of Wikipedia conducted by Roy Rosenzweig for *The Journal of American History* actually found that many Wikipedia entries, while inconsistent overall, were "as accurate or more accurate than more traditional encyclopedias" (Jaschik, 2007). But, Rosenzweig stresses that despite these findings, Wikipedia should be a regarded as a starting point, as college level students should be using more advanced, primary sources for research instead of relying on Wikipedia. Even Wikipedia founder Jimmy Wales cautions against relying on the site as a primary source: "People shouldn't be citing encyclopedias in the first place. [Rather,] Wikipedia and other encyclopedias should be solid enough to give good, solid background information to inform your studies for a deeper level" (Helm, 2005).

Many university librarians suggest that instead of simply banning its use, today's college students need to be taught to develop information literacy skills that will help them navigate an increasingly complex information environment. Steven Bell, associate librarian for research and instructional services at Temple University, says students should be taught "how to 'triangulate' a source like Wikipedia, so they could use other sources to tell whether a given entry could be trusted" (Jaschik, 2007). For example, instead of simply accepting the Wikipedia entry as "fact," students should, at the very least, verify the information by clicking on the sources in the "Notes" section at the end of an entry to see if it comes from a primary and trusted source, such as books, magazine, newspaper, and journal articles, original interviews, and court decisions. Darren Crovitz and W. Scott Smoot (2009) write, "Talking with [students] about how the site operates is essential in helping them move from passive acceptors of information to practicing analyzers and evaluators." Many university libraries have answered this call and offer a range of online and offline options to help students move their research beyond Wikipedia. So before you click on Wikipedia, check out your library's Web site to see what they offer!

Questions to Ponder

1. Do you use Wikipedia? Why or why not?

2. Do you use it as a primary source? Or as the starting point for research?

2. *Books* If your topic has been around for awhile, there are likely to be books written about it. Although books are excellent sources of in-depth material about a topic, keep in mind that most of the information in a book is likely to be at least two years old by the time it is published. So books are not a good resource if you're looking for the latest information on a topic.

3. *Articles* Articles, which may contain more current or highly specialized information on your topic than a book would, are published in **periodicals**—magazines and journals that appear at regular intervals. The information in periodical articles is often more current than that published in books because many periodicals are published weekly, biweekly, or monthly. So a periodical article is likely to be a better source if a topic is one that's "in the news." Most libraries subscribe to electronic databases that index periodical articles. Check with your librarian to learn what electronic indexes your college or university subscribes to. Four frequently available databases that index many popular magazines, such as *Time* and *Newsweek*, as well as some of the popular academic journals, such as *Communication Quarterly* and *Journal of Psychology*, are **InfoTrac College Edition** (that you can access this semester through the resources that accompany this textbook), **InfoTrac University Library**, **Periodical Abstract**, and **EBSCO**.

> **periodicals**
>
> *magazines and journals that appear at regular intervals*

4. *Newspapers* Newspaper articles are excellent sources of facts about and interpretations of both contemporary and historical issues and provide information about local issues and perspectives. Keep in mind, however, that most authors of newspaper articles are journalists who are not experts themselves on the topics they write about. So, it is best not to rely solely on

THE AUDIENCE *BEYOND*

Lauren typed the subject "prescription drug abuse" into the "subject" prompt on the home page of the EBSCO database. The search revealed 108 references from a variety of highly respected periodicals, including the *National Review*, the *Journal of the American Medical Association*, and *American Medical News*.

Tetra Images/Jupiter Images

Have you ever taken a course in online research, perhaps at your library? If not, consider doing so. You will save yourself a lot of time and will locate great sources of useful information.

newspaper articles for your speech. Today, most newspapers are available online, which makes them very accessible. Two electronic newspaper indexes that are most useful if they are available to you are the *National Newspaper Index*, which indexes five major newspapers: the *New York Times*, the *Wall Street Journal*, the *Christian Science Monitor*, the *Washington Post*, and the *Los Angeles Times*—as well as *Newsbank*, which provides not only the indexes but also the text of articles from more than 450 U.S. and Canadian newspapers. If you don't have access to an electronic newspaper index, you may be able to access articles about your topic at the Web sites of specific newspapers.

5. ***Statistical Sources*** Statistical sources present numerical information on a wide variety of subjects. When you need facts about demography, continents, heads of state, weather, or similar subjects, access one of the many single-volume sources that report such data. *The Statistical Abstract of the United States*, which provides numerical information on various aspects of American life, is available online.

6. ***Biographies*** When you need an account of a person's life, from thumbnail sketches to reasonably complete essays, you can use a biographical reference source. Although you can access some biographical information online, you will find information of more depth and breadth by reading full-length biographies and by consulting biographical references such as *Who's Who in America* and *International Who's Who*. Your library is also likely to carry *Contemporary Black Biography, Dictionary of Hispanic Biography, Native American Women, Who's Who of American Women, Who's Who Among Asian Americans,* and many more.

7. ***Quotation Books and Web sites*** A good quotation can be especially provocative as well as informative, and there are times you want to use a quotation from a respected person. *Bartlett's Familiar Quotations* is a popular source of quotes from historical as well as contemporary figures. But many other collections of quotations are also available. Some others include *The International Thesaurus of Quotations; Harper Book of American Quotations; My Soul Looks Back, 'Less I Forget: A Collection of Quotations by People of Color; The New Quotable Woman;* and *The Oxford Dictionary of Quotations*. Some popular quotation Web sites include *The Quotations Page* and *Quoteland.com*.

8. ***Government Documents*** If your topic is related to public policy, government documents may provide useful information. The *Federal Register* publishes daily regulations and legal notices issued by the executive branch of the United States and all federal agencies. It is divided into sections, such as rules and regulations and Sunshine Act meetings. Of special interest are announcements of hearings and investigations, committee meetings, and agency decisions and rulings. The *Monthly Catalog of United States Government Publications* covers publications of all branches of the federal government.

Skimming

rapidly viewing a work to determine what is covered and how

Skim sources Because your search of secondary sources is likely to uncover far more information than you can use, you will want to skim sources to determine whether or not to read them in full. **Skimming** is a method of rapidly viewing a work to determine what is covered and how.

As you skim an article, think about whether it really presents information on the area of the topic you are exploring and whether it contains any documented statistics, examples, meaningful visuals, or quotable opinions. You can start by reading the **abstract**—a short paragraph summarizing the research findings. As you skim a book, read the table of contents carefully, look at the index, and review the headings and visuals in pertinent chapters, asking the same questions as you would for a magazine article. A few minutes spent skimming will save hours of time.

Surfing the Internet is actually a form of skimming that you can also use with articles and books.

abstract

a short paragraph summarizing the research findings

valid sources

report factual information that can be counted on to be true

accurate sources

present unbiased information that includes a balanced discussion of controversial ideas

reliable sources

those sources with a history of presenting accurate information

Evaluate sources The validity, accuracy, and reliability of secondary sources vary. **Valid sources** report factual information that can be counted on to be true. Tabloid magazines and tabloid newspapers are generally considered less valid sources for information on celebrities than mainline news organizations that use "fact-checkers" before publishing an article. **Accurate sources** present unbiased information that often includes a balanced discussion of controversial ideas. For example, the *Congressional Record* provides an accurate account of what each member of U.S. Congress has said on the House or Senate floor. A newspaper account of a member's speech, however, may only report part of what was said and may distort the remark by taking it out of context. **Reliable sources** are those with a history of presenting accurate information. For example, the *Bureau of Labor Statistics* is an accurate source for information about U.S. employment. A union newsletter, on the other hand, may sometimes report accurate information about employment trends and other times pick and choose to use only information that supports its case. Four criteria can help you assess the validity, accuracy, and reliability of sources.

1. **Authority.** The first test of a source is the expertise of its author and/or the reputation of the publishing or sponsoring organization. When an author is listed, you can check the author's credentials through biographical references or by seeing if the author has a home page listing professional qualifications. Use the electronic periodical indexes or check the Library of Congress to see what else the author has published in the field.

   On the Internet, you will sometimes find information that is anonymous or credited to someone whose background is not clear. In these cases, your ability to trust the information depends on evaluating the qualifications of the sponsoring organization. URLs ending in ".gov" (governmental), ".edu" (educational), and ".org" are noncommercial sites with institutional publishers. The URL ".com" indicates that the sponsor is a for-profit organization. If you do not know whether you can trust the sources, do not use the information.

2. **Objectivity.** Although all authors have a viewpoint, be wary of information that seems excessively slanted. Documents that have been published by business, government, or public interest groups should be carefully scrutinized for obvious biases or good public relations fronts. To evaluate the potential biases in articles and books, read the preface or identify the thesis statement. These often reveal the author's point of view. When evaluating a Web site with which you are unfamiliar, look for its purpose. Most

home pages contain a purpose or mission statement (sometimes in a link called "About"). Armed with this information, you are in a better position to recognize potential biases in the information.

3. **Currency.** In general, newer information is more accurate than older information (unless, for example, you are documenting a historical event). So when evaluating your sources, unless doing a speech on a historical event, be sure to consult the latest information you can find. One of the reasons for using Web-based sources is that they can provide more up-to-date information than printed sources. But just because a source is found online does not mean that the information is timely. To determine how current the information is, you will need to find out when the book was published, the article was written, the study was conducted, or the article was placed on the Web or revised. Web page dates are usually listed at the end of the article. If there are no dates listed, you have no way of judging how current the information is.

4. **Relevance.** During your research, you will likely come across a great deal of interesting information. Whether that information is appropriate for your speech is another matter. Relevant information is directly related to your topic and supports your main points, making your speech easier to follow and understand. Irrelevant information will only confuse listeners, so you should avoid using it no matter how interesting it is.

Primary Research

When there is little secondary research available on your topic or on a main idea you want to develop in your speech, or when you wonder whether what you are reading about is true in a particular setting, consider doing primary research. Recall that *primary research* is conducting your own study in the real world. But keep in mind that primary research is much more labor intensive and time consuming than secondary research—and, in the professional world, much more costly. You can conduct fieldwork observations, surveys, interviews, original artifact or document examinations, or experiments.

Fieldwork observations You might choose to learn about a group of people and their practices by conducting **fieldwork observations**, which is a method focused on careful observation of people or groups of people while immersed in their community. You can conduct fieldwork as a *participant observer* by engaging in interactions and activities with the people you are studying or a *non-participant observer* by observing but not engaging with them. If, for instance, you are planning to talk about how social service agencies help the homeless find shelter and job training, or the process involved in adopting a pet, you can learn more by visiting or even volunteering for a period of time at a homeless shelter or humane society. By focusing on specific behaviors and taking notes on your observations, you will have a record of specifics that you can use in your speech.

Surveys Recall that a survey is an examination to get information about peoples' ideas and opinions. Surveys may be conducted in person, over the phone, via the Internet, or in writing.

Interviews Like media reporters, you may get some of your best information from an **interview**—a planned, structured conversation where one person asks questions and another answers them. Appendix A provides information and guidelines for conducting effective interviews.

fieldwork observations

a research method focused on careful observations of people or groups of people while immersed in their community

interview

a planned, structured conversation where one person asks questions and another answers them

ACTION STEP 2.A

Locate and Evaluate Information Sources

The goal of this activity is to help you compile a list of potential sources for your speech.

1. Brainstorm a list of key words related to your speech goal.

2. Identify gaps in your knowledge that you would like to fill.

3. Using a search engine like *Google*, identify Internet-sponsored and personal Web sites that may be information sources for your speech.

4. Search electronic databases to identify library resources.

5. Gather and skim the resources you have found to identify potentially useful information.

6. Evaluate the validity, accuracy, and reliability of each source.

7. If needed, conduct primary research to find answers to questions you couldn't find from your secondary research.

Original artifact or document examinations Sometimes the information you need has not been published. Rather, it may exist in an original unpublished source, such as an ancient manuscript, a diary, personal correspondence, or company files. Or you may need to view an object to get the information you need, such as a geographic feature, a building, a monument, or an artifact in a museum.

Experiments You can design an experiment to test a **hypothesis**, which is an educated guess about a cause-and-effect relationship between two or more things. Then you can report the results of your experiment in your speech. Keep in mind that experiments take time, and you must understand the principles of the scientific process to be able to trust the results of a formal experiment. However, sometimes you can conduct an informal experiment to test the results of a study you learn about elsewhere.

hypothesis

an educated guess about a cause and effect relationship between two or more things

Identify and Evaluate a Variety of Information

Once you have collected a variety of sources, you need to identify different types of information or evidence to use in your speech. These include factual statements, expert opinions, and elaborations. You may find the information written in narrative form or presented as a graphic in visual form.

Factual Statements

Factual statements are those that can be verified. *A recent study confirmed that preschoolers watch an average of 28 hours of television a week* and *The microprocessor, which was invented by Ted Hoff at Intel in 1971, made the creation of personal computers possible* are both statements of fact that can be verified. One way to verify whether a statement is accurate is to check it against other sources on the same

factual statements

statements that can be verified

THE AUDIENCE *BEYOND*

Because distance prohibited Betty from doing her interview in person, she conducted it via *Skype*.

subject. Never use any information that is not carefully documented unless you have corroborating sources. Factual statements may come in the form of statistics or real examples.

statistics

numerical facts

1. **Statistics. Statistics** are numerical facts. *Only five of every ten local citizens voted in the last election* or *The national unemployment rate for March 2010 was 9.7 percent* can provide impressive support for a point, but when statistics are poorly used in a speech, they may be boring and, in some instances, downright deceiving. Here are some ethical guidelines for using statistics:

   - Use only statistics you can verify to be reliable and valid. Taking statistics from only the most reliable sources and double-checking any startling statistics with another source will guard against the use of faulty statistics.
   - Use only recent statistics so your audience will not be misled.
   - Use statistics comparatively. You can show growth, decline, gain, or loss by comparing two numbers. For example, according to the U.S. Department of Labor, the national unemployment rate for March 2010 was 9.7 percent. This statistic is more meaningful when you also mention that this figure has held steady for three months or when you compare it to 8.5 percent in March 2009 and to 5.1 percent in March 2008.
   - Use statistics sparingly. A few pertinent numbers are far more effective than a battery of statistics.
   - Remember that statistics can be biased. Mark Twain once said there are three kinds of lies: "lies, damned lies, and statistics." Not all statistics are lies, of course, but consider the source of statistics you'd like to use, what that source may have been trying to prove with these data, and how the data were collected and interpreted. So statistics, like other types of information, must be thoughtfully evaluated and cross-checked for validity, accuracy, and reliability (Frances, 1994).

> **CONSIDER *THIS*....**
>
> Have you ever listened to a professor or speaker who used a lot of statistics? Did the statistics help or hurt your understanding of his or her main points? Why?

examples

specific instances that illustrate or explain a general factual statement

2. **Examples. Examples** are specific instances that illustrate or explain a general factual statement. One or two short examples like the following ones provide concrete detail that makes a general statement more meaningful to the audience:

   "One way a company increases its power is to buy out another company. Recently, Delta bought out Northwest and thereby became the world's largest airline company."

   "Professional figure skaters practice many long hours every day. Adam Rippon, 2010 Olympic Gold medalist, practices 20 to 25 hours per week."

Expert Opinions

expert opinions

interpretations and judgments made by authorities in a particular subject area

expert

a person who has mastered a specific subject, usually through long-term study

Expert opinions are interpretations and judgments made by an expert in a subject area. They can help explain what facts mean or put them into perspective. *Watching 28 hours of television a week is far too much for young children, but may be OK for adults* and *Having a firewire port on your computer is absolutely necessary* are opinions. Whether they are expert opinions depends on who made the statements. An **expert** is a person who has mastered a specific subject, usually through long-term study, and who is recognized by other people in the field as being a knowledgeable and trustworthy authority. When you use expert opinions in your speech, remember to cite their credentials.

Elaborations

Both factual information and expert opinions can be elaborated upon through anecdotes and narratives, comparisons and contrasts, or quotable explanations and opinions.

1. **Anecdotes and narratives. Anecdotes** are brief, often amusing stories; **narratives** are accounts, personal experiences, tales, or lengthier stories. Because holding audience interest is important and because audience attention is likely to be captured by a story, anecdotes and narratives are worth looking for or creating. The key to using them is to be sure the point of the story directly addresses the point you are making in your speech. Good stories and narratives may be humorous, sentimental, suspenseful, or dramatic.

anecdotes

brief, often amusing stories

narratives

accounts, personal experiences, tales, or lengthier stories

2. **Comparisons and contrasts.** One of the best ways to give meaning to new ideas or facts is through comparison and contrast. **Comparisons** illuminate a point by showing similarities, whereas **contrasts** highlight differences. Although comparisons and contrasts may be literal, like comparing and contrasting the murder rates in different countries or during different eras, they may also be figurative.

comparisons

illuminate a point by showing similarities

contrasts

highlight differences

- *Figurative comparison*: "In short, living without health insurance is as much of a risk as having uncontrolled diabetes or driving without a safety belt" (Nelson, 2006, p. 24).
- *Figurative contrast:* "If this morning you had bacon and eggs for breakfast, I think it illustrates the difference. The eggs represented 'participation' on the part of the chicken. The bacon represented 'total commitment' on the part of the pig!" (Durst, 1989, p. 325).

3. **Quotations.** At times, information you find will be so well stated that you want to quote it directly in your speech. Because the audience is interested in listening to your ideas and arguments, you should avoid using quotations that are too long or too numerous. But when you find that an author or expert has worded an idea especially well, quote it directly and then verbally acknowledge the person who said or wrote it. Using quotations or close paraphrases without acknowledging their source is **plagiarism**, the unethical act of representing another person's work as your own.

plagiarism

the unethical act of representing a published author's work as your own

Seek Information from Multiple Cultural Perspectives

With many topics, how we perceive facts as well as what opinions we hold are influenced by our cultural background. Therefore, it is important to seek information from a variety of cultural perspectives by drawing from sources with different cultural orientations and by interviewing experts with diverse cultural backgrounds. For example, when Carrie was preparing her speech on proficiency testing in grade schools, she purposefully searched for articles written by noted Hispanic, Asian American, African American, and

European American authors. In addition, she interviewed two local school superintendents—one from an urban and another from a suburban district. Doing so boosted Carrie's confidence that her speech would accurately reflect multiple sides of the debate on proficiency testing.

Record Information

As you find information to use in your speech, you need to record it accurately and keep a careful account of your sources so you can cite them appropriately during your speech. How should you keep track of the information you plan to use? One way to do so is to compile an annotated bibliography of the sources you believe are relevant and create a research card for each individual item of information you plan to cite in the speech.

Annotated Bibliography

annotated bibliography

a preliminary record of the relevant sources you find as you conduct your research

An **annotated bibliography** is a preliminary record of the relevant sources you find as you conduct your research that includes a short summary of information in that source. You can compile an annotated bibliography on your computer as you work. When identifying the exact information you want to use in the speech, your bibliography can be edited to create your speech reference list. A good annotated bibliography for speech planning includes:

- A complete bibliographic citation for each source based on the type of source (such as book, article, or Web site) and the style guide (such as APA or MLA) you are using;

- Two or three sentences summarizing the information in the source;

- Two or three sentences explaining how the source is related to your speech topic; and

- Any direct quotations you might want to include verbatim in your speech.

Research Cards

research cards

individual cards or facsimiles that record one piece of relevant information for your speech

Research cards are individual 3×5- or 4×6-inch index cards or electronic facsimiles that record one piece of information relevant to your speech along with a key word or main idea and the bibliographic information identifying where you found it. Recording each piece of information using a key word or main idea identifier on a unique research card allows you to easily find, arrange, and rearrange individual pieces of information as you prepare your speech.

As your stack of research cards grows, you can sort the material and place each item under the heading to which it is related. Figure 11.7 provides a sample research card.

Figure 11.7

A sample research card

Brown, Valerie J. (February 2007). "Industry Issues: Putting the Heat on Gas". Environmental Health Perspectives (US National Institute of Environmental Health Sciences),115, 2.

> **Topic:** Fracking
>
> **Key Term/Main idea:** Health Issues
>
> Theo Colborn, president of The Endocrine Disruption Exchange in Paonia, Colorado, believes that some drilling and fracking additives that can end up in produced water are neurotoxic; among these are 2-butoxyethanol. "If you compare [such chemicals] with the health problems the people have," Colborn says, "they match up."

ACTION STEP 2.B

Prepare Research Cards: Record Facts, Opinions, and Elaborations

The goal of this step is to review the source material you identified in Action Step 2.a and to record specific items of information that you might wish to use in your speech.

1. Carefully read all print and electronic sources (including Web site material) you have identified and evaluated as appropriate sources for your speech. Review your notes and any tapes from interviews and observations.

2. As you read an item (fact, opinion, example, illustration, statistic, anecdote, narrative, comparison/contrast, quotation, definition, or description) that you think might be useful in your speech, record it on a research card or on the appropriate electronic note card form available on the Speech Communication CourseMate Web site for *Communicate!* If you are using an article from a periodical that you read online, use the periodical research card form.

Go to the Speech Communication Course-Mate at cengagebrain.com to access this activity online. Look for it in the Action Steps for Chapter 11. There you can view samples of research cards prepared by another student, use online forms to prepare your own research cards, print them out to use as you prepare your speech, and if requested, email them to your instructor.

Cite Sources

In your speeches, as in any communication in which you use information that is not your own, you need to acknowledge the sources of it. Specifically mentioning your sources not only helps the audience evaluate them but also enhances their perception of you as knowledgeable. Frankly, failure to cite sources constitutes plagiarism. Just as you would provide internal citations or footnotes in a written document, you must provide oral footnotes during your speech. **Oral footnotes** are references to an original source, made at the point in the speech where information from that source is presented. The key to preparing oral footnotes is to include enough information for listeners to access the sources themselves and to offer enough credentials to enhance the credibility of the information you are citing.

oral footnote

references to an original source, made at the point in the speech where information from that source is presented

ACTION STEP 2.C

Citing Sources

On the back of each research card, write a short phrase that you can use in your speech as an oral footnote.

"Thomas Friedman, noted columnist for *The New York Times*, stated in his book *The World Is Flat...*"

"In an interview with *New Republic magazine*, Governor Chris Christie stated..."

"According to an article in last week's *Newsweek* magazine, the average college graduate..."

"In the latest Gallup poll cited in the February 10 issue of *The New York Times* Online..."

"But to get a complete picture, we have to look at the statistics. According to the 2012 *Statistical Abstracts*, the level of production for the European Economic Community fell from...."

"During the Indo-US Strategic Dialogue in Afghanistan in 2012, Secretary of State Hillary Clinton stated..."

Figure 11.8

Appropriate oral footnotes

© Cengage Learning

WHAT WOULD YOU DO?

A Question of Ethics

Alessandra decided to do her speech on the limited educational opportunities for women in the developing world. This topic was close to her heart, as her mother had struggled for years to improve education for women in her native country of Eritrea before immigrating to the United States. Moreover, Alessandra had already done quite a bit of reading on the topic.

As chance would have it, Alessandra came down with the flu the week before her speech was due and was flat on her back for four days so she didn't begin working on her speech until the afternoon before it was due. Still, by midnight, she had completed what she felt was a strong draft.

The next morning she cleaned up a few typos and errors in her outline and then practiced delivering it for the next two hours. Just before leaving for school, she read the instructions one last time to double-check that she had done everything correctly. Were her eyes playing tricks on her? The speech needed to be supported by no fewer than five published sources, yet she had cited only four. How could she have overlooked this detail? Alessandra thought frantically. She could ask for an extension, but she had too much other schoolwork to do in the coming days and needed to complete this project now. She could leave her speech as it was, but Mr. Allen was a stickler for little details and he'd certainly lower her grade over the missing source.

Alessandra had, of course, read other books on her topic in the past, even if she hadn't cited them in her speech. Although she couldn't remember the specific details of these books, she recalled their general message well enough. That was the solution! She would write a few quotations from one of the books based on her memory, drop them into her speech—she knew just the spot—and then update her references with credit information pulled from the Internet.

In less than a half hour, Alessandra completed her emergency revisions to her speech and was on her way to class.

1. Although blatantly fabricating information from a source is clearly unethical, what do you think about someone like Alessandra writing quotations based on her memory of earlier reading?

2. What ethical obligations does Alessandra have to her sources?

COMMUNICATE ON YOUR FEET

Speech Assignment

Citing Oral Footnotes

The Assignment

Do secondary research on a topic assigned to the class by your instructor. For that topic, create research cards and oral footnotes for the following kinds of sources:

- One newspaper article
- One journal or magazine article

- One book
- One Internet source

Be prepared when called on in class to present the information on your research card with an appropriate oral footnote. You should be equally prepared to critique the oral footnotes your classmates present and to hear critiques of yours.

Summary

This chapter focused on the first two action steps in the speechmaking process: selecting a specific speech goal that is adapted to the rhetorical situation, and gathering and evaluating information to develop the speech. To accomplish the first step, begin identifying a topic by listing subjects you are interested in and know something about. Then for each subject, generate topic ideas by brainstorming or concept mapping. To select an appropriate topic, gather and analyze demographic and subject-related data about your audience. You can gather the data by conducting a survey, informally observing, questioning an audience representative, or making educated guesses. You will also want to analyze the occasion in order to select an appropriate topic. Based on your audience and occasion analyses, through a process of elimination, select one topic that addresses the rhetorical situation. Once you have a topic, identify whether your general goal is to entertain, inform, or persuade, and construct a specific goal statement that identifies the desired response you want from your audience.

The second action step is to gather and evaluate information or evidence to develop your speech. To find material, begin by exploring your personal knowledge and experience. Then work outward by looking on the Internet for Web sites, blogs, and videos, as well as in libraries (online and in person) for secondary sources such as encyclopedias, books, articles, newspapers, statistical sources, biographical references, and government documents. By skimming written material, you can quickly evaluate sources to determine whether or not to read them in full. Four criteria for judging sources are authority, relevance, objectivity, and currency. You may also need to conduct primary research if secondary sources are insufficient. You may conduct fieldwork observations, surveys, interviews, original artifact or document examinations, or experiments. Two major types of evidence for speeches are factual statements and expert opinions. Factual statements are presented in narrative or as graphic illustrations in the form of examples, statistics, and definitions. Expert opinions are interpretations of facts and judgments made by qualified authorities. Depending on your topic and speech goal, you may use facts and opinions and elaborate them with examples, anecdotes, narratives, comparisons, contrasts, and quotations.

As you review your sources, you will want to record the information you find in an annotated bibliography and on research cards. Be sure to record pertinent information related to your topic, as well as complete bibliographic citations. Finally, be sure to cite sources as oral footnotes where appropriate throughout your speech.

COMMUNICATE!

RESOURCE AND ASSESSMENT CENTER

Now that you have read Chapter 11, go to the Speech Communication Course-Mate at cengagebrain.com where you'll find an interactive eBook and interactive learning tools including quizzes, flashcards, sample speech videos, audio study tools, skill-building activities, action step activities, and more. Student Workbook, Speech Builder Express 3.0, and Speech Studio 2.0 are also available.

Applying What You've Learned

Impromptu Speech Activity

1. Draw an information source from a box in the front of the room. It might be a book, a magazine or academic journal article, or a printout from a discussion board or blog or Web site. Read or skim the source. Then prepare a proper APA reference citation. Go to the front of the room and write the citation on the board. Then present a 2- to 3-minute informative speech on how well the source meets each of the four evaluation criteria for a speech on a related topic. Provide evidence for your assessments. Be sure to quote something from the information source using a proper oral footnote during the speech.

Assessment Activities

1. Go to VS Video Productions Web site at www.vsvideoproductions.com and click on the "demo reels" link. What kinds of information and information sources are used to compel viewers to use this company's services? Which are most compelling to you and why?

Attend a public speech delivered outside your school. If your schedule makes going to a live speech difficult, you may watch a speech delivered on TV or cable (try C-SPAN). When watching the speech, give close consideration to the audience and occasion and evaluate how they might have influenced the speaker. Was the speech pitched directly at the immediate interests of the audience? If not, did the speaker attempt to draw connections between his or her topic and the audience's interests? Did the speaker use any particular words or gestures to connect better with the audience? What about the manner in which the speaker was dressed; how might this have played with the audience? Can you discern any influence the setting might have played on the speaker?

2. Recognizing a Specific Goal Find a speech online about a topic that interests you. (Try sites such as AmericanRhetoric.com or www.whitehouse.gov/briefing_ room.) Then read that speech to identify the speaker's goal. Was the goal clearly stated in the introduction? Was it implied but nevertheless clear? Was it unclear? Note how this analysis can help you clarify your own speech goal. Write a paragraph explaining what you have learned.

3. Evaluating Sources Compare the definitions of *fracking* presented on these two Web pages:

    a) http://energyanswered.org/questions/how-does-hydraulic-fracturing-work

    b) http://www.foodandwaterwatch.org/water/fracking/

Note the specific wording of each definition. Use the concept of source bias to explain this difference. Locate a third source that defines fracking that is less biased than the two provided. On what basis did you decide it was less biased?

Organizing Your Speech

What you'll know

- The components of an effective speech outline

- How to determine the main points of your speech

- Elements of an effective speech introduction

- Elements of an effective speech conclusion

What you'll be able to do

- Construct an effective thesis statement for your speech

- Craft clear main points related to your specific speech goal

- Prepare a complete speech outline

- Create effective transitions

- Create an effective introduction

- Create an effective conclusion

- Prepare an accurate reference list

"Troy, Mareka gave an awesome speech on recycling paper. I haven't heard so many powerful stories in a long time."

"Yeah, Brett, I agree; the stories were interesting. But, you know, I had a hard time following the talk. I couldn't really get a hold of what the main ideas were. Could you?"

"Well, she was talking about recycling and stuff, . . . but now that you mention it, I'm not sure what she really wanted us to think or do about it. I mean, it was really interesting, but kind of confusing, too."

CONSIDER *THIS*....

Have you ever had trouble
following the main ideas in
a professor's lecture? What
do you do to try to stay
focused? Does it help?

Troy and Brett's experience is not that unusual. Even well-known speakers sometimes give speeches that are hard to follow. Yet, when your speech is well organized, you are far more likely to achieve your goal. A well-organized speech has three identifiable parts: an introduction, a body, and a conclusion. When these parts are constructed effectively, our speeches will have lasting impact. In other words, when the speech is over, audience members will remember not only an opening joke or a compelling story, but also the goal and main ideas. In this chapter, we describe the third of the five speech plan action steps: organizing ideas into a well-structured outline.

ACTION STEP 3

Organize Ideas Into a Well-Structured Outline

organizing

the process of structuring the material to be presented in the speech

Organizing, the process of structuring the material you will present in your speech, is guided by what you learned when you conducted your audience analysis. When the audience's expectations are violated or when they can't understand your goal or follow your main points, they may get frustrated, "tune out," or even become hostile. The *Pop Comm!* feature "Raise a Glass: Giving a Toast," illustrates the negative consequences of a poorly organized speech. To turn your ideas into a well-organized outline, begin by developing the body, then the introduction, and finally, the conclusion.

POP COMM!

Raise a Glass: Giving a Toast

Purestock/Jupiter Images

Public speaking is not just for business events or classroom presentations. People are often asked to give short speeches at a variety of social events, including weddings, funerals, and even birthday parties. The wedding toast (often referred to as the best man's speech or maid of honor's speech) is a traditional part of most wedding receptions in the United States and one of the most common "real-life" examples of public speaking. It's also a speech where a person's *lack* of public speaking skills becomes readily apparent. Many Hollywood films, particularly comedies, play off the awkward situations that arise from poorly delivered wedding toasts. While it is fun to chuckle at Alan's (Zach

Galifianakis's) ridiculous "wolf pack" speech from *The Hangover*, cringe at the awkward one-upmanship between Annie (Kristen Wiig) and Helen (Rose Byrne) during the engagement party in *Bridesmaids*, or laugh at Steve Buscemi's drunken rant in *The Wedding Singer*, chances are you don't want to follow these models should you ever be called upon to give a toast. But how do you prepare for this sort of speech?

It may seem like a social occasion is not the place for a prepared and structured speech, but most experts suggest it's best to prepare your remarks ahead of time. This will give you a chance to gather your thoughts and help you manage your nerves when you actually give the toast. Practicing aloud in advance will also help you to sound more natural and conversational because you are less likely to simply read it. But that doesn't mean you need to prepare something lengthy. Renowned etiquette expert Emily Post says "[Y]ou can never go wrong if you keep it short and sweet" ("Vermont Vows: The Toast!," 2010). The fundamental goal of the wedding toast is to honor the bride and groom, and some of the best toasts accomplish this goal in just one or two minutes.

When considering how to structure your toast, begin by writing down your thoughts about the bride and groom. Consider how you know them, how you would describe them, how you would describe their relationship, and any advice you might want to offer as they begin their new life together. You might also find inspiration from traditional toasts or famous quotes about love or marriage, easily found on the Internet. From this brainstorming list, you can begin to structure your speech by pairing your research with your personal experience and your personal knowledge about the bride and groom.

Having outside research is helpful, but ultimately a toast should focus on the personal and emotional. About.com Weddings writer Nina Calloway suggests beginning your speech by introducing yourself and indicating how you know the couple. Humorous or heartfelt anecdotes about the couple can be a great way to personalize the speech and keep your audience interested. In fact, including a joke or a poignant memory about the bride or groom can be an effective way to start your toast and set the tone for the entire speech. Most experts recommend keeping such personal anecdotes positive rather than embarrassing. Lisa B. Marshall and Trent Armstrong (2010) say, "[T]his is not the time to bring up past relationships or the time she got drunk and lost her lunch in your backseat. That is a sure-fire way to lose a friend and sour a nice moment." Be mindful of your audience, too, as it's unlikely that Grandma wants to hear a raunchy story about the bride's single days. Choosing an appropriate anecdote can help you structure the entire speech, as the emotions brought out in the anecdote can set up the well-wishes you use to end your toast. You can end with your own words or turn again to popular quotations for traditional wedding blessings that exemplify the positive emotions you've expressed during your toast.

Weddings are meant to be joyous occasions, and your toast should ultimately be celebratory and focused on the couple, not on you. Slate.com writer Troy Patterson (2011) offers succinct and humorous advice: "[K]eep it brief. Stand up straight. In a wedding toast—unlike in marriage itself—love is all you need."

Questions to Ponder

1. If you have you ever given a wedding toast, did you follow this advice?

2. How did it go?

3. What are some things you will be sure to do (and NOT do) if you ever find yourself responsible for giving a toast, and why?

Developing the Body

Once you have completed the first two Action Steps (identified your general and specific speech goal and assembled a body of information on your topic), you are ready to plan the body of your speech by (a) choosing the main points; (b) crafting them into a well-phrased thesis statement; (c) outlining the body of the speech; and (d) creating transitions.

Choose Main Points

Begin to organize the body of your speech by identifying the main ideas you want to share. The **main points** are complete sentence statements of the two to four central ideas your audience needs to understand if you are to achieve your speech goal. You will then develop each main idea with

main points

complete sentence representations of the main ideas used in your thesis and preview statement

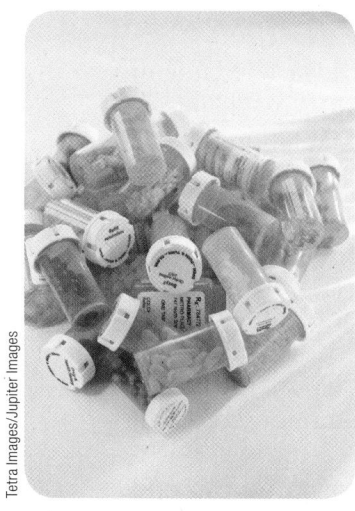

You want to limit the body of your speech to two to four main points so that your audience can follow along easily.

supporting material. Usually, the difference between a 5-minute speech and a 25-minute speech with the same speech goal is not the number of main points, but the extent to which each one is developed with supporting material.

For some goals, determining the main points is easy. For example, if your goal is to teach your audience how to create a Web site, your main points will likely be the steps involved in developing a very basic one. Most times, however, identifying main points that achieve your speech goal is more complex. How can you identify the main ideas when they aren't obvious? First, begin by listing the ideas you believe relate to your specific goal. You will probably find it easy to list as many as nine or more. Second, eliminate ideas that your analysis suggests this audience already understands. Third, eliminate any ideas that might be too complicated or too broad for this audience to comprehend in the time allotted for your speech. Fourth, check to see if some of the ideas can be grouped together under a broader concept. Finally, from the ideas that remain, choose two to four that are most central to your specific speech goal.

Let's look at how Katie used these steps to identify the main points for a speech whose goal was to "inform my classmates of the growing problem of Adderall abuse among college students." To begin, Katie listed ideas she had discovered while doing her research.

What is a prescription drug?

What is Adderall?

What are the ingredients in Adderall?

How is Adderall made?

What is the history of Adderall?

Who takes Adderall?

Why is it prescribed?

What are its benefits?

What are its risks?

How many college students take Adderall without a prescription?

What are the demographics of college students who take Adderall without a prescription?

Why do college students who don't have a prescription take it (perceived benefits)?

What are the benefit myths?

What are actual results or consequences of this behavior?

Second, Katie eliminated the idea "what is a prescription drug" because she knew her audience already understood this. Third, Katie noticed that several of the ideas seemed to be related. What is Adderall, why is it prescribed, who takes it, as well as its risks and benefits seemed to go together. How many people take it, demographics, and perceived benefits of college students who take Adderall without a prescription also seemed to be related. And benefit myths and actual results/consequences could be grouped together. Fourth, Katie decided the ingredients, history, and how Adderall is made were too broad to cover adequately in the time she was allotted for the speech and were not directly related to her goal. Based on this examination, Katie decided her main points would be: (1) Adderall is a prescription drug developed for a specific purpose;

(2) Adderall's ability to increase memory retention has made it a popular drug among college students looking for an edge; and (3) Using Adderall as a study aid can cause serious problems. These main points became the framework for the body of Katie's speech. When she finished her analysis and synthesis, Katie's list looked like this:

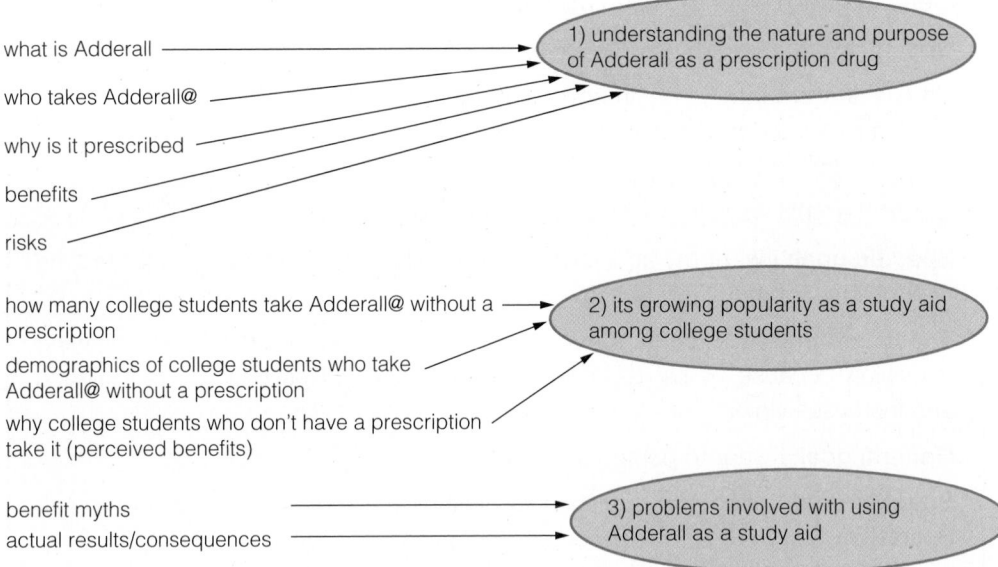

Write the Thesis Statement

A **thesis statement** is a one- or two-sentence summary that incorporates your general and specific goals and previews the main points of your speech. Katie crafted the following thesis statement for her speech on Adderall: "I want to inform my audience about the growing problem of college students taking Adderall without a prescription by explaining the nature and purpose of Adderall as a prescription drug, its growing popularity as a study aid among college students, and problems associated with using Adderall without a prescription." Review Figure 12.1 for several additional examples.

thesis statement

a one- or two-sentence summary of your speech that states your general and specific goals and previews the main points of your speech

Outline the Speech Body

Once you have a chosen your main points and written a thesis statement, you can begin to organize the information you want to present under each main point. The most effective way to do this is to outline your speech. **Speech outlines** are full-sentence written frameworks of the sequential and hierarchical relationships among the ideas we plan to present. In most speeches, three levels of hierarchy are all you will need: main points (numbered with Roman numerals), subpoints that support a main point (ordered under each main point with capital letters), and sometimes sub-subpoints (numbered under the relevant subpoint with Arabic numbers). Figure 12.2 shows the general form of most speech outlines. Notice that it proposes between two and four main points and offers at least two subpoints under each main point.

speech outline

a sentence representation of the sequential and hierarchical relationships between the ideas presented in a speech

General goal: I want to inform my audience.

Specific goal: I want my audience to understand how to improve their grades in college.

Thesis statement: Three proven techniques for improving test scores in college are to attend classes regularly, develop a positive attitude, and study efficiently.

General goal: I want to inform my audience.

Specific goal: I want the audience to understand the benefits of volunteering.

Thesis statement: Some important benefits of volunteering include helping underprivileged populations, supporting nonprofit organizations, and improving your own self-esteem.

General goal: I want to persuade my audience.

Specific goal: I want my audience to believe that parents should limit the time their children spend viewing television.

Thesis statement: Parents should limit the time their children spend viewing television because heavy television viewing desensitizes children to violence and increases violent tendencies in children.

General goal: I want to persuade my audience.

Specific goal: I want my audience to believe that they should learn to speak Spanish.

Thesis statement: You should learn to speak Spanish because it will benefit you personally, economically, and practically.

Figure 12.1

Goal and thesis statement examples

© Cengage Learning

Writing your main points and subpoints in complete sentences will help you clarify the relationships between main points and subpoints. Once you have worded each main point and determined its relevant subpoints, you are ready to choose an organizational pattern that fits your thesis. Let's look at how Katie developed her outline.

ACTION STEP 3.A

Choose Main Points

The goal of this activity is to help you determine two to four main ideas or main points that you can use as the framework for your speech.

1. List all the ideas you have found that relate to the specific goal of your speech.

2. If you have trouble limiting the number, do the following:

a. Draw a line through each idea that you believe the audience already understands, that you have no supporting information for, or that just seems too complicated.

b. Combine ideas that can be grouped together under a single heading.

3. From the ideas that remain, choose the two to four you will use as main points in your speech.

ACTION STEP 3.B

Write a Thesis Statement

The goal of this activity is to use your specific goals and the main points you have identified to develop a well-worded thesis statement for your speech.

1. Write the general and specific goals you developed in Chapter 11 with Action Step 1.e.

2. List the main points you determined in Action Step 3.a.

3. Now write a complete sentence that combines your specific goal with your main point ideas.

 You can complete this activity online using Speech Builder Express, view a student sample of this activity, and, if requested, e-mail your completed activity to your instructor. Use the Speech Communication CourseMate at cengagebrain.com to access the Action Step activities for Chapter 12.

Limit your speech to two, three or four main points.
Use at least two subpoints to support each main point.
If you support any subpoints with a sub-subpoint, be sure to offer at least two.

I. Main point one

  A. Subpoint A for main point one

    1. Sub-subpoint one (optional)

    2. Sub-subpoint two (optional)

  B. Subpoint B for main point one

II. Main point two

  A. Subpoint A for main point two

    1. Sub-subpoint one (optional)

    2. Sub-subpoint two (optional)

  B. Subpoint B of main point two

  C. Subpoint C of main point two

    1. Sub-subpoint one (optional)

    2. Sub-subpoint two (optional)

    3. Sub-subpoint three (optional)

III. Main point three

  A. Subpoint A for main point three

    1. Sub-subpoint one (optional)

    2. Sub-subpoint two (optional)

  B. Subpoint B of main point three

    . . . and so on.

© Cengage Learning

Figure 12.2

General form for a speech outline

Word Main Points

Recall that Katie's main points would be understanding the nature and purpose of Adderall as a prescription drug, its growing popularity as a study aid among college students, and the risks involved in doing so. Her thesis statement was: "Today I want to alert you to the uses and abuses of Adderall among college students. We'll do so by, first, discussing its nature and legal uses as a prescription drug, then its growing popularity as a study aid among college students, and, finally, the problems associated with abusing Adderall." Suppose she wrote her first draft of main points as follows:

I. What exactly is Adderall, and why is it prescribed?
II. College student use
III. Risks

From this wording, Katie would have drafted some ideas of the main points she was going to talk about and then create complete sentences for each. So she might clarify her main points like this:

I. What exactly is Adderall?
II. An increasing number of American college students are using Adderall.
III. Abusing Adderall is risky.

Study these statements. Do they seem a bit vague? Notice that we have emphasized that this is a first draft. Sometimes, the first draft of a main point is well expressed and doesn't need additional work. More often, however, we find that our first attempt doesn't quite capture what we want to say. So we need to rework our points to make them clearer. Let's consider Katie's draft statements more carefully. Katie has made a pretty good start. Her three main points are complete sentences. Now let's see how Katie might use two test questions to assure herself that she has achieved the best wording for her points.

1. **Is the relationship between each main point and the goal statement clearly specified?** Katie's first main point statement doesn't indicate what purposes Adderall serves as a prescription medicine. So she could improve this statement by saying:

   What exactly is Adderall, and what is it prescribed for?

   Similarly, she can improve the second main point statement by saying:

   Adderall abuse is becoming increasingly popular among American college students.

   The third point might be redrafted to state:

   Abusing Adderall as a study aid is dangerous.

Time order is appropriate when you are showing others how to do something or make something, or how to understand the way something works.

Linda Kennedy/Alamy

2. **Are the main points wordings parallel in structure?** Main points are *parallel* to one another when their wording follows the same structural pattern. Parallel structure is not a requirement, but it can help the audience recognize main points when you deliver your speech. Katie notices that she could make her main points parallel with a small adjustment:

   I. First, what exactly is Adderall, and why is it prescribed?
   II. Second, a growing number of American college students are using Adderall.
   III. Third, abusing Adderall as a study aid is dangerous.

Parallelism can be achieved in many ways. Katie used numbering: "first . . . second . . . third." Another way is to start each sentence with an active verb. Suppose Adam wants his audience to understand the steps involved in writing an effective job application cover letter. He might write the following first draft of his main points:

I. Format the heading elements correctly.
II. The body of the letter should be three paragraphs long.
III. When concluding, use "sincerely" or "regards."
IV. Then you need to proofread the letter carefully.

Narrative order is a way to organize your ideas as a story or series of stories.

After further consideration, Adam might revise his main points to make them parallel in structure by using active verbs (italicized):

I. *Format* the heading elements correctly.
II. *Organize* the body into three paragraphs.
III. *Conclude* the letter with "sincerely" or "regards."
IV. *Proofread* the letter carefully.

Notice how the similarity of structure clarifies the message. The audience can immediately identify the key steps in the process and the parallel structure makes the main points easier to remember.

Select an Organizational Pattern A speech can be organized in many different ways. An **organizational pattern** is a logical way to structure information that makes it easy for an audience to follow what is being said. Although speeches may use many different organizational patterns, four fundamental patterns are time (a.k.a. sequential or chronological) order, narrative order, topical order, and logical reasons order.

1. **Time order**, sometimes called *sequential order* or *chronological order*, arranges main points in sequence or by steps in a process. When you are explaining how to do something, how to make something, how something works, or how something happened, you will use time order. Adam's speech on the steps in writing a job application and cover letter followed a time order pattern. Let's look at another example of time order.

   Thesis statement: The four steps involved in developing a personal network are to analyze your current networking potential, to position yourself in places for opportunity, to advertise yourself, and to follow up on contacts.
   I. First, analyze your current networking potential.
   II. Second, position yourself in places for opportunity.
   III. Third, advertise yourself.
   IV. Fourth, follow up on contacts.

2. **Narrative order** structures your ideas through a story or series of stories. Narrative order is rooted in narrative theory, which suggests that one important way people communicate is through storytelling. We use stories to teach and learn, to entertain, and to make sense of the world around us (Fisher, 1987). While a narrative may be presented in chronological order, it may also use a series of flashbacks or flash forwards to increase the dramatic effect. The main points in a narrative may be the events in a single story that highlights the thesis, or the main points may be individual stories, each of

organizational pattern

a logical way to structure information that makes it easy for an audience to follow what is said

time (a.k.a. sequential or chronological) order

organizing the main points by a chronological sequence or by steps in a process

narrative order

dramatizes the thesis using a story or series of stories that includes characters, settings, and a plot which dramatizes the thesis. Lonna shared her story about having anorexia to help listeners understand the impact of the condition on someone's life.

Thesis statement: Today, I want to share my story as a person living with anorexia. I'll start by describing what a typical day is like for me as a recovering anorexic, then how I became anorexic and, finally, who saved my life.

I. Let me begin by telling you a story about what a typical day is like for me today as a recovering anorexic.

II. Becoming anorexic was a gradual process that began when I was a high school gymnast.

III. When I nearly died as a college sophomore, I got the help I needed thanks to two people I consider to be angels on earth.

topical order

structures the main points using some logical relationship among them

3. **Topical order** structures the main points using some logical relationship among them. Main points may be organized to progress from general to specific, least to most important, most to least familiar, and so forth. In the following example, the most important point is presented last and the second most important point is presented first, which is the order that the speaker believes is most suitable for the audience and speech goal.

Thesis statement: To maintain good health, let's discuss three proven methods for ridding our bodies of harmful toxins: staying hydrated, reducing animal foods, and eating natural whole foods.

I. One proven method for ridding our bodies of harmful toxins is reducing our intake of animal products.

II. A second proven method for ridding our bodies of harmful toxins is eating more natural whole foods.

III. A third proven method for ridding our bodies of harmful toxins is keeping well hydrated.

logical reasons order

structures the main points as reasons for accepting the thesis as desirable or true

4. **Logical reasons order** structures the main points as reasons for accepting the thesis as desirable or true. Logical reasons order is usually used when your goal is to persuade.

Thesis statement: Donating to the United Way is appropriate because your one donation can be divided among many charities, you can stipulate which specific charities you wish to support, and a high percentage of your donation goes to charities.

I. When you donate to the United Way, your one donation can be divided among many charities.

II. When you donate to the United Way, you can stipulate which charities you wish to support.

III. When you donate to the United Way, you know that a high percentage of your donation will go directly to the charities you've selected.

These four organizational patterns are the most basic ones. In Chapters 16 and 17, you will be introduced to several additional patterns for structuring the main points of informative and persuasive speeches.

subpoints

statements that elaborate on a main point

Identify Subpoints Subpoints are statements that elaborate on a main point. A main point may have two, three, or even more subpoints depending on the

THE AUDIENCE *BEYOND*

Chris decided to use topical reasons order to explain why soldiers create blogs about their combat experiences. He decided to post a link to his recorded speech to each soldier blog he referenced during it.

ACTION STEP 3.C

Outline the Main Points

The goal of this activity is to help you phrase and order your main points.

1. Write your thesis statement (Action Step 3.b).

2. Using the thesis statement you wrote in Action Step 3.b, underline the two to four main points for your speech.

3. Review the main points as a group.

   a. Is the relationship of each main point statement to the goal statement clearly specified? If not, revise.

   b. Are the main points parallel in structure? If not, revise.

4. Choose an organizational pattern for your main points.

5. Write your main points down in this order. Place a "I." before the main point you will make first, a "II." before your second point, and so on.

You can complete this activity online using Speech Builder Express, view a student sample of this activity, and, if requested, e-mail your completed activity to your instructor. Use the Speech Communication CourseMate at cengagebrain.com to access the Action Step activities for Chapter 12.

complexity of it. Subpoints use **supporting material**—developmental material you gathered through secondary and primary research. Subpoints and/or sub-subpoints may be elaborated with definitions, examples, statistics, personal experiences, stories, quotations, and other items.

As a first step, you can sort the research cards you prepared earlier into piles that correspond to each of your main points. Or color-code your annotated bibliography to indicate which sources relate to which main points. After categorizing each piece of information by main points, make a list of the subpoints that belong to each main point. Then, look for relationships between and among ideas. As you analyze, you can draw lines connecting items of information that fit together logically, cross out information that seems less important or doesn't really fit, and combine similar ideas using different language. One subpoint in each main point should be a **listener relevance link**, a piece of information that alerts listeners to why the main point is related to them or why they should care about this point.

supporting material

developmental material you gathered through secondary and primary research

listener relevance link

a piece of information that informs listeners why the main point is related to them or why they should care about the topic or point

If you were giving a speech on the phenomenon of soldiers creating blogs about their combat experiences, what organizational pattern do you think would best suit your speech?

Outline Subpoints Subpoints should also be represented on the outline in full sentences. It helps to include internal references for items of information you found in secondary sources. Doing so will remind you to cite them during the speech, which will enhance listeners' perception of you as an authority on the subject and help you avoid unintentional plagiarism. As with main points, subpoints should be revised until they are clearly stated. Katie developed her first main point this way:

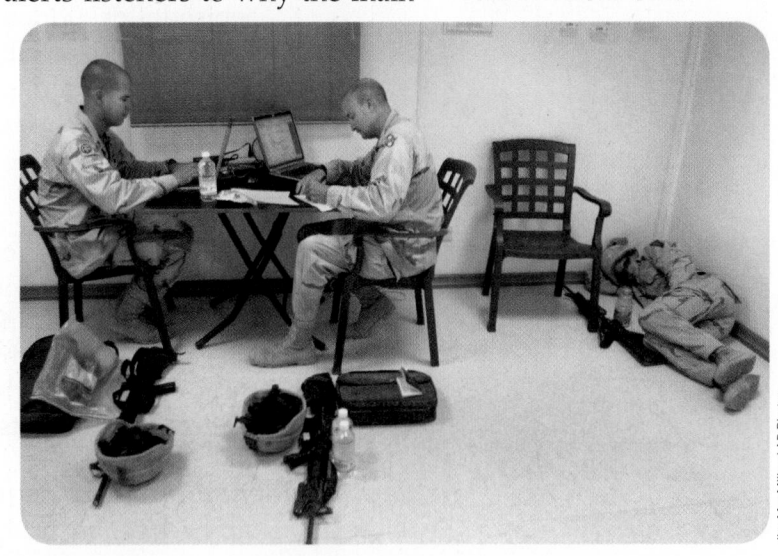

Jim MacMillan/ AP Photos

I. Adderall is a psychostimulant prescribed to treat three conditions.

   A. Adderall, the brand name for amphetamikne-dextroamphetamine is a psychostimulant, one of a class of drugs intended to promote concentration, suppress hyperactivity, and promote healthy social experiences for patients.

      1. Adderall stimulates the central nervous system by increasing the amount of dopamine and norepinephrine in the brain. These chemicals are neurotransmitters that help the brain send signals between nerve cells.

      2. Mentally, Adderall brings about a temporary improvement in alertness, wakefulness, endurance, and motivation.

      3. Physically, it can increase heart rate and blood pressure and decrease perceived need for food or sleep.

   B. Adderall is prescribed for the medical treatment of attention deficit hyperactivity disorder (ADHD) in children and adults as well as for narcolepsy and clinical depression.

      1. ADHD is a neurobehavioral developmental disorder characterized by problems of attention coupled with hyperactivity.

         a. Since the mid-1990s, there has been a documented increase in the number of American children diagnosed and treated for ADHD.

         b. According to the *Diagnostic and Statistical Manual of Mental Disorders (2000)*, symptoms must be present for at least six months for diagnosis, and symptoms must be excessive for medicinal treatment.

         c. The drugs Ritalin® and Dexedrine® are also used to treat ADHD. Adderall, however, remains the most widely prescribed of these drugs.

         d. According to the Centers for Disease Control and Prevention, approximately 4.4 million American children have been diagnosed with ADHD, and more than 2.5 million of those patients have been prescribed medicine to treat the condition.

      2. Adderall is also prescribed to treat narcolepsy, which occurs when the brain can't normally regulate cycles of sleep and waking, so sufferers experience excessive daytime sleepiness that results in episodes of suddenly falling asleep.

      3. Adderall can also be used to treat clinical depression, a disorder that is characterized by low mood, a loss of interest in normal activities, and low self-esteem.

Create Transitions

transitions

words, phrases, or sentences that show the relationship between or bridge ideas

section transition

complete sentence that shows the relationship between or bridges major parts of the speech

Transitions are words, phrases, or sentences that allow you to move smoothly from one point to another by showing the relationship between the two ideas. Good transitions are important in writing, but they are even more important in speaking. If listeners get lost or think they have missed something, they cannot go back and check as they can when reading. Transitions can come in the form of section transitions or signposts.

Section Transitions Section transitions are complete sentences that show the relationship between or bridges major parts of the speech. They typically

ACTION STEP 3.D

Identify and Outline Subpoints

The goal of this activity is to help you develop and outline your subpoints. Complete the following steps for each of your main points.

1. List the main point.

2. Using your research cards or annotated bibliography, list the key information related to that main point.

3. Analyze that information and cross out items that seem less relevant or don't fit.

4. Look for items that seem related and can be grouped under a broader heading.

5. Try to group information until you have between two and four supporting points for the main point.

6. Write those supporting subpoints in full sentences.

7. Repeat this process for all main points.

8. Write an outline using Roman numerals for main points, capital letters for supporting points, and Arabic numbers for material related to supporting points.

You can complete this activity online using Speech Builder Express, view a student sample of this activity, and, if requested, e-mail your completed activity to your instructor. Use the Speech Communication CourseMate at cengagebrain.com to access the Action Step activities for Chapter 12.

summarize what has just been said in one main point and preview the next main idea. Essentially, section transitions are the "glue" that links the main points of your speech together.

For example, suppose Adam just finished his introduction on creating a cover letter and is now ready to launch into his main points. Before stating his first main point, he might say, "Creating a good cover letter is a process that has four steps. Now, let's consider the first one." When his listeners hear this transition, they are signaled to listen to and remember the first main point. When he finishes his first main point, he will use another section transition to signal that he is finished speaking about the first main point and is moving on to the second main point: "Now that we understand what is involved in creating the heading elements, let's move on to discuss what to include in the body of the letter."

You might be thinking that this sounds repetitive or patronizing, but section transitions are important for two reasons. First, they help the audience follow the organization of ideas in the speech. Second, they help audience members remember information. To help remember and use section transitions, write them in complete sentences between the appropriate main points on your speech outline.

Signposts **Signposts** are words or phrases that connect pieces of supporting material to the main point or sub point they address. Sometimes signposts number ideas: *first*, *second*, *third*, and *fourth*. Sometimes they help the audience focus on a key idea: *foremost*, *most important*, or *above all*. Signposts can also be used to

signposts

short word or phrase transitions that connect pieces of supporting material to the main point or subpoint they address

Sometimes signposts are used to highlight numerical order.

AP Photo/Jacques Brinon

ACTION STEP 3.E

Prepare Section Transitions

The goal of this exercise is to help you prepare section transitions. Section transitions appear as parenthetical statements before or after each main point. Using complete sentences:

1. Write a transition from your first main point to your second.

2. Write a transition from each remaining main point to the one after it.

3. Add these transitional statements to your outline.

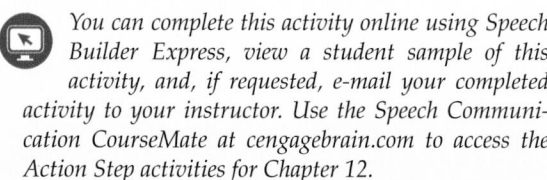 *You can complete this activity online using Speech Builder Express, view a student sample of this activity, and, if requested, e-mail your completed activity to your instructor. Use the Speech Communication CourseMate at cengagebrain.com to access the Action Step activities for Chapter 12.*

introduce an explanation: *to illustrate, for example, in other words, essentially,* or *to clarify.* Signposts can also signal that a lengthy anecdote, or even the speech itself, is coming to an end: *in short, finally, in conclusion,* or *to summarize.* Just as section transitions serve as the glue that holds your big-picture main points together, signposts connect your subpoints and supporting material together within each main point.

Developing the Introduction

Once you have developed the body of the speech, you can decide how to introduce it. Because the introduction is so important to your success, you will want to develop two or three different introductions and then select the one that seems best for your specific goal and the audience you will be addressing. An introduction is generally about 10 percent of the length of the entire speech, so for a five-minute speech (approximately 750 words), an introduction of about 30 seconds (approximately 60–85 words) is appropriate.

An effective introduction achieves four primary goals: It gets the audience's attention, it identifies the relevance of the topic to the audience, it begins to establish speaker credibility, and it states the thesis (speech goal and main point preview).

Get Attention

An audience's physical presence does not guarantee people will actually listen to your speech. Your first goal, then, is to create an opening that will win your listeners' attention by arousing their curiosity and motivating them to want to know more about your topic. Let's look at several strategies for getting attention: startling statements, questions, stories, jokes, personal references, quotations, action, and suspense.

startling statement

a shocking expression or example used to arouse the audience's interest

Startling Statements A **startling statement** is a shocking expression or example. Chris used this startling statement to get his listeners' attention for his speech about how automobile emissions contribute to global warming:

Look around. Each one of you is sitting next to a killer. That's right. You are sitting next to a cold-blooded killer. Before you think about jumping up and running out of this room, let me explain. Everyone who drives an automobile is a killer of the environment. Every time you turn the key to your ignition, you are helping to destroy our precious surroundings.

© 1983 Cathy Guisewite. Reprinted by permission of Universal Press Syndicate. All rights reserved.

Questions Questions are requests for information that encourage the audience to think about something related to your topic. Questions can be *rhetorical* or *direct*. A **rhetorical question** is one that doesn't require an overt response. Notice how a student began her speech on counterfeiting with three short, rhetorical questions:

> *What would you do with this $20 bill if I gave it to you? Would you take your friend to a movie? Or would you treat yourself to pizza and drinks? Well, if you did either of these things, you could get in big trouble—this bill is counterfeit!*

Notice that the speaker didn't ask the question to find out what her audience members would actually do with the money, but to set up the speech on counterfeiting. Unlike a rhetorical question, a **direct question** demands an overt response from the audience. It might be a "yea" or "nay" or a show of hands. For example, here's how author and motivational speaker, Harvey MacKay, started his commencement address at the University of Southern California in 2009:

> *Let me start by asking all of you in the audience this question: How many people talk to themselves? Please raise your hands. I count approximately 50 percent. To the other 50 percent who didn't raise your hands, I can just hear you now, saying to yourself: "Who me? I don't talk to myself!"*
>
> *Well I think all of you will be talking to yourself about the day's events on your way home this evening. This is an unforgettable moment among many fine hours you will have in your career and life. (Mackay, 2009)*

questions

requests for information that encourage the audience to think about something related to your topic

rhetorical question

a question that doesn't require an overt response

direct question

a question that demands an overt response from the audience

CONSIDER *THIS....*

Would you ever try to get attention by asking a direct question? Why or why not?

Speakers typically ask for a show of hands when getting attention with a direct question.

AP Photo/Hani Mohammed

Direct questions get audience attention because they require a physical response. However, getting listeners to actually comply with your request can
also pose a challenge.

story

*an account of something that
has happened or could happen*

Stories A **story** is an account of something that has happened (actual) or could
happen (hypothetical). Most people enjoy a well-told story, so it makes a good
attention getter. One drawback is that stories can sometimes take more time to
tell than is appropriate for the length of your speech. Use a story only if it is
short or if you can abbreviate it so that it is just right for your speech length.
Yash Gupta, dean of the Carey Business School at Johns Hopkins University,
used a story to get attention about assumptions, prejudices, and policies about
older people:

> *Imagine this.*
>
> *You are boarding a routine business flight. As you get on the plane you notice the
> pilot looks perhaps a bit . . . grandfatherly. In fact, he is only two years away from
> his FAA-mandated retirement age.*
>
> *You sit and open a magazine. You know, in advertisements flight attendants
> always look like the champagne they are pouring: fresh and bubbly. But look-
> ing around the cabin at the flight crew the words that instead come to mind are
> mature and no-nonsense. All three flight attendants are in their 50s.*
>
> *You are belted comfortably, your seat is in the upright position, and you have just
> felt the wheels lift off the runway from LaGuardia Airport.*
>
> *Only a couple minutes into your flight there is a loud bang, followed by another
> loud bang. Flames shoot out from the plane's two jet engines, and then they both
> go silent. Less than three minutes later, the pilot makes one terse announcement:
> prepare for impact.*
>
> *The next thing you know you're floating on the Hudson River and the flight crew
> is quickly and efficiently moving you onto the wings of the aircraft. They know
> their jobs.*
>
> *Flight attendant Doreen Welsh is 58. She's been flying since 1970—almost
> 40 years' experience. Sheila Daily is 57. She's been flying since 1980, and the
> other flight attendant, 51-year-old Donna Dent, has been flying since 1982.*
>
> *As you watch the rescue boats approach, one thought goes through your mind: At
> moments like this, who needs fresh and bubbly?*
>
> *The story of Flight 1549 suggests that, in our society, perhaps we have been
> too quick to praise youth, too ready to underestimate the value of age, wisdom,
> and experience. One thing is certain: As we look forward to the middle years
> of the 21st century, we are going to have ample opportunity to discover if our
> assumptions, our prejudices, and our policies about older people are valid—or
> if perhaps we have some serious reconsidering to do. (Gupta, 2010)*

joke

*anecdote or a piece of
wordplay designed to be funny
and make people laugh*

Jokes A **joke** is an anecdote or a piece of wordplay designed to make people
laugh. A joke can be used to get attention when it meets the *three R's test*: It
must be realistic, relevant, and repeatable (Humes, 1988). In other words, the
joke can't be too far-fetched, unrelated to the speech purpose, or potentially

offensive to some listeners. In his speech about being a person of integrity, for example, Joel Osteen offered this joke to get attention:

> A kindergarten teacher asked one of her students what she was drawing a picture of. The little girl said, "I'm drawing a picture of God." The teacher replied, "Oh honey, nobody knows what God looks like. Without missing a beat, the little girl replied, "They will in a minute . . .". (Osteen, 2012)

Personal references

A **personal reference** is a brief account of something that happened to you or a hypothetical situation that listeners can imagine themselves in. In addition to getting attention, a personal reference can engage listeners as active participants. A personal reference like the one that follows is suitable for a speech of any length:

> Were you panting when you got to the top of those four flights of stairs this morning? I'll bet there were a few of you who vowed you're never going to take a class on the top floor of this building again. But did you ever stop to think that maybe the problem isn't that this class is on the top floor? It just might be that you are not getting enough exercise.

Quotations A **quotation** is a comment made by and attributed to someone other than the speaker. A particularly vivid or thought-provoking quotation can make an excellent introduction as long as it relates to your topic. For instance, notice how Sally Mason, provost at Purdue University, used a quotation to get the attention of her audience, the Lafayette, Indiana, YWCA:

> There is an ancient saying, "May you live in interesting times." It is actually an ancient curse. It might sound great to live in interesting times. But interesting times are times of change and even turmoil. They are times of struggle. They are exciting. But, at the same time, they are difficult. People of my generation have certainly lived through interesting times and they continue today. (Mason, 2007, p. 159)

Action An **action** is an attention-getting act designed to highlight and arouse interest in your topic. You can perform an action yourself, just as Juan did when he split a stack of boards with his hand to get attention for his speech on karate.

As long as your joke adheres to the Three R's test, you can use it to get the attention of your audience.

personal reference
a brief account of something that happened to you or a hypothetical situation that listeners can imagine themselves in

quotation
a comment made by and attributed to someone other than the speaker

action
an act designed to highlight and arouse interest in a topic

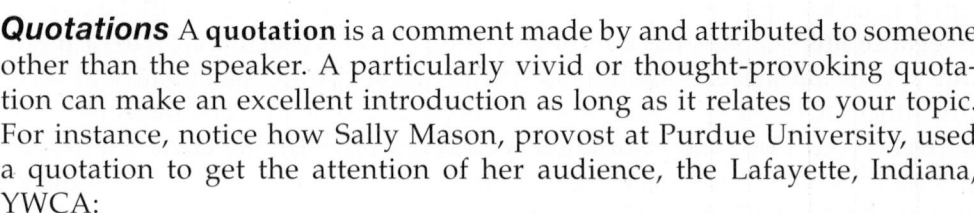
THE AUDIENCE *BEYOND*

Rather than cite the lyrics of a song opening as an attention getter, Jerry found it online and played it for his audience.

Or you can ask volunteers from the audience to perform the action. For example, Cindria used three audience members to participate in breaking a piñata to create interest in her speech on the history of the piñata. If you choose to use audience members, consider soliciting participants ahead of time to avoid the possibility of having no volunteers when you ask during your speech. Finally, you can ask your entire audience to perform some action related to your speech topic. If you'd like to ask your whole audience to perform an action, realistically assess whether what you are asking is something your audience is likely to comply with.

Suspense To create **suspense**, you word your attention-getter so that what is described generates uncertainty or mystery and excites the audience. When your audience wonders, "What is she leading up to?" you have created suspense. A suspenseful opening is especially valuable when your audience is not particularly interested in hearing about your topic. Consider this suspenseful statement:

> *It costs the United States more than $116 billion per year. It has cost the loss of more jobs than a recession. It accounts for nearly 100,000 deaths a year. I'm not talking about drug abuse—the problem is alcoholism. Today I want to show you how we can avoid this inhumane killer by abstaining from alcohol.*

By putting the problem, alcoholism, at the end, the speaker encourages the audience to try to anticipate the answer. And because the audience may well be thinking the problem is drugs, the revelation that the answer is alcoholism is likely to be that much more effective.

Establish Relevance

Even if you successfully get the attention of your listeners, to *keep* their attention you will need to motivate them to listen to your speech. You can do this by offering a clear listener relevance link in the introduction. Recall that a listener relevance link is a statement of how and why your speech relates to or might affect your audience. Sometimes your attention-getting statement will serve this function, but if it doesn't, you will need to provide a personal connection between your topic and your audience. Notice how Tiffany created a listener relevance link for her speech about being a vegetarian by asking her audience to consider the topic in relation to their own lives:

> *Although a diet rich in eggs and meat was once the norm in this country, more and more of us are choosing a vegetarian lifestyle to help lower blood pressure, reduce cholesterol, and even help prevent the onset of some diseases.*

When creating a listener relevance link, answer these questions: Why should my listeners care about what I'm saying? In what way(s) might they benefit from hearing about it? How might my speech address my listeners' needs or desires for such things as health, wealth, well-being, self-esteem, success, and so forth?

Establish Credibility

If someone hasn't formally introduced you, audience members are going to wonder who you are and why they should pay attention to what you say. So, another goal of the introduction is to begin to build your credibility. **Credibility** is the perception your audience has about your competence and character. You want to provide some indication that you are an authority on the subject of your speech and that you care about the audience and the occasion. Remember, though, that your goal is to highlight that you are a credible speaker on this topic, one who respects the audience and occasion, not that you are *the* or even *a* final authority on the subject. Carmen Mariano, president of Archbishop Williams High School, established credibility and goodwill in a "welcome back, students" speech this way:

> *Ladies and gentlemen, you will hear one word many times this morning. That word is welcome. Please know how much we mean that word. Please know how much I mean that word.*
>
> *Why will we mean that word so much?*
>
> *Because without you, this is just a building on 80 Independence Avenue. And with you, this is Archbishop Williams High School. That's right. When you walked through those doors this morning, you made this building a school again.*
>
> *So welcome back.*
>
> *And welcome to your school.*

State the Thesis

Because audiences want to know what the speech is going to be about, it's important to state your thesis. After Miguel gained the audience's attention and established relevance and credibility, he introduced his thesis, "In the next five minutes, I'd like to explain to you that romantic love consists of three elements: passion, intimacy, and commitment."

Stating main points in the introduction is necessary unless you have some special reason for not revealing the details of the thesis. For instance, after getting the attention of his audience, Miguel might say, "In the next five minutes, I'd like to explain the three aspects of romantic love," a statement that specifies the number of main points, but leaves specifics for transition statements immediately preceding the main points. In a commencement address at Stanford

---

ACTION STEP 3.F

Write Speech Introductions

The goal of this activity is to create choices for how you will begin your speech.

1. For the speech body you outlined earlier, write three different introductions that you believe meet the goals of effective introductions and that you believe would set an appropriate tone for your speech goal and audience.

2. Of the three you drafted, which do you believe is the best? Why?

3. Write that introduction in outline form.

You can complete this activity online using Speech Builder Express, view a student sample of this activity, and, if requested, e-mail your completed activity to your instructor. Use the Speech Communication CourseMate at cengagebrain.com to access the Action Step activities for Chapter 12.

The conclusion offers you one final chance to leave a lasting impression.

University, Steve Jobs stated the main points in his introduction in this way: "Today I want to tell you three stories from my life. That's it. No big deal. Just three stories" (Jobs, 2005).

Developing the Conclusion

Shakespeare once said, "All's well that ends well." Effective conclusions heighten the impact of a good speech by summarizing the main ideas and leaving the audience with a vivid impression. Even though the conclusion is a relatively short part of the speech—seldom more than 5 percent (35 to 40 words for a 5-minute speech)—your conclusion should be carefully planned. As with your speech introduction, you should prepare two or three conclusions and then choose the one you believe will be the most effective with your audience.

Summarize Main Points

An effective speech conclusion includes an abbreviated restatement of your thesis. An appropriate summary for an informative speech on how to improve your grades might be "So I hope you now understand [informative goal] that three techniques to help you improve your grades are to attend classes regularly, to develop a positive attitude toward the course, and to study systematically [main points]." A short ending for a persuasive speech on why you should exercise might be "So you should exercise for at least 30 minutes each day [persuasive goal] to improve your appearance, as well as your physical and mental health [main points]."

Clinch

CONSIDER *THIS....*

Can you recall conclusions from any of the speeches you have heard? What made each of them memorable?

clincher

a one- or two-sentence statement that provides a sense of closure by driving home the importance of your speech in a memorable way

Although a good summary helps the audience remember your main points, a good clincher leaves the audience with a vivid impression. A **clincher** is a short memorable statement that provides a sense of closure by driving home the importance of your speech goal in a memorable way. If you can, try to devise a clincher that refers back to the introductory comments in some way. Two effective strategies for clinching are using vivid imagery and appealing to action.

Vivid Imagery To develop vivid imagery, you can use any of the devices we discussed for getting attention (startling statement, question, story, joke, personal reference, quotation, action, or suspense). For example, in Tiffany's speech about being a vegetarian, she referred back to the personal reference she had made in her introduction about a vegetarian Thanksgiving meal:

> *So now you know why I made the choice to become a vegetarian and how this choice affects my life today. As a vegetarian, I've discovered a world of food I never knew existed. Believe me, I am salivating just thinking about the meal I have planned for this Thanksgiving: fennel and blood orange salad; followed by baked polenta layered with tomato, Fontina, and Gorgonzola cheeses; an acorn squash tart; marinated tofu; and with what else but pumpkin pie for dessert!*

Sounds good doesn't it? Clinchers with vivid imagery are effective because they leave listeners with a picture imprinted in their minds.

Appeal to Action The appeal to action is a common clincher for persuasive speeches. The **appeal to action** describes the behavior that you want your listeners to follow after they have heard your arguments. Notice how Matthew Cossolott, president and founder of Study Abroad Alumni International, concludes his speech on global awareness and responsibility with a strong appeal to action:

appeal to action

describes the behavior you want your listeners to follow after they have heard your arguments

> *So, yes, you should have this re-entry program. Yes, you should network and explore international career opportunities. That's all good.*
>
> *But I also encourage you to Globalize Your Locality. I urge you to Think Global. . . . Act Global. . . . Be Global.*
>
> *This is an urgent call to action . . . for you and other study abroad alumni . . . to help us reduce the global awareness deficit.*
>
> *You can do so by becoming involved with SAAI . . . and other organizations such as the National Council for International Visitors, Sister Cities, or Rotary International.*
>
> *You can speak to local schools and community organizations about your study abroad experience and the need for more global awareness.*
>
> *When you studied abroad, I'm sure you were told many times that you would be serving as unofficial ambassadors of the United States . . . your campus . . . and even your community back home.*
>
> *Now that you're home again, I hope you'll become ambassadors for the value of the study abroad experience and for the need for greater international awareness.*
>
> *In wrapping up . . . I'd like to leave you with this image . . . just picture in your mind's eye that iconic photograph of planet earth. I'm sure you've seen it. Taken over four decades ago . . . in December 1968 . . . on the Apollo 8 mission to the moon.*
>
> *The photograph—dubbed Earthrise—shows our small, blue planet rising above a desolate lunar landscape. This photo was a true watershed in human history . . . marking the first time earthlings . . . fellow global citizens had traveled outside earth's orbit and looked back on our lonely planet.*
>
> *The widespread publication of Earthrise had a lot to do with launching the world-wide environmental movement. It's no accident that the first Earth Day—on April 22, 1970—took place so soon after the publication of this remarkable photograph.*
>
> *We're all privileged to inhabit this same planet—truly an island in space. And voices to the contrary notwithstanding . . . whether we want to admit it or not . . . we are all, undeniably and by definition, citizens of the worlds.*
>
> *The only question is: will we accept the responsibilities of global citizenship?*
>
> *Your future . . . and perhaps the survival of the planet . . . just may depend on how many of us answer yes to that question. (Cossolotto, 2009)*

THE AUDIENCE *BEYOND*

Darius wanted to reach more people than just his classmates to encourage them to eat organic food. So he posted his speech on YouTube and his Facebook page.

ACTION STEP 3.G

Create Speech Conclusions

The goal of this activity is to help you create choices for how you will conclude your speech.

1. For the speech body you outlined earlier, write three different conclusions that review important points you want the audience to remember and leave the audience with a vivid impression.

2. Which do you believe is the best? Why?

3. Write that conclusion in outline form.

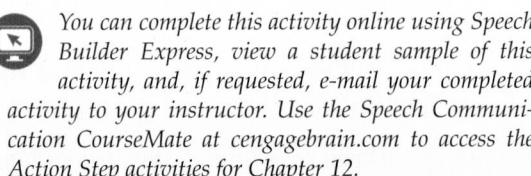 *You can complete this activity online using Speech Builder Express, view a student sample of this activity, and, if requested, e-mail your completed activity to your instructor. Use the Speech Communication CourseMate at cengagebrain.com to access the Action Step activities for Chapter 12.*

COMMUNICATE ON YOUR FEET

Speech Assignment

The Assignment

1. Identify a favorite toy, game, food, or hobby you had as a child.

2. Come up with a thesis statement and three main points you could talk about for that toy, game, food, or hobby.

3. Prepare an introduction, section transitions, and conclusion for a "speech" about that toy, game, food, or hobby. But do not prepare any supporting material.

4. At your instructor's request, come to the front of the room and deliver the introduction, section transitions, and conclusion for a speech on that topic.

5. Be prepared to hear critiques from your classmates and to offer suggestions on theirs as well.

Compiling the Reference List

Regardless of the type or length of your speech, you'll want to prepare a list of the sources you use in it. This list will enable you to direct audience members to the specific source of any information you used, and will allow you to quickly find the information at a later date. The two standard methods of organizing source lists are (1) alphabetically by author's last name or (2) by content category, with items listed alphabetically by author within each category. For speeches with a short list, the first method is efficient. But for long speeches with a lengthy source list, it is helpful to group sources by content categories.

	MLA style	APA style
Book	Jones, Phillip March. *Points of Departure: Roadside Memorial* Polaroids. Lexington, KY: The Jargon Society, 2011.	Jones, P. M. (2011). *Points of departure: Roadside memorial polaroids.* Lexington, KY: The Jargon Society.
Academic Journal	Von Burg, Ron. "Decades Away or *The Day After Tomorrow?*: Rhetoric, Film, and the Global Warming Debate." *Critical Studies in Media Communication*, 29.1(2012): 7–26.	Von Burg, R. (2012). Decades away or *The Day After Tomorrow?*: Rhetoric, film, and the global warming debate. *Critical Studies in Media Communication, 29*(1) 7-26.
Magazine	Abrahamson, Rachel Paula. "Destroyed by Plastic Surgery." *US Weekly*, 19 Mar., 2012: 54–55.	Abrahamson, R. P. (2012, March19). Destroyed by plastic surgery. *US Weekly, 892*, 54–55.
Web Site	"Supplier Responsibility at Apple."Apple.com. n.d. Web. 01 June 2012.	Apple. (n.d.). Supplier responsibility at Apple. Retrieved from http://www.apple.com /supplierresponsibility/
Blog Post	Ramsey, G. "UK Hoops Dominates SEC Awards." Cat Scratches: The Official Blog of UK Athletics. ukathletics. com. 29 February 2012. Web. 01 June 2012.	Ramsey, G. (2012, February 29). UK hoops dominates SEC awards [Web log post]. Retrieved from http://www.ukathletics.com /blog/2012/02/uk-hoops -dominates-sec-awards.html
Movie	*The Iron Lady*. Dir. Phyllida Lloyd. Prod. Damien Jones. Pathe, 2011. DVD.	Jones, D. (Producer), & Lloyd, P. (Director). (2011). *The iron lady* [Motion picture]. United Kingdom: Pathe.
Online Video	"Barry Schwartz: The Paradox of Choice." TEDtalks. *YouTube*. 2007. Web. 01 June 2012.	TEDtalksDirector. (2007, January 16). *Barry Schwartz: The paradox of choice* [Video file]. Retrieved from http://www.youtube.com /watch?v=VO6XEQIsCoM

Figure 12.3

Examples of MLA and APA citation forms for speech sources

© Cengage Learning

Many formal bibliographic style formats can be used (e.g., MLA, APA, Chicago, CBE). The "correct" form differs by professional or academic discipline. Check to see if your instructor has a preference about which style you use for this class. Figure 12.3 gives examples of Modern Language Association (MLA) and American Psychological Association (APA) citations for the most commonly used sources.

ACTION STEP 3.H

Compiling a List of Sources

The goal of this activity is to help you record the list of sources you used in the speech.

1. Review your research cards and/or annotated bibliography, separating those with information you used in your speech from those you did not use.

2. List the sources of information used in the speech by copying the bibliographic information recorded into a "references" or "works cited" list using the format required by your instructor.

3. Arrange your entries alphabetically by the last name of the first author.

You can complete this activity online using Speech Builder Express, view a student sample of this activity, and, if requested, e-mail your completed activity to your instructor. Use the Speech Communication CourseMate at cengagebrain.com to access the Action Step activities for Chapter 12.

COMMUNICATION SKILL

Organizing the Speech

Skill	Use	Procedure	Example
The process of identifying main points, constructing a thesis statement, outlining the body of the speech, creating an introduction, crafting a conclusion, and cataloguing a list of sources.	To create a hierarchy and sequence of ideas that help a particular audience to easily understand the speaker's goal and main ideas in the speech.	1. Identify your main ideas. 2. Write a thesis statement. 3. Outline the body of the speech by carefully wording main points, selecting an organizational pattern, selecting and organizing subpoints, and preparing transitions. 4. Create three introductions and select the best one. 5. Create three conclusions and select the best one. 6. List sources.	The **three aspects** of romantic love are passion, intimacy, and commitment. I. Passion is the first aspect of romantic love to develop. II. Intimacy is the second. III. Commitment is the third. **Example** for "passion": A. Passion is a compelling feeling of love. B. (Focus on function.) C. (Discuss maintenance.) **Transition from I to II:** Although passion is essential to a relationship, passion without intimacy is just sex. **Possible introduction:** What does it mean to say "I'm in love"? And how can you know whether what you are experiencing is not just a crush? **Possible conclusion:** Developing romantic love involves passion, intimacy, and commitment. **Sample entry:** Sternberg, Robert J., and Michael L. Barnes, eds. *The Psychology of Love.* New Haven, CT: Yale University Press, 1988.

Reviewing the Outline

Now that you have created all of the parts of the outline, it is time to put them together in complete outline form and edit them to make sure the outline is well organized and well worded. Use this checklist to complete the final review of your outline.

1. **Have I used a standard set of symbols to indicate structure?** Main points are indicated by Roman numerals, major subpoints by capital letters, sub-subpoints by Arabic numerals, and further subdivisions by lowercase letters.

2. **Have I written main points and major subpoints as complete sentences?** Complete sentences help you to see (1) whether each main point actually develops your speech goal and (2) whether the wording makes your intended point.

3. **Do main points and major subpoints each contain a single idea?** This guideline ensures that the development of each part of the speech will be relevant to the point. Thus, rather than:

   Organically produced food is good for the environment and good for animals and good for you.

   divide the sentence so that each part is stated separately:

   I. Organically produced food is good for the environment.

   II. Organically produced food is good for animals.

   III. Organically produced food is good for you.

4. **Does each major subpoint relate to or support its major point?** This principle, called subordination, insures that you don't wander off point and confuse your audience. For example:

   I. Proper equipment is necessary for successful play.

   A. Good gym shoes are needed for maneuverability.

   B. Padded gloves will help protect your hands.

   C. A lively ball provides sufficient bounce.

   D. A good attitude doesn't hurt either.

   Notice that the main point deals with equipment. Subpoints A, B, and C (shoes, gloves, and ball) all relate to the main point. But D, attitude, is not equipment and should appear under some other main point, if at all.

5. **Are potential subpoint elaborations indicated?** Recall that subpoint elaborations help build the speech. Because you don't know how long it might take you to discuss these elaborations, you should include more than you are likely to use. During rehearsals, you may discuss each a different way.

   Now that we have considered the various parts of an outline, let us put them together for a final look. The outline in Figure 12.4 illustrates the principles in practice.

Using and Abusing Adderall: What's the Big Deal?
by Katie Anthony University of Kentucky

General goal: I want to inform my audience.

Specific goal: I would like the audience to understand the uses and abuses of Adderall by college students.

Thesis statement: I want to inform you about the growing problem of off-label Adderall usage by college students, explaining the nature and legal uses of Adderall, its growing popularity as a study aid for college students, and the problems associated with abusing Adderall.

Introduction

I. *Attention getter:* Raise your hand if anyone you know has taken the drug Adderall. Keep your hand raised if the person you know to be taking Adderall is doing so without a prescription for the drug.

II. *Listener relevance:* The illegal use of stimulants like Adderall among college students has increased dramatically over the past decade. The latest National Study on Drug Use and Health found that nearly 7 percent of full-time college students reported using Adderall without a prescription. So if you know ten people who are in college, it is likely that you know someone who is abusing Adderall.

III. *Speaker credibility:* I became interested in this topic my freshman year when my roommate received a call from her mother telling her that her best friend, who was a sophomore at a different college, had died suddenly from an Adderall-induced heart attack. Because I had several friends who were also using Adderall without a prescription but who thought it was safe to do so, I began to read all I could about the drug, its use, and its risks. Not only have I become versed in the written information on Adderall, but I have also interviewed several faculty here who are studying the problem, and I have become an undergraduate research assistant helping one faculty member to collect data on this problem. Today, I want to share with you some of what I have learned.

IV. *Thesis statement:* Specifically, I want to inform you about the growing problem of off-label Adderall usage by college students, explaining the nature and legal uses of Adderall, its growing popularity as a study aid for college students, and the problems associated with abusing Adderall.

Body

I. Adderall is a psychostimulant prescribed to treat three conditions.

    Listener relevance link: Understanding the intended medical uses of the drug Adderall may help you understand why the drug is so widely abused by collegians.

    A. Adderall, the brand name for amphetamikne-dextroamphetamine, is a psychostimulant, one of a class of drugs intended to promote concentration, suppress hyperactivity, and promote healthy social experiences for patients (Willis, 2001).

        1. Adderall stimulates the central nervous system by increasing the amount of dopamine and norepinephrine in the brain. These chemicals are neurotransmitters that help the brain send signals between nerve cells (Daley, 2004, April 20).

        2. Mentally, Adderall brings about a temporary improvement in alertness, wakefulness, endurance, and motivation.

Figure 12.4

Sample complete formal outline

3. Physically, it can increase heart rate and blood pressure and decrease perceived need for food or sleep.

B. Adderall is prescribed for the medical treatment of attention deficit hyperactivity disorder (ADHD) in children and adults as well as for narcolepsy and clinical depression.

   1. ADHD is a neurobehavioral developmental disorder characterized by problems of attention coupled with hyperactivity.

      a. Since the mid-1990s, there has been a documented increase in the number of American children diagnosed and treated for ADHD (McCabe, Teter, & Boyd, 2004).

      b. According to the *Diagnostic and Statistical Manual of Mental Disorders* (2000), symptoms must be present for at least six months for diagnosis and symptoms must be excessive for medicinal treatment.

      c. The drugs Ritalin and Dexedrine are also used to treat ADHD. Adderall, however, remains the most widely prescribed of these drugs (Willis, 2001).

      d. According to the Centers for Disease Control, approximately 4.4 million American children have been diagnosed with ADHD, and over 2.5 million of those patients have been prescribed medicine to treat the condition (2005).

   2. Adderall is also prescribed to treat narcolepsy, which occurs when the brain can't normally regulate cycles of sleep and waking.

      a. Sufferers of narcolepsy experience excessive daytime sleepiness that results in episodes of suddenly falling asleep.

      b. A chronic sleep disorder, narcolepsy affects between 50,000 and 2.4 million Americans. (National Heart, Lung, and Blood Institute, 2008).

   3. Adderall can also be used to treat clinical depression.

      a. Clinical depression is a disorder characterized by low mood, a loss of interest in normal activities, and low self-esteem.

      b. According to the National Institute of Mental Health, 9.5% of the adult population—that is nearly 1.8 million American adults—suffer from clinical depression.

Transition: Now that we understand the basic properties and medical uses of the drug Adderall, let's assess the increasing level of abuse of the drug by college students.

II. Unfortunately, Adderall has become popular among college students who use it as a study aid and for recreational purposes.

   Listener relevance link: As college students, we need to be aware of what students believe about Adderall and why they are abusing it.

   A. College students who don't suffer ADHD, narcolepsy, or depression will take it with no prescription because they believe that it will improve their focus and concentration, allowing them to perform better on academic tasks (Teter, McCabe, Crandford, Boyd, & Gunthrie, 2005).

      1. Adderall abuse among college students occurs especially at stressful times of the semester when students get little sleep.

         a. DeSantis, Webb, and Noar (2008) found that 72 percent of the students they surveyed reported using the drug to stay awake

Figure 12.4

(Continued)

so that they could study longer when they had many assignments due.

    b. Katherine Stump, a Georgetown University student, reported in the school newspaper: "During finals week here at Georgetown, campus turns into an Adderall drug den. Everyone from a cappella singers to newspaper writers become addicts, while anyone with a prescription and an understanding of the free market becomes an instant pusherman" (Jaffe, 2006, January 1).

    c. Collegians report using the drug frequently during stressful times of the semester. One student said, "I use it every time I have a major paper due" (Daley, 2004, April 20).

B. Students also use Adderall for purposes other than academic ones.

    1. A survey of undergraduate and graduate students revealed that students engage in Adderall abuse for partying at a frequency just slightly less than taking the drug for academic purposes (Prudhomme White, Becker-Blease, & Grace-Bishop, 2006).

    2. DeSantis, Webb, and Noar (2007) report that students take the drug for its energizing effects. Other students report taking the drug to make them more social and outgoing at parties.

    3. Some college students, especially women, report using the drug for its use as an appetite suppressant for dieting purposes (Daley, 2004, April 20).

Transition: Now that we understand that Adderall abuse is prevalent on university campuses among students, it is important to understand the detrimental effects that can accompany the illegal use of Adderall.

III. Whether students acknowledge the dangers or not, there are great risks involved in illegally using Adderall.

    Listener relevance link: As we have now discussed the pervasiveness of Adderall abuse, statistically, it is likely that several of you have used this substance without a prescription to either enhance your academic performance or your social outings. Thus, it is important that we all recognize the adverse effects that result from taking Adderall without a prescription.

A. Adderall abuse can cause negative health effects for individuals not diagnosed with ADHD (Daley, 2004, April 20).

    1. Adderall is reported to cause a heightened risk for heart problems when used inappropriately. Problems include sudden heart attack or stroke, sudden death in individuals with heart conditions, and increased blood pressure and heart rate (FDA, 2010).

    2. Adderall abuse also can result in a myriad of mental problems, including manifestation of bipolar disorder, an increase of aggressive thoughts, and a heightened risk for psychosis similar to schizophrenia (FDA, 2010).

B. Adderall is highly addictive.

    1. Adderall is an amphetamine, and while amphetamines were once used to treat a variety of ailments including weight loss in the 1950s and '60s, the drugs began to be much more closely regulated once their addictive nature was realized (Daley, 2004, April 20).

Figure 12.4

(Continued)

2. Adderall has similar properties to cocaine, and, as a result, abuse of the drug can lead to substance dependence (FDA, 2010).

C. Though clear risks are associated with the illegal use of Adderall, unlike other drugs, collegians do not view the inappropriate use of Adderall as harmful or illegal.

1. College students typically view stimulant abuse as morally acceptable and physically harmless. In a 2010 study, DeSantis and Hane found that students were quick to justify their stimulant abuse by claiming its use was fine in moderation.

2. The *Kentucky Kernel*, the student newspaper at the University of Kentucky, published an editorial of a student who flippantly described the use of Adderall among college students. He states, "If you want to abuse ice cream, amphetamines or alcohol, then there are going to be serious problems; however, let's not pretend a person using Adderall twice a semester to help them study is in any way likely to die a horrible death or suffer terrible side effects" (Riley, 2010, May 3).

3. In a study assessing the attitudes of college students toward the inappropriate use of stimulants, the authors found that "the majority of students who reported misuse or abuse were not concerned about the misuse and abuse of prescription stimulants, and a number of students thought that they should be more readily available (Prudhomme White, Becker-Blease, & Grace-Bishop, 2006, p. 265).

Conclusion

I. **Restatement of thesis:** Adderall is a prescription stimulant that is increasingly being abused by college students primarily as a study aid.

II. **Main point review:** We have examined today what the drug Adderall is, its growing popularity among college students especially as a study aid, and the risks associated with using the drug illegally.

III. **Clincher:** The next time you or a friend considers taking Adderall as a study aid, think again. The potential harm that the drug could cause to your body is not worth even a perfect grade point average.

References

American Psychiatric Association. (2000). *Diagnostic and statistical manual of mental disorders*. Arlington, VA: Author.

Centers for Disease Control and Prevention. (2005, September 2). *Morbidity and Mortality Weekly Report (MMWR)*. Retrieved from http://www.cdc.gov

Daley, B. (2004, April 20). Perspective: Miracle drug? Adderall is prescribed for individuals with ADD and ADHD; for nonprescribed users there can be some serious risks. *Daily Pennsylvanian*. Retrieved from http://www.vpul.upenn.edu

DeSantis, A. D., & Hane, A. C. (2010). "Adderall is definitely not a drug": Justifications for the illegal use of ADHD stimulants. *Substance Use & Misuse, 45*, 31–46.

DeSantis, A. D., Webb, E. M., & Noar, S. M. (2008). Illicit use of prescription ADHD medications on a college campus: A multimethodological approach. *Journal of American College Health, 57*, 315–324.

Food and Drug Administration. (2010). *Drugs @ FDS: FDA approved drug products*. Retrieved from http://www.accessdata.fda.gov

Figure 12.4

(Continued)

National Heart, Blood, and Lung Insitute (2008). "What is narcolepsy?" *National Heart, Blood, and Lung Institute Diseases and Conditions Index*. Retrieved from http://www.nhlbi.nih.gov/health/dci/Diseases/nar/nar_what.html

Jaffe, H. (2006, January 1). ADD and abusing Adderall. *The Washingtonian*. Retrieved from http://www.washingtonian.com

McCabe, S. E., Teter, C. J., & Boyd, C. J. (2004). The use, misuse and diversion of prescription stimulants among middle and high school students. *Substance Use and Misuse*, 39, 1095–1116.

Prudhomme White, B., Becker-Blease, K. A., & Grace-Bishop, K. (2006). Stimulant medication use, misuse, and abuse in an undergraduate and graduate student sample. *Journal of American College Health, 54*, 261–268.

Riley, T. (2010, May 3). Prescription drug abuse is a personal choice. *Kentucky Kernel*. Retrieved from http://kykernel.com

Substance Abuse and Mental Health Services Administration, Office of Applied Studies. (April 7, 2009). *The NSDUH Report: Nonmedical Use of Adderall among Full-Time College Students*. Rockville, MD.

Teter, J. C., McCabe, S. E., Crandford, J. A., Boyd, C. J., & Gunthrie, S. K. (2005). Prevalence and motives for illicit use of prescription stimulants in an undergraduate student sample. *Journal of American College Health, 53*, 253–262.

Willis, F. (2001). Attention deficit disorder. *Modern Drug Discovery, 4*, 84–86.

Figure 12.4

(Continued)

WHAT WOULD YOU DO?

A Question of Ethics

As Marna and Gloria were eating lunch together, Marna happened to ask Gloria, "How are you doing in Woodward's speech class?"

"Not bad," Gloria replied. "I'm working on this speech about product development. I think it will be really informative, but I'm having a little trouble with the opening. I just can't seem to get a good idea for getting started."

"Why not start with a story? That always worked for me in class."

"Thanks, Marna; I'll think on it."

The next day when Marna ran into Gloria again, she asked, "How's that introduction going?"

"Great. I've prepared a great story about Mary Kay—you know, the cosmetics entrepreneur? I'm going to tell about how she was terrible in school and no one thought she'd amount to anything. But she loved dabbling with cosmetics so much that she decided to start her own business—and the rest is history."

"That's a great story. I really like that part about being terrible in school. Was she really that bad?"

"I really don't know—the material I read didn't really focus on that part of her life. But I thought that angle would get people listening right away. And after all, I did it that way because you suggested starting with a story."

"Yes, but . . ."

"Listen, she did start the business. So what if the story isn't quite right? It makes the point I want to make—if people are creative and have a strong work ethic, they can make it big."

1. What are the ethical issues here?

2. Is anyone really hurt by Gloria's opening the speech with this story?

3. What are the speaker's ethical responsibilities?

Summary

Organizing is the process of arranging your ideas in a way that will help your audience follow along and remember your speech.

You begin by identifying two to four main points and crafting them into a well-phrased thesis statement. Then you develop the body of the speech. Once identified, main points and their related subpoints and sub-subpoints are written in complete sentences and arranged using a formal organizational pattern. The four organizational patterns we discussed in this chapter are time, narrative, topical, and logical reasons order. Subpoints support each main point with definitions, examples, statistics, personal experiences, stories, quotations, and so on. Finally, transitions are inserted between the introduction and the body, between main points within the body, and between the body and the conclusion. Similarly, signposts are placed appropriately to connect subpoints and supporting material together.

The organization process is completed by creating (1) an introduction that gets attention, establishes listener relevance and speaker credibility, and introduces the thesis; (2) a conclusion that summarizes the main points and creates a vivid impression; and (3) a list of sources compiled from the bibliographic information used in the speech.

The complete draft outline should be reviewed and revised to make sure that you have used a standard set of symbols, used complete sentences for main points and major subpoints, limited each point to a single idea, and related minor points to major points.

COMMUNICATE!

RESOURCE AND ASSESSMENT CENTER

Now that you have read Chapter 12, go to the Speech Communication CourseMate at cengagebrain.com where you'll find an interactive eBook and interactive learning tools including quizzes, flashcards, sample speech videos, audio study tools, skill-building activities, action step activities, and more. Student Workbook, Speech Builder Express 3.0, and Speech Studio 2.0 are also available.

Applying What You've Learned

Impromptu Speech Activity

1. From a basket of thesis statements provided by your instructor, create two introductions and two conclusions based on the guidelines offered in this chapter. Deliver both versions to the class as though you were giving an actual speech on the topic. Ask for feedback regarding which version the class likes better and why.

Assessment Activities

1. Identifying Structural Elements of the Speech Body Access the American Rhetoric Online Speech Bank (http://www.americanrhetoric.com/speechbank.htm). Select a speech and listen to the audio recording of it following along with its transcript. As you listen, identify and write down what you believe is the thesis statement. If you feel any one of the speeches does not contain an explicit thesis statement, identify its implied thesis. Now try to identify and write down the main points. What organizational pattern is being used? What types of supporting material does the speaker use? Does the speaker cite the sources for his or her supporting material? Identify and write down the transitions used in each speech. Were transitions missing and, if so, did it make following along more difficult? Why or why not?

2. Access the American Rhetoric Online Speech Bank by visiting http://www .americanrhetoric.com/speechbank.htm. Select a speech and listen to the audio recording of it following along with the transcript of it. As you listen, identify what the speaker uses to get attention. Is it effective? Why or why not? Does the speaker offer listener relevance and speaker credibility? Explain. What is the thesis statement? Based on the guidelines suggested in this chapter, is it an effective thesis statement? Why or why not? Does the speaker summarize the main points in his or her conclusion? How does the speaker clinch? Is it effective? Why or why not?

Skill-Building Activity

1. Create a thesis statement for each of the following:

    a. General goal: To inform

    b. Specific goal: I want my audience to understand the pros and cons of spanking as a form of discipline.

    c. Thesis statement:

a. General goal: To persuade

b. Specific goal: I want my audience to agree with my prediction that (insert name) is the best team in baseball.

c. Thesis statement: _____

a. General goal: To inform

b. Specific goal: I want my audience to know how to change a flat tire.

c. Thesis statement: _____

a. General goal: To persuade

b. Specific goal: I want to convince my audience to enroll in an auto mechanics class.

c. Thesis statement: _____

Presentational Aids

What you'll know

- Why you should incorporate presentational aids into your speech

- Different types of presentational aids you can choose from

- Various media you can use to display your presentational aids

What you'll be able to do

- Identify effective presentational aids for your speech

- Create effective presentational aids for your speech

- Display presentational aids effectively for your speech

As Scott and Carrie drove home, Carrie exclaimed, "Wow! Dominic's speech was really great. I learned so much about what we can do to develop more sustainable electronics."

"Yeah, I know what you mean," Scott replied. "I've even got some ideas for reducing the e-waste he talked about."

"You know, what's really amazing to me is how much I learned from such short talks!"

"I know what you mean. When I heard these were going to be PowerPoint presentations, all I could think was 'Oh no! Here we go again! Beer or no beer, it's going to be Death by PowerPoint: a darkened room and a faceless speaker talking to an oversized screen.' Thank goodness I was wrong. Dominic's visuals really helped me visualize what he was explaining and actually reinforce the important points he was making. My manager could benefit from watching someone like Dominic."

"I know. I can't believe we learned so much in five minutes! Tomorrow when I get into the office, I'm going to check out Dominic's blog."

13

Music + Video

This conversation might have occurred between two people who attended the Ignite Seattle 6 event when industrial designer Dominic Muren gave a 5-minute PowerPoint-aided presentation titled "Humblefacturing a Sustainable Electronic Future."[1] Begun by Brady Forrest of O'Reilly Radar in 2006, Ignite has become a worldwide public speaking movement. During an Ignite event, speakers give 5-minute presentations, often on technical topics, aided by 20 PowerPoint slides. Unlike the "death by PowerPoint" speeches Scott alluded to and we've all had to suffer through, the speeches given at these events are adapted to people today—people for whom online social networking, talking or texting on mobile phones, and eating dinner are simultaneous activities. You can read more about this contemporary approach to public speaking in the *Pop Comm!* feature in this chapter.

ACTION STEP   4

Identify, Prepare, and Use Appropriate Presentational Aids

presentational aid

any visual, audio, audiovisual, or other sensory material used to enhance a verbal message

visual aids

enhance a speech by allowing audience members to see what it is you are describing or explaining

audio aids

enhance a verbal message through sound

audiovisual aids

enhance a verbal message through a combination of sight and sound

other sensory aids

enhance a verbal message through smell, touch, or taste

We live in an era when the written, oral, visual, and digital modes of communicating are merging. Whether it is a TV news program, your professor's lecture, or a motivational speech, audiences have come to expect messages to be enhanced with presentational aids. This means that as you prepare your speech, you will need to decide what presentational aids will enhance your verbal message and motivate your audience to both pay attention and remember it. In fact, presentational aids have become so important to public speeches that they are essentially a form of supporting material you should be looking for when conducting your research. Ultimately, you might use them to get attention in the introduction, to support a main point in the body, or to clinch the conclusion.

A **presentational aid** is any visual, audio, audiovisual, or other sensory material used to enhance a verbal message. **Visual aids** enhance a speech by allowing audience members to see what it is you are describing or explaining. Examples of visual aids include actual objects, models, photographs, drawings and diagrams, maps, charts, and graphs. **Audio aids** enhance the speaker's verbal message through sound. Some examples include musical clips from CDs and iTunes, recorded clips from conversations, interviews, famous speeches, and recordings of nature sounds like bird calls and whale songs. **Audiovisual aids** enhance the speech using a combination of sight and sound. Examples of audiovisual aids include clips from movies and television, YouTube videos, and podcasts, as well as other events or observations captured on video. **Other sensory aids** include materials that enhance your ideas by appealing to smell,

POP COMM!

Ignite: The Power(Point) of eXtreme Audience Adaptation

Ignite Baltimore/Mike Subelsk

Ignite asks speakers, "If you had five minutes on stage, what would you say? What if you only had 20 slides and they rotated automatically after 15 seconds?" ("What Is Ignite?"). Ignite challenges speakers to engage in what could be called extreme audience adaptation, sharing information in a timely and relevant manner so that audiences can easily comprehend it. Created in 2006 by Brady Forrest, of technology publisher O'Reilly Media, and Bre Pettis, of DIY technology guide *Make* magazine, Ignite is an event featuring specifically styled presentations tied to the creators' roots in Seattle's "geek" culture. It started as a way to provide fun, free, informal conferences for people working in the technology industry, but was quickly adopted by other groups as way to "unite disparate communities of innovators in business, art and science" as a way to share creative ideas in a condensed form (Guzman, 2009). Since its 2006 inception, the events have spread to cities all over the United States and beyond, including Sydney, Australia, and Buenos Aires, Argentina (Guzman, 2009).

Speeches at Ignite events range from "Fighting Dirty in Scrabble" and "Causal Inference Is Hard" to "How I Learned to Appreciate Dance: Being Married to a Ballerina," "Geek Generation," and "How to Buy a Car Without Getting Screwed" ("Ignite Seattle 7," 2009; Guzman, 2009). The emphasis on extreme brevity as a way to share ideas is reflected in Ignite Seattle's tagline: "Enlighten us, but make it quick," and reveals the importance of well-designed visual aids to successful public speaking (*Ignite Seattle*, n.d.). Since Ignite presenters are given just 20 slides, each slide must be carefully crafted to concisely and creatively express an idea in only a few seconds. The organizers of Ignite Phoenix offer guidelines for creating better presentations, including focusing on one idea per slide, limiting the amount of text on each slide, avoiding animations and sound, and using pictures instead of words when appropriate ("Tips," n.d.).

This condensed yet creative use of visual aids is part of what makes Ignite a great model for public speaking. Event organizer Jason Prothero says, "[Ignite is] a deliberate attempt to avoid what sucks about presentations. They're boring" (Neznanski, 2008). An online review of Ignite Seattle recommends that "all presentations should be five minutes long," explaining: "Anyone who knows PowerPoint presentations knows that a 'five-minute presentation,' after including setup time, switching between

applications, waiting for your Web browser demo to respond, etc., lasts a half hour but feels like an eternity. Ignite's presentation style is a slap in the face to convention" (Weill, 2006). Another online reviewer wrote, "The messages were succinct and powerful because the speakers knew they didn't have time for the clutter that normally pops up in conferences" (Raybould, 2007).

Another part of Ignite's success has been its ability to adapt to the interests of its various audiences. For example, cocreator Brady Forrest attempts to balance the gender of the speakers and to keep topics only moderately tech-oriented so that more audience members can relate (Guzman, 2009). Ignite Bend, in Oregon, has applied the established presentation style to community organization; Ignite Change, in Boston, focuses on social justice; and Ignite Phoenix includes a group dedicated to presentations about food (Guzman, 2009; IgnitePhoenix.com). Ignite presentations are even finding their way into college classrooms. Journalism and mass communication professor Greg Downey won a teaching award in 2010 for his use of Ignite assignments as part of his Information Literacy courses at the University of Wisconsin–Madison ("Digital Media Assignments," n.d.). Tailoring assignments to Ignite's short presentation style helps students develop as speakers by honing their ability to analyze and distill research into its most important points as well becoming comfortable with creating and delivering presentations using digital media.

Extreme audience adaptation? Perhaps for now—sounds like pretty soon *everybody* will be doing it. If you'd like to see for yourself what Ignite is all about, visit the Ignite Seattle Web site at www.igniteseattle.com.

Questions to Ponder

1. What do you think about the role of presentational aids in public speaking?

2. Do you think the Ignite approach takes it too far? Why or why not?

3. Do you think public speeches that don't use presentational aids are becoming a thing of the past? Why or why not?

touch, or taste. For example, a speaker can enhance the verbal description of the fragrance of a particular perfume by allowing audience members to smell it and the flavor of a particular entrée by allowing audience members to taste it.

Benefits of Presentational Aids

Research documents several benefits for using presentational aids. First, they clarify and dramatize your verbal message. Second, they help audiences remember information (Tversky, 1997). Third, they allow you to address the diverse learning style preferences of your audience (Kolb, 1984). Fourth, they increase persuasive appeal. In fact, some research suggests that speakers who use presentational aids are almost two times more likely to convince listeners than those who do not (Hanke, 1998). Finally, using presentational aids may help you feel more competent and confident (Ayres, 1991).

Today, presentational aids are usually developed into computerized slide shows using presentation software such as PowerPoint, MediaPro, Adobe Acrobat, or Photodex and projected onto a large screen via a computer and LCD projector. These programs allow you to embed audio and audiovisual links from local files and the Internet, which makes it fairly simple to create effective multimedia presentations. Whether creating multimedia presentations or developing simpler presentational aids, your purpose for using them is the same: to enhance your message without overpowering it. Speakers who violate this purpose end up with what Scott called "death by PowerPoint" in the chapter opener, a situation where the audience is overwhelmed by the aids and the message gets lost. In this chapter, we describe various types of presentational aids, criteria to consider when choosing and preparing them, and methods for displaying them during your speech.

Types of Presentational Aids

Presentational aids range from those that are readily available from existing sources to those that are custom produced for a specific speech.

Visual Aids

Visual aids enhance your verbal message by allowing listeners to see what it is you are describing or explaining. They include actual objects and models, photographs, drawings and diagrams, maps, charts, and graphs.

Actual objects **Actual objects** are inanimate or animate physical samples of the idea you are communicating. Inanimate objects make good visual aids if they are (1) large enough to be seen by all audience members, (2) small enough to transport to the speech site, (3) simple enough to understand visually, and (4) safe. A volleyball or a Muslim prayer rug would be appropriate in size for most classroom audiences. An iPhone or Blackberry might be OK if the goal is to show what a smartphone looks like, but it might be too small if you want to demonstrate how to use any of the phone's specialized functions.

On occasion, *you* can be an effective visual aid. For instance, you can use descriptive gestures to show the height of a tennis net; you can use posture and movement to show the

actual objects

inanimate or animate physical samples of the idea being communicated

Why might a speaker use an animal as a presentational aid? Would you? Why or why not?

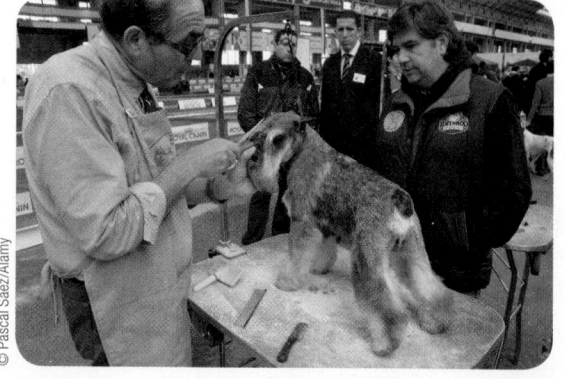
© Pascal Saez/Alamy

motions involved in a golf swing; or you can use your attire to illustrate the traditional attire of a particular country. Sometimes it can be appropriate to use another person as a visual aid, such as when Jenny used a friend to demonstrate the Heimlich maneuver. Animals can also be effective visual aids. For example, Josh used his AKC Obedience Champion dog to demonstrate the basics of dog training. But keep in mind that some animals placed in unfamiliar settings can become difficult to control and can distract from your message.

Using a model as a visual aid can help the audience understand your topic. This model of a wind turbine helps the speaker clarify his explanation of how it works to harness the wind and convert it into power.

Models When an actual object is too large or too small for the room where you'll be speaking, too complex to understand visually, or potentially unsafe or uncontrollable, a model of it can be an effective visual aid. A **model** is a three-dimensional scaled-down or scaled-up version of an actual object that may also be simplified to aid understanding. In a speech on the physics of bridge construction, a scale model of a suspension bridge would be an effective visual aid. Likewise, in a speech on genetic engineering, a scaled-up model of the DNA double helix might help the audience understand what happens during these microscopic procedures.

model

a three-dimensional scaled-down or scaled-up version of an actual object

Photographs If an exact reproduction of material is needed, enlarged photographs can be excellent visual aids. In a speech on smart weapons, enlarged before-and-after photos of target sites would be effective in helping the audience understand the pinpoint accuracy of these weapons. When choosing photographs, be sure that the image is large enough for the audience to see, that the object of interest in the photo is clearly identified, and ideally, that the object is in the foreground. For example, if you are giving a speech about your grandmother and show a photo of her with her college graduating class, you might circle her image so that she can easily be seen.

Simple drawings and diagrams Simple drawings and **diagrams** (a type of drawing that shows how the whole relates to its parts) are easy to prepare and can be effective because you can choose how much detail to include. To make sure they look professional, you can prepare them using a basic computer software program or find them already prepared in a book, an article, or on the Internet. If you do this, however, be sure to credit the source during your speech to enhance your credibility and avoid plagiarism. Andria's diagram of the human body and its pressure points, for example, worked well to clarify her message visually (see Figure 13.1).

diagram

a type of drawing that shows how the whole relates to its parts

Maps Like drawings and diagrams, maps are relatively easy to prepare or find on the Internet. Simple maps allow you to orient audiences to landmarks (mountains, rivers, and lakes), states, cities, land routes, weather systems, and so on. Remember to include only the details that are relevant to your purpose. Figure 13.2 shows a map that focuses on weather systems.

THE AUDIENCE *BEYOND*

After finishing his speech about "places to visit in Italy," Paolo decided to post the photographs, maps, and other visual aids he used in his speech to his Facebook page, so that more people could see them.

Figure 13.1

Sample diagram

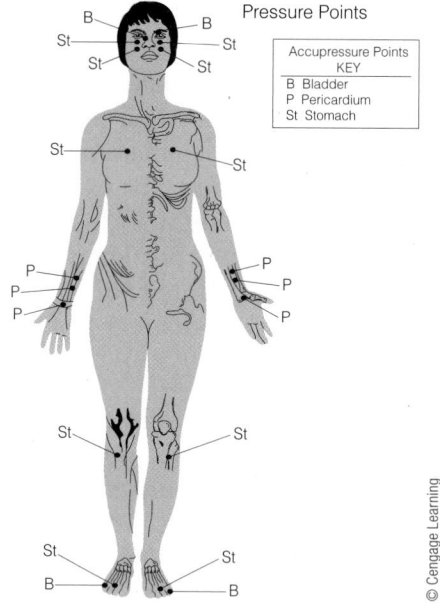

Figure 13.2

Sample map

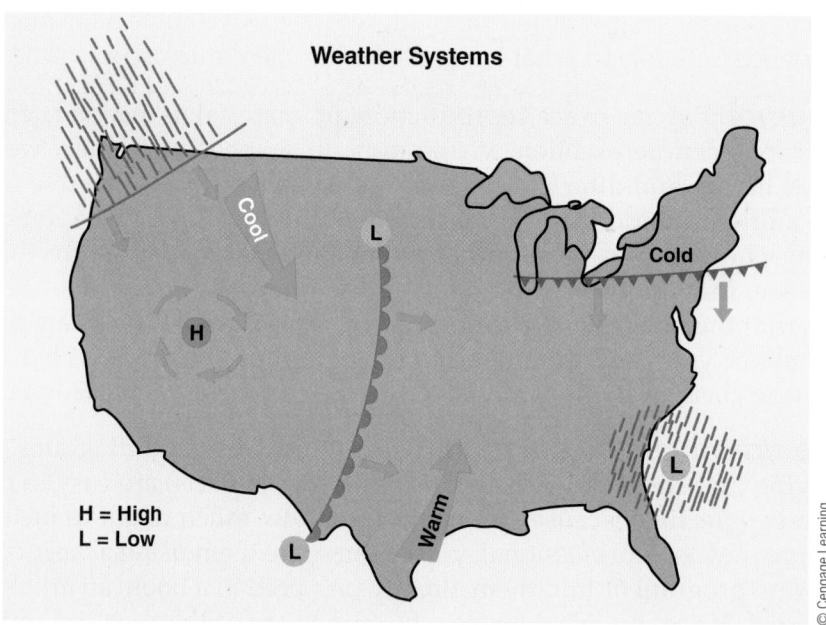

chart

a graphic representation that distills a lot of information into an easily interpreted visual format

flow chart

uses symbols and connecting lines to diagram the progression through a complicated process

organizational chart

shows the structure of an organization in terms of rank and chain of command

pie chart

shows the relationships among parts of a single unit

Charts A **chart** is a graphic representation that distills a lot of information and presents it in an easily interpreted visual format. Flow charts, organizational charts, and pie charts are the most common. A **flow chart** uses symbols and connecting lines to diagram the progression through a complicated process. Tim used a flow chart to help listeners move through the sequence of steps to assess their weight (Figure 13.3) An **organizational chart** shows the structure of an organization in terms of rank and chain of command. The chart in Figure 13.4 illustrates the organization of a student union board. A **pie chart** shows the relationships among parts of a single unit. Ideally, pie charts have two to five "slices," or wedges—more than eight wedges clutter a pie chart. If your chart includes too many wedges, use another kind of chart unless you can consolidate several of the less important wedges into the category of "other," as Tim did to show the percentage of total calories that should come from the various components of food (see Figure 13.5).

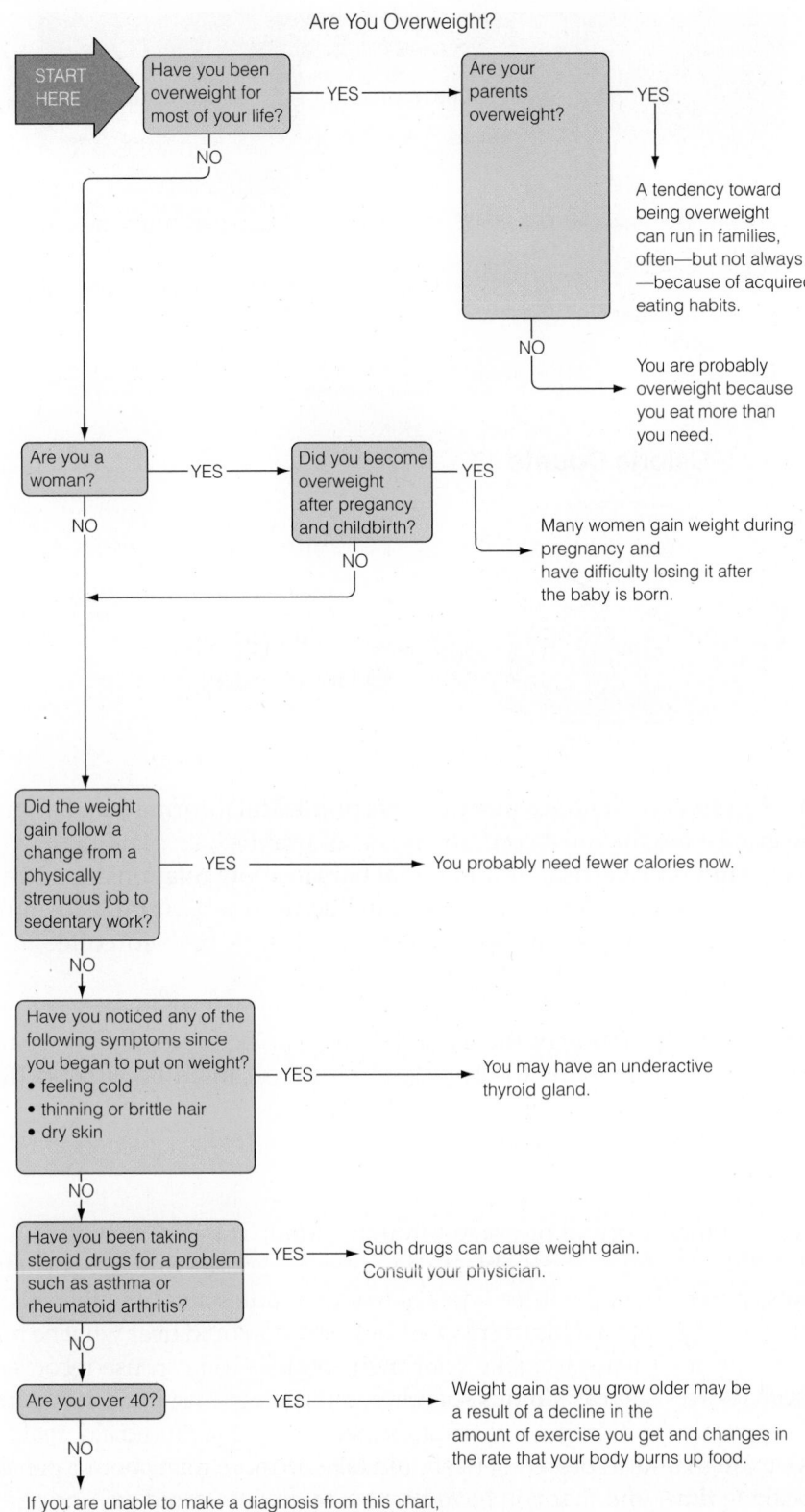

Are You Overweight?

START HERE

Have you been overweight for most of your life? —YES→ Are your parents overweight? —YES→ A tendency toward being overweight can run in families, often—but not always—because of acquired eating habits.

NO

Are your parents overweight? —NO→ You are probably overweight because you eat more than you need.

Are you a woman? —YES→ Did you become overweight after pregancy and childbirth? —YES→ Many women gain weight during pregnancy and have difficulty losing it after the baby is born.

NO

NO

Did the weight gain follow a change from a physically strenuous job to sedentary work? —YES→ You probably need fewer calories now.

NO

Have you noticed any of the following symptoms since you began to put on weight?
• feeling cold
• thinning or brittle hair
• dry skin
—YES→ You may have an underactive thyroid gland.

NO

Have you been taking steroid drugs for a problem such as asthma or rheumatoid arthritis? —YES→ Such drugs can cause weight gain. Consult your physician.

NO

Are you over 40? —YES→ Weight gain as you grow older may be a result of a decline in the amount of exercise you get and changes in the rate that your body burns up food.

NO

If you are unable to make a diagnosis from this chart, your excess weight is probably due only to overeating.
If, after a month of dieting, you fail to lose weight, consult your physician.

© Cengage Learning

Figure 13.3

Sample flow chart

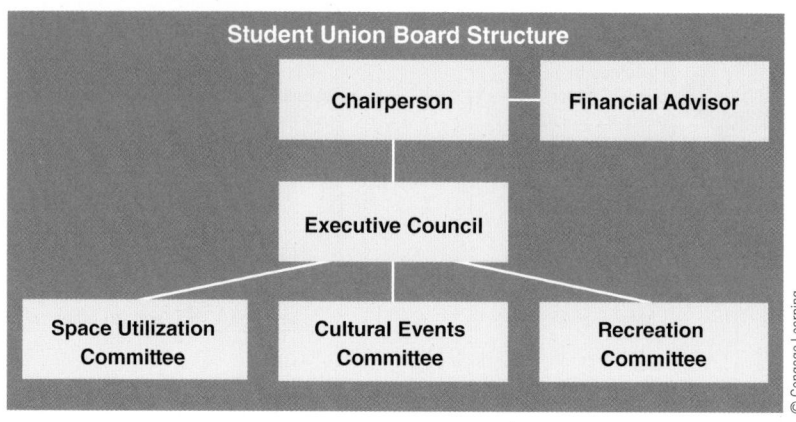

Figure 13.4

Sample organizational chart

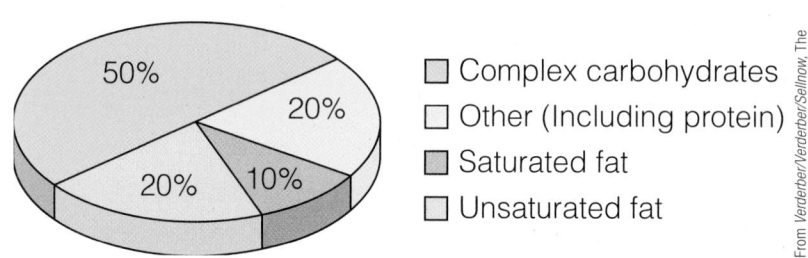

Figure 13.5

Sample pie chart

graph

a diagram that presents numerical information

bar graph

uses vertical or horizontal bars to show relationships between two or more variables

line graph

indicates the changes in one or more variables over time

Graphs A **graph** is a diagram that presents numerical information. Bar graphs and line graphs are the most common forms of graphs.

A **bar graph** uses vertical or horizontal bars to show relationships between two or more variables. For instance, Jacqueline used a bar graph to compare the amounts of caffeine found in one serving each of brewed coffee, instant coffee, tea, cocoa, and cola (see Figure 13.6).

A **line graph** indicates the changes in one or more variables over time. In a speech on the population of the United States, for example, the line graph in Figure 13.7 helps by showing the population increase, in millions, from 1810 to 2010 (308,745,538).

Audio Aids

Audio aids enhance a verbal message through sound. They are especially useful when it is difficult, if not impossible, to describe a sound in words. For example, in David's speech about the three types of trumpet mutes and how they alter the trumpet's sound, he played his trumpet so that listeners could hear what he meant. If you can't or don't want to make your own sounds, you can use recorded excerpts from sources such as famous speeches, radio programs, interviews, and recordings of music or environmental sounds. Before using an audio aid, make sure you have enough time to present it (it should take no more than about 5 percent of your speaking time) and that you have access to a quality sound system.

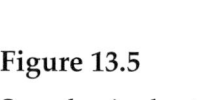

THE AUDIENCE *BEYOND*

Chas wrote a song and used a snippet from it as an attention catcher and clincher in his speech. Afterward, he posted a link to it on his Facebook page, which he referenced in his speech in case others would like to hear it in its entirety.

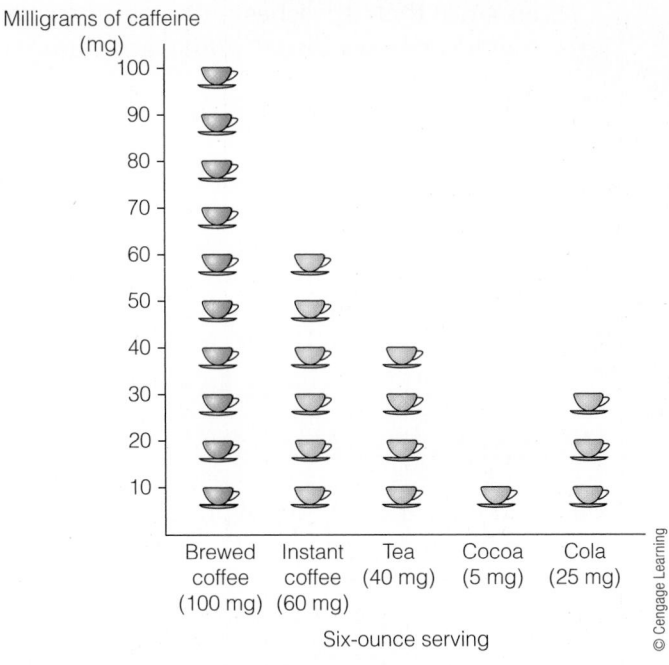

Figure 13.6

Sample bar graph

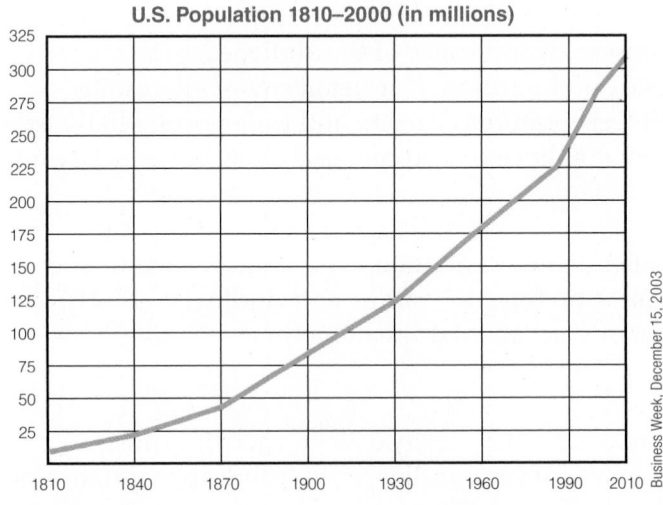

Figure 13.7

Sample line graph

Audiovisual Aids

Audiovisual aids enhance a verbal message using a combination of sight and sound. You can use short clips from films and videos to demonstrate concepts or processes or to expose audiences to important people. They are relatively easy to access on Internet sites such as YouTube. For example, in his speech about the use of robots in automobile production, Chad, who worked as a technician at the local Ford plant, showed a 20-second video clip of a car being painted in a robotic paint booth. As with audio aids, your audiovisual aid should take no more than 5 percent of your speaking time.

It can be challenging to keep clips this short, particularly in short classroom speeches, so choose clips that are to the point and really enhance your message. Because computerized slide show software programs like PowerPoint make it so easy to import sounds and visual images, as well as to insert

Zak Waters/Alamy

Celebrity chefs often ask observers to sample their dishes to confirm that they really do taste good.

hyperlinks to Web sites, most effective speakers today enhance their speeches with computerized slide shows that incorporate visual, audio, and audiovisual material.

Other Sensory Aids

Depending on your topic, *other sensory aids* that appeal to smell, touch, or taste may effectively enhance your speech. For example, a speech about making perfume might benefit from allowing your audience to smell scented swatches as you describe the ingredients used to make the scents. In a speech about Braille, Javier handed out copies of his outline written in Braille for audience members to touch.

Choosing Presentational Aids

Now that you understand the various types of presentational aids, you need to consider what content to highlight and how. Some simple guidelines can help you make good choices.

1. Choose aids that

    - will illustrate the most important ideas for your audience to understand and remember.
    - will convey complex ideas that are difficult to explain verbally.
    - are appropriate for the size of the audience.
    - will make dull information or details more interesting.
    - you will feel comfortable using and transporting to the speech site.
    - you know you have or you can easily get the necessary equipment.

2. Limit

    - the number of aids to about one per minute of your speech.
    - the amount of time for audio and audiovisual aids to no more than 5 percent of your allotted speaking time.

3. Consider

    - preparation time and expense when choosing aids.
    - cultural norms of your audience regarding appropriate aids make choices accordingly. (To understand why, read the *Diverse Voices* feature by Neil Payne, below.)

DIVERSE VOICES

Public Relations Across Cultures

by Neil Payne

Director, Kwintessential (a cross-cultural communication consultancy)

The public relations (PR) industry is responsible for creating and maintaining relationships between clients and customers. PR practitio-

ners are aware of how best to foster interest, trust and belief in a product or company when dealing within their own nations and cultures, however, when dealing with a foreign audience analysis is critical.

To illustrate the impact cross-cultural awareness can have on the success or failure of a PR campaign, consider these examples: Pepsodent tried to sell its toothpaste in Southeast Asia by emphasizing that it "whitens your teeth." They found out that the local natives chew betel nuts to blacken their teeth because they found it attractive. Had the PR company behind this campaign analyzed the cross-cultural issues related to Pepsodent's product, the failure of this PR campaign could have been avoided.

When Ford launched the Pinto in Brazil they were puzzled as to why sales were dead. They eventually found out that Brazilians did not want to be seen driving a car meaning "small male genitals" and promptly changed the name.

Finally, PR campaign materials such as logos, slogans, pictures, colors, and designs must all be cross culturally examined. Pictures of seemingly innocuous things in one culture could mean something different in another. For example, a company advertised eyeglasses in Thailand by featuring a variety of cute animals wearing glasses. The ad failed as animals are considered to be a low form of life in Thailand and no self-respecting Thai would wear anything worn by animals. Similarly, logos or symbols are culturally sensitive. A soft drink was introduced into Arab countries with an attractive label that had a six-pointed star on it. The Arabs interpreted this as pro-Israeli and refused to buy it. (Payne, n.d.)

Payne, N. (n.d.). Public relations across cultures: Building international communication bridges. All About Public Relations with Steven R. Van Hook. Retrieved on April 26, 2012 at: http://www.aboutpublicrelations.net/ucpayne.htm

Preparing Presentational Aids

However simple your presentational aids, you still need to produce them carefully. You may need to find or create charts, graphs, diagrams, maps, or drawings. You may need to search for and prepare photographs. You may look for audio or audiovisual snippets and then convert them to a format that you can use at your speech site.

The goal is to prepare professional-looking presentational aids that will enhance your ethos (perceived competence, credibility, and character) in addition to clarifying your message and making it more memorable. You will want to prepare your presentational aids with the following guidelines in mind.

CONSIDER THIS....

Think of a time when a speaker or teacher used visual aids that required you to read a lot of information. How much do you remember about their speech or lecture, and why?

1. **Limit the reading required of the audience.** The audience should be listening to you not reading the presentational aid. So use key words and short phrases rather than complete sentences.

2. **Customize presentational aids from other sources.** If you get an idea from another source, be sure to simplify the aid to include only the information that is relevant to your purpose or audience. For example, Jia Li was preparing a speech on alcohol abuse by young adults. During her research she found a graph showing statistics on "Current, Binge, and Heavy Alcohol Use among Persons Aged 12 or Older by Age." Since this graph presented more information than Jia Li needed, she simplified it for her presentation and used only the information for young adults aged 16 to 29.

3. **Use a photo, print, or type size that can be seen easily and a volume and sound quality that can be heard easily by your entire audience.** Check your photo, charts, and lettering for size by moving as far away

from the presentational aid as the farthest person in your audience will be sitting. If you can see the image, read the lettering, and see the details from that distance, your aid is large enough; if not, create another and check it again. Check audio materials for volume and quality in a similar manner.

4. **Use a consistent print style that is easy to read.** Avoid fancy print styles and stick to one print style throughout the aid or computerized slide show. In addition, some people think that printing in all capital letters creates emphasis, but the combination of uppercase and lowercase letters is easier to read than uppercase only—even when the ideas are written in short phrases.

5. **Make sure information is laid out in a way that is aesthetically pleasing.** Leave sufficient white space around the whole visual so that it's easy to identify each component. Also, use typefaces and indenting to visually represent relationships between ideas.

6. **Use pictures or other visual symbols to add interest.** To truly enhance a verbal message, a presentational aid should consist of more than just words (Booher, 2003). Visual symbols can increase retention by appealing to diverse learning styles (Kolb, 1984; Long, 1997). If you are working with computer graphics, consider adding clip art. Most computer graphics packages have a wide variety of clip art that you can import to your document. You can also buy relatively inexpensive software packages that contain thousands of clip art images. A relevant piece of clip art can make the image look both more professional and more dramatic. But be careful; clip art can be overdone. Don't let your message be overpowered by unnecessary pictures or animations.

7. **Use color strategically.** Although black and white can work well for your visual aids, consider using color strategically to emphasize points. Here are some suggestions for incorporating color in your presentational aids:

   • Use the same background color for all your presentational aids and theme for the slides on your computerized slide show.
   • Use the same color to show similarities, and use opposite colors (on a color wheel) to show differences between ideas.
   • Use bright colors, such as red, to highlight important information. Be sure to avoid using red and green together, however, because audience members who are color-blind may not be able to distinguish between them.
   • Use dark colors for lettering on a white background and a light color for lettering on black or deep blue backgrounds.
   • Use no more than two or three colors on any presentational aid that is not a photograph or video clip.
   • Pretend you are your audience. Sit as far away as they will be sitting, and evaluate the colors you have chosen for their readability and appeal.

Let's see if we can put all of these principles to work. Figure 13.8 contains a lot of important information, but notice how unpleasant it is to the eye. As you can see, this visual aid ignores all the principles we've discussed. However, with

I WANT YOU TO REMEMBER THE THREE R'S OF RECYCLING

Reduce the amount of waste people produce, like overpacking or using material that won't recycle.

Reuse by relying on cloth towels rather than paper towels, earthenware dishes rather than paper or plastic plates, and glass bottles rather than aluminum cans.

Recycle by collecting recyclable products, sorting them correctly, and getting them to the appropriate recycling agency.

© Cengage Learning

Figure 13.8

A cluttered and cumbersome visual aid

© Cengage Learning 2014

Figure 13.9

A simple but effective visual aid

some thoughtful simplification, this speaker could produce the visual aid shown in Figure 13.9, which sharpens the focus by emphasizing the key words (*reduce, reuse, recycle*), highlighting the major details, and adding clip art for a professional touch.

Displaying Presentational Aids

Once you have decided on the specific presentational aids for your speech, you will need to choose the method to display them. Methods for displaying aids vary in the type of preparation they require, the amount of specialized training needed to use them effectively, and the professionalism they convey. Hand-drawn charts and graphs that are hastily or sloppily developed mark you as an amateur; whereas professional-looking and -sounding presentational aids enhance your credibility. Speakers can choose from the following methods for displaying presentational aids.

Posters

The easiest method for displaying simple drawings, charts, maps, photos, and graphs is by mounting them on stiff cardboard or foam core. Then the visual can be placed on an easel when it is referred to during the speech. Because posters tend to be fairly small, use them only with smaller audiences (30 people or less).

Posterboards are often used by professionals to help explain research projects.

© Jeff Greenberg/Alamy

Whiteboards or Chalkboards

Because a whiteboard or chalkboard is a staple in every college classroom, many novice (and ill-prepared) speakers rely on this method for displaying their visual aids. Unfortunately, a whiteboard or chalkboard is easy to misuse and to overuse. Moreover, they are not suitable for depicting complex material. Writing on a whiteboard or chalkboard is appropriate only for very short items of information that can be written in a few seconds. Nevertheless, being able to use a whiteboard or chalkboard effectively should be a part of any speaker's repertoire.

Whiteboards or chalkboards should be written on prior to speaking or during a break in speaking. Otherwise, the visual is likely to be either illegible or partly obscured by your body as you write. Or you may end up talking to the board instead of to the audience. Should you need to draw or write on the board while you are talking, you should practice doing it. If you are right-handed, stand to the right of what you are drawing. Try to face at least part of the audience while you work. Although it may seem awkward at first, your effort will allow you to maintain contact with your audience and will allow the audience to see what you are doing while you are doing it.

"Chalk talks" are easy to prepare, but they are the most likely to result in damage to speaker credibility. It is the rare individual who can develop well-crafted visual aids on a whiteboard or chalkboard. More often, they signal a lack of preparation.

Flip Charts

flip chart

a large pad of paper mounted on an easel

A **flip chart**, a large pad of paper mounted on an easel, can be an effective method for presenting visual aids. Flip charts (and easels) are available in many sizes. For a presentation to four or five people, a small tabletop version works well; for a larger audience, a larger-size pad (30″ × 40″) is needed.

As with whiteboards and chalkboards, you should prepare them prior to giving the speech. In some situations, you may write down some information before the speech begins and then add information while speaking.

For flip charts to be effective, handwritten information must be neat and appropriately sized to be seen by all audience members. Flip chart visuals that are not neatly done detract from speaker credibility. Flipcharts can be comfortably used with smaller audiences (less than one hundred people) but are not appropriate for larger settings.

Handouts

handout

material printed on sheets of paper

At times it may be useful for each member of the audience to have a personal copy of the visual aid. In these situations, you can prepare a **handout** (material printed on sheets of paper). The benefit is that everyone in the audience can have a copy to refer to and take with them after the speech. The drawback is that distributing handouts is distracting and has the potential for losing audience members' attention when you want them to be looking at you.

Before you decide to use handouts, carefully consider why they would be better than some other method. Handouts are effective for information you want listeners to refer to after the speech, such as a set of steps to follow later, useful telephone numbers and addresses, or mathematical formulas.

If you decide on handouts, distribute them at the end of the speech. If you want to refer to information on the handout during the speech, create another visual aid that you can reveal when discussing it during your speech.

Document Cameras

Another simple way to project drawings, charts, photos, and graphs is using a document camera, such as an Elmo. An Elmo is a document camera that allows you to project images without transferring them to an acetate film. Be sure to transfer drawings, charts, photos, and graphs from their source onto a sheet of 8½″ × 11″ piece of paper so that you can display them smoothly and professionally.

Computers, CD/DVD Players, and LCD Projectors

Most people today prefer to present audio recordings, audiovisual recordings, and computerized slide shows using an LCD projector connected to an onsite computer. Because you can't always anticipate problems with computer and projection equipment, you should always prepare back-up aids such as handouts or any of the other methods described earlier. Also, to ensure that audience members focus their attention on you when you're not talking about one of your slides or clips, insert blank screens between slides or press the "B" key on your computer to display a blank screen.

ACTION STEP 4

Identifying Presentational Aids

The goal of this activity is to help you decide which visual aids you will use in your speech.

1. Identify the key ideas you could emphasize with a presentational aid to increase audience interest, understanding, or retention.

2. For each idea you have identified, list the type of presentational aid you think would be most appropriate to develop and use.

3. For each idea you plan to enhance with an aid, decide on the method you will use to display it.

4. Write a brief paragraph describing why you chose the types of presentational aids and display methods that you did. Be sure to consider how your choices will affect your preparation time and the audience's perception of your credibility.

You can complete this activity online using Speech Builder Express, view a student sample of this activity, and, if requested, e-mail your completed activity to your instructor. Use the Speech Communication CourseMate at cengagebrain.com for Communicate! to access the Action Step activities for Chapter 13.

THE AUDIENCE *BEYOND*

After presenting her speech about why college students should engage in volunteer or service-learning projects, Alyssa decided to re-mix it into a narrated computerized slideshow and post it to the Community Engagement Club's Web site. She figured doing so might reach more people and convince them to get involved.

COMMUNICATE ON YOUR FEET

Speech Assignment

Battle of the Visual Aids

The Assignment

Form groups of four or five people. Your instructor will provide you with three sample visual aids that might be used in a speech. Based on the criteria and guidelines you learned in this chapter, evaluate each visual aid and select the best one. At your instructor's request, one member of each team should go to the front of the room and give a 2- to 3-minute speech that makes a case for why the visual aid you selected is the best of the three. After all groups have made their presentations, vote as a class on the best one and discuss why.

WHAT WOULD YOU DO?

A Question of Ethics

As Oscar and Max were finishing dinner, Max asked:

"Have you figured out what you're going to use for presentational aids in your speech next week in Professor Gilman's class? I'm totally stumped."

Oscar replied, "Yeah, I am so ready and actually pretty pumped about mine."

"What are you going to use?" inquired Max.

"Well, you know I'm going to try to persuade the class to agree with me that the death penalty is wrong. Well, I got ahold of an audio clip of someone writhing in pain during an execution. I'm going to play it while I show several photographs of people who have been executed. THAT should really make my speech memorable and my argument convincing!"

"Yikes," exclaimed Max. "Are you sure that's such a good idea?"

"Yeah, why not?"

1. Is it ethical to use potentially offensive presentational aids if doing so will make your speech more memorable or your argument more convincing? Why or why not?

2. Could Oscar achieve his goal using different presentational aids? If so, what might they be?

Summary

Presentational aids are useful when they help audience members understand and remember important information. The most common types of visual aids are objects, models, photographs, simple drawings and diagrams, maps, charts, and graphs. Audio aids include recordings of music, speeches, and environmental sounds. Audio aids include recordings of music, speeches, interviews, and nature sounds. Audiovisual aids include clips from movies, television programs, commercials, and YouTube. Other sensory aids enhance the verbal message by focusing on taste, smell, or touch. Methods that speakers can use to present presentational aids include posters, flipcharts, whiteboards and chalkboards, handouts, and computers with LCD projectors.

Before you start collecting or preparing your presentational aids, consider a number of questions. What ideas are most important in helping me achieve my speech goal? Are there ideas that are complex or difficult to explain verbally but would be easier to explain with the help of a presentational aid? How many presentational aids should I consider? How large is the audience? Is the necessary equipment readily available? Is the time involved in making or getting the visual aid or equipment cost-effective? What cultural norms of your audience might influence your choice of aids?

Take time to design your visual aids with the following principles in mind: Use a print or font size that can be seen easily and read by your entire audience. Use upper- and lowercase type; Include only items of information that you will emphasize in your speech; Make sure information is laid out in a way that is aesthetically pleasing; Add clip art where appropriate; Use color strategically; With audio and audiovisual aids, be sure they take no more than 5 percent of your allotted speaking time.

With regard to methods for displaying your aids, you might use a flip chart or posterboard, whiteboard or chalkboard, handouts, or a computer and LCD projector. If you use electronic media, however, be sure to always prepare a back-up plan to account for potential equipment malfunctions.

COMMUNICATE!

RESOURCE AND ASSESSMENT CENTER

Now that you have read Chapter 13, go to the Speech Communication Course-Mate at cengagebrain.com where you'll find an interactive eBook and interactive learning tools including quizzes, flashcards, sample speech videos, audio study tools, skill-building activities, action step activities, and more. Student Workbook, Speech Builder Express 3.0, and Speech Studio 2.0 are also available.

Applying What You've Learned

Impromptu Speech Activity

1. Locate one magazine advertisement that seems to do a good job of following the guidelines of effective visual aids and one that does not according to what you've read in this chapter. Prepare a short 2- to 3-minute speech articulating why you think one is effective and the other is not.

Assessment Activity

1. Locate a visual, audio, and audiovisual aid example that you believe represents an effective and ineffective presentational aid based on the information and guidelines offered in this chapter. Prepare a two- to three-page paper explaining why you assessed them as you did.

Skill-Building Activity

1. Choosing Appropriate Presentational Aids For each of the following, identify what type of presentational aid you would use and why:

(a) the Great Wall of China

(b) how to bake cookies

(c) energy comparison between fluorescent and incandescent light bulbs

(d) college tuition rate trends

(e) time management in one typical day of a college student

(f) members and roles in a campus club

Language

Nathan had asked his friend George to listen to one of his speech rehearsals. He finished the final sentences of the speech, "So, now you know what a Meckel's diverticulum is, who is most susceptible, and what its symptoms are. And now I'd like to end as I began with the rules of 2s. But I'd like to add one more. Please don't blow off acute abdominal pain as only a stomachache because doing so could lead '2' death." Then, he asked George, "So, what do you think?"

"You're giving the speech to your classmates, right?"

"Yeah."

"And they're mostly mass media majors?"

"Uh-huh."

"Well, it was a good speech, but it was awfully technical and I didn't hear anything that showed that you had media majors in mind. Why would they want to know about this?"

P14

Mel Yates/Cultura/Jupiter Images

audience adaptation

the process of tailoring your speech to your specific audience

Nathan may have chosen his topic and main points with his audience in mind, but as he prepared, he forgot that an effective speech is one that is verbally adapted to the specific audience. Recall from Chapter 11 that **audience adaptation** is the process of tailoring your speech to your specific audience. In this chapter, we turn our focus to tailoring your language and oral style to the audience.

We begin by clarifying how oral style differs from written style, as well as how the formal oral style we use in public speeches differs from the informal oral style we use in conversations with friends and family members. Then, we review several aspects of semantic, pragmatic, and sociolinguistic word meanings we introduced in chapter four as they relate specifically to public speaking.

ACTION STEP 5

Practice Oral Language and Delivery Style

Oral Style

oral style

the manner in which one conveys messages through the spoken word

Oral style refers to how we convey messages through the spoken word. An effective oral style differs quite a bit from written style, though when giving a speech your oral style is still more formal than everyday talk. Your goal is to adapt your language to your purpose, the audience, and the occasion. For example, although your language when speaking to a small audience of colleagues at a business meeting will be more formal than when conversing with a friend at dinner, it will not be as formal as when speaking to an audience of 100 or more at a professional conference or workshop. Still, even in a formal public speaking situation, you must *establish a relationship* with your listeners. Although your oral style is slightly more formal than in everyday conversations, it should still reflect a personal tone that encourages listeners to perceive you to be *having a conversation with them*. Four primary characteristics distinguish an effective oral style from an effective written style.

1. **An effective oral style tends toward short sentences and familiar language.** Because listeners have only one opportunity to hear your speech, make sure you use words your audience is likely to understand. Likewise, opt for short, simple sentences rather than complex ones, which would require additional time for audience members to decipher.

2. **An effective oral style features plural personal pronouns.** Using personal pronouns such as "we," "us," and "our" creates a sense of relationship with the audience, fostering an impression of respect for them as participants in the rhetorical situation. Remember your goal is to create a perception of conversing *with* your audience rather than presenting *to* or *in front of* them. Personal pronouns help foster that perception.

3. **An effective oral style features descriptive words and phrases that appeal to the ear in ways that sustain listener interest and promote retention.** By using colorful adjectives and adverbs that appeal to the senses, as well as rhetorical figures of speech we will discuss later in this chapter, you will capture the interest of your audience to pay attention and motivate them to stay focused on it throughout.

4. **An effective oral style incorporates clear structural elements (e.g., main point preview, section transitions, and signposts as discussed**

in Chapter 12). Unless your public speech is being recorded and posted for additional viewing, listeners will be afforded the opportunity to hear it only once. Consequently, you need to intentionally articulate a preview of your main points so listeners can conceptualize the framework for your main ideas at the outset. Similarly, you need to provide section transitions that verbally signal when you are moving from one major idea to the next, as well as signposts such as "first," "second," "third," and "fourth" to help listeners follow your train of thought as the speech progresses.

Now that you have a sense of the nature of oral style as it differs from written style, let's turn our attention to some specific actions to take regarding language semantics, pragmatics, and sociolinguistics when preparing and presenting public speeches. These include speaking appropriately, clearly, and vividly.

Speaking Appropriately

Speaking appropriately means using language that adapts to the needs, interests, knowledge, and attitudes of your listeners and avoiding language that alienates any audience members. In the communication field, we use the term **verbal immediacy** to describe language used to reduce the psychological distance between you and your audience (Witt, Wheeless, & Allen, 2004). In other words, speaking appropriately means making language choices that enhance a sense of connection between you and the audience members. Speaking appropriately demonstrates that we respect others, even those who differ from us. If we speak inappropriately, on the other hand, we are likely to offend some listeners and fail to achieve our speech goal because, from that moment on, offended audience members are likely to stop listening. Speaking appropriately during a speech means highlighting the relevance of your topic and purpose to the interests and needs of audience members, establishing common ground, underscoring your credibility, demonstrating linguistic sensitivity, and adapting to cultural diversity.

Relevance

Your first challenge is to help the audience see the relevance of your topic to them. Listeners pay attention to and are interested in ideas that have a personal impact (when they can answer the question, "What does this have to do with me?"); they are bored when they don't see how the speech relates to them. You can help the audience perceive your topic and purpose as relevant by highlighting its timeliness, proximity, and personal impact for them.

Establish Timeliness Listeners are more likely to be interested in information they perceive as **timely**—they want to know how they can use the information *now*. For example, in a speech about the hazards of talking or texting while driving, J. J. quickly established the topic's relevance in his introduction:

> *Most of us in this room, as many as 90 percent in fact, are a danger to society. Why? Because we talk or text on our cell phones while driving. Although driving while phoning (DWP) seems harmless, a recent study conducted by the Nationwide Mutual Insurance Company reports that DWP is the most common cause of accidents today–even more common than driving under the*

CONSIDER THIS....

Consider a time when you attended a lecture or other public speaking event where the speaker read the manuscript to you using long sentences and unfamiliar vocabulary. How effective was the speaker in maintaining your interest? Helping you understand the point? Why?

speaking appropriately

using language that adapts to the needs, interests, knowledge, and attitudes of the audience

verbal immediacy

language used to reduce the psychological distance between you and your audience

timeliness

how the information can be used now

Solaria/Shutterstock.com

How can you establish relevance in a speech about driving while phoning or texting?

proximity

information in relation to listeners' personal space

common ground

background, knowledge, attitudes, experiences, and philosophies shared by speaker and audience

influence (DUI)! Did you know that when you talk on the phone when you're driving—even if you do so on a hands-free set—you're four times more likely to get into a serious crash than if you're not doing so? That's why several states have actually banned the practice. So this issue is far from harmless and is one each of us should take seriously.

Establish Proximity Your listeners are more likely to be interested in information that has **proximity**, a relationship to their personal "space." Psychologically, we pay more attention to information that is related to our "territory"—to our family, our neighborhood, or our city, state, or country. You have probably heard speakers say something like this: "Let me bring this closer to home by showing you . . ." and then make their point by using a local example. As you review the supporting material you collect for your speech, look for statistics and examples that have proximity for your audience. For example, J. J. shared a story reported in the local paper of a young mother who was killed while texting and driving.

Demonstrate Personal Impact When you present information that can have a serious physical, economic, or psychological impact on audience members, they are more likely to be interested in what you have to say. For example, notice how your classmates' attention picks up when your instructor says that what is said next "will definitely be on the test." Your instructor understands that this "economic" impact (not paying attention can "cost") is enough to refocus most students' attention on what is being said.

Common Ground

Common ground is the background, knowledge, attitudes, experiences, and philosophies that you share with your audience. You should use audience analysis to identify areas of similarity; then speak using personal pronouns, rhetorical questions, and common experiences to help establish common ground.

Use Personal Pronouns The simplest way to establish common ground between yourself and your audience is to use *personal pronouns: we, us,* and *our.* For example, in a speech given to an audience whose members are known to

THE AUDIENCE *BEYOND*

Gerry had finished his senior thesis on the importance of regular screenings for prostate cancer and wanted to reach a broader audience than just his thesis committee. He decided to tweet about it and provide a link to the American Medical Association's Web site.

be concerned about violence in children's TV programming, notice the effect of different language choices:

> *I know that most* people *worry about the effects violence on TV is having on young children. In the next few minutes, I will describe several negative effects, explain their implications, and propose a solution.*

> *I know that most of* us *worry about the effects violence on TV is having on young children. In the next few minutes, <u>let's discuss</u> several negative effects. Then <u>we</u> can explore their implications as we* work together *to find a solution.*

In what ways do you think the speaker in this situation can create common ground with the audience?

By using *us, let's,* and *we* instead of *most people* and *I will,* the speaker includes the audience members in the conversation in a way that gives them a role in the communication exchange that is to follow. You can easily replace "I'" and "you" language in your introductory remarks and section transitions. In your thesis statement, for example, you can say "let's discuss . . ." rather than "I will inform you . . ." and in your section transitions, you can say "Now that we all have a clearer understanding of . . .," rather than, "Now that I've explained . . ." and so on.

Ask Rhetorical Questions Recall that a *rhetorical question* is one whose answer is obvious to audience members and to which they are not expected to reply. Rhetorical questions create common ground by alluding to information that is shared by audience members and the speaker. They are often used in speech introductions but can also be effective as transitions and in other parts of the speech. For instance, notice how this transition, phrased as a rhetorical question, creates common ground:

> *When watching a particularly violent TV program, have you ever asked yourself, "Did they really need to be this graphic to make the point"?*

Draw from Common Experiences You can also develop common ground by sharing personal experiences, examples, and illustrations that embody what you and the audience have in common. For instance, in a speech about the effects of television violence, you might allude to a common viewing experience:

> *Remember how sometimes at a key moment when you're watching a really frightening scene in a movie, you may quickly shut your eyes? I vividly remember closing my eyes shut over and over again during the scariest scenes in* The Shining, The Blair Witch Project, *and* Halloween.

Speaker Credibility

Credibility is the confidence an audience places in the truthfulness of what a speaker says. Some people are widely known experts in a particular area and don't have to adapt their remarks to establish their credibility. However, most of us—even if we are given a formal introduction to acquaint the audience with our credentials—will still need to adapt our remarks to demonstrate our knowledge and expertise.

credibility

the confidence an audience places in the truthfulness of what a speaker says

You can verbally share your formal education, special study, demonstrated skill, and personal examples and stories. You can also share high-quality examples and illustrations from external sources you discovered through research. Determining what is "high-quality" material can sometimes be difficult, particularly with the advent of Web 2.0 technology. The *Pop Comm!* feature illustrates some of the pros and cons of this new "collective intelligence" phenomonon.

POP COMM!

Where Have All the Experts Gone?

Web 2.0 is the term used to describe the quickly evolving information exchange on the Internet that is replacing the old Web 1.0, in which the status quo dictated that Web site content changed more slowly and was strictly controlled by Web masters. The advent of Web 2.0 has been heralded as a democratizing force that not only opens up access to knowledge and information to everyone with an online connection, but also expands the range of individuals who can contribute to the body of knowledge that defines our world. From editing a *Wikipedia* entry or writing a book review on Amazon.com to creating a blog about any topic imaginable, more of us are becoming "prosumers" in that we not only consume Web content but share in producing it as well. However, critics argue that this "collective intelligence" phenomenon has diluted true expertise without any sense of distinction between facts and opinions or recognition of the validity of a piece of information.

The idea of collective expertise is rooted in the belief that knowledge is a shared resource, that "[N]o one knows everything, everyone knows something, all knowledge resides in humanity," according to cybertheorist Pierre Lévy (1997, p. 20). By collectively, and largely anonymously, pooling our intellectual resources, no single individual is the master of any set of knowledge; rather, we all utilize and contribute to a global knowledge community and Web 2.0 has greatly accelerated our ability to share.

However, drawing from a multitude of voices does not automatically improve the quality or truth-value of information, according to digital theorist Jaron Lanier (2006). Lanier says, "[Y]ou get to include all sorts of material without committing to anything. You can be superficially interesting without having to worry about the possibility of being wrong. . . . [T]he collective can be stupid, too." Furthermore, given that Internet search engines place the most popular sources at the top of a search, rather than the most authoritative, those with the most popular viewpoints are often held up as "right" without scrutiny of their information. Although *Wikipedia* frequently comes up as a top result in an Internet search, does that make it the best and most authoritative source?

The problem is not the broadening of the knowledge base to include more perspectives, but the fact that certain voices, both online and off, are using their place in the public sphere to act as experts despite having little claim to such a title. For example, media watchdog group *Media Matters* reported that during the height of the debt-ceiling debate in July 2011, only 4.1 percent of the 1,258 guests on Fox, CNN, and MSNBC news programs were actually economists "with an advanced degree in economics" or who have served as an "economics professor at a college or university level." Cable news programs have the ability to reach a large number of people and frame our knowledge about current events. The lack of actual experts hinders rather than helps our understanding of issues, and in the case of the debt-ceiling issue, it resulted in much of the public adopting beliefs that differed from most economists ("Economists shut out of debt-ceiling debate").

Ultimately, there are pros and cons to this practice of collective intelligence. On one hand, knowledge is generated through discussion among several sources rather than delivered top-down from a single source. On the other, holding up less informed voices as equal to those with more expertise can produce dangerous consequences, particularly when non-experts are afforded a larger platform to spread misinformation in the name of knowledge.

Questions to Ponder

1. Do you think the pros of collective intelligence afforded us via Internet technologies outweigh the potential consequences? Why or why not?

2. As consumers, what should we do to ensure that the information we gain from various Internet sources are true, valid, and reliable?

3. Do you think fact-checking should be required before information can be posted on Internet sites such as *Wikipedia*? Why or why not?

Linguistic Sensitivity

Recall from chapter four that we demonstrate *linguistic sensitivity* by choosing words that are respectful of others and by avoiding potentially offensive language. Just as this is crucial to effective interpersonal and group communication, so is it imperative in public speaking sitautions. To demonstrate linguistic sensitivity, avoid using generic language, nonparallel language, potentially offensive humor, as well as profanity and vulgarity.

Generic Language **Generic language** uses words that apply only to one sex, race, or other group as though they represent everyone. In the past, English speakers used the masculine pronoun *he* to stand for all humans regardless of sex. This example of generic language excludes 50 percent of the audience. The best way to avoid using generic language in public speeches is to use plurals: "When we shop, we should have a clear idea of what we want to buy" (Stewart, Cooper, Stewart, & Friedley, 2003).

generic language

words used that apply to one co-cultural group as though they represent everyone

Nonparallel Language **Nonparallel language** is a term that describes when terms are changed because of the sex, race, or other group characteristics of the individual. Two common forms of nonparallelism are marking and irrelevant association.

Marking is the *addition* of sex, race, age, or other group designations to a description. For instance, a doctor is a person with a medical degree who is licensed to practice medicine. Notice the difference between the following two sentences:

Jones is a good doctor.

Jones is a good black doctor.

In the second sentence, use of the marker "black" has nothing to do with doctoring. Marking is inappropriate because it trivializes the subject's role by introducing an irrelevant characteristic (Treinen & Warren, 2001). The speaker may be intending to praise Jones, but listeners may interpret the sentence as

nonparallel language

words that are changed because of the sex, race, or other group characteristics of the individual

marking

the addition of sex, race, age, or other group designations to a description saying that Jones is a good doctor for a black person (or a woman or an old person) but not that Jones is as good as a good white doctor (or a male doctor or a young doctor).

A second form of nonparallelism is **irrelevant association**, which is when one person's relationship to another is emphasized, even though that relationship is irrelevant to the point. For example, it is inappropriate to introduce a speaker by saying, "Gladys Thompson, whose husband is CEO of Acme Inc., is the chairperson for this year's United Way campaign." Mentioning her husband's status implies that Gladys Thompson is chairperson because of her *husband's* accomplishments, not her own.

Offensive Humor Dirty jokes and racist, sexist, or other "-ist" remarks may not be intended to be offensive, but if some listeners are offended, you will have lost verbal immediacy. To be most effective with your formal public speeches, avoid humorous comments or jokes that may be offensive to some listeners. Being inclusive means demonstrating respect for all listeners.

Profanity and Vulgarity Appropriate language avoids profanity and vulgar expressions. Fifty years ago, a child was punished for saying "hell" or "damn," and adults used profanity and vulgarity only in rare situations to express strong emotions. Today, "casual swearing"—profanity injected into regular conversation—is an epidemic in some language communities, including college campuses (Lehman & Dufrene, 2008).

Despite the growing, mindless use of crude speech, many people are still shocked and offended by swearing. And people who casually pepper their formal speeches with profanity and vulgar expressions are often perceived as abrasive and lacking in character, maturity, intelligence, manners, and emotional control (O'Connor, 2000). Recall how actress Melissa Leo's credibility was damaged by her use of the "F" word in her Academy Award acceptance speech for Best Supporting Actress in *The Fighter*.

Cultural Diversity

When you address an audience composed of people from ethnic and language groups different from your own, you should make extra effort to ensure that you are being understood. When the first language spoken by audience members is different from yours, they may not be able to understand what you are saying because you may speak with an accent, mispronounce words, choose inappropriate words, and misuse idioms. Speaking in a second language can make you anxious and self-conscious. But most audience members are more tolerant of mistakes made by a second-language speaker than they are of those made by a native speaker. Likewise, they will work hard to understand a second-language speaker.

Nevertheless, when you are speaking in a second language, you have an additional responsibility to make your speech as understandable as possible. You can help your audience by speaking more slowly and articulating as clearly as you can. By slowing your speaking rate, you give yourself additional time to pronounce difficult sounds and choose words

---

irrelevant association

when one emphasizes one person's relationship to another when doing so is not necessary to make the point

How might this speaker adapt verbally to address the diversity in his or her audience?

Michelle Pemberton/Rapport Press/Newscom

whose meanings you know. You also give your audience members additional time to adjust their ears so that they can more easily process what you are saying. You can also use visual aids to reinforce key terms and concepts as you move through the speech. Doing so assures listeners that they've heard you correctly.

One of the best ways to improve when you are giving a speech in a second language is to practice the speech in front of friends and associates who are native speakers. Ask them to take note of words and phrases that you mispronounce or misuse. Then they can work with you to correct the pronunciation or to choose other words that better express your idea. Also, keep in mind that the more you practice speaking the language, the more comfortable you will become with the language and with your ability to relate to the audience members.

In the *Diverse Voices* feature, Ann Neville Miller provides insights into public speaking practices in Kenya and how Kenyans must adapt their speeches to appeal to their audiences' shared experiences and knowledge.

DIVERSE VOICES

Public Speaking Patterns in Kenya

by Ann Neville Miller

One of the major differences in adapting to different groups is understanding their expectations and their reactions to your words. In this excerpt, Ann Neville Miller describes the different purposes of public speaking in Kenya and how those purposes influence how Kenyan speakers adapt their words to the expectations of their audiences.

Much public speaking in the United States is informative or persuasive in purpose; ceremonial occasions for public speaking are less common. This is due, in part, to the stress that mainstream U.S. culture places on informality. The average Kenyan, in contrast, will give far more ceremonial speeches in life than any other kind of speech. These may be speeches of greeting, introduction, tribute, and thanks, among others. Life events, both major and minor, are marked by ceremonies, and ceremonies occasion multiple public speeches.

This means that, unlike the majority of people in the United States, who report that they fear speaking in public, possibly even more than they fear death (Richmond & McCroskey, 1995), for most Kenyans, public speaking is an unavoidable responsibility.

For example, when a Kenyan attends a church service or other event away from home, he or she will often be asked to stand up and give an impromptu word of greeting to the assembly. In more remote areas, where literacy rates are low and there is little access to electronic media, this word of greeting also can serve an informative purpose because the one who has traveled often brings news of the outside world. The *harambee*, a kind of community fund-raising event peculiar to Kenya, is characterized by the presence of both a guest of honor and various dignitaries of a stature appropriate to the specific occasion, all of whom are likely at some point to address the gathering. Weddings and funerals overflow with ceremonial speeches; virtually any relative, friend, or business associate of the newly married or deceased may give advice or pay tribute. Older members of the bride's family, for example, may remind her how important it is to feed her husband well, or warn the groom that in their family men are expected never to abuse their wives, but to settle marital disputes with patience. Even the woman selected to cut the cake expects to give a brief word of exhortation before performing her duty. The free dispensing of advice, a hallmark of Kenyan wedding celebrations, would be out of place at most receptions in the United States, where the focus of speeches is normally more on remembrances and well-wishing.

In fact, when it comes to marriage, speech making begins long before the actual wedding day, at bridal negotiations where up to 40 or 50 people from the two families attempt to settle on a bride price. At these negotiations especially, but also in other ceremonial speeches, "deep" language replete with proverbs and metaphors is expected. The family of the man may explain that their son has seen a beautiful flower, or a lovely she-goat, or some other item in the compound of the family of the young lady and that they would like to obtain it for their son. In a negotiation of this type that I recently attended, the speaker for the bride's relatives explained that the family would require 20 goats as a major portion of the bride price. Because both parties were urban dwellers and would have no space to keep that many animals, the groom's family conferred with each other and determined that the bride's family really wanted cash. They settled on what they considered to be a reasonable price per goat, multiplied it by 20, and presented the total amount through a designated spokesperson to the representative of the bride. The original speaker from the bride's family looked at the money and observed dryly that goats in the groom's area were considerably thinner than those the bride's family were accustomed to! This type of indirect communication, the subtlety of which affords immense satisfaction and sometimes amusement to both speaker and listener, is a form of the high-context communication described by [Edward T.] Hall. A full appreciation of the speech requires extensive knowledge of shared experiences and traditions.

Excerpted from Ann Neville Miller, "Public Speaking Patterns in Kenya." In Larry A. Samovar, Richard E. Porter, & Edwin R. McDaniel, eds., Intercultural Communication: A Reader *(11th ed., pp. 238–245). Belmont, CA: Wadsworth, 2006.*

Speaking Clearly

speaking clearly

using words that convey your meaning precisely

Speaking clearly means using words that convey your meaning precisely. Remember from our discussion in Chapter Four that words are arbitrarily chosen symbols to represent our thoughts and feelings (Saeid, 2003). In communication studies, we often simply say the *word* is NOT the *thing*. In their influential book, *The Meaning of Meaning: A Study of the Influence of Language upon Thought and the Science of Symbolism,* I. A. Richards and C. K. Ogden (1923) clarify this idea using the semantic triangle. As depicted in Figure 14.1, a "referent" is the *thing* or object we refer to with a word, which is the "symbol" we use to refer to it. Our audience then attaches meaning to that symbol, which is what Richards and Ogden label the "thought of referent." For example, when you hear the word *dog*, what image forms in your mind? Do you visualize a poodle? A sheepdog? A mutt? There is so much variation in what the word *dog* conjures in our minds because the word *dog* is not the actual animal. The word is a symbol you use to represent the animal. So if you use the word *dog* in a speech, each member of your audience may picture something different. Because the *word* is not the *thing,* as a public speaker you should use words that most closely match the thing or idea you want your audience to see or understand. By doing so, your meaning is more likely to be understood as you intended. Let's review four strategies for improving clarity that are crucial for effective public speakers: use specific language, choose familiar terms, provide details and examples, and limit vocalized pauses.

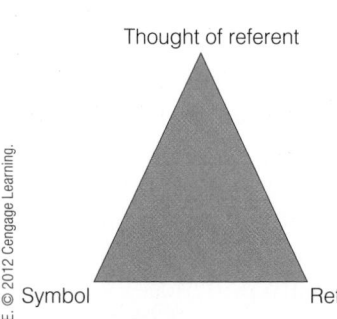

Figure 14.1

The semantic triangle

From Verderber/Verderber/Sellnow, The Challenge of Effective Speaking, 15E. © 2012 Cengage Learning.

Specific Language

Specific language refers to using precise words that clarify meaning by narrowing what is understood from a general category to a particular item or group within that category. For instance, if in her speech Nevah refers to a "blue-collar worker," you might picture any number of occupations that fall within this broad category. If, instead, she says he's a "construction worker," the number of possible images you can picture is reduced. Now you select your image from the subcategory of construction worker, and your meaning is likely to be closer to the one she intended. If she is even more specific, she may say "bulldozer operator." Now you are even clearer on the specific occupation.

specific language

words that narrow what is understood from a general category to a particular item or group within it

Choosing specific language is easier when you have a large working vocabulary. As a speaker, the larger your vocabulary, the more choices you have from which to select the word you want. Some speakers think that to be effective they must impress their audience with their extensive vocabularies. As a result, instead of looking for specific and *precise words*, they use words that appear pompous, affected, or stilted to the listener. Speaking precisely and specifically does not mean speaking obscurely. The following story illustrates the problem with pretentious words:

> *A plumber e-mailed a government agency, saying he found that hydrochloric acid quickly opened drainpipes, but he wasn't sure whether it was a good thing to use.*
>
> *A scientist at the agency replied, "The efficacy of hydrochloric acid is indisputable, but the corrosive residue is incompatible with metallic permanence."*
>
> *The plumber wrote back thanking him for the assurance that hydrochloric acid was all right.*
>
> *Disturbed by this, the scientist showed the e-mail to his boss, another scientist, who then e-mailed the plumber: "We cannot assume responsibility for the production of toxic and noxious residue with hydrochloric acid and suggest you use an alternative procedure."*
>
> *The plumber e-mailed back that he agreed. Hydrochloric acid worked fine.*
>
> *Greatly disturbed by this misunderstanding, the scientists took their problem to the top boss. She wrote to the plumber: "Don't use hydrochloric acid. It eats the hell out of pipes."*

As a general rule, use a more difficult word *only* when you believe that it is the very best word for a specific context. Let's suppose you wanted to use a more precise or specific word for *building*. Using the guideline of familiarity, you might select *house, apartment, high-rise,* or *skyscraper,* but you would avoid *edifice*. Each of the other choices is more precise or more specific, but *edifice* is neither more precise nor more specific, and in addition to being less commonly understood, it will be perceived as affected or stilted.

Familiar Terms

Using familiar terms is just as important as using specific words in public speeches. Avoid jargon, slang, abbreviations, and acronyms unless (1) you define them clearly the first time they are used and (2) using them is central to your speech goal.

Watterson. Reprinted with permission of Universal UCLICK

jargon

the unique technical terminology of a trade or profession

Jargon is the unique technical terminology of a trade or profession that is not generally understood by outsiders. We might forget that people who are not in our same line of work or who do not have the same hobbies may not understand the jargon that seems such a part of our daily communication. For instance, when Jenny, who is sophisticated in the use of cyberlanguage, starts talking with her computer-illiterate friend Sarah about "social MUDs based on fictional universes," Sarah is likely to be totally lost. If, however, Jenny recognizes Sarah's lack of familiarity with cyberlanguage, she can make her message clear by discussing the concepts in words her friend understands. In short, limit your use of jargon in speeches to general audiences and always define jargon in simple terms the first time you use it.

slang

informal, nonstandard vocabulary and definitions assigned to words by a social group or subculture

Slang refers to informal, nonstandard vocabulary and nonstandard definitions assigned to words by a social group or subculture. For example, today the word *wicked,* which has a standard definition denoting something wrong or immoral, can mean quite the opposite in some social groups and co-cultures (Rader, 2007). You should generally avoid slang in your public speeches not only because you risk being misunderstood but also because slang doesn't sound professional and it can hurt your credibility. Slang is so pervasive that there are special dictionaries devoted to the specialized vocabulary of different communities. You can even find slang dictionaries online.

Overusing and misusing abbreviations and acronyms can also hinder clarity. Even if you think the abbreviation or acronym is a common one, to ensure intelligibility, always define it the first time you use it in the speech. For example, in a speech about NASCAR, refer to it initially by the organization's full name and then provide the acronym: "National Association for Stock Car Auto Racing, or NASCAR." Providing the full and abbreviated forms of the name will ensure clarity for all listeners. If you are assuming right now that everyone knows what NASCAR is, it might benefit you to know one of your authors had to look it up to include it in this book!

Details and Examples

Sometimes, the word we use may not have a precise synonym. In these situations, clarity can be achieved by adding details or examples.

Saying "He lives in a really big house" can be clarified by adding, "He lives in a fourteen-room Tudor mansion on a six-acre estate."

 **THE AUDIENCE** *BEYOND*

To be sure her blog readers would know what she meant by "dicing the carrots," she provided details about the size and shape each individual piece should be.

Vocalized Pauses

Vocalized pauses are unnecessary words interjected into sentences to fill moments of silence. Words commonly used for this purpose are "like," "you know," "really," and "basically," as well as "um" and "uh." We sometimes refer to vocalized pauses as "verbal garbage" because they do not serve a meaningful purpose and actually distract audience members from the message. Although a few vocalized pauses typically don't hinder clarity, practicing your speech aloud will help you eliminate them.

vocalized pauses

unnecessary words interjected to fill moments of silence

Speaking Vividly

Because listeners cannot "reread" what you have said, you must speak in ways that help them remember your speech. Speaking vividly is one effective way to maintain your audience's interest and help them remember what you say. **Vivid language** is full of life—vigorous, bright, and intense. For example, a mediocre baseball announcer might say, "Jackson made a great catch," but a better commentator's vivid account might be, "Jackson leaped and made a spectacular one-handed catch just as he crashed into the center field wall." The words *leaped, spectacular, one-handed catch,* and *crashed* paint an intense verbal picture of the action. You can make your ideas come to life by using sensory language and by using rhetorical figures and structures of speech.

vivid language

words that are full of life

Sensory Language

Sensory language is language that appeals to the senses of seeing, hearing, tasting, smelling, and feeling. Vivid sensory language begins with vivid thought. You are much more likely to express yourself vividly if you can physically or psychologically sense the meanings you are trying to convey. If you feel the "bite of the wind" or "the sting of freezing rain," if you hear and smell "the thick, juicy sirloin steaks sizzling on the grill," you will be able to describe these sensations. Does the cake "taste good"? Or do your taste buds "quiver with the sweet double-chocolate icing and velvety feel of the rich, moist cake"?

sensory language

words that appeal to seeing, hearing, tasting, smelling, and feeling

To develop vivid sensory language, begin by considering how you can re-create what something, someone, or some place *looks like*. Consider, too, how you can help listeners imagine how something *sounds*. How can you use language to convey the way something *feels* (textures, shapes, temperatures)? How can language re-create a sense of how something *tastes* or *smells*? To achieve this in your speech, use colorful descriptors. They make your ideas more concrete and can arouse emotions. They invite listeners to imagine details. Here's an example about downhill skiing:

Sight: *As you climb the hill, the bright winter sunshine glistening on the snow is blinding.*

Touch and feel: *Just before you take off, you gently slip your goggles over your eyes. They are bitterly cold and sting your nose for a moment.*

Taste: *You start the descent and, as you gradually pick up speed, the taste of air and ice and snow in your mouth invigorates you.*

Credit line to come

You can help listeners remember by appealing to the senses.

Sound: *An odd* silence *fills the air. You hear nothing but the swish of your skis against the snow beneath your feet. At last, you arrive at the bottom of the slope. Reality hits as you hear the hustle and bustle of other skiers and instructors directing them to their next session.*

Smell and feel: *You enter the warming house. As your fingers thaw in the warm air, the aroma from the wood stove in the corner comforts you as you ready yourself to drift off into sleep.*

By using colorful descriptors that appeal to the senses, you arouse and maintain listener interest and make your ideas more memorable.

Rhetorical Figures and Structures of Speech

rhetorical figures of speech

make striking comparisons between things that are not obviously alike

rhetorical structures of speech

combine ideas in a particular way

simile

a direct comparison of dissimilar things using the word like or as

metaphor

an implied comparison between two unlike things, expressed without using like or as

analogy

an extended metaphor

Rhetorical figures of speech make striking comparisons between things that are not obviously alike to help listeners visualize or internalize what you are saying. **Rhetorical structures of speech** combine ideas in a particular way. Any of these devices can serve to make your speech more memorable as long as they aren't overused. Let's look at some examples.

A **simile** is a direct comparison of dissimilar things using the word *like* or *as.* Clichés such as "He walks like a duck" and "She's as busy as a bee" are similes. If you've seen the movie *Forrest Gump,* you might recall Forrest's use of the simile: "Life is like a box of chocolates. You never know what you're going to get." An elementary school teacher used a simile by saying that being back at school after a long absence "was like trying to hold 35 corks under water at the same time"(Hensley, 1995). Similes can be effective because they make ideas more vivid in listeners' minds. But they should be used sparingly or they lose their appeal. Clichés should be avoided because their predictability reduces their effectiveness.

A **metaphor** is an implied comparison between two unlike things, expressed without using *like* or *as*. Instead of saying that one thing is *like* another, a metaphor says that one thing *is* another. Thus, problem cars are "lemons," and the leaky roof is a "sieve." Metaphors can be effective because they make an abstract concept more concrete, strengthen an important point, or heighten emotions. Notice how one speaker used a metaphor effectively to conclude a speech: "It is imperative that we weave our fabric of the future with durable thread"(Schertz, 1977).

An **analogy** is an extended metaphor. Sometimes, you can develop a story from a metaphor that makes a concept more vivid. If you were to describe a family member as the "black sheep in the barnyard," that's a metaphor. If you went on to talk about the other members of the family as different animals on the farm and the roles ascribed to them, you would be extending the metaphor into an analogy. Analogies can be effective for holding your speech together in a creative and vivid way. Analogies are particularly useful to highlight the similarities between a complex and unfamiliar concept with one that is familiar.

Alliteration is the repetition of consonant sounds at the beginning of words that are near one another. Tongue twisters such as "She sells seashells by the seashore" use alliteration. In her speech about the history of jelly beans, Sharla used alliteration when she said, "And today there are more than fifty fabulous fruity flavors from which to choose." Used sparingly, alliteration can catch listeners' attention and make the speech memorable. But overuse can hurt the message because listeners might focus on the technique rather than the content of your message.

Assonance is the repetition of vowel sounds in a phrase or phrases. "How now brown cow" is a common example. Sometimes, the words rhyme, but they don't have to. As with alliteration, assonance can make your speech more memorable as long as it's not overused.

Onomatopoeia is the use of words that sound like the things they stand for, such as "buzz," "hiss," "crack," and "plop." In the speech about skiing, the "swish" of the skis is an example of onomatopoeia.

Personification attributes human qualities to a concept or an inanimate object. When Madison talked about her truck, "Big Red," as her trusted friend and companion, she used personification. Likewise, when Rick talked about flowers dancing on the front lawn, he used personification.

Repetition is restating words, phrases, or sentences for emphasis. Martin Luther King Jr.'s "I Have a Dream" speech is a classic example:

> I say to you today, my friends, so even though we face the difficulties of today and tomorrow, I still have a dream. It is a dream deeply rooted in the American dream.
>
> I have a dream that one day this nation will rise up and live out the true meaning of its creed: "We hold these truths to be self-evident: that all men are created equal."
>
> I have a dream that one day on the red hills of Georgia the sons of former slaves and the sons of former slave owners will be able to sit down together at the table of brotherhood.
>
> I have a dream that one day even the state of Mississippi, a state sweltering with the heat of injustice, sweltering with the heat of oppression, will be transformed into the oasis of freedom and justice.
>
> I have a dream that my four little children will one day live in a nation where they will not be judged by the color of their skin but by the content of their character. I have a dream today.

Reprinted by arrangement with the Estate of Martin Luther King, Jr. c/o Writers House as agent for the proprietor New York, NY. Copyright 1963 Dr. Martin Luther King, Jr., copyright renewed 1991 Coretta Scott King.

Antithesis is combining contrasting ideas in the same sentence, as when John F. Kennedy said, "My fellow Americans, ask not what your country can do for you. Ask what you can do for your country." Likewise, astronaut Neil Armstrong used antithesis when he first stepped on the moon: "That's one small step for man, one giant leap for mankind." Speeches that offer antithesis in the concluding remarks are often very memorable.

alliteration
the repetition of consonant sounds at the beginning of words that are near one another

assonance
The repetition of vowel sounds in a phrase or phrases

onomatopoeia
the use of words that sound like the things they stand for

personification
attributing human qualities to a concept or an inanimate object

repetition
restating words, phrases, or sentences for emphasis

antithesis
combining contrasting ideas in the same sentence

ACTION STEP 5.A

Adapting Oral Language and Style

The goal of this activity is to help you plan how you will adapt your language and style to the specific audience..

Write your thesis statement:

_____

Review the audience analysis that you completed in Action Steps 1 through 4. Now, verbally adapt to your audience by answering the following questions:

1. How can I adapt my language to foster verbal immediacy with this audience?

2. How can I adapt my language choices to demonstrate respect for this audience?

3. Where can I adapt my language to be most intelligible for this audience?

4. How can I use sensory language and rhetorical figures of speech to make my ideas more vivid for this audience?

WHAT WOULD YOU DO?

A Question of Ethics

"Kendra, I heard you telling Jim about the speech you're giving tomorrow. You think it's a winner, huh?"

"You got that right, Omar. I'm going to have Bardston eating out of the palm of my hand."

"You sound confident."

"This time I have reason to be. See, Professor Bardston's been talking about the importance of audience adaptation. These last two weeks that's all we've heard—adaptation, adaptation."

"What does she mean?"

"Talking about something in a way that really relates to people personally."

"OK—so how are you going to do that?"

"Well, you see, I'm giving this speech on abortion. Now here's the kick. Bardston let it slip that she's a supporter of Right to Life. So what I'm going to do is give this informative speech on the Right to Life movement. But I'm going to discuss the major beliefs of the movement in a way that'll get her to think that I'm a supporter. I'm going to mention aspects of the movement that I know she'll like."

"But I've heard you talk about how you're pro-choice."

"I am—all the way. But by keeping the information positive, she'll think I'm a supporter. It isn't as if I'm going to be telling any lies or anything."

1. In a speech, is it ethical to adapt in a way that resonates with your audience but isn't in keeping with what you really believe?

2. Could Kendra have achieved her goal using a different method? How?

Summary

Audience adaptation is the process of customizing your speech to your specific audience. Audience adaptation begins with topic selection and development and continues throughout the speechmaking process. In this chapter, we focused on how to adapt your language and oral style to address the needs and expectations of the audience and occasion. First, we discussed the nature of effective oral style as it differs from written style. Then we examined some specific guidelines to consider when preparing your public speeches.

Appropriate language fosters verbal immediacy between you and your audience. In other words, you choose words that enhance a sense of connection with your listeners by demonstrating relevance, common ground, credibility, and linguistic sensitivity, and by adapting to cultural diversity. To ensure clarity, use specific language and familiar terms, provide details and examples, and limit vocalized pauses. To speak vividly, use language that appeals to the senses of seeing, hearing, tasting, smelling, and feeling, as well as rhetorical figures and structures of speech. Some examples include simile, metaphor, analogy, alliteration, assonance, onomatopoeia, personification, repetition, and antithesis.

COMMUNICATE!

RESOURCE AND ASSESSMENT CENTER

Now that you have read Chapter 14, go to the Speech Communication Course-Mate at cengagebrain.com where you'll find an interactive eBook and interactive learning tools including quizzes, flashcards, sample speech videos, audio study tools, skill-building activities, action step activities, and more. Student Workbook, Speech Builder Express 3.0, and Speech Studio 2.0 are also available.

Applying What You've Learned

Impromptu Speech Activity

1. Draw a card from a stack provided by your instructor. The card will have a rhetorical figure of speech printed on it. Create a short 2–3 minute speech about a local event that uses that particular figure of speech at least twice.

Assessment Activity

1. Search online for the article "A Question of Real American Black Men," by Bailey B. Baker Jr., *Vital Speeches*, April 15, 2002. Analyze how this speaker uses personal pronouns, rhetorical questions, common experiences, and personalized information to create common ground. Write a short essay describing the conclusions of your analysis.

Skill-Building Activity

1. Practice Using Sensory Language Create a description of each of the following events appealing to each of the five senses: sight, touch/feel, taste, sound, smell.

(a) lawn mowing

(b) tacos

(c) traffic congestion

(d) babysitting

2. Rhetorical Figures of Speech Describe a circus using each of the following figures of speech: simile, metaphor, analogy, alliteration, assonance, onomatopoeia, personification, repetition, and antithesis.

Delivery

When Gwen finished speaking, virtually everyone in the audience burst into spontaneous applause.

Miguel turned to his friend Justin and said, "That was a great speech. I can see why people are excited; the information was good and easy to follow. I thought it was excellent."

Justin replied, "Miguel, I've heard many speeches that had excellent information and were well organized, but what made Gwen's speech so much better was her delivery. She sounded conversational and convincing. She was poised and animated—and she didn't appear to be nervous at all!"

15

Mel Yates/Cultura RF/Jupiter Images

As Justin and his classmates recognized, the difference between a good speech and a great speech is often how well it is delivered. In fact, research suggests that listeners are often influenced more by speech delivery than content (Decker, 1992; Gardner, 2003; Towler, 2003). Although some people seem to be naturally fluent and comfortable speaking to a group, most of us are actually a bit nervous and maybe even downright frightened. What you'll learn in this chapter will help you manage your nervousness as you deliver effective speeches.

ACTION STEP   5

Practice Oral Language and Delivery Style

CONSIDER *THIS*....

Think about the experiences you had with public speaking when you were growing up. Did people praise or criticize your efforts? How did that influence your apprehension?

In the last chapter, we focused on one aspect of the fifth action step: oral language style. In this chapter, we turn our attention to the other aspect: delivery style. We begin by discussing stage fright and ways to manage it effectively. Then we explain how to use your voice and body effectively, as well as three common methods for delivering a speech. We then introduce a process designed to make your practice sessions productive and some delivery guidelines to consider while giving the actual speech. Finally, we offer several criteria you can use to evaluate your speeches and apply that criteria to a sample student speech.

Public Speaking Apprehension

Most of us feel some fear about public speaking. In fact, as many as 76 percent of experienced public speakers feel some fear before presenting a speech (Hahner, Sokoloff, & Salisch, 2001). Did you know, for example, that award-winning actors Meryl Streep and Kim Basinger, entertainers Barbra Streisand and Donny Osmond, professional football player Ricky Williams, and evangelist Billy Graham all experience a fear of public speaking? In spite of their fear, they are all effective public speakers.

public speaking apprehension

the level of fear you experience when anticipating or actually speaking to an audience

Many famous speakers feel some apprehension about public speaking.

Public speaking apprehension is the level of fear we experience when anticipating or actually speaking to an audience. Fortunately, we can benefit from the results of a good deal of research about managing public speaking apprehension effectively. We say *manage* because having some fear actually makes us better speakers. Just as an adrenaline boost helps athletes, musicians, and actors perform better, it can also help us deliver better public speeches (Kelly, Duran, & Stewart, 1990; Motley, 1997; Phillips, 1977).

Symptoms and Causes

The symptoms of pubic speaking apprehension vary from individual to individual and range from mild to debilitating. Symptoms can be cognitive, physical, or emotional. Cognitive symptoms stem from negative self-talk (e.g., "I'm going to blow it" or "I just know I'll make a fool of myself"), which is also the most common cause of speech apprehension (Richmond & McCroskey, 2000). Physical symptoms may be stomach upset (or butterflies), flushed skin, sweating, shaking, light-headedness, rapid or pounding heartbeats, stuttering, and vocalized pauses ("like," "you know," "ah," "um," and so on). Emotional symptoms include feeling anxious, worried, or upset.

In addition to negative self-talk, previous experience, modeling, and negative reinforcement can also cause public speaking apprehension.

Kevin Winter/Getty Images

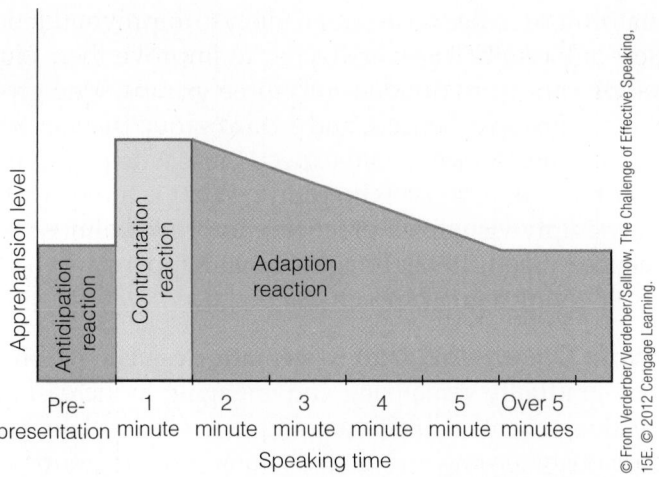

© From Verderber/Verderber/Sellnow, *The Challenge of Effective Speaking,* 15E. © 2012 Cengage Learning.

Figure 15.1

Phases of public speaking apprehension

Previous experience has to do with being socialized to fear public speaking as a result of modeling and negative reinforcement (Richmond & McCroskey, 2000). Modeling has to do with observing how your friends and family members react to speaking in public. If they tend to be quiet and reserved and avoid public speaking, your fears may stem from modeling. Negative reinforcement concerns how others have responded to your public speaking endeavors. If you experienced negative reactions, you might be more apprehensive about speaking in public than if you had been praised for your efforts (Motley, 1997).

Luckily, our apprehension gradually decreases for most of us as we speak. Researchers have identified three phases we proceed through: anticipation, confrontation, and adaptation (Behnke & Carlile, 1971). Figure 15.1 illustrates these phases. The **anticipation phase** is the anxiety we experience before giving the speech, both while preparing it and waiting to speak. The **confrontation phase** is the surge of anxiety we feel as we begin delivering the speech. The **adaptation phase** is the period during which our anxiety level gradually decreases. It typically begins about one minute into the presentation and tends to level off after about five minutes (Beatty & Behnke, 1991).

Management Techniques

We propose five techniques you can use to help manage your apprehension effectively: communication orientation, visualization, systematic desensitization, cognitive restructuring, and public speaking skills training.

Communication Orientation Motivation Communication orientation motivation (COM) techniques reduce anxiety by helping us adopt a *communication* rather than *performance* orientation toward speeches (Motley, 1997). When we have a **performance orientation**, we believe we must *impress* a hypercritical audience with our knowledge and delivery. On the other hand, when we have a **communication orientation**, we focus on talking with our audience about an important topic and *getting a message across to them*—not about how they might be judging our performance.

Visualization Visualization helps us reduce anxiety by developing a mental picture of ourselves giving a masterful speech. If we visualize ourselves going through an entire speech-making process successfully, we are more likely to be successful when we actually deliver the speech (Ayres & Hopf, 1990; Ayres, Hopf, & Ayres, 1994).

anticipation phase

anxiety we experience before giving the speech

confrontation phase

the surge of anxiety we experience when beginning to deliver the speech

adaptation phase

the period during which our anxiety gradually decreases

performance orientation

believing we must impress a hypercritical audience with our knowledge and delivery

communication orientation

seeing a speech situation as an opportunity to talk with a number of people about a topic that is important to the speaker and to them

visualization

a method to reduce apprehension by developing a mental picture of yourself giving a masterful speech

Do you use positive self-talk to pump yourself up before you have an important event? Do the same before you speak. If you believe you can perform well, you will.

systematic desensitization

a method to reduce apprehension by gradually visualizing and then engaging in more frightening speaking events

cognitive restructuring

replacing anxiety-arousing negative self-talk with anxiety-reducing positive self-talk

public speaking skills training

the systematic teaching of the skills associated with preparing and delivering an effective public speech, with the intention of improving speaking competence and thereby reducing public speaking apprehension

Visualization has been used extensively to improve athletic performances. In a study of basketball players trying to improve their foul-shooting percentages, players were divided into three groups. One group never practiced, another group practiced, and a third group visualized practicing and making foul shots. As we would expect, those who physically practiced improved far more than those who didn't. What is amazing, however, is that those who simply visualized practicing improved almost as much as those who practiced (Scott, 1997). Imagine what happens when you both visualize yourself giving a great speech *and* practice!

Systematic Desensitization **Systematic desensitization** can help reduce anxiety by gradually visualizing and engaging in increasingly more frightening speaking events while remaining in a relaxed state. The process starts with consciously tensing and then relaxing muscle groups in order to learn how to recognize the difference between the two states. Then, while in a relaxed state, you first imagine yourself and then engage in successively more stressful situations—for example, researching a speech topic in the library, practicing the speech out loud to a roommate, and finally, giving a speech. The ultimate goal of systematic desensitization is to transfer the calm feelings we attain while visualizing to the actual speaking event. Calmness on command—it works.

Cognitive Restructuring **Cognitive restructuring** helps reduce anxiety by changing negative thoughts about public speaking. In other words, we replace anxiety-arousing negative self-talk with anxiety-reducing positive self-talk through a four-step process.

1. **Identify your fears.** Write down all the fears that come to mind when you know you must give a speech.

2. **Determine whether or not these fears are rational.** Most are irrational because public speaking is not life threatening.

3. **Develop positive coping statements to replace each negative self-talk statement.** There is no list of coping statements that will work for everyone. Psychologist Richard Heimberg of the State University of New York at Albany reminds his clients that most listeners don't notice or even care if the clients do what they're afraid of doing when giving a speech. Ultimately, he asks them, "Can you cope with the one or two people who [notice or criticize or] get upset?"

4. **Incorporate positive coping statements into your life so they become second nature.** You can do this by writing your statements down and reading them aloud to yourself each day, as well as before you give a speech. The more you repeat your coping statements, the more natural they will become (see Figure 15.2).

Public Speaking Skills Training **Public speaking skills training** is systematically practicing the skills involved in preparing and delivering an effective public speech. Skills training is based on the assumption that some public speaking anxiety is caused by not knowing how to be successful. So

THE AUDIENCE *BEYOND*

Justin posted each of his negative self-talk statements on Facebook and Twitter and asked friends and followers to help him come up with positive coping statement alternatives.

Here are the positive statements Beth developed to counter her negative self-talk:

Negative self-talk
1. I'm afraid I'll stumble over my words and look foolish.
2. I'm afraid everyone will be able to tell that I am nervous.
3. I'm afraid my voice will crack.
4. I'm afraid I'll sound boring.

Positive coping statements
1. Even if I stumble, I will have succeeded as long as I get my message across.
2. They probably won't be able to tell I'm nervous, but as long as I focus on getting my message across, that's what matters.
3. Even if my voice cracks, as long as I keep going and focus on getting my message across, I'll succeed at what matters most.
4. I won't sound bored if I focus on how important this message is to me and to my audience. I don't have to do somersaults to keep their attention, because my topic is relevant to them.

Figure 15.2

Negative self-talk versus positive coping statements

if we learn the skills associated with effective speech making (e.g., audience analysis, topic selection and development, organization, oral language, and delivery style), then we will be less anxious (Kelly, Phillips, & Keaten, 1995).

Effective Delivery Style

Think about the best speaker you have ever heard. What made this person stand out in your mind? In all likelihood, how the speaker delivered the speech had a lot to do with it. **Delivery** is how a message is communicated orally and visually through the use of voice and body. So we achieve effective delivery by adapting the types of nonverbal communication introduced in Chapter 5 to a public speaking situation. An effective public speaking delivery style is both conversational and animated.

delivery

how a message is communicated orally and visually through the use of voice and body

Conversational

You have probably heard ineffective speakers whose delivery was overly dramatic and affected or stiff and mechanical. In contrast, effective delivery is **conversational.** The audience perceives you as *talking with* them and not performing *in front of* or *reading to* them. The hallmark of a conversational style is spontaneity. **Spontaneity** is the ability to sound natural—as though you are really thinking about the ideas and getting them across to your audience—no matter how many times you've practiced.

conversational style

presenting a speech so that your audience feels you are talking with them

spontaneity

a naturalness that seems unrehearsed and unmemorized

Animated

Have you ever been bored by a professor reading a well-structured lecture while looking at the lecture notes rather than the students and making few gestures other than turning the pages? Even a well-written speech given by an expert can bore an audience unless its delivery is **animated**, that is, lively and dynamic.

How can you sound conversational and animated at the same time? The secret is to focus on conveying the passion you feel about the topic through your voice and body. When we are passionate about sharing something with someone, almost all of us become more animated in our delivery. Your goal

animated

lively and dynamic

"LADIES AND GENTLEMEN... IS *THAT MY VOICE?*... I NEVER HEARD IT AMPLIFIED BEFORE. IT SOUNDS SO WEIRD. HELLO. HELLO. I CAN'T BELIEVE IT'S ME. WHAT A STRANGE SENSATION. ONE, TWO, THREE... HELLO. WOW..."

intelligible

understandable

articulation

using the tongue, palate, teeth, jaw movement, and lips to shape vocalized sounds that combine to produce a word

pronunciation

the form and accent of various syllables of a word

accent

the articulation, inflection, tone, and speech habits typical of the native speakers of a language

CONSIDER *THIS*....

Think of someone you know personally or an actor you're familiar with who has a very distinguishable vocal quality. Do you think they are difficult to understand? Why or why not?

is to duplicate this level of liveliness when you deliver your speeches. The next two sections focus more closely on how you can use your voice and your body to achieve effective conversational and animated delivery.

Use of Voice

Recall from Chapter 5 that your *voice* is the sound you produce using your vocal organs. How your voice sounds depends on its pitch, volume, rate, and quality. As a public speaker, you can achieve a conversational and animated delivery style by varying your pitch, volume, rate, and quality in ways that make you more intelligible and expressive.

Intelligibility

To be **intelligible** means to be understandable. All of us have experienced situations in which we couldn't understand what was being said because the speaker was talking too softly or too quickly. If you practice your speech using appropriate pitch, volume, rate, and vocal quality, you can improve the likelihood that you will be intelligible to your audience.

Most of us speak at a pitch that is appropriate for us and intelligible to listeners. However, some people naturally have voices that are higher or lower in register or become accustomed to talking in tones that are either above or below their natural pitch. Speaking at an appropriate pitch is particularly important if your audience includes people who have hearing loss because they may find it difficult to hear a pitch that is too high or too low.

Appropriate volume is key to intelligibility. You must speak loudly enough, with or without a microphone, to be heard easily by the audience members in the back of the room but not so loudly as to cause discomfort to listeners seated in the front. You can also vary your volume to emphasize important information. For example, you may speak louder when you introduce each main point or when imploring listeners to take action.

The rate at which you speak can also influence intelligibility. Speaking too slowly gives your listeners time to let their minds wander after they've processed an idea. If you speak too quickly, especially when sharing complex ideas and arguments, listeners may not have enough time to process the information completely. Because nervousness may cause you to speak more quickly than normal, monitor your rate and adjust if you are speaking more quickly than normal.

In addition to vocal characteristics, articulation and accent can affect intelligibility. **Articulation** is using the tongue, palate, teeth, jaws, and lips to shape vocalized sounds that combine to produce a word. Many of us suffer from minor articulation and **pronunciation** problems such as adding an extra sound ("athalete" for *athlete*), leaving out a sound ("libary" for *library*), transposing sounds ("revalent" for *relevant*), and distorting sounds ("troof " for *truth*).

Accent is the inflection, tone, and speech habits typical of native speakers of a language. When you misarticulate or speak with a heavy accent during a conversation, your listeners can ask you to repeat yourself until they understand you. But in a speech setting, audience members are unlikely to interrupt to ask you to repeat what you have just said.

Accent can be a major concern for second language speakers or even speakers from various regions of the United States. Everyone speaks with some kind of accent, since "accent" means any tone or inflection that differs from the way others speak. Natives of a particular city or region in the U.S. will speak with inflections they believe are "normal" spoken English—for instance, people from the Northeast who drop the *r* sound (saying "cah" for *car*) or people from the South who elongate their vowels and "drawl," or people from the upper Midwest who elongate certain vowels (e.g., "Min-ne-SOOO-ta"). But when they visit a different city or region, they are perceived as having an accent. If your accent is "thick" or very different from that of most of your audience, practice pronouncing key words so that you are easily understood, speak slowly to allow your audience members more time to process your message, and consider using visual aids to reinforce key terms, concepts, and important points.

Vocal Expression

Vocal expression is achieved by changing your pitch, volume, and rate, stressing certain words, and using pauses. Doing so clarifies the emotional intent of your message and helps animate your delivery. Generally, speeding up your rate, raising your pitch, or increasing your volume reinforces emotions such as joy, enthusiasm, excitement, anticipation, and a sense of urgency or fear. Slowing down your rate, lowering your pitch, or decreasing your volume can communicate resolution, peacefulness, remorse, disgust, or sadness.

A total lack of vocal expression produces a **monotone**—a voice in which the pitch, volume, and rate remain constant, with no word, idea, or sentence differing significantly in sound from any other. Although few people speak in a true monotone, many severely limit themselves by using only two or three pitch levels and relatively unchanging volume and rate when giving public speeches. An actual or near monotone not only lulls an audience to sleep but, more importantly, diminishes the chances of audience understanding. For instance, if the sentence "Congress should pass laws limiting the sale of pornography" is presented in a monotone, listeners will be uncertain whether the speaker is concerned with *who* should be taking action, what Congress should *do*, or *what* the laws should be.

Pauses, moments of silence strategically used to enhance meaning, can also mark important ideas. If you use one or more sentences in your speech to express an important idea, pause before each sentence to signal that something important is coming or pause afterward to allow the idea to sink in. Pausing one or more times within a sentence can also add impact. Nick included several short pauses within and a long pause after his sentence "Our government has no compassion (*pause*), no empathy (*pause*), and no regard for human feeling" (*longer pause*).

vocal expression
the contrasts in pitch, volume, rate, and quality that affect the meaning an audience gets from the sentences you speak

monotone
a voice in which the pitch, volume, and rate remain constant, with no word, idea, or sentence differing significantly from any other

pauses
moments of silence strategically used to enhance meaning

Use of Body

Because your audience can see as well as hear you, how you use your body also contributes to how conversational and animated your audience perceives you to be. Body language elements that affect speech delivery include appearance, posture, poise, eye contact, facial expressions, gestures, and movement.

Appearance

Some speakers think that what they wear doesn't or shouldn't affect the success of their speech. But studies show that a neatly groomed and professional appearance sends important messages about a public speaker's commitment to the topic and occasion, as well as about the speaker's credibility (ethos) (Bates, 1992; Hammer, 2000; Sellnow & Treinen, 2004). Your appearance should complement your message, not detract from it. Three guidelines can help you decide how to dress for your speech.

1. **Consider the audience and occasion.** Dress a bit more formally than you expect members of your audience to dress. If you dress too formally, your audience is likely to perceive you to be untrustworthy and insincere and if you dress too casually, your audience may view you as uncommitted to your topic or disrespectful of them or the occasion (Morris, Gorham, Cohen, & Huffman, 1996).

2. **Consider your topic and purpose.** In general, the more serious your topic, the more formally you should dress. For example, if your topic is AIDS and you are trying to convince your audience to be tested for HIV, you will want to look like someone who is an authority by dressing the part. But if your topic is yoga and you are trying to convince your audience to take a yoga class at the new campus recreation center, you might dress more casually, or even in sportswear.

3. **Avoid extremes.** Your attire shouldn't detract from your speech. Avoid gaudy jewelry, over- or undersized clothing, and sexually suggestive attire. Remember you want your audience to focus on your message, so your appearance should be neutral, not distracting.

Posture

Recall from Chapter 5 that *posture* is how you hold your body. When giving a public speech, an upright stance and squared shoulders communicate a sense of confidence. Speakers who slouch may be perceived as lacking self-confidence and not caring about the topic, audience, and occasion. As you practice, be aware of your posture and adjust it so that you do not slouch; keep your weight equally distributed on both feet.

Poise

poise

graceful and controlled use of the body

Poise is a graceful and controlled use of the body that gives the impression that you are self-assured, calm, and dignified. Mannerisms that convey nervousness, such as swaying from side to side, drumming fingers on the lectern, taking off or putting on glasses, jiggling pocket change, smacking the tongue, licking the lips, or scratching the nose, hand, or arm should be noted during practice sessions and avoided during the speech.

Eye Contact

When giving a public speech, effective *eye contact* involves looking at people in all parts of an audience throughout the speech. As long as you are looking at someone (those in front of you, in the left rear of the room, in the right center of the room, and so on) and not at your notes or the ceiling, floor, or

THE AUDIENCE *BEYOND*

Because she knows how important appearance is to potential employers, Allison posted on her *LinkedIn* page three photographs taken by a professional photographer. One was a head and shoulders shot wearing a navy suit. Another was of her leading a meeting. The other was of her giving a formal presentation wearing a black pinstriped suit.

window, everyone in the audience will perceive you as having good eye contact with them. Generally, you should look at your audience at least 90 percent of the time, glancing at your notes only when you need a quick reference point. Maintaining eye contact is important for several reasons.

1. **Maintaining eye contact helps audiences concentrate on the speech.** If you do not look at audience members while you talk, audience members are unlikely to maintain eye contact with you. This break in mutual eye contact often decreases concentration on the message.

2. **Maintaining eye contact bolsters ethos.** Just as you are likely to be skeptical of people who do not look you in the eye as they converse, so too audiences will be skeptical of speakers who do not look at them. In the United States, eye contact is perceived as a sign of sincerity. Speakers who fail to maintain eye contact with audiences are perceived almost always as ill at ease and often as insincere or dishonest (Burgoon, Coker, & Coker, 1986; Levine, Asada, & Park, 2006).

3. **Maintaining eye contact helps you gauge the audience's reaction to your ideas.** Because communication is two-way, audience members communicate with you while you are speaking to them. In conversation, the audience's response is likely to be both verbal and nonverbal. In public speaking, the audience's response is likely to only be through nonverbal cues. Bored audience members might yawn, look out the window, slouch in their chairs, and even sleep. Confused audience members might look puzzled by furrowing their brows or shaking their head. Audience members who understand or agree with something you say might nod their heads. By monitoring your audience's behavior, you can adjust by becoming more animated, offering additional examples, or moving more quickly through a point.

When speaking to large audiences of 100 or more people, you must create a *sense* of looking listeners in the eye even though you actually cannot. This process is called **audience contact**. You can create audience contact by mentally dividing your audience into small groups. Then, tracing the letter Z with your gaze, talk for four to six seconds with each group as you move through your speech.

audience contact

when speaking to large audiences, create a sense of looking listeners in the eye even though you actually cannot

nonverbal immediacy

communicating through body language that you are personable and likeable

Facial Expressions

Recall from Chapter 5 that *facial expression* is the arrangement of facial muscles to express emotions. For public speakers, effective facial expressions can convey **nonverbal immediacy** by communicating that you are personable and likable. They can also help animate your speech. Speakers who do not vary their facial expressions during their speech but instead wear a deadpan expression, perpetual grin, or permanent scowl tend to be perceived as boring, insincere, or stern. To assess whether you are using effective facial expressions during your speech, practice delivering it to yourself in a mirror or record your rehearsal and evaluate your facial expressions as you watch it.

Effective speakers use facial expressions that complement the emotional intent of their verbal message

Gestures

As we discussed in Chapter 5, *gestures* are the movements of your hands, arms, and fingers. You can use gestures when delivering speeches to describe or emphasize what you are saying, refer to presentational aids, or clarify structure. For example, as Aaron began to speak about the advantages of smart phone apps, he said, "on one hand" and lifted his right hand face up. When he got to the disadvantages, he lifted his left hand face up as he said, "on the other hand." Recall from Chapter 5, however, that certain gestures mean different things in different cultures. Gestures may also create confusion between cultures as Bill French illustrates this in the *Diverse Voices* feature in this chapter. Figure 15.3 illustrates some examples of

- The supine hand with palm upward to express good humor, frankness, and generalization.

- The prone hand with palm downward to show superposition or the resting of one thing upon another.

- The vertical hand with palm outward to indicate warding off, putting from, or a disagreeable thought.

- The clenched hand to reinforce anger or defiance or to emphasize an important point.

- The index finger to specialize or reinforce the first in a sequence of events.

Figure 15.3

Common hand gestures used by speakers

gestures you might use to enhance intelligibility and expressiveness in your speeches.

Some people who are nervous when giving a speech clasp their hands behind their backs, bury them in their pockets, or grip the lectern. Unable to pry their hands free gracefully, they wiggle their elbows or appear stiff, which can distract listeners from the message.

As with facial expressions, effective gestures must appear spontaneous and natural even though they are carefully planned and practiced. When you practice and then deliver your speech, leave your hands free so that they will be available to gesture as you normally do.

> **CONSIDER THIS....**
>
> Do you ever engage in distracting behaviors when you are nervous? What are they? How can you work to eliminate them when giving a public speech?

DIVERSE VOICES

"Language Barriers" Are Not Necessarily Verbal

By Bill French

Co-Founder, MyST Technology

I was asked to present a 90-minute database programmer productivity session in many cities in Asia; starting in Singapore and ending in Taipei. All along the route, the conference promoters indicated there were no language translation issues or requirements; English and the programming languages of the products I was speaking about, dBase and Clipper would be enough.

Throughout Asia the presentations went exceedingly well; the turnout was phenomenal and the venues and presentation technology was extremely advanced with multiple large projection screens and high-quality audio-visual systems. In addition, the quality and depth of questions demonstrated deep understanding of the technologies and mastery of the English language.

When we arrived in Taipei, as was customary, I presented first. Also as customary, I started my session with a few questions to get to know the general knowledge and programmer demographics of the audience. It went something like this:

"How many of you use Ashton-Tate's dBASE?" (On asking the question, I raised my own hand.) The Taipei audience was almost unanimous in raising their own hands. I continued.

"How many here use Nantucket's Clipper compiler for dBASE development?" (Again, I raised my hand first.) And once again, nearly 100% of the attendees raised their hands.

"How many of you use dBRIEF, the most productive editing system for dBASE programming?" Amazingly, nearly everyone in the audience raised his hand! Either I was staring at 700 copyright infringers who unabashedly proclaim their theft in public, or I was simply engaged in a monkey-see, monkey-do early morning exercise program for my right arm and 700 or so other arms. In a blink, I knew exactly what to ask next:

"How many of you want to be a fire engine?" Fearfully, I watched as everyone's hands went up. I might as well have been speaking to an alien society from Alpha Centauri—nearly 100 percent of the audience spoke Chinese, and only Chinese. It was very easy to see who in the auditorium spoke English, since they were the ones practically rolling on the floor laughing.

French, B. (n.d.). Language barriers. Public Speaking International. *Retrieved on May 3, 2012 from http://www.publicspeakinginternational.com/funny-stories/*

Using appropriate facial expressions, gestures, and motivated movement enhances your intelligibility and effectiveness.

motivated movement

movement with a specific purpose

impromptu speech

a speech that is delivered with only seconds or minutes of advance notice for preparation

Movement

Recall that *movement* refers to changing your body position. During your speech, it is important to engage only in **motivated movement**, movement with a specific purpose such as emphasizing an important idea, referencing a presentational aid, or clarifying structure. To emphasize a particular point, you might move closer to the audience. To create a feeling of intimacy before telling a personal story, you might walk out from behind a lectern and sit down on a chair placed at the edge of the stage. Each time you begin a new main point, you might take a few steps to one side of the stage or the other. To use motivated movement effectively, you need to practice when and how you will move so you can do so in a way that appears spontaneous and natural while remaining "open" to the audience (not turning your back to them).

Avoid such unmotivated movement as bobbing, weaving, shifting from foot to foot, or pacing from one side of the room to the other because unplanned movements distract the audience from your message. Because many unplanned movements result from nervousness, you can minimize them by paying mindful attention to your body as you speak. At the beginning of your speech, stand up straight on both feet. If you find yourself fidgeting, readjust and position your body with your weight equally distributed on both feet.

Delivery Methods

Speeches vary in the amount of content preparation and practice you do ahead of time. The three most common delivery methods are impromptu, scripted, and extemporaneous.

Impromptu Speeches

An **impromptu speech** is one that is delivered with only seconds or minutes of advance notice for preparation and is usually presented without referring to notes of any kind. Because impromptu speakers must quickly gather their thoughts just before and while they speak, carefully organizing and developing ideas can be challenging. As a result, they may leave out important information or confuse audience members. Delivery can suffer as speakers often use "ahs," "ums," "like," and "you know" to buy time as they scramble to collect their thoughts. That's why the more opportunities you have to organize and deliver your thoughts using an impromptu method, the better you'll become at doing so.

Some of the most common situations you may find yourself in that will require you to speak using the impromptu method are during employment and performance review interviews, during business meetings, in class, at social ceremonies, and to the media. In each situation, having practiced organizing ideas quickly and conveying them intelligibly and expressively will bolster your ethos and help you succeed in business and in life.

You can improve your impromptu performances by practicing mock impromptu speeches. For example, if you are taking a class in which the professor calls on students at random to answer questions, you can prepare by anticipating the questions that might be asked on the readings for the day and practice giving your answers aloud. Over time, you will become more adept at organizing your ideas and thinking on your feet.

Scripted Speeches

At the other extreme, a **scripted speech** is one that is prepared by creating a complete written manuscript and then delivered by reading from or memorizing a written copy. Obviously, effective scripted speeches take a great deal of time to prepare because both an outline and a word-for-word transcript must be prepared, practiced, and delivered in a way that sounds both conversational and animated. When you memorize a scripted speech, you face the increased anxiety of forgetting your lines. When you read a scripted speech, you must become adept at looking at the script with your peripheral vision so that you don't appear to be reading and sound conversational and animated.

scripted speech

a speech that is prepared by creating a complete written manuscript and delivered by rote memory or by reading a written copy

Because of the time and skill required to effectively prepare and deliver a scripted speech, they are usually reserved for important occasions that have important consequences. Political speeches, keynote addresses at conventions, commencement addresses, and CEO remarks at annual stockholder meetings are examples of occasions when a scripted speech might be appropriate and worth the extra effort.

Extemporaneous Speeches

Most speeches, whether in the workplace, in the community, or in class, are delivered extemporaneously. An **extemporaneous speech** is researched and planned ahead of time, but the exact wording is not scripted and will vary somewhat from presentation to presentation. When speaking extemporaneously, you may refer to speaking notes reminding you of key ideas, structure, and delivery cues as you speak. Some speakers today use their computerized slideshows as speaking notes. If you choose to do so, however, be careful not to include too many words on any given slide, which will ultimately distract listeners from focusing on you as you speak.

extemporaneous speech

a speech that is researched and planned ahead of time, although the exact wording is not scripted and will vary from presentation to presentation

Extemporaneous speeches are the easiest to give effectively. Unlike impromptu speeches, when speaking extemporaneously, you are able to prepare your thoughts ahead of time and have notes to prompt you. Unlike scripted speeches, extemporaneous speeches do not require as lengthy a preparation process to be effective.

Choosing the most effective delivery method and style can be particularly challenging for public figures who are attempting to influence public opinion and win elections. Read the *Pop Comm!* feature, "Politics, Politicians, and Public Speech Delivery," to think about what style you find most compelling and why.

Politics, Politicians, and Public Speech Delivery

Jose Gil/Shutterstock.com

In political speeches, as with most moments of public speaking, delivery style is as important and sometimes even more important than the message itself. In other words, it is not always *what* you say that resonates with audiences, but *how* you say it. Politicians are often criticized for exhibiting an overly rehearsed speaking style that rarely deviates from a pre-determined set of talking points. This leaves some audiences with the impression that the speaker is simply saying what he or she thinks we want to hear, rather than using the speech to convey his or her actual beliefs. For example, although President Barack Obama is often held up as an example of a successful public speaker, some criticize his use of a teleprompter. Republican politician Rick Santorum, a presidential candidate at the time, took a swipe at Obama, suggesting it "should be illegal" for candidates to read from a teleprompter as they deliver speeches "because all you're doing is reading someone else's words to people" (Cillizza, 2012).

However, presidents and candidates, including some of Obama's detractors, have been using teleprompters to deliver speeches since the technology's invention over 50 years ago. Presidential historian Doris Kearns Goodwin argues that many presidents have relied on teleprompters, particularly for important speeches, to ensure the clarity of the message when the stakes are high. She says, "if a president says something that is not what he meant to say, it could be an international situation" (quoted in Rucker, 2011). Skilled use of use of a teleprompter—or speaking notes—may not only help focus one's message, it may also aid in delivery because it allows the speaker to connect with the audience through eye contact and delivery style (Rucker, 2011). Therefore, even though President Obama may be critiqued

for *using* a teleprompter, such critiques rarely assert that he is just "reading" his speech. In fact, the president is often celebrated for employing an oratory style that uses emotional range and intensity to bring his carefully crafted speeches to life. Drawing on an African-American oratory style that recognizes the "power of the word . . . as a source of inspiration," Obama uses crisp articulation, a nimble sense of timing, and a musical presentation of his voice to arouse the emotions of the audience and convince them of his ideas (Dilliplane, 2012; Frenkel, 2011).

Another politician whose contrasting delivery style has helped elevate him to the national political stage is New Jersey governor Chris Christie. Christie is often celebrated for using a blunt and straightforward speaking style that contrasts with the scripted style exhibited by Obama. When Hurricane Irene was barreling down on the eastern seaboard in August 2011, for example, Governor Christie used a news briefing to call for those who had not yet evacuated to "[G]et the hell off the beach in Asbury Park and get out — you're done. . . . Do not waste any more time working on your tan" (Barron, 2011). He is well known for routinely using words like "stupid," "crap," and "insane" in news briefings, town hall meetings, and even more formal political speeches (Ibid). Christie supporters champion his spirited style as evidence of his real commitment to his goals of political reform and his rejection of political pandering. For example, when many prominent Republicans, such as Sarah Palin and Newt Gingrich, decried the construction of an Islamic mosque and cultural center in New York City two blocks away from ground zero, Christie publicly warned that the party was overreacting. He said "We cannot paint all of Islam with that brush. . . . We have to bring people together. And what offends me the most about all this, is that it's being used as a political football by both parties" (Haberman, 2010). In an era when Americans are increasingly frustrated with Washington political bickering, Christie's straightforward style seems like a welcome alternative.

However, not everyone is a fan of Christie's frank and confrontational style. Some critics suggest that his combative delivery style makes him come off as a bully. For example, while speaking at a town hall meeting on education reform in New Jersey, Christie scolded a teacher who accused him of unfairly criticizing teachers and teachers unions. He said, "If what you want to do is put on a show and giggle every time I talk, well then I have no interest in answering your question" (Shear, 2012). At a different town hall meeting, Christie called a Navy veteran an "idiot" after the man questioned Christie's plan to merge two of New Jersey's public universities into a single school (Mandell, 2012). When the man interrupted Christie's explanation, the governor became agitated, saying, "Let me tell you something, after you graduate from law school, you conduct yourself like that in a courtroom, your rear end is going to be thrown in jail, idiot" (Ibid.). Though both men were combative in their style during this exchange, some suggest Christie's tendency to allow his emotions get the better of him during his public speeches does not fit with the need for rational and measured debate within the political realm. But his supporters say it is exactly this heartfelt and authentic expression of his ideas that makes Christie appealing as a politician.

Questions to Ponder

1. Does a scripted and teleprompted or an extemporaneous style better serve our politicians and our democracy?

2. Which style do you prefer and why?

Rehearsals

Rehearsing is the iterative process of practicing your speech aloud. A speech that is not practiced out loud is likely to be far less effective than it would have been had you given yourself sufficient time to revise, evaluate, and mull over all aspects of the speech (Menzel & Carrell, 1994). Figure 15.4 provides a useful timetable for preparing a classroom speech.

rehearsing
practicing the presentation of your speech aloud

In this section, we describe how to rehearse effectively by preparing speaking notes, handling presentational aids, and recording, analyzing, and refining delivery.

Preparing Speaking Notes

Prior to your first rehearsal session, prepare a draft of your speaking notes. **Speaking notes** are a key word outline of your speech including hard-to-remember

speaking notes
word or phrase outlines of your speech

8 days before	Select topic; begin research
7 days before	Continue research
6 days before	Outline body of speech
5 days before	Work on introduction and conclusion
4 days before	Finish outline; find additional material if needed; have all presentational aids completed
3 days before	First rehearsal session
2 days before	Second rehearsal session
1 day before	Third rehearsal session
Due date	Deliver speech

Figure 15.4

Timetable for preparing a speech

© Cengage Learning

information or quotations and delivery cues. The best notes contain the fewest words possible written in lettering large enough to be seen instantly at a distance.

To develop your notes, begin by reducing your speech outline to an abbreviated outline of key phrases and words. Then, if there are details you must cite exactly accurately—such as a specific example, a quotation, or a set of statistics—add these in the appropriate spots. You might also put these on a separate card as a "Quotation Card" to refer to when delivering direct quotations during the speech, which is what Alyssa did (see Figure 15.5). Next, indicate exactly where you plan to share presentational aids. Finally, incorporate delivery cues indicating where you want to make use of your voice and body to enhance intelligibility or expressiveness. For example, indicate where you want to pause, gesture, or make a motivated movement. Capitalize or underline

---

NOTE CARD 1: Introduction

PLANT FEET. . . . DIRECT EYE CONTACT. . . . POISE/ETHOS! ☺

I. Famous Indian peace activist Mahatma Gandhi: "We must become the change we seek in the world."
    Tall order. . . . We can make a difference right here in Lexington, KY

II. Think for a moment. . . . child/homework, neighbor/leaves, stranger/groceries. . . . It's easy for college students like us to get involved.

III. I volunteer at LRM and reaped benefits **(Slide 1)**

IV. Benefits volunteering. . . .

    a. get acquainted

    b. responsibility & privilege

    c. resumé-building skills

BLANK SLIDE, WALK RIGHT, EYE C.: Let's begin by explaining the ways volunteering can help us connect to our local community.

NOTE CARD 2: Body

I. GREAT WAY to become acquainted ☺ ☺

    LR: Comforts of home. . . . unfamiliar city. . . . volunteering. . . . easy and quick way. . . .

    Natalie Cunningham—May 2nd (Q. CARD #1)

    Social issues and conditions

    Acc. to a 1991 article published in **the *J. of Prevention and Intervention in the Community*** by Cohen, Mowbray, Gillette, and Thompson raise awareness. . . .

    My experience at LRM (SLIDES 2 & 3)

    BLANK SLIDE, WALK LEFT, EYE C.: Not only is volunteering important. . . . familiar and social issues. . . . FRANKLY. . . . dem society. . . .

II. Civic responsibility AND privilege. . . . LR: We benefit college. . . . give back.

    I agree with Wilson and Musick who said in their 1997 article in ***Social Forces active participation or deprived.*** (SLIDES 4 & 5)

    Also a privilege. . . . make a difference. . . . feel good. . . . self-actualization (SLIDE #6)

Figure 15.5

Alyssa's speaking notes

NOTE CARD 3: Body & Conclusion

BLANK SLIDE, WALK RIGHT, EYE C: privilege & responsibility. . . . resume-building. . . .

III. Life skills

Article "Employability Credentials: A Key to Successful Youth Transition to Work" by I. Charner—1988 issue of the *Journal of Career Development*. . . . (Q. CARD #2)

Laura Hatfield. . . . leadership, teamwork, and listening skills

Andrea Stockelman, volunteer (SLIDE #7) (Q. CARD #3)

MY RESUMÉ (SLIDE #8)

BLANK SLIDE, WALK TO CENTER, EYE C: Today, we've discussed. . . . get acquainted, responsibility & privilege, resumé-building life skills help after grad.

CL: So, I'm hoping the next time you recall. . . . not distant past. Instead, I hope you'll be thinking bout how you **ARE** being the change you seek in the world by **volunteering right here //in Lexington///right now!**

PAUSE, EYE CONTACT, POISE, NOD ☺

Quotation Card

#1: "My first group of students needed rides to all the various volunteer sites b/c they had no idea where things were in the city. It was really easy for the students who lived on campus to remain ignorant of their city, but while volunteering they become acquainted with Lexington and the important issues going on here."

#2: "Employers rely on credentials to certify that a young person will become a valuable employee. Credentials that document the experiences and employability skills, knowledge, and attitude."

#3: "I learned that there was a lot more that went into preparing food for the homeless than I ever thought possible. It was neat to be a part of that process."

Figure 15.5
(Continued)

words you want to stress. Use slash marks (//) to remind yourself to pause. Use an upward-pointing arrow to remind yourself to increase rate or volume.

For a 3- to 5-minute speech, you should need no more than three 3 × 5-inch note cards to record your speaking notes. For longer speeches, you might need one card for the introduction, one for each main point, and one for the conclusion. If your speech contains a particularly important and long quotation or a complicated set of statistics, you can record this information in detail on a separate card. Speakers who use computerized slideshows often use the "notes" feature on the program for their speaking notes.

Use your notes during practice sessions as you will when you actually give the speech. If you will use a lectern, set the notes on the speaker's stand or, alternatively, hold them in one hand and refer to them only when needed. How important is it to construct good speaking notes? Speakers often find that the act of making the notes is so effective in helping cement ideas in the mind that during practice, or later during the speech itself, they rarely refer to them at all.

Handling Presentational Aids

Many speakers think that once they have prepared good presentational aids, they will have no trouble using them in the speech. However, many speeches with good aids have become a shambles because the aids were not well handled. You can avoid problems by following these guidelines:

1. **Carefully plan when to use presentational aids.** Indicate in your speaking notes exactly when you will reveal and conceal each aid. Practice introducing and using your aids until you can use them comfortably and smoothly.

2. **Consider audience needs carefully.** As you practice, eliminate any presentational aid that does not contribute directly to the audience's attention to, understanding of, or retention of the key ideas in the speech.

3. **Position presentational aids and equipment before beginning your speech.** Make sure your aids and equipment are where you want them and that everything is ready and in working order. Test electronic equipment to make sure everything works and that excerpts are cued correctly.

4. **Reveal a presentational aid only when talking about it.** Because presentational aids will draw audience attention, practice sharing them only when you are talking about them, and then concealing them when they are no longer the focus of attention.
   Because a single presentational aid may contain several bits of information, practice revealing only the portion you are currently discussing. On computerized slideshows, you can do so by using the "custom animation" feature to allow only one item to appear at a time. You can also strike the "B" key for a black screen when you aren't directly referencing the aid and insert blank slides where ideas in your speech are not being supplemented with something on the slideshow.

5. **Display presentational aids so that everyone in the audience can see and hear them.** The inability to see or hear an aid is frustrating. If possible, practice in the space where you will give your speech so you can adjust equipment accordingly. If you cannot practice in the space ahead of time, then arrive early enough on the day of the presentation to practice quickly with the equipment you will use.

6. **Reference the presentational aid during the speech.** Because you already know what you want your audience to see in a visual aid, tell your audience what to look for, explain the various elements in it, and interpret figures, symbols, and percentages. For an audio or audiovisual aid, point out what you want your audience to listen for before you play the excerpt. When showing a visual or audiovisual aid, use the "turn-touch-talk" technique.

   • When you display the visual, walk to the screen—that's where everyone will look anyway. Slightly turn to the visual and touch it—that is, point to it with an arm gesture or a pointer if necessary. Then, with your back to the screen and your body still facing the audience at a slight forty-five-degree angle, talk to your audience about it.
   • When you finish making your comments, return to the lectern or your speaking position and conceal the aid.

7. **Talk to your audience, not to the presentational aid.** Although you will want to acknowledge the presentational aid by looking at it occasionally, it is important to maintain eye contact with your audience as much as possible. As you practice, resist the urge to stare at your presentational aid.

8. **Resist the temptation to pass objects through the audience.** People look at, read, handle, and think about whatever they hold in their hands. While they are so occupied, they are not likely to be listening to you. If you have handouts or objects to distribute, do so after the speech rather than during it.

Effective speakers use gestures to reference their visual aids while discussing them.

Rehearsing and Refining Delivery

As with any other activity, effective speech delivery requires practice, and the more you practice, the better your speech will be. During practice sessions, you have three major goals. First, practice wording your ideas so that they are appropriate, accurate, clear, and vivid. Second, practice your speech aloud until your voice and body convey your ideas conversationally, intelligibly, and expressively. Third, practice using presentational aids. As part of each practice, analyze how well it went and set goals for the next practice session.

Let's look at how you can proceed through several practice rounds.

First Practice Your initial rehearsal should include the following steps:

1. Record (audio and video) your practice session. You may also want to have a friend sit in on it.

2. Read through your complete sentence outline once or twice to refresh your memory. Then put the outline out of sight and practice the speech using only your speaking notes.

3. Make the practice as similar to the speech situation as possible, including using the presentational aids you've prepared. Stand up and face your imaginary audience. Pretend that the chairs, lamps, books, and other objects in your practice room are people.

4. Write down the time that you begin.

5. Begin speaking. Regardless of what happens, keep going until you have presented your entire speech. If you goof, make a repair as you would have to do if you were actually delivering the speech to an audience.

6. Write down the time you finish. Compute the length of the speech for this first rehearsal.

Analysis Watch and listen to the recorded performance while reviewing your complete outline. How did it go? Did you leave out any key ideas? Did you talk too long on any one point and not long enough on another? Did you clarify each of your points? Did you adapt to your anticipated audience? (If you had a friend or relative watch and listen to your practice, have him or her help with your analysis.) Were your speaking notes effective? How well did you do with your presentational aids? Make any necessary changes before your second rehearsal.

Second Practice Repeat the six steps outlined for the first rehearsal. By practicing a second time right after your analysis, you are more likely to make the kind of adjustments that begin to improve the speech.

Additional Practices After you have completed one full rehearsal session—consisting of two practices and the analysis in between them—put the speech away until that night or the next day. Although you should rehearse the speech at least a couple more times, you will not benefit if you cram all the practices into one long rehearsal time. You may find that a final practice right before you go to bed will be very helpful; while you are sleeping, your subconscious will continue to work on the speech. As a result, you are likely to find significant improvement in your mastery of the speech when you practice again the next day.

Adapting While Delivering the Speech

Even when you've practiced your speech to the point that you know it inside and out, you must be prepared to adapt to your audience and possibly change course a bit as you give your speech. Remember that your primary goal as a public speaker is to generate shared understanding with your listeners, so pay attention to the audience's feedback as you speak and adjust accordingly. Here are six tips for adapting to your audience.

1. **Be aware of and respond to audience feedback.** As you make eye contact with members of your audience, notice how they react to what you say. For instance, if you see quizzical looks on the faces of several listeners, you may need to explain a particular point in a different way, perhaps by providing an additional example to clarify the point. On the other hand, if you see listeners nodding impatiently, recognize that you don't need to belabor your point and move on. If you notice that many audience members look bored, adjust your voice and try to rekindle their interest by showing your enthusiasm for what you are saying.

2. **Be prepared to use alternative developmental material.** Your ability to adjust to your audience's needs depends on how much additional alternative information you have to share. If you have prepared only one example, you wouldn't be ready if your audience is confused and needs another. If you have prepared only one definition for a term, you may be unable to rephrase an additional definition if needed. As you prepare, try to anticipate where your audience may be confused or already knowledgeable and practice adding or dropping examples and other details.

3. **Correct yourself when you misspeak.** Every speaker makes mistakes. They stumble over words, mispronounce terms, forget information, and mishandle presentational aids. It's normal. What's important is what you do when you make that mistake. If you stumble over a phrase or mispronounce a word, correct yourself and move on. Don't make a big deal of it by laughing, rolling your eyes, or in other ways drawing unnecessary attention to it. If you suddenly remember that you forgot to provide some

information, consider how important it is for your audience to have that information. If what you forgot to say will make it difficult for your audience to understand a point that comes later, figure out how and when to provide the information later in your speech. Usually, however, information we forgot to share is not critical to the audience's understanding and its better to leave it out and move on.

Effective speakers handle questions respectfully even when they don't know the answer.

4. **Adapt to unexpected events.** Maintain your composure if something unexpected happens, such as a cell phone ringing or someone entering the room while you're speaking. Simply pause until the disruption ceases and then move on. If the disruption causes you to lose your train of thought or has distracted the audience, take a deep breath, look at your speaking notes, and continue your speech at a point slightly before the interruption occurred. This will allow both you and your audience to refocus on your speech. You might acknowledge that you are backtracking by saying something like, "Let's back up a bit and remember where we were. . . ."

5. **Adapt to unexpected audience reactions.** Sometimes, you'll encounter listeners who disagree strongly with your message. They might show their disagreement by being inattentive, heckling you belligerently, or rolling their eyes when you try to make eye contact with them. If these behaviors are limited to one or only a few members of your audience, ignore them and focus on the rest of your listeners. If, however, you find that your audience analysis was inaccurate and that the majority of your audience is hostile to what you are saying, try to anticipate and address their concerns. You might begin by acknowledging their feedback and then try to convince your audience to suspend their judgment while they listen. For example, you could say something like, "I can see that most of you don't agree with my first point. But let me ask you to put aside your initial reaction and think along with me on this next point. Even if we end up disagreeing, at least you will understand my position."

6. **Handle questions respectfully.** It is rare for audience members to interrupt speakers with questions during a speech. But if you are interrupted, be prepared to deal respectfully with the question. If the question is directly related to understanding the point you are making, answer it immediately. If it is not, acknowledge the question, indicate that you will answer it later, and then do so.

In most professional settings, you will be expected to answer questions when you've finished your speech. Some people will ask you to clarify information. Some will ask you for an opinion or to draw conclusions beyond what you have said. Whenever you answer a question, be honest about what you know and don't know. If an audience member asks a question you don't know the answer to, admit it by saying something like, "That's an excellent question. I'm not sure of the answer, but I would be happy to follow up on it later if you're interested." Then move on to the next question. If someone asks you to state an opinion about a matter you haven't thought much about, it's okay to say, "You know, I don't think I have given that enough thought to have a valid opinion."

Be sure to monitor how much time you have to answer questions. When the time is nearly up, mention that you'll entertain one more question to warn listeners that the question-and-answer period is almost over. You might also suggest that you'll be happy to talk more with individuals one on one later—this provides your more reserved listeners an opportunity to follow up with you.

Evaluating Speeches

In addition to learning to prepare and present speeches, you are learning to evaluate (critically analyze) the speeches you hear. From an educational standpoint, critical analysis of speeches provides the speaker with an analysis of where the speech went right and where it went wrong, and it also gives you, the critic, insight into the methods that you can incorporate or avoid in your own speeches. In this section, we look at some general criteria for evaluating public speeches.

The critical assumption is that if a speech has good content that is adapted to the audience, is clearly organized, and is delivered well, it is likely to achieve its goal. Thus, you can evaluate any speech by answering questions that relate to the basics of content, structure, and delivery. Figure 15.6 is a speech critique checklist. You can use this checklist to analyze your first speech during your rehearsal period and to critique sample student speeches at the end of this chapter as well as speeches delivered by your classmates.

Thinking Critically About Speeches
Check all items that were accomplished effectively.

Content
_____ 1. Was the goal of the speech clear?
_____ 2. Did the speaker offer breadth and depth to support each main point?
_____ 3. Did the speaker use high-quality information and sources?
_____ 4. Did the speaker provide appropriate listener relevance links?
_____ 5. Were presentational aids appropriate?

Structure
_____ 6. Did the introduction gain attention, establish relevance and listener relevance, and lead into the speech using a thesis with main point preview?
_____ 7. Were the main points clear, parallel, and in meaningful complete sentences?
_____ 8. Did section transitions lead smoothly from one point to another?
_____ 9. Was the language appropriate, accurate, clear, and vivid?
_____ 10. Did the conclusion tie the speech together by summarizing the goal and main points and providing a clincher?

Figure 15.6

Speech critique checklist

Delivery

_____ 11. Did the speaker appear and sound conversational?
_____ 12. Did the speaker appear and sound animated?
_____ 13. Was the speaker intelligible?
_____ 14. Was the speaker vocally expressive?
_____ 15. Was the speaker's appearance appropriate?
_____ 16. Did the speaker have good posture and poise?
_____ 17. Did the speaker look directly at and throughout the audience at least 90% of the time?
_____ 18. Did the speaker have good facial expressions?
_____ 19. Were the speaker's gestures and movement appropriate?
_____ 20. Did the speaker handle the presentational aids effectively?

Based on these criteria, evaluate the speech as (check one):
_____ excellent _____ good _____ satisfactory _____ fair _____ poor

Figure 15.6
(Continued)

ACTION STEP 5

Rehearsing Your Speech

The goal of this activity is to rehearse your speech, analyze it, and rehearse it again. One complete rehearsal includes a practice, an analysis, and a second practice.

1. Find a place where you can be alone to practice your speech. Follow the six points for the first practice explained earlier.

2. Review your outline as you watch and listen to the recording and then answer the following questions.

Are you satisfied with how well

The introduction got attention and led into the speech? ___

Main points were clearly stated? ___ And well developed? ___

Material adapted to the audience? ___

Section transitions were used? ___

The conclusion summarized the main points? ___
Left the speech on a high note?___

Presentational aids were used? ___

Ideas were expressed vividly? ___ And clearly? ___

Sounded conversational throughout? _____

Sounded animated? ___ Sounded intelligible? ___

Used natural gestures and movement ? ___ Used effective eye contact? _____Facial expression? ___ Posture? ___ Appearance? ___

List the three most important changes you will make in your next practice session:

One: _____

Two: _____

Three: _____

3. Go through the six steps outlined for the first practice again.

Then assess: Did you achieve the goals you set for the second practice?

_____

Reevaluate the speech using the checklist and continue to practice until you are satisfied with all parts of your presentation.

COMMUNICATE ON YOUR FEET

Speech Assignment

Presenting Your First Speech

The Assignment

1. Follow the Action Steps to prepare an informative or persuasive speech. Your instructor will provide you with the time limit and other parameters for this assignment.

2. Criteria for evaluation include all the essentials of topic and purpose, content, organization, and presentation, but special emphasis will be placed on clarity of goal, clarity and appropriateness of main points, and delivery (items that are grouped under the boldface headings in the Speech Critique Checklist in Figure 15.6). As you practice your speech, you can use the checklist to ensure that you are meeting the basic criteria in your speech. In addition, you may want to refer to the sample student outline and speech that follow this assignment box.

3. Prior to presenting your speech, prepare a complete sentence outline and a written plan for adapting your speech to the audience. If you have used Speech Builder Express to complete the action step activities online, you will be able to print out a copy of your completed outline. Your adaptation plan should describe how you plan to verbally and visually adapt your material to the audience.

If you completed the Action Step activities in Chapter 13, you can use them for the basis of your written adaptation plan.

SAMPLE SPEECH PLAN AND OUTLINE

Informative Speech with Presentational Aids

This section presents a sample informative speech given by a student, including an adaptation plan, an outline, and a transcript.

College Student Volunteering and Civic Engagement[1]

By Alyssa Grace Millner

Read the speech adaptation plan, outline, and transcript of a speech given by Alyssa Grace Millner. You can access a video clip of Alyssa's speech through the Chapter 15 resources of your CourseMate for *Communicate!* You can also use your CourseMate to identify some of the strengths of Alyssa's speech by preparing an evaluation checklist and an analysis. You can then compare your answer with those of the authors.

Adaptation Plan

1. Key aspects of audience. The majority of listeners know what volunteering is in a general sense, but they probably don't know the ways it can benefit them as college students.

2. Establishing and maintaining common ground. I'll use personal pronouns throughout the speech, as well as specific examples about volunteering from volunteers right here in Lexington.

3. Building and maintaining interest. I'll insert listener relevance links in the introduction and for each main point that point out how volunteering is directly related to improving the lives of college students in some way.

4. Building credibility. I will point out right away that I volunteer and that I've done a good deal of research on it. I'll insert examples of my own experiences throughout the speech, as well as cite credible research to support my claims.

5. Audience attitudes. Some may be indifferent, but according to the research I've found, most will probably be open to the idea of volunteering. They might not know how easy it can be to get started though.

6. Adapting to audiences from different cultures and language communities. Although most of my classmates are U.S. citizens, there are a couple of international students in the class. So, when I talk about volunteering being a civic responsibility, I'll make sure to talk about how all of us are reaping the benefits of a U.S. education; that's why we are all responsible for giving back in some way. I'll talk about it as an ethical responsibility.

7. Use presentational aids. I will show photographs of people engaged in volunteer work throughout the speech. I think this will make my ideas very concrete for the audience and will enhance pathos (emotional appeal). I'll also show some graphs about homelessness in Lexington and the percentage of college students who believe in volunteering. I think these will bolster my ethos as the audience will see I've done research. Finally, I'll show my résumé with elements highlighted that I've been able to include because I've volunteered. I think this will drive home my point about the future benefits for college students who volunteer while still in school.

Formal Speech Outline

General goal: I want to inform my audience.

Specific goal: I want my audience to realize the benefits of volunteering in Lexington while we are still students at the University of Kentucky.

Introduction

I. The famous Indian peace activist and spiritual leader Mahatma Gandhi is known for saying "We must become the change we seek in the world." That sounds at first like an awfully tall order, but today I'd like to show you how each of us can do just that and make a difference right here in Lexington, Kentucky. — *Attention getter*

II. Think for a moment of a time in your life when you did something kind for someone else. Maybe you helped a child do homework, or a neighbor rake leaves, or even a stranger get groceries from the store to the car. Do you remember how that made you feel? Well, that feeling can be a normal part of your week when you choose to be a volunteer. And for college students like us, it's easy to get involved as volunteers in our local community. — *Listener relevance link*

III. Personally, I volunteer at the Lexington Rescue Mission and have reaped many benefits by doing so. *(Show slide 1: picture of me volunteering at the Mission)* I've also done extensive research on volunteering and civic engagement. — *Speaker credibility*

Thesis statement with main point preview

IV. So, let's spend the next few minutes discussing the benefits volunteering can have for us as college students by focusing on how volunteering helps us get acquainted with the local community, why civic engagement is the responsibility of every one of us, and what volunteering can do to teach us new skills and build our résumés.

Transition

Let's begin by explaining the ways volunteering can connect each of us to our local community.

Body

I. Volunteering is a great way to become acquainted with a community beyond the university campus.

Listener relevance link

Most college students move away from the comforts of home to a new and unfamiliar city. Not knowing what there is to do or even how to get around can be overwhelming and isolating. Volunteering is an easy way to quickly become familiar with and begin to feel a part of this new city in addition to the campus community.

A. Volunteering allows you to learn your way around town.

   1. In an interview I had with Natalie Cunningham, the volunteer coordinator of the Lexington Rescue Mission, she said, "My first group of students needed rides to all the various volunteer sites because they had no idea where things were in the city. It was really easy for the students who lived on campus to remain ignorant of their city, but while volunteering they become acquainted with Lexington and the important issues going on here" (personal communication, May 2, 2010).

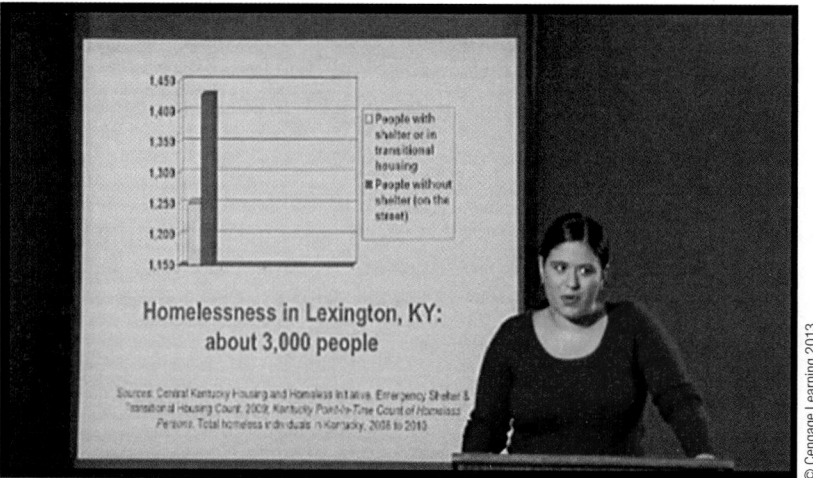

   2. It seems like a silly thing, but knowing your way around town starts to make any city feel like home. Volunteering gets you out into the local area and helps you begin to get acquainted with new people and places.

B. Volunteering can also open your eyes to local social issues and conditions.

1. Many nonprofit organizations strive to raise awareness of important social issues, things like hunger and homelessness (Cohen, Mowbray, Gillette, & Thompson, 1991).

2. The second time I showed up to volunteer at the Lexington Rescue Mission, I served food to the homeless. *(Show slide 2: group of volunteers in the kitchen)*

   a. I served soup and hung out with other volunteers and local homeless people. One of the "veteran" volunteers explained to me that Lexington has approximately 3,000 homeless people. *(Show slide 3: homelessness statistics in Lexington)*

   b. I was shocked to learn that we had such a large number of men, women, and children without a regular place to sleep. I wouldn't have known about this problem or the organizations working to end homelessness if I hadn't been a volunteer.

Not only is volunteering important because it helps us become familiar with a town and its social issues; frankly, as members of a democratic society, volunteering is our civic responsibility. Transition

II. Giving back to the community through volunteer work is our civic responsibility and a privilege. Listener relevance link

Each of us in this room—whether as U.S. citizens or international students—are reaping the benefits of earning college degrees in this democratic society. With that benefit comes the responsibility and privilege of giving back.

A. Volunteering is our civic responsibility.

1. Wilson and Musick (1997) explain that, without active participation in the local community, civil society becomes deprived.

2. I agree. Giving back by volunteering helps the community in so many ways. *(Show slides 4 and 5: volunteers sorting clothes at the mission and then volunteers playing cards with people served at the shelter)*

B. Volunteering is also a privilege. Making a difference by volunteering ends up making us feel better about ourselves and our role in the world we live in.

1. In fact, college students aged 16 to 24 represent the largest growth in percentages of volunteers across the country (Corporation for National and Community Service, 2006). *(Show slide 6: bar graph of growth)*

2. A study of first-year college students done by the Higher Education Research Institute published in January 2009 revealed that 69.7 percent of students believe it is *essential or very important* to volunteer in order to help people in need (Pryor et al., 2009).

Certainly, the privilege of giving back as volunteers is our civic responsibility and helps our local community, but we can also reap valuable résumé-building life skills by volunteering. Transition

III. Volunteering helps teach us new skills.

These new skills and talents can actually make us more marketable for better jobs once we graduate. Listener relevance link

A. Being a consistent volunteer at a nonprofit organization while attending college can strengthen your résumé.

  1. "Employers rely on credentials to certify that a young person will become a valuable employee. Credentials that document the experiences and employability skills, knowledge, and attitude" (Charner, 1988, p. 30).

  2. Laura Hatfield, director of the Center for Community Outreach at the University of Kentucky, points out that volunteers can include leadership, teamwork, and listening skills on their résumés because they can document the experiences where they had to use them effectively in the real world.

  3. Andrea Stockelman, another volunteer at the Lexington Rescue Mission, explained some of the new skills she picked up with volunteering. She said, "I learned that there was a lot more that went into preparing food for the homeless than I ever thought possible. It was neat to be a part of that process" (personal communication, April 28, 2010). *(Show slide 7: photo of Andrea preparing food)*

B. Volunteering at the Lexington Rescue Mission taught me new skills that bolstered my résumé. *(Show slide 8: résumé with skills highlighted)*

  1. I learned to coordinate the schedules of other volunteers.

  2. I also practiced important people skills such as teamwork, empathy, conflict management, and listening.

Conclusion

Thesis restatement with main point summary

I. Today we've discussed why volunteering is beneficial to college students by focusing on how volunteering can connect us quickly and easily to our local community, why it's both our responsibility and a privilege to do so, and how volunteering will benefit us after we graduate.

Clincher

II. So, I'm hoping the next time you recall a time you really enjoyed making a difference by helping someone, that memory won't come from the distant past. Instead, I hope you'll be thinking about how you are being the change you seek in the world by volunteering right here in Lexington right now.

[1]*From Verder/Verderber/Sellnow, The Challenge of Effective Speaking, 15E. © 2012 Cengage Learning.*

References

Charner, I. (1988). Employability credentials: A key to successful youth transition to work. Journal of Career Development, 15(1), 30–40.

Cohen, E., Mowbray, C. T., Gillette, V., & Thompson, E. (1991). Religious organizations and housing development. Journal of Prevention and Intervention in the Community, 10(1), 169–185.

Corporation for National and Community Service. (2006). College students helping America. *Washington, DC: Author.*

Pryor, J. H., Hurtado, S., DeAngelo, L., Sharkness, J., Romero, L., Korn, W. S., & Tran, S. (2009). The American freshman: National norms for fall 2008. *Los Angeles, CA: Higher Education Research Institute.*

Wilson, J., & Musick, M. A. (1997). Work and volunteering: The long arm of the job. Social Forces, 76(1), 251–272.

SPEECH AND ANALYSIS

Speech

Analysis

The famous Indian peace activist and spiritual leader Mahatma Gandhi is known for saying "We must become the change we seek in the world." That sounds at first like an awfully tall order, but today I'd like to show you how each of us can do just that and make a difference right here in Lexington, Kentucky. Think for a moment of a time in your life when you did something kind for someone else. Maybe you helped a child do homework, or a neighbor rake leaves, or even a stranger get groceries from the store to the car. Do you remember how that made you feel? Well, that feeling can be a normal part of your week when you choose to be a volunteer. And for college students like us, it's easy to get involved as volunteers in our local community. Personally, I volunteer at the Lexington Rescue Mission and have reaped many benefits by doing so. (*Show slide 1: picture of me volunteering at the Mission*) I've also done extensive research on volunteering and civic engagement. So, let's spend the next few minutes discussing the benefits volunteering can have for us as college students by focusing on how volunteering helps us get acquainted with the local community, why civic engagement is the responsibility of every citizen, and what volunteering can do to teach us new skills and build our résumés. Let's begin by explaining the ways volunteering can connect each of us to our local community.

Volunteering is a great way to become acquainted with a community beyond the university campus. Most college students move away from the comforts of home to a new and unfamiliar city. Not knowing what there is to do or

Notice how Alyssa uses a famous quotation to get the attention of her audience in a way that also piques interest about the topic.

Here, Alyssa establishes listener relevance by pointing out that helping others makes us feel good and volunteering can be easy.

Alyssa mentions that she volunteers, which bolsters ethos and establishes her credibility to speak on the topic.

Notice how Alyssa's thesis with main point preview gives us a sense of the organizational framework for her ideas.

Again, as Alyssa introduces the first main point, she gets us to tune in because we all know how

even how to get around can be overwhelming and isolating. Volunteering is an easy way to quickly become familiar with and begin to feel a part of this new city in addition to the campus community.

Volunteering allows you to learn your way around town. In an interview I had with Natalie Cunningham, the volunteer coordinator of the Lexington Rescue Mission, she said, "My first group of students needed rides to all the various volunteer sites because they had no idea where things were in the city. It was really easy for the students who lived on campus to remain ignorant of their city, but while volunteering they become acquainted with Lexington and the important issues going on here." It seems like a silly thing, but knowing your way around town starts to make any city feel like home. Volunteering gets you out into the local area and helps you begin to get acquainted with new people and places.

Volunteering can also open your eyes to local social issues and conditions. According to Cohen, Mowbray, Gillette, and Thompson, many nonprofit organizations strive to raise awareness of important social issues, things like hunger and homelessness. The second time I showed up to volunteer at the Lexington Rescue Mission, I served food to the homeless. *(Show slide 2: group of volunteers in the kitchen)* I served soup and hung out with other volunteers and local homeless people. One of the "veteran" volunteers explained to me that Lexington has approximately 3,000 homeless people. *(Show slide 3: homelessness statistics in Lexington)* I was shocked to learn that we had such a large number of men, women, and children without a regular place to sleep. I wouldn't have known about this problem or the organizations working to end homelessness if I hadn't been a volunteer. Not only is volunteering important because it helps us become familiar with a town and its social issues; frankly, as members of a democratic society, volunteering is our civic responsibility.

Giving back to the community through volunteer work is our civic responsibility and a privilege. Each of us in this room—whether as U.S. citizens or international students—are reaping the benefits of earning college degrees in this democratic society. With that benefit comes the responsibility and privilege of giving back. Volunteering is our civic responsibility. Wilson and Musick explain that, without active participation in the local community, civil society becomes deprived. I agree. Giving back by volunteering helps the community in so many ways. *(Show slides 4 and 5: volunteers sorting clothes at the mission and then volunteers playing cards with people served at the shelter)*

Volunteering is also a privilege. Making a difference by volunteering ends up making us feel better about ourselves and our role in the world around us. In fact, research con-

overwhelming and isolating we can feel when we move to a new place.

Quoting the volunteer coordinator is a great piece of developmental material that encourages us to trust that Alyssa's message is trustworthy. (Note that interviews are not included in the reference section but are cited in the text of the outline.)

Alyssa intersperses actual photos of her and others volunteering throughout the speech. Doing so enhances her verbal message but doesn't replace it. The photos also provide pathos, making her ideas more emotionally compelling.

Here and throughout the speech, notice how Alyssa uses effective section transitions to verbally tie the point she is wrapping up with an introduction of the point to come. This makes her speech flow smoothly so listeners can follow her train of thought and bolsters her ethos because she sounds prepared.

Alyssa's careful audience analysis reveals itself here as she reminds her audience that even those who are not American citizens are benefiting as students in our educational system and, thus, have a responsibility to give back in some way.

ducted by the Corporation for National and Community Service from 2002 to 2005 shows that college students age sixteen to twenty-four represent the fastest growing demographic of volunteers in this country. *(Show slide 6: bar graph showing growth)* Not only that, a study done by the Higher Education Research Institute published in January of 2009 shows that a whopping 69.7 percent of first-year college students believe it is essential or very important to volunteer to help people in need. Certainly, the privilege of giving back as volunteers is our civic responsibility and helps our local community, but we can also reap valuable résumé-building life skills by volunteering.

Volunteering helps teach us new skills. These new skills and talents can actually make us more marketable for better jobs once we graduate. Being a consistent volunteer at a non-profit organization while attending college can strengthen your résumé. According to Charmer, in the *Journal of Career Development,* "Employers rely on credentials to certify that a young person will become a valuable employee. Credentials that document the experiences and employability skills, knowledge, and attitude." Laura Hatfield, director of the Center for Community Outreach at the University of Kentucky, points out that volunteers can include leadership, teamwork, and listening skills on their résumés because they can document the experiences where they had to use them effectively in the real world. Andrea Stockelman, another volunteer at the Lexington Rescue Mission, explained some of the new skills she picked up with volunteering. She said, "I learned that there was a lot more that went into preparing food for the homeless than I ever thought possible. It was neat to be a part of that process." *(Show slide 7: photo of Andrea preparing food)*

Volunteering at the Lexington Rescue Mission taught me new skills that bolstered my résumé. *(Show slide 8: résumé with skills highlighted)* I learned to coordinate the schedules of other volunteers. I also practiced important people skills such as teamwork, empathy, conflict management, and listening.

Today we've discussed why volunteering is beneficial to college students by focusing on how volunteering can connect us quickly and easily to our local community, why it's both our responsibility and privilege to do so, and how volunteering will benefit us after we graduate. So, I'm hoping the next time you recall a time you really enjoyed making a difference by helping someone, that memory won't come from the distant past. Instead, I hope you'll be thinking about how you are being the change you seek in the world by volunteering right here in Lexington right now.

Alyssa's choice to include national statistics of college student volunteers bolsters her credibility and provides listener relevance by reinforcing that college students are doing this, want to do this, and feel good about doing this kind of work.

Students want to know how to market themselves to get good jobs. So this main point will help maintain listener interest at a point when minds might tend to wander.

By including a quotation from another volunteer, we don't have to take Alyssa's word alone.

This very clear thesis restatement with main point summary signals a sense of closure.

Notice how Alyssa ties back to her opening quotation in her clincher. This provides a sense of wrapping up without saying thank you that helps listeners feel like the speech is complete in a memorable way.

WHAT WOULD YOU DO?

A Question of Ethics

Nalini sighed loudly as the club members of Toastmasters International took their seats. It was her first time meeting with the public speaking group, and she didn't want to be there, but her mom had insisted that she join the club in the hopes that it would help Nalini transfer from her community college to the university. It wasn't that the idea of public speaking scared Nalini. She had already spent time in front of an audience as the lead singer of the defunct emo band Deathstar. To Nalini's mind, public speaking was just another type of performance—like singing or acting—albeit a stuffy one, better suited to middle-aged men and women than people her age, a sentiment that explained why she wanted to be elsewhere at the moment.

After the club leader called the meeting to order, he asked each of the new members to stand, introduce themselves, and give a brief speech describing their background, aspirations, and reasons for joining the club. "Spare me," Nalini muttered loud enough for those next to her to hear. The club leader then called on a young woman to Nalini's left, who rose and began to speak about her dream of becoming a lawyer and doing public advocacy work for the poor. After the young woman sat down, the club members applauded politely. Nalini whistled and clapped loudly and kept on clapping after the others had stopped.

The club leader, somewhat taken aback, called on Nalini next. She rose from her seat and introduced herself as the secret love child of a former president and a famous actress. Nalini then strung together a series of other fantastic lies about her past and her ambitions. She concluded her speech by saying that she had joined the club in the hopes that she could learn how to hypnotize audiences into obeying her commands. After Nalini sat, a few of the club members applauded quietly, while others cast glances at each other and the club leader.

1. Is mocking behavior in a formal public speaking setting, either by an audience member or a speaker, an ethical matter? Explain your answer.

2. What ethical obligations does an audience member have to a speaker? What about a speaker to his or her audience?

Summary

Effective speeches must not only provide strong and relevant content that is clearly organized, they must also be presented using an effective delivery that is both conversational and animated.

Even though almost all of us experience public speaking apprehension, only 15 percent or less experience high levels of fear. The signs of speaking apprehension vary from individual to individual. You can learn to manage apprehension by adopting a communication orientation, practicing visualization, systematic desensitization, and cognitive restructuring techniques, and by preparing carefully and rehearsing your speech.

The major elements of speech delivery are embedded within your use of voice (pitch, volume, rate, quality, articulation, and pronunciation) and use of body (appearance, poise, posture, eye contact, facial expression, gestures, and movement).

Three of the most common types of speech delivery are impromptu speaking (talking on the spot), scripted speeches (completely written manuscripts), and extemporaneous speaking (speeches that are researched and planned but not scripted).

Effective delivery requires rehearsal. Experienced speakers schedule and conduct rehearsal sessions. Once their outline is complete, effective speakers usually rehearse at least twice, often using speech notes on cards that include key words, phrases, and delivery cue reminders. In many cases, speakers may use presentational aids to help audiences understand and remember the material. To be effective, presentational aids need to be carefully planned, shared only when being talked about, and displayed so that all can see and hear them.

In addition to preparing and presenting, you should also evaluate speeches, focusing on content, structure, and delivery.

COMMUNICATE!

RESOURCE AND ASSESSMENT CENTER

Now that you have read Chapter 15, go to the Speech Communication Course-Mate at cengagebrain.com where you'll find an interactive eBook and interactive learning tools including quizzes, flashcards, sample speech videos, audio study tools, skill-building activities, action step activities, and more. Student Workbook, Speech Builder Express 3.0, and Speech Studio 2.0 are also available.

Applying What You've Learned

Impromptu Speech Activity

1. Pick a slip of paper from a container provided by your instructor. The slip of paper will identify an element we've discussed about effective speech preparation (identifying a topic and writing a speech goal, audience analysis and adaptation, locating and evaluating secondary research sources, types of developmental material, conducting primary research, elements of an effective macrostructure, elements of effective microstructure, constructing presentational aids, effective delivery, use of voice, use of body, delivery methods, rehearsal sessions, etc.). Prepare and present a 2- to 3-minute impromptu speech explaining the element with specific examples.

Assessment Activity

2. Controlling Nervousness Interview one or two people who give frequent speeches (such as a minister, a politician, a lawyer, a businessperson, or a teacher). Ask what is likely to make them more or less nervous about giving the speech. Find out how they cope with their nervousness. Write a short paragraph summarizing what you have learned from the interviews. Then identify the behaviors used by those people that you believe might work for you.

3. Evaluating Speaker's Vocal and Body Action Behaviors Attend a public speech event on campus or in your community. Watch and evaluate the speaker's use of vocal characteristics (voice and articulation), body action (facial expressions, gestures, movement, poise, and posture), animation, spontaneity, and eye contact. Which vocal or body action behaviors stood out and why? How did the speaker's use of voice, body actions, animation, spontaneity, and eye contact contribute to or detract from the speaker's message? What three things could the speaker have done to improve the delivery of the speech?

Skill-Building Activities

1. Articulation Practice The goal of this activity is to practice articulating difficult word combinations. To find a list of sentences that are difficult to articulate, go to http://jimpowell.com, click on "Directing Tips," and then on "Articulation Exercises." Practice saying each of these sentences until you can do so without error.

2. Cognitive Restructuring Prepare and practice your personal cognitive restructuring by following the process outlined in this chapter.

Informative Speaking

What you'll know

- The characteristics of informative speaking

- Some of the major methods of informing

- Two of the most common informative speech patterns

- The major elements of process speeches

- The major elements of expository speeches

What you'll be able to do

- Create an informative process speech

- Create an informative expository speech

- Evaluate informative speeches based on key criteria

The campus had been fortunate to hear a number of excellent speakers at this year's Future of Energy series and tonight would be no different. Interested students, faculty, and invited guests had taken their seats and listened as the speaker was introduced by the director of the university's Center for the Study of the Environment. Then Susan Cischke, Vice President of Sustainability, Environment and Safety Engineering for Ford Motor Company, walked to the microphone to begin her speech entitled "Sustainability, Environment, and Safety Engineering."

16

This is but one of many scenes played out every day when experts deliver speeches to help others understand complex information. In this chapter, we focus specifically on the characteristics of good informative speaking and the methods you can use to develop an effective informative speech.

An **informative speech** is one whose goal is to explain or describe facts, truths, and principles in a way that stimulates interest, facilitates understanding, and increases the likelihood of remembering. In short, informative speeches are designed to educate audiences. Informative speeches answer questions about a topic, such as those beginning with who, when, what, where, why, how to, and how does. For example, your informative speech might describe who popular singer-songwriter Adele is, define Scientology, compare and contrast the similarities and differences between Twitter and Facebook, tell the story of golf professional Rory McIlroy's rise to fame, or demonstrate how to create and post a video on a Web site like YouTube. Informative speaking differs from other speech forms (such as speaking to persuade, to entertain, or to celebrate) in that your goal is simply to achieve mutual understanding about an object, person, place, process, event, idea, concept, or issue.

In this chapter, we discuss five distinguishing characteristics of informative speeches and five methods of informing. Then, we discuss two common types of informative speeches (process and expository speeches) and provide an example of an informative speech.

Characteristics of Effective Informative Speaking

Effective informative speeches are intellectually stimulating, relevant, creative, memorable, and address diverse learning styles.

Intellectually Stimulating

Your audience will perceive information to be **intellectually stimulating** when it is new to them and when it is explained in a way that piques their curiosity and interest. By *new*, we mean information that most of your audience is unfamiliar with or fresh insights into a topic with which they are already familiar.

If your audience is unfamiliar with your topic, you should consider how you might tap their natural curiosity. Imagine you are an anthropology major who is interested in prehistoric humans, which is not an interest shared by most members of your audience. You know that in 1991, the 5,300-year-old remains of a man, now called Ötzi, were found surprisingly well preserved in an ice field in the mountains between Austria and Italy. Even though the discovery was big news at the time, your audience today probably doesn't know much about it. You can draw on their natural curiosity, however, as you present "Unraveling the Mystery of the Iceman," describing scientists' efforts to understand who Ötzi was and what happened to him ("Ötzi, the Ice Man," n.d.).

If your audience is familiar with your topic, you will need to identify fresh insight about it. Begin by asking yourself, "What things about my topic do listeners probably not know?" Then consider depth and breadth as you answer the question. *Depth* has to do with going into more detail than people's general knowledge of the topic. If you watch programs on the Food Network, that's what you'll find. Most people know basic recipes, but these programs show new ways to cook the same foods. *Breadth* has to do with looking at how your topic relates to associated topics. Trace considered breadth when he informed his audience about Type 1 diabetes. He discussed not only the physical and emotional effects of the disease on a diabetic person, but also the emotional and relational effects on family and friends, as well as the financial effects on society.

informative speech

a speech whose goal is to explain or describe facts, truths, and principles in a way that increases understanding

CONSIDER *THIS....*

Identify several public figures that you find interesting (e.g., actors, singers, athletes, politicians). Which of them (if any) do you think you could do a speech about and why?

intellectually stimulating

information that is new to audience members and piques interest

You can make familiar topics intellectually stimulating by sharing fresh insight focused on depth and breadth.

J. Pat Carter/Associated Press

Relevant

A general rule to remember when preparing your informative speeches is this: Don't assume that your listeners will recognize how the information is relevant to them. Remember to incorporate *listener relevance links* throughout the speech. As you prepare each main point, ask and answer the question: How would knowing this information make my listeners happier, healthier, wealthier, wiser, and so forth?

Creative

Your audience will perceive your information to be **creative** when it yields innovative ideas. You may not ordinarily consider yourself to be creative, but that may be because you have never recognized or fully developed your own innovative ideas. Contrary to what you may think, creativity is not a gift that some have and some don't; rather, it is the result of hard work. Creativity comes from doing good research, taking time, and practicing productive thinking.

creative
using information in a way that yields innovative ideas and insights

Creative informative speeches begin with *good research*. The more you learn about a topic, the more you will have to work with in order to develop it creatively. Speakers who present information creatively have given themselves lots of supporting material to work with.

Rarely do creative ideas come when we are in a time crunch. Instead, they are likely to come when we least expect it—when we're driving our car, preparing for bed, or daydreaming. The creative process depends on having time to mull over ideas. If you complete a draft of your outline several days before you speak, you'll have time to consider how to present your ideas creatively.

For the creative process to work, you also have to *think productively*. **Productive thinking** occurs when we contemplate something from a variety of perspectives. Then, with numerous ideas to choose from, we can select the ones that are best suited to our particular audience. In the article "A Theory about Genius," Michael Michalko (1998) describes several tactics you can use to become better at productive thinking. They include:

productive thinking
contemplating something from a variety of perspectives

1. Rethink a problem, issue, or topic from many perspectives. Albert Einstein actually came up with the theory of relativity doing this. As you brainstorm, try to think about a possible topic as it might be perceived by many different groups and co-cultural groups. Then as you conduct research, try to find sources that represent a variety of viewpoints and perspectives, as well.

2. Make your thoughts visible by sketching drawings, diagrams, and graphs. Galileo revolutionized science by doing this. Concept mapping is an example of doing so when generating possible topics.

3. Produce. Set regular goals to produce *something*. The great NHL hockey player, Wayne Gretzky, put it this way: "You miss every shot you don't take." So take some shots! Thomas Edison actually set a goal to produce an invention every 10 days. J. S. Bach wrote one cantata a week. And T. S. Eliot's many

THE AUDIENCE *BEYOND*

To nurture creative thinking about transnational celebrity activism in global politics, Anne Marie not only conducted an extensive library search on several databases, but she also researched the topic by reading celebrity gossip magazines and visiting the Web sites of celebrities known for practicing it (e.g., Angelina Jolie, Matt Damon, George Clooney, Madonna).

drafts of *The Waste Land* eventually became a masterpiece. Don't let writer's block keep you from drafting an initial outline. You need to start somewhere. Getting ideas out of your head and onto the paper or computer screen gives you something to work with and revise. After all, you can't edit air.

4. Combine and recombine ideas, images, and thoughts in different ways. The Austrian monk, Gregor Mendel, combined mathematics and biology to come up with the laws of heredity, which still ground the modern science of genetics today. Jennifer's list of possible speech topics included gardening, something she loved to do, and the issue of rising college tuition costs. She put the two ideas together and came up with the idea of doing an informative speech about how to use gardening (services, produce, and products) to raise money to help pay for college.

Let's look at how productive thinking can help to identify different approaches to a topic. Suppose you want to give a speech on volunteering in the United States, and in your research, you ran across the data shown in Figure 16.1. With

| State | General adult Population | | College students, ages 16–24 | |
	Volunteering rate (in %)	State rank	Volunteering rate (in %)	State rank
Alabama	28.9	32	34.8	16
Alaska	38.9	5	40.1	7
Arizona	24.9	45	30.8	32
Arkansas	25.6	43	31.7	22
California	26.1	40	28.5	38
Colorado	32.8	17	38.3	10
Connecticut	30.8	21	31.5	23
Delaware	26.7	37	26.4	42
District of Columbia	30.8	22	31.0	30
Florida	24.1	48	25.9	43
Georgia	25.9	41	21.4	51
Hawaii	25.4	44	29.6	35
Idaho	35.5	14	44.4	2
Illinois	29.7	28	31.2	27
Indiana	29.5	29	37.3	13
Iowa	39.2	4	31.1	29
Kansas	38.6	8	31.5	24
Kentucky	29.8	27	30.4	33
Louisiana	22.7	49	27.8	40
Maine	33.2	16	31.4	25
Maryland	30.3	25	30.2	34
Massachusetts	27.0	36	24.0	47
Michigan	32.1	18	37.4	12
Minnesota	40.7	3	39.9	8
Mississippi	26.4	39	33.1	20
Missouri	31.9	20	38.9	9
Montana	37.9	10	34.6	17
Nebraska	42.8	2	41.5	5
Nevada	18.8	51	23.6	49
New Hampshire	32.0	19	32.0	21
New Jersey	26.5	38	25.0	45
New Mexico	28.5	33	31.3	26
New York	21.3	50	23.4	50
North Carolina	29.1	30	28.8	37
North Dakota	36.5	13	33.7	19
Ohio	30.7	24	34.4	18
Oklahoma	30.0	26	43.0	3
Oregon	33.6	15	31.1	28
Pennsylvania	30.8	23	35.1	15
Rhode Island	24.9	46	25.8	44
South Carolina	28.0	35	28.3	39
South Dakota	38.8	6	31.0	31
Tennessee	25.9	42	24.0	48
Texas	28.3	34	29.2	36
Utah	48.0	1	62.9	1
Vermont	38.1	9	41.5	4
Virginia	29.0	31	24.6	46
Washington	36.8	12	37.6	11
West Virginia	24.6	47	27.4	41
Wisconsin	37.0	11	36.2	14
Wyoming	38.8	7	40.3	6

Figure 16.1

Volunteering rates across the U.S.

Dote, Cramer, Dietz, and Grimm (2006). College students helping America. Washington, D. C.: Corporation for National and Community Service.

productive thinking, you can identify several ways to develop your speech. For instance, notice that roughly two-thirds of the state's college students (ages 16 to 24) volunteer as much as or more than the general adult population. You could investigate why this is so and do a speech about it. Looking at the data from another perspective, you might notice that the percentage of both the general adult and college student populations that volunteer in three states (Minnesota, Nebraska, and Utah) is 40 percent or more. You might examine what types of volunteer work people do in those states and why. Looking at these data yet another way reveals that Utah ranks first for the percentage of the general adult population that volunteers and Nevada ranks last. You could do a speech comparing volunteerism in those two states. Or you might notice that a majority of the states that rank lowest in terms of percentages who volunteer are in the east, and many of the states that tend to rank highest are in the Midwest and mountain west. Again, you could do a speech comparing volunteerism in these regions.

If you take a shot and write something down, even if it's not very good, you have something to revise. If you don't take a shot, you most assuredly have nothing to work with.

Productive thinking can also help us find alternative ways to make the same point. Using the information in Figure 16.1, we can quickly create two ways to support the point "On average, about 30 percent of the U.S. general adult population volunteers."

Alternative A: *Eighteen of the fifty states plus the District of Columbia had volunteering rates between 25 and 30 percent. Twelve of them had volunteering rates between 30 and 35 percent. In other words, thirty of the fifty states plus D.C. (or 60 percent) report volunteering rates between 25 and 35 percent.*

Alternative B: *If we exclude Nevada with its very low volunteering rate of 18.8 percent and Utah, Nebraska, and Minnesota with very high rates of 48 percent, 42.8 percent, and 40.7 percent, respectively, then we see that most states (forty-seven) reported volunteering rates between 20 and 40 percent.*

Memorable

If your speech is really informative, your audience will hear a lot of new information but will need help remembering what is most important. Emphasizing your specific goal, main points, and key facts are good starting points. Figure 16.2 summarizes several memory-enhancing techniques you might use.

Address Diverse Learning Styles

Because audience members differ in how they prefer to learn, you will be most successful when you address diverse learning styles. You can appeal to people who prefer to learn through the feeling dimension by providing concrete, vivid images, examples, stories, and testimonials. Address the watching dimension by using visual aids. Address the thinking dimension by including definitions, explanations, and statistics. Address the doing dimension by encouraging your listeners to do something during the speech or afterward. Rounding the learning cycle in this way ensures that you address the diverse learning style preferences of your audience and make the speech understandable, meaningful, and memorable for all.

CONSIDER *THIS....*

Are you more compelled to learn and remember when you can see, feel, think about, or practice doing something? Why?

Technique	Use	Example
Presentational aids	To provide audience members with a visual, audio, or audiovisual conceptualization of important information	A diagram of the process of making ethanol
Repetition	To give the audience a second or third chance to retain important information by repeating or paraphrasing it	"The first dimension of romantic love is passion; that is, it can't really be romantic love if there is no sexual attraction."
Transitions	To help the audience understand the relationship between the ideas, including primary and supporting information	"So the three characteristics of romantic love are passion, intimacy, and commitment. Now let's consider five ways to keep love alive."
Humor and other emotional anecdotes	To create an emotional memory link to important ideas	"True love is like a pair of socks, you have to have two, and they've got to match. So you and your partner need to be mutually committed and compatible."
Mnemonics and acronyms	To provide an easily remembered memory prompt for a series or a list	"You can remember the four criteria for evaluating a diamond as the four Cs: carat, clarity, cut, and color." "As you can see, useful goals are SMART: S for specific, M for measurable, A for action-oriented, R for reasonable, and T for time-bound. That's SMART."

Figure 16.2

Techniques for making informative speeches memorable

© Cengage Learning

Methods of Informing

We can inform through description, definition, comparison and contrast, narration, and demonstration. Let's look at each of these methods more closely.

Description

description

method of informing used to create an accurate, vivid, verbal picture of an object, geographic feature, setting, person, event, or image

Description is an informative method used to create an accurate, vivid, verbal picture of an object, geographic feature, setting, event, person, or image. This method usually answers an overarching who, what, or where question. If the thing to be described is simple and familiar (like a light bulb or a river), the description may not need to be detailed. But if the thing to be described is complex and unfamiliar (like a sextant or holograph), the description will need to be more exhaustive. Descriptions are, of course, easier if you have a presentational aid, but vivid verbal descriptions can also create informative mental pictures. To describe something effectively, you can explain its size, shape, weight, color, composition, age, condition, and spatial organization. You can describe size subjectively as large or small and objectively by noting specific numerical measures. For example, you can describe New York City subjectively as the largest in the United States or more objectively as home to more than 8 million people with more than 26,000 people per square mile.

You can describe shape by reference to common geometric forms like round, triangular, oblong, spherical, conical, cylindrical, or rectangular, or by reference to common objects such as a book or a milk carton. For example, the Lower Peninsula of Michigan is often described as being shaped like a left-hand mitten. Shape is made more vivid by using adjectives, such as *smooth* or *jagged*.

You can describe weight subjectively as heavy or light and objectively by pounds and ounces or kilograms, grams, and milligrams. As with size, you can clarify weight with comparisons. For example, you can describe a Humvee (Hummer) as weighing about 7,600 pounds, or about as much as three Honda Civics.

You can describe color by coupling a basic color (such as black, white, red, or yellow) with a common object. For instance, instead of describing something as puce or ochre, you might describe the object as "eggplant purple" or "clay-pot orange."

You can describe the composition of something by indicating what it is made of, such as by saying the building was made of brick, concrete, or wood. Sometimes, you might be clearer by describing what it looks like rather than what it is. For example, you might say something looks metallic, even if it is made of plastic rather than metal.

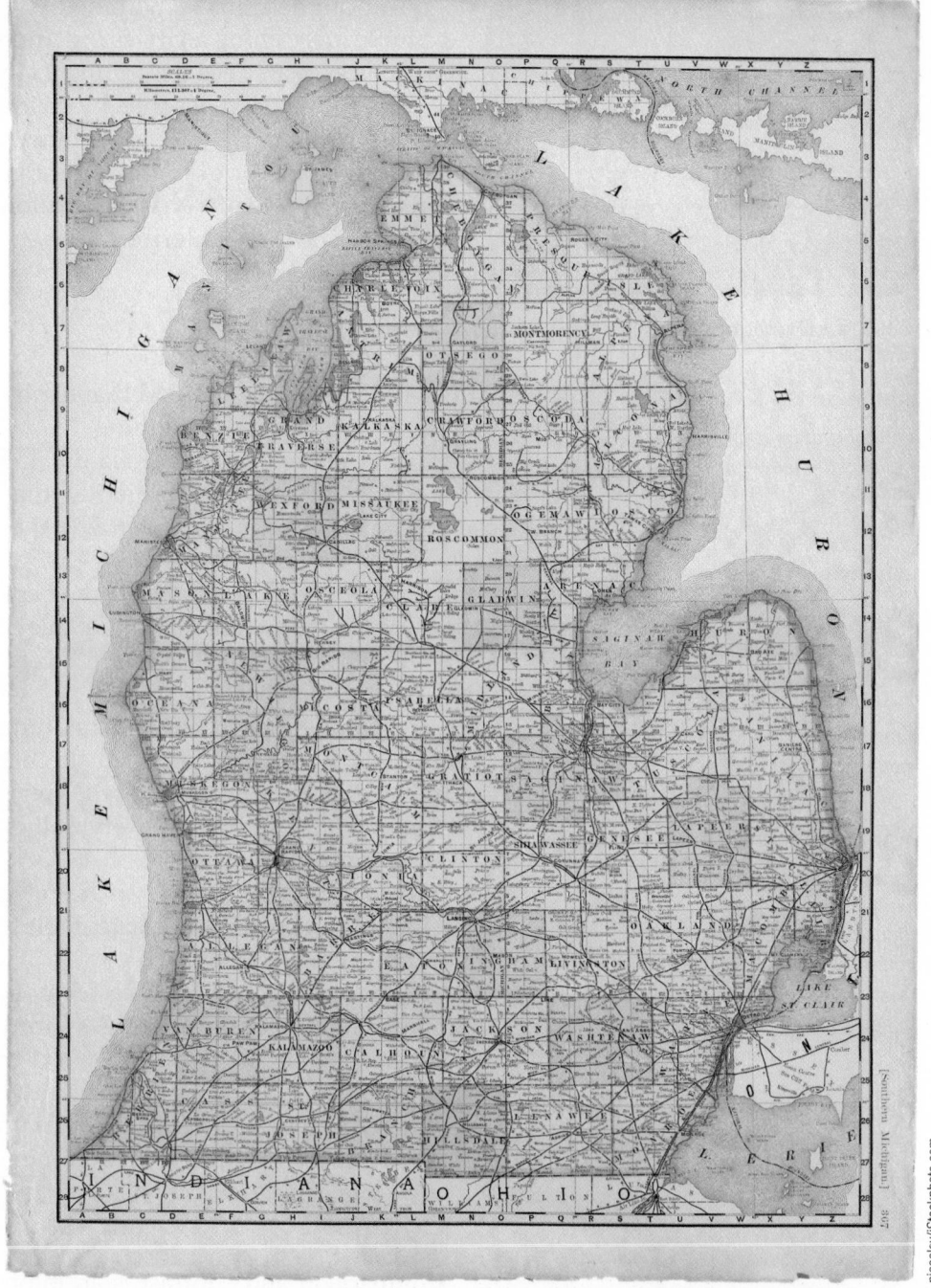

The shape of the Lower Peninsula of Michigan can be described as looking like the left hand of a mitten.

nicooley/iStockphoto.com

You can describe something by its age and by its condition. For example, describing a city as old and well kept gives different mental pictures than does describing a city as old and war torn.

Finally, you can describe by spatial organization going from top to bottom, left to right, outer to inner, and so on. A description of the Sistine Chapel, for example, might go from the floor to the ceiling, and a description of a NASCAR automobile might go from the body to the engine to the interior.

How might you describe a NASCAR automobile?

definition

a method of informing that explains the meaning of something

synonym

word that has the same or similar meaning

antonym

word that has the opposite meaning

comparison and contrast

a method of informing that explains something by focusing on how it is similar and different from other things

Definition

Definition is an informative method that explains the meaning of something. There are four ways to define something.

First, you can define a word or idea by classifying it and differentiating it from similar words or ideas. For example, in a speech on vegetarianism, you might use information from the Vegan Society's Web site (www.vegansociety .com) to develop a definition of a vegan: "A vegan is a vegetarian who is seeking a lifestyle free from animal products for the benefit of people, animals, and the environment. Vegans eat a plant-based diet free from all animal products including milk, eggs, and honey. Vegans also don't wear leather, wool, or silk and avoid other animal-based products."

Second, you can define a word by explaining its derivation or history. For instance, the word *vegan* is made from the beginning and end of the word *vegetarian* and was coined in the United Kingdom in 1944, when the Vegan Society was founded. Offering this etymology will help your audience to remember the meaning of *vegan*.

Third, you can define a word by explaining its use or function. For example, in vegan recipes, you can use tofu or tempeh to replace meat and almond or soy milk to replace cow's milk.

The fourth, and perhaps the quickest way you can define something, is by using a familiar synonym or antonym. A **synonym** is a word that has the same or a similar meaning; an **antonym** is a word that has the opposite meaning. So you could define a *vegan* by comparing it to the word *vegetarian*, which is a synonym with a similar although not identical meaning, or to the word *carnivore*, which is an antonym.

Comparison and Contrast

Comparison and contrast is an informative method that focuses on how something is similar to and different from other things. For example, in a speech on veganism, you might tell your audience how vegans are similar and different from other types of vegetarians. You can point out that like vegetarians, vegans don't eat meat. In contrast, semi-vegetarians eat fish or poultry. Like lacto vegetarians, vegans don't eat eggs, but unlike this group and lacto-ovo vegetarians, vegans don't use dairy products. So of all vegetarians, vegans have the most restrictive

How might a presentational aid help enhance your informative speech about veganism?

THE AUDIENCE *BEYOND*

Although Randi used vivid language to describe the ancient ruins of Pompeii, Italy, she also downloaded several images from the Internet, which she includes as visual aids while describing them.

diet. Because comparisons and contrasts can be figurative or literal, you can use metaphors and analogies as well as making direct comparisons.

Narration

Narration is an informative method that recounts an autobiographical or biographical event, a myth, a story, or some other account. Narrations usually have four parts. First, the narration orients the listener by describing when and where the event took place and by introducing the important people or characters. Second, the narration explains the sequence of events that led to a complication or problem, including details that enhance the development. Third, the narration discusses how the complication or problem affected the key people in the narrative. Finally, the narration recounts how the complication or problem was solved. The characteristics of a good narration include a strong story line; use of descriptive language and detail that enhance the plot, people, setting, and events; effective use of dialogue; pacing that builds suspense; and a strong voice (Baerwald, n.d.).

Narrations can be presented in a first-, second-, or third-person voice. When you use first person, you report what you have personally experienced or observed, using the pronouns *I*, *me*, and *my* as you recount the events. "Let me tell you about the first time I tried to water-ski" might be the opening for a narrative story told in first person. When you use second person, you place your audience at the scene by using the pronouns *you* and *your*. You might say, for example, "Imagine that you have just gotten off the plane in Hong Kong. You look at the signs, but can't read a thing. Which way is the terminal?" When you use third person, you describe to your audience what has happened, is happening, or will happen to other people by using pronouns like *he, she, his, her,* and *they*. "When the students arrived in Venice for their study-abroad experience, the first thing they saw was . . .""

Demonstration

Demonstration is an informative method that shows how something is done, displays the stages of a process, or depicts how something works. Demonstrations range from very simple with a few easy-to-follow steps (such as how to iron a shirt) to very complex (such as explaining how a nuclear reactor works). Regardless of whether the topic is simple or complex, effective demonstrations require expertise, developing a hierarchy of steps, and using vivid language and presentational aids.

In a demonstration, your experience with what you are demonstrating is critical. Expertise gives you the necessary background to supplement bare-bones instructions with personally lived experiences. Why are TV cooking shows so popular? Because the chef doesn't just read the recipe and do what it says. Rather, while performing each step, the chef shares tips that aren't mentioned in any cookbook. It is the chef's experience that allows him or her to say that one egg will work as well as two, or how to tell if the cake is really done.

In a demonstration, you organize the steps from first to last so that your audience will be able to remember the sequence of actions accurately. Suppose you want to demonstrate the steps in using a touch-screen voting machine. If you present 14 separate points, your audience is unlikely to remember them. However, if you group them under the following four headings, chances are much higher that your audience will be able to remember most of the items: I. Get ready to vote; II. Vote; III. Review your choices; and IV. Cast your ballot.

Although you could explain a process with only words, most demonstrations show the audience the process or parts of the process. That's in part why

The first-person narrative method used in the TV program *How I Met Your Mother* is an example of informing. How does this technique capture and maintain audience interest?

narration
a method of informing that explains something by recounting events or stories

demonstration
a method of informing that explains something by showing how it is done, by displaying the stages of a process, or by depicting how something works

COMMUNICATE ON YOUR FEET

Speech Assignment

A Process Speech

1. Follow the speech plan Action Steps in Chapters 11–15 to prepare a process speech. Your instructor will announce the time limit and other parameters for this assignment.

2. Criteria for evaluation include the general criteria of topic and purpose, content, organization, and presentation, but special emphasis will be placed on how intellectually stimulating the topic is made for the audience, how creatively ideas are presented, and how clearly the important information is emphasized.

3. Prior to presenting your speech, prepare a complete sentence outline and source list (bibliography) as well as a written plan for adapting your speech to the audience.

process speech

an informative speech that demonstrates how something is done or made, or how it works

TV shows like *What Not to Wear* and *Flip This House* are so popular. If what you are explaining is relatively simple, you can demonstrate the entire process from start to finish. However, if the process is lengthy or complex, you may choose to pre-prepare the material for some of the steps. Although you will show all stages in the process, you will not have to take the time for every single step as the audience watches. For example, many of the ingredients used by TV chefs are already cut up, measured, and separated into little bowls.

Effective demonstrations require practice. Remember that under the pressure of speaking to an audience, even the simplest task can become difficult. (Have you ever tried to thread a needle with 25 people watching you?) As you practice, you will want to consider the size of your audience and the configuration of the room. Be sure that all of the audience will be able see what you are doing.

Common Informative Patterns

Two of the most common patterns for organizing informative speech ideas are process patterns and expository patterns.

Process Speeches

The goal of a **process speech** is to demonstrate how something is done, is made, or works. Effective process speeches require you to carefully delineate the steps and the order in which they occur. These steps typically become the main points and explanations of each step become the subpoints. Process speeches rely heavily on the demonstration method of informing.

Although some process speeches require you to demonstrate, others are not suited to demonstrations. For these, you can use visual or audiovisual aids to help the audience see the steps in the process. In a speech on remodeling a kitchen, it would not be practical to demonstrate the process; however, you could greatly enhance the verbal description by showing pictures before, during, and after the remodeling.

CONSIDER THIS....

Identify several hobbies you enjoy. Which of them could you develop a process speech on? What steps would you use as main points?

expository speech

an informative presentation that provides carefully researched, in-depth knowledge about a complex topic

Expository Speeches

The goal of an **expository speech** is to provide carefully researched, in-depth knowledge about a complex topic. For example, "understanding the health care debate," "the origins and classification of nursery rhymes," "the socio-biological theory of child abuse," and "viewing rap as poetry" are all topics on which you could give an interesting expository speech. Lengthy expository speeches are known as lectures.

All expository speeches require speakers to draw from an extensive research base, choose an organizational pattern best suited to the material and specific speech goal, and use a variety of informative methods (e.g., descriptions, definitions, comparisons and contrasts, narration, and short demonstrations) to sustain the audience's attention and help them understand the material presented.

Expository speeches include speeches that explain a political, economic, social, religious, or ethical issue; forces of history; a theory, principle, or law; and a creative work.

Exposition of Political, Economic, Social, Religious, or Ethical Issues In an expository speech, you have the opportunity to help the audience understand the background or context of an issue, including the forces that gave rise to and continue to affect it. You may also present the various positions held about the issue and the reasoning behind these positions. Finally, you may discuss various ways that have been presented for resolving the issue.

The general goal of your speech is to inform, not to persuade. So you will want to present all sides of controversial issues, without advocating which side is better. You will also want to make sure that the sources you draw from are respected experts and are objective in what they report. Finally, you will want to present complex issues in a straightforward manner that helps your audience understand them, while refraining from oversimplifying knotty issues. Figure 16.3 provides examples of topic ideas for an expository speech about a political, economic, social, religious, or ethical issue.

For example, while researching a speech on fracking—the controversial method for extracting natural gas deposits, you need to be careful to consult articles and experts on all sides of this issue and fairly represent and incorporate their views in your outline. You should discuss not only the technology that is used, but also the controversies that surround its use. If time is limited, you might discuss just one or two of these issues, but you should at least inform the audience of others.

job search strategies	cyber bullying	fracking
global warming	digital remixing	capital punishment
teacher accountability	right to bear arms	Occupy Wall Street
patterns of immigration	media bias	cleaning up oil spills
Sikhism	celebrity culture	consequences of Arab Spring
stem cell research	European debt crisis	

Figure 16.3

Topic ideas for expository speeches about political, economic, social, religious, or ethical issues

© Cengage Learning

 THE AUDIENCE *BEYOND*

After doing her speech about the nature and prevalence of domestic abuse, Jen created a mashup (digitally remixed recording) of Matchbox 20's "Push," the Dresden Dolls' "Delilah," and the Crystals' "He Hit Me (It Felt Like a Kiss)," which she posted to YouTube with a link to the transcript of her speech.

We often think of broadcast news programs as unbiased. However, as you read the *Pop Comm!* feature, "Coloring the News: Is the Information Provided by the Media Biased?" you can see it is difficult to simply provide information.

POP COMM!

Coloring the News: Is the Information Provided by the Media Biased?

NBCUniversal/Getty Images

When you watch a newscast or read an online news article, do you expect the information to be reported objectively? Or do you assume that the news media is biased in some way? If you do think the mainstream media is biased, you are not alone. The Pew Research Center for the People and the Press (2011) found that 77 percent of Americans across political affiliations think news organizations "tend to favor one side" and 66 percent believe news organizations are politically biased in their reporting.

What makes us think that the news we receive is biased or unbiased? One of the factors is presentation. One journalist who personifies a professional, unbiased delivery—even almost thirty years after his final broadcast as a news anchor—is Walter Cronkite. Cronkite anchored and reported for the *CBS Evening News* from 1962 to 1981 and was so admired and respected that he was named "the most trusted man in America" in a 1972 poll. He delivered the news in a calm, straightforward manner no matter what he was reporting, betraying emotion only rarely, such as when he announced the death of President John F. Kennedy. He also took pains to ensure that he would be clearly understood by listeners, training himself to speak 124 words per minute, which is 40 words per minute slower than the average American speaks (Hinckley, 2009). And he always made it very clear when he was veering from reporting the news to expressing an opinion. A tireless advocate of objective journalism, he once said, "[The journalist's] job is only to hold up the mirror—to tell and show the public what has happened" (Leopold, 2009).

Television newscasts remain an important news source in today's media culture. Research has shown that nearly two thirds of Americans name television as their main source for national and international news, and 63 percent of those surveyed suggest cable news outlets like CNN and Fox News are the outlets that "first come to mind when they think of news organizations" (Pew Research Center, 2011). These outlets clearly play a central role in Americans' knowledge of current events, but are they upholding the standards of journalistic objectivity that made Walter Cronkite the most trusted man in America? In an effort to fulfill cable TV's demand for 24-hour-a-day programming, even respected news organizations such as CNN must present not only the "hard news" but also news analysis, sensational graphics, and chitchat among program hosts. As a result, the news many people watch blurs the lines between opinion, entertainment, and the straightforward presentation of facts. In addition, some cable news anchors and show hosts have become the subject of controversy for their on-air rants, partisan attacks, and melodramatic grandstanding, including Bill O'Reilly, Keith Olbermann, and Geraldo Rivera—all of whom are reporters who were trained in the principles of fair reporting.

Another factor that makes us suspect that the information in news reports is biased is how events are covered. News coverage during presidential campaigns tends to generate a lot of interest and analysis. During the 2008 presidential race, some charged the media was showing bias in support of

Democratic candidate Barack Obama. *The Washington Post's* Deborah Howell (2008) reported that during the first week of June 2008, Obama dominated political stories by 142 to Republican candidate John McCain's 96, a 3-to-1 advantage. Although she acknowledged that numbers weren't everything and that Obama generated a lot of coverage because he was the first African American nominee and initially less well known than McCain, she argued that readers deserved comparable coverage of both candidates.

Though many Americans agree that media bias is a problem, there is little consensus about how to determine the nature of such bias or which side it even favors. For example, National Public Radio (NPR) has long been accused of having a liberal bias in its reporting and some conservative critics have called for an end to federal funding of the organization. Some, like respected journalist Bill Moyers, have defended NPR as an independent news source that practices journalistic objectivity and balanced reporting because they don't take explicit stands on controversial issues like abortion and gay marriage (Moyers & Winship, 2011). Conservative critics, such as Bernard Goldberg (2011), counter that the partiality of NPR and other news organizations is rooted in ideological biases that shape what stories they choose to cover and how they are reported, such as the choice of sources and amount of time given to sources on each side of an issue. At times bias may be as subtle as the language used to describe people on different sides of controversial issues. For example, consider how the pragmatics of messages change depending on whether a reporter chooses to label opponents as pro-choice vs. pro-life, pro-choice vs. anti-abortion; anti-life vs. anti-abortion, or anti-life vs. pro-life. By choosing nonparallel labels to opposing sides, the reporter subtly colors the perceptions of unsophisticated audience members.

Whatever your thoughts about media bias, you'll be a better-informed consumer if you learn how to evaluate news source bias critically. Fairness and Accuracy in Reporting (FAIR) provides a helpful list of factors that can contribute to bias in news reporting ("What's Wrong with the News?," n.d.):

- Corporate ownership
- Advertiser influence
- Official agendas
- Telecommunications policy
- The public relations industry
- Pressure groups
- The narrow range of debate
- Censorship
- Sensationalism

FAIR also recommends asking the following critical questions when evaluating news information ("How to Detect Bias," n.d.):

- Who are the sources?
- Is there a lack of diversity?
- From whose point of view is the news reported?
- Are there double standards?
- What are the unchallenged assumptions?
- Is the language loaded?
- Is there a lack of context?
- Do the headlines and stories match?
- Are stories on important issues featured prominently?

Questions to Ponder

1. Do you think biased news reporting is a problem? Why or why not?
2. Do you think news satire programs such as The Daily Show and the Colbert Report are more or less ethical than those proclaiming to be reporting news objectively? Why or why not?

genocide	the colonization of Africa	Irish immigration
women's suffrage	Ghandi and his movement	the War on Terror
the Olympics Pakistan	the Spanish Flu Epidemic	the Ming Dynasty
the New Madrid Earthquake	the Industrial Revolution	the Balfour Declaration
the papacy		

Figure 16.4

Topic ideas for expository speeches about historical events and forces

© Cengage Learning

Exposition of Historical Events and Forces It has been said that those who don't understand history may be destined to repeat it. So an expositional speech about historical events and forces can be fascinating for its own sake, but it can also be relevant for what is happening today. Unfortunately, some people think history is boring. So, you have an obligation to seek out stories and narratives that can enliven your speech. And you will want to analyze the events you describe and their impact at the time they occurred, as well as the meaning they have today. Figure 16.4 proposes examples of topic ideas for an expository speech about historical events and forces.

Exposition of a Theory, Principle, or Law The way we live is affected by natural and human laws and principles and is explained by various theories. Yet there are many theories, principles, and laws that we do not completely understand—or, at least, we don't understand how they affect us. The main challenge is to find material that explains the theory, law, or principle in language that is understandable to the audience. You will want to search for or create examples and illustrations that demystify complicated concepts and terminology. Effective examples and comparing unfamiliar ideas with those that the audience already knows are techniques that can help you with this kind of speech. In a speech on the psychological principles of operant conditioning, a speaker can help the audience understand the difference between continuous reinforcement and intermittent reinforcement by providing the following explanation:

> *When a behavior is reinforced continuously, each time the person performs the behavior, a reward is given, but when the behavior is reinforced intermittently, the reward is not always given when the behavior is displayed. Behavior that is learned by continuous reinforcement disappears quickly when the reward no longer is provided, but behavior that is learned by intermittent reinforcement continues for long periods of time, even when not reinforced. Every day you can see the effects of how a behavior was conditioned. For example, take the behavior of putting a coin in a machine. If the machine is a vending machine, you expect to be rewarded every time you "play." And if the machine doesn't dispense the item, you might wonder if the machine is out of order and "play" just one more coin, or you might bang on the machine. In any case, you are unlikely to put in more than one more coin. But suppose the machine is a slot machine or a machine that dispenses instant-winner lottery tickets. How many coins will you "play" before you stop and conclude that the machine isn't going to give you what you want? Why the difference? Because you were conditioned to a vending machine on a continuous schedule, but a slot machine or automatic lottery ticket dispenser "rewards" you on an intermittent schedule.*

Figure 16.5 provides some examples of topic ideas for an expository speech about a theory, principle, or law.

natural selection	Boyle's law	Maslow's hierarchy of needs
gravity	number theory	
Murphy's Law	the Law of Diminishing Returns	intelligent design
the Peter Principle		social cognitive theory
feminist theory	color theory	
diminishing returns	psychoanalytic theory	

Figure 16.5

Topic ideas for expository speeches about theories, principles, or laws

Exposition of a Creative Work Courses in art, theatre, music, literature, and film appreciation give students tools by which to recognize the style, historical period, and quality of a particular piece or group of pieces. Yet most of us know very little about how to understand a creative work, so presentations designed to explain creative works like poems, novels, songs, or even famous speeches can be very instructive for audience members.

When developing a speech that explains a creative work, you will want to find information on the work and the artist who created it. You will also want to find sources that educate you about the period in which this work was created and inform you about the criteria that critics use to evaluate works of this type. For example, if you wanted to give an expository speech on Fredrick Douglass's Fourth of July Oration given in Rochester, New York in 1852, you might need to orient your audience by first reminding them of who Douglass was. Then you would want to explain the traditional expectations for Fourth of July speakers in the mid-1800s. After this, you might want to summarize the speech and perhaps share a few memorable quotes. Finally, you would want to discuss how speech critics view the speech and why the speech is considered great.

Figure 16.6 presents examples of topics for expository speeches about creative works. Figure 16.7 is a checklist you can use to analyze any informative speech you rehearse or to critique the speeches of others.

hip-hop music	the love sonnets of Shakespeare	the *Hunger Games* trilogy
Impressionist painting	Kabuki theater	iconography
salsa dancing	graphic novels	Spike Lee's *Mo' Better Blues*
women in cinema	the Martin Luther King National memorial	
the films of Alfred Hitchcock		

Figure 16.6

Topic ideas for expository speeches about creative works

You can use this form to critique informative speeches you hear in class. As you listen, outline the speech and identify which informative speech framework the speaker is using. Then answer the questions that follow.

Informative Speech Critique

Process Speech:
__ How something is done
__ How something is made
__ How something works

Figure 16.7

Informative speech evaluation checklist

Expository Speech:
___ Exposition of political, economic, social, religious, or ethical issue
___ Exposition of historical events or forces
___ Exposition of a theory, principle, or law
___ Exposition of creative work

General Criteria
___ 1. Was the specific goal clear?
___ 2. Were the main points developed with breadth and depth of appropriate supporting material?
___ 3. Was the introduction effective in creating interest and introducing the main points?
___ 4. Was the speech organized and easy to follow?
___ 5. Was the language appropriate, clear, and vivid?
___ 6. Was the conclusion effective in summarizing the main points and providing closure?
___ 7. Was the vocal delivery intelligible, conversational, and expressive?
___ 8. Did the body actions appear poised, natural, spontaneous, and appropriate?

Specific Criteria for Process Speeches
___ 1. Was the introduction clear in previewing the process to be explained?
___ 2. Was the speech easy to follow and organized in a time order?
___ 3. Were presentational aids used effectively to clarify the process?
___ 4. Did the process use a demonstration method effectively?

Specific Criteria for Expository Speeches
___ 1. Was the specific goal of the speech to provide well-researched information on a complex topic?
___ 2. Did the speaker effectively use a variety of methods to convey the information?
___ 3. Did the speaker emphasize the main ideas and important supporting material?
___ 4. Did the speaker present in-depth, high-quality, appropriately cited information?

Figure 16.7
(Continued)

COMMUNICATE ON YOUR FEET

Speech Assignment

An Expository Speech

1. Follow the speech plan Action Steps in Chapters 11–15 to prepare a 5- to 8-minute informative speech in which you present carefully researched, in-depth information about a complex topic. Your instructor will announce other parameters for this assignment.

2. Criteria for evaluation include all the general criteria of topic and purpose, content, organization, and presentation, but special emphasis will be placed on how intellectually stimulating the topic is made for the audience, how creatively ideas are presented, and how clearly the important information is emphasized. Use the informative speech evaluation checklist in Figure 16.7 to critique yourself as you practice your speech.

3. Prior to presenting your speech, prepare a complete-sentence outline, a reference list (bibliography), and a written plan for adapting your speech to the audience.

SAMPLE SPEECH PLAN AND OUTLINE

Sample Informative Speech

This section presents a sample informative speech given by a student, including an adaptation plan, an outline, and a transcript.

Making Ethanol[1]

By Louisa Greene

Read the speech adaptation plan, outline, and transcript of a speech given by Louisa Greene in an introductory speaking course. You can access a video clip of Louisa's speech through the Chapter 16 resources of your CourseMate for *Communicate!* You can also use CourseMate to identify some of the strengths of Louisa's speech by preparing an evaluation checklist and an analysis. You can then compare your answers with those of the authors.

© Cengage Learning 2013

Adaptation Plan

1. Key aspects of audience. Most people in my audience have probably heard of ethanol as an alternative to fossil fuels but don't know exactly what it is or how it's produced.

2. Establishing and maintaining common ground. I will begin my speech by asking the audience a question. Throughout the speech, I will refer to the audience's previous knowledge and experience.

3. Building and maintaining interest. Because my audience is initially unlikely to be interested in how to produce ethanol, I will have to work hard to interest them and to keep their interest through the speech. I will try to gain interest in the introduction by relating the production of ethanol, the fuel, to the production of "white lightning," the illegal alcohol, which might be of more interest to the average college student. Throughout the speech, I will use common analogies and metaphors to explain the complex chemical processes. Finally, I will use a well-designed PowerPoint presentation to capture attention.

4. Audience knowledge and sophistication. Because most of the class is not familiar with ethanol, I will introduce them to the four-part process of making ethanol. I believe that by relating the process to that of making alcohol that people can drink, my audience will be more likely to be interested in and retain the information.

5. Building credibility. Early in the speech, I will tell the audience about how I got interested in ethanol when I built a still as a science fair project in high school. I will also tell them that I am now a chemical engineering major and am hoping to make a career in the alternative fuel industry.

6. Audience attitudes. My audience is likely to be indifferent to my topic, so I need to capture their attention by using interesting examples. I then need to keep them interested by relating the topic to things they're familiar with.

7. Adapting to audiences from different cultures and language communities. I will use visual and audiovisual aids in my PowerPoint presentation to help those listeners from different cultures understand what I'm talking about even if English is not their native language.

8. Using presentational aids to enhance understanding and memory. Throughout the speech, I will use color-coded PowerPoint slides with headers to reinforce the steps being discussed.

Outline

General goal: To inform

Specific goal: I want my audience to understand the process for making ethanol from corn.

Introduction

I. Did you know that the first Model T cars were originally designed to run on ethanol or that Henry Ford said that ethanol was the fuel of the future? Did you know that in World War II about 75 percent of the German and American military vehicles were powered by ethanol since oil for gasoline was difficult to attain?

II. The process for making ethanol is actually very similar to the process used to make moonshine, which may be why—during the first Arab oil embargo in 1978—when Robert Warren built a still to produce ethanol, he called the product "liquid sunshine" (Warren, 2006). Ethanol is an easy-to-make, inexpensive, and nearly pollution-free renewable alternative to gasoline.

III. I became interested in ethanol in high school when I built a miniature ethanol still as a science fair project. I'm now a chemical engineering major and hope to make a career in the alternative fuel industry.

IV. Today, I'm going to explain the commercial process that turns corn into ethanol. The four steps include, first, preparing the corn by making a mash; second, fermenting the mash by adding yeast to make beer; third, distilling the ethanol from the beer; and fourth, processing the remaining whole stillage to produce co-products such as animal feed (Ethanol Business, 2004). *(Slide 1. Shows the four-step flow process.)*

Body

I. The first step in the commercial process of making ethanol, preparing the mash, has two parts: milling the corn and breaking the starch down into simple sugars (DENCO, n.d.). *(Slide 2. Title: Preparation. Shows corn flowing from a silo into a hammer mill and then into a holding tank where yeast is added.)*

In your saliva, you have enzymes that begin to break the bread and other starches you eat into sugar. In your stomach, you have other enzymes that finish this job of turning starch to simple sugar so your body can use the energy in the food you eat. In the commercial process of making ethanol, a similar transformation takes place.

  A. The corn is emptied into a bin and passes into a hammer mill, where it is ground into coarse flour.

B. After milling, the corn flour, a starch, must be broken down so that it becomes simple sugar by mixing in water and enzymes to form a thick liquid called slurry.

    1. First the water and corn flour are dosed with the enzyme alpha-amylase and heated.

    2. Then the starchy slurry is heated to help the enzyme do its work.

    3. Later gluco-amylase is added to finish the process of turning the starch to simple sugar.

Once this mixture of sugar, water, and residual corn solids is turned into slurry or mash, it is ready to be fermented.   **Transition**

II. The second step of the commercial process for making ethanol is fermenting the slurry or mash by adding yeast (DENCO, n.d.). *(Slide 3. Title: Fermentation. Shows yeast added to the mash in a fermenter and carbon dioxide being released to form beer.)*

This step works in much the same way yeast is used to make bread dough rise. But in bread the carbon dioxide is trapped in the dough and causes it to rise, and the alcohol is burned off when the bread is baked. In making ethanol, carbon dioxide bubbles out of the mash and is released into the air.   **Listener relevance**

A. The mash remains in the fermenters for about fifty hours.

B. As the mash ferments, the sugar is turned into alcohol and carbon dioxide.

C. The carbon dioxide bubbles out into the air.

D. What remains after the carbon dioxide is released is called "beer."

Once the yeast has done its job and the fermentation process is complete, we move on to distillation.   **Transition**

III. The third step of the commercial process for making ethanol is distilling the fermented mash, now called "beer," by passing it through a series of columns where the alcohol is removed from the mash (Tham, 1997–2006). *(Slide 4. Title: Distillation of Ethanol. Animated slide showing beer flowing into distillation tank, heat being applied to the beer, and ethanol vapors being released and captured in a condenser.)*

If you've ever seen moonshine cookers in real life or in the movies, that's basically the same process as what I'm explaining here (DENCO, n.d.).   **Listener relevance**

A. Distillation is the process of boiling a liquid and then condensing the resulting vapor in order to separate out one component of the liquid.

B. In most ethanol production, distillation occurs through the use of cooling columns.

C. Once the ethanol has reached the desired purity or proof, it is denatured to be made undrinkable by adding gasoline to it.

D. The ethanol is ready to be transported from the plant.

Once this step is complete, you've successfully produced ethanol, but we aren't done until we complete step 4.   **Transition**

IV. The fourth step in commercial production is converting the remaining whole stillage into co-products (DENCO, n.d.). *(Slide 5. Title: Co-product. Shows a tank with remaining whole solids flowing into a condenser with output flowing into a bin of animal feed.)*

Listener relevance

Not only is ethanol a renewable resource, but even its byproducts get put to good use!

Conclusion

Thesis restatement with main point summary

I. As you can see, producing ethanol is a simple four-step process: preparing the corn into a slurry or mash, fermenting the slurry into beer, distilling the beer to release the ethanol, and processing the remaining water and corn solids into co-products. *(Slide 6: Same as slide 1.)*

Clincher

II. In 1980, when Robert Warren was operating his still, only 175 million gallons of ethanol were being commercially produced in the United States. Twenty-five years later, 4.85 billion gallons were produced (Renewable Fuels Association, 2007). That's a whopping 2,674 percent increase! And it is a trend that is continuing. With today's skyrocketing gasoline prices and our increasing concerns about preserving our environment, you can see why this simple process of making liquid sunshine is getting more and more popular. I don't know about you, but I'm glad it is!

[1]*From Verderber/Verderber/Sellnow, The Challenge of Effective Speaking, 15E. © 2012 Cengage Learning.*

References

DENCO, LLC. (n.d.) Tour the plant. *Retrieved July 2, 2007, from http://www.dencollc.com/DENCO%20WebSite_files/Tour.htm*

Ethanol Business and Industry Center. (2004, May). Module 2: Ethanol science and technology. *Retrieved July 3, 2007, from http://www.nwicc.com/pages/continuing/business/ethanol/Module2.htm*

Renewable Fuels Association. (2007). Industry statistics: The ethanol industry. *Retrieved July 9, 2007, from http://www.ethanolrfa.org/industry/statistics/*

Tham, M. T. (1997–2006). Distillation: An introduction. *Retrieved July 5, 2007, from http://lorien.ncl.ac.uk/ming/distil/distil0.htm*

Warren, R. (2006, August). Make your own fuel. *Retrieved July 3, 2007, from http://running_on_alcohol.tripod.com/ index.html*

SPEECH AND ANALYSIS

Speech	Analysis

Read the following aloud at least once. Then, analyze it on the basis of the criteria in the checklist on page 401–402.

Did you know that the first Model T's were designed to run on ethanol and that Henry Ford said that ethanol was the fuel of the future? Or that in World War II about 75 percent of the German and American military vehicles were powered by

Louisa begins this speech with rhetorical questions designed to pique the audience's interest. At the time she prepared the speech,

ethanol since oil for gasoline was difficult to obtain? In 1978, during the first Arab oil embargo, when gas soared from 62 cents a gallon to $1.64, Californian Robert Warren and others built stills to produce what he called—no, not "white lightning"—but "liquid sunshine," which we call ethanol.

I became interested in ethanol in high school when I built a miniature ethanol still as a science fair project. I'm now a chemical engineering major and hope to make a career in the alternative fuel industry. So, today, I'm going to explain to you the simple process that takes corn and turns it into liquid sunshine. Specifically, I want you to understand the process that is used to make ethanol from corn.

According to the Ethanol Business and Industry Center at Northwest Iowa Community College, the four steps in the commercial process of making ethanol are, first, preparing the corn by making a mash; second, fermenting the mash by adding yeast to make beer; third, distilling the ethanol from the beer; and fourth, processing the remaining whole stillage to produce co-products like animal feed. *(Slide 1)*

As this slide taken from the DENCO, LCC, "Tour the Plant" Web site depicts, the first step in the commercial process of making ethanol, preparing the mash, has two parts: milling the corn and breaking the starch down into simple sugars. *(Slide 2)*

The corn, which has been tested for quality and stored in a silo, is emptied into a bin and passes into a hammer mill, where it is ground into coarse flour. This is done to expose more of the corn's starchy material so that these starches can be more easily broken down into sugar.

In your saliva, you have enzymes that begin to break the bread and other starches you eat into sugar. In your stomach, you have other enzymes that finish this job of turning starch to simple sugar so your body can use the energy in the food you eat. In the commercial production of ethanol, a similar transformation takes place.

To break the milled corn flour starch into sugar, the milled flour is mixed with water and alpha-amylase, the same enzyme that you have in your saliva, and is heated. The alpha-amylase acts as Pacman and takes bites out of the long sugar chains that are bound together in the starch. What results are broken bits of starch that need further processing to become glucose. So later, gluco-amylase, which is like the enzyme in your stomach, is added, and these new Pacmen bite the starchy bits into simple glucose sugar molecules. Now this mixture of sugar, water, and residual corn solids, called slurry or mash, is ready to be fermented.

The second step in the commercial production of ethanol is to ferment the mash by adding yeast in an environment that has no oxygen and allowing the mixture to "rest" while the yeast "works." *(Slide 3)* This is accomplished by piping the slurry into an oxygen-free tank called a fermenter,

gasoline prices were again soaring, so these questions—coupled with the example of Warren's solution—provide a provocative introduction to her topic.

At this point, Louisa personalizes the topic with a self-disclosure that also establishes her credibility.

One thing Louisa could do better throughout the speech is to offer listener relevance links that more directly remind the audience of the speech's relevance to them whenever possible.

Notice how Louisa has nested two steps, milling and breaking starch into sugars, under the more general heading of "Preparation." This grouping keeps the main points at a manageable number and will help her audience remember the steps. Her second slide is simple but effective because it reinforces the two substeps.

Louisa helps the audience understand the unfamiliar starch-to-sugar conversion by comparing it to the familiar process of digestion.

The Pacman analogy also helps the audience visualize what occurs during the starch-to-sugar conversion.

The last sentence, mentioning slurry, is an excellent transition between the two main points.

Louisa helps the audience stay with her by using the signpost "second step." Her third slide, a visual of

adding the yeast, and allowing the mixture to sit for about fifty hours. Without oxygen, the yeast feeds on the sugar and gives off ethanol and carbon dioxide as waste products. Eventually, deprived of oxygen, the yeast dies.

This is similar to what happens when we add yeast to bread dough. But in bread the carbon dioxide is trapped in the dough and causes it to rise, while the alcohol is burned off when the bread is baked.

In ethanol production, the carbon dioxide is not trapped in the watery slurry. Because it is a gas, it bubbles out of the mixture and is captured and released into the outside air. The ethanol, however, remains in the mixture, which is now called "beer," with the water and the nonfermentable corn solids. At the end of the fermentation process, it is the ethanol in the mixture that retains much of the energy of the original sugar. At this point, we are now ready to separate or distill the ethanol from the other parts of the beer.

The third step in the commercial production of ethanol is distillation, which, according to M. T. Tham's book *Distillation: An Introduction*, is the process of purifying a liquid by heating it and then condensing its vapor. So, for example, if you boiled your tap water and condensed the steam that was produced, you would have purified water with no minerals or other impurities. But distilling ethanol is a bit more complicated since both the ethanol and the water in the beer are liquids and can be vaporized into steam by adding heat.

Luckily, different liquids boil at different temperatures, and since ethanol boils at 173°F while water boils at 212°F, we can use this boiling point difference to separate the two. So to simplify what is really a more complex process, *(Slide 4)* in the commercial distillation of ethanol, a column or series of columns are used to boil off the ethanol and the water and then to separate these vapors so that the ethanol vapors are captured and condensed back into pure liquid ethanol. The liquid ethanol is then tested to make sure that it meets the specifications for purity and proof. At this point, ethanol is drinkable alcohol and would be subject to a $20 per gallon federal excise tax. To avoid this, it is "denatured"—made undrinkable by adding gasoline to it. After this, the ethanol is ready to be transported from the plant.

The fourth step in the commercial production process is converting the whole stillage into co-products. *(Slide 5)* One of the greatest things about producing ethanol is that the water and nonfermentable corn solids that are left after the ethanol is distilled aren't just thrown out as waste. Instead, the remaining water and nonfermentable corn solids can also be processed to make co-products that are primarily used as animal feed.

So as you have seen, the process of making ethanol is really quite simple. *(Slide 6)* One, prepare the corn by milling and breaking its starch into sugar. Two, ferment the mash

the "fermentation equation," nicely simplifies the complex chemistry that underlies fermentation.

Here she uses an effective transition statement to signal to her audience that she will be moving to the third step.

Her fourth slide is much more elaborate than the others. The animation in the slide helps the audience visualize how distillation works. It would have been more effective had she been able to control the motion so that each stage was animated as she talked about it.

The last sentence serves as an internal conclusion to the third step.

The slide for the fourth main point is so simple that it really isn't needed to aid audience understanding, but it is a visual reinforcement of this step, and the audience has been conditioned to expect one slide per point, so it would seem odd if there were not a slide for this step.

Louisa begins the conclusion with a summary of her main points. The sixth slide, a repetition of the first slide, visually "closes the loop" and reinforces the four steps.

The conclusion includes a circular reference back to Robert Warren who was introduced at the beginning of the speech. In the conclusion, she uses statistics to drive

using yeast. Three, distill off the ethanol from the beer, and four, process the co-products.

In 1980, when Robert Warren was operating his still, only 175 million gallons of ethanol were being commercially produced in the United States. Twenty-five years later, according to the Renewable Fuels Association, 4.85 billion gallons were produced. That's a whopping 2,674 percent increase! And it is a trend that is continuing. With today's skyrocketing gasoline prices and our increasing concerns about preserving our environment, you can see why this simple process of making liquid sunshine is getting more and more popular. I don't know about you, but I'm glad it is!

home the point that ethanol is an important fuel source and that in the near future ethanol may be a fuel used by members of the audience.

Louisa could have offered a better clincher by tying her final sentence back to her introductory comments about Henry Ford. For example, she might have said, "Almost a century later, it seems that what Henry Ford said will be coming true. Look for a green-handled pump coming soon to a gas station near you."

WHAT WOULD YOU DO?

A Question of Ethics

After class, as Gina and Paul were discussing what they intended to talk about in their process speeches, Paul said, "I think I'm going to talk about how to make a synthetic diamond."

Gina was impressed. "That sounds interesting. I didn't know you had expertise with that."

"I don't. But the way I see it, Professor Henderson will really be impressed with my speech because my topic will be so novel."

"Well, yeah," Gina replied, "but didn't he stress that for this speech we should choose a topic that was important to us and that we knew a lot about?"

"Sure," Paul said sarcastically, "he's going to be impressed if I talk about how to maintain a blog? Forget it. Just watch—everyone's going to think I make diamonds in my basement, and I'm going to get a good grade."

1. Is Paul's plan ethical? Why or why not?

2. What should Gina say to challenge Paul's last statement?

Summary

An informative speech is one whose goal is to explain or describe facts, truths, and principles in a way that stimulates interest, facilitates understanding, and increases the likelihood that audiences will remember. In short, informative speeches are designed to educate.

Effective informative speeches are intellectually stimulating, relevant, creative, memorable, and address diverse learning styles. Informative speeches will be perceived as intellectually stimulating when the information is new and when it is explained in a way that excites interest. We can inform by describing something, defining it, comparing and contrasting it with other things, narrating a story about it, or demonstrating it.

Two common patterns for informative speeches are process speeches, in which the steps of something are shown, and expository speeches, which are well-researched explanations of complex ideas. Expository speeches can explain political, economic, social, religious, or ethical issues; events or forces of history; a theory, principle, or law; or a creative work.

COMMUNICATE!

RESOURCE AND ASSESSMENT CENTER

Now that you have read Chapter 16, go to the Speech Communication CourseMate at cengagebrain.com where you'll find an interactive eBook and interactive learning tools including quizzes, flashcards, sample speech videos, audio study tools, skill-building activities, action step activities, and more. Student Workbook, Speech Builder Express 3.0, and Speech Studio 2.0 are also available.

Applying What You've Learned

Impromptu Speech Activity

1. Pick three slips of paper from a container offered by your instructor. Each slip will identify a historical event or historical figure on it. Select one event you'd like to experience or one figure you'd like to meet if you could travel back in time. Do a 2- to 3-minute impromptu speech about why you'd like to experience that historical event or meet that historical figure if you could travel back in time.

Assessment Activities

1. Evaluating Demonstrations Watch an informative speech involving a demonstration, and evaluate how effectively the speaker performs the demonstration. (Do-it-yourself and home improvement TV programs, like those on the cable channels DIY and HGTV, often feature demonstrations as do programs on the Food Network.) Did the speaker perform a complete or modified demonstration? Did the speaker use only the tools and equipment needed to perform the demonstrated task, or did he or she also use other items, such as visual aids? How effective was the demonstration overall? Were there any areas of the demonstration the speaker could have improved?

2. Evaluating Demonstrations Identify a contemporary celebrity (e.g., television or movie actor, sports star, or musician). Learn more about that person by visiting his or her personal Web site or blog, a social networking site devoted to him or her, and an entertainment magazine. How does the information differ in each source? Why might he or she be an appropriate person to do an expository speech on (or not)? How trustworthy do you think the information you have discovered is and why? What might you do to verify the truth of your information and credibility of your sources?

Skill-Building Activity

1. Creating Through Productive Thinking Use the data in the following table to practice productive thinking. Create a list of all of the speech ideas suggested by these data.

Total tuition, room and board rates charged for full-time undergraduate students in degree-granting institutions, by type and control of institution: Selected years, 1980–81 to 2009–10

Year and control of institution	Constant 2008–09 dollars[1]			Current dollars		
	All institutions	Four-year institutions	Two-year institutions	All institutions	Four-year institutions	Two-year institutions
All institutions						
1980–81	$7,685	$8,672	$5,526	$3,101	$3,499	$2,230
1990–91	10,518	12,185	6,300	6,562	7,602	3,930
2000–01	13,263	15,843	6,693	10,818	12,922	5,460

Year and control of institution	Constant 2008–09 dollars[1]			Current dollars		
	All institutions	Four-year institutions	Two-year institutions	All institutions	Four-year institutions	Two-year institutions
2001–02	13,709	16,430	6,888	11,380	13,639	5,718
2002–03	14,161	17,020	7,370	12,014	14,439	6,252
2003–04	14,942	17,855	7,734	12,953	15,505	6,705
2004–05	15,444	18,487	7,935	13,792	16,509	7,086
2005–06	15,780	18,820	7,800	14,629	17,447	7,231
2006–07	16,281	19,423	7,850	15,483	18,471	7,466
2007–08	16,385	19,592	7,744	16,159	19,323	7,637
2008–09	17,012	20,385	8,238	17,012	20,385	8,238
2009–10	17,464	20,986	8,451	17,633	21,189	8,533
Public institutions						
1980–81	$5,881	$6,320	$5,023	$2,373	$2,550	$2,027
1990–91	7,625	8,403	5,558	4,757	5,243	3,467
2000–01	9,300	10,609	5,933	7,586	8,653	4,839
2001–02	9,633	11,078	6,189	8,022	9,196	5,137
2002–03	10,021	11,537	6,603	8,502	9,787	5,601
2003–04	10,666	12,312	6,935	9,247	10,674	6,012
2004–05	11,046	12,795	7,139	9,864	11,426	6,375
2005–06	11,277	13,062	7,003	10,454	12,108	6,492
2006–07	11,618	13,457	7,166	11,049	12,797	6,815
2007–08	11,735	13,616	7,073	11,573	13,429	6,975
2008–09	12,256	14,262	7,568	12,256	14,262	7,568
2009–10	12,681	14,870	7,629	12,804	15,014	7,703
Private institutions						
1980–81	$13,555	$13,861	$10,663	$5,470	$5,594	$4,303
1990–91	20,693	21,218	14,911	12,910	13,237	9,302
2000–01	26,197	26,795	18,130	21,368	21,856	14,788
2001–02	27,000	27,581	19,064	22,413	22,896	15,825
2002–03	27,512	28,039	20,926	23,340	23,787	17,753
2003–04	28,404	28,918	22,560	24,624	25,069	19,558
2004–05	28,903	29,403	22,500	25,810	26,257	20,093
2005–06	29,006	29,467	22,836	26,889	27,317	21,170
2006–07	29,905	30,409	21,329	28,439	28,919	20,284
2007–08	30,680	31,207	21,988	30,258	30,778	21,685
2008–09	31,532	32,090	22,726	31,532	32,090	22,726
2009–10	31,876	32,475	24,248	32,184	32,790	24,483

[1]Constant dollars based on the Consumer Price Index, prepared by the Bureau of Labor Statistics, U.S. Department of Labor, adjusted to a school-year basis.

NOTE: Data are for the entire academic year and are average total charges for full-time attendance. Room and board were based on full-time students. Data through 1995–96 are for institutions of higher education, while later data are for degree-granting institutions. Degree-granting institutions grant associate's or higher degrees and participate in Title IV federal financial aid programs. The degree-granting classification is very similar to the earlier higher education classification, but it includes more two-year colleges and excludes a few higher education institutions that did not grant degrees.

SOURCE: U.S. Department of Education, National Center for Education Statistics. (2011). *Digest of Education Statistics, 2010* (NCES 2011-015)

Retrieved on May 6, 2012 from: http://nces.ed.gov/fastfacts/display.asp?id=76

Persuasive Speaking

What you'll know

- How people listen to and evaluate persuasive messages

- Three types of persuasive speaking goals or propositions

- How the target audience's initial attitude toward your topic affects your proposition

- Several common fallacies to avoid when developing arguments

What you'll be able to do

- Incorporate logos, pathos, and ethos effectively in your persuasive speeches

- Organize your persuasive speeches using an appropriate pattern

- Evaluate persuasive messages from others

Rick lives in an apartment downtown and enjoys taking his golden retriever, Trini, for walks twice a day. He wishes there was a place nearby where he could let Trini off her leash to run. He decided to try to convince the city council to fence off an area within a large inner-city park for a dog park where owners can let their dogs run free. He learned he needed to circulate a petition about the idea, get at least 500 others to sign it, and collect $1000 in donations to help pay for the fence. Rick easily gathered more than enough signatures in a few weeks of knocking on doors, but raised less than half of the $1000. He wonders what he can do to convince more people to actually donate money for the cause.

PART 17

This scenario is not unusual. Whether we are attempting to influence others or others are attempting to influence us, we are constantly involved in persuasion. For example, friends might convince us to see a particular movie or to eat at a certain restaurant. We are bombarded with advertisements to buy different products whenever we turn on the radio or television or surf the Internet. **Persuasion** is the word we use to label this process of influencing people's attitudes, beliefs, values, or behaviors. **Persuasive speaking** is the process of doing so in a public speech.

In this chapter, we begin by describing the nature of persuasive messages and how people process them. Then, we explain how to form an effective persuasive speech goal and develop it with logos, ethos, and pathos. Finally, we discuss several persuasive speech patterns you can use to organize your speech.

The Nature of Persuasion

Persuasive messages are fundamentally different from informative ones. Whereas the goal of an informative message is to teach, the goal of a persuasive message is to lead. So persuasive speakers are only successful when their audience members are convinced to agree, change their behavior, or take action. Persuasive speaking can actually be traced to its roots in ancient Greece, where men used it to debate public issues and make important decisions. Thinkers like Aristotle and Plato used the word **rhetoric** to mean using any and all "available means of persuasion" in public speeches (Solmsen, 1954, p. 24). Persuasive speakers do so by developing solid arguments. An argument, in this context, is not synonymous with "quarrel" as we sometimes define it today. Rather, **argument** means articulating a position with the support of logos, ethos, and pathos (Perloff, 2010). **Logos** is a persuasive strategy of constructing logical arguments that support your position. **Ethos** is a persuasive strategy of highlighting your competence, credibility, and good character as a means to convince others to support your position (Kennedy, 1980). And **pathos** is a persuasive strategy of appealing to emotions in order to convince others to support your position.

Now that we have a basic understanding of the nature of persuasion, let's look more closely at how people think about the persuasive messages they receive.

Processing Persuasive Messages

Do you remember times when you listened carefully and thoughtfully about something someone was trying to convince you to agree with before making a deliberate decision? Do you remember other times when you only half-listened and made up your mind quickly based on your gut feeling? What determines how closely we listen to and how carefully we evaluate the hundreds of persuasive messages we hear each day? Richard Petty and John Cacioppo (1996) developed the Elaboration Likelihood Model (ELM) to explain how likely people are to spend more or less time critically evaluating information before making their decisions.

This dual processing model that we introduced in Chapter 2 suggests that people process information in one of two ways. Sometimes we use the "central route" in which we listen carefully, reflect thoughtfully, and maybe even mentally elaborate on the message before making a decision. In doing so, we base our decision primarily on appeals to logic and reasoning (logos). The second way, called the "peripheral route," is a shortcut that relies on simple cues, such as a quick evaluation of the speaker's competence, credibility, and character (ethos), or a gut check about what we feel (pathos) about the message.

persuasion
the process of influencing people's attitudes, beliefs, values, or behaviors

persuasive speech
a speech attempting to influence the attitudes, values, beliefs, or behavior of others

rhetoric
use of all available means of persuasion

argument
articulating a position with the support of logos, ethos, and pathos

logos
a persuasive strategy of constructing logical arguments supported with evidence and reasoning

ethos
a persuasive strategy of highlighting competence, credibility, and good character

pathos
a persuasive strategy of appealing to emotions

We choose a route based on how important we perceive the issue to be for us. When we believe the issue is important, we will expend the energy necessary to process it using the central route. When we don't, we take the peripheral route. For example, if you have a serious chronic illness that is expensive to treat, you are more likely to pay attention to and evaluate carefully any proposals to change health care benefits. If you are healthy, you are more likely to quickly agree with suggestions from someone you perceive to be credible or with a proposal that seems compassionate. The ELM also suggests that when we form attitudes as a result of central processing, we are less likely to change our minds than when we base our decisions on peripheral cues.

Scott Olson/Getty Images

Imagine you are a speaker whose goal is to convince your audience that U.S. armed forces should pull out of Afghanistan. What type of audience do you suppose this would be, and why?

When you prepare a persuasive speech, you will want to use strategies that address both the central and peripheral routes. You can address the central route by using rhetorical strategies that appeal to logos (logic and reasoning). And you can address the peripheral route by using rhetorical strategies that appeal to both ethos (competence, credibility, and good character) and pathos (emotions). Before doing so, however, you need to form your speech goal as a proposition.

Persuasive Speech Goals

Persuasive speech goals are stated as propositions. A **proposition** is a declarative sentence that clearly indicates the position you advocate. For example, "I want to convince my audience that pirating copyrighted media (downloading music and movies without paying for it) is wrong." Notice how a persuasive proposition differs from an information speech goal on the same subject: "I want to inform my audience about the practice of pirating copyrighted media." In the informative speech, you will achieve your goal if the audience understands and remembers what you talk about. In the persuasive speech, however, they must not only understand and remember, but also agree with your position and possibly even take action. The three types of propositions are fact, value, and policy.

CONSIDER THIS....

Think of a time when you were persuaded because somebody seemed "really smart." How much do you recall about the actual evidence and reasoning they offered?

proposition

a declarative sentence that clearly indicates the speaker's position on the topic

Types of Propositions

A **proposition of fact** is a statement designed to convince your audience that something: (1) did, probably did, probably did not, or did not exist or occur; (2) is, probably is, probably is not, or is not true; or (3) will, probably will, probably will not, or will not occur. Although propositions of fact may or may not be true—both positions are arguable—they are stated as though they are, in fact, true. For example, whether or not Princess Diana's death was an unfortunate car accident or an assassination is debatable. So you could argue a proposition of fact in two ways: "Princess Diana's death was nothing more than a tragic car accident" or "Princess Diana's death was, in fact, a successful assassination attempt." Examples of propositions of fact concerning the present include "God exists" or "There is no God"; and "Mobile phone use causes brain cancer" or "Mobile phone use does not cause brain cancer." Propositions of fact concerning the future are predictions. For example, "Thanks to the Internet, iPads, and Kindles, paperbound books will eventually cease to exist," and "The New York Yankees will surely win the World Series next year" are propositions of fact concerning the future.

A **proposition of value** is a statement designed to convince your audience that something is good, bad, desirable, undesirable, fair, unfair, moral, immoral, sound, unsound, beneficial, harmful, important, or unimportant (Hill &

proposition of fact

a statement designed to convince the audience that something did or did not occur, is or is not true, or will or will not occur

proposition of value

a statement designed to convince the audience that something is good, fair, moral, sound, etc., or its opposite

Propositions of fact	Propositions of value	Propositions of policy
Mahatma Gandhi was the father of passive resistance	Mahatma Gandhi was a moral leader.	Mahatma Gandhi should be given a special award for his views on and practices of passive resistance.
Pharmaceutical advertising to consumers increases prescription drug prices.	Advertising of new prescription drugs on TV is better than marketing new drugs directly to doctors.	Pharmaceutical companies should be prohibited from advertising prescription drugs on TV.
Using paper ballots is a reliable method for voting in U.S. elections.	Paper ballots are better than electronic voting machines.	Using paper ballots should be required for U.S. elections.

© Cengage Learning

Figure 17.1

Examples of persuasive speech propositions

Leeman, 1997). You can attempt to convince your audience that something has more value than something else, or you can attempt to convince them that something meets valued standards. "Running is a better form of exercise than bicycling" is an example of the former, and "The real value of a college education is that it creates an informed citizenry" is an example of the latter.

A **proposition of policy** is a statement designed to convince your audience that a particular rule, plan, or course of action should be taken. Propositions of policy implore listeners using phrases such as *do it/don't do it, should/shouldn't,* and *must/must not.* "All college students should be required to take an oral communication skills course in order to graduate," "The U.S. must stop deep-sea oil drilling," and "We must not text while driving" are propositions of policy. Figure 17.1 provides several examples of how propositions of fact, value, and policy can be developed from the same topic idea.

proposition of policy

a statement designed to convince the audience that a specific course of action should be taken

Tailoring Propositions to Your Target Audience

Because it is very difficult to convince people to change their minds, what you can hope to accomplish in one speech depends on where your audience stands on your topic. So you'll want to analyze your audience and tailor your proposition based on their initial attitude toward the topic. An **attitude** is "a general or enduring positive or negative feeling about some person, object or issue" (Petty & Cacioppo, 1996, p. 7).

attitude

general or enduring positive or negative feeling about some person, object, or issue

Audience members' attitudes can range from highly favorable to strongly opposed and can be visualized on a continuum like the one in Figure 17.2. Even though your audience will include individuals with opinions at nearly every point along the continuum, generally audience members' opinions tend to cluster in one area of it. For instance, most of the audience members represented in Figure 17.2 are "mildly opposed," even though a few people are more highly opposed and a few have favorable opinions. This cluster point represents your **target audience,**

target audience

the group of people a speaker most wants to persuade

Figure 17.2

Sample speech continuum

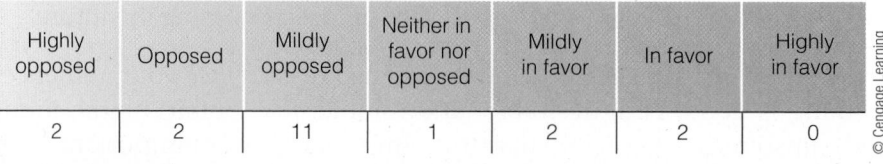

Highly opposed	Opposed	Mildly opposed	Neither in favor nor opposed	Mildly in favor	In favor	Highly in favor
2	2	11	1	2	2	0

© Cengage Learning

the group of people you most want to persuade. Based on your target audience, you can classify your audience's initial attitude toward your topic as "in favor" (already supportive), "no opinion" (uninformed, neutral, or apathetic), or "opposed" (against a particular belief).

Opposed It is unrealistic to believe that you will change your target audience's attitude from "opposed" to "in favor" in only one short speech. Instead, seek **incremental change**, that is, attempt to move them only a small degree in your direction, hoping for additional movement later. For example, if your target audience is opposed to the goal "I want to convince my audience that gay marriage should be legalized," you might rephrase it to "I want to convince my audience that committed gay couples should be afforded the same legal protection as committed heterosexual couples through state-recognized civil unions." Then brainstorm potential objections, questions, and criticisms that might arise and shape your speech to address them.

When trying to convince people to give money to a cause, is it more challenging when your audience is apathetic, or when they are neutral?

incremental change
attempt to move audience only a small degree in the speaker's direction

No Opinion If your target audience has no opinion for or against your topic, you should consider whether they are uninformed, neutral, or apathetic about your topic. If they are **uninformed**, that is, they do not know enough about a topic to have formed an opinion, you will need to provide the basic arguments and information needed for them to become informed. For example, if your target audience is uninformed about the topic of gay marriage, you might need to begin by highlighting the legal benefits of marriage in general. If your target audience is **neutral**, that is, they know the basics about your topic but not enough to have formed an opinion, you will want to provide evidence and reasoning illustrating why your position is superior to others. Perhaps your audience knows the legal benefits of marriage in general but needs to understand how committed gay couples who do not have these benefits are disadvantaged. When target audience members have no opinion because they are **apathetic**, you will need to find ways to show how it relates to them or their needs. In other words, you need to provide answers to a question such as, "I'm not gay, so why should I care?" You can do this by including strong listener relevance links for each main point in your speech.

uninformed
not knowing enough about a topic to have formed an opinion

neutral
knowing the basics about a topic but still having no opinion about it

apathetic
having no opinion because one is uninterested, unconcerned, or indifferent to a topic

In Favor If your target audience is only mildly in favor of your proposal, your task is to reinforce and strengthen their beliefs. Audience members who favor your topic may become further committed to the belief by hearing new reasons and more recent evidence that support it. When your target audience strongly agrees with your position, then you can consider a proposition that moves them to act on it. For example, if the topic is gay marriage and your target audience is in favor of the idea, then your goal may be "I want my audience members to e-mail or write letters to their state representatives urging them to support legislation extending the right to marry to gay couples."

THE AUDIENCE *BEYOND*

Jeff knew his classmates agreed that course fees for college classes are way too high. He wanted to get them to join his campaign to lobby the state legislature, the university's Board of Trustees, and the campus president, so he created a *Facebook* campaign page, which he updated daily with information about where and when to join him.

Viktor1/Shutterstock

Logos is making an argument by drawing inferences from factual information to support your conclusion.

claim

the conclusion the speaker wants the audience to agree with

support

evidence offered as grounds to accept the claim

warrant

reasoning process that connects the support to the claim

inductive reasoning

arriving at a general conclusion based on several pieces of evidence

deductive reasoning

arguing that if something is true for everything in a certain class, then it is true for a given item in that class

Once you have identified your topic and tailored your proposition to your target audience, you are ready to develop content that addresses both the central and peripheral persuasive processing routes. You do so by using rhetorical strategies appealing to logos, ethos, and pathos.

Rhetorical Appeals to Logos

Audience members who process on the central route will evaluate the logic and reasoning of your arguments. Stephen Toulmin (1958) developed a model to explain the form of everyday arguments that has stood the test of time. His model has three major elements: the claim, the support, and the warrant.

The **claim** is the conclusion the speaker wants the audience to agree with. For example, you might *claim:* "Jim's car needs a tune-up." The **support** is the evidence offered as grounds for accepting the claim. You can support a claim with facts, opinions, experiences, and observations. In our car example, we might support our claim with observations that the engine is "missing at slow speeds" and "stalling at stoplights." The **warrant** is the reasoning process that connects the support to the claim. Sometimes, the warrant is verbalized and sometimes it is implied. For instance, if you claim that "the car needs a tune-up" on the basis of "missing" and "stalling at stoplights," you might also say "Missing at slow speeds and stalling at lights *are common indications* that a car needs a tune-up." Or you might assume that others see these as signs that a car needs a tune-up.

Using C for claim (conclusion) S for support (reasons and evidence), and W for warrant (explanation of the reasoning process), we can write the reasoning for the proposition in our example in outline form as follows:

C I want Jim to believe that the car needs a tune-up.

S I. The engine misses at slow speeds.

S II. The car stalls at stoplights.

W (I believe this reasoning is sound because missing and stalling are *major indicators—signs—*of the need for a tune-up.) (The warrant is written in parentheses because it may not be verbalized when the speech is given.)

You can use inductive or deductive reasoning in your warrant. **Inductive reasoning** is arriving at a general conclusion based on several pieces of specific evidence. When we reason inductively, how much our audience agrees with our conclusion depends on the number, quality, and typicality of each piece of evidence you offer. For Jim's car, an inductive argument might look like this:

Evidence: Jim's car is missing at slow speeds.

Evidence: Jim's car is stalling at stoplights.

Logical Conclusion: Jim's car needs a tune-up.

Deductive reasoning is arguing that if something is true for everything that belongs to a certain class (major premise) and a specific instance is part of that class (minor premise), then we must conclude that what is true for all members of the class must be true in the specific instance (logical conclusion). This three-part form of deductive reasoning is called a **syllogism**. For Jim's car, a syllogism might look like this:

> Major Premise: Cars need a tune-up when the engine misses consistently at slow speeds.
>
> Minor Premise: Jim's car is missing at slow speeds.
>
> Conclusion: Jim's car needs a tune-up.

With this introduction in mind, let's look at some different types of logical arguments.

Types of Logical Arguments

Although a logical argument *always* includes a claim and support, different types of warrants can be used to illustrate the relationship between the claim and the support on which it is based. Four common types of logical arguments are sign, example, analogy, and causation.

Arguing from Sign If certain events, characteristics, or situations usually or always accompany something, those events, characteristics, or situations are signs. You **argue from sign** when you support a claim by providing evidence that the events that signal the claim have occurred.

The general warrant for reasoning from sign can be stated as follows: When phenomena that usually or always accompany a specific situation occur, then we can expect that specific situation is occurring (or will occur). For example: "Hives and a slight fever are indicators (signs) of an allergic reaction."

Signs should not be confused with causes; signs accompany a phenomenon but do not bring about, lead to, or create the claim. In fact, signs may actually be the effects of the phenomenon. In the allergy example, a rash and fever don't *cause* an allergic reaction; they are indications, or effects, of a reaction.

When arguing from sign, you can make sure that your argument is valid by answering the following questions.

1. Do the signs cited always or usually indicate the conclusion drawn?
2. Are a sufficient number of signs present?
3. Are contradictory signs in evidence?

If your answer to the first two questions is "no" or your answer to the third is "yes," then your reasoning is not sound.

Arguing from Example You **argue from example** when the evidence you use as support are examples of the claim you are making. For almost any topic, it is easy to find examples. So you are likely to use arguing from example quite frequently. The warrant for an argument from example—its underlying logic—is, "What is true in the examples provided is (or will be) true in general or in other instances."

Suppose you are supporting Juanita Martinez for president of the local neighborhood council. One of the reasons you suggest is the claim that "Juanita is electable." In examining her résumé to find support for this claim, you find several examples of her previous victories. She was elected treasurer of her high school junior class, chairperson of her church youth group, and president of her college sorority. Each of these is an example that gives support

---

syllogism

the three-part form of deductive reasoning

arguing from sign

supports a claim by citing information that signals the claim

arguing from example

supports a claim by providing one or more individual examples

to the claim. What would the warrant statement for this argument look like? "What was true in several instances (Juanita has been elected in three previous races) is true or will be true in general or in other instances (she will be electable in this situation)."

When arguing from example, you can make sure your argument is valid by answering the following questions.

1. Are enough instances or examples cited so that listeners understand they are not isolated or handpicked examples?

2. Are the examples typical and representative?

3. Are negative examples really atypical?

If the answer to any of these questions is "no," then your reasoning is not sound.

arguing from analogy

supports a claim with a single comparable example that is significantly similar to the subject of the claim

Arguing from Analogy You **argue from analogy** when you support a claim with a single comparable example that is so significantly similar to the subject of the claim as to be strong proof. The general statement of a warrant for an argument from analogy is, "What is true for situation A will also be true in situation B, which is similar to situation A" or "What is true for situation A will be true in all similar situations."

Suppose you wanted to argue that the Cherry Fork Volunteer Fire Department should conduct a raffle to raise money for three portable defibrillator units (claim). You could support the claim with an analogy to a single comparable example like this: The Jefferson City Fire Department, which is very similar to that of Cherry Fork, conducted a raffle and raised enough money to purchase four units.

When arguing from analogy, you can make sure that your argument is valid by answering the following questions.

1. Are the subjects being compared similar in every important way? If they are not, then your reasoning is not sound.

2. Are any of the ways in which the subjects are dissimilar important to the conclusion? If so, then your reasoning is not sound.

arguing from causation

supports a claim by citing evidence that shows one or more events always or almost always brings about, leads to, creates, or prevents another event or effect

Arguing from Causation You **argue from causation** when you support a claim by citing events that have occurred that result in the claim. Reasoning from causation says that one or more of the events cited always (or almost always) brings about, leads to, or creates or prevents a predictable effect or set of effects.

The general warrant for arguments from cause can be stated as follows: If an event comes before another event and is associated with that event, then we can say that it is the cause of the event. "If A, which is known to bring about B, has been observed, then we can expect B to occur." Let's return to Juanita's election campaign for an example.

In researching Juanita's election campaign, you might discover that (1) she has campaigned intelligently and (2) she has won the endorsement of key community leaders. If these two events are usually associated with victory, then you can form the argument that Juanita has engaged in key behaviors that lead to campaign victories. So your causal argument supports your claim that she is electable.

When arguing from causation, you can make sure that your argument is valid by answering the following questions.

1. Are the events alone sufficient to cause the stated effect?

2. Do other events accompanying the cited events actually cause the effect?

3. Is the relationship between the causal events and the effect consistent?

If the answer to any of these questions is "no," then your reasoning is not sound.

Michael Siluk/The Image Works

CSIL1603000 St. Paul, Minnesota. Anti-smoking billboard: reads "smoking can cause impotence in young men" June 2000 ©Michael Siluk / The Image Works   NOTE: The copyright notice must include "The Image Works" DO NOT SHORTEN THE NAME OF THE COMPANY

How would you evaluate the causal claim made on this billboard?

Reasoning Fallacies

As you develop your arguments, you will want to be sure to avoid **fallacies**, or errors in reasoning. Five common fallacies are hasty generalization, false cause, either/or, straw man, and ad hominem arguments.

1. A **hasty generalization** occurs when a claim is either not supported with evidence or is supported with only one weak example. Because the supporting material that is cited should represent all the supporting material that could be cited, enough supporting material must be presented to satisfy the audience that the instances are not isolated or handpicked. For example, someone who argued, "All Akitas are vicious dogs," whose sole piece of evidence was, "My neighbor had an Akita and it bit my best friend's sister," would be guilty of a hasty generalization. It is hasty to generalize about the temperament of a whole breed of dogs based on a single action of one dog.

2. A **false cause** occurs when the alleged cause fails to be related to, or to produce, the effect. The Latin term for this fallacy is *post hoc, ergo propter hoc*, meaning "after this, therefore because of this." Just because two things happen one after the other does not mean that the first necessarily caused the second. Unlike people who blame monetary setbacks and illness on black cats or broken mirrors, be careful that you don't present a coincidental event as a cause unless you can prove the causal relationship. An example of a false cause fallacy is when a speaker claims that school violence is caused only by television violence, the Internet, a certain song or musical group, or lack of parental involvement. When one event follows another, there may be no connection at all, or the first event might be just one of many causes that contribute to the second.

3. An **either/or** fallacy occurs by suggesting there are only two alternatives when, in fact, others exist. Many such cases are an oversimplification of a complex issue. For example, when Robert argued that "we'll either have to raise taxes or close the library," he committed an either/or fallacy. He reduced a complex issue to one oversimplified solution when there were many other possible solutions.

fallacies

flawed reasoning

hasty generalization

a fallacy that presents a generalization that is either not supported with evidence or is supported with only one weak example

false cause

a fallacy that occurs when the alleged cause fails to be related to, or to produce, the effect

either/or

a fallacy that occurs when a speaker supports a claim by suggesting there are only two alternatives when, in fact, others exist

THE AUDIENCE *BEYOND*

Josh knew a lot of classmates who used or abused drugs like marijuana, Adderall, and anabolic steroids. To make sure he didn't make a hasty generalization that a growing percentage of young adults are doing so throughout the United States, he did an online search for statistics from credible sources such as the National Institute on Drug Abuse (NIDA), National Institute of Health (NIH), and the U.S. Department of Health and Human Services.

This ad suggests that, if you like the Kardashians, you should also like Shape-Ups.

straw man

a fallacy that occurs when a speaker weakens the opposing position by misrepresenting it in some way and then attacks that weaker (straw person) position

ad hominem

a fallacy that occurs when one attacks the person making the argument, rather than the argument itself

4. A **straw man** fallacy occurs when a speaker weakens the opposing position by misrepresenting it in some way and then attacks that weaker (straw man) position. For example, in her speech advocating a seven-day waiting period to purchase handguns, Colleen favored regulation, not prohibition, of gun ownership. Bob argued against that by claiming "It is our constitutional right to bear arms." However, Colleen did not advocate abolishing the right to bear arms. Hence, Bob distorted Colleen's position, making it easier for him to refute.

5. An **ad hominem** fallacy attacks or praises the person making the argument rather than addressing the argument itself. *Ad hominem* literally means "to the man." For example, if Jamal's support for his claim that his audience should buy an Apple computer is that Steve Jobs, the founder and former president of Apple Computer, was a genius, he is making an ad hominem argument. Jobs's intelligence isn't really a reason to buy a particular brand of computer. Unfortunately, politicians sometimes resort to ad hominem arguments when they attack their opponent's character rather than their platforms while campaigning for office. Bullying in person, over the Internet, and via text messaging is another example of ad hominem attacks that can have dire consequences. TV commercials that feature celebrities using a particular product are often guilty of ad hominem reasoning. For example, Robert De Niro and Jerry Seinfeld have both appeared in American Express commercials, and Gwyneth Paltrow has done ads for Estée Lauder. What makes any of these celebrities experts about the products they are endorsing?

Have you ever watched an infomercial and been convinced to purchase the product? If so, did the product live up to your expectations? Probably not. Infomercials attempt to develop arguments that convince consumers to buy their products. Although these arguments may seem compelling, a student of persuasion will quickly identify common reasoning fallacies. You can read more about the history of infomercials, how they've changed over time, and what we can expect of them in the future in the *Pop Comm!* feature, "You Too Can Have Six-Pack Abs in Only Three Weeks!"

POP COMM!

You Too Can Have Six-Pack Abs in Only Three Weeks!

Body by Jake, Body Dome, Bun & Thigh Max, and Smart Abs all promise that you can trim and tone your way to a better body in just minutes a day. Besides promising to be the most effective exercise equipment ever, what do all these products have in common? They're the subject of infomercials. Infomercials are television and online programs designed to look like 30- or 60-minute talk shows, but they're actually extended advertisements that focus on a product's extraordinary features and offer testimonials of its effectiveness.

Until 1984 the Federal Communications Commission banned program-length commercials, and the ban is still in effect for products that are marketed to children (Head, Spann, & McGregor, 2001). Although some view infomercials with skepticism and derision, others view them as "an example of capitalism at its best" ("Billy Mays," 2009) and their presence and use is growing. In 2009, Fox Broadcasting chose to cancel its Saturday morning children's programming and give over two hours of that time block to "longform commercials" (Schneider, 2008). Though the network hopes to eventually attract "more traditional programming that weaves in advertising messages," the initial programs scheduled are infomercials (Ibid). While fringe candidates had used the infomercial format for several decades, in 2008 Barack Obama used the infomerical format extensively, culminating in his 30-minute advertisement, which played on seven networks and was watched by 33.55 million viewers (Carter, 2008). Democratic strategist Joe Lockhart defended Obama's strategy as wise: "The benefit is you get to make your closing argument in a dramatic way without the filter of the media. It gives you more context and texture than a 30-second or 60-second ad" (Cummings, 2008).

Infomercials have even become sources of entertainment. In 2008 and 2009, the Snuggie— "A blanket with sleeves!"—and a similar product, the Slanket, were frequently referenced in popular culture, from You Tube parodies ("The Cult of Snuggie") to *30 Rock* storylines (with Liz Lemon asserting, "It's not product placement; I just like it!"). When "infomercial king" Billy Mays passed away unexpectedly in June 2009, many were inspired to affectionately celebrate his influence. A "Billy Mays Gangsta Remix" grew to quick popularity on YouTube (Mastamokei, 2008), and a Facebook page "RIP Billy Mays" gained 175,000 fans, some of whom posted about their favorite Billy Mays product. Despite the fun we like to have with infomercials, they have come under criticism in recent

years. Many Americans put at least part of the blame for the economic recession on advertising, claiming that it often causes people to buy things they don't need and can't afford (Crain, 2009). But consumer suspicion of the ability of infomercials in particular to deceive is nothing new. For example, in 2002 Guthy-Renker, the largest producer of television infomercials, whose products include the popular Proactiv Solution acne treatment, became the subject of a class-action lawsuit, which claimed Guthy-Renker made exaggerated claims of profitability and promoted an Internet "shopping mall" that was simply a scam ("Timothy D. Naegele & Associates," 2002). The case is ongoing, but the online consumer complaint sites like complaints.com and pissedcustomer.com are full of testimonials from disgruntled customers who believe the products did not deliver what they promised.

Because advertisements are inherently persuasive, it's important to view them with a critical eye, although certainly not all ads and infomercials make false claims. If you suspect that an infomercial is making questionable claims, be careful before you buy. A good strategy is to first contact the Better Business Bureau (www.bbb.org) or other reputable consumer watchdog groups and see if there have been any complaints lodged about the company advertising the product. If there have, buyer beware!

Questions to Ponder

1. Do you think calling these advertisements "info"-mercials is ethical? Why or why not?

2. Have you or someone you know ever purchased a product based on claims made about it on an infomercial, only to discover later that the claims were false?

Rhetorical Appeals to Ethos

Not everyone will choose the central processing route to make his or her decision to your proposition. One important cue people use when they process information by the peripheral route is ethos. So, you will also want to demonstrate good character, as well as say and do things to convey competence and credibility.

Conveying Good Character

We turn again to the ancient Greek philosopher Aristotle (384–322 b.c.e.) who first observed that perceived credibility is dependent on the audience's perception of the speaker's goodwill. Today, we define **goodwill** as a perception the audience forms of a speaker who they believe (1) understands them, (2) empathizes with them, and (3) is responsive to them. When audience members believe in the speaker's goodwill, they are more willing to believe what the speaker says.

goodwill

the audience perception that the speaker understands, empathizes with, and is responsive to them

One way to demonstrate that you understand your audience is by personalizing your information. For example, in his speech at the annual conference of the Property Casualty Insurers Association of America (PCI), Julian James, director of Worldwide Markets for Lloyds, demonstrated understanding by referencing membership facts from the previous year.

> *I would certainly contend that, following two consecutive record hurricane seasons, we have passed a key financial test. Debate after Katrina was largely about the detail of how we can do things better, and not about whether the industry could survive—as it was after 9/11. Not bad progress for an industry that faced almost double the value of claims from catastrophes in 2005 as it did for 9/11. . . . If we come out of this year intact, U.S. insurance industry profits in 2006 are forecast to be the best in a generation at $55 to 460 billion. (James, 2007, pp. 26–29)*

You can also demonstrate goodwill by empathizing with your audience. **Empathy** is the ability to see the world through the eyes of someone else. Empathizing with the views of the audience doesn't necessarily mean that you accept their views as your own. It does mean that you acknowledge them as valid. Although your speech may be designed to change audience members' views, the sensitivity you show to audience members' feelings will demonstrate goodwill. Julian James demonstrates empathy for the reputation of business and industry today:

empathy

the ability to see the world through the eyes of someone else

> *So far the industry's finances have rarely looked better. But not everyone is celebrating. With success in business comes greater scrutiny—just ask the oil industry.*
>
> *In recent weeks we have seen a growing vilification of insurers that is unprecedented and, I believe, wholly unwarranted. Take these recent headlines I came across:*
>
> *From* USA Today: *"Insurance rates pummel Florida homeowners"*
>
> *From* Dow Jones Market Watch: *"Sweet are the uses of adversity: Are insurers reeling from disaster or reeling in the profits?" (No prizes for guessing which side the authors came down on in that one.)*
>
> *And from the* Niagara Falls Reporter: *"Insurance companies real villains in Hurricane Katrina's aftermath"*
>
> *If that is the kind of press the industry is getting in Niagara Falls, in upstate New York, you might wonder how we are being portrayed in the Gulf States. (James, 2007, pp. 26–29)*

Finally, you can demonstrate goodwill by being responsive. Speakers who are **responsive** show that they care about the audience by acknowledging feedback, especially subtle negative cues. This feedback may occur during the presentation, but it also may have occurred prior to the speech. Let's turn again to Julian James's speech as an example:

responsive

show that you care about the audience by acknowledging feedback

When I spoke to you at this conference, I posed a challenge and asked, "Do you want to take control of the insurance cycle . . . or do you want to stay a passenger?" The reaction was very interesting. One group said, "That's so obvious, why hasn't anyone said that before?" Others said, "Ah, but you're very young, you don't understand, insurance cycles are a fact of life, and you can't do anything about them." . . . Ladies and gentlemen, four years ago, it may have felt like we were standing at the cliff edge, looking into the abyss.

The good news is that, in the intervening period, we have made important progress. . . . But we put our future in grave danger if we stop here. . . . The challenges we face today may be different, but the message from 2002 remains the same: "Our thinking and behaviour must change if the insurance industry is to be a stable, secure industry for our policy holders and shareholders of the future." Let's not mess it up again. (pp. 26–29)

Effective persuasive speakers make extra efforts to convey competence, credibility, and goodwill.

Conveying Competence and Credibility

Not surprisingly, we are more likely to be persuaded when we perceive a speaker to be competent and credible. We propose the following strategies so that your **terminal credibility**, the audience's perception of your expertise at the end of your speech, is greater than your **initial credibility**, their perception of your expertise at the beginning of your speech.

1. **Explain your competence.** Unless someone has formally introduced you and your qualifications to your audience, your initial credibility will be low, and as you speak, you will need to tell your audience about your expertise. Sending these types of messages during the speech results in your achieving a level of **derived credibility** with your audience. You can interweave comments about your expertise into introductory comments and at appropriate places within the body of the speech.

2. **Use evidence from respected sources.** You can also increase your derived credibility by using supporting material from well-recognized and respected sources. So, if you have a choice between using a statistic from a known partisan organization or from a dispassionate professional association, choose the professional association. Likewise, if you can quote a local expert who is well known and respected by your audience or an international scholar with limited name recognition with your audience, use the local expert's opinion.

3. **Use nonverbal delivery to enhance your credibility.** Your audience assesses your credibility not only from what it hears about you before you begin speaking but also from what it observes by looking at you. Although professional attire enhances credibility in any speaking situation, it is particularly important for persuasive speeches. Persuasive speakers dressed more formally are perceived as more credible than those dressed casually or sloppily (Sellnow & Treinen, 2004).

    The audience will also notice how confident you appear as you prepare to address them. From the moment you rise to speak, you will want to convey through your nonverbal behavior that you are competent. Plant your feet firmly, glance at your notes, then make eye contact or audience contact with one person or group before taking a breath and beginning to speak. Likewise, pause and establish eye contact upon finishing the speech. Just as pausing

terminal credibility

perception of a speaker's expertise at the end of the speech

initial credibility

perception of a speaker's expertise at the beginning of the speech

derived credibility

perception of a speaker's expertise during the speech

CONSIDER *THIS*....

Think of a professional speaker you've observed who you would describe as really well informed. Identify several ways the speaker conveyed competence, credibility, and good character to you.

emotions

buildup of action-specific energy

and establishing eye contact or audience contact before the speech enhance credibility, doing so upon delivering the closing lines has the same result.

4. **Use vocal expression to enhance your credibility.** Research shows that credibility is strongly influenced by how you sound. Speaking fluently, using a moderately fast rate, and expressing yourself with conviction makes you appear more intelligent and competent.

Rhetorical Appeals to Pathos

We are more likely to be involved with a topic when we have an emotional stake in it. **Emotions** are the buildup of action-specific energy (Petri & Govern, 2012). You can increase audience involvement by evoking negative or positive emotions during your speech (Nabi, 2002).

Evoking Negative Emotions

Negative emotions are disquieting, so when people experience them, they look for ways to eliminate them. Although you can tap numerous negative emotions, we describe five of the most common and how you might use them in a persuasive speech.

Fear We experience *fear* when we perceive ourselves to have no control over a situation that threatens us. We may fear physical harm or psychological harm. If you use examples, stories, and statistics that evoke fear in your audience, they will be more motivated to hear how your proposal can eliminate the source of their fear or allow them to escape from it. For example, in a speech whose goal was to convince the audience that they are at risk of developing high blood pressure, the speaker might use a fear appeal in this way:

> *One of every three Americans aged 18 and older has high blood pressure. It is a primary cause of stroke, heart disease, heart failure, kidney disease, and blindness. It triples a person's chance of developing heart disease, boosts the chance of stroke seven times, and the chance of congestive heart failure six times. Look at the person on your right; look at the person on your left. If they don't get it, chances are, you will. Today, I'd like to convince you that you are at risk for developing high blood pressure.*

Guilt We feel *guilt* when we personally violate a moral, ethical, or religious code that we hold dear. We experience guilt as a gnawing sensation that we have done something wrong. When we feel guilty, we are motivated to "make things right" or to atone for our transgression. For example, in a speech designed to motivate the audience to take their turn as designated drivers, a speaker might evoke guilt like this:

> *Have you ever promised your mom that you wouldn't ride in a car driven by someone who had been drinking? And then turned around and got in the car with your buddy even though you both had had a few? You know that wasn't right. Lying to your mother, putting yourself and your buddy at risk . . . (pause) but what can you do? Well, today I'm going to show you how to avoid all that guilt, live up to your promises to Mom, and keep both you and your buddy safe.*

Shame We feel *shame* when a moral code we violate is revealed to someone we think highly of. The more egregious our behavior or the more we admire the person who finds out, the more shame we experience. When we feel shame, we are motivated to "redeem" ourselves in the eyes of that person. Likewise, we can be convinced to refrain from doing something to avoid feelings of shame. If in your speech you can evoke feelings of shame and then demonstrate how your proposal can either redeem someone after a violation has occurred or prevent feelings of shame, then you can motivate the audience to carefully consider your arguments. For example, in a speech advocating thankfulness, the speaker might use a shame-based approach by quoting the old saying, "I cried because I had no shoes until I met a man who had no feet."

Anger When we are faced with an obstacle that stands in the way of something we want, we experience *anger*. We may also experience anger when someone demeans us or someone we love. Speakers who choose to evoke anger must be careful not to incite so much anger that reasoning processes are short-circuited.

In your speeches, if you can rouse your audience's anger and then show how your proposal will enable them to achieve their goals or stop or prevent the demeaning that has occurred, you can motivate them to listen to and really consider your arguments. For example, suppose you want to convince the audience to support a law requiring the active community notification when a convicted sex offender moves into the neighborhood. You might arouse the audience's anger to get their attention by personalizing the story of Megan Kanka.

> *She was your little girl, just seven years old, and the light of your world. She had a smile that could bring you to your knees. And she loved puppies. So when that nice man who had moved in down the street invited her in to see his new puppy, she didn't hesitate. But she didn't get to see the puppy, and you didn't ever see her alive again. He beat her, he raped her, and then he strangled her. He packaged her body in an old toy chest and dumped it in a park. Your seven-year-old princess would never dig in a toy chest again or slip down the slide in that park. And that hurts. But what makes you really angry is that she wasn't his first. But you didn't know that. Because no one bothered to tell you that the guy down the street was likely to kill little girls. The cops knew it. But they couldn't tell you. You, the one who was supposed to keep her safe, didn't know. Angry? You bet. Yeah, he's behind bars again, but you still don't know who's living down the street from you. But you can. There is a law before Congress right now that will require active notification of the community when a known sex offender takes up residence, and today I'm going to tell how you can help to get this passed. ("Megan's Law," n.d.)*

Sadness When we fail to achieve a goal or experience a loss, we feel *sadness*. Unlike other negative emotions, we tend to withdraw and become isolated when we feel sad. Because sadness is an unpleasant feeling, we look for ways to end it. Speeches that help us understand and find answers for what has happened can comfort us and help relieve this unpleasant feeling. For example, after 9/11, many Americans were sad. Yes, they were also afraid and angry, but overlaying it all was profound sadness for those who had been lost and what had been lost. The questions "Why? Why did they do this? Why do they hate us so?" capture the national melancholy. So, when politicians suggest that they understand the answers to these questions and can repair the relationships that led to 9/11, Americans tend to listen to and think about what they say.

Evoking Positive Emotions

Just as evoking negative emotions can cause audience members to internalize your arguments, so too can you tap *positive emotions*, which are feelings that people enjoy experiencing. We discuss five of them here.

CONSIDER *THIS*....

Think of a movie you've watched that appealed to one or more of the emotions we've discussed. What are some specific examples of how the film did so?

Happiness or Joy *Happiness* or *joy* is the buildup of positive energy we experience when we accomplish something, when we have a satisfying interaction or relationship, or when we see or possess objects that appeal to us. Think of how you felt when you won that ribbon in grade school or when you found out that you got an "A" on that volcano project in fourth grade. Think of how you felt when you heard that special someone say "I love you" for the very first time. Or think about the birthday when you received that toy you had been dreaming about. In each of these cases, you were happy, maybe even so happy that you were joyous. As a speaker, if you can show how your proposal will lead your audience members to be happy or joyful, then they are likely to listen and to think about your proposal. For example, suppose you want to motivate your audience to attend a couples encounter weekend where they will learn how to "rekindle" their relationship with a partner. If you can remind them about how they felt early in their relationship and then prove that they can reignite those feelings, they may be more motivated to listen.

Pride When we experience satisfaction about something we or someone we care about accomplishes, we feel *pride*. "We're number one! We're number one!" is the chant of the crowd feeling pride in the accomplishment of "their" team. Whereas happiness is related to feelings of pleasure, pride is related to feelings of self-worth. So, if you can demonstrate how your proposal will help audience members to feel good about themselves, they will be more motivated to support your proposition. For example, suppose you want to convince your audience to volunteer to work on the newest Habitat for Humanity house being constructed in your community. You might allude to the pride they will feel when they see people moving into the house they helped to build, which stands where there was once nothing but a vacant lot.

Relief When a threatening situation has been alleviated, we feel the positive emotion of *relief*. We relax and put down our guard. As a speaker, you use relief to motivate audience members by combining it with the negative emotion of fear. For example, suppose your goal is to convince the audience that they are not at risk for high blood pressure. You might use the same personalization of statistics that was described in the example of fear appeals, but instead of stopping at convincing the audience that they are at risk, you could also promise relief if they hear you out and do what you advocate.

Hope The emotional energy that stems from believing something desirable is likely to happen is called *hope*. Whereas relief causes you to relax and let down your guard, hope energizes you to take action to overcome the situation. Hope empowers. As with relief, hope appeals are usually accompanied by fear appeals. So you can motivate audience members to listen by showing them how your proposal provides a plan for overcoming a difficult situation. For example, if you propose adopting a low-fat diet to reduce the risk of high blood pressure, you can use the same personalization of statistics cited in the example of fear but change the ending to state: "Today, I'm going to convince you to beat the odds by adopting a low-fat diet."

Compassion When we feel selfless concern for the suffering of another person and that concern energizes us to try to relieve that suffering, we feel *compassion*. Speakers can evoke audience members' feelings of compassion by vividly describing the suffering endured by someone. The audience will then be motivated to listen to see how the speaker's proposal can end that suffering. For example, when a speaker whose goal is to gather donations to Project Peanut Butter displays a slide of an emaciated child, claims that 13 percent of all Malawi children die of malnutrition, and states that for $10 you can save a child, he or she is appealing to compassion.

You can evoke negative emotions, positive emotions, or both as a way to encourage listeners to internalize your message. You can do so by telling vivid stories and testimonials, offering startling statistics, using striking presentational aids and provocative language, as well as through an animated and expressive delivery style.

THE HUMANE SOCIETY
OF THE UNITED STATES
humanesociety.org

Speakers appeal to compassion when they show us how someone is suffering and that we can help.

Persuasive Speech Patterns

The most common patterns for organizing persuasive speeches include statement of reasons, comparative advantages, criteria satisfaction, refutative, problem–solution, problem–cause–solution, and motivated sequence. In this section, we describe and illustrate each pattern by examining the same topic with slightly different propositions.

Statement of Reasons

The **statement of reasons pattern** is used to confirm propositions of fact by presenting the best-supported reasons in a meaningful order. For a speech with three reasons or more, place the strongest reason last because this is the reason you believe the audience will find most persuasive. Place the second strongest reason first because you want to start with a significant point. Place the other reasons in between.

> **Proposition:** *I want my audience to believe that passing the proposed school tax levy is necessary.*
>
> I. *The income will enable the schools to restore vital programs.* [second strongest]
>
> II. *The income will enable the schools to give teachers the raises they need to keep up with the cost of living.*
>
> III. *The income will allow the community to maintain local control and will save the district from state intervention.* [strongest]

statement of reasons pattern

used to confirm propositions of fact by presenting best-supported reasons in a meaningful order

Comparative Advantages

The **comparative advantages pattern** attempts to convince others that something has more value than something else. A comparative advantages approach to a school tax proposition would look like this:

> **Proposition:** *I want my audience to believe that passing the school tax levy is better than not passing it.* [compares the value of change to the status quo]
>
> I. *Income from a tax levy will enable schools to reintroduce important programs that had to be cut.* [advantage 1]
>
> II. *Income from a tax levy will enable schools to avoid a tentative strike by teachers who are underpaid.* [advantage 2]
>
> III. *Income from a tax levy will enable us to retain local control of our schools, which will be lost to the state if additional local funding is not provided.* [advantage 3]

comparative advantages pattern

attempts to convince that something is of more value than something else

Criteria Satisfaction

The **criteria satisfaction pattern** seeks agreement on criteria that should be considered when evaluating a particular proposition and then shows how the proposition satisfies the criteria. A criteria satisfaction pattern is especially useful when your audience is opposed to your proposition, because it approaches the proposition indirectly by first focusing on the criteria that the audience should agree with before introducing the specific solution. A criteria satisfaction organization for the school levy would look like this:

Proposition: *I want my audience to believe that passing a school levy is a good way to fund our schools.*

I. *We can all agree that a good school funding method must meet three criteria:*

A. *A good funding method results in the reestablishment of programs that have been dropped due to budget constraints.*

B. *A good funding method results in fair pay for teachers.*

C. *A good funding method generates enough income to maintain local control, avoiding state intervention.*

II. *Passage of a local school tax levy is a good way to fund our schools.*

A. *A local levy will allow us to re-fund important programs.*

B. *A local levy will allow us to give teachers a raise.*

C. *A local levy will generate enough income to maintain local control and avoid state intervention.*

Refutative

The **refutative pattern** arranges main points according to opposing arguments and then both challenges them and bolsters your own. This pattern is particularly useful when the target audience opposes your position. Begin by acknowledging the merit of opposing arguments and then provide evidence of their flaws. Once listeners understand the flaws, they will be more receptive to the arguments you present to support your proposition. A refutative pattern for the school tax proposition might look like this:

Proposition: *I want my audience to agree that a school levy is the best way to fund our schools.*

I. *Opponents of the tax levy argue that the tax increase will fall only on property owners.*

A. *Landlords will recoup property taxes in the form of higher rents.*

B. *Thus, all people will be affected.*

II. *Opponents of the tax levy argue that there are fewer students in the school district, so schools should be able to function on the same amount of revenue.*

A. *Although there are fewer pupils, costs continue to rise.*

1. *Salary costs are increasing.*

2. *Energy costs are increasing.*

3. *Maintenance costs are increasing.*

4. *Costs from unfunded federal and state government mandates are rising.*

B. *Although there are fewer pupils, there are many aging school buildings that need replacing or retrofitting.*

III. *Opponents of the tax levy argue that parents should be responsible for the excessive cost of educating their children.*

A. *Historically, our nation has flourished under a publicly funded educational system.*

B. *Parents today are already paying more than previous generations.*

1. *Activity fees*

2. *Lab fees*

3. *Book fees*

4. *Transportation fees*

C. *Of school-age children today in this district, 42 percent live in families that are below the poverty line and have limited resources.*

Problem–Solution

The **problem–solution pattern** explains the nature of a problem and proposes a solution. This organization is particularly effective when the audience is neutral or agrees only that there is a problem but has no opinion about a particular solution. A problem–solution organization for the school tax proposition might look like this:

> **problem–solution pattern**
>
> *explains the nature of a particular problem and then proposes a solution*

Proposition: *The current fiscal crisis in the school district can be solved through a local tax levy.*

I. *The current funding is insufficient and has resulted in program cuts, labor problems resulting from stagnant wages, and a threatened state takeover of local schools.* [statement of problem]

II. *The proposed local tax levy is large enough to solve these problems.* [solution]

Problem–Cause–Solution

The **problem–cause–solution pattern** is similar to the problem–solution pattern, but differs from it by adding a main point that reveals the causes of the problem and a solution designed to alleviate those causes. This pattern is particularly useful for addressing seemingly intractable problems that have been dealt with unsuccessfully in the past as a result of treating symptoms rather than underlying causes. A problem–cause–solution organization for the school tax proposition might look like this:

> **problem–cause–solution pattern**
>
> *demonstrates that there is a problem caused by specific things that can be alleviated with the proposed solution that addresses the causes*

Proposition: *The current fiscal crisis in the school district can be solved through a local tax levy.*

I. *The current funding is insufficient and has resulted in program cuts, labor problems, and a threatened state takeover of local schools.* [statement of problem]

II. *These problems exist due to dwindling government support and increasing costs for operating expenses.* [causes]

III. *The proposed local tax levy will solve these problems by supplementing government support and enhancing operating budgets.* [solution]

Motivated Sequence

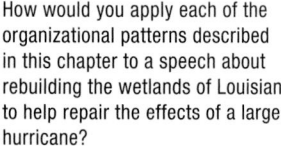

motivated sequence pattern

a form of organization that combines the problem–solution pattern with explicit appeals designed to motivate the audience to act

The **motivated sequence pattern** combines a problem–solution pattern with explicit appeals designed to motivate the audience to act. The motivational sequence pattern is a unified five-point sequence that replaces the normal introduction-body-conclusion model with (1) an attention step, (2) a need step that fully explains the nature of the problem, (3) a satisfaction step that explains how the proposal solves the problem in a satisfactory manner, (4) a visualization step that provides a personal application of the proposal, and (5) an action appeal step that emphasizes the direction that audience action should take. A motivational pattern for the school tax levy proposition would look like this:

Proposition: *I want my audience to vote in favor of the school tax levy on the November ballot.*

I. *Comparisons of worldwide test scores in math and science have refocused our attention on education.* [attention]

II. *The shortage of money is resulting in cost-cutting measures that compromise our ability to teach basic academic subjects well.* [need, statement of problem]

III. *The proposed increase is large enough to solve those problems in ways that allow for increased emphasis on academic need areas.* [satisfaction, how the proposal solves the problem]

IV. *Think of the contribution you will be making to the education of your children and also to efforts to return our educational system to the world-class level it once held.* [visualization of -personal application]

V. *Here are "Vote Yes" buttons that you can wear to show you are willing to support this much-needed tax levy.* [action appeal showing specific direction]

How would you apply each of the organizational patterns described in this chapter to a speech about rebuilding the wetlands of Louisiana to help repair the effects of a large hurricane?

Yann Arthus-Bertrand/Terra/Corbis

Because motivational patterns are variations of problem–solution patterns, the underlying assumption is similar: When the current means are not solving the problem, a new solution that does solve the problem should be adopted. Figure 17.3 is a checklist that you can use to analyze any persuasive speech you rehearse or to critique the speeches of others.

THE AUDIENCE *BEYOND*

Mary Ann wanted to reach to an audience beyond her classmates with her persuasive message about the negative implications of reality TV programs on healthy teen behaviors. So she posted her speech to YouTube with a blog for comments from viewers.

You can use this form to critique a persuasive speech to convince that you hear in class. As you listen to the speaker, outline the speech, paying close attention to the reasoning process the speaker uses. Also note the claims and support used in the arguments and identify the types of warrants being used. Then answer the questions that follow.

General Criteria

_____ 1. Was the proposition clear? Could you tell the speaker's position on the issue?

_____ 2. Was the introduction effective in creating interest and involving the audience in the speech?

_____ 3. Was the speech organized using an appropriate persuasive pattern?

_____ 4. Was the language clear, vivid, inclusive, and appropriate?

_____ 5. Was the conclusion effective in summarizing what had been said and mobilizing the audience to act?

_____ 6. Was the speech delivered conversationally and expressively?

7. Did the speaker establish credibility by demonstrating:

_____ expertise?

_____ personableness?

_____ trustworthiness?

Primary Criteria

_____ 1. Was the specific goal phrased as a proposition (were you clear about the speaker's position on the issue)?

_____ 2. Did the proposition appear to be adapted to the initial attitude of the target audience?

_____ 3. Were emotional appeals used to involve the audience with the topic?

4. Were the reasons used in the speech

_____ directly related to the proposition?

_____ supported by strong evidence?

_____ persuasive for the particular audience?

5. Was the evidence [*support*] used to back the reasons [*claims*]

_____ from well-respected sources?

_____ recent and/or still valid?

_____ persuasive for this audience?

_____ typical of all evidence that might have been used?

_____ sufficient [*enough evidence cited*]?

6. Could you identify the types of arguments that were used?

_____ Did the speaker argue from example? _____ If so, was it valid?

_____ Did the speaker argue from analogy? _____ If so, was it valid?

_____ Did the speaker argue from causation? _____ If so, was it valid?

_____ Did the speaker argue from sign? _____ If so, was it valid?

Figure 17.3

Persuasive speech evaluation checklist

Figure 17.3

(Continued)

7. Could you identify any fallacies of reasoning in the speech?

_____ hasty generalizations

_____ arguing from false cause

_____ ad hominem attacks

_____ straw person

_____ either-or

_____ 8. Did the speaker demonstrate goodwill?

9. If the speech called for the audience to take action,

_____ did the speaker describe incentives and relate them to audience needs?

_____ did the speaker acknowledge any costs associated with the action?

10. Did the speaker use an appropriate persuasive organizational pattern?

_____ statement of reasons

_____ comparative advantages

_____ criteria satisfaction

_____ refutative

_____ problem-solution

_____ problem-cause-solution

_____ motivated sequence

Overall evaluation of the speech (check one):

_____ excellent _____ good _____ average _____ fair _____ poor

Use the information from this checklist to support your evaluation.

COMMUNICATE ON YOUR FEET

Speech Assignment

A Persuasive Speech

1. Follow the speech plan Action Steps to prepare a speech in which you change audience belief. Your instructor will announce the time limit and other parameters for this assignment.

2. Criteria for evaluation include all the general criteria of topic and purpose, content, organization, and presentation, but special emphasis will be placed on the primary persuasive criteria of how well the speech's specific goal was adapted to the audience's initial attitude toward the topic, the soundness of the reasons, the evidence cited in support of them, and the credibility of the arguments.

3. Use the persuasive speech evaluation checklist in Figure 17.3 to critique yourself as you practice your speech.

4. Prior to presenting your speech, prepare a complete sentence outline and source list (bibliography).

SAMPLE SPEECH PLAN AND OUTLINE

Sample Actuation Persuasive Speech

This section presents a sample speech to actuate given by a student, including an adaptation plan, an outline, and a transcript.

© Cengage Learning 2013

Together, We Can Stop Cyber-Bullying[1]

By Adam Parrish

 Read the speech adaptation plan, outline, and transcript of a speech given by Adam Parrish in an introductory speaking course. You can access a video clip of Adam's speech through the Chapter 17 resources of your CourseMate for *Communicate!* You can also use your CourseMate to identify some of the strengths of Adam's speech by preparing an evaluation checklist and an analysis. You can then compare your answers with those of the authors.

Adaptation Plan

1. Target audience initial attitude and background knowledge: My audience is composed of traditional-aged college students with varying majors and classes. Most are from middle-class backgrounds. The initial attitude about bullying for most will be to agree with me already that it's a bad thing. So I will try to get them to take action. My perception is that my audience knows about cyber-bullying but not the nuances of it.

2. Organizational framework: I will organize my speech using a problem-cause-solution framework because my audience already agrees that bullying is bad but may not know what they can and should do to help stop it.

3. Arguments (logos): I will demonstrate what widespread (breadth) and harmful (depth of effects) cyber-bullying is and why it persists (causes). Once I've convinced my audience, I will propose solutions that must be taken and cite specifically what we must do to help stop this horrible practice.

4. Building competence, credibility, and good character (ethos): I will use credible sources to support my claims and cite them using oral footnotes. I will also offer personal stories to create goodwill.

5. Creating and maintaining interest (pathos): I will involve my audience by appealing to several emotions, including guilt, sadness, relief, hope, and compassion.

Outline

General goal: To persuade

Specific goal: To convince my audience to take action to help stop cyber-bullying.

Introduction

Attention catcher

I. "I'll miss just being around her." "I didn't want to believe it." "It's such a sad thing." These quotes are from the friends and family of 15-year-old Phoebe Prince, who, on January 14, 2010, committed suicide by hanging herself. Why did this senseless act occur? The answer is simple: Phoebe Prince was bullied to death.

Listener relevance

II. Many of us know someone who has been bullied in school. Perhaps they were teased in the parking lot or in the locker room. In the past, bullying occurred primarily in and around schools. However, with the advent of new communication technologies such as cell phones with text messaging capability, instant messaging, e-mails, blogs, and social networking sites, bullies can now follow their victims anywhere, even into their own bedrooms. Using electronic communications to tease, harass, threaten, and intimidate another person is called cyber-bullying.

Speaker credibility

III. As a tutor and mentor to young students, I have witnessed cyber-bullying firsthand, and by examining current research, I believe I understand the problem, its causes, and how we can help end cyber-bullying.

Thesis statement (stated as a proposition)

IV. Cyber-bullying is a devastating form of abuse that must be confronted and stopped.

Preview

V. Today, we will examine the widespread and harmful nature of cyber-bullying, discover how and why it persists, and propose some simple solutions that we must engage in to thwart cyber-bullies and comfort their victims.

Transition

Let's begin by tackling the problem head on.

Body

The problem
Listener relevance

I. Cyber-bullying is a pervasive and dangerous behavior.

Many of us have read rude, insensitive, or nasty statements posted about us or someone we care about on social networking sites like MySpace and Facebook. Whether or not those comments were actually intended to hurt another person's feelings, they are perfect examples of cyber-bullying.

A. Cyber-bullying takes place all over the world through a wide array of electronic media.

1. According to an article in the winter 2005 edition of *Reclaiming Children and Youth*, 57 percent of American middle-school students have experienced instances of cyber-bullying ranging from hurtful comments to threats of physical violence (Keith & Martin, 2005).

2. Females are just as likely as males to engage in cyber-bullying, although women are 10 percent more likely to be victimized (Li, 2007).

3. While the number of students who are targets of cyber-bullies decreases as students age, data from the Youth Internet Safety Survey indicate that the instances of American high school students being cyber-bullied increased nearly 50 percent from 2000 to 2005 (Ybarra, Mitchell, Wolak, & Finkelhor, 2006).

4. Quing Li (2007), a researcher of computer-mediated communication, noted that Internet and cell-phone technologies have been used by bullies to harass, torment, and threaten young people in North America, Europe, and Asia.

5. A particularly disturbing incident occurred in Dallas, Texas, where an overweight student with multiple sclerosis was targeted on a school's social networking page. One message read, "I guess I'll have to wait until you kill yourself, which I hope is not long from now, or I'll have to wait until your disease kills you" (Keith & Martin, 2005, p. 226).

Clearly, cyber-bullying is a widespread problem. What is most disturbing about cyber-bullying, however, is its effects upon victims, bystanders, and perhaps even upon the bullies themselves.   **Transition**

B. Cyber-bullying can lead to traumatic physical psychological injuries upon its victims.

1. According to a 2007 article in the *Journal of Adolescent Health*, 36 percent of the victims of cyber-bullies are also harassed by their attackers in school (Ybarra, Diener-West, & Leaf, 2007).

2. For example, the Dallas student with MS had eggs thrown at her car and a bottle of acid thrown at her house (Keith & Martin, 2005).

3. Ybarra et al. (2007) reported that victims of cyber-bullying experience such severe emotional distress that they often exhibit behavioral problems such as poor grades, skipping school, and receiving detentions and suspensions.

4. Smith et al. (2008) suggested that even a few instances of cyber-bullying can have these long-lasting and heartbreaking results.

5. What is even more alarming is that victims of cyber-bullying are significantly more likely to carry weapons to school as a result of feeling threatened (Ybarra et al., 2007). Obviously, this could lead to violent, and perhaps even deadly, outcomes for bullies, victims, and even bystanders.

Now that we realize the devastating nature, scope, and effects of cyber-bullying, let's look at its causes.   **Transition**

II. Cyber-bullying is perpetuated because victims and bystanders do not report their abusers to authorities.   **The cause**

Think back to a time when you may have seen a friend or loved one being harassed online. Did you report the bully to the network administrator or other authorities? Did you console the victim? I know I didn't. If you are like me, we may unknowingly be enabling future instances of cyber-bullying.   **Listener relevance**

A. Cyber-bullies are cowards who attack their victims anonymously.

1. Ybarra et al. (2007) discovered that 13 percent of cyber-bullying victims did not know who was tormenting them.

2. This is an important statistic because, as Keith and Martin (2005) point out, traditional bullying takes place face to face and often ends when students leave school. However, today, students are subjected to bullying in their own homes.

3. Perhaps the anonymous nature of cyber-attacks partially explains why Li (2007) found that nearly 76 percent of victims of cyber-bullying and 75 percent of bystanders never reported instances of bullying to adults.

B. Victims and bystanders who do not report attacks from cyber-bullies can unintentionally enable bullies.

1. According to De Nies, Donaldson, and Netter of *ABCNews.com* (2010) several of Phoebe Prince's classmates were aware that she was being harassed but did not inform the school's administration.

2. Li (2007) suggested that victims and bystanders often do not believe that adults will actually intervene to stop cyber-bullying.

3. However, *ABCNews.com* (2010) reports that 41 states have laws against bullying in schools, and 23 of those states target cyber-bullying specifically.

Transition

Now that we realize that victims of cyber-bullies desperately need the help of witnesses and bystanders to report their attacks, we should arm ourselves with the information necessary to provide that assistance.

The solution

III. Cyber-bullying must be confronted on national, local, and personal levels.

Listener relevance

Think about the next time you see a friend or loved one being tormented or harassed online. What would you be willing to do to help?

A. There should be a comprehensive national law confronting cyber-bullying in schools. Certain statutes currently in state laws should be amalgamated to create the strongest protections for victims and the most effective punishments for bullies as possible.

1. According to Limber and Small's (2003) article titled *State Laws and Policies to Address Bullying in Schools,* Georgia law requires faculty and staff to be trained on the nature of bullying and what actions to take if they see students being bullied.

2. Furthermore, Connecticut law *requires* school employees to report bullying as part their hiring contract (Limber & Small, 2003). Washington takes this a step further by protecting employees from any legal action if a reported bully is proven to be innocent (Limber & Small, 2003).

3. When it comes to protecting victims, West Virginia law demands that schools must ensure that a bullied student does not receive additional abuse at the hands of his or her bully (Limber & Small, 2003).

4. Legislating punishment for bullies is difficult. As Limber and Small (2003) noted, zero-tolerance polices often perpetuate violence because at-risk youth (bullies) are removed from all of the benefits of school, which might help make them less abusive.

5. A comprehensive anti-cyber-bullying law should incorporate the best aspects of these state laws and find a way to punish bullies that is both punitive and has the ability to rehabilitate abusers.

B. Local communities must organize and mobilize to attack the problem of cyber-bullying.

1. According to Greene (2006), communities need to support bullying prevention programs by conducting a school-based bullying survey for individual school districts. We can't know how to best protect victims in our community without knowing how they are affected by the problem.

2. It is critical to know this information. As Greene noted, only 3 percent of teachers in the United States perceive bullying to be a problem in their schools (Greene, 2006).

3. Local school districts should create a Coordinating Committee made up of "administrators, teachers, students, parents, school staff, and community partners" to gather bullying data and rally support to confront the problem (Greene, 2006, p. 73).

4. Even if your local school district is unable or unwilling to mobilize behind this dire cause, there are some important actions you can take personally to safeguard those you love against cyber-bullying.

C. Take note of these warning signs that might indicate a friend or loved one is a victim of a cyber-bully.

1. Victims of cyber-bullies often use electronic communication more frequently than do people who are not being bullied.

2. Victims of cyber-bullies have mood swings and difficulty sleeping (Keith & Martin, 2005).

3. Victims of cyber-bullies seem depressed and/or become anxious (Keith & Martin, 2005).

4. Victims of cyber-bullies become withdrawn from social activities and fall behind in scholastic responsibilities (Keith &/Martin, 2005).

D. If you see a friend or loved one exhibiting any of these signs, I implore you not to ignore them. Rather, take action. Get involved. Do something to stop it.

1. According to Raskauskas and Stoltz (2007), witnesses of cyber-bullying should inform victims to take the attacks seriously, especially if the bullies threaten violence.

2. Tell victims to report their attacks to police or other authority figures (Raskauskas & Stoltz, 2007).

3. Tell victims to block harmful messages by blocking e-mail accounts and cell phone numbers (Raskauskas & Stoltz, 2007).

4. Tell victims to save copies of attacks and provide them to authorities (Raskauskas & Stoltz, 2007).

5. If you personally know the bully and feel safe confronting him or her, do so! As Raskauskas and Stoltz (2007) noted, bullies will often back down when confronted by peers.

6. By being a good friend and by giving good advice, you can help a victim report his or her attacks from cyber-bullies and take a major step toward eliminating this horrendous problem.

Transition

So, you see, we are not helpless to stop the cyber-bulling problem as long as we make the choice NOT to ignore it.

Conclusion

Thesis restatement

I. Cyber-bullying is a devastating form of abuse that must be reported to authorities.

Main point summary

II. Cyber-bullying is a worldwide problem perpetuated by the silence of both victims and bystanders. By paying attention to certain warning signs, we can empower ourselves to console victims and report their abusers.

Call to action and clincher

III. Today, I implore you to do your part to help stop cyber-bullying. I know that you agree that stopping cyber-bullying must be a priority. First, although other states have cyber-bullying laws in place, ours does not. So I'm asking you to sign this petition that I will forward to our district's state legislators. We need to make our voices heard that we want specific laws passed to stop this horrific practice and to punish those caught doing it. Second, I'm also asking you to be vigilant in noticing signs of cyber-bullying and then taking action. Look for signs that your friend, brother, sister, cousin, boyfriend, girlfriend, or loved one might be a victim of cyber-bullying and then get involved to help stop it! Phoebe Prince showed the warning signs, and she did not deserve to die so senselessly. None of us would ever want to say, "I'll miss just being around her," "I didn't want to believe it," "It's such a sad thing" about our own friends or family members. We must work to ensure that victims are supported and bullies are confronted nationally, locally, and personally. I know that, if we stand together and refuse to be silent, we can and will stop cyber-bullying.

[1]*From Verderber/Verderber/Sellnow, The Challenge of Effective Speaking, 15E.*
© 2012 Cengage Learning.

References

De Nies, Y., Donaldson, S., & Netter, S. (2010, January 28). *Mean girls: Cyberbullying blamed for teen suicides.* ABCNews.com. *Retrieved from http://abcnews.go.com/GMA/Parenting/girls-teen-suicide-calls-attention-cyberbullying/story?id=9685026*

Greene, M. B. (2006). *Bullying in schools: A plea for measure of human rights.* Journal of Social Issues, 62(1), *63–79.*

Keith, S., & Martin, M. (2005). *Cyber-bullying: Creating a culture of respect in the cyber world.* Reclaiming Children and Youth, 13(4), 224–228.

Li, Q. (2007). *New bottle of old wine: A research of cyberbullying in schools.* Computers in Human Behavior, 23, 1777–1791.

Limber, S. P., & Small, M. A. (2003). *State laws and policies to address bullying in schools.* School Psychology Review, 32(3), 445–455.

Raskauskas, J., & Stoltz, A. D. (2007). *Involvement in traditional and electronic bullying among adolescents.* Developmental Psychology, 43(3), 564–575.

Smith, P. K., Mahdavi, J., Carvalho, M., Fisher, S. Russel, S., & Tippett, N. (2008). *Cyberbullying: Its nature and impact in secondary school pupils.* Journal of Child Psychology and Psychiatry, 49(4), 374–385.

Ybarra, M. L., Diener-West, M., & Leaf, P. J. (2007). Examining the overlap in internet harassment and school bullying: Implications for school intervention. Journal of Adolescent Health, 41, S42–S50.

Ybarra, M. L., Mitchell, K. J., Wolak, J., & Finkelhor, D. (2006). Examining characteristics and associated distress related to Internet harassment: Findings from the second Youth Internet Safety Survey. Pediatrics, 118, 1169–1177.

SPEECH AND ANALYSIS

Speech	Analysis

Speech

"I'll miss just being around her." "I didn't want to believe it." "It's such a sad thing." These quotes are from the friends and family of 15-year-old Phoebe Prince, who, on January 14, 2010, committed suicide by hanging herself. Why did this senseless act occur? The answer is simple. . . . Phoebe Prince was bullied to death.

Many of us know someone who has been bullied in school. Perhaps they were teased in the parking lot or in the locker room. In the past, bullying occurred primarily in school. However, with the advent of new communication technologies such as cell phones, text messaging, instant messaging, blogs, and social networking sites, bullies can now follow and terrorize their victims anywhere, even into their own bedrooms. Using electronic communications to tease, harass, threaten, and intimidate another person is called cyber-bullying.

As a tutor and mentor to young students, I have witnessed cyber-bullying firsthand, and by examining current research, I believe I understand the problem, its causes, and how we can help end cyber-bullying. What I know for sure is that cyber-bullying is a devastating form of abuse that must be confronted on national, local, and personal levels.

Today, we will examine the widespread and harmful nature of cyber-bulling, uncover how and why it persists, and pinpoint some simple solutions we must begin to enact in order to thwart cyber-bullies and comfort their victims. Let's begin by tackling the problem head on.

Many of us have read rude, insensitive, or nasty statements posted about us or someone we care about on social networking sites like MySpace and Facebook. Well, whether or not those comments were actually intended to hurt another person's feelings, if they did hurt their feelings, then they are perfect examples of cyber-bullying.

Cyber-bullying is a pervasive and dangerous behavior. It takes place all over the world and through a wide array of electronic media. According to Keith and Martin's article in the winter 2005 edition of *Reclaiming Children and Youth*, 57 percent of American middle-school students had experienced instances of cyber-bullying ranging from hurtful

Analysis

Adam uses quotes from family and friends of cyber-bullying victim Phoebe Prince to get attention and lead into his proposition.

Here Adam further entices his listeners to pay attention by offering listener relevance that we all can relate to.

Using the vivid term "terrorize," Adam appeals to negative emotions (pathos).

Adam begins to establish ethos by mentioning why he has credibility about this topic. Mentioning that he is a tutor and mentor also conveys goodwill. Listeners are likely to think he must have good character if he volunteers as a tutor and mentor.

Adam does a nice job of previewing his problem-cause-solution organizational framework, but his thesis statement phrased as a proposition is somewhat lost and could be made more overtly here.

Again, Adam's use of a listener relevance helps keep listeners tuned in and interested in hearing more.

Here Adam bolsters his ethos (and avoids plagiarism) by citing an oral footnote for his statistics.

comments to threats of physical violence. Quing Li's article published in the journal *Computers in Human Behavior* noted that cyber-bullying is not gender biased. According to Li, females are just as likely as males to engage in cyber-bullying, although women are 10 percent more likely to be victimized.

While the number of students who are targets of cyber-bullies decreases as students age, data from the *Youth Internet Safety Survey* indicates that the instances of American high school students being cyber-bullied had increased nearly 50 percent from 2000 to 2005. The problem does not exist in the United States alone.

Li noted that Internet and cell-phone technologies have been used by bullies to harass, torment, and threaten young people in North America, Europe, and Asia. However, some of the most horrific attacks happen right here at home.

According to Keith and Martin, a particularly disturbing incident occurred in Dallas, Texas, where an overweight student with multiple sclerosis was targeted on a school's social networking page. One message read, "I guess I'll have to wait until you kill yourself which I hope is not long from now, or I'll have to wait until your disease kills you." Clearly, cyber-bullying is a worldwide and perverse phenomenon. What is most disturbing about cyber-bullying is its effects upon victims, bystanders, and perhaps even upon bullies themselves.

Cyber-bullying can lead to physical and psychological injuries upon its victims. According to a 2007 article in the *Journal of Adolescent Health,* Ybarra and colleagues noted that 36 percent of the victims of cyber-bullies are also harassed by their attackers in school. For example, the Dallas student with MS had eggs thrown at her car and a bottle of acid thrown at her house.

Ybarra et al. reported that victims of cyber-bullying experience such severe emotional distress that they often exhibit behavioral problems such as poor grades, skipping school, and receiving detentions and suspensions. Furthermore, Smith et al. suggested that even a few instances of cyber-bullying can have these long-lasting negative effects.

What is even more alarming is that, according to Ybarra and colleagues, victims of cyber-bullying are significantly more likely to carry weapons to school as a result of feeling threatened. Obviously, this could lead to violent outcomes for bullies, victims, and even bystanders.

Now that we have heard about the nature, scope, and effects of cyber-bullying, let's see if we can discover its causes. Let's think back to a time when we may have seen a friend or loved one being harassed online. Did we report the bully to the network administrator or other authorities? Did we console the victim? I know I didn't. If you are like me, we may unknowingly be enabling future instances of cyber-bullying.

Cyber-bullying occurs because of the anonymity offered to bullies by cell phone and Internet technologies, as well as

Although this statistic is interesting, it would be more compelling to know more recent statistics and the trends since 2005.

Notice Adam's word choices (harass, torment, threaten, horrific) to enhance pathos.

This example provides an emotional appeal by offering a real example of a real victim in Dallas, Texas.

This vivid example enhances pathos.

Now that Adam has established the breadth of the problem as widespread, he moves into a discussion about the depth of the effects it can have on victims.

Here Adam helps pique listener interest by pointing out how bystanders could also be hurt if we don't do something to stop this form of terrorism.

Notice how Adam's transition verbally ties the point he is finishing (problem) to the next point (causes) clearly using inclusive "we" language. This, too, bolsters a sense of goodwill and uses a conversational style that keeps listeners engaged.

the failure of victims and bystanders to report incidents of cyber-bullying. You see, unlike schoolyard bullies, cyber-bullies can attack their victims anonymously.

Ybarra and colleagues discovered that 13 percent of cyber-bullying victims did not know who was tormenting them. This devastating statistic is important because, as Keith and Martin noted, traditional bullying takes place face to face and often ends when students leave school. However, today, students are subjected to nonstop bullying, even when they are alone in their own homes.

Perhaps the anonymous nature of cyber-attacks partially explains why Li found that nearly 76 percent of victims of cyber-bullying and 75 percent of bystanders never reported instances of bullying to adults. Victims and bystanders who do not report attacks from cyber-bullies can unintentionally enable bullies.

According to De Nies, Donaldson, and Netter of *ABC-News.com* (2010), several of Phoebe Prince's classmates were aware that she was being harassed but did not inform the school's administration. Li suggested that victims and bystanders often do not believe that adults will actually intervene to stop cyber-bullying. However, *ABCNews.com* reports that 41 states have laws against bullying in schools, and 23 of those states target cyber-bullying specifically.

Now that we know that victims of cyber-bullies desperately need the help of witnesses and bystanders to report their attacks, we should arm ourselves with the information necessary to provide that assistance. Think about the next time you see a friend or loved one being tormented or harassed online. What would you be willing to do to help?

Again, Adam does a nice job with his transition.

Cyber-bullying must be confronted on national, local, and personal levels. There should be a comprehensive national law confronting cyber-bullying in schools. Certain statutes currently in state laws should be amalgamated to create the strongest protections for victims and the most effective punishments for bullies as possible.

Notice how Adam gets right to the point about needing to take action on a variety of levels to stop this practice.

According to Limber and Small's article titled State *Laws and Policies to Address Bullying in Schools*, Georgia law requires faculty and staff to be trained on the nature of bullying and what actions to take if they see students being bullied.

Adam gives credence to his policy statement by pointing to several states that have already succeeded in creating such laws.

Furthermore, Connecticut law *requires* school employees to report bullying as part of their hiring contract. Washington takes this a step further by protecting employees from any legal action if a reported bully is proven to be innocent. When it comes to protecting victims, West Virginia law demands that schools must ensure that a bullied student does not receive additional abuse at the hands of his or her bully.

Legislating punishment for bullies is difficult. As Limber and Small noted, zero-tolerance polices often perpetuate violence because at-risk youth, i.e., bullies, are removed from all of the benefits of school, which might help make them less abusive. A comprehensive anti-cyber-bullying law should incorporate the best aspects of these state laws and find a way to punish bullies that is both punitive and has the ability to rehabilitate abusers. However, for national laws to be effective, local communities need to be supportive.

Local communities must organize and mobilize to attack the problem of cyber-bullying. According to Greene's 2006 article published in the *Journal of Social Issues,* communities need to support bullying prevention programs by conducting a school-based bullying survey for individual school districts. We can't know how to best protect victims in our community without knowing how they are affected by the problem. It is critical to know this information. As Greene noted, only 3 percent of teachers in the United States perceive bullying to be a problem in their schools.

Local school districts should create a Coordinating Committee made up of administrators, teachers, students, parents, school staff, and community partners to gather bullying data and rally support to confront the problem. Even if your local school district is unable or unwilling to mobilize behind this dire cause, there are some important actions you can take personally to safeguard those you love against cyber-bullying.

There are several warning signs that might indicate a friend or loved one is a victim of a cyber-bully. If you see a friend or loved one exhibiting these signs, the decision to get involved can be the difference between life and death.

According to Keith and Martin's article *Cyber-Bullying: Creating a Culture of Respect in a Cyber World,* victims of cyber-bullies often use electronic communication more frequently than do people who are not being bullied. Victims of cyber-bullies have mood swings and difficulty sleeping. They seem depressed and/or become anxious. Victims can also become withdrawn from social activities and fall behind in scholastic responsibilities. If you witness your friends or family members exhibiting these symptoms, there are several ways you can help.

According to Raskauskas and Stoltz's 2007 article in *Developmental Psychology,* witnesses of cyber-bullying should inform victims to take the attacks seriously, especially if the bullies threaten violence. You should tell victims to report their attacks to police or other authorities, to block harmful messages by blocking e-mail accounts and cell phone numbers, and to save copies of attacks and provide them to authorities.

If you personally know the bully and feel safe confronting him or her, do so! As Raskauskas and Stoltz noted, bullies will often back down when confronted by peers. By being a good friend and by giving good advice, you can help a victim report his or her attacks from cyber-bullies and take a major step toward eliminating this horrendous problem. So, you see, we are not helpless to stop the cyber-bulling problem as long as we make the choice NOT to ignore it.

Here Adam points to the need for consequences for bullying behavior when it is caught.

Adam offers specific action steps that communities ought to do to help stop cyber-bullying.

Here Adam gets personal, pointing out that each person in the room has an ethical responsibility to help stop cyber-bullying.

Adam could make this statement more compelling by offering a specific example of what one might tell the police, as well as how to install blockers on e-mail and mobile phones.

To conclude, cyber-bullying is a devastating form of abuse that must be reported to authorities. Cyber-bullying is a worldwide problem perpetuated by the silence of both victims and bystanders. By paying attention to certain warning signs, we can empower ourselves to console victims and report their abusers.

Today, I'm imploring you to do your part to help stop cyber-bullying. I know that you agree that stopping cyber-bullying must be a priority. First, although other states have cyber-bullying laws in place, ours does not. So I'm asking you to sign this petition that I will forward to our district's state legislators. We need to make our voices heard that we want specific laws passed to stop this horrific practice and to punish those caught doing it.

Second, I'm also asking you to be vigilant in noticing signs of cyber-bullying and then taking action. Look for signs that your friend, brother, sister, cousin, boyfriend, girlfriend, or loved one might be a victim of cyber-bullying, and then get involved to help stop it! Phoebe Prince showed the warning signs, and she did not deserve to die so senselessly. None of us would ever want to say, "I'll miss just being around her," "I didn't want to believe it," "It's such a sad thing" about our own friends or family members. We must work to ensure that victims are supported and bullies are confronted nationally, locally, and personally.

I know that, if we stand together and refuse to be silent, we can and will stop cyber-bullying.

Here Adam restates his proposition, but it actually could be more comprehensive (beyond just our need to report bullying to authorities).

Adam reminds us of his specific call to action and even asks listeners to sign a petition today. His approach encourages listeners to follow through with his goal, that is, to actuate.

Adam does a nice job with his clincher in terms of tying back to the Phoebe story in his attention catcher. Doing so also appeals to emotions (pathos) in a way that should make his speech very memorable.

Summary

Persuasive speeches are designed to influence the attitudes, beliefs, values, and/or behavior of audience members. They do so by developing strong arguments using logos, ethos, and pathos. The elaboration likelihood model (ELM) suggests that when people hear an argument, they can process it one of two ways. They can listen carefully, reflect thoughtfully, and elaborate on its implications for themselves; or they can make decisions based on simple cues about the speaker's credibility and gut reactions to the message. So in preparing a persuasive speech, you must formulate a proposition (goal) that takes into account the target audience's initial attitude. A target audience may be opposed to, have no opinion (because they are uninformed, neutral, or apathetic), or be in favor of your proposition. You must develop logical arguments to support your proposition, which are what Aristotle referred to as rhetorical appeals to logos. As you do so, be sure you avoid common reasoning fallacies including hasty generalizations, false cause, straw man, either/or, and ad hominem. You must also provide rhetorical appeals to ethos by conveying good character, competence, and credibility, as well as to pathos (motivational appeals to negative and positive emotions).

Effective persuasive speeches can be organized following one of several patterns, which include the statement of reasons pattern, the comparative advantages pattern, the criteria satisfaction pattern, the refutative pattern, the problem–solution pattern, the problem–cause–solution pattern, and the motivational sequence pattern. The same elements that can guide you to create effective persuasive speeches can be used to evaluate the persuasive messages you receive from others.

COMMUNICATE!

RESOURCE AND ASSESSMENT CENTER

Now that you have read Chapter 17, go to the Speech Communication CourseMate at cengagebrain.com where you'll find an interactive eBook and interactive learning tools including quizzes, flashcards, sample speech videos, audio study tools, skill-building activities, action step activities, and more. Student Workbook, Speech Builder Express 3.0, and Speech Studio 2.0 are also available.

Applying What You've Learned

Impromptu Speech Activities

1. Draw a common household product from a box of products your instructor provides. Some products in the box might be nonperishable foods (soup, cereal, snacks, etc.), cleaning supplies (window wash, hand soap, dishwashing liquid), and paper products (toilet paper, paper towels, napkins). Prepare a 2- to 3-minute speech identifying how the product you selected appeals to logos, ethos, and pathos.

2. You and a partner will draw a slip of paper from a container provided by your instructor. The paper will identify competing topics (e.g., superman versus batman, butter versus margarine, eggs versus egg substitutes, flying versus driving, running versus biking). Each of you will prepare a 1- to 2-minute persuasive impromptu speech advocating opposing positions (point/counterpoint).

Assessment Activities

1. Watch a television commercial for a similar product that airs on a cable news network, sports network, and family channel. Who is the target audience for each and why? Identify similar and different rhetorical appeals used in them. Would you rate them as effective for the target audience? Why or why not? Prepare a 1- to 2-page reflection paper describing what you discovered and the assessment you drew from it.

2. Consider an interaction you had in the last week with a friend or family member who convinced you (a) *to do something* you hadn't planned on doing (e.g., go to a movie, attend an event) or (b) *not to do something* you had intended to do (e.g., a household chore, homework). What rhetorical strategies can you identify that influenced your decision? Prepare a 1- to 2-page paper documenting examples of logos, ethos, and pathos that persuaded you.

Skill-Building Activities

1. Forming Propositions Create a proposition of fact, value, and policy for each of the following topics.

    (a) TV violence

    (b) obesity

    (c) illiteracy

    (d) civility

    (e) sexuality

2. Practicing Pathos Identify a negative and positive emotional appeal statement for each of the propositions of fact, value, and policy you created in Skill Builder #1.

UNIT 4 SEQUEL

WHAT'S TECHNOLOGY GOT TO DO WITH IT?
Technology, Digital Media, and Public Speaking

As Cameron watched the rain pouring down, he realized his boss wasn't going to need him to mow greens at the golf course today. This was certainly turning out to be a soggy summer break!

After calling in to confirm with his boss, Cam texted Geoff, "Up for a movie to-day?"

"Can't," Geoff replied. "Gotta do a speech in class at 3."

"Huh?" remarked Cam. "School's 400 miles away!"

"Taking speech class online this summer."

"RUS? LOL." Cam responded.

Geoff chuckled a bit as he replied, "Yup, seriously. Gotta practice now. CU."

When great orators like Plato, Aristotle, and Cicero engaged in public speaking to conduct business, debate public issues, and gain and maintain power, the communication event occurred in real time with both the speaker and audience physically present. Thanks to technology, however, public speeches today may be delivered in both face-to-face and virtual environments. In the opening scenario, for instance, Geoff would present his speech virtually to an audience of classmates watching and listening to him on their computers. Technology also makes it possible to record public speeches and watch them again and again. Geoff's speech was being recorded and uploaded to the class Web site. So later he would watch it, critique himself, and prepare a reflective assessment explaining what he would do to improve next time.

Technology also makes it possible to speak publicly to multiple audiences across the country and around the world. For example, Geoff planned to earn extra credit by posting one of his speeches to YouTube. That speech would reach an audience far beyond his classmates; an audience comprised of people he would probably never meet. Although public speaking certainly still occurs in traditional face-to-face settings, it is no longer limited by place and time—far from it!

President Franklin Delano Roosevelt (FDR) is credited as one of the first public figures to capitalize on the benefits of technology to break through the *place* limitation to reach a wider audience. Throughout his presidency in the 1930s and 1940s, FDR delivered *fireside chats*, weekly radio addresses about important issues facing the country (Mankowski & Jose, 2012). These speeches could be heard by anyone who chose to tune in. U.S. presidents have been offering weekly addresses ever since! In fact, today President Obama even posts weekly addresses on YouTube and the White House Web site (Obama, *Your Weekly Address*).

Perhaps one of the most significant examples of technology overcoming the limitation of *time* comes from Martin Luther King, Jr. Over 200,000 people were at the political rally in Washington, D.C., on August 28, 1963, to hear his famous "I Have a Dream" speech live and in person. More than 50 years later, we can join the 200,000 who made up that first audience to hear him deliver this powerful oration by clicking on any number of Web sites where it is archived. In fact, a quick *Google* search of "I Have a Dream speech" yields more than 37,400,000 *hits*.

The benefits of overcoming *place* and *time* barriers also come with some new challenges, particularly regarding *audience analysis and adaptation*. While many fundamentals of effective public speaking remain true, today speakers must also adapt to multiple audiences and to some unique demands of a mediated platform.

To reach multiple audiences successfully, we must consider not just those who are informed about the topic and issue, but also those who may not be informed, may be apathetic, and perhaps may even be hostile toward it. Those who have analyzed Dr. King's speech, for instance, claim he did so by using the rhetorical devices common to the black preacher style, and at the same time, transcending the typical Civil Rights–era speeches that were aimed at supportive audiences. In the first half of the speech, King addressed his remarks to the assembled throng, but he then moved from addressing the grievances of black Americans to focus on the bedrock of American values. Linking civil rights to the American Dream appealed not only to the audience present on the Washington Mall, but also to the millions of noncommitted Americans who watched the speech on TV. Today, more than 50 years later, it continues to resonate as representing American values and the American dream.

Technology today brings with it a challenge to address mediated audiences that we intentionally target, as was the case with King. However, because speeches today may be easily uploaded to websites like YouTube with or without our permission and then quickly go viral, we also must always be cognizant of possible audiences we never intended to target. Not doing so can result in devastating consequences. For example, in 2011 Texas governor and then–GOP presidential hopeful Rick Perry discovered this when a speech he delivered to a group of supporters in New Hampshire went viral. Blog posts and newspaper editorials blamed his giggling and rambling remarks on being "drunk" or "drugged" (Camia, 2011).

Guidelines for Public Speaking in a Virtual World

The benefits of mediated public speaking to overcome *place* and *time* barriers can be traced to FDR's fireside chats in the 1930s. However, the unique challenges it poses are only beginning to surface. So, the following list of

guidelines provides a starting point that will inevitably grow as we learn more about the role technology and digital media play in effective public speaking.

1. **Adapt your speech to address multiple audiences.** Assume that any speech you give may be recorded and made available to those who are not in your immediate target audience. Always consider how you might adapt your content, structure, and delivery to accurately and respectfully address uninformed, apathetic, and oppositional audiences who may view your speech virtually.

2. **Adapt your speech to account for unintended audiences.** Don't say anything to one specific audience that you would not want broadcast to a wider audience. With just a few clicks of an iPhone or Blackberry, an audience member can record a video and post it online. So make sure your content, language, and humorous anecdotes are accurate and respectful.

3. **Choose presentational aids carefully.** Make sure the visuals and audiovisuals you use can be easily viewed and heard in an online format. Also, be sure to explain them so that those who only have audio access or who view them on a small smartphone screen can understand the information on them.

4. **Become proficient with technology.** Consult with communication technology experts at your university, college, place of business, or professional organization to learn how to use the technologies effectively. Consider taking a course or seminar devoted to developing these competencies.

5. **Employ the fundamentals of effective public speaking.** Although this might seem to go without saying, be sure to adhere to the strategies of effective public speaking even when delivering your speech online to mediated audiences. In other words, use an attention getter to pique curiosity, thesis statement with preview to frame what is to come, and transitions to help your audience follow along. Use accurate, clear, and vivid language, and employ verbal and nonverbal techniques that are intelligible, conversational, and animated.

Appendix: Interviewing

What you'll know

- The types of questions used in interviews

- Ways to find job openings

- Best practices for information-gathering interviews

- Best practices for employment interviews

- Best practices for media interviews

What you'll be able to do

- Prepare for and conduct an information-gathering interview

- Prepare for and conduct an employment interview

- Present yourself successfully in a job interview

- Communicate effectively in a media interview

Terrence, the manager at *Qwik In and Out*, a convenience store and gas station, needed a new night cashier and was interviewing applicants. His first candidate arrived on time, and after taking a tour around the store, they retired to Terrence's office for the interview.

Terrence began, "Take a seat. What did you say your name was again?"

"Bobby. And, um. . . . I'm not sure where you want me to sit."

"Oh, well, just sit on that box over there. Sorry for the mess, but, you know, I've had a lot to do. So, Bobby, you want to work here at *Qwik In and Out*?"

"Yeah."

"Well, you understand that you will be working alone at night, right?"

"Yeah."

"So, it says on your application that you went to Highlands High School. Is that right?"

"Uh-huh."

"And now you're a student at CSCTU?"

"Yeah."

"Will school interfere with your work schedule?"

"Nope."

"Is there anything else I should know?"

"No."

"Well, I've got several other people to talk to, and I'll let you know by Monday what I decide."

"Okay."

After Bobby left the store, Terrence turned to Mary, the day cashier, and said, "Boy, that guy was sure a loser. He just wasn't at all prepared for the interview. I sure hope the next one's better."

What do you think about Terrence's assessment of Bobby? What do you think about how Terrence conducted the interview? Interviewing is a powerful method of collecting or presenting firsthand information that may be unavailable elsewhere. So, it is an important communication skill to master. An **interview** is a highly structured conversation in which one person asks questions and another person answers them. By *highly structured*, we mean that the purpose and the questions to be asked are determined ahead of time. Because interviews are highly structured, they can be used to make comparisons. For example, an interviewer may ask two potential employees the same set of questions, compare the answers, and hire the person whose answers fit best with the needs of the organization and responsibilities of the position. Although we all find ourselves doing interviews, only a few of us have been educated about how to do so effectively as the interviewer or interviewee.

Because the heart of effective interviewing is developing a series of good questions, we begin by describing how to do so. Then we propose some guidelines to follow when engaged in information-gathering, employment, and media interviews.

The Interview Protocol

The **interview protocol** is the list of questions used to elicit desired information from the interviewee. An effective interviewer always prepares a protocol in advance. How many questions you plan to ask depends on how much time you will have for the interview. Begin by listing the topics you want to cover. Then prioritize them. Figure A.1 presents a list of topics for an interview with a music producer when the goal is to learn about how producers find and sign new talent.

Just as the topics in a well-developed speech are structured in an outline with main points, subpoints, and supporting material, an effective interview protocol is structured into primary and secondary questions. The questions should be a mix of open-ended and closed questions, as well as neutral and leading questions. Let's briefly examine each type.

interview

a planned, structured conversation in which one person asks questions and another person answers them

CONSIDER *THIS*....

Think of a time when you were interviewed. How did you feel before the interview began and once it was over? Did you feel you were effective? Why or why not?

interview protocol

the list of questions used to elicit desired information from the interviewee

Figure A.1

Music producer interview topics

- Finding artists
- Decision process
- Criteria
- Stories of success and failure

© Cengage Learning

(1) How do you find artists to consider for contract?

(2) Once an artist has been brought to your attention, what course of action do you follow?

(3) What criteria do you use when deciding to offer a contract?

(4) Can you tell me the story of how you came to sign one of your most successful artists and then one about an unsuccessful artist?

© Cengage Learning

Figure A.2

Music producer primary questions

Primary and Secondary Questions

Primary questions are introductory questions about each major interview topic. Figure A.2 illustrates what the primary questions might be for the music producer interview.

Secondary questions are follow-up questions that probe the interviewee to expand on the answers given to primary questions. The interviewee may not realize how much detail you want or may be purposely evasive. Some follow-up questions probe by simply encouraging the interviewee to continue ("And then?" or "Is there more?"); some probe into a specific detail the person mentioned or failed to mention ("What does 'regionally popular' mean?" and "You didn't mention genre. What role might that play in your decision to offer a contract?"); and some probe into their feelings ("How did it feel when her first record went platinum?").

primary questions

introductory questions about each major interview topic

secondary questions

follow-up questions that probe the interviewee to expand on the answers given to primary questions

Open and Closed Questions

Open questions are broad-based queries that allow freedom about to the specific information, opinions, or feelings that can be divulged. Open questions encourage the interviewee to talk and allow the interviewer an opportunity to listen and observe. Since open questions give respondents more control, interviewers need to intentionally redirect the interviewee to focus on the original purpose (Tengler & Jablin, 1983). For example, in a job interview you might be asked, "What one accomplishment has best prepared you for this job?" In a customer service interview, a representative might ask, "What seems to be the problem?" or "Can you tell me the steps you took when you first set up this product?"

By contrast, **closed questions** are narrowly focused and require very brief (one- or two-word) answers. Closed questions range from those that can be answered yes or no, such as "Have you had a course in marketing?" to those that require only a short answer, such as "Which of the artists that you have signed have won Grammys?" By asking closed questions, interviewers can control the interview and obtain specific information quickly. But the answers to closed questions cannot reveal the nuances behind responses, nor are they likely to capture the complexity of the story.

open questions

broad-based that freedom about what specific information, opinions, or feelings to divulge

closed questions

narrowly focused questions that require very brief (one- or two-word) answers

Neutral and Leading Questions

Open and closed questions may also be either neutral or leading. **Neutral questions** do not direct a person's answer. "What can you tell me about your work with Habitat for Humanity?" and "What criteria do you use in deciding whether to offer an artist a contract?" are neutral questions. The neutral question gives the respondent free rein to answer the question without any knowledge of what the interviewer thinks or believes.

neutral questions

questions that do not direct a person's answer

Rapport-Building Opener

How did you get interested in becoming a music producer?

Major Topic Questions

Primary Question #1: How do you find artists to consider for contract?

   Secondary Question: Is this different from the methods used by other producers?

   Secondary Question: Do artists ever come to you in other ways?

Primary Question #2: Once an artist has been brought to your attention, what course of action follows?

   Secondary Question: Do you ever just see an artist or band and immediately sign them?

   Secondary Question: What's the longest period of time you "auditioned" an artist or band before signing them?

Primary Question #3: What criteria do you use in deciding to offer a contract?

   Secondary Question: How important are the artist's age, sex, or ethnicity?

Primary Question #4: Can you tell me the story of how you came to sign one of your most successful artists?

   Secondary Question: What do you think made the artist so successful?

Primary Question #5: Can you tell me the story of an artist you signed that was not successful?

   Secondary Question: Why do you think this artist failed?

   Secondary Question: Do you think it was a mistake to sign this artist?

   Secondary Question: In retrospect, what could you or the artist have done differently that might have helped him or her succeed?

From *VERDERBER/VERDERBER/SELLNOW, The Challenge of Effective Speaking*, 15E. © 2012 Cengage Learning.

Figure A.3

Sample music producer interview protocol

leading questions

questions that guide respondents toward providing certain types of information and imply that the interviewer prefers one answer over another

By contrast, **leading questions** guide respondents toward providing certain types of information and imply that the interviewer prefers one answer over another. "What do you like about working for Habitat for Humanity?" steers respondents to describe only the positive aspects of their volunteer work. "Having a 'commercial sound' is an important criteria, isn't it?" directs the answer by providing the standard for comparison. In most types of interviews, neutral questions are preferable because they are less likely to create defensiveness in the interviewee. In the opening interview, which of Terrence's questions were neutral and which were leading?

A good interview protocol will use a combination of open, closed, neutral, and leading questions. With this in mind, look again at the opening interview. What kinds of questions did Terrence ask Bobby? How did this affect what happened? Figure A.3 provides a sample interview protocol for the music producer interview.

Information-Gathering Interviews

Interviewing is a valuable method for obtaining information on nearly any topic. Lawyers and police interview witnesses to establish facts; health care providers interview patients to obtain medical histories before making diagnoses; reporters interview sources for their stories; managers interview employees to receive updates on projects; and students interview experts to obtain information for research projects. Once you have prepared a good interview protocol, you need to choose an appropriate person to interview, conduct the interview effectively, and follow up respectfully.

Choosing the Interviewee

Sometimes the choice is obvious, but other times, you will have to do research to identify the right person to interview. Suppose your purpose is to learn about how to get a recording contract. You might begin by asking a professor in the music department for the name of a music production agency in the area. Or you could find the name of an agency by searching online. Once you find a Web site, you can usually find an "About Us" or "Contact Us" link on it, which will offer names, titles, e-mail addresses, and phone numbers. You should be able to identify someone appropriate to your purpose from this list. Once you have identified the person or people to be interviewed, you should contact them to make an appointment. Today, it is generally best to do so by both e-mail and telephone if possible. When you contact them, be sure to clearly state the purpose of the interview, how the interview information will be used, and how long you expect the interview to take. When setting a date and time, suggest several dates and time ranges and ask which would be best for them. As you conclude, thank the person for agreeing to be interviewed and confirm the date, time, and location you have agreed to for the interview. If you make the appointment more than a few days in advance, call or e-mail the day before the interview to confirm the appointment.

You don't want to bother your interviewee with information you can get elsewhere. So to prepare appropriate protocol questions, do some research on the topic in advance. This includes learning about what the interviewee may have written about the topic and his or her credentials. Interviewees will be more responsive if you appear informed and being informed will ensure that you ask good questions. For instance, if you are going to interview a music producer, you will want to do preliminary research about what a music producer is and does, whether any general "best practices" exist for signing artists, and whether this particular producer has published any criteria. You can usually do so by carefully reading the information posted on their Web site. Then, during the interview, you can ask about additional criteria, different criteria, or to expand on how the criteria is used in making judgments.

Conducting the Interview

To guide you in the process of conducting effective and ethical interviews, we offer this list of best practices.

1. **Dress professionally.** Doing so sends a message to the interviewee that you *respect them* and the time they are giving you and that you take the interview seriously.

2. **Be prompt.** You also *demonstrate respect* by showing up prepared to begin at the time you have agreed to. Remember to allow enough time for potential traffic and parking problems.

THE AUDIENCE *BEYOND*

Kira decided she wanted to interview the director of the local food bank as research for her speech about homelessness in the local community. She spent a good deal of time learning specifics about the director and the food bank before contacting him to request an interview.

3. **Be courteous.** Begin by introducing yourself and the purpose of the interview and by thanking the person for taking the time to talk to you. Remember, although interviewees may enjoy talking about the subject, may be flattered, and may wish to share knowledge, they most likely have nothing to gain from the interview. So, you should let them know you are grateful for their time. Most of all, *respect* what the interviewee says regardless of what you may think of his or her responses.

4. **Ask permission to record.** If the interviewee says no, *respect* his or her wishes and take careful notes instead.

5. **Listen carefully.** At key points in the interview, paraphrase what the interviewee has said to be sure that you really understand. This will assure the interviewee that you will report the answers *truthfully* and *fairly* in your paper, project, or speech.

6. **Keep the interview moving.** You do not want to rush the person, but you do want to behave *responsibly* by getting your questions answered during the allotted time.

7. **Monitor your nonverbal reactions.** Maintain good eye contact with the person. Nod to show understanding, and smile occasionally to maintain the friendliness of the interview. How you look and act is likely to determine whether the person will warm up to you and give you an informative interview.

8. **Get permission to quote.** Be sure to get permission for exact quotes. Doing so demonstrates that you *respect* the interviewee and want to report his or her ideas *honestly* and *fairly.* Doing so also communicates that you have *integrity* and strive to act *responsibly.* You might even offer to let the person see a copy of what you prepare before you share it with others. That way, he or she can double-check the accuracy of direct quotations.

9. **Confirm credentials.** Before you leave, be sure to confirm your interviewee's professional title and the company or organization he or she represents. To do so is to act *responsibly* because you will need these details when explaining why you chose to interview this person.

10. **End on time.** As with arriving promptly, ending the interview when you said you would demonstrates *respect* for the interviewee and that you act *responsibly* and with *integrity.*

11. **Thank the interviewee.** Thanking the interviewee leads to positive rapport, should you need to follow up later, and demonstrates that you appreciate his or her valuable time. You may even follow up with a short thank-you note after you leave.

Following Up

Because your interview notes were probably taken in outline or shorthand form, the longer you wait to translate them the more difficult doing so will be. So you'll need to sit down with your notes as soon as possible after the interview to make more extensive notes of the information you may want to use later. If you recorded the interview, take some time to **transcribe** the responses by translating them word for word into written form. If at any point you are not sure whether you have accurately transcribed what the person said or meant, telephone or e-mail them to double-check. When you have

transcribe

translate oral interview responses word for word into written form

completed a draft of your paper, project, or speech outline, you can demonstrate *respect* for the person and *integrity* as a reporter by providing him or her with a copy of the product if it is a written paper or report, a link to it if it is an online document, or an invitation to attend if it is a public speech or performance.

Employment Interviews

Believe it or not, in the past 50 years, the average amount of time an employee stays with one company or organization has gone from over 23 years to about 4 years (Employee Tenure, 2010; Taylor & Hardy, 2004)! Not only that, but between 15 and 20 million Americans find themselves changing jobs each year (Bashara, 2006). What this means is that we spend more time doing employment interviews both as interviewers and interviewees than ever before. Employment interviews help interviewers assess which applicants have the knowledge, experience, and skills that best fit the responsibilities of the position and culture of the organization—characteristics and skills that cannot be judged from a résumé. And employment interviews help employment-seekers make an educated guess about whether the organization is one they would enjoy working in. So let's look at some best practices for both employment interviewers and employment seekers.

Employment Interviewers

Historically, human resource professionals have conducted most employment interviews on behalf of a firm, but today more and more workplaces rely on co-workers as interviewers. You may have already helped conduct employment interviews, or you may be asked to do so in the near future. As with any interview, you will need to follow some guidelines as you both prepare for and conduct the interview.

Preparing for the Interview As with information interviews, you begin by doing research. In the case of employment interviewing, this means becoming familiar with the knowledge, skills, and aptitudes someone must have to be successful in the job. It also means studying the résumés, reference letters, and other application materials to narrow the applicant pool to the short list of applicants you will interview. Before interviewing each candidate on the short list, prepare by reviewing their materials again, making notes about topics to address with probing secondary questions.

In most employment interviewing situations, you will see several candidates. It's important to make an interview protocol to make sure that all applicants are asked the same (or very similar) questions about characteristics and skills. Be sure to identify primary questions and secondary questions that will probe knowledge, skills, characteristics, and experiences relevant to the position and the culture of your organization. Using a protocol will also help you avoid questions that violate fair employment practice legislation. The Equal Opportunity Commission has detailed guidelines that spell out what questions are unlawful.

Conducting the Interview As with the information-gathering interview, begin with introductions and a question or two designed to establish rapport and to help the interviewee relax. What follows are some best-practice tips to follow when conducting employment interviews.

CONSIDER *THIS*....

Have you ever received a thank-you note you didn't expect? If so, how did it make you feel about the person? Why might you want to send a thank-you note to the person you interview for information-gathering purposes?

1. **Greet the applicant.** Warmly greet the applicant by name, shake hands, and introduce yourself. If you will be taking notes or recording the interview, you should explain that as well. Ask a couple of rapport-building "warm-up" questions to put the applicant at ease. For example, you might ask how the traffic was, whether it was difficult to find parking, or something about the weather. Once the applicant seems comfortable, you can proceed.

2. **Ask a series of prepared protocol questions.** Here is where you ask your well-planned questions to determine whether the applicant's knowledge, skills, experiences, personal characteristics, and interpersonal style fit the demands of the job and the organizational culture. It is important to keep the interview moving. You want to give the applicant sufficient time to answer your questions, but don't waste time by allowing the applicant to over-answer questions.

3. **Consider your verbal and nonverbal cues.** As you ask questions, strive to sound spontaneous and to speak in a voice that is easily heard. Be sensitive to the nonverbal messages you are sending. Be careful that you are not leading applicants to answer in certain ways through your nonverbal cues.

4. **Use secondary follow-up questions.** You should probe the applicant to expand on answers that are vague or too brief. Remember, your goal is to understand the applicant, which includes his or her strengths, weaknesses, and potential fit with the position and your organization.

5. **Conclude with a clarification of next steps.** As the interview comes to an end, tell the applicant what will happen next. Explain how and approximately when the hiring decision will be made, as well as how the applicant will be notified. Unless you are the person with hiring authority, remain neutral about the applicant. You don't want to mislead the applicant with false hope or discouragement.

Following Up Once you have hired one of the interviewees, be sure to follow up with a short e-mail or letter informing each of the other candidates that the position has been filled. You can do so *respectfully* by thanking them for their interest in the position and taking the time to participate in the interview, reminding them that they were a strong candidate in a strong applicant pool, and wishing them well in their future employment-seeking endeavors.

Employment Seekers

An **employment seeker** is anyone who is looking for a job or considering a job change. Some may be unemployed and dedicating 100 percent of their time to finding a job. Others may be happily employed and recruited to apply for another position. Still others could be employed, but seeking a more rewarding position. As many employment experts will tell you, "As a rule, the best jobs do *not* go to the best-qualified individuals—they go to the best job seekers" (Graber, 2000, p. 29). Successful employment seekers are obviously the ones who get the job. To be successful, you need to follow guidelines searching for job openings, as well as when applying and interviewing.

Locating Job Openings At this point in your life, you have probably been through the hiring process at least once and perhaps many times. So you know how stressful it can be. You also probably know that sometimes

> **CONSIDER *THIS*....**
>
> Have you ever interviewed for a job and wondered whether it had been filled? How did you find out? Why is it important to let candidates who were not selected know a position has been filled?

employment seeker

anyone who is looking for a job or considering a job change

the most difficult part is finding out about job openings. Sometimes openings are easily accessible by searching the Internet, newspaper, career fairs, and career centers. We call this the **visible job market.** Other times, however, job openings are not readily apparent and require you to use other methods to locate and apply for them. We call this the **hidden job market** (Yena, 2011). We focus here on locating jobs in both the visible and hidden job markets by searching published resources (in print and online), using referral services, and networking.

Published Resources When employers want to cast a wide net for applicants, they will publish in a variety of outlets that are read most widely by employment seekers. These range from Web sites such as CareerBuilder.com, Monster.com, HotJobs.com, USAJOBS.gov (dedicated to government jobs), CollegeJobBank.com (dedicated to recent college graduates), as well as classified sections of online newspapers and newsletters. Some sites allow you to post your résumé online and will forward it to potential employers when your credentials fit their needs. Although employers often use these sites, they also very often publish openings on their own Web sites. So, even if you find an announcement posted on another site, you can improve your chances of landing an interview if you actually apply through the company's own Web site (Light, 2011).

Referral Services Some employers like to use referral services to do the initial screening of applicants. Most colleges and universities have an on-site career center that serves this purpose. Your tuition dollars pay for this service, so it's one of the first places you should look. They post and publish local, regional, national, and international openings in a variety of for-profit, non-profit, and government organizations. In addition to doing initial screenings for employers, career service officers also provide applicants helpful advice about writing cover letters, preparing résumés, selecting references, and doing interviews. Finally, they often facilitate on-campus **career fairs** to help bring potential employers and applicants together to learn about the company and make contacts.

Some employers also have in-house **employee referral programs** that reward current employees for referring strong candidates to the company. If you are interested in working for a particular company, you might seek an opportunity to ask a current employee to recommend you.

Networking Networking is the process of using developing or established relationships to make contacts with people who can help you discover and apply for positions that may or may not be accessible through the *visible job market.* In fact, some research suggests that the majority of jobs are filled this way (Betty, 2010). Your **network** consists of the people you know, people you meet, and the people who are known to the people you know. These people may include teachers, counselors, your friends, family friends, relatives, service club members, mentors, classmates, colleagues, and even people you meet at sporting events, country clubs, and health clubs. We offer two guidelines to help make networking work for you.

1. **Reach out to people you know and tell them you are in the job market.** Speak up and tell the people you know that you are looking for a job. Bring it up during a conversation you may be having with them or intentionally seek them out to let them know. Prepare business cards with your contact information on them and give them to the people you

---

visible job market

easily accessible job opening announcements

hidden job market

job openings that are not readily apparent and require alternative methods to locate

career fairs

events that bring potential employers and applicants together to foster networking and create awareness about opportunities

employee referral programs

in-house reward programs for employees who refer strong candidates to the company

networking

the process of using developing or established relationships to make contacts regarding job openings

network

the people you know, people you meet, and people who are known to the people you know

elevator speech

a 60-second oral summary of the type of job you are seeking and your qualifications for it

talk to. Similarly, don't assume they know your résumé. In addition to business cards, be prepared to provide them with an **elevator speech**—a 60-second oral summary of the type of job you're seeking and your qualifications for it. Ask them if they know of (1) any job opportunities that might be appropriate, and (2) anyone you might contact to help you find such opportunities. Finally, ask them to keep their eyes and ears open about anything that might be of interest to you and to share such information with you.

2. **Grow your network.** Attend networking events in your area that may be hosted by your college or university career center, the local chamber of commerce, and alumni association. Join professional and civic organizations. Volunteer. The more people you know, the more people you will have to ask about potential opportunities on the *hidden job market*. You should also join online networking groups such as *LinkedIn, Facebook,* and *Twitter.* Remember the key here is to develop and nurture relationships. People will make a special effort to help you if they believe you are a friend and a good person.

CONSIDER *THIS....*

When you think about networking and growing your network, what thoughts and feelings come to mind? What will you do to ensure that you network effectively?

Preparing Application Materials

Because interviewing is time consuming, most organizations do not interview all the people who apply for a job. Rather, they use a variety of screening devices to eliminate people who don't meet their qualifications. Chief among them are evaluating the qualifications you highlight on your résumé and in your cover letter (Kaplan, 2002). A **résumé** is a summary sheet highlighting your related experience, educational background, skills, and accomplishments. A **cover letter** is a short well-written letter or e-mail expressing your interest in the position and piquing curiosity about why your application materials deserve a closer look. The goal of your cover letter and résumé is to land an interview (Farr, 2009). Whether you send your application materials electronically or through regular postal mail, the guidelines for preparing them effectively are the same. Before you can even begin, you need to know something about the company and about the job requirements so that you can tailor them to highlight how and why you are the best candidate. Today you can learn a lot about an organization by visiting its Web site and reading online material thoroughly. You can also talk to people you know who work or worked there, or acquaintances of employees. Let's look at three guidelines to follow when tailoring your résumé and cover letter.

résumé

a summary sheet highlighting your related experience, educational background, skills, and accomplishments

cover letter

a short, well-written letter or e-mail expressing your interest in a particular job and piquing curiosity about you as an applicant

Tailoring Your Résumé **Tailor your résumé to highlight your skills and experiences related to the position and its responsibilities.** There are two types of résumés. In both, you begin by supplying basic contact information (name, address, e-mail, phone number), educational degrees or certificates earned, and career objective. In a **chronological résumé**, you list your job positions and accomplishments in reverse chronological order. Chronological résumés are most appropriate if you have held jobs in the past that are clearly related to the position you are applying for. In a **functional résumé** you focus on highlighting the skills and experiences you have that qualify you for the position. You may find a functional résumé best for highlighting your skills and accomplishments if you are changing careers, have

chronological résumé

listing your job positions and accomplishments in reverse chronological order

functional résumé

focuses on highlighting the skills and experiences that qualify you for the position

Elisa C. Vardin

2326 Tower Place
Cincinnati, OH 45220
(513) 861-2497
ECVardin@yahoo.com

Professional Objective:

An entry-level marketing research position where I can use my quantitative train-ing to create and analyze marketing data and use my organizing, writing and public speaking skills to communicate technical findings to decision makers.

Educational Background:

University of Cincinnati, Cincinnati, OH, B.A. June 2001.

Major: Applied Mathematics, Minor: Marketing.

GPA 3.36. Dean's List.

Work and Other Relevant Experience:

Marketing Solutions, Inc., Cincinnati, OH. Summer 2011.

Intern at marketing research firm. Provided administrative support to marketing research team. Created a new method for tracking internal project workflow. Analyzed Survant generated data with Mentor. Helped prepare client reports.

McMicken College of Arts and Sciences, U.C. Student Ambassador. 2008–2011. Chair, Activities Committee 2010–2011. Responsible for planning social events and scheduling over 6,000 student visits. Over 45 presentations to groups.

Strategic Planning Committee, Summit Country Day School, Cincinnati, OH. Fall 2006–2007. One of two student members. Worked with the board of directors developing the first strategic plan for a 1,000-student independent school (pre-K through 12).

AYF National Leadership Conference, Miniwanca Conference Center, Shelby, MI. Summer 2005–2006. Participant in conference sponsored by American Youth Foundation.

Technical Skills and Training:

MINITAB, SAS, SPSS, MatLab, MATHSTAT, MicroSoft Office, Survant, Mentor. Coursework in statistics, regression analysis, math stats, nonparametric stats, applied complex analysis, marketing research.

© Cengage Learning 2014

Figure A.4

Sample chronological résumé

a gap in your work history, or have limited formal job experience, but have acquired job-related skills in other ways (courses you have taken, clubs you have belonged to, service-learning and volunteer work, etc.). Figures A.4 and A.5 are examples of a chronological and functional résumé for the same college student.

THE AUDIENCE *BEYOND*

Jill wasn't sure what to highlight in her résumé so she visited the business's Web site to read its mission and values statement and get an idea of the implicit norms the company seemed to hold. Then she made sure to highlight her experiences that related to similar values and norms.

Elisa C. Vardin

2326 Tower Place
Cincinnati, OH 45220
(513) 861-2497
ECVardin@yahoo.com

Professional Objective:

Entry-level marketing research position allowing me to use my quantitative training to create and analyze marketing data and use my organizing, writing and public speaking skills to communicate technical findings to decision makers.

Educational Background:

University of Cincinnati, Cincinnati, OH, B.A. June 2011.

Major: Applied Mathematics, Minor: Marketing.

GPA 3.36. Dean's List.

Relevant Coursework: Multivariate Stats, Regression Analysis, Math Stats, Non Parametric Stats, Applied Complex Analysis, Marketing Research.

Technical Skills: MINITAB, SPSS, SAS, MatLab, MATHSTAT, MicroSoft Office

Professional Skills:

Statistical and Analytical

- Proficient with various statistical software packages used to analyze marketing research data.
- Hands-on experience cleaning marketing research data sets.
- Analyzed complex statistical output from a multisite marketing research study under extreme time pressure.

Organizing/Leadership Skills

- Created and coordinated a schedule for over 6,000 client visits.
- Participated in strategic planning process for an independent private school.
- Graduated from two-year national leadership development program.

Communication Skills

- Presented over 45 10- to 30-minute presentations using PowerPoint.
- Drafted marketing research report and PowerPoint presentation for client.
- Public speaking, persuasion, and technical writing coursework.

Experience:

Marketing Solutions, Inc., Cincinnati, OH. Summer 2011. Intern.

McMicken College of Arts and Sciences, U.C. Student Ambassador. 2008–2011. Chair, Activities Committee 2010–2011.

Strategic Planning Committee, Summit Country Day School, Cincinnati, OH. Fall 2006–2007. Student Representative. Strategic Planning Committee.

National Leadership Conference, American Youth Foundation. Summer 2005–2006.

Figure A.5

Sample functional résumé

Tailoring Your Cover Letter **Tailor your cover letter to the position.** Be sure to highlight your qualifications for *a specific job and its responsibilities.* You can learn some of this information in the job description, but you may also need to make inferences about it by visiting the company's Web site and talking to people associated with the organization or familiar with the type of position described in the advertisement.

Your cover letter should be short, no more than four or five paragraphs. If you prepare your cover letter in the body of an e-mail message, it should be even shorter. These paragraphs should highlight your job-related skills and experiences *using key words that appeared in the posting*. Many employers use software programs that scan e-mails and résumés for job-relevant key words. Using them in your cover letter will increase the likelihood that someone will actually look at your application materials. Use a spell-checker and carefully proofread for errors such programs don't catch. Your cover letter must be 100% error free to serve as a catalyst for getting an interview. Figures A.6 and A.7 provide a sample cover letter and sample cover e-mail.

2326 Tower Place
Cincinnati, OH 45220
April 8, 2013

Mr. Kyle Jones
Acme Marketing Research Associates
P.O. Box 482
Cincinnati, OH 45201

Dear Mr. Jones:

I am applying for the position of first-year associate at Acme Marketing Research Associates, which I learned about through the Office of Career Counseling at the University of Cincinnati. I am a senior mathematics major at the University of Cincinnati who is interested in a career in marketing research. I am highly motivated, eager to learn, and I enjoy working with all types of people. I am excited by the prospect of working for a firm like Acme Marketing Research Associates, where I can apply my leadership and problem-solving skills in a professional setting.

As a mathematics major, I have developed the analytical proficiency that is necessary for working through complex problems. My courses in statistics have especially prepared me for data analysis, and my more theoretical courses have taught me how to construct an effective argument. My leadership training and experiences have given me the ability to work effectively in groups and have taught me the benefits of both individual and group problem solving. My work on the Strategic Planning Committee has given me an introduction to market analysis by teaching me skills associated with strategic planning. Finally, from my theatrical experience, I have gained the poise to make presentations in front of small and large groups alike. I believe these experiences and others have shaped who I am and have helped me to develop many of the skills necessary to be successful. I am interested in learning more and continuing to grow.

I look forward to having the opportunity for an interview with you. I have enclosed my résumé with my school address and phone number. Thank you for your consideration. I hope to hear from you soon.

Sincerely,
Elisa C. Vardin

Figure A.6

Sample cover letter

Dear Mr. Jones:

I am applying for the position of research assistant at Acme Marketing Research Associates. Professor Robert Carl at the University of Cincinnati suggested that I might be a good fit for your company.

As an applied mathematics major at the University of Cincinnati with a minor in marketing I have prepared myself for a career in marketing research. I have worked hard to develop a comprehensive background in statistics and am equipped with the skills to use the major statistical packages required to analyze market research data. In addition to these technical qualifications I have also developed my organizational, leadership, and communication skills though a variety of paid and volunteer positions.

I am excited by the prospect of beginning my career at AMRA because your company is known for its cutting-edge marketing research programs as well as high ethical standards. I look forward to having the opportunity to speak with you. I have attached both a .txt and a .rtf formatted copy of my résumé for your consideration. I look forward to hearing from you about the next steps I can take to become a member of your marketing research team.

Sincerely,
Elisa C. Vardin

© Cengage Learning 2014

Figure A.7

Sample cover e-mail

Tailoring Materials for Online Submissions **Tailor your application materials for a variety of online submission programs.** Because you will apply for most jobs online, make sure your materials can be submitted in several formats. Some of them are illustrated in Figure A.8 along with their advantages and disadvantages.

Conducting the Employment Interview

employment interview

a conversation or set of conversations between a job candidate and a representative or representatives of a hiring organization

An **employment interview** is a conversation or set of conversations between a job candidate and a representative or representatives of a hiring organization. Your goal is to convince the interviewer that you are the best qualified candidate and the best fit for the position and company. Successful interviewing begins with thorough preparation, then with the actual interview, and finally with appropriate follow up.

Preparing Once you submit your application materials, you need to prepare for the interview you hope to get. In this section, we offer four suggestions to prepare for a job interview.

1. **Do your homework.** Although you should have already done extensive research on the position and the organization to prepare your application materials, you should review what you've learned before going to the interview. Be sure you know the organization's products and services, areas of operation, ownership, and financial health. Nothing puts off interviewers more than applicants who arrive at an interview knowing little about the organization. Be sure to look beyond the "Work for Us" or "Frequently Asked Questions" links on the company's Web site. Find more specific information such as pages that target potential investors, report company

TYPE	USE	FILE EXTENTION	ADVANTAGES	DISADVANTAGES
Formatted	For print résumé or e-mail attachments	.doc .wpd .wps	• Visually attractive	• Vulnerable to viruses • Inconsistencies in formatting from computer to computer
Text	• Posting to job boards • Conversion to scannable résumé	.txt	• Key word searchable • Consistent formatting computer to computer • Not vulnerable to viruses	• Not visually appealing
Rich Text	• When sending résumé as an attachment • When you don't know employer's format preference	.rft	• Good for résumé attachment because it is compatible with all platforms and word processing programs • Formatting of original résumé holds up pretty well • Less vulnerable to viruses	None
Portable Document	• When you want to retain the exact identical formatting and pagination • When employers request it	.pdf	• Invulnerable to viruses • Compatible across computer systems	• Hard to do key word search • If prepared by others, can not make revisions without expensive software
Web Based	• For passive job searching • To post resume to your Web site or a hosted	.html .htm	• Employer can find your résumé • Available 24/7	• Need a host site

Adapted from: Hansen, K. Your e-résumé's file format aligns with its delivery method. Accessed at Quintessential Careers.com: http://www.quintcareers.com/e-resume_format.html.

Figure A.8

Online application submission variations

stock performance, and describe the organization's mission (Slayter, 2006). Likewise, pictures can suggest the type of organizational culture you can expect—formal or informal dress, collaborative or individual work spaces, diversity, and so on. Researching these details will help you decide whether the organization is right for you, as well as help you form questions to ask during the interview.

2. **Prepare a self-summary.** You should not have to hesitate when an interviewer asks you why you are interested in the job. You should also be prepared to describe your previous accomplishments. Form these statements as personal stories with specific examples that people will remember (Beshara, 2006). Robin Ryan (2000), one of the nation's foremost career authorities, advises job seekers to prepare a 60-second general statement they can share with a potential employer. She advises job

seekers to identify which aspects of their training and experience would be most valued by a potential employer. She suggests making a five-point agenda that can (a) summarize your most relevant experience and (b) "build a solid picture emphasizing how you *can* do the job" (p. 10). Once you have your points identified, practice communicating them fluently in 60 seconds or less.

3. **Prepare a list of questions about the organization and the job.** The employment interview should be a two-way street, where you size up the company as they are sizing you up. So you will probably have a number of specific questions to ask the interviewer. For example, "Can you describe a typical workday for the person in this position?" or "What is the biggest challenge in this job?" Make a list of your questions and take it with you to the interview. It can be difficult to come up with good questions on the spur of the moment, so you should prepare several questions in advance. One question we do not advise asking during the interview, however, is "How much money will I make?" Save salary, benefits, and vacation-time negotiations until after you have been offered the job.

4. **Rehearse the interview.** Several days before the interview, spend time outlining the job requirements and how your knowledge, skills, and experiences meet those requirements. Practice answering questions commonly asked in interviews, such as those listed in Figure A.9.

Interviewing The actual interview is your opportunity to sell yourself to the organization. Although interviews can be stressful, your preparation should give you the confidence you need to relax and communicate effectively. Believe it or not, the job interview is somewhat stressful for the interviewer as well. Most companies do not interview potential employees every day. Moreover, the majority of interviewers have little or no formal training in the interview process. Your goal is to make the interview a comfortable conversation for both of you.

Use these guidelines to help you have a successful interview.

1. **Dress appropriately.** You want to make a good first impression, so it is important to be well groomed and neatly dressed. Although "casual" or "business casual" is common in many workplaces, some organizations still expect employees to be more formally dressed. If you don't know the dress code for the organization, call the human resources department and ask.

Figure A.9

Frequently asked interview questions

- In what ways does your transcript reflect your ability?
- Can you give an example of how you work under pressure?
- What are your major strengths? Weaknesses?
- Can you give an example of when you were a leader and what happened?
- Tell me about a time when you tried something at work that failed. How did you respond to the failure?
- Tell me about a time you had a serious conflict with a co-worker. How did you deal with the conflict?
- What have you done that shows your creativity?
- What kind of position are you looking for?

2. **Arrive on time.** The interview is the organization's first exposure to your work behavior, so you don't want to be late. Find out how long it will take you to travel by making a dry run at least a day before. Plan to arrive 10 or 15 minutes before your appointment.

3. **Bring supplies.** Bring extra copies of your résumé, cover letter, business cards, and references, as well as the list of questions you plan to ask. You might also bring a portfolio of previous work you have done. You will also want to have paper and a pen so that you can make notes.

4. **Use active listening.** When we are anxious, we sometimes have trouble listening well. Work on paying attention to, understanding, and remembering what is asked. Remember that the interviewer will be aware of your nonverbal behavior, so be sure to make and keep eye contact as you listen.

5. **Think before answering.** If you have prepared for the interview, make sure that as you answer the interviewer's questions, you also tell your story. Take a moment to consider how your answers portray your skills and experiences.

6. **Be enthusiastic.** If you come across as bored or disinterested, the interviewer is likely to conclude that you would be an unmotivated employee.

7. **Ask questions.** As the interview is winding down, be sure to ask any questions you prepared that have not already been answered. You may also want to ask how well the interviewer believes your qualifications match the position, and what your strengths are.

8. **Thank the interviewer and restate your interest in the position.** As the interview comes to a close, shake the interviewer's hand and thank him or her for the opportunity. Finally, restate your interest in the position and desire to work on the company team.

Following Up

Once the interview is over, you can set yourself apart from the other applicants by following these important steps:

1. **Send a thank-you note.** It is appropriate to write a short note thanking the interviewer for the experience and again expressing your interest in the job.

2. **Self-assess your performance.** Take time to critique your performance. How well did you do? What can you do better next time?

3. **Contact the interviewer for feedback.** If you don't get the job, you might call the interviewer and ask for feedback. Be polite and indicate that you are only calling to get some help on your interviewing skills. Actively listen to the feedback, using questions and paraphrases to clarify what is being said. Be sure to thank the interviewer for helping you.

Media Interviews

Today we live in a media-saturated environment in which any individual may be approached by a newsperson and asked to participate in an on-air interview. For example, the authors have a friend who became the object of media interest when the city council refused to grant him a zoning variance so that he could complete building a new home on his property. In the course of three days, his story became front-page news in his town, and reports about his situation made the local radio and TV news shows. You might be asked for an interview at public meetings, at the mall, or within the context of your work or community service. For example, you may be asked to share your knowledge of your organization's programs, events, or activities. Because media interviews are likely to be edited in some way before they are aired and because they reach a wide audience, there are specific strategies you should use to prepare for and participate in them.

Before the Interview

The members of the media work under very tight deadlines, so it is crucial that you respond immediately to media requests for an interview. When people are insensitive to media deadlines, they can end up looking like they have purposefully evaded the interview and have something to hide. When you speak with the media representative, clarify what the focus of the interview will be and how the information will be presented. At times, the entire interview will be presented; however, it is more likely that the interview will be edited or paraphrased and not all of your comments will be reported.

As you prepare for the interview, identify three or four **talking points**, that is, the central ideas you want to present as you answer questions during a media interview. For example, before our friend was interviewed by the local TV news anchor, he knew that he wanted to emphasize that he was a victim of others' mistakes: (1) he had hired a licensed architect to draw the plans; (2) the city inspectors had repeatedly approved earlier stages of the building process; (3) the city planning commission had voted unanimously to grant him the variance; and (4) he would be out half the cost of the house if he were forced to tear it down and rebuild. Consider how you will tailor your information to the specific audience in terms they can understand. Consider how you will respond to tough or hostile questions.

During the Interview

Media interviews call for a combination of interviewing, nonverbal communication, and public speaking skills (Boyd, 1999). Follow these strategies during a media interview:

1. **Present appropriate nonverbal cues.** Inexperienced interviewees can often look or sound tense or stiff. By standing up during a phone interview, your voice will sound more energetic and authoritative. With on-camera interviews, when checking your notes, move your eyes but not your head. Keep a small smile when listening. Look at the interviewer, not into the camera.

2. **Make clear and concise statements.** It is important to speak slowly, to articulate clearly, and to avoid technical terms or jargon. Remember that the audience is not familiar with your area of expertise.

3. **Realize that you are always "on the record."** Say nothing as an aside or confidentially to a reporter. Do not say anything that you would not want quoted. If you do not know an answer, do not speculate, but indicate that

talking points

the three or four central ideas you will present as you answer the questions asked during a media interview

CONSIDER THIS....

Have you or someone you know ever been interviewed by the media? If so, what were the circumstances and how did it go? If you were to be interviewed by the media now—after reading this chapter—how would you go about it and why?

the question is outside of your area of expertise. Do not ramble during the interviewer's periods of silence. Do not allow yourself to be rushed into an answer.

4. **Learn how to bridge.** Media consultant Joanna Krotz (2006) defines a **bridge** as a transition you create so that you can move from the interviewer's subject to the message you want to communicate. To do this, you first answer the direct question and then use a phrase such as "What's important to remember, however . . . ," "Let me put that in perspective . . . ," or "It's also important to know. . . ." With careful preparation, specific communication strategies during the interview, and practice, one can skillfully deliver a message in any media interview format.

bridge

the transition you create in a media interview so that you can move from the interviewer's subject to the message you want to communicate

WHAT WOULD YOU DO?

A Question of Ethics

Ken shifted in his chair as Ms. Goldsmith, his interviewer, looked over his résumé.

"I have to tell you that you have considerably more experience than the average applicant we usually get coming straight out of college," Ms. Goldsmith said. "Let's see, you've managed a hardware store, been a bookkeeper for a chain of three restaurants, and were the number-one salesman for six straight months at a cell phone store."

"That's right," Ken said. "My family has always stressed the value of hard work, so I have worked a full-time job every summer since I entered junior high school, right through my last year of college. During the school year, I usually worked four to six hours a day after class."

"Very impressive," Ms. Goldsmith said. "And still you managed to get excellent grades and do a considerable amount of volunteer work in your spare time. What's your secret?"

"Secret?" said Ken nervously. "There's no secret—just a lot of hard work."

"Yes, I see that," said Ms. Goldsmith. "What I mean is that there are only 24 hours in a day and you obviously had a lot on your plate each day, especially for someone so young. How did you manage to do it?"

Ken thought for a moment before answering. "I only need five hours of sleep a day." He could feel Ms. Goldsmith's eyes scrutinizing his face. He hadn't exactly lied on his résumé—just exaggerated a little bit. He had, in fact, helped his father run the family hardware store for a number of years. He had helped his aunt, from time to time, keep track of her restaurant's receipts. He had also spent one summer selling cell phones for his cousin. Of course, his family always required him to do his schoolwork first before they let him help at the store, so Ken often had little time to help at all, but there was no reason Ms. Goldsmith needed to know that.

"And you can provide references for these jobs?" Ms. Goldsmith asked.

"I have them with me right here," said Ken, pulling a typed page from his briefcase and handing it across the desk.

1. Are the exaggerated claims Ken made in his résumé ethical? Do the ethics of his actions change at all if he has references (family members) who will vouch for his claims?

2. Many people justify exaggerating or even lying on their résumés by saying that everybody does it and then rationalizing that, if they don't do it too, they will be handicapping their chances to get a good job. If the consequences of acting ethically diminish your economic prospects, are you justified in bending the rules? Explain your answer.

Summary

Interviewing can be a productive way to obtain information from an expert for a paper, an article, or a speech. The key to effective interviewing begins with a highly structured interview protocol identifying a series of good questions. Primary questions stimulate response; follow-up questions probe for additional information. Open questions allow for flexible responses; closed questions require very brief answers. Neutral questions allow the respondent free choice; leading questions require the person to answer in a particular way. When you are interviewing for information, you will want to define the purpose, select the best person to interview, develop a protocol, and conduct the interview according to the protocol.

When you are interviewing a prospective applicant for a job, become familiar with the data contained in the interviewee's application form, résumé, reference letters, and other application materials. Be careful how you present yourself, do not waste time, do not ask questions that violate fair employment practice legislation, and give the applicant an opportunity to ask questions. At the end of the interview, explain to the applicant what will happen next in the process.

If you are an employment seeker, your first goal is to submit a résumé and cover letter that will get you an interview. Begin by taking the time to learn about the company and prepare your cover letter and résumé to highlight strengths you have that match the company's needs. For the interview itself, you should dress appropriately, be prompt, be alert, look directly at the interviewer, give yourself time to think before answering difficult questions, ask intelligent questions about the company and the job, and show enthusiasm for the position.

If you are asked for an interview from the media, prepare by understanding the focus and format of the interview and considering the few main points you want to convey. During the media interview, you should present appropriate nonverbal cues, make clear and concise statements, realize everything you say is on the record, and learn to use bridges as transitions to your message.

> **Note:**
> Activities for this chapter can be found on the Speech Communication CourseMate at cengagebrain.com.

References

UNIT 1 PREQUEL

Robert M. Hutchins (n.d.). *FinestQuotes.com*. Retrieved November 25, 2011, from FinestQuotes.com Web site: http://www.finestquotes.com/author_quotes -author- Robert M. Hutchins-page-0.htm.

CHAPTER 1

Beebe, S., & Masterson, J. (2006). *Communicating in groups: Principles and practices* (8th ed.). Boston: Pearson.

Berger, C. (1997). *Planning strategic interaction: Attaining goals through communicative action.* Mahwah, NJ: Lawrence Erlbaum.

Burgoon, J. K., Bonito, J. A., Ramirez, Artemio, Dunbar, N. E., Kam, K., & Fisher, J. (1998). The interactivity principle: Effects of mediation, propinquity, and verbal and nonverbal modalities in interpersonal interaction. *Journal of Communication, 48,* 657–677.

Burleson, B. R. (2009). Understanding the outcomes of supportive communication: A dual-processing approach. *Journal of Social and Personal Relationships, 26,* 21–38.

College learning for the new global century. (2007). *A Report from the National Leadership Council for Liberal Education and America's Promise.* Washington, DC: Association of American Colleges and Universities.

Darling, A.L., & Dannels, D. P. (2003). Practicing engineers talk about the importance of talk: A report on the role of oral communication in the workplace. *Communication Education, 52,* 1–16.

Hansen, R. S., & Hansen, K. What do employers really want? Top skills and values employers seek from job-seekers. Retrieved from Quintessential Careers Web site: http://www.quintcareers.com/job_skills _values.html

Hart Research Associates. (2010, January 10). Raising the bar: Employers' views on college learning in the wake of the economic downturn. Washington, DC: Association of American Colleges and Universities.

Hart Research Associates. (2006, December 28). How should colleges prepare students to succeed in today's global economy? Washington, DC: Association of American Colleges and Universities.

Hirokawa, R., Cathcart, R., Samovar, L., & Henman, L. (Eds.). (2003). *Small group communication theory and practice* (8th ed.). Los Angeles: Roxbury.

Kellerman, K. (1992). Communication: Inherently strategic and primarily automatic. *Communication Monographs, 59,* 288–300.

Knapp, M., & Daly, J. (2002). *Handbook of interpersonal communication.* Thousand Oaks, CA: Sage.

Littlejohn, S. W., & Foss, K. A. (2008). *Theories of human communication* (9th ed.). Belmont, CA: Thomson Wadsworth.

Littlejohn, S. W., & Foss, K. A. (2011). *Theories of human communication* (10th ed). Long Grove, IL: Waveland Press.

McCroskey, J. C. (1977). Oral communication apprehension: A review of recent theory and research. *Human Communication Research, 4,* 78–96.

Millar, F. E. & Rogers, L. E. (1987). Relational dimensions of interpersonal dynamics. In M. E. Roloff & G. E. Miller (Eds.), Interpersonal processes: New directions in communication research. (pp. 117–139). Newbury Park, CA: Sage.

Pajares, F., Prestin, A., Chen, J., & Nabi, R. L. (2009). Social cognitive theory and media effects. In R. L. Nabi and M. B. Oliver (eds.) *The SAGE handbook of media processes and effects* (pp. 283–297). Los Angeles, CA: Sage.

Samovar, L. A., Porter, R. E., & McDaniel, E. R. (2007). *Communication between cultures* (6th ed.). Belmont, CA: Thomson Wadsworth.

Spitzberg, B. H. & Cupach, W. R. (Eds.). (2011). *The dark side of close relationships II.* New York: Routledge.

Spitzberg, B. H. (2000). A model of intercultural communication competence. In L. A. Samovar & R. E. Porter (Eds.), *Intercultural communication: A reader* (9th ed., pp. 375–387). Belmont, CA: Wadsworth.

Terkel, S. N., & Duval, R. S. (Eds.). (1999). *Encyclopedia of ethics.* New York: Facts on File.

Richmond, V. P., & McCroskey, J. C. (2000). *Communication: Apprehension, avoidance, and effectiveness* (5th ed.). Scottsdale, AZ: Gorsuch Scarisbrick.

Wright, J. W. (2002). New York Times *almanac.* New York: New York Times.

Young, M. (2003). Integrating communication skills into the marketing curriculum: A case study. *Journal of Marketing Education, 25,* 57–70.

CHAPTER 2

Aron, A., Mashek, D., & Aron, E. (2004). Closeness as including other in the self. In D. Mashek & A. Aron (Eds.), Handbook of closeness and intimacy (pp. 27–41). Mahwah, NJ: Lawrence Erlbaum.

Bandura, A. (1977). Self-efficacy: Toward a unifying theory of behavioral change. *Psychological Review, 84,* 191–215.

Baron, R. A., Byrne, D., & Branscombe, N. R. (2006). *Social psychology* (11th ed.). Boston: Allyn & Bacon.

Benet-Martinez, V., & Haritatos, J. (2005). Bi-cultural identity integration: Components and socio-personality antecedents. *Journal of Personality, 73,* 1015–1049.

Berger, C.R., & Bradac, J.J. (1982). *Language and social knowledge.* London: Edward Arnold Publishers Ltd.

Centi, P. J. (1981). *Up with the positive—out with the negative.* Upper Saddle River, NJ: Prentice Hall.

Chen, G., & Starosta, W. (1998). *Foundations of intercultural communication.* Boston: Allyn & Bacon.

Demo, D. H. (1987). Family relations and the self-esteem of adolescents and their parents. *Journal of Marriage and the Family, 49,* 705–715.

Downey, G., Freitas, A. L., Michaelis, B., & Khouri, H. (2004). The self-fulfilling prophecy in close relationships: Rejection sensitivity and rejection by romantic partners. In H. T. Reis & C. E. Rusbult (Eds.), *Close relationships* (pp. 153–174). New York: Psychology Press.

Engel, B. (2005). *Breaking the cycle of abuse: How to move beyond your past to create an abuse-free future.* Hoboken, NJ: John Wiley and Sons.

Gangestad, S. W., & Snyder, M. (2000). Self-monitoring: Appraisal and reappraisal. *Psychological Bulletin, 126,* 530–555.

Gibson, J. J. (1966). *The senses considered as perceptual systems.* Boston: Houghton Mifflin.

Guerrero, L., Anderson, P., Afifi, W. (2007). *Close encounters: Communication in relationships (2nd ed.).* Los Angeles: Sage Publications.

Hinduja, S., & Patchin, J. W. (2010). Bullying, cyberbullying, and suicide. *Archives of Suicide Research, 14,* 206–221.

Jones, M. (2002*). Social psychology of prejudice.* Upper Saddle River, NJ: Prentice-Hall.

"Lady Gaga discusses her struggles and connections to fans in *Rolling Stone* cover story" (2011, May 25). Retrieved from http://www.rollingstone.com/music/news /lady-gaga-discusses-her-struggles-and-connection -to-fans-in-rolling-stone-cover-story-20110525

Leary, M. R. (2002). When selves collide: The nature of the self and the dynamics of interpersonal relationships. In A. Tesser, D. A. Stapel, & J. V. Wood (Eds.), *Self and motivation: Emerging psychological perspectives* (pp. 119–145). Washington, DC: American Psychological Association.

Littlejohn, S. W., & Foss, K. A. (2011). *Theories of human communication* (10th ed). Long Grove, IL: Waveland Press.

Markus, H., & Kitayama, S. (1991). Culture and the self: Implications for cognition, emotion, and motivation. *Psychological Review, 98,* 224–253.

Merton, R. K. (1968). *Social theory and social structure.* New York: Free Press.

Mruk, C. J. (2006). *Self-esteem research, theory, and practice: Toward a positive psychology of self-esteem.* New York: Springer.

Mruk, C. (1999). *Self-esteem: Research, theory, and practice* (2nd ed.). New York: Springer.

Rayner, S. G. (2001). Aspects of the self as learner: Perception, concept, and esteem. In R. J. Riding & S. G. Rayner (Eds.), *Self-perception: International perspectives on individual differences* (Vol. 2). Westport, CN: Ablex.

Sampson, E. E. (1999). *Dealing with differences: An introduction to the social psychology of prejudice.* Fort Worth, TX: Harcourt Brace.

Shedletsky, L. J., & Aiken, J. E. (2004). *Human communication on the Internet.* Boston: Pearson.

Schillaci, S. (2011, Feb 14). Lady Gaga on *60 Minutes:* 'I'm a master of the art of fame.' Zap2It. Retrieved from http://blog.zap2it.com/pop2it/2011/02 /lady-gaga-on-60-minutes-im-a-master-of-the-art -of-fame.html

Weiten, W. (1998). *Psychology: Themes and variations* (4th ed.). Pacific Grove, CA: Brooks/Cole.

Willis, J. and Todorov, A (2006). First impressions: making up your mind after a 100-ms exposure to a face. *Psych Sci.* 17, 592–598.

Wood, J. T. (2007). *Gendered lives: Communication, gender, and culture* (7th ed.). Belmont, CA: Wadsworth.

CHAPTER 3

Andersen, P. A., Hecht, M. L., Hoobler, G. D., & Smallwood, M. (2003). Nonverbal communication across cultures. In W. B. Gudykunst (Ed.), *Cross-cultural and intercultural communication*. Thousand Oaks, CA: Sage.

A Ruby Films, Gerson Saines Production in association with HBO Films Leo Trombetta, A.C.E., *Editor*.

Association of Black Women Historians. (2011, Aug 7). *An open statement to the fans of* The Help. Retrieved from http://www.abwh.org

Bonvillain, N. (2003). *Language, culture and communication: The meaning of messages* (4th ed.). Upper Saddle River, NJ: Prentice-Hall.

Bornstein, M. H., & *Bradley*, R. H. (Eds.). (2003). *Socioeconomic status, parenting, and child development*. Mahwah, NJ: Lawrence Erlbaum Associates.

Carlo-Casellas, J. R. (2002). *Marketing to U.S. Hispanic population requires analysis of cultures*. National Underwriter: Life & Health/Financial Services Edition.

Chen, G., & Starosta, W. (1998). *Foundations of intercultural communication*. Boston: Allyn and Bacon.

Ellis, R. (1999). *Learning a second language through interaction*. Amsterdam: John Benjamins.

Gleiberman, O. (2011, Aug 14). Is 'The Help' a condescending movie for white liberals? Actually, the real condescension is calling it that. *EW.com*. Retrieved from http://insidemovies.ew.com/2011/08/14/is-the-help-a-movie-for-white-liberals/

Hotz, R. L. (April 15, 1995). Official racial definitions have shifted sharply and often. *Los Angeles Times*, p. A14.

Hall, E. T. (1976). *Beyond culture*. New York: Random House.

Haviland, W. A. (1993). *Cultural anthropology*. Fort Worth, TX: Harcourt, Brace, Jovanovich.

Hofstede, G. (2000). Masculine and feminine cultures. In A. E. Kazdin (Ed.), *Encyclopedia of psychology, vol. 5*. Washington, DC: American Psychological Association.

Hofstede, G. (1998). *Masculinity and femininity: The taboo*. Thousand Oaks, CA: Sage.

Jackson, M. (Director). (2010). *Temple Grandin* [Motion picture]. USA: Home Box Office.

Jackson, R. L., II (Ed.). (2004). *African American communication and identities*. Thousand Oaks, CA: Sage.

Kim, Y. Y. (2001). *Becoming intercultural: An integrative theory of communication and cross-cultural adaptation*. Thousand Oaks, CA: Sage.

Kim, M. (2005). Culture-based conversational constraints theory: Individual- and culture-level analyses. In W. B. Gudykunst (Ed.), *Theorizing about intercultural communication*, (pp. 93–117). Thousand Oaks, CA: Sage.

Klyukanov, I. E. (2005). *Principles of intercultural communication*. New York: Pearson.

Kraus, M. W., & Keltner, D. (2009). Signs of socioeconomic status: A thin-slicing approach. *Psychological Science, 20,* 99–106.

Leonhardt, D. (2005, May 24). Class matters: The college dropout doom. *New York Times*. Retrieved from http://www.nytimes.com/2005/05/24/national/class/EDUCATION-FINAL.html?pagewanted=all

Luckmann, J. (1999). *Transcultural communication in nursing*. New York: Delmar.

Neuliep, J. W. (2006). *Intercultural communication: A contextual approach* (3rd ed.). Thousand Oaks, CA: Sage.

Pew Research Center. (2007). *A portrait of "Generation Next": How young people view their lives, futures, and politics* (survey report). Retrieved from http://people-press.org/report/300/a-portrait-of-generation-next

Pierce, W. (2011, Aug 15). The movie *The Help* was painful to watch. This passive segregation lite was hurtful. I kept thinking of my grandmother who was The Help [Twitter post]. Retrieved from http://twitter.com/#!/WendellPierce/status/103257666805170176

Pierce, W. (2011, Aug 16). Watching the film in Uptown-NewOrleans to the sniffles of elderly white people while my 80year old mother was seething, made clear distinction [Twitter post]. Retrieved from http://twitter.com/#!/WendellPierce/status/103351421965041665

Prensky, M. (2001). Digital natives, digital immigrants. From *On the Horizon* (MCB University Press, Vol. 9 No. 5, October 2001).

Turner, P. A. (2011, Aug 28). Dangerous white stereotypes. *New York Times*. Retrieved from http://www.nytimes.com/2011/08/29/opinion/dangerous-white-stereotypes.html

Renard, J. (2011). *Islam and Christianity: Theological themes in comparative perspective*. Berkeley, CA: University of California Press.

Samovar, L., Porter, R. E., & McDaniel, E. R. (2009). *Communication between cultures*. Boston: Wadsworth Cengage.

Ting-Toomey, S., Yee-Jung, K., Shapiro, R., Garcia, W., Wright, T., & Oetzel, J. G. (2000). Cultural/ethnic identity salience and conflict styles. *International Journal of Intercultural Relations, 23*, 47–81.

2010 Census: State Population Profile Maps. *2010 Census*: State Population Profile Maps. At: www .census.gov/

Wallis, C. (2006), "The multitasking generation", *Time*, Vol. 167 No. 13, pp. 48–55.

Wood, J. T. (2007). *Gendered lives: Communication, gender, and culture* (7th ed.). Belmont, CA: Wadsworth.

Zemke, R., Raines, C., & Filipczak (2000). *Generations at work*. New York: AMACOM Books.

CHAPTER 4

Aronoff, M. and Rees-Miller, J (Eds.). 2001. *The handbook of linguistics*. Blackwell Handbooks in Linguistics. Oxford: Blackwell.

Burke, K. (1968). *Language as symbolic action*. Berkeley, CA: University of California Press.

Chaika, E. (2008). *Language: The social mirror (4th ed.)*. Boston: Heinle ELT/Cengage.

Cvetkovic, L. (February 21, 2009) *Serbian, Croatian, Bosnian, or Montenegrin, or "Just our language."* Radio Free Europe/Radio Liberty Web site. Retrieved from http://www.rferl.org/content/Serbian_Croatian _Bosnian_or_Montenegrin_Many_In_Balkans_Just _Call_It_Our_Language_/1497105.html

Freed, A. F. (2003). Reflections on language and gender research. In J. Holmes & M. Meyers, (Eds.) *The handbook of language and gender* (699–721). Malden, MA: Blackwell Publishing.

Grice, H. P. (1975). Logic and conversation. In P. Cole & J. L. Morgan (Eds.) *Syntax and Semantics (Vol. 3, Speech Acts)*. New York, NY: Academic Press.

Higginbotham, J. (2006). Languages and idiolects: Their language and ours. In E. Lepore & B.C. Smith (Eds.), *The Oxford handbook of philosophy of language*. Oxford, UK: Oxford University Press.

Korta, K. and Perry, J. (2008). Pragmatics. In Edward N Zalta (Ed.), *The Stanford Encyclopedia of Philosophy (Fall 2008 Edition)*. Retrieved from http://plato.stanford .edu/archives/fall2008/entries/pragmatics/

Langer, E. J. & Moldoveanu, M. (2000). The construct of mindfulness. *Journal of Social Issues, 56*(1), 1–9.

Lewis, M. P. (Ed.). (2009). *Ethnologue: Languages of the world* (16th ed.). Dallas: SIL International.

Maresca, R. (2012, Jan 18). Jennifer Aniston's pregnancy rumors through the years. [Blog post]. Retrieved from http:// www.celebuzz.com/2012-01-18/jennifer -aniston-pregnancy-rumors-through-the-years-photos/

O'Grady, W., Archibald, J., Aronoff, M., & Rees-Miller, J. (2001). *Contemporary linguistics* (4th ed.). Boston: Bedford/St. Martin's.

Saeid, J. I. (2003). *Semantics* (2nd ed.). Malden, MA: Blackwell.

Slattery, K., Doremus, M., & Marcus, L. (2001). Shifts in public affairs reporting on the network evening news: A move toward the sensational. *Journal of Broadcasting & Electronic Media 45*(2), 295–298.

Stewart, L. P., Cooper, P. J., Stewart, A. D., & Friedley, S. A. (1998). *Communication and gender* (3rd ed.). Boston: Allyn & Bacon.

Ting-Toomey, S., & Chung, L. C. (2005). *Understanding Intercultural Communication*. Los Angeles: Roxbury Publishing.

Washington, L. Jr. (1999, Nov.). Facts, fallacies, and fears of tabloidization. *USA Today*. Retrieved from http://findarticles.com/p/articles/mi_m1272 /is_2654_128/ai_57564088/

Wright, R. (2010). Chinese language facts. Retrieved from http://www.languagehelpers.com /languagefacts/chinese.html

CHAPTER 5

African neck stretching. (2008–2009). Retrieved from http://www.african-tribes.org/african -neck-stretching.html

American Museum of Natural History. (1999). Exhibition highlights. *Body art: Marks of identity*. Retrieved from http://www.amnh.org/exhibitions/bodyart /exhibition_highlights.html

Australian Museum. (2009). Shaping. *Body art*. Retrieved from http://amonline.net.au/bodyart /shaping/

Axtell, R. E. (1998). *Gestures: The Do's and Taboos of body language around the world*. Hoboken, NJ: John Wiley and Sons.

Birdwhistell, R. (1970). *Kinesics and context*. Philadelphia: University of Pennsylvania Press.

Burgoon, J. K., & Bacue, A. E. (2003). Nonverbal communication skills. In J. O. Greene & B. R. Burleson (Eds.), *Handbook of communication and social interaction skills* (pp. 179–220). Mahwah, NJ: Erlbaum.

Burgoon, J. K., Blair, J. P., & Strom, R. E. (2008). Cognitive biases and nonverbal cue availability in detecting deception. *Human Communication Research, 34,* 572–599.

Gudykunst, W. B., & Kim, Y. Y. (1997). *Communicating with strangers: An approach to intercultural communication.* New York: McGraw-Hill.

Hall, E. T. (1959). *The silent language.* Greenwich, CT: Fawcett.

Hall, E. T. (1968). Proxemics. *Current Anthropology, 9,* 83–108.

Hall, E. T. (1969). *The hidden dimension.* Garden City, NY: Doubleday.

Knapp, M., & Hall, J. (2006). *Nonverbal communication in human interaction (6th ed.)* Belmont, CA: Thomson Wadsworth.

Jacobs, B. (2005, June). *Adolescents and self-cutting (self-harm): Information for parents* (Bringing Science to Your Life, Guide I-104). Retrieved from http://aces .nmsu.edu/pubs/_i/I-104.pdf

Knapp, M. L., & Hall, J. A. (2006). *Nonverbal communication in human interaction* (5th ed.). Belmont, CA: Thomson Wadsworth.

Lim, L. (2007, March 19). Painful memories for China's footbinding survivors [Radio broadcast story]. *Morning Edition.* Retrieved from http://www.npr .org/templates/story/story.php?storyId=8966942

Martin, J. N., & Nakayama, T. K. (2000). *Intercultural communication in contexts* (2nd ed.). Mountain View, CA: Mayfield.

Mehrabian, A. (1972). *Nonverbal communication.* Chicago: Aldine.

Neuliep, J. W. (2006). *Intercultural communication: A contextual approach* (3rd ed.). Thousand Oaks, CA: Sage.

Olaniran, B. (2002–2003). Computer-mediated communication: A test of the impact of social cues on the choice of medium for resolving misunderstandings. *Journal of Educational Technology Systems, 31*(2), 205–222.

Pearson, J. C., West, R. L., & Turner, L. H. (1995). *Gender & communication* (3rd ed.). Dubuque, IA: Brown & Benchmark.

Samovar, L. A., Porter, R. E., & McDaniel, E. R. (Eds.). (2009). *Intercultural communication: A reader* (12th ed.). Belmont, CA: Cengage.

Schurman, A. (n.d.). A brief and rich body piercing history. *Life 123.* Retrieved from http://www.life123.com /beauty/style/piercings/body-piercing-history .shtml

Walther, J. B., & Parks, M. R. (2002). Cues filtered out, cues filtered in: Computer-mediated communication and relationships. In M. C. Knapp & J. A. Daly (Eds.), *Handbook of interpersonal communication* (3rd ed.; pp. 529–563). Thousand Oaks, CA: Sage.

Watzlawick, P., Bavelas, J. B., & Jackson, D. D. (1967). *Pragmatics of human communication.* New York: Norton.

Wilson, C. (2002). The history of corsets. *eSSORTMENT: Information and advice you want to know.* Retrieved from http://www.essortment.com/all /historyofcors_rmue.htm

Wood, J. T. (2007). *Gendered lives: Communication, gender, and culture* (7th ed.). Belmont, CA: Wadsworth.

CHAPTER 6

Bostrom, R. N. (2006). The process of listening. In O. Hargie (Ed.), *Handbook of communication skills* (3rd ed., pp. 267–291). New York: Routledge.

Brownell, J. (2006). *Listening: Attitudes, principles, and skills* (3rd ed.). Boston: Allyn & Bacon.

Burleson, B. R. (2003). Emotional support skills. In J. O. Green & B. R. Burleson (Eds.), *Handbook of communication and social interaction skills* (pp. 551–594). Mahwah, NJ: Erlbaum.

Donoghue, P. J., & Siegel, M. E. (2005). *Are you really listening?: Keys to successful communication.* Notre Dame, IN: Sorin Books.

Estes, W. K. (1989). Learning theory. In A. Lesgold & R. Glaser (Eds.), *Foundations for a psychology of education* (pp. 1–49). Hillsdale, NJ: Erlbaum.

Greenwald, G. (2011, Sept 8). Cheering for state-imposed death. *Salon.* Retrieved from http://www .salon.com/2011/09/08/death_17/

Halone, K. K. & Pecchioni, L. L. (2001). Relational listening: A grounded theoretical model. *Communication Reports, 14,* 5.

Harris, J. A. (2003). Learning to listen across cultural divides. *Listening Professional, 2,* 4–21.

International Listening Association. (1996). http:// www.listen.org/

Janusik, L. A., & Wolvin, A. D. (2006). *24 hours in a day: A listening update to the time studies.* Paper presented at the meeting of the International Listening Association, Salem, OR.

Johnson, P. (2006, September 24). Cable rantings boost ratings. *USA Today.* Retrieved from http://www

.usatoday.com/life/columnist/mediamix/2006-09-24-media-mix_x.htm

Kiewitz, C., Weaver, J. B., Brosius, H. B., & Weimann, G. (1997). Cultural differences in listening style preferences. *International Journal of Public Opinion Research, 9*, 233–247.

Listening factoid. (2003). International Listening Association. Retrieved from http://www.listen.org/pages/factoids.html

Maguire, J. (2007, February 22). Cicero's rules of rhetoric and our own shout-fest. *Maguire Online*. Retrieved from http://www.maguireonline.com/2007/02/ciceros_rules_of_rhetoric_and.php

Morrison, J. A. (2011, October 20). GOP debate audience booed bickering and interrupting. *Las Vegas Review-Journal*. Retrieved from http://www.lvrj.com/news/gop-debate-audience-booed-bickering-and-interrupting-132224143.html

Mutz, D., Reeves, B., & Wise, K. (2003, May 27). *Exposure to mediated political conflict: Effects of civility of interaction on arousal and memory.* Paper presented at the annual meeting of the International Communication Association, San Diego, CA. Retrieved from http://www.allacademic.com/meta/p111574_index.html

Omdahl, B. L. (1995). *Cognitive appraisal, emotion, and empathy.* Mahwah, NJ: Erlbaum.

O'Shaughnessey, B. (2003). Active attending or a theory of mental action. *Consciousness and the world, 29*: 379–407.

Pew Research Center for the People and the Press. (2011, Dec 15). Frustration with Congress could hurt Republican incumbents. [Press release] Retrieved from http://www.people-press.org/2011/12/15/frustration-with-congress-could-hurt-republican-incumbents/

Purpose. (n.d.) National Institute for Civil Discourse. Retrieved from http://nicd.arizona.edu/node/1

Romney, Cain under fire at feisty GOP debate. (2011, October 19). *Fox News*. Retrieved from http://www.foxnews.com/politics/2011/10/18/romney-cain-under-fire-as-feisty-gop-debate-begins/

Salisbury, J. R. & Chen, G. M. (2007). An examination of the relationship between conversational sensitivity and listening styles. *Intercultural Communication Studies, XVI*(1) 251–262.

Sargent, S. L. & Weaver, J. B. (2007). The listening styles profile. In R.A. Reynolds, R. Woods, & J. D. Baker (Eds.), *Handbook of research on electronic surveys and measurements* (pp. 335–338). Hershey, PA: Idea Group References.

Steil, L. K., Barker, L. L., & Watson, K. W. (1983). *Effective listening.* Reading, MA: Addison-Wesley.

Stiff, J. B., Dillard, J. P., Somera, L., Kim, H., & Sleight, C. (1988). Empathy, communication and prosocial behavior. *Communication Monographs, 55*, 198–213.

Watson, K. W., Barker, L. L., & Weaver, J. B., III (1995). The listening styles profile (LSP-16): Development and validation of an instrument to assess four listening styles. *International Journal of Listening, 9*, 1–13.

Weaver, J. B. III, & Kirtley, M. D. (1995). Listening styles and empathy. *The Southern Communication Journal, 60*(2): 131–140.

Wheeless, L. R. (1975). An investigation of receiver apprehension and social context dimensions of communication apprehension. *The Speech Teacher, 24*, 261–268.

Wolf, Z.B. (2011, September 23). Debate crowd booed gay soldier. *ABCNews*. Retrieved from http://abcnews.go.com/blogs/politics/2011/09/debate-crowd-booed-gay-soldier/

Wolvin, A. D., & Coakley, C. G. (1992). *Listening.* Dubuque, IA: Wm. C. Brown.

UNIT 1 SEQUEL

Biocca, F., & Harms, C. (2002). Defining and measuring social presence: Contribution to the Networked Minds theory and measure. Proceedings of Presence 2002: 7–36.

Biocca, F., & Nowak, K. (2001). Plugging your body into the telecommunication system: Mediated embodiment, media interfaces, and social virtual environments. In C. Lin & D. Atkin (Eds.), *Communication technology and society* (pp. 407–447). Waverly Hill, VI: Hampton Press.

Condon, S. L. & Čech, C. G. (2010). Discourse management in three modalities. *Language@Internet, 7*. Retrieved from http://www.languageatinternet.org/articles/2010/2770

Daft, R. L. & Lengel, R. H. (1984). Information richness: a new approach to managerial behavior and organizational design. In: Cummings, L.L. & Staw, B.M. (Eds.), *Research in organizational behavior 6*, (pp. 191–233). Homewood, IL: JAI Press.

Heeter, C. (1992). Being there: The subjective experience of presence. *Presence, 1*(2), 262–271.

Kiesler, S., Zubrow, D., Moses, A., & Geller, V. (1985). Affect in computer-mediated communication: An experiment in synchronous terminal-to-terminal discussion. *Human-Computer Interaction, 1,* 77–104.

Short, J., Williams, E., & Christie, B. (1976). *The social psychology of telecommunications.* London: John Wiley & Sons, Ltd.

Spitzer, M. (1986, January). Writing style in computer conferences. *IEEE Transactions on Professional Communications, 29:* 19–22.

UNIT 2 PREQUEL

Berger, C. R. (2005). Interpersonal communication: Theoretical perspectives, future prospects. *Journal of Communication, 55*(3), 415–447.

Carnegie, D. (1936). *How to win friends and influence people.* New York: Simon and Schuster.

Knapp, M. L., & Daly, J. A. (2011). *The SAGE handbook of interpersonal communication* (4th ed.). Thousand Oaks, CA: Sage.

Knapp, M. L., & Miller, G. R. (1985). *Handbook of interpersonal communication.* Beverly Hills, CA: Sage.

LeBaron, C. D., Mandelbaum, J., & Glenn, P. J. (2003). An overview of language and social interaction research. In P. J. Glenn, C. D. LeBaron, & J. Mandelbaum (Eds.), *Studies in language and social interaction in honor of robert hopper* (pp. 1–44). Mahwah, NJ: Lawrence Erlbaum.

Littlejohn, S. W., & Foss, K. A. (2011). *Theories of human communication* (10th ed). Long Grove, IL: Waveland Press.

Wazlawick, P., Bavelas, J., & Jackson, D. (1967). *Pragmatics of human communication. A study of interactional patterns, pathologies, and paradoxes.* New York: Norton.

CHAPTER 7

Alsever, J. (2007, March 11). In the computer dating game, room for a coach. *New York Times.* Retrieved from http://www.nytimes.com/2007/03/11 /business/yourmoney/11dating.html

Altman, I., & Taylor, D. (1973). *Social penetration: The development of interpersonal relationships.* New York: Holt.

Aron, A., Aron, E. N., Tudor, M., & Nelson, G. (2004). Close relationships as including other in the self. In H. T. Reis & C. E. Rusbult (Eds.). *Close relationships* (pp. 365–379). New York: Psychology Press.

Baxter, L. (1982). Strategies for ending relationships: Two studies. *Western Journal of Speech Communication, 46,* 223–241.

Baxter, L. A., & Montgomery, B. M. (1996). *Relating: Dialogues and dialectics.* New York: Guilford.

Baxter, L. A., & West, L. (2003). Couple perceptions of their similarities and differences: A dialectical perspective. *Journal of Social and Personal Relationships, 20,* 491–514.

Berger, C. (1987). Communicating under uncertainty. In M. Roloff & G. Miller (Eds.), *Interpersonal processes: New directions in communication research* (pp. 39–62). Newbury Park, CA: Sage.

Boon, S. D. (1994). Dispelling doubt and uncertainty: Trust in romantic relationships. In S. Duck (Ed.), *Dynamics of relationships* (pp. 86–111). Thousand Oaks, CA: Sage.

Bowman, J. M. (2008). Gender role orientation and relational closeness: Self-disclosive behavior in same-sex male friendships. *Journal of Men's Studies, 16,* 316–330.

Brooks, M. (2011, February 14). How has internet dating changed society? An insider's look. *Courtland Brooks.* Retrieved from http://internetdating.typepad.com /courtland_brooks/2011/02/how-has-internet -dating-changed-society.html

Bryner, J. (2011, November 4). You gotta have friends? Most have just 2 true pals. *Live Science.* Retrieved from http://vitals.msnbc.msn.com /_news/2011/11/04/8637894-you-gotta-have -friends-most-have-just-2-true-pals?lite

Buber, M. (1970). *I and thou* (W. Kaufman, Trans.). New York: Scribner.

Burleson, B. R. (2003). Emotional support skills. In J. O. Green & B. R. Burleson (Eds.), *Handbook of communication and social interaction skills* (pp. 551–594). Mahwah, NJ: Erlbaum.

Burleson, B. R., & Goldsmith, D. J. (1998). How the comforting process works: Alleviating emotional distress through conversationally induced reappraisals. In P. A. Andersen & L. K. Guerrero (Eds.), *Handbook of communication and emotion: Research, theory, applications, and contexts* (pp. 248–280). San Diego, CA: Academic Press.

Carnegie, D. (1936). *How to win friends and influence people.* New York: Simon and Schuster.

Cupach, W. R., & Metts, S. (1986). Accounts of relational disclosure: A comparison of marital and non-marital relationships. *Communication Monographs, 53,* 319–321.

Dindia, K. (2003). Definitions and perspectives on relational maintenance communication. In D. J. Canary and M. Dainton (Eds.), *Maintaining relationships through communication.* Mahwah, NJ: Erlbaum.

Dindia, K. (2000). Sex differences in self-disclosure, reciprocity of self-disclosure, and self-disclosure and liking: Three meta-analyses reviewed. In S. Petronio (Ed.), *Balancing disclosure, privacy, and secrecy.* Mahwah, NJ: Erlbaum.

Dindia, K., & Timmerman, L. (2003). Accomplishing romantic relationships. In J. O. Greene & B. R. Burleson (Eds.), *Handbook of communication and social interaction* (pp. 685–722). Mahwah, NJ: Erlbaum.

Duck, S. (1982). A topography of relationship disengagement and dissolution. In S. Duck (Ed.). *Personal relationships 4: Dissolving personal relationships* (pp. 1–30). New York: Academic Press.

Duck, S. (1999). *Relating to others.* Philadelphia: Open University Press.

Duck, S. (2007). *Human relationships* (4th ed.). Thousand Oaks, CA: Sage.

Fiske, S. T., Gilbert, D. T., & Lindzey, G. (Eds.). (2010). *Handbook of social psychology* (5th ed.). Hoboken, NJ: John Wiley and Sons.

Hatfield, E., & Rapson, R. L. (2006). Passionate love, sexual desire, and mate selection: Cross-cultural and historical perspectives. In P. Noller & J. A. Feeney (Eds.). *Close relationships: Functions, forms and processes* (pp. 227–243). Hove, UK: Psychology Press/Taylor & Francis.

Ianotti, L. (2010, Sept 13). Do you need a professional to write your online dating profile? *Marie Claire.* Retrieved from http://www.marieclaire.com /sex-love/relationship-issues/online-dating-profile -ghostwriters?click=main_sr

King, A. E., Austin-Oden, D., & Lohr, J. M. (2009). Browsing for love in all the wrong places: Does research show that Internet matchmaking is more successful than traditional dating? *Skeptic* 15 i1 48(8). Retrieved from Infotrac.

Knapp, M. L., & Vangelisti, A. L. (2000). *Interpersonal communication and human relationships* (4th ed.). Boston: Allyn & Bacon.

Littlejohn, S. W., & Foss, K. A. (2011). *Theories of human communication* (10th ed). Long Grove, IL: Waveland Press.

McCarthy, E. (2008, September 24). Matchmakers, matchmakers, making a mint. *Washington Post.* Retrieved from http://www.washingtonpost .com/wp-dyn/content/article/2008/09/23 /AR2008092303669.html

Luft, J. (1969). *Of human interaction.* Palo Alto, CA: National Press.

McPherson, M., Smith-Lovin, L., & Brashears, M. E. (2006). Social isolation in America: Changes in core discussion networks over two decades. *American Sociological Review,* 71(3): 353–375.

Moore, D. W. (2003, January 3). Family, health most important aspects of life. *Gallup.* Retrieved from http://www.gallup.com/poll/7504/family -health-most-important-aspects-life.aspx

Morman, M. T., & Floyd, K. (1999). Affection communication between fathers and young adult sons: Individual and relational-level correlates. *Communication Studies, 50,* 294–309.

Morman, M. T., & Floyd, K. (2002). A "changing culture of fatherhood:" Effects of affectionate communication, closeness, and satisfaction in men's relationships with their fathers and their sons. *Western Journal of Communication, 66,* 395–411.

Parks, M. R. (2006). *Personal relationships and personal networks.* Mahwah, NJ: Erlbaum.

Patterson, B. R., Bettini, L., & Nussbaum, J. F. (1993). The meaning of friendship across the life-span: Two studies. *Communication Quarterly, 41,* 145.

Peterson, C. (2006). *A primer in positive psychology.* New York: Oxford.

Petronio, S. (2002). *Boundaries of privacy: Dialectics of disclosure.* Albany: State University of New York Press.

Prager, K. J., & Buhrmester, D. (1998). Intimacy and need fulfillment in couple relationships. *Journal of Social and Personal Relationships, 15,* 435–469.

Rabby, M., & Walther, J. B. (2003). Computer mediated communication effects in relationship formation and maintenance. In D. J. Canary & M. Dainton (Eds.), *Maintaining relationships through communication* (pp. 141–162). Mahwah, NJ: Erlbaum.

Rusbult, C. E., Olsen, N., Davis, J. L., & Hannon, P. A. (2004). Commitment and relationship maintenance mechanisms. In H. T. Reis & C. E. Rusbult (Eds.), *Key readings on close relationships* (pp. 287–304). Washington, DC: Taylor & Francis.

Samter, W. (2003). Friendship interaction skills across the lifespan. In J. O. Greene & B. R. Burleson (Eds.), *Handbook of communication and social interaction skills* (pp. 637–684). Mahwah, NJ: Erlbaum.

Stafford, L., Dainton, M., & Haas, S. (2000). Measuring routine and strategic relational maintenance: Scale revision, sex versus gender roles, and the prediction of relational characteristics. *Communication Monographs, 67*, 306–323.

Swain, S. (1989). Covert intimacy in men's friendships: Closeness in men's friendships. In B. J. Risman & P. Schwartz (Eds.). *Gender in intimate relationships: A microstructural approach.* Belmont, CA: Wadsworth.

Taylor, D., & Altman, I. (1987). Communication in interpersonal relationships: Social penetration processes. In Roloff, M. E., and Miller, G. R. *Interpersonal processes: New directions in communication research.* pp. 257–277. Newbury Park, CA: Sage.

Ting-Toomey, S. (2004). The matrix of face: An updated face-negotiation theory. In W. Gudykunst (Ed.), *Theorizing about intercultural communication* (pp. 71–92). Thousand Oaks, CA: Sage.

Triandis, H. C. (1994). *Culture and social behavior.* New York: McGraw-Hill.

Wang, J. (2011, January 25). A marketer coaches online daters on personal branding. *Entrepreneur.* Retrieved from http://www.entrepreneur.com/article/217911

Walther, J. B., & Parks, M. R. (2002). Cues filtered out, cues filtered in: Computer-mediated communication and relationships. In M. C. Knapp & J. A. Daly (Eds.), *Handbook of interpersonal communication* (3rd ed.; pp. 529–563). Thousand Oaks, CA: Sage.

Ward, C. C., & Tracy, T. J. G. (2004). Relation of shyness with aspects of online relationship involvement. *Journal of Social and Personal Relationships, 21,* 611–623.

Wood, J.T. (2000). *Relational communication: Continuity and change in personal relationships* (2nd ed.). Belmont, CA: Wadsworth.

CHAPTER 8

Alberti, R. E., & Emmons, M. L. (2008). *Your perfect right: Assertiveness and equality in your life and relationships* (9th ed.). Atascadero, CA: Impact Publishers.

Altman I. (1993). Dialectics, physical environments, and personal relationships. *Communication Monographs, 60,* 26–34.

Bilton. N. (2012, February 28). Apple loophole gives developers access to photos. *New York Times.* Retrieved from http://bits.blogs.nytimes.com /2012/02/28/tk-ios-gives-developers-access-to -photos-videos-location/

Brake, T., Walker, D. M., & Walker, T. (1995*). Doing business internationally: The guide to cross-cultural success.* New York: Irwin.

Burleson, B. R. (2003). Emotional support skills. In J. O. Greene & B. R. Burleson (Eds.), *Handbook of communication and social interaction skills* (pp. 551–594). Mahwah, NJ: Erlbaum.

Burleson, B. R., & Goldsmith, D. J. (1998). How the comforting process works: Alleviating emotional distress through conversationally induced reappraisals. In P. A. Andersen & L. K. Guerrero (Eds.), *Handbook of communication and emotion: Research, theory, applications, and contexts* (pp. 248–280). San Diego, CA: Academic Press.

Chen, A. (2011, November 10). Facebook is the final frontier in amateur porn. *Gawker* [Blog post]. Retrieved from http://gawker.com/5858485 /facebook-is-the-final-frontier-in-amateur-porn

Cissna, K., & Seiberg, E. (1995). Patterns of interactional confirmation and disconfirmation. In M. V. Redmond (Ed.), *Interpersonal communication: Readings in theory and research.* Fort Worth, TX: Harcourt Brace.

Cloud, H., & Townsend, J. (2007). *Boundaries: When to say YES, when to say NO—to take control of your life.* Grand Rapids, MI: Zondervan.

Cupach, W. R., & Canary, D. J. (1997). *Competence in interpersonal conflict.* New York: McGraw-Hill.

Dailey, R. M. (2006). Confirmation in parent-adolescent relationship and adolescent openness: Toward extending confirmation theory. *Communication Monographs, 73,* 434–458.

Dindia, K. (2000b). Sex differences in self-disclosure, reciprocity of self-disclosure, and self-disclosure and liking: Three metaanalyses reviewed. In S. Petronio (Ed.), *Balancing the secrets of private disclosures* (pp. 21–36). Mahwah, NJ: Erlbaum.

Dindia, K., Fitzpatrick, M. A., & Kenny, D. A. (1997). Self-disclosure in spouse and stranger interaction: A social relations analysis. *Human Communication Research, 23,* 388–412.

Gold, D. (2011, November 10). The man who makes money publishing your nude pics. *The Awl* [Blog post]. Retrieved from http://www.theawl

.com/2011/11/the-man-who-makes-money-publishing-your-nude-pics

Hample. D. (2003). Arguing skill. In J.O. Greene & B. R. Burleson (Eds.) *Handbook of communication and social interaction skills.* Mahwah, NJ: Lawrence Erlbaum.

Hendrick, S. S. (1981). Self-disclosure and marital satisfaction. *Journal of Personality and Social Psychology, 40,* 1150–1159.

Hess, N. H., & Hagen, E. H. (2006). Psychological adaptations for assessing gossip veracity. Human Nature, 17, 337–354.

Holt, J. L., & DeVore, C. J. (2005). Culture, gender, organizational role, and styles of conflict resolution: A meta-analysis. *International Journal of Intercultural Relations, 29,* 165–196.

Itzkoff, D. (2009, February 20). Police investigate photo in Chris Brown case. *New York Times.* Retrieved from http://www.nytimes.com/2009/02/21/arts/music/21arts-POLICEINVEST_BRF.html

Kleinman, S. (2007). *Displacing place: Mobile communication in the twenty-first century.* New York, NY: Peter Lang Publishing.

Margulis, S. T. (1977). Concepts of privacy: Current status and next steps. *Journal of Social Issues 33*(3), 5–21.

Maul, K. (2009, February 25). Rihanna aftermath rouses ethics debate. *PR Week.* Retrieved from http://www.prweekus.com/Rihanna-aftermath-rouses-ethics-debate/article/127824

McCartney, A. (2009, February 20). Rihanna won't discuss Chris Brown, but thanks fans [Television story]. Retrieved from http://abcnews.go.com/Entertainment/wireStory?id=6918527

Petronio, S. (2002). *Boundaries of privacy: Dialectics of disclosure.* Albany: State University of New York Press.

Rancer, A. S., & Avtgis, T. A. (2006). *Argumentative and aggressive communication: Theory, research, and application.* Thousand Oaks, CA: Sage.

Roloff, M.E., & Ifert, D.E. (2000). Conflict management through avoidance: Withholding complaints, suppressing arguments, and declaring topics taboo. In S. Petronio (Ed.), *Balancing the secrets of private disclosures* (pp. 151–163). Mahwah, NJ: LEA.

Samovar, L. A., Porter, R. E., & McDaniel, E. R. (Eds.). (2012). *Intercultural communication: A reader* (13th ed.). Belmont, CA: Cengage. Tate, R. (2009, February 20). Battered Rihanna picture a media ethics lightning rod. *Gawker* [Blog post]. Retrieved from http://gawker.com/5157078/battered-rihanna-picture-a-media-ethics-lightning-rod

Thomas, K. W. (1976). Conflict and conflict management. In M. D. Dunnette (Ed.). *Handbook of industrial and organizational psychology* (pp. 889–935). Chicago, IL: Rand McNally.

Thomas, K. W., & Kilmann, R. H. (1978). Comparison of four instruments measuring conflict behavior. *Psychological Reports, 42,* 1139–1145.

Thomas, K. W. (1992). Conflict and conflict management: Reflections and update. *Journal of Organizational Behavior, 13,* 265–274.

Ting-Toomey, S. (2006). Managing intercultural conflicts effectively. In L. A. Samovar & R. E. Porter (Eds.), *Intercultural communication: A reader,* 11th ed. Belmont, CA: Wadsworth. 366–377.

Ukashah, A., Arboleda-Flórez, J., & Sartorius, N. (2000). *Ethics, culture, and society: International perspectives.* Arlington, VA: American Psychiatric Publishing.

Ting-Toomey, S., & Chung, L. C. (2005). *Understanding intercultural communication.* Los Angeles, CA: Roxbury.

TMZ responds to LAPD internal investigation on battered Rihanna photo [Television story]. (2009, February 22). In *On the Record.* Retrieved from http://www.foxnews.com/story/0,2933,498157,00.html

Wilmot, W., & Hocker, J. L. (2010). *Interpersonal conflict* (8th ed.). New York: McGraw-Hill.

UNIT 2 SEQUEL

Baym, N. K. (2010). *Personal connections in the digital age.* Malden, MA: Polity Press.

Baym, N. K. & Ledbetter, A. (2009). Tunes that bind? Predicting friendship strength in music-based social networks. *Information, Community, and Society, 12*(3) 408–427.

Clark, L.S. (1998). Dating on the net: Teens and the rise of "pure" relationships. In S. Jones (Ed.). *Cybersociety 2.0: Revisiting computer-mediated communication and community* (pp. 159-183). Thousand Oaks, CA: Sage.

Giddens, A. (1993). *The transformation of intimacy.* Palo Alto, CA: Stanford University Press.

Gilbert, E., Karahalios, K. & Sandvig, C. (2008). The network in the garden: An empirical analysis of social media in rural life. Paper presented at the Computer Human Interaction Conference. Florence, Italy. Retrieved from http://social.cs.uiuc.edu/papers/pdfs/chi08-rural-gilbert.pdf

Golder, S.A., Wilkinson, D. & Huberman, B.A. (2007). Rhythms of social interactions: Messaging within a massive online network. In C. Steinfield, B. Pentland, M. Ackerman, & N. Contractor (Eds.), *Proceedings of the third International Conference on Communities and Technologies*, (pp. 41–66). London: Springer.

Greshon, I. (2010). *The Breakup 2.0: Disconnecting over new media*. Ithaca, NY: Cornell University Press.

Haythornthwaite, C. Strong, weak, and latent ties and the impact of new media. *Information Society, 8*(2) 385–401.

McKenna, K. Y. A., Green, A. S., & Gleason, M. E. J. (2002). Relationship formation on the Internet: What's the big attraction. *Journal of Social Issues, 58*(1) 9–31.

Mesch G. & Talmud, I. (2006). The quality of online and offline relationships. *The Information Society, 22,* 137–148.

Raine, L., Lenhart, A., Fox, S., Spooner, T. & Horrigan, J. (2000). Tracking online life: How women use the Internet to cultivate relationships with family and friends. Pew Internet and American Life Project. Retrieved from www.pewinternet.org/Reports/2000/Tracking-Online-Life.aspx

Rawlins, W. K. (1992). *Friendship matters: Communication, dialectics and the life course*. New York: Aldine de Gruyter.

Walther, J. B. (1996). Computer-mediated communication: Impersonal, interpersonal, and hyperpersonal interaction. *Communication Research, 23,* 3–43.

UNIT 3 PREQUEL

Cartwright, D., & Zander, A. (1968). *Group dynamics: Research and theory*. New York: Harper and Row.

Dewey, J. (1933). *How we think*. Boston: Heath.

Ettin, M. F. (1992). *Foundations and applications of group psychotherapy: A sphere of influence*. Needham Heights, MA: Allyn and Bacon.

Forsyth, D. R. & Burnette, J. L. (2005). The history of group research. In S. A Wheelen (Ed.), *The handbook of group research and practice*. Thousand Oaks, CA: Sage.

Mead, M. (n.d.). "Never doubt…" Retrieved from http://www.quoteland.com/author/Margaret-Mead-Quotes/390/

Tuckman, B. W. (1965). Developmental sequence in small groups. *Psychological Bulletin, 63,* 384–399.

Tuckman, B.W., & Jensen, M. A. C. (1977). Stages of small group development revisited. *Group and Organizational Studies, 2,* 419–427.

CHAPTER 9

Anderson, J. (1988). Communication competency in the small group. In R. Cathcart & L. Samovar (Eds.), *Small group communication: A reader*. Dubuque, IA: Brown.

Balgopal, P. R., Ephross, P. H., & Vassil, T. V. (1986). Self-help groups and professional helpers. *Small Group Research, 17,* 123–137.

Becker-Beck, U., Wintermantel, M., & Borg, A. (2005). Principles regulating interaction in teams practicing face-to-face communication versus teams practicing computer-mediated communication. *Small Group Research, 36,* 499–536.

Bonito, J. (2000). The effect of contributing substantively on perceptions of participation. *Small Group Research, 31,* 528–553.

Bordia, P., DiFonzo, N., & Chang, A. (1999). Rumor as group problem-solving: Development patterns in informal computer-mediated groups. *Small Group Research, 30,* 8–28.

Croucher, M. (2008, February 29.) I just want to be thin. If it takes dying to get there—so be it. *The Epoch Times*. Retrieved from http://en.epochtimes.com/news/8-2-29/66794.html

Eisenberg, J. (2007). Group cohesiveness. In R. F. Baumeister & K. D. Vohs (Eds.), *Encyclopaedia of social psychology* (pp. 386–388). Thousand Oaks, CA: Sage.

Evans, C., & Dion, K. (1991). Group cohesion and performance: A meta-analysis. *Small Group Research, 22,* 175–186.

Galvin, K. M., Byland, C. L., & Brommel, B. J. (2007*). Family communication: Cohesion and change* (7th ed.). Boston: Allyn & Bacon.

Giles, D. (2006). Constructing identities in cyberspace: The case of eating disorders. *British Journal of Social Psychology 45*(3): 463–477. Retrieved from http://www.brown.uk.com/eatingdisorders/giles2.pdf

Henley, A. B., & Price, K. H. (2002). Want a better team? Foster a climate of fairness. *Academy of Management Executive, 16,* 153–154.

Henman, L. D. (2003). Groups as systems: A functional perspective. In R. Y. Hirokawa, R. S. Cathcart, L. A. Samovar, & L. D. Henman (Eds.), *Small group communication theory and practice: An anthology* (8th ed., pp. 3–7). Los Angeles: Roxbury.

Janis, I. L. (1982). *Groupthink: Psychological studies of policy decisions and fiascoes*. Boston: Houghton Mifflin.

Jiang, L., Bazarova, N. N., & Hancock, J. T. (2011). The disclosure-intimacy link in computer-mediated communication: An attributional extension of the hyperpersonal model. *Human Communication Research, 371*(1), 58–77.

Johnson, D., & Johnson, F. (2003). *Joining together: Group theory and group skills* (8th ed.). Boston: Allyn & Bacon.

Katz, N., & Koenig, G. (2001). Sports teams as a model for workplace teams: Lessons and liabilities. *Academy of Management Executive, 15*, 56–67.

Katzenbach, J. R., & Smith, D. K. (2003). *The wisdom of teams: Creating the high-performance organization.* New York: Harper Business Essentials.

Koerner, A. F., & Fitzpatrick, M. A. (2002). Understanding family communication patterns and family functioning: The roles of conversation orientation and conformity orientation. In W. B. Gudykunst (Ed.), *Communication yearbook 26* (pp. 36–68). Mahwah, NJ: Erlbaum.

Kraus, G. (1997). The psychodynamics of constructive aggression in small groups. *Small Group Research, 28*, 122–145.

LaFasto, F. M., & Larson, C. E. (2001). *When teams work best: 6,000 team members and leaders tell what it takes to succeed.* Thousand Oaks, CA: Sage.

Li, J., & Hambrick, D. C. (2005). Factional groups: A new vantage on demographic faultlines, conflict, and disintegration in work teams. *Academy of Management Journal, 48*, 794–813.

Midura, D. W., & Glover, D. R. (2005). *Essentials of teambuilding*. Champaign, IL: Human Kinetics.

Nussbaum, M., Singer, M., Rosas, R., Castillo, M., Flies, E., Lara, R., & Sommers, R. (1999). Decisions support system for conflict diagnosis in personnel selection. *Information and Management, 36*, 55–62.

Pascoe, C. J. (2008, January 22). Interview in Growing up online [Television series episode]. In D. Fanning. (Executive producer) *Frontline*. Boston, MA: WGBH. Retrieved from http://www.pbs.org/wgbh/pages/frontline/kidsonline/interviews/pascoe.html

Renz, M. A., & Greg, J. B. (2000). *Effective small group communication in theory and practice*. Boston: Allyn & Bacon.

Sell, J., Lovaglia, M. J., Mannix, E. A., Samuelson, C. D., & Wilson, R. K. (2004). Investigating conflict, power, and status within and among groups. *Small Group Research, 35*, 44–72.

Shaw, M. E. (1981). *Group dynamics: The psychology of small group behavior* (3rd ed.). New York: McGraw-Hill.

Shimanoff, M. (1992). Group interaction and communication rules. In R. Cathcart & L. Samovar (Eds.), *Small group communication: A reader*. Dubuque, IA: William C. Brown.

Stokes, P. (2008, November 26). Perfectionist school girl hanged herself while worried about appearance. *Telegraph.co.uk*. Retrieved from http://www.telegraph.co.uk/news/uknews/3525738/Perfectionist-schoolgirl-hanged-herself-while-worried-about-appearance.html

Sundstrom, E., DeMeuse, K. P., & Futrell, D. (1990, February). Work teams: Applications and effectiveness. *American Psychologist*, 120–133.

Timmerman, C. E., & Scott, C. R. (2006). Virtually working: Communicative and structural predictors of media use and key outcomes in virtual work teams. *Communication Monographs, 73*, 108–136.

Thompson, L. L. (2003). *The social psychology of organizational behavior: Key readings*. New York: Taylor & Francis.

Ting-Toomey, S., & Oetzel, J. (2003). Cross-cultural face concerns and conflict styles: Current status and future directions. In W. B. Gudykunst and W. B. Mody (Eds.). *Handbook of international and intercultural communication* (2nd ed.; pp. 143–163). Thousand Oaks, CA: Sage.

Tuckman, B. W. (1965). Developmental sequence in small groups. *Psychological Bulletin, 6393*, 384–399.

Valacich, J. S., George, J. F., Nonamaker, J. F., Jr., & Vogel, D. R. (1994). Idea generation in computer based groups: A new ending to an old story. *Small Group Research, 25*, 83–104.

Wang, Z., Walther, J. B., & Hancock, J. T. (2009). Social identification and interpersonal communication in computer mediated communication: What you do versus who you are in virtual groups. *Human Communication Research, 35*(1), 59–85.

"What Is the It Gets Better Project?" Retrieved from http://www.itgetsbetter.org/pages/about-it-gets-better-project/

Widmer, W. N., & Williams, J. M. (1991). Predicting cohesion in a coacting sport. *Small Group Research, 22*, 548–570.

Wilmot, W. W., & Hocker, J. L. (2007). *Interpersonal conflict*. New York: McGraw-Hill.

Wilson, G. L. (2005). *Groups in context: Leadership and participation in small groups* (7th ed.). New York: McGraw-Hill.

CHAPTER 10

Drummond, D. (2004). *Miracle meetings* [e-book]. Retrieved from http://www.superteams.com.

Duch, B. J., Groh, S. E., & Allen, D. E. (Eds.). (2001). *The power of problem-based learning*. Sterling, VA: Stylus.

Ebeling, R. (2008, March 6). So long, Dungeon Master. *Newsweek*. Retrieved from http://www.newsweek.com/id/119782

Edens, K. M. (2000). Preparing problem solvers for the 21st century through problem-based learning. *College Teaching, 48*, 55–60.

Fairhurst, G. T. (2001). Dualism in leadership. In F. M. Jablin & L. M. Putnam (Eds.), *The new handbook of organizational communication* (pp. 379–439). Thousand Oaks, CA: Sage.

Frey, L., & Sunwulf. (2005). The communication perspective on group life. In S. A. Wheelen (Ed.), *The handbook of group research and practice* (pp. 159–186). Thousand Oaks, CA: Sage.

Gardner, H. (1995/2011). *Leading minds: An anatomy of leadership*. Basic Books.

Huling, R. (2008, May 27). "Dungeons & Dragons" owns the future. *The Escapist*. Retrieved from http://www.escapistmagazine.com/articles/view/issues/issue_151/4931-Dungeons-Dragons-Owns-the-Future.2

Jensen, A. D., & Chilberg, J. C. (1991). *Small group communication: Theory and application*. Belmont, CA: Wadsworth.

Katzenbach, J. R., & Smith, D. K. (2003). *The wisdom of teams: Creating the high-performance organization*. New York: Harper Collins.

Kippenberger, T. (2002). *Leadership styles*. New York: John Wiley and Sons.

Levin, B. B. (Ed.). (2001). *Energizing teacher education and professional development with problem-based learning*. Alexandria, MN: Association for Supervision and Curriculum Development.

"MIT's Education Arcade uses online gaming to teach science." (2012, Jan 17). [Press release]. Retrieved from http://education.mit.edu/blogs/louisa/2012/pressrelease

Newman, H. (2007). "World of Warcraft" players: Let's slay together. *Detroit Free Press*. Retrieved from InfoTrac.

Northouse, G. (2007). *Leadership theory and practice* (4th ed.). Thousand Oaks, CA: Sage.

"MIT's Education Arcade uses online gaming to teach science" (2012, Jan 17). [Press release]. Retrieved from http://education.mit.edu/blogs/louisa/2012/pressrelease

Rahim, M. A. (2001). *Managing conflict in organizations* (4th ed.). Westport, CT: Greenwood Press.

Schiesel, S. (2008, March 5). Gary Gygax, game pioneer, dies at 69. *New York Times*. Retrieved from http://www.nytimes.com/2008/03/05/arts/05gygax.html

Seely Brown, J., & Hagel, J. (2009). How "World of Warcraft" promotes innovation. *Business Week Online*. Retrieved from Infotrac.

Snyder, B. (2004). Differing views cultivate better decisions. *Stanford Business*. Retrieved from http://www.gsb.stanford.edu/NEWS/bmag/sbsm0405/feature_workteams_gruenfeld.shtml

Sultanoff, S. (1993). Tickling our funny bone: Humor matters in health. *International Journal of Humor Research, 6*, 89–104.

Teams that succeed (2004). *Harvard Business Review*. Boston: Harvard Business School Press.

Tullar, W., & Kaiser, P. (2000). The effect of process training on process and outcomes in virtual groups. *Journal of Business Communication, 37*, 408–427.

Weiten, W., Dunn, D. S., & Hammer, E. Y. (2011). *Psychology applied to modern life: Adjustment in the 21st century*. Boston, MA: Cengage.

Williams, J. P., Hendricks, S. Q., & Winkler, W. K. (Eds.). (2006). *Gaming as culture: Essays on reality, identity and experience in fantasy games*. Jefferson, NC: McFarland.

Young, K. S., Wood, J. T., Phillips, G. M., & Pedersen, D. J. (2007). *Group discussion: A practical guide to participation and leadership* (4th ed.). Long Grove, IL: Waveland Press.

UNIT 3 SEQUEL

Andres, H. P. (2002) A comparison of face-to-face and virtual software development teams. *Team Performance Management: An International Journal, 8-1/2*, 39–48.

Bouas, K. S. & Arrow, H. (1996). The development of group identity in computer and face-to-face groups with membership change. *CSCW, 4,* 153–178.

Burke, K., Aytes, K. & Chidambaram, L. (2001) Media effects on the development of cohesion and process satisfaction in computer-supported workgroups. *Information Technology & People, 14*(2)122–141.

Chidambaram, L. (1996). Relational development in computer-supported groups. *MIS Quarterly, 20*(2), 143–163.

Hightower, R. T., & Sayeed, L. (1996). Effects of communication mode and prediscussion information distribution characteristics on information exchange in groups. *Information Systems Research, 7*(4) 451–465.

Huang, W. W., Wei, K.-K., Watson, R. T. & Tan, B. C. Y. (2003). Supporting virtual team-building with a GSS: An empirical investigation. *Decision Support Systems, 34*(4), 359–367.

McGrath, J. E., & Hollingshead, A. B. (1994). *Groups interacting with technology: Ideas, evidence, issues and an agenda.* London: Sage.

Olson, J., & Teasley, S. (1996) Groupware in the wild: Lessons learned from a year of virtual collocation. In *Proceedings of the ACM Conference, Denver, CO, USA,* 419–427.

Shoemaker-Galloway, J. (2007, August 6). Top 10 netiquette guidelines. *Suite 101.* Retrieved from http://jace-shoemaker-galloway.suite101.com/netiquette-guidelines-a26615#ixzz1HIIIhsZn

Siegel, J., Dubrovsky, V., Kiesler, S. & McGuire, T. W. (1986) Group processes in computer-mediated communication. *Organizational Behavior and Human Decision Processes, 37*(2), 157–188.

Warkentin, M. E., Sayeed, L., & Hightower, R. (1997) Virtual teams versus face-to-face teams: An exploratory study of a Web-based conference system. *Decision Sciences 28*(4) 957–996.

Weisband, S., & Atwater, L. (1999) Evaluating self and others in electronic and face-to-face groups. *Journal of Applied Psychology, 84*(4) 632–639.

UNIT 4 PREQUEL
CHAPTER 11

Berger, C. R., & Calabrese, R. J. (1975). Some exploration in initial interaction and beyond: Toward a developmental theory of communication. *Human Communication Research, 1,* 99–112.

Bitzer, L. F. (1968). The rhetorical situation. *Philosophy and Rhetoric, 1*(1) 1–14.

Callison, D. (2001). Concept mapping. *School Library Media Activities Monthly, 17*(10) 30–32.

Cohen N. (2009, August 24). Wikipedia to limit changes to articles on people. *New York Times.* Retrieved from http://www.nytimes.com/2009/08/25/technology/internet/25wikipedia.html?_r=1

Cohen, N. (2011, May 23) Wikipedia. *The New York Times.* Retrieved from http://topics.nytimes.com/top/news/business/companies/wikipedia/index.html

Crovitz, D., & Smoot, W. S. (2009, January). Wikipedia: Friend, not foe. *English Journal, 98*(3), 91–97. Retrieved from http://www.nytimes.com/learning/teachers/archival/EnglishJournalArticle2.pdf

Durst, G. M. (1989, March 1). The manager as a developer. *Vital Speeches of the Day* (pp. 309–314).

Gallagher, M. P. (2009, April 27). Wikipedia held too malleable to be reliable as evidence. *New Jersey Law Journal.* n.p. Retrieved from Infotrac.

Gregoire, S. W. (2009, December 8). Considering cultural differences when speaking. *Becoming a Christian women's speaker: With author and speaker Sheila Wray Gregoire.* Retrieved from http://christianwomensspeaker.wordpress.com/2009/12/08/considering-cultural-differences-when-speaking/

Helm, B. (2005, December 14). Wikipedia: "A work in progress." *Business Week.* Retrieved from http://www.businessweek.com/technology/content/dec2005/tc20051214_441708 .htm?chan=db

Jaschik, S (2007, January 26). A stand against Wikipedia. *Inside Higher Ed.* Retrieved from http://www.insidehighered.com/news/2007/01/26/wiki

Kirkpatrick, M. (2011, November 2). Wikipedia is a mess, wikipedians say: 1 in 20 articles bare of references. *ReadWiteWeb.* Retrieved from http://www.readwriteweb.com/archives/wikipedia_is_a_mess_wikipedians_say_1_in_20_articl.php

Manguard, S. (2011, October 31). The monster under the rug. *The Signpost.* Retrieved from http://en.wikipedia.org/wiki/Wikipedia:Wikipedia_Signpost/2011-10-31/Opinion_essay

Nelson J. C. (2006). *Leadership.* Utah School Boards Association 83rd Annual Conference, Salt LakeCity, Utah. Retrieved from http://www.ama-assn.org/ama/pub/category/15860.html

Seigenthaler J. (2005, November 29). A false Wikipedia "biography." *USA Today*. Retrieved from http://www.usatoday.com/news/opinion/editorials/2005-11-29-wikipedia-edit_x.htm

CHAPTER 12

Aristotle. (1954). *Rhetoric* (W. Rhys Roberts, Trans.). New York: Modern Library.

Calloway, N. (n.d.) Tips for the best man on writing a wedding toast. *About.com Weddings*. Retrieved from http://weddings.about.com/od/theweddingparty/a/toastwriting.htm

Cossolotto, M. (2009, December). An urgent call to action for study abroad alumni to help reduce our global awareness deficit. *Vital Speeches*, pp. 564–568.

Coyne, S. (n.d.) A child's song. Retrieved from http://scoyne.weebly.com/the-shock-of-a-childs-song.html

Fisher, W. (1987). *Human communication as narration: Toward a philosophy of reason, value, and action.* Columbia, SC: University of South Carolina Press.

Gupta, Y. (February 2010). Beyond wisdom: Business dimensions of an aging America. *Vital Speeches*, pp. 69–75.

Humes, J. C. (1988). *Standing ovation: How to be an effective speaker and communicator.* New York: Harper and Row.

Jobs, S. (2005, June 15). You've got to find what you love. *Stanford University News*. Retrieved from http://news.stanford.edu/news/2005/june15/jobs-061505.html

Mackay, H. (July 2009). Changing the world: Your future is a work in progress. *Vital Speeches of the Day*, pp. 319–323.

Mariano, C. (January 2010). Unity, quality, responsibility: The real meaning of the words. *Vital Speeches of the Day*, pp. 20–22.

Marshall, L. B., & Armstrong, T. (2010, July 16). How to make a wedding toast. *The Public Speaker: Quick and Dirty Tips*. Retrieved from http://publicspeaker.quickanddirtytips.com/Making-Wedding-Toast.aspx

Mason, S. (2007, April). Equality will someday come. *Vital Speeches of the Day*, pp. 159–163.

Osteen, J. (2012). Best jokes of Joel Osteen. *Better Days TV*. Retrieved on April 6, 2012 from http://www.betterdaystv.net/play.php?vid=247

Patterson, T. (2010, June 20). How to give a wedding toast. *Slate*. Retrieved from http://www.slate.com/articles/news_and_politics/weddings/2011/06/how_to_give_a_wedding_toast.html

Post, A. (2010). Vermont vows: The toast!. *Emily Post Etipedia*. Retrieved from http://www.emilypost.com/weddings/your-day/719-toasts

CHAPTER 13

Ayers, J. (1991). Using visual aids to reduce speech anxiety. *Communication Research Reports*, 73–79.

Booher, D. D. (2003). *Speak with confidence [electronic resources]: Powerful presentations that inform, inspire, and persuade.* New York, NY: McGraw-Hill.

Brandt, J. R. (2007, January). Missing the (Power) point: When bullet points fly, attention spans die. *Industry Week*. Retrieved from http://www.industryweek.com

"Digital Media Assignments: Ignite Presentations for the Information Society (Comm-B course)" (n.d.). Retrieved from http://engage.wisc.edu/dma/awards/downey/index.html

Dwyer, K. (1991). *Conquer your speechfright.* Orlando, FL: Harcourt Brace.

Guzman, M. (2009, April 16). A Seattle geek fest spreads its wings. *Seattle PI*. Retrieved from http://www.seattlepi.com/business/405192_IGNITE16.html

Hanke, J. (1998). The psychology of presentation visuals. *Presentations, 12*(5), 42–47.

Ignite Seattle. (n.d.). Retrieved from http://www.igniteseattle.com/

Ignite Seattle 7 is happening on 8/3. (2009). *Ignite.* Retrieved from http://ignite.oreilly.com/2009/07/ignite-seattle-7-is-happening-on-83.html

Kolb, D. (1984). *Experiential learning: Experience as the source of learning and development.* Englewood Cliffs, NJ: Prentice Hall; Gallo, C. (2006, December 5). Presentations with something for everyone. *Business Week Online.* Retrieved from http://www.businessweek.com/smallbiz/content/dec2006/sb20061205_454055.htm

Long, K. (1997, August 12). *Visual aids and learning.* Retrieved from http://www.mech.port.ac.uk/av/AVALearn.htm

Maun, K. (2009, May 7). Anti-abortion protesters disturbing communities: Anti-choice activists' graphic images in protests upsetting many. *Suite101.com.* Retrieved from http://activism.suite101.com/article.cfm/have_antichoice_protestors_gone_too_far_yes

Muren, D. (2009). *Humblefacturing a sustainable electronic future*. Presentation at Ignite Seattle 6. Retrieved from http://www.youtube.com /watch?v=FIoU1pemi18

Muren, D. (2009). *Humblefacturing a sustainable electronic future*. Presentation at Ignite Seattle 6. Retrieved from http://www.youtube.com/watch?v=FIoU1pemi18

Neznanski, M. (2008, November 14). Sharing ideas quickly. *Gazette Times*. Retrieved from http://www .gazettetimes.com/articles/2008/11/14/news /community/3loc01_tech.txt

O'Connor, J. V. (2000). *FAQs #1*. Retrieved from http://www.cusscontrol.com/faqs.html

Payne, N. (n.d.). Public relations across cultures: Building international communication bridges. *All About Public Relations with Steven R. Van Hook*. Retrieved from http://www.aboutpublicrelations.net /ucpayne.htm

Raybould, B. (2007, August 11). Gnomedex: Ignite Seattle. *Bold Words*. Retrieved from http://boldwords. wordpress.com/2007/08/11/gnomedex-ignite-seattle/

"Tips—Special instructions for presenters" (n.d.) Retrieved from http://ignitephoenix.com/tips/

Tversky, B. (1997). Memory for pictures, maps, environments, and graphs. In D. G. Payne & F. G. Conrad (Eds.), *Intersections in basic and applied memory research* (pp. 257–277). Hillsdale, NJ: Erlbaum.

Wahl, A. (2003, November 23). PowerPoint of no return. *Canadian Business*, 76 p. 22.

Weill, J. (2006, December 18). All presentations should be five minutes long. *Jason Weill Web Productions*. Retrieved from http://weill.org/2006/12/08/all -presentations-should-be-five-minutes-long/

CHAPTER 14

DuFrene, D. D., & Lehman, C. M. (2002). Persuasive appeal for clean language. *Business Communication Quarterly, 65* (March), 48–56.

Gastil, J. (1990). Generic pronouns and sexist language: The oxymoronic character of masculine generics. *Journal of Applied Social Psychology, 22,* 423–450.

Hensley, C. W. (1995, September 1). Speak with style and watch the impact. *Vital Speeches of the Day*, p. 703.

Pierre Lévy (1997). *Collective intelligence: Mankind's emerging world in cyberspace*. (p. 20). Cambridge, MA: Perseus Books.

Jaron Lanier (2006). Digital Maoism: The hazards of the new online collectivism. *Edge The Third Culture*. Retrieved at: http://www.edge.org/3rd_culture /lanier06/lanier06_index.html

Rader, W. (2007). The online slang dictionary. Retrieved from http://www.ocf.berkeley.edu/~wrader /slang/b.html

Richards, I. A., & Ogden, C. K. (1923). *The meaning of meaning: A study of the influence of language upon thought and the science of symbolism*. Orlando, FL: Harcourt.

Saeid, J.I. (2003). *Semantics* (2nd ed.). Malden, MA: Blackwell Publishing Ltd.

Schertz, R. H. (1977, November 1). Deregulation: After the airlines, is trucking next? *Vital Speeches*, p. 40.

Stewart, L. P., Cooper, P. J., Stewart, A. D., & Friedley, S. A. (1998). *Communication and gender* (3rd ed.). Boston: Allyn & Bacon. **[1998 OR 2003]**

Treinen, K. P., & Warren, J. T. (2001). Anti-Racist Pedagogy in the Basic Course: Teaching Cultural Communication as if Whiteness Matters. *Basic Communication Course Annual 13*, 46–75.

Witt, P., Wheeless, L., & Allen, M. (2004). A meta-analytical review of the relationship between teacher immediacy and student learning. *Communication Monographs*, 71(2), 184–207.

CHAPTER 15

Ayres, J., & Hopf, T. S. (1990, January). The long-term effect of visualization in the classroom: A brief research report. *Communication Education, 39*, 75–78.

Ayres, J., Hopf, T. S., & Ayres, D. M. (1994, July). An examination of whether imaging ability enhances the effectiveness of an intervention designed to reduce speech anxiety. *Communication Education, 43*, 252–258.

Barron, J. (2011, August 26). With Hurricane Irene near, 370,000 in New York City get evacuation order. *New York Times*. Retrieved from http://www.nytimes .com/2011/08/27/nyregion/new-york-city-begins -evacuations-before-hurricane.html? _r=2&pagewanted=all

Bates, B. (1992). *Communication and the sexes*. Prospect Heights, IL: Waveland Press.

Beatty, M. J., & Behnke, R. R. (1991). Effects of public speaking trait anxiety and intensity of speaking task on heart rate during performance. *Human Communication Research, 18*, 147–176.

Burgoon, J. K., Coker, D. A., & Coker, R. A. (1986). Communicative effects of gaze behavior: A test of two contrasting explanations. *Human Communication Research, 12*, 495–524.

Cizillia, C. (2012, March 12). Republicans war on the TelePrompter—and its limits. *The Washington Post.* [Blog post] Retrieved from http://www.washingtonpost.com/blogs/the-fix/post/republicans-war-on-the-teleprompter--and-its-limits/2012/03/12/gIQAjuMV7R_blog.html

Decker, B. (1992). *You've got to be believed to be heard.* New York: St. Martin's Press.

Dilliplane, S. (2012). Race, rhetoric, and running for President: Unpacking the significance of Barack Obama's "A More Perfect Union" speech. *Rhetoric & Public Affairs, 15*(1), 127–152.

Dwyer, K. K. (2000, January). The multidimensional model: Teaching students to self-manage high communication apprehension by self-selecting treatments. *Communication Education,* 72-81.

French, B. (n.d.). Language barriers. *Public Speaking International.* Retrieved from http://www.publicspeakinginternational.com/funny-stories/

Gardner, W. L. (2003). Perceptions of leader charisma, effectiveness, and integrity: Effects of exemplification, delivery, and ethical reputation. *Management Communication Quarterly, 16*(4), 502–527.

Griffin, K. (1995, July). Beating performance anxiety. *Working Woman, 76*, 62–65.

Haberman, M. (2010, August 16). Chris Christie warns GOP on mosque. *Politico* [Blog post]. Retrieved from http://www.politico.com/news/stories/0810/41141.html#ixzz1pHr4SS14

Hahner, J. C., Sokoloff, M. A., & Salisch, S. L. (2001). *Speaking clearly: Improving voice and diction* (6th ed.). New York: McGraw-Hill.

Hammer, D. P. (2000). Professional attitudes and behaviors: The "As" and "Bs" of professionalism. *American Journal of Pharmaceutical Education, 64*, 455–464.

Frenkel, D. (2011, November 16). Public speaking 101: A lesson in leadership from Barack Obama. *The Drum* [Blog post]. Retrieved from http://www.abc.net.au/unleashed/3674660.html

Kelly, L., Duran, R. L., & Stewart, J. (1990). Rhetoritherapy revisited: A test of its effectiveness as a treatment for communication problems. *Communication Education, 39*, 207–226.

Kelly, L., Phillips, G. M., & Keaten, J. A. (1995). *Teaching people to speak well: Training and remediation of communication reticence.* Cresskill, NJ: Hampton.

Levine, T., Asada, K. J. K., & Park, H. S. (2006). The lying chicken and the gaze avoidant egg: Eye contact, deception, and causal order. *Southern Communication Journal, 71*, 401–411.

Mandell, N. (2012, March 9). New Jersey Governor Chris Christie calls Navy veteran an "idiot." *New York Daily News.* Retrieved from http://articles.nydailynews.com/2012-03-09/news/31141625_1_chris-christie-town-hall-meeting-law-school

Menzel, K. E., & Carrell, L. J. (1994). The relationship between preparation and performance in public speaking. *Communication Education, 43*, 17–26.

Morris, T. L., Gorham, J., Cohen, S. H., & Huffman, D. (1996). Fashion in the classroom: Effects of attire on student perceptions of instructors in college classes. *Communication Education, 45*, 135–148.

Motley, M. (1997). COM therapy. In J. A. Daly, J. C. McCroskey, J. Ayres, T. Hopf, & D. M. Ayres (Eds.) *Avoiding communication: Shyness reticence, and communication apprehension* (2nd ed.). Cresskill, NJ: Hampton Press.

Phillips, G. M. (1977). Rhetoritherapy versus the medical model: Dealing with reticence. *Communication Education, 26*, 34–43.

Richmond, V. P., & McCroskey, J. C. (2000). *Communication: Apprehension, avoidance, and effectiveness* (5th ed.). Scottsdale, AZ: Gorsuch Scarisbrick.

Rucker, P. (October 20, 2011). Republicans mock Obama's teleprompters. *The Washington Post.* Retrieved at: http://www.thehawkeye.com/story/WPBLOOM-101811--bc-teleprompter

Scott, P. (1997, January–February). Mind of a champion. *Natural Health, 27*, 99.

Sellnow , D. D., & Treinen, K. P. (2004). The role of gender in perceived speaker competence: An analysis of student peer critiques. *Communication Education, 53*(3), 286–296.

Shear, M. D. (2011, September 30). Imagining a Christie campaign for president. *New York Times.* Retrieved from http://www.nytimes.com/2011/10/01/us/politics/imagining-a-christie-campaign-for-president.html?pagewanted=all

Towler, A. J. (2003). Effects of charismatic influence training on attitudes, behavior, and performance. *Personnel Psychology, 56*, 363–381.

CHAPTER 16

Baerwald, D. (n.d.). Narrative. Retrieved from Northshore School District Web site: http://ccweb.norshore.wednet.edu/writingcorner/narrative.html.

Dote, L., Kramer, K., Dietz, N., & Grimm, R. Jr. (2006). *College students helping America.* Washington, DC: Corporation for National and Community Service.

Goldberg, B. (2011, March 14). No liberal bias at NPR—just ask NPR. [Blog post] Retrieved from http://www.bernardgoldberg.com/no-liberal -bias-at-npr-just-ask-npr/

Hinckley, D. (2009, July 18). Walter Cronkite remains gold standard for journalists. *NYDailyNews.com.* Retrieved from http://www.nydailynews.com /entertainment/tv/2009/07/18/2009-07-18_he _remains_the_gold_standard_among_all.html

How to detect bias in news media. (n.d.) Retrieved from FAIR (Fairness and Accuracy in Reporting) Web site: http://www.fair.org/index.php?page=121

Howell, D. (2008, August 17). Obama's edge in the coverage race. *Washington Post.* Retrieved from http://www.washingtonpost.com /wp-dyn/content/article/2008/08/15 /AR2008081503100.html?sub=AR

Leopold, T. (2009, July 18). Former CBS anchor '"Uncle Walter" Cronkite dead at 92. *CNN.com.* Retrieved from http://www.cnn.com/2009/US/07/17 /walter.cronkite.dead/index.html

Moyers, B., & Winship M. (2011, March 25). What the right means when it calls NPR "liberal." *Salon.* Retrieved from http://www.salon.com/2011/03/25 /moyers_winship_npr/

Pew Research Center for the People & The Press. (2011, September 22). Press widely criticized, but trusted more than other information sources. [Press Release] Retrieved from http://www.people-press.org/2011/09/22/press-widely-criticized -but-trusted-more-than-other-institutions/

Ötzi, the ice man. (n.d.). *Dig: The archaeology magazine for kids.* Retrieved from http://www.digonsite.com /drdig/mummy/22.html.

U.S. Department of Education, National Center for Education Statistics. (2011). *Digest of Education Statistics, 2010* (NCES 2011–015).

What's wrong with the news? (n.d.). Retrieved from FAIR (Fairness and Accuracy in the News) Web site: http: //www.fair.org/index.php?page=101

CHAPTER 17

Billy Mays, the infomercial king; Death of a great American salesman; Want to know the secret of America's innovation edge? Call now! (2009, July 1). *Global Agenda.* Retrieved from InfoTrac College Edition.

Carter, B. (2008, October 31). Infomercial for Obama is big success in ratings. *New York Times, 158*(54480), A19. Retrieved from InfoTrac College Edition.

Crain, R. (2009, May 4). Deceitful financial infomercial tars entire advertising industry. *Advertising Age, 80*(16), 17. Retrieved from InfoTrac College Edition.

Cummings, J. (2008, October 29). Obama infomercial: Smart or overkill? *Politico.* Retrieved from http: //www.politico.com/news/stories/1008/15056 _Page2.html

Head, S. W., Spann, T., & McGregor, M. A. (2001). *Broadcasting in America: A survey of electronic media* (9th ed.). Boston: Houghton Mifflin.

Hill, B., & Leeman, R. W. (1997). *The art and practice of argumentation and debate.* Mountain View, CA: Mayfield.

James, J. (2007, January). No time for complacency. *Vital Speeches of the Day, 73,* pp. 26–29.

Kennedy, G. A. (1999). *Classical rhetoric and its Christian and secular tradition from ancient to modern times* (2nd ed). Chapel Hill, NC: University of North Carolina Press. Please update this to the 1999 2nd edition.

Mastamokei. (2008, April 30). Billy Mays gangsta remix [Video file]. Retrieved from www.youtube.com /watch?v=_tyct9l-fD8

Megan's Law. (n.d.). *Parents for Megan's Law.* Retrieved from http://www.parentsformmeganslaw.com /html/questions.lasso.

Nabi, R. L. (2002). Discrete emotions and persuasion. In James P. Dillard and Michael Pfau (Eds.), *The persuasion handbook: Developments in theory and practice.* (pp. 291–299). Thousand Oaks, CA: Sage.

Perloff, R. M. (2010). *The dynamics of persuasion: Communication and attitudes in the 21st century* (4th ed.). New York: Taylor & Francis.

Petri, H. L., & Govern, J. M. (2012). *Motivation: Theory, research, and application* (6th ed.). Belmont, CA: Wadsworth.

Petty, R. E., & Cacioppo, J. (1996). *Attitudes and persuasion: Classic and contemporary approaches.* Boulder, CO: Westview.

Schneider, M. (2008, November 23). Longform ads replace kids fare on Fox. *Variety*. Retrieved from http://www.variety.com/article/VR1117996360?refCatId=14

Sellnow, D., & Treinen, K. (2004). The role of gender and physical attractiveness in perceived speaker competence: An analysis of student peer critiques.*Communication Education*, 53(3) 286-296.

Solmsen, F. (Ed). (1954). *The rhetoric and the poetics of Aristotle.* New York: The Modern Library.

Timothy D. Naegele & Associates announces class action lawsuit against Guthy-Renker. (2002, June 26). *All Business.* Retrieved from http://www.allbusiness.com/crime-law/criminal-offenses-cybercrime/5968871-1.html

Toulmin, S. (1958). *The uses of argument.* Cambridge, England: Cambridge University Press.

UNIT 4 SEQUEL

Camia, C. (2011, October 31). Rick Perry's speech video goes viral. *USA Today.* Retrieved from http://content.usatoday.com/communities/onpolitics/post/2011/10/rick-perry-viral-video-new-hampshire-/1#.T7jPKY57ipI

Mankowski, D., & Jose, R. (2012). MBC flashback: The 70th anniversary of FDR's fireside chats. *The Museum of Broadcast Communications.* Retrieved at: http://www.museum.tv/exhibitionssection.php?page=79

Obama, B. (n.d.). Your weekly address. *The White House.* Retrieve at: http://www.whitehouse.gov/briefing-room/weekly-address/

Presentation Revolution. Retrieved from http://info.sliderocket.com/rs/sliderocket/images/Death-By-PowerPoint-Infographic.jpg

Thomas, W. G. (2004). Television news and the civil rights struggle: The views in Virginia and Mississippi. *Southern Spaces.* Retrieved from http://southernspaces.org/2004/television-news-and-civil-rights-struggle-views-virginia-and-mississippi#section6

APPENDIX

Beshara, T. (2006). *The Job Search Solution.* New York: AMACOM.

Betty, K. (2010, July 1). The math behind the networking claim. Retrieved from http://blog.jobfully.com/2010/07/the-math-behind-the-networking-claim/

Boyd, A. (1999). *How to handle media interviews.* London: Mercury.

Employee Tenure in 2010. (2012, September 14). Bureau of labor statistics economic news release. *U.S. Department of Labor,* Washington, DC. Retrieved from http://www.bls.gov/news.release/tenure.nr0.htm

Farr, J. M. (2009). *Top 100 careers without a four-year degree: Your complete guidebook to major jobs in many fields.* Indianapolis, IN: JIST.

Graber, S. (2000). *The everything get-a-job book: From resume writing to interviewing to finding tons of job openings.* Avon, MA: Adams Media.

Hansen, K. (n.d.). Your e-resume's file format aligns with its delivery method. *Quintessential Careers.com.* Retrieved from http://www.quintcareers.com/e-resume_format.html.

Kaplan, R. M. (2002). *How to say it in your job search: Choice words, phrases, sentences and paragraphs for résumés, cover letters and interviews.* Paramus, NJ: Prentice-Hall.

Krotz, J. (2006). *6 tips for taking control in media interviews.* Retrieved from http://www.microsoft.com/smallbusiness/resources/management/leadership-training/6-tips-for-taking-control-in-media-interviews.aspx#tipsfortakingcontrolinmediainterviews

Light, J. (2011, April, 4). For job seekers, company sites beat online job boards, social media. *Wall Street Journal.* Retrieved from http://online.wsj.com/article/SB1000142405274870380630457623673131318345282.html?KEYWORDS=JOE+LIGH

Ryan, R. (2000). *60 seconds & you're hired.* New York: Penguin Books.

Slayter, M. E. (2006, January 14). Rehearse, rehearse, repeat: Have a rock-solid plan when preparing for an interview. *The Forum,* p. E3.

Taylor, J., & Hardy D. (2004). *Monster careers: How to land the job of your life.* New York: Penguin Books.

Tengler, C. D., & Jablin, F. M. (1983). Effects of question type, orientation, and sequencing in the employment screening interview. *Communication Monographs,* 50, 261.

Yena, D. J. (2011). *Career directions: The path to your ideal career.* New York: McGraw-Hill.

Index

Italicized page numbers indicate materials in figures

A

Able-ism, 43
Abstract, 265
Accents, 356–357
Accommodating/accommodation (lose-win), *179, 180*
Accountability, 205–206
Accuracy, 34, 43
Accurate sources, 265
Acoustic space, 101, 102
Acquaintances, 140–142
Acronyms, 11
Action, definition of, 293–294
Action-oriented listeners, 115
Active listening, 118–119, 126
Actual objects, 314–315
Adaptation phase, 353
Adaptors, 97
Ad hominem fallacies, 422
Adjourning, 208
Adult Survivors of Child Abuse (ASCA), 197
Age/generation, 54–55
Ageism, 43
Agendas, *222,* 222
Aggressive communication style, 176–177
Alcoholics Anonymous (AA), 197
Ali, Saba, 151, 153–154
Alliteration, 345
Altman, Irwin, 148
Altruism, 67
Ambiguity, 66, 96, 174
American Psychological Association (APA), 298–299, *299*
Americans with Disabilities Act, 55
Analogy, 344
Analogy, arguing from, 420
Analysis, critical. *See* Critical analysis
Analytical skills, 6
Anecdotes, 254, 269
Anger, 427
Animation, in delivery, 355–356
Annotated bibliography, 270
Anthony, Katie, *302–306*
Anticipation phase, 353
Antithesis, 345
Antonyms, 394
Anxiety
  in communicating, 19, 20, 63
  high uncertainty-avoidance cultures and, 58
  intercultural communication competence and, 63
  managing, 353–355
  in public speaking (*See* Public speaking apprehension)
  scripted speeches and, 363
APA citation style, 298–299, *299*
Apathetic audiences, 417, 450
Appeal to action, 297
Appearance
  nonverbal communication and, 96, 104–105, 107, 108
  self-perceptions and, 33, 41
  in speech presentation, 358–359
Apprehension. *See* Anxiety; Communication apprehension (CA); Public speaking apprehension
Argumentation skills, 56
Arguments (persuasive). *See also* Persuasive speaking
  audience adaptation and, 371, 416–418
  definition of, 414
  emotional appeal and, 441– 445
  fallacies in, 421–422
  main points, 430, 431
  persuasive goals and, 415–418
  supporting evidence, 418–419
  types of, 419–421
Articles, 263
Articulation, 356
Artifacts, 55, 102
(ASCA) Adult Survivors of Child Abuse, 197
Assertive communication style, 177, 178
Assertiveness, 56, *179,* 179
Assonance, 345
Assumed similarity, 41
Assumptions, 9, 55, 66
Asynchronous channels, 134
Attending, 118–119
Attention, 28–29, 42
Attention, gaining, in speeches, 290–294, 302, 323–325
Attitudes
  of audiences, 416–418
  common ground and, 334
  intercultural communication and, 50, 51, 55, 66
  topic selection and, 251
Attributions, 41–42
Audience adaptation
  common ground and, 334, 371
  attitudes and, 416–418
  audience analysis and, 248, 250–255, *251*
  cultural diversity and, 338–340
  definition of, 248, 332
  intellectual stimulation and, 388
  interest and, 290, 294
  memory aids and, 391
  occasion of speech and, 255–256
  presentational aids and, 315, 319, 320, 323–325, 368–369
  propositions and, 415–416
  relevance and, 294, *302–306*

sample plans, 374–375, 403–406
    topic selection and, 248, 249, 250, 253
Audience analysis, 248, 250–255, *251.*
        See also Audience adaptation
Audience-based communication apprehension, 20
Audience contact, 358–359
Audience diversity, 253–254
Audiovisual aids, 312, 319–320
Authority, 265
Automatic processing, 30, 43
Autonomy, 157
Average group opinion method, 229
Avoidance, uncertainty, 58, 61, 66
Avoiding (Lose-Lose), 155, 179–180

B

Baby Boomers, 54
Bar graphs, 318, *319*
Barriers, 63–65
Beginning relationship, 150–151
Behavior, 172–173, 181, 400
Bias, media, *397,* 398–399
Biased reporting, 83, 84–85
Bibliographic style formats, 299
Biographies, 264
Blended family, 196
Blind pane, *149,* 149
Blogs, 66, 74, 78, 84, 201
Body actions, 119
Body art, 104–105
Body language. *See* Kinesics
Body movement, 99
Body orientation, 98–99
Books, 263
Boundary, establishing personal, 175
Brainstorming, 228–229, 249–250
Breadth, 388
Bridge, 471
Briefs, 232, 234
Buffering messages, 165
Bullying, self-esteem and, 32
Bureau of Labor Statistics, *265*

C

CA. *See* Communication apprehension (CA)
Cameras, document, 325
Canned plan, 7–8
Career fairs, 461
Causation, arguing from, 420–421
Causes, false, 421
CD/DVD players, 325
Chalkboards, 324
Change
    language and, 78–79

perceptions and, 38–39, 44
    of subject, 174
Channels, 11–12
Charts, *316,* 316
Chronemics (use of time), 57–58, 102–104
Chronological order, 285
Chronological résumé, 462, *463*
Circumscribing stage, 155
Citing sources, 271–272, 298–300, *299*
Claim, 418
Clinchers, 297–298
Clip art, 322, 323
Closedness, 157, 159, 166
Clothing, nonverbal communication and, 104
Co-cultures, 51–55
    communication behavior and, 52
    communication styles and, 178
    intimacy and, 144–148
    listening style and, 115
Codes, communication, 63–64
Code switch, 52, 89
Cognitive restructuring, 354, 382, 385
Cohesiveness, 203, 217, 234
Collaborating (win-win), 56, *179,* 180, 181
Collaborativeness, 147
Collectivism/Collectivist cultures
    definition of, 56
    interdependent self-perceptions and, 33
    listening styles and, 115
    passive behavior and, 178
Color, in presentational aids, 322
Comforting, 164–166. *See also* Listening
Commitment, 144, 147, 152, 220
Common ground, 333, 334–335, 374
Communication, 4–22
    anxiety and, 19, 20, 63
    characteristics of, 14–17
    codes, 63–64
    competence in, 19–20, 63–69
    cultural influences on, 17
    definition of, 7
    ethics and, 17–19
    in groups (*See* Group communication)
    intercultural (*see* Intercultural communication)
    learning and, 16
    nature of, 7–8
    nonverbal (*See* Nonverbal messages)
    paraphrasing, 121
    process model, 12, *13*
    in relationships (*See* Interpersonal communication)
    self-perception and, 35–38
    skills, improving, 14–17
    verbal (*See* Verbal messages)
Communication apprehension (CA), 9, 18, 20. *See also*
        Public speaking apprehension

Communication climate, definition of, 164
Communication competence, 19–20, 63–69
Communication contexts, 8–10
Communication orientation motivation (COM), 353
Communication settings, 9–10
Communication skills
    assertive communication style, 178
    feelings, describing, 174
    paraphrasing, 122
    perception checking, 44
    specific language, using, 81
    speech goals, 259
    speech organization, 300
Comparative advantages pattern, 429
Comparisons, 269, 319, 394–495
Compassion, 428–429
Competence, 19–20, 63–69, 425
Competent communication strategies, 65–69
Competing (win-lose), 180
Competitiveness, 59
Complementary feedback, 16
Comprehensive reports, 232
Compromising (partial lose-lose), 179, 180
Computer-mediated presentational aids, 233
Computers, 325
Concept mapping, 249–250, 250
Conclusions, speech, 296–298
Concrete language, 81
Concrete words, 80
Confidentiality, 166. See also Privacy
Confirming communication messages, definition of, 164
Conflict
    collaboration in managing, 147
    in groups, 208–211
    individualistic cultures and, 56
    interpersonal, managing, 179–182
    management of, 143, 179–182, 221
    relationships and, 152–153
Confrontation phase, 353
Connection, 157
Connotation, 79–80
Conscious processing, 30, 43
Consensus method, 230
Constructed messages, 17
Constructive criticism, 173, 174
Content-oriented listeners, 115
Content paraphrases, 121
Context-based communication apprehension, 20
Continuity of communication, 15
Continuous reinforcement, 400
Continuum, speech, 416
Contrasts, 269, 394–395
Control, 16
Controversial topics, 397–398

Conversational style, 355
Coping statements, 354, 355
Cover letters, 462, 464–466, 465–466
Creative works, expository speeches on, 401, 401
Creativity, in expository speeches, 389–391
Credentials, 260
Credibility, 295–296, 302
    communication competence and, 19
    definition of, 19
    goodwill and, 424, 425
    of speakers, 335–336, 358, 374, 375, 425–426
    in speeches, 295–296, 403, 425–426
    trustworthiness and, 19, 266–267, 308, 375
Criteria, solutions, 228
Criteria satisfaction pattern, 430
Critical analysis, 372–373, 379–381, 441–445
Critique response guidelines, 127, 128
Cronkite, Walter, 398
Cross-cultural adaptation, 60–62
Cultural context, 9, 57
Cultural diversity, 338–339
Cultural identity, 115, 146
Cultural immersion, 66
Cultural norms, 17, 32–33, 204–205
Culture-centered skills, 68–69
Cultures
    assertiveness and, 177–178
    barriers to communication between, 63–64
    co-cultures and, 51–55, 115
    communication and, 50–55
    communication competence and, 19–20, 63–69
    conflict and, 209–210
    cultural identity of, 51–55, 115
    definition of, 17, 50
    eye contact and, 97–98
    gestures and, 96–97
    intimacy and, 144–148
    nonverbal communication and, 96
    norms and values of, 50, 86–87
    physical contact and, 151
    time orientation and, 57–58
    touch and, 99
    vocal tone and, 100
Culture shock, 50
Curiosity, intellectual, 290, 388
Currency of information, 266
Cyberbullying, 32, 78

D

Dark side messages, 18, 18–19
Data-gathering methods, 252–253
Decision making, 224, 229–230
Decoding, 7, 17
Deductive reasoning, 418–419

Definitions, 394
Deliverables, 232
Delivery, 350–383. *See also* Speech presentation
Demographic data, 251
Demonstrations, 395–396
Denotation, 79
Dependability, intimacy and, 147
Depth, 388
Derived credibility, 425
Describing behavior, 172–173
Describing feelings, 171–172, 174
Descriptions, 392–394
Descriptive language, 81
Desensitization, 354
Desires, expressing, 176–178
Deteriorating relationships, 159
Developing relationships, 151–152
Developmental material, 370
Diagrams, 315, *316*
Dialect, 75
Dialectics, 156–159
Dimensions (learning cycle), 391
Direct body orientation, 98
Direct questions, 291
Direct verbal style, 87
Disability, 55
Disclosure
    definition of, 148
    feedback and, 150, 151, 172–173
    of feelings, 171–172
    guidelines for, 169–170
    intimacy and, 144
    managing privacy and, 166–167
    other-, 146, 149
    of personal information, 171
    reciprocity and, 169
    in relationship lifecycles, 148–150, 168–169
Disconfirming communication messages,
        definition of, 164
Discrimination, 43
Dispositional attribution, 42
Dissolving relationships, 155–156
Distortion, self-perception and, 34–35, 42–43
Distractions, 12, 119
Diverse Voices
    changing times, 103–104
    cross-cultural adaptation, 61–62
    cultural differences and speaking, 254
    dialect, 76–77
    disclosure of information, 167–168
    interpersonal relationships, 153–154
    language barriers, 361
    managing competing group norms, 204–205
    problem solving and cultural diversity, 218–219

public relations across cultures, 320–321
public speaking patterns, 339–340
self-perception struggles, 39–40
value of listening, 116–117
Diversity, 253, 338–339
Document cameras, 325
Doing dimension, 391
Dominant cultures, 51–55
Drawings, 315
Drummond, Mike, 221
Dual processing, 30
DVD players, 325

E

EBSCO, 263
e-Communication, 8
Educated guesses, 253
Egocentricity, 67
Either-or fallacies, 421
Elaboration Likelihood Model (ELM), 414
Elaborations, 269
Electronic resources, 263
Elevator speech, 462
ELM. *See* Elaboration Likelihood Model (ELM)
Emblems, 96
Emoticons, 11–12
Emotional support, 143, 164–166. *See also* Listening
Emotional support response, 126–127
Emotions, 95, 98, 172, 174, 426–429
Empathic responsiveness, 122
Empathy, 69, 122, 424–425
Employee referral programs, 461
Employment interviews, 459–469
    conducting, 466–469
    employment interviewers, 459–460
    employment seekers and, 460–462
    following up with, 469
    preparing application materials, 462–466
Encoding, 7, 17
Encyclopedias, 261
Ethical dilemmas, 19
Ethics
    definition of, 17
    implications on communication, 17–19
    in speeches, 271–272, 308, 329, 382, 409
Ethics issues
    audience adaptation, 346
    audience ethical obligations to speakers, 382
    developing culture-centered skills, 68
    ethical listening, 128
    expository speech topics, 409
    group communication, 210
    group decision making, 221, 237, 245
    interpersonal communication, 182

linguistic sensitivity, 80, 81–82
nonverbal communication, 109
online ethics, 158
presentation aids, 326
résumé, exaggerating in, 471
source citations in speeches, 272
speaker/audience obligations, 382
standards for communication, 22
truthfulness in speeches, 306
Ethnicity, 52–53, 147
Ethnocentrism, 43, 63
Ethos, 414, 436, 441
Etymology, 394
Evaluating. *See* Critical analysis
Evidence, to support reasons, 418
Example, arguing from, 419–420
Examples, 268
Executive summaries, 232
Exigence, 248
Expectations, *29,* 29, 176–178
Expediting (meetings), 220, 232
Experiences, perception and, 30, 31
Experiments, 267
Expert, definition of, 268
Expert opinion method, 229
Expert opinions, 268
Expository speeches, 396–402
Extemporaneous speeches, 363
Extended family, 196
Eye contact, 97–98, 358–359, 369, 370, 371

F

Face, 165
Facebook, 55, 85
Face-to-face relationship, 151, 152
Facial expressions, 96, 98, 107, 119, 359, 361
Fact, 125, 415
Factual statements, 124–125, 267–268
Fairness, 18, 23
Faithfulness, intimacy and, 148
Fallacies, reasoning, 421–422
False causes, 421
False perception, 34
Familiar language, 81, 332
Families, 196–197
Fear, 9, 20, 426
Feedback, 7, 16, 148–150, 172–174, 370
Feedback cues, 126
Feelings, 171–172, 174
Feelings paraphrases, 121–123
Feminine co-culture, 115, 146
Feminine culture, 59
Fieldwork observations, 266
Figurative comparisons/contrasts, 269

Filtering messages, 35
First impressions. *See* Social perceptions
Flattery, 172
Flexibility, 69
Flip charts, 324
Flow charts, 316, *317*
Forced consistency, 42
Formal leader, 216
Forming, 207
French, Bill, 361
Friends, 142–143, 156, 197
Functional résumé, 462, *464*

G

Gatekeepers, 220, 223
Gaur, Raj, 76–77
Gaze (eye contact), 97–98, 359
Gender, 53, 146
Gender differences, 53, 164
General speech goal, 257
Generic language, 337
Gestures, 96–97, *236–237,* 359–361, *360*
Giving advice, 165–166
Goals
    with acquaintances, 140–141
    communication improvement, 21–23, *23*
    in constructive criticism, 173
    in groups, 198, 199–200
    informative, *258*
    language clarification, 332, 334
    listening, 126, 127
    persuasive, *258,* 415–418
    in relationships, 140–141, 150
    in responding, 173
    of speeches (*See* Speech goals)
Goodwill, 295, 424, 425
Gossip, 166
Government documents, 264
Grandin, Temple, 55
Graphs, 318
Grave-dressing, 156
"The Great Man Theory of Leadership"
    (Kippenberger), 216
Gregoire, Sheila Wray, 254
Grieving, 13–14
Grooming, 95, 104
Ground rules, 203–204
Group communication, 194–213
    conflicts in, 208–211
    of decisions, 232–234
    definition of, 196
    group development and, 206–208
    healthy groups and, 201–206
    humor in, 218, 292–293

problem solving and (*See* Problem solving)
in small groups, definition of, 10
types of groups and, 196–201
Groups
  accountability in, 205
  cohesiveness in, 203
  collectivist cultures and, 56, 209
  communicating in (*See* Group communication)
  conflict management in, 221
  cultural influences on, 58
  decision methods in, 229–230
  definition of, 196
  development stages of, 206–208
  dynamics of, 234–236, *235–236*
  ethics and, 210
  goals of, 198 , 199–200
  healthy, 201–206
  interdependence in, 202–203
  leadership in, 216–217, 220–221
  perceptions of, 42–43
  problem solving in (*See* Problem solving)
  small, 10
  status in, 53, 54, 59
  trust and, 203, 207, 208
  types of, 198–201
  working in, 206
Groupthink, 207
Guilt, 426

H

Habermas, Jürgen, 8
Hall, Edward T., 55
Handouts, 324–325
Happiness or Joy, 428
Haptics (touch), 99, 107, 108
Harmonizers, 217–218, 223
Hasty generalizations, 421
Healthy groups, 201–206
Healthy relationship, 140
Herakova, Lily, 217, 218–219
Heterogeneous groups, 199
Heterosexism, 43
Heuristic, 30
Hidden job market, 461
High-context communicators, 57
High-context cultures, 57, 89
High power-distance cultures, 59
High uncertainty-avoidance cultures, 58
Historical context, 9
Historical topics, 370
Hofstede, Gerard Henrik (Geert), 55, 59
Home pages, 265, 266
Homogeneous groups, 199
Honesty, 18. *See also* Truthfulness

assertiveness and, 177
groups and, 197, 207
managing conflict and, 143
trust and (*See* Trust)
trustworthiness and (*See* Trustworthiness)
Hope, 428
Humor
  in group communication, 218, 292–293
  as memory aid, *392*
  offensive, 337, 338
  as speech opener, 279
  in speech presentation, 279,392, 450
  as tension reliever, 218, 223
Hyperpersonal communication, 189
Hypothesis, 267

I

"I"-centered messages, 175
Ideal self-concept, 31
Ideal values, definition of, 50
Idiolect, 77
Idioms, 87
Ignite (presentation style), 312–313
Illustrators, 96
Immersion, cultural, 66
Impersonal communication, 140–142
Implementing solutions, 230
Implicit personality theory, 41
Impression formation, 41
Impromptu speeches, 24, 362–363
Improvement plan, 21–23, *23*
Incentives, 434
Inclusive language, 81
Incongruence, 34
Incremental change, 417
Independent self-perceptions, 33
Index, 16
Indexical communication, 16
Indirect body orientation, 98
Indirect verbal style, 87
Individualistic cultures, 56, 177–178
Inductive reasoning, 418
Inferences, 124–125
Infomercials, 422–423
Informal emergent leaders, 216
Information co-ownership, 169
Information-gathering interviews, 456–459
Information givers/seekers/analyzers, 217
Information sources, locating and evaluating, 260–267
Informative methods, 392–396, 397
Informative speaking, 386–411
  characteristics of, 388–391, *392*
  definition of, 388
  evaluation checklist, *401–402*

methods of, 392–396
  sample speech, 374–379, 403–406
  speech frameworks of, 396–402
Informative speech goals, *258*
InfoTrac College Edition, 263
InfoTrac University Library, 263
Initial credibility, 425
Initiation, in relationships, 142
Instant messaging (IMs), 15
Integrity, 18
Intellectual stimulation, 388
Intelligible speaking, 356–357
Interaction coordination, 11
Intercultural communication, 48–71
  barriers to, 63–69
  basic skills, 68
  co-cultures and, 51–55
  competence in, 63–69
  cultural differences in, 55–62, 76–77
  cultural identity and, 51–55
  cultural norms and values and, 64
  definition of, 50
  dominant cultures and, 51–55
  listening and, 68–69
  sex and gender, 53
Intercultural competence, 89
Interdependence, group, 202–203
Interdependent self-perceptions, 33
Interest groups, 198
Interests, 28–29
Interference (noise), 12
Intermittent reinforcement, 400
Internal noise, 12
Interpersonal communication, 162–191
  comforting, 164–166
  definition of, 10, 140
  disclosure guidelines for, 169–174
  expressing desires and expectations, 176–178
  intimacy and, 144
  managing interpersonal conflict, 179–182
  managing privacy and disclosure, 166–176
  mediated, in relationships, 188–191
  providing emotional support, 164–166
Interpersonal conflict, managing, 179–182
Interpersonal relationships, 138–161
  communication skills for (*See* Interpersonal communication)
  conflict in, 143, 179–182, 221
  definition of, 140
  dialectics in, 156–159
  life cycles of, 148–150
  stages of, 150–156
  trust in, 144, 147
  types of, 140–148

Interpreters, 217
Interpreting, 29–30
Interviews, 452–472
  employment, 459–469
  information-gathering, 458–459
  with media, 469–471
  protocols for, *454–455*, 454–456, *456*
  questions for, 455–456
Intimacy, 16, 144–148, 169
Intimate distance, 101
Intimates, 144–148
Intonation, 100. *See also* Vocalics
Intrapersonal communication, 9
Introductions, speech, 290–296
Irrelevant association, 338
Irreversibility of communication, 15
Issue-related group conflict, 209

J

Jargon, 52, 81, 342
Job interviews. *See* Employment interviews
Job market, hidden and visible, 461
Job openings, locating, 460–461
Johari window, *149*, 149–150
Jokes. *See* Humor

K

Kinesics, 96–99, 357–362. *See also* Nonverbal messages
Knowledge, 19, 20, 66

L

Language
  appropriate use of, 0, 372
  audience adaptation and, 332
  characteristics of, 77–79
  clarity of, 340–343
  definition of, 75
  ethnicity and, 52–53
  linguistic sensitivity and, 80, 81–82, 337–338
  meaning and, 79–89
  nature of, 74–79
  nonparallel, 337–338
  oral style, 332–333
  sensory, 343–344
  speaking vividly, 343–346
Language communities, 75, 78, 79
LCD projectors, 325
Leaders/governors, guidelines for meeting, 221–224
Leadership, 34, 216–217, 220–221
Leading questions, 456
Learning styles, 391
Lectures. *See* Expository speeches

Legal issues, in speeches, 400
Lexicon, 75
Line graphs, 318, *319*
Linguistic sensitivity, 80, 81–82, 337–338
Lion Club International, 198, 203, 204, 205– 206
Listener relevance links, 287, 302, 303, 304, 407
Listeners, challenges to, 115–118
Listening, 112–135
    active listening, 118–129
    challenges to effective listeners, 115–118
    comforting and, 164–166
    common ground and, 333, 334–335
    definition of, 114
    evaluating and (*See* Critical analysis)
    intercultural communication and, 68–69
    interference with, 12
    nonverbal communication and, 115, 119
    practice, 68
    relevance and, 266, 294, 333–334
    relevance links and, 287
    remembering and, 123–124
    responding and, 125–129
Listening apprehension, 116
Listening style, 115–118
Liu, Min, 61–62
Logical reasons order, 286
Logistics (meetings), 220, 223, 224–226
Logos, 414, 415, 418–422
Long-term oriented culture, 60
Low-context communicators, 57
Low-context cultures, 57, 89
Low power-distance cultures, 59
Low uncertainty-avoidance cultures, 58
Luft, Joe, 148

M

"Machismo," 178
MADD (Mothers against Drunk Driving), 198
Main points
    choosing, 279–281, 282
    definition of, 279
    organizing, 285–287
    writing, 281
Maintaining relationships, 152, 155
Maintenance leadership roles, 217–219
Majority rule method, 230
Maps, 315, *316*
Marginalizing, 253
Mariano, Carmen, 295
Marking, 337
Masculine co-culture, 115, 146
Masculine culture, 59
Masculinity/femininity, 32, 33
Mask feelings, 174

Mass communication, 10
Meaning, 10, 11, 82, 83, 86–88
Media bias, *397*, 398–399
Media images, 35
Media interviews, 469–471
Media multiplexity, 190
Mediators, 218
Meetings, 221–226
Memory aids, 391, *392*
Mendel, Gregor, 390
Message interpretation, 11
Message production, 10
Messages
    comforting and, 165
    dark side, *18*, 18–19
    definition of, 7
    filtering, 35
    persuasive (*See* Persuasive speaking)
    types of, 17
Metaphor, 344
Miller, Ann Neville, 339–340
Milliner, Alyssa Grace, 374–379
Mindfulness, 89
MLA citation style, 298–299, *299*
Mnemonic devices, 124, *392*
Modeling, 352
Models, scale, 315
Modern Language Association (MLA), 298–299, *299*
Monochronic cultures, 57
Monochronic time orientation, 57
Monotone, 100, 357
Mother language, 53
Mothers against Drunk Driving (MADD), 198
Motivated movement, 362
Motivated sequence pattern, 432
Motivation, communication competence and, 19
Mourning, 13–14
Movement, 96, 99, 362
Multi-channeled nonverbal communication, 95–96, 107
Multiple-response items, 252
Multitasking, 4, 6

N

Narrative order, 285–286
Narratives, 269, 395
National Association of Colleges and Employers, 6, 196
Native language (mother tongue), 53
Nativization, 76–77
Needs, 28
Negative face needs, 165
Negative reinforcement, 352, 353
Negative self-perception, 32, 35–36

Nervousness. *See* Anxiety
Network, 461–462
Networking, 461
Neutral attitudes, 417
Neutralization, 159
Neutral questions, 455
Newspapers, 263–264
New York Times, 54
New York Times Almanac, 17
Noise, 12
Nonparallel language, 337–338
Nonparticipant observation, 66
Nonverbal behavior, observing, 119
Nonverbal immediacy, 359
Nonverbal messages, 92–111
    appearance and, 94, 95, 96, 104–105
    body, use of (*See* Kinesics)
    characteristics of, 95–96
    definition of, 94
    gender differences in, 96, 107
    guidelines for improving, 107–109
    interpreting messages, 107–109
    listening and, 115, 119
    personal space and, 101
    sending, 107
    time use and, 102–103
    types of, 96–106
    vocal characteristics of, 96, 107, 356–357
Norming stage, 207–208
Norms, 32–33, 50, 64, 86–87, 146, 203–204
Notes, speaking, 356–357, *356– 357*
Note-taking, 124
Novelty, 157
Nuclear family, 196
Nye, Naomi Shihab, 167–168

O

Objectivity, 265–266
Observation, 66, 266
Observing
    cultural differences, 50
    as data source, 252–253
    nonverbal behavior, 119
Occasion, 255–256
Oculesics (eye contact), 97–98, 358–359, *366, 367,* 369
Offensive humor, 337, 338
Offensive language, 337
Okigbo, Charles, 103–104
Online relationship, 151, 152
Onomatopoeia, 345
Open-ended items, 252
Open-mindedness, 67
Openness, 157, 158–159
Open pane, in Johari window, *149,* 149
Open questions, 455

Operant conditioning, 400
Opinion givers/seekers/analyzers, 217
Opposing attitudes, 417
Oral brief, 232
Oral footnote, 271
Oral reports, 233
Oral style, 332–333
Organizational charts, 316, *318*
Organizational patterns
    for expository speeches, 397
    for main points, 285–286
    for persuasive speeches, 432, *434*
Organizing, 278. *See also* Speech organization
Orientation, long-term/short-term, 60
Other-centered messages, 165
Other-disclosure, 148
Other-imposed prophecies, 34–35
Other sensory aids, 312, 320
Outlining speeches. *See* Speech organization

P

Panel discussions, 233, 234
Paralanguage, 95, 99–101. *See also* Vocalics
Paralinguistics. *See* Paralanguage
Parallel, 284
Paraphrasing, 121–122, 182
Participant observation, 66
Participants, 8, 9, 17, 224–226
Passive-aggressive communication style, 177
Passive communication style, 176
Passive listening, 118
Passive observation, 66
Pathos, 414, 435
Pattern, 29
Pauses, in speech, 343, 357, 366, *367. See also* Vocalics
Payne, Neil, 320–321
People-oriented listeners, 115
Perception
    checking, 44, 109
    of communication competence, 23
    definition of, 28
    false, 34
    of others, 41–45
    process, 28–30
    of self (*See* Self-perceptions)
    stereotypes and, 42–43
Performance orientation, 353
Performing stage, in group development, 208
Periodical Abstract, 263
Periodicals, 263
Personal distance, 101
Personal experiences, 30, 31
Personal feelings, sharing, 171–172
Personal impact, on audiences, 334
Personality-related group conflict, 209

Personality theories, implicit, 41

Personal references, 290, 293

Personal space, 101–102

Personas, 37–38

Personification, 345

Perspective taking, 122

Persuasive speaking, 412–450

  conveying competence and credibility, 425–426

  definition and nature of persuasion, 414

  demonstrating goodwill, 424–425

  developing logic and arguments, 418–422

  evaluation checklist, *434–435*

  evoking emotions, 426–429

  goals, 415–418, *416*

  organizational patterns, 429–432

  processing persuasive messages, 414–415

  sample speech, *416*, 435–441

Persuasive speech goals, *258*, 415–418

Persuasive speech propositions, *391*, 415–418

Phonology, 75

Photographs, 315

Photos, in presentational aids, 321

Physical appearance, 41, 104–105

Physical contact, 151

Physical context, 8

Physical environment, listening and, 118–119

Physical space, 102

Pictures, in presentational aids, 322

Pie chart, 318, *318*

Pitch, vocal, 100, 356, 357

Plagiarism, 269

Platonic relationship, 144

Poise, 358, *366, 367*

Policy, proposition of, 416, *416*

Polychronic cultures, 57–58

Pop Comm!

  audience adaptation, 312–313

  body art, 105–106

  "collective intelligence" phenomonon, 336–337

  ghostwritten online dating profiles, 145–146

  giving a toast, 278–279

  infomercials, 422–423

  mourning, 13–14

  online gaming, 231–232

  online social groups, 201–202

  political debates and listening, 120–121

  politics, politicians, and public speech delivery, 364–365

  pragmatics of tabloid and mainstream journalism, 84–85

  race and stereotypes in popular culture, 64–65

  right to privacy in mediated society, 170–171

  self-monitoring and celebrity culture, 37–38

  Wikipedia, 262–263

Positive communication climate, definition of, 164

Positive face needs, 165

Posters, 323

Posture, 98–99, 358

Power distance, 59

Practicing speeches. *See* Speech presentation

Pragmatic meaning, 82, 83

Pragmatics, 82–86

Praise, 172

Predictability, 157

Predictions, 34, 42

Prejudice, 42

Presentational aids

  benefits of, 314

  computer-mediated aids, 233

  criteria for choosing, 320

  definition of, 312

  displaying methods, 323–325

  handling during speech, 323, 368–369

  preparing, 321–323

  in process speeches, 396

  types of, 314–320

Presentations. *See* Speech presentation

Pride, 428

Primary questions, 455

Primary research, 260, 266–267

Principles, 400

Print style, in presentational aids, 322

Privacy

  definition of, 166

  disclosure rules and, 169

  information co-ownership and, 169

  intimacy and, 169

  management guidelines, 174–175

  personal feedback and, 172–173

  personal information and, 171

  reciprocity and, 169

  self-disclosure and, 157

  sharing feelings and, 171–172

Privacy management, 166–167, 174–176

Probing for information, 125

Problem analysis, *227*, 227

Problem-cause-solution pattern, 431–432

Problem definition, 226

Problem-solution pattern, 431

Problem solving, 214–242

  brainstorming, 228–229

  communicating solutions in, 232–234

  decision making, 229–230

  effective meetings for, 221–226

  problem analysis, 227, *227–228*

  problem definition, 226

  shared leadership in, 216–217, 220–221

  solutions, 228–230

  systematic, 226–232

Procedural leadership roles, 220

Processing approach, 118

Process speeches, 396

Productive thinking, 410–411
Profanity, 338
Projectors, 325
Pronouns, personal, 332, 334, 374
Pronunciation, 339, 356
Prophecies, self-fulfilling, 34–35
Propositions, 415–418, *416*
Prosocial behaviors, 152
Proxemics (use of space), 95, 101–102
Proximity, 334
Pseudo-conflict, 208
Psychological context, 9
Public communication, 10
Public distance, 101
Public speaking
    action steps for, 248
    apprehension and (*See* Public speaking apprehension)
    audience and (*See* Audience analysis)
    developing speech content (*See* Speech content)
    organizing speeches (*See* Speech organization)
    practicing/presenting (*See* Speech presentation)
Public speaking apprehension, 352–355, *353. See also* Speech presentation
Public speaking skills training, 354–355
Published resources, employment seekers and, 461
Purpose, 14–15, 107, 199

Q

Quality (Timber), 100
Question(s), 119, 121, 291
    of fact, 226
    handling, speeches and, 371
    interview, 455–456
    of policy, 227
    rhetorical, 335
    survey, sample of, *252*
    of value, 226
Quotation books, 264
Quotations, 269, 293

R

Race, 52, 147
Racism, 43
RAR. *See* Remote access reports (RAR)
Rate, speaking, 100, 356
Reacting, 99. *See also* Feedback
Reactions, self-concept and, 31
Reading to audience, presentational aids and, 321
Real time, 201
Real values, definition of, 50
Reason/reasoning, 418–419, 429
Reciprocity, 169
Recorders, 220

Recording information, 270–271
References, 124–125
Referral services, 461
Reframing, 159
Reframing the situation, 165
Refutative pattern, 430–431
Rehearsing speeches, 365–370, 373. *See also* Speech presentation
Relational dialectics, 156–157
Relational message, 16
Relationship Filtering Model, 150
Relationship life cycle, 148
Relationship maintenance, 152–155
Relationships, 144, 150–156, 168–169. *See also* Interpersonal relationships
Relationship transformation, 156
Relevance, 266, 294, 333–334
Reliable sources, 265
Relief, 428
Religion, 54, 147
Remembering, 123–124, 391
Remote access reports (RAR), 233, *234*
Repetition, 124, 345
Reports, 232–234
Research cards, *270*, 270–271
Respect, 18, 89, 128
Responding, 94, 104, 126–129, 182. *See also* Feedback
Responses, 31, 172
Responsibility, 18
Responsiveness, 142, 147, 425–426
Restructuring, cognitive, 354, 382, 385
Résumé, 462, *463*, 464
Rewards, 60
Rhetoric, 414
Rhetorical figures of speech, 332, 344, 346, 349
Rhetorical questions, 335
Rhetorical situation, *248*, 248–249, 291
Rhetorical structures of speech, 344
Ritualized touch, 99
Roles, 198, 199, 200, 207
Romantic relationships, 144, 156

S

Sacrifice, 152
Sadness, 427
Salvation Army, 198
Saving face, 141
Scaled items, 252
Script, definition of, 7–8
Scripted speeches, 363
Secondary research, 260–266
Secret pane, in Johari Window, *149*, 149
Section transitions, 288–289, 290

Selection, 28–29
Selective perception, 42
Self-concept, 30–31
Self-created prophecies, 34–35
Self-disclosure, 157, 148, 149, 159, 171
Self-esteem, 30, 32, 35, 38, 56
Self-fulfilling prophecies, 34–35
Self-monitoring, 37
Self-perceptions, 30–40
    accuracy and distortion of, 34–35, 43
    changing, 38–40
    cultural norms and, 32–33
    effects on communication, 35–38
    process, 28–30
Self-talk, 35–36, 352, 354, 355
Semantic meaning, 79, 80, 83
Semantic noises, 12
Semantics, 79–82
Sense of self, communication and, 14
Sensory language, 343–344
Sensory stimuli, 28
Sequential order, 285
Service groups, 198–199
Sex, 53
Sexism, 43
Sexual orientation, 53–54
Shame, 426–427
Shared leadership, 220–221
Shared leadership functions, 216–217
Short-term oriented culture, 60
Sign, arguing from, 419
Signposts, 289–290
Simile, 344
Simplicity, 29
Single parent family, 196
Situated communication, 15
Situational attribution, 42
Situational communication apprehension, 20
Skill Building, 44, 121–122, 130, 185
Skills, communication, 44
Skimming, 264–265
Slang, 52, 342
Slide, example of RAR, 234
Slide shows, 314, 319–320, 325
Small group communication. See Group communication
Smith, Eileen, 116–117
Social construction of self, 36
Social context, 9
Social distance, 101
Social ease, 19
Social environment, 38, 39
Social friendship groups, 197
Social media, nonverbal messages and, 94
Social networking sites, 201

Social penetration, 148–149, 149
Social penetration theory, 148
Social perceptions, 28, 45
Social presence, 133
Socioeconomic status (SES), 54, 147
Sociolinguistic meaning, 86–89
Solution criteria, 227, 228
Solution evaluation, 229–230
Sources, citing, 271, 272, 298–300, 299
Space, use of, 101–102
Speaking anxiety. See Public speaking apprehension
Speaking appropriately, 333–340
Speaking clearly, 340–343
Speaking notes, 365–367, 366–367
Specific language, 81, 341
Specific speech goal, 248, 257–260
Speech, critiquing, 129
Speech act, 82–83
Speech adaptation. See Audience adaptation
Speech assignments
    acquiring cultural knowledge, 67
    active listening and evaluating speech, 126
    the assignment, 298
    citing oral footnotes, 273
    encoding and decoding skill and practice, 108
    expository speech, 402
    introducing a classmate, 20–21
    meaning clarification, 82
    panel discussion, 234
    personal narrative, 175
    persuasive speech, 434
    process speech, 396
    relationships speech, 147
    self-concept, 40
    speech presentation, 374
    visual aids, 326
Speech communities, 75
Speech content
    citing sources, 271–272
    cultural differences and, 254–255
    gathering and evaluating information, 260–267
    identifying and evaluating information, 267–270
    recording information, 270
Speech continuum, 391
Speech critiques, 129
Speech goals
    audience and, 250–253, 251, 258
    examining the occasion, 255–256
    generating list of topics, 249–250, 256–257
    rhetorical situation, 248, 248–249
    writing, 257–260
Speech organization, 276–309
    audience analysis and, 278
    compiling reference list, 298–300, 299

conclusions, 296–298
introductions, 290–296
main points, identifying, 279–281, 282
organization patterns and, 283–287
outlines, 278, 281, *283*, 287, 289, *302–306*
section transitions, 288–289, 290
signposts, 289–290
speech body, outlining, 281–288
supporting materials, 287
thesis statement, 281, 283
Speech outlines. *See* Speech organization
Speech practicing. *See* Speech presentation
Speech presentation, 355–356
body language and, 357–362, *360*
critiquing, *372–373, 379–381,* 441–445
delivery, 355–357, 362–365
humor in, 279, 392, 450
rehearsing, 365–370, 373
skills training for, 354–355
speech samples, 374–379, 403–406, *416,* 435–440
voice and, 356–357
Speech rehearsing, 365–370. *See also* Speech presentation
Speech research
citing sources, 271, *272*
experiments, 267
locating information sources, 260–267
recording information, 270–271
selecting relevant information, 267–270
sources, evaluating, 267–270
sources, types of, 261–264
Speech topics
audience analysis and, 248, 250– 255
brainstorming/concept mapping, 249–250, *250*
content development of (*See* Speech content)
examining the occasion, 255–256
for expository speeches, *401*
goals of (*See* Speech goals)
identifying, 249–250
selecting, 256–257
Spontaneity, 355, 361
Spontaneous expressions, 17
Spontaneous touch, 99
Stagnating stage, in relationships, 155
Startling statements, 290–291
Statement of reasons pattern, 429
Statistical sources, 264, 268
Stereotypes, 42, 63, 253
Stimuli, 29, 30
Stories, in speeches, 292
Storming stage, in group development, 207–208
Straw man fallacies, 422
Streaming videos, 233–234
Subject lists, *249*
Subject-related data, 251–252
Subjects, 249. *See also* Topics
Subpoints, identifying and outlining, 289
Support, definition of, 418
Supporters, 217
Support groups, 197–198
Supporting material, 280, 287, 289, 290, 312
Supportive attitudes, 418–419
Supportive responses, 126, *127*
Surveys, *252,* 252–253, 266
Suspense, in speeches, 294
Syllogism, 419
Symbols, 17
Symmetrical feedback, 16
Sympathetic responsiveness, 123
Sympathy, in responding, 123
Symposium, 233
Synchronous channels, 135
Synergy, 206
Synonyms, 394
Syntax and grammar, 75
Systematic desensitization, 354
Systematic problem solving, 226–232

T

Talking points, 153, 470
Target audiences, 416–418, 430, 435
Task leadership roles, 217
Task-related touch, 99
Taylor, Dalmas, 148
Team-building activities, 203
Teamwork skills, 6
Temporal selection, 158
Tension relievers, 218, 223
Terminal credibility, 425
Terminating stage, in relationships, 145, 155–156
Territorial space, 102
Territory, marking of, 102
Texting, 6, 10, 59
Theoretical topics, 400
Therapy, self-concept and, 38
Thesis statements, 281, *282,* 283, 295
Timbre, quality, 100
Timeliness, 333–334
Time order, 285
Time orientation, differences in, 57–58
Time-oriented listeners, 115
Timetable, speech preparation, *365*
Topical segmentation, 158–159
Topic order, 286
Topics, 249–250. *See also* speech topics
Touch, 99
Toulmin, Stephen, 418
Traitlike communication apprehension, 20

Transcribe, 458
Transformation, relationship, 156
Transforming, 208
Transitions, 289
Transparency, intimacy and, 148
Trust, 19, 124. *See also* Honesty
    definition of, 16, 144
    disclosure and, 171
    in groups, 203, 207, 208
    in interpersonal relationships, 144, 147
    intimacy and, 144, 147
Trustworthiness, 265, 358, 374–375. *See also* Truthfulness
Truthfulness, 19, 124, 335. *See also* Honesty; Trust
Tsay, Mina, 204–205
Turn-taking, 74, 141
Two-sided items, 252

U

Unanimous decision method, 230
Uncertainty avoidance, 58, 61, 66
Uncertainty reduction, 41–42, 140, 150
Uncertainty reduction theory, 248–249
Understanding, 119–123, 165, 388, 396, 404
Uninformed audiences, 417
Unknown pane, in Johari window, *149*, 149–150
Utterance, 74

V

Valid sources, 265
Values
    cultural, 56, 66,
    definition of, 50
    proposition of, 415–416
Vegans, 394
Verbal immediacy, 333, 338, 346
Verbal messages, 72–91
    appropriate language use, 333–339
    clarity of, 80–82
    meaning and, 79–89
    nature of language, 74–79
Video reports, 233–234
Virtual group communication, 200–201

Virtual groups, 200, 210–211
Virtual reports, 233–234
Visible job market, 461
Visual aids, *323*
    choosing, 320
    computer-mediated aids, 233
    definition of, 312
    display methods for, 323–325
    preparing, 321–323
    in process speeches, 396
    types of, 314–320
Visualization, 353–354
Vividness, 293, 296, 343–345
Vocal characteristics, 356–357
Vocal expression, 357
Vocalics, 99–101, 356–357
Vocalized pauses, 100–101, 343
Vocal pitch and rate, 96
Vocal quality, 100, 356, 357
Voice, tone of, 94, 119, 129
Voice characteristics, 356–457
Volume, vocal, 100, 356, 357

W

Warrant, 418
Watching dimension, 391
Web sites, 201, 264
Whiteboards, 324
White lies, 175
Wikipedia, 261, 262–263
Willingness, intimacy and, 148
Withdrawal, 156, 180
Words, 57, 78
Work group team goal, 199–200
Work group teams, 199
Workplace humor, 218
Written brief, 232
Written reports, 232

Y

YouTube, 261, 319